To Love An Enemy

To Love An Enemy

❖

To Ann Lloyd —
A dear friend.
May the Lord bless you.
Dovye A. Culpepper
11-10-2012

Dovye Ann Culpepper

To order additional copies of this book, contact:
Xlibris Corporation
1-888-795-4274
www.Xlibris.com
Orders@Xlibris.com
25472

Dedication

To Ernie

*who is my husband
and my Nathan.*

With all my love,

D.A.C.

CHAPTER 1

The sky of Ireland had never been more beautiful. It was a deep blue and served as a backdrop to the gulls that circled and occasionally swooped and skimmed the ocean surface. Their gray and white plumage blended with the blue. There was no threat of the rain that came often to the island, and the ceaseless breaking of the waves against a rock seawall added to the perfection of the day. The date was April 2, 1812.

Hannah stood on the dock in Cork Harbor with a wide-brimmed hat in one hand and a small book in the other. Wind blew wisps of dark red hair around the sides of her face. Her hair was long and thick, but had been combed back on top and was held by a silver clasp at the back of her head.

She shaded her eyes with the small book and looked toward the green hills of her beloved Ireland that had been home for all of her nineteen years. She wanted her eyes to absorb their beauty that she might see them forever because she never expected to return. Only the future could tell if she did the right thing.

Although the sky was beautiful and the sun was bright, a slight chill in the wind made her glad she'd worn a long-sleeved blouse that fit high around her neck. Her mother's brooch was pinned at her throat. It matched the clasp in her hair and her long dark-green skirt. Her shoes were comfortable as she walked back and forth, while waiting beside three large trunks.

The trunks contained all that she would take to America. One was filled with winter clothes and another with summer clothes. The third trunk held memorabilia that meant more to her than any of her other possessions. After giving most of her belongings to friends or to the church, the rest had been carefully wrapped and placed inside the trunk. Her mother's Bible and her father's watch were among the things she could not part with. A set of China dishes had been a wedding gift to her parents, and a teapot had belonged to her grandmother. She feared that some of the things that held memories of her past would be broken on the long voyage ahead.

The trunk that held the memorabilia was heavy, and she hoped that whoever came for her was strong enough to lift it. The man who had bought her horse and wagon had unloaded it from the wagon onto the dock. A bag that held her personal things set on top of it.

Hannah worried that Captain Barrington had forgotten her. His ship, the *Monarch*, was moored at the end of the dock, and she had watched earlier as seamen had unloaded goods from it and then loaded other cargo to be transported across the Atlantic. The seamen were now gone, either into town or back to the ship, and she was left alone on the dock. It had been almost two months since she'd received a letter from the captain, stating the time of their next departure from Liverpool, England, to America. He had written that the seaport of Cork was on their route and for her to wait on the dock on this day. And he had agreed in the letter that he would wait to receive the fare for her voyage from the owner of a Tidewater plantation near Charleston, South Carolina.

She heard the sound of squeaking wheels. A young seaman pushed a large cart with bars at both ends of it down the gangplank. She hoped that he came for her and tried to think what she should say. She'd seldom talked to men her own age; most of the men she knew were her father's age.

As he came closer, she saw that the young man was tall, at least six feet, and had a slender physique. The wind tousled his short light-brown hair. Narrow sideburns seemed uncontrollable and stuck out from the sides of his cheeks like tiny wires. His handsome face was slightly tanned, even in April, and brown eyes twinkled under his heavy eyebrows. She kept silent and he spoke the first words.

"Since no one else is on the dock, you must be Miss Hannah Thornton." He had a pleasant voice and smiled as he spoke. His teeth were perfect.

"Yes, I'm Hannah Thornton. Did Captain Barrington send you to help me aboard?"

"He did, Ma'am, and he sends his apologies for being so long about it. We took on more cargo that had to be stowed away before it was safe for you to come on deck. The *Monarch* is a merchant ship, but has a few cabins for passengers; it'll be a pleasure to have you aboard."

"Thank you."

"I hope the trip won't be too difficult, but the North Atlantic can be pretty rough this time of the year. By the way, I'm Nathan Lee."

She smiled. "I'm glad to meet you, Nathan. Please call me Hannah and thanks for the warning."

He lifted the two trunks that contained her clothes onto the cart without any trouble, but when he tried to lift the third one, she heard a soft whistle. "What do you have in here—bricks?" He held his hand to his back as though it was broken.

He only joked, but she reached for one end of the trunk and made an effort to help. When the small book slipped from her hand and fell to the dock, the young man reached to pick it up. He noticed its title, *Comforting Scriptures from the Protestant Bible*. Since he knew that Catholicism was the predominant religion of Ireland, he was surprised to see that she was a Protestant. He was of the same faith.

Together, they lifted the heavy trunk onto the cart, and the young seaman walked to the opposite end of it to push it down the dock. He waited as Hannah turned and gazed one last time at the hills of her homeland. A tear trickled down one side of her face. It was plain to see that she struggled within, but he pretended not to notice. She quickly wiped the tear away, and they started down the dock with the wheels squeaking on the cart.

He was curious as to why a girl so young would depart from Ireland alone and thought it strange there was no one to see her off. Perhaps her family had come and gone before he got there, but most families would not have left her alone as he had found her on the dock.

They walked in silence. As they approached the ship, Hannah thought how much larger it appeared to be from this end of the dock. She was fearful of its gangplank, but excited that the moment had finally arrived. It was hard to leave Ireland, but she'd made up her mind to look to the future and decided that once on the ship she would not look back, although she knew there would be times of despair.

Nathan was glad that his friend, Jason, didn't go for the passenger when he asked him to. He smiled to himself, for he could just hear him say the expression that he used quite often when he saw Hannah. She was young and attractive, although he'd expected a fat middle-aged or older lady and had given no thought to his own appearance. Hannah walked in front of him, giving him an opportunity to really look at her. She was slender, and he estimated her height to be five feet, five inches. He thought her hair was gorgeous on her back over her white blouse and had never known anyone with hair that color before.

"I can't push the cart up the gangplank with all three trunks on it," he said, as they neared the end of the dock. "If you'll wait here, I'll get someone to help me take them to your cabin, one at a time."

She agreed to wait, as she didn't want any of the China or glassware to break. Nathan ran up the gangplank, but soon returned with another seaman.

Hannah had no idea what the second young man meant when she overheard him say "Awe man!" as the two of them came down the plank. When Nathan looked at her and laughed, she suspected the expression had something to do with her. She felt her face grow warm.

Nathan noticed the pinkish color of her cheeks when he introduced her to his friend. "Hannah, this is Jason Williams." He then turned to Jason. "And this is Hannah Thornton who was all alone on the dock."

"It's sure a pleasure to meet someone so pretty, Ma'am. You're welcome aboard the *Monarch*."

"Thank you, Jason. I'm pleased to meet you." Her soft voice revealed her shyness.

As the seamen lifted each trunk and took it to her cabin, Hannah waited beside the cart. She thought how magnificent the ship looked with the blue sky behind it. It had three tall masts from which a shroud of rigging hung, and the flag of England flew atop her mainmast. It appeared to have been recently constructed. Hannah marveled at who could design and build such an object of strength and beauty.

She wanted to push the empty cart up the gangplank, but decided against it and shuddered at the thought of her and the cart falling into the water. When the seamen returned, they seemed in a hurry. "Hop on the cart, Ma'am," Jason said, "and we'll give you a ride."

Hannah hesitated. She looked at the seaman who had come to get her. He seemed amused as he waited for her decision, so taking a chance, she plopped her hat on her head and jumped onto the cart with her legs stretched in front of her. She laid the small book on her lap and held to each side of the cart.

With Nathan in front and Jason at the rear, they ran as fast as they could, giving Hannah a wild ride up the gangplank. She was frightened and cried out when the wind almost blew her hat from her head. She let go with one hand to catch the hat just as they went over the end of the gangplank and a big bump that bounced her off the cart and onto the quarterdeck in a most awkward position. Thus was her "graceful" boarding of the *Monarch*; the ship that would be home for almost three months.

When the laughter of other seamen filled the air, Hannah felt her cheeks burn and knew they were scarlet red. As she reached for one end of the cart to pull herself from the deck, Nathan offered her his hand, but she refused his help.

She straightened her skirt, regained her composure as much as possible, and even waved to those still laughing. They applauded her as she turned to the two who had caused her to completely lose her dignity. "If you could be so kind as to show me to my cabin," she said in an icy voice.

Jason looked at Nathan. "I'll put the cart away," he mumbled, and left with it quickly.

Hannah waited, but the seaman was no longer in a hurry. "I'm sorry you fell," he said. "I hope you're not hurt."

"Only my dignity. I'll surely recover from that."

"Jason always gets me in trouble."

"And you had nothing to do with it?"

"Hey," he laughed, "I didn't tell you to get on the cart."

"You didn't tell me not to, either."

He opened his mouth, but his words were drowned out by the voice of the captain. "**All hands on deck. All hands on deck. Prepare for sailing.**"

"That's why we were in a hurry," he explained. "We knew the captain wanted to sail as soon as you were aboard. Follow me to your cabin, and please stay inside until the crew has readied the *Monarch* for sailing."

She followed him to the first door on their right. "This is your room," he said, then pointed toward the stern of the ship. "The last door is the galley and dining hall where the evening meal is served at six o'clock." He left in a hurry, but as he ran across the deck, he saw Hannah's small book lying where she had fallen. He picked it up and put it in his pocket to give to her later; there wasn't time to take it to her now. The captain wanted them under way as soon as possible.

Hannah stepped inside the cabin and closed the door behind her. The room was dark until her eyes adjusted from the bright sunlight. A small round window let in enough light to see, and her eyes slowly surveyed the room. At one side, a bed had been neatly made; beside it was a table that could be used for dining or as a desk. It had only one chair. Across the room, her trunks set against the wall.

A white curtain over the window matched the cover on the bed, and both appeared to have been freshly washed. An oil lamp attached to the wall burned so low that it gave no light at all. Two other doors in the room opened to a small water closet and into a corridor.

After viewing everything in the room, Hannah lay down on the bed and found it comfortable and the pillow was soft, but she realized how exhausted she was. Her legs and feet ached; she'd been on them since early morning. The present time was near four o'clock in the afternoon. She heard the seamen on the deck, shouting to each other about sails and rigging, then the noise became muffled and all seemed to run together. It became farther and farther away until she no longer heard it.

Darkness fell, but the small crew of the *Monarch* worked on into the night. The rigging was tightened, but sails were loosed and set to make as much speed as possible. The wind was just right when they cast off, and the mighty *Monarch* began to sail across Cork Harbor toward the open sea.

They had not stopped to eat the evening meal, but each knew he could go by the galley for food before going to his quarters. All were in a jovial mood as they headed that way.

Scott Hogan was the youngest among them, being only seventeen years of age, but Stuart Anderson and Billy Stevenson were not much older. The three were close friends and called on often to complete a job together. Mark Monroe and Jefferson "Jeff" Adams were two others who worked well together. The older and more experienced of the crew were Robert Moore, George Thomas, and Murray Mills. Murray, the *Monarch's* main pilot, and Robert, the ship's navigator, had worked for Captain Barrington many years. Some members of the crew were trained in warfare and had fought in battles, while the others, although less experienced, had proven to be worthy seamen.

Nathan made sure that a watch was set before joining the others in the galley. He stayed long enough to eat a small amount of food and then left for his cabin, next door to the captain's.

He entered his room and began to empty his pockets before undressing for bed. He'd forgotten the small book that he picked up from the deck and belonged to the passenger whom they had taken aboard that evening. Inside the front cover, he found words written in a neat handwriting. "To my precious Hannah. I will always love you. Collin." On the second page, a scripture had been underlined. It read, "And, lo, I am with you always, even unto the end of the world." Matthew 28:20.

He laid the book in the middle of his desk, where he would be sure to see it and not forget to return it, then finished getting ready for bed and lay down on his back with his hands under his head. He felt the *Monarch* heeling from one side to the other and heard the wind in her sails.

He closed his eyes and saw the girl who had stood tall and erect at the far end of the dock, silhouetted against the blue sky as gulls circled over her. The wind blew her hair that was the color of a late evening sunset. It was a scene he would never forget. Before he went to sleep, he wondered about the person who had written the message in her book.

CHAPTER 2

Hannah awoke during the night and at first was somewhat disoriented. She had not meant to fall asleep when she lay down on the bed the evening before, but there had been little time for rest the last three months. It had been a relief to be finished with everything and on the ship. She would be forever indebted to her father's friend, John Dudley, who practiced law in Cork and had helped settle her father's small estate. He'd found a buyer for the house and property and even arranged her passage across the ocean with Captain Barrington.

Awake in the night, she sat alone in the darkness, and fear dug deep into her soul, causing her to shiver. The sound of the wind against the sails was as unfamiliar to her as was the swaying of the *Monarch* back and forth on the waves. Neither brought the comfort that she sought for her burdened heart.

Having found that God's word written in the Holy Scriptures was her greatest weapon against fear, she rose from the bed to read from her small book. Her hands moved down the wall of the dark room until they touched the warm whale-oil lamp. She slowly turned it up. The dim light brought a degree of consolation, but she became distraught when she could not find the book of comforting scriptures. As her mind thought back, she realized she must have dropped it on the quarterdeck when she fell from the cart. She hoped it would still be there when morning came.

Hannah took her mother's Bible from the trunk and opened it to the book of Genesis. She read about Joseph who was sold to the Ishmeelites by his brothers and taken to Egypt. Later, his brothers had to depend on him for grain during a time of famine. God had taken care of Joseph in Egypt, and after the Bible was closed, she asked Him to take care of her in a new land.

As she put the Bible back inside the trunk, she noticed a tint of light outside the window. The dawn had come. Soon the sun would rise, bringing forth her first day at sea.

To freshen herself for the day, she washed her face and combed her hair. As she slipped a favorite cotton dress over her head, she was reminded of how her father had enjoyed buying pretty clothes for her. She picked a ribbon that matched her dress and tied it in her hair, then looked in the small water-closet mirror to apply a touch of color to her face.

When satisfied with her appearance, she opened the door and walked out onto the deck. The sun had begun to peep over the eastern horizon. Only a small portion of it could be seen, but it cast a fan-shaped glow in the sky that reflected brilliant colors on the water below. Hannah had watched many sunrises by the sea, but had never seen one more beautiful than today.

The wind, mingled with a slight mist of salt water, blew across the *Monarch* and sprinkled her face. It had lost some of its force in the early morning hours and brought calmer waters off the southern tip of Ireland.

She walked to the quarterdeck where she had fallen the evening before. Jeff Adams stood guard that morning and recognized her as the new passenger. He'd seen her fall from the cart. She didn't see him, but he gazed at her, while the sun rose and turned darkness into light. The wind blew her hair over one side of her shoulder and whipped her dress around the calf of her legs. Jeff wondered why she was on the deck at dawn. He noticed that she seemed to be searching for something and went to see if he could help.

"Good morning, Ma'am. Did you lose something?"

"Good morning," Hannah responded. "Yes, I had a book on my lap when I fell here, yesterday, and now I can't find it. I thought that perhaps I dropped it when I fell, but it doesn't seem to be here."

"Things get kicked around when we're all working on the deck as we were last night. If I find it, I'll see that you get it."

"Thank you. My name is Hannah."

"I'm Jeff Adams, and I'm sorry we laughed when you fell."

Hannah smiled. "I suppose it was a funny sight to see. If it gave you pleasure, I'm glad it happened."

"That's a good way to look at it."

"Well, I don't think my book is here, but it was nice to meet you."

"The same here, Ma'am—uh—Hannah."

As she walked toward her cabin, Hannah noticed the wind had picked up. The *Monarch* was headed into the swell; its bow rose high above the water. As it plunged forward, it gave the sensation of walking on air and made her dizzy.

Since she'd skipped the evening meal the day before, she was hungry and was glad when she heard people in the corridor, going toward the dining hall. She opened her door and followed them, as they would be familiar with the ship's routine of the day. With a tray of food in her hands, she went to a corner of the small dining hall and sat alone, but noticed the people around her as she ate.

A man and a lady who appeared to be about forty years of age were seated at a table nearby with three children. The man was tall, but thin, and thick sideburns on each side of his face came together under his chin. The lady was pretty, but her face showed signs of stress and her shoulder-length hair had a trace of gray in it. The oldest of the children was a boy, about twelve years of age; two younger girls were, perhaps, six and ten. The smallest child could not sit still, and the mother kept saying, "Eat your breakfast, Jenny." They were the only children in the dining hall.

An older couple was engaged in a conversation. They smiled at each other often and appeared to be very much in love. Were they going to America on a wedding trip? The couple was dressed nicely, yet comfortably. The lady was somewhat plump with dimples in her cheeks, but he was thin and had a bald spot on his head.

A sophisticated lady with a neat hairstyle was dressed nicer than the other passengers. Her appearance led Hannah to believe she was a lady of great wealth. A man whom the other passengers seemed to know came in and sat down at her table. He looked Hannah's way, but she glanced down at her plate quickly and was embarrassed that he'd caught her staring. He was tall and very handsome, dressed in a white officer's uniform that had a gold-colored epaulet across each shoulder. Brown hair that had begun to gray at the temple made him more distinguished. Was this Captain Barrington? If so, who was the lady? Could it be his wife?

Hannah remembered hearing John Dudley say that Captain Barrington owned a large shipping company in Liverpool. He was a British Aristocrat. Her father had never liked aristocratic people, especially British. His strong dislike stemmed from British rule over Ireland and their persecution of Catholics since the time of the first Norman invaders in 1170.

A young couple sat near the door of the dining hall, and anyone could see that the lady was with child. Hannah judged her to be between six and seven months along. She thought how scary it must be to cross the ocean while expecting a baby and hoped that nothing went wrong, for she didn't think there was a doctor on board. The young girl seemed about her own age, perhaps a year or so older. She was small, but her stomach was large, making it difficult for her to get close to the table. Her dark blonde hair curled around the sides of her pretty face. The husband, who looked to be a few years older than his wife, was medium size and had a pale complexion.

The couple with the children came by Hannah's table as they were leaving. The man held out his hand. "Hello," he said, "we're the Hartmans. I'm John, and this is my wife, Rachel; our son, Steven, and our daughters, Mary and Jenny."

Hannah stood. "It's a pleasure to meet all of you," she said. "I'm Hannah Thornton of County Cork, Ireland. I hope we get to know each other well during the voyage."

"I'm sure we will," said the wife. "We're in the cabin next to yours. If we can be of any help, let us know."

"Thank you; I will."

Hannah left the dining hall at the same time as the young couple. Since they walked out together, they introduced themselves. Their names were Elizabeth and Michael Sutterfield, but Elizabeth said everyone called her "Lizzy."

As the three of them walked down the hallway together, Hannah asked, "When is your baby due?"

"The last of June." Lizzy rubbed her hand over her stomach. "We should have plenty of time to get there."

"I'm sure we will. Are you going to the United States to live?"

"Yes . . . at least until the war is over. Many people fear that the French will invade England. What do you plan to do there?"

"Teach children on a plantation for five years, but after that, I don't know." Hannah laughed softly and added, "My future is somewhat uncertain."

"Well, we hope everything works out for you," said Michael.

"Thank you."

A friendship developed instantly between them. Hannah thought both displayed a humble attitude, having no pomp about them, and their cabin was right across the hall. To know they were there made her feel safe.

By the time she reached her room, something was wrong. The dizziness she'd felt earlier was worse, and now she was nauseated. She wished she'd not eaten such a large breakfast, but thought fresh air would make her feel better and went outside to stand by the guardrail.

Jeff remained on guard duty and saw her come outside. "Did you find your book, Hannah?" he raised his voice that she might hear him from where he stood.

"No," she replied.

"I looked for it, but didn't find it."

"Don't worry about it. I could have dropped it on the gangplank." Jeff seemed like a nice young man and was certainly nice-looking with blonde hair and blue eyes, but she was glad he stayed at a distance, for she felt very ill.

The swells were higher now, and Hannah made a mistake by looking down at the churning water. Everything began

to spin. She leaned her head over the rail and lost all her breakfast . . . . She was seasick.

She looked around her and was glad that she saw no one. Her stomach felt better after the breakfast came up, but the sickness soon returned, and she leaned over the rail again. She couldn't remember ever being so sick and sank to the deck with her head between her knees. After sitting in this position for quite some time, she took hold of the rail and pulled herself from the deck. With weak knees and her eyes closed, she braced her back against the rail and placed her elbows on top of it. She leaned her head backward and drew in a deep breath of air and then released it slowly. The wind felt good against the back of her neck as it blew her mass of hair toward her face.

She opened her eyes and looked upward . . . right into the eyes of the young seaman who had come to the dock to get her. He mended a sail over her cabin. When their eyes met, he leaned his head slightly and one corner of his mouth twitched. Hannah felt the blood rush to her face, and she turned quickly toward the water.

She was terribly embarrassed, as she knew he had watched when she lost her breakfast and while she rolled on the deck with her head between her knees. At first, she wished she could disappear, but then became angry because he'd not made his presence known to her.

As another wave of sickness came over her, she made a dash for her cabin, just as he swung down from the sail with a wooden bucket in his hand and landed on the deck between her and the door. He quickly dumped tools from the bucket and held it up to her, and she threw up in it. Drops of perspiration ran down her face and fell into the bucket. She feared she would lose consciousness because she had fainted often in her lifetime.

He took her arm and led her to a bench near her cabin and forced her to sit down with the bucket between her legs. Not wanting anyone to see her in such a state, she gasped, "Please go away."

Nathan had thought she would be embarrassed, and for that reason, he'd hoped she wouldn't see him. He purposely mended

the sail over her cabin that morning in hopes of seeing her, but not like this. As she leaned forward with her head over the bucket, retching arduously, he squatted down beside her and held her hair back.

"Hannah," he spoke softly in her ear, "let me help you. I know you're alone, and you need someone right now. Most people are seasick on their first ocean voyage, so it's nothing to be embarrassed about. I remember how awful it was on my first trip across. I can help you if you'll let me."

His kind voice was so sympathetic, she could not stay angry. "What can you do?" she asked.

"The cook makes a tea from ginger root. It'll settle your stomach and make you feel better. May I get you some?"

"Yes—please," she gasped.

He left, but soon returned with fresh water for her to wash the awful taste from her mouth. With a wet cloth, he gently wiped perspiration from her face, then sat down beside her and held a mug of hot tea to her lips. She sipped it. The warm liquid felt wonderful to her throat. She drank more; it really did seem to settle her stomach and to soothe her frazzled nerves. She took the mug from him and drank all the tea.

"I do feel better," she said. "I appreciate your help."

"I'm sorry I didn't let you know I was over your cabin. I waited for a chance to get down without you seeing me."

"Well, now that you have seen me fall on my fanny and roll on the deck with my head between my legs, I can imagine what you must think of me."

He laughed, but answered seriously, "I think you're pretty and awfully sweet."

She leaned her head and looked at him out of the corner of her eyes as if to say she didn't believe he thought either. "I certainly don't feel pretty, or sweet, right now." However, when the tea took its full effect, she felt much better and thanked him again for his help.

"Was everything all right in the dining hall this morning?" he asked.

"Yes. I met other passengers. Do you know the Hartmans and the Sutterfields?"

"I've known Michael Sutterfield for years. We went to the same boarding school."

"An older couple seemed to be very much in love."

"They've been in love for forty years," he mumbled. Then in a more distinct voice, "They're the Butlers. George was Captain Barrington's bookkeeper for twenty-five years. He just retired and received a nice bonus for his faithfulness and free passage to America for him and his wife, Alice. They have six grandchildren there whom they've never seen, so the trip is a dream-come-true."

"How long have you known them?"

"A long time."

"Where were you this morning? I didn't see you."

"I ate in the mess hall with the rest of the crew, but I'd rather eat with a pretty girl if she'd allow me to."

Hannah felt her face become warm again. She wasn't sure how to answer. Did he mean her?

Nathan chuckled when her cheeks blushed. "You have the most sensitive face of any girl I know."

"And you know quite a few, I suppose?" she spoke rashly.

"I've been around awhile."

"That doesn't answer my question."

"Maybe you ask too many."

"Forgive me. It's an Irish characteristic."

"I will if you'll agree to share a table with me."

"I'd be happy to have someone join me for meals."

"Then I shall look forward to each one."

"Nathan, do you know Captain Barrington very well?"

He turned and looked into her eyes before nodding his head slowly. "Yes—why do you ask?"

"There was another couple in the dining hall this morning. Could it have been the captain and his wife?"

"It had to be, for you've named everyone else. His wife is aboard."

"Why is she going to the United States?"

"Man, you ask a lot of questions! They own a home in North Carolina; she'll spend the summer there." He didn't mention her fear of a French invasion.

"They must be very rich. My father didn't like wealthy British Aristocrats."

"Why not?" Nathan quickly asked defensively.

"Their wealth gives them power to rule the Irish people. The rulers of Great Britain have persecuted Irish Catholics for hundreds of years."

"The Barringtons have nothing to do with ruling the Irish; besides, you're not a Catholic . . . are you?"

"No."

He remembered there had been no one on the dock to see her off the day before. "Maybe your father is just an old fuddy-duddy," he said.

Hannah was shocked. There was a pause in their conversation. She'd not expected him to take her words so personally, and would he have said what he did, had he known about her father? She wanted to tell him, but couldn't.

Nathan heard her sigh and thought he saw tears in her eyes. She stood, but in a kind voice, said, "I must lie down for I feel weak. I really do appreciate your help. Perhaps if I eat only a little at a time, I won't get so sick again."

He suddenly jumped to his feet. "Hannah, wait!" He wanted to apologize for what he'd called her father, but she had already gone through her door, and she closed it behind her. They had neither understood the other's reaction to their conversation.

Nathan was exasperated and wanted to bite his tongue for what he had said. Hannah seemed sad about something. He suspected she struggled with leaving home, or was her sadness caused by her reason for leaving? He knew she'd not meant to offend him with her remark about wealthy British. To make matters worse, he'd forgotten to give her the book that he picked up from the deck. He overheard her conversation with Jeff and understood that she had looked for it.

He waited for her at noon, but she didn't come for the meal. Since she had gotten up before dawn and was left weak after the seasickness, she went to sleep and slept for several hours. When she awoke, she felt better and went to the dining hall, but by then everyone had left. She had missed the noon meal. She returned to her cabin, and had not been there long when someone knocked on her door. It was Nathan and he held her small book in his hand.

"Where did you find it?" She was delighted.

"On the quarterdeck where you fell from the cart. I've carried it in my pocket all day. I meant to give it to you this morning."

"I thought I would never see it again. I'm so glad you found it; thanks for returning it."

"I waited for you at noon. Did you eat in your room?"

"No. I went to sleep and didn't wake up in time. I'm sorry you waited."

"Then you haven't eaten. Come with me. The cook always leaves something in the galley."

"That's okay. I'm not hungry."

"Hannah, you didn't eat last night, and you lost your breakfast this morning, so you need something. Please come with me."

"Is it your job to take care of passengers?"

"Yes, and one of them makes it difficult for me."

"Which one?" she giggled.

He squinted his eyes at her, but insisted that she come with him.

She finally agreed to follow him to the galley where he found some potatoes that had been baked in the skins. He peeled one and put salt and pepper on it. To go with it was fresh baked bread and warm tea. They sat together in the dining hall, and while she ate, Nathan told her how sorry he was for what he had said about her father. "I just said it before I thought," he apologized.

"Oh, that's all right. I certainly should not have said what I did about British Aristocrats. I know you're British. Please forgive me."

"Hannah . . ." Nathan wanted to tell her something, but didn't know how.

"Yes?"

He hesitated, then said, "I hope you like the food."

She knew it was not what he had intended to say.

"It's good, especially the potato," she answered, not wanting to press him.

"That's because it's from Ireland," he laughed.

"I should have known."

"They were part of the cargo we took on yesterday."

When she finished eating, Nathan walked her to her cabin and lingered at her door. He wanted to get to know her right away. The trip across the ocean would take only eight weeks, and from New York Harbor to Charleston would take only half that time.

"I have to go," he muttered under his breath. "A seaman's job is never finished." Before he left, he reminded her of the promise to share a table with him. "I'll see you at six o'clock," he said.

"Do you know what time it is?"

"The clock in the galley just now showed two o'clock."

After he left, Hannah opened the trunk that held her treasures and took out an old clock. She set its hands to show the right time and then put it on the floor by her bed, so she could be ready at six.

She spent the evening exploring the main deck and saw that the cabins were built together at the ship's stern, but were divided by a hallway down the middle of them. At the far end of the hallway, a staircase led to a lower deck.

On the right, facing the stern, the first cabin was hers, then the Hartman's, the dining hall, the galley, and mess hall, but the only cabin she could identify on the left was the Sutterfield's. A walkway ran between the cabins and the guardrail at each side of the ship, and a cover that extended from the roof of the cabins covered half of it; beneath it, a narrow partition divided one cabin from another.

On her exploration, Hannah found Jason coiling a pile of ropes. He looks about the same age as Nathan, she thought, and wondered how long they had been friends. She stopped to talk.

"Good morning, Ma'am," he said. "I heard you were pretty sick this morning."

"Yes, I was, but Nathan brought me tea that made me feel better."

"Sometimes the ship pitches so badly everyone on it gets sick."

"Do you?"

"I feel dizzy when the weather is rough, but I don't get real sick like I did when I first started sailing. This is my second trip on the *Monarch* with Nathan."

"Jason, how old is Nathan?"

"He's twenty-two, Ma'am."

"Please call me Hannah. It makes me feel like an old woman when you call me ma'am."

"All right, Hannah, but if you're not an old woman, how old are you, or is that an improper question to ask a young lady?"

"I'm nineteen, and I don't think it's improper at all."

"Awe Man!"

"What?"

"You and Nathan are the right age for each other."

Hannah's face blushed. "That doesn't matter. I'm just another passenger to him. He helped me this morning because it's his job to take care of the passengers."

Jason laughed out loud. "Is that what he told you?"

"Yes."

Did she really believe it was Nathan's job to take care of passengers? If so, how naïve could she be, thought Jason? Didn't she realize she wasn't an ordinary passenger? Most women who crossed the ocean were married, and some had children. Not many made the voyage alone and certainly not many who looked like her. Was Nathan's interest in her for real, or was he merely infatuated by her beauty? It was easy for girls to fall in love with him, but up until now, he'd not seemed attracted to any of them.

"Any man could be interested in a girl as pretty as you," he said, "so I don't think you're just another passenger to Nathan."

"You're just being nice. The owner of the *Monarch* is fortunate to have two sailors like you and Nathan to work for him."

Jason looked at her strangely. He suddenly seemed upset and refused to carry the conversation any further.

"Did I say something that offended you?"

"No, Hannah, but British would rather be called seamen instead of sailors."

"I'm sorry. I'll remember that."

On the way to her room, Hannah noticed a small two-story cabin near the middle of the bow with a narrow flight of stairs that ascended almost straight up to the second floor. A handrail accommodated one side of the stairs, and at the top, a small platform suspended from the wall underneath a door. On the door at the lower level were the words "Captain Barrington." She assumed it was the captain's office, but what was the room at the top?

Back inside her cabin, Hannah read until it was time to get ready for the evening meal. She wanted to look her best since she would have it with Nathan, but used as little water as possible to bathe and wash her hair. With a towel wrapped around her, she opened her trunk and took out a gingham blouse that had tiny blue and white checks and a blue denim skirt that hung to her ankles.

By now, it was almost six o'clock. She quickly made touches to her face and combed her hair back in its usual style. With a narrow blue ribbon, she made a bow at the top of her head and let the ends of the ribbon hang down. She hoped Nathan would like the way she looked. As she tried to decide if she should meet him in the dining hall or wait for him to come to her cabin, there was a knock at her door. It was Nathan.

He had changed clothes and looked fresh and clean in a white shirt and black vest with dark colored pants that were quite different from his white seaman pants. His complete attire was of the latest fashion that young men wore in Europe. He had even gotten a hair cut, and his sideburns had been trimmed and combed neatly. He gazed at her from the doorway and she was the first to speak.

"Nathan, you look fantastic! Any girl would be elated to share a table with you."

"Hannah, it's your beauty that has made me speechless. I shall be forever grateful to you for allowing me the honor of having this meal with you."

"Please be yourself."

"I **am** being myself and meant every word that I said."

"Then it is I who should feel honored," she insisted.

The cook had prepared a tasty meal, but Hannah was afraid to eat. She had not regained her appetite, and after the late noon meal, she really wasn't hungry. Nathan noticed that she ate very little, but said nothing about it.

She wished to know his interests that she might talk about them, but hated to ask. He must like sailing, she thought, or he wouldn't work on a ship.

"I'd enjoy sailing if I didn't get seasick," she opened the subject, and he began to tell her all the things he loved about it.

"I love to sail the seas," he said. "It takes me from a routine in life and gives me a chance to realize what's really important. There's work to be done, but it's worth it to see the sun go down between the sky and the water and then watch the moon rise. When on a small ship in the middle of the ocean, I'm reminded of how much I depend on God. I tend to forget that in my everyday life. There's always one adventure after another and never a dull day. It can get lonely, and it helps to have people that you care about on board. I think it would be wonderful to have someone special with you."

Their eyes gazed into each other's until she blinked and looked down without answering. When he asked, "Don't you, Hannah?" their eyes met again.

"Yes, I suppose it would be," she nodded her head and softly agreed and then turned her attention to her plate.

"Do I talk too much?" he asked.

"Oh, no."

"Come on, I'll introduce you to the ship's cook."

"Sam, I want you to meet Hannah Thornton who came aboard in Ireland, yesterday." Sam was a large man with a jolly face. He smiled and held out a sweaty hand to Hannah. She took it in both of hers and told him how delicious the meal was.

"Hannah," Nathan warned her, "if you brag on Sam's cooking, he'll get lazy, and we won't get a decent meal for a week."

Sam threw back his head and laughed. "It's a pleasure to meet you, Miss Hannah," he said. "I'll bake you a special pie."

By the time they finished talking to Sam, everyone had left the dining hall except Michael and Lizzy Sutterfield. They stopped at their table, and the Sutterfields insisted they sit down and visit. Michael and Nathan talked about Michael's new job in the United States at Norfolk, Virginia. Captain Barrington had talked to a shipbuilder who agreed to hire him. Hannah and Lizzy shared each other's thoughts as to what it would be like in America. Both agreed that not knowing what to expect was scary.

"You have a husband to go with you," Hannah said. "I wish I had someone to go with me. If I allow myself to think how alone I am, I become frightened, so I try not to think of it. Instead, I remember that I'm never really alone. God is with me and I know He'll take care of me."

"Yes, He will," Lizzy agreed. Nevertheless, she felt sorry for Hannah and thought of how scary it would be to go to a new country alone. Why had she left Ireland?

The four of them left the dining hall together with the Sutterfields in front. Michael held Lizzy's hand. Hannah was surprised when Nathan reached for hers and squeezed it gently. She felt a warm feeling spread over her entire body instead of just her face.

When the Sutterfields returned to their cabin, Nathan said, "Let me show you the deck below," and on the way, he told Hannah to whom each room belonged.

He laughed quietly when they passed the room across the hall from the galley. "That's where the crew bunks," he said. "They'd rather be near the galley than in the forecastle. It's located at the bow under the deck, but the captain allows them to sleep here since they're so few in number. They call it the "little forecastle" and he pronounced it slowly, "fo'c's'le'."

If the crew sleeps here, Hannah thought, why does he have a room to himself?

The stairs at the end of the hallway descended to a large room under the main deck; a row of cannons flanked each side of it. "This is the gun deck," he said, "and down below is the hold where cargo is stowed."

Hannah was amazed at all the cannons. "Why is the ship so heavily armed?" she asked.

"We never know when we'll be attacked by pirates or a French ship. We could be forced to fight a battle before we reach America."

Her silence told him that he had frightened her, and he wanted to take her mind off what he'd said. He pulled a rope that hung from the ceiling over a cannon and a window flew open. He quickly pushed the cannon to the edge of the opening and yelled, **"Fire the cannon! Boom! Boom!"** He then stepped backward and fell to the deck, shouting, "I've been hit! Oh, no, I'm dying!" He reached out his arms to Hannah and said, "Kiss me, my darling, before I die."

He meant to make her laugh and she did smile. His performance was amusing, but his words were not funny.

"Please get up."

"Not until you kiss me."

His eyes gazed at her from the deck, and after a long pause, she slowly sank to her knees beside him and kissed him lightly on the forehead.

His arm went around her. "Is that the best you can do for a dying man?"

"You're not dying."

"Yes, I am. I'm dying to kiss you." He pulled her closer.

"Please, Nathan . . . let's go back up the stairs."

His eyes held hers a moment before he answered, "All right."

She waited for him to pull the cannon in place and close the window. When he turned, his eyes twinkled and he smiled at her. He took her hand, and they returned to the main deck and walked by the rail until they came to her cabin. She started toward the door, but he held to her hand.

"Don't go in yet. It's still early," he reminded her, "and since tomorrow is Sunday, we can sleep late. It's a day of rest on the ship; breakfast is served later than usual. If you're interested, there is a Christian worship service in the dining hall at ten o'clock."

"I am interested. Who will lead the service?"

"My . . . uh . . . the captain," he answered.

"The captain?"

"Does that surprise you?"

"Yes."

"You'll find the captain is not such a bad person when you get to know him."

"My father and I always attended church in Ireland." She disregarded his statement, as she didn't want conflict between them again. "I had no idea there would be a service on the ship. Will you be there?"

There was a rumbling of thunder in the sky and a light rain began to fall.

"Yes," he answered, as he pulled her under the covered part of the walkway. He thought of something that had been on his mind since he met her. He stood quietly and watched the raindrops fall.

"Is something wrong," she asked.

He sighed lightly and then began, "Hannah, I'm sure you know that England is at war with France. Napoleon wants to control all of Europe, and he has to be stopped. I must help fight for my country. Jason and I enlisted in the Royal Navy, but asked for and were granted a deferment to make this voyage. We have our papers and will report for duty as soon as we return. Commerce is important to England, but with so many men fighting the war, it's hard to enlist crews for merchant ships.

"Our relationship with the United States is not good. Their neutrality between England and France has expanded their commercial trade, hurting British merchants and shipping companies. Since their trade industry is doing so well, they can pay higher wages and the food is better. Many British seamen work on American ships. I hope this crew will be loyal when we drop anchor in American ports and that we'll be allowed to unload our cargo.

"A war of commerce has existed between England, the United States, and France for several years. Two years ago the United States cut off all imports from our country, so we might not be allowed to unload any goods. I'm hoping we can unload most of them and bring back some needed products to England. The captain plans to raise his company's flag under the British flag, because it's recognized in many ports.

"The British Navy's impressment of American sailors has many Americans upset. Life on a British naval ship is harsh, and many from the Royal Navy have deserted to the American Navy. I'll have to admit that I don't look forward to serving on a British man-of-war, but with my training and experience, that is where I can serve best.

"British officers go on board American ships to look for deserters. Sometimes they make mistakes and take American citizens as well as British. Both are dealt with severely, but with desertion rates so high they're forced to do something. However, if the naval seaman's living conditions were better the desertion rates wouldn't be so high. The Americans also claim that British are arming hostile Indians in their Northwest. I'm sorry, but all of this is on my mind, and I wanted to tell you about it."

"I'm glad you did."

Neither spoke for a moment as each thought of the war. Nathan knew he was forced to put his life on hold. He'd not planned on meeting someone like Hannah; it was because of her that he thought of the future. They would have such little time together, but she hardly knew him. She'd let him know on the gun deck that she would not be rushed, so he said nothing about it. He wished he'd not spoken of the war at all.

He didn't blame her when she said she had better go in. As they walked to her door, he said, "It's been a wonderful evening for me. I hope you have enjoyed it if only half as much as I."

"It's meant just as much to me. You've been kind and I'm grateful. If you take care of other passengers half as well, it will be a good trip for everyone."

"Hannah, you're not just another passenger to me. You must know that. It's not really my job to take care of passengers, but I wanted to spend time with you."

"I'm glad you wanted to."

"I heard you talk to Jeff Adams this morning, while I worked over your cabin."

"Is that bad?"

"It could be for me . . . considering his blonde hair and blue eyes."

"What do you mean?"

"You know what I mean." His lips brushed her hair. "Please remember that I'm the one who found you on the dock."

"I will," she whispered. "And I'm glad you found me. Nathan . . ." she felt she should tell him that she was indentured and of her uncertain future.

"Huh-h-h?" he more or less groaned in her ear and waited for her to speak.

But she couldn't find the words, and she didn't want to spoil their wonderful evening, so instead, she said, "I really must go in."

He kissed her lightly on the forehead, the way she had kissed him when they were on the gun deck.

"Good night, Nathan," she whispered and went inside.

He lingered on the deck, wondering what she had wanted to tell him, but couldn't. The rain had stopped and the clouds had passed; stars shined overhead. He put one foot on the bottom rail and crossed his arms on his knee as he watched the moon rise over the horizon. It was almost full, and the path of light it cast across the water seemed to point the way for the *Monarch*. It reminded him of when God parted the waters of the Red Sea and provided a path for the Children of Israel to cross safely out of the hands of the Egyptian Pharaoh.

With the war with France and conflict with the United States, he felt burdened for everyone on the *Monarch*. He bowed his head and prayed that God would be with them, as He had been with the Israelites, and lead them safely across the Atlantic. He thanked Him for the smooth beginning and for a wind that carried them west. He also thanked Him for the special person He had brought into his life. He prayed for Hannah and asked God to show him how to help her with the burden that she carried. He hoped that she would trust him enough to share it with him. He prayed for his friend, Michael Sutterfield, and his wife and unborn child. Michael had asked him to pray for them. He asked God to give him the knowledge to know what to do if Lizzy got in trouble with the baby. He asked a special blessing for everyone, including Jason and all the crew. "And, Lord, please be with my parents. Help me to lighten their load in life." Then Nathan prayed for himself. "Direct me, Lord, in all things, and give me strength that I might be strong for others. And I pray for the war to end. In the name of Jesus, Amen."

The words from a Psalm of David came to his mind. "The Lord is my rock, and my fortress, and my deliverer; my God, my strength, in whom I will trust." Psalm 18:2.

Jason had guard duty on the night watch and saw Nathan with his head bowed. He left him alone until he lifted his head and stood on both feet again. Then he walked to where he stood and asked, "How did everything go tonight?"

Nathan sighed, expressing his weariness. "Everything was perfect until I began to think about the war. I hadn't thought that much about it, but now that I've met Hannah, life has a different perspective."

"Maybe it'll be over by the time we return to England," said Jason.

They stood silently a moment, both knowing there was little chance that the war would end soon.

Jason remembered Hannah's words about Nathan and him working on the *Monarch*. "You didn't tell Hannah who you are, did you?"

"No . . . not yet."

"What if she falls in love with you? Don't you think she has a right to know who you are before that happens? She thinks we're both just a couple of common seamen."

"Well, we are right now," Nathan laughed. "Does that hurt your ego?"

"Doesn't help it any, but I'm more concerned about you and Hannah than I am my ego. You know she's Irish. That could cause a problem. Do her feelings mean nothing to you?"

"Her feelings mean everything to me, Jason, but I'm afraid if I tell her, she won't have anything to do with me, and I'm already in love with her."

"How can you know so soon?"

"I just know. I knew when I saw her standing on the dock."

"Awe man!"

"Her father doesn't like certain British, because he believes they all have a hand in ruling Ireland. I don't know if he plans to come to America or not. And I'm afraid that someone else is in love with her; I found a message written in her book. I know she's burdened about something, but she won't tell me what. There's so much that I want to know about her, but how can I ask when I can't tell her anything about myself? I've never felt this way about anyone before, but you're right, I must tell her who I am, and I will when the time is right."

Jason understood the situation that Nathan was in, but he still thought that Hannah had a right to know who he was. He understood British laws and the conflict between England and Ireland far more than Nathan did. He knew how the Irish yearned for their freedom and the hatred that some felt for the British.

"What did you tell her your name is?" he asked.

"Nathan Lee."

"Awe man! You better tell her the truth before someone else on the ship tells her and you find yourself in a battle before you get to the war."

Nathan looked at Jason who had been his best friend all of his life. "You won't tell her, will you?"

"Oh, no, Mate, not me! That's something you've got to do."

Nathan had nothing more to say. He looked down at the water and bit his bottom lip as he thought of what Jason had said. What if someone did tell Hannah about him and who he really was?

CHAPTER 3

Later that night, Hannah lay in her bed and thought of the war between England and France. Conflict between the two nations had been on and off for many years. The military genius, Napoleon Bonaparte, had crowned himself Emperor of France with intent to control all of Europe, including the British Isles. Her father had feared Napoleon, but he hated British control over Ireland and had hoped to see it an independent country.

Napoleon was one of two reasons why he'd advised her to go to America; the other reason had to do with her religion. Catholics far outnumbered Protestants in Ireland, but her father had remembered his wife's hope for her to walk in the faith of her mother's forefathers. Since Protestantism was the most widespread religion in the United States, he believed that there she would be more likely to marry within her faith.

It saddened Hannah to think of Nathan going to war. She had been attracted to him by his handsomeness and pleasant manner from the very first, and now his kindness had given her a deeper feeling for him. As her eyelashes slowly fell over her eyes, his words came to her again. "You're not just another passenger to me. You must know that." They made her feel warm inside and were comforting until she remembered her uncertain future. Would it permit her to fall in love?

She fell asleep and dreamed that she stood on a hill that overlooked a vast body of water. Large billowing clouds floated low in the sky, and Nathan's face suddenly appeared among them. He called her name from the clouds. When she awoke, she raised her head from the pillow and listened to be sure that it was a dream and not really him calling.

The next morning, Hannah gulped down lukewarm tea and a slice of bread with jam, then rushed to her cabin to change for the worship service. She fastened a pink pin to the front of her white dress and tied her hair back with a wide pink ribbon. With her arms stretched high, she made a large bow at the back of her head.

When she returned to the dining hall, the tables had been pushed to one side, and five rows of chairs had been put in order. Several people were there. She quietly took a seat on the back row behind the Hartmans. Nathan wasn't there, but other members of the crew were. She saw Jeff and wanted to be sure to tell him that Nathan had found her book. His friend, Mark Monroe, was with him, and Scott Hogan sat with them. Others came in and most of the seats were filled.

The Hartman children were dressed neatly and sat very still. Hannah thought how difficult the trip must be for them with no room to run and play. Their mother was afraid to let them play alone on the deck, so most of their day was spent inside the small cabin. How could she help them pass the time?

Just as the captain stood with his Bible opened, Nathan and Jason slipped quietly into the room, and Nathan sat down beside her with Jason at his other side. She smiled at him and worded silently with her lips, "You're late."

"You're beautiful," he worded back.

Both turned their attention to the captain as he began to read from the fourth chapter of Mark. After reading the story of when Jesus calmed a great storm at sea, he closed the Bible and talked about some storms he had encountered. He said he'd experienced, firsthand, the powerful force that could sink a ship, yet Jesus had spoken to the wind and it became calm. He closed his sermon by saying, "If Jesus can take care of something as powerful as a storm at sea, He can surely take care of the storms in our lives." They sang a hymn and were dismissed.

The message brought encouragement to Hannah, and at first, she thought God had put it on the captain's heart just for her because of all that had happened in her life the last three months. She took notice of the small group, however, and realized that she wasn't alone in her somewhat perilous journey. She had only herself to worry about, but the Hartmans had three young children, and the Sutterfields, an unborn child. No, she wasn't alone, and God had not sent the message just to her. The captain, she decided, was aware of the fears and concerns of each one aboard.

She wished to tell him how much his sermon had meant, but Rachel stopped to talk, and Hannah took the opportunity to ask if she could read the children a story after their noon meal. Rachel said "yes" and seemed delighted.

While she talked, Nathan and Jason joined the captain and his wife. Mrs. Barrington looked remarkable in a blue silk dress with fine jewelry that matched. Hannah heard her laugh and saw her reach to tousle Nathan's hair. He must know the Barringtons well, she thought.

Others gathered around the captain, but she was too shy to go alone and was about to leave when Jeff walked by.

"Good morning, Jeff."

"Good morning, Hannah. You look pretty this morning."

"Thank you. I hoped I would get a chance to tell you that I found my book."

"Where?"

"Well, actually, I didn't find it. Nathan had picked it up from the quarterdeck where I dropped it the evening before. He returned it to me that afternoon."

"I'm glad you got it back."

"I appreciate you helping me look for it."

"Hannah, are you and Nathan . . . uh . . ."

"Yes." She knew what he wanted to ask.

"Well, he's a nice fellow, but I'll be around if you need someone to talk to."

"I'll remember that." She smiled at Jeff just as Nathan looked their way. Her eyes met his. His lips came together and his head bent forward.

Jeff left the dining hall and Nathan lifted his head. Hannah stood alone with her hands on the back of the chair in front of her. She stood straight with her chin up and smiled warmly at him, but he didn't smile back.

To Hannah's disappointment, he left the room. She was puzzled at his behavior until she remembered what he had said about Jeff the night before.

While others in the room talked, she circled around them and walked out, unnoticed. She turned in the same direction as Nathan had gone and saw him with his arms crossed on top of the guardrail.

"Nathan," she said his name softly.

He stood straight and turned to face her.

"Nathan, I'm sorry if I upset you."

He stared into her eyes before he turned back to the water. She walked closer and stood beside him. "I'm sorry," she said again.

"It's okay, Hannah. You did nothing to be sorry about. It's just that I've never felt this way before; I suppose it's jealousy. Whatever it is, I don't like it."

"You have no reason to feel that way."

"I know you have a right to talk to whomever you want to, but I've never felt this way because no one has ever mattered that much to me."

"Please don't be upset."

"All right." He smiled. "Come on; let's go eat."

When they finished eating, Hannah told him of her promise to read to the children.

"That's good," he said, and left the dining hall without her. While waiting for the children, she talked to Sam.

"It was a good meal, Sam. I wish I could cook like you."

"Thank you, Miss Hannah." He reached under the counter and brought out the pie he'd promised her.

"Sam, I thought you were joking! You didn't have time to do this!"

"I make time for special people. You're special to Nathan and that makes you special to me."

"Thank you, Sam. I'll share this with Nathan and with the Hartman children."

When the children finished eating, she took them to her cabin and cut each a slice of the cream-filled pie. Afterward, she opened the trunk filled with her treasures and unwrapped several things for them to see. Jenny especially liked some small stuffed animals, and Mary liked an old music box. Her eyes lit up when she carefully lifted its top and heard a pretty melody. Steven held her father's watch to his ear to see if it ticked.

When they grew tired of looking at her things, she put each back inside the trunk and let them select a book to read. They chose one about the ancient civilization of Egypt that had drawings of the pyramids, the Great Sphinx, and felucca boats on the Nile River.

They took the book outside, and when seated on blocks of wood in the shade of the sails, Hannah opened it. She knew the story by heart and told it in her own words to make it more interesting; nevertheless, Jenny's head soon began to nod. She laid it across Hannah's lap and went to sleep.

Hannah found it difficult to turn the pages of the book, while holding Jenny, and was glad when Nathan came to her rescue. He'd kept an eye on them as he talked to other seamen on the deck and now knelt beside her. "Let me have Jenny," he said. "I'll take her to their cabin."

"Thank you, Nathan."

She finished the book and then walked Steven and Mary to the Hartmans' cabin where Nathan talked to John. When the children began to tell Rachel about all the things in her trunk, Hannah slipped quietly out the door and walked the length of the ship to stand at the tip of its bow.

Waves beat against the ship's hull and a British flag fluttered overhead. She was suddenly overcome with homesickness and grief. It was as if she realized for the first time that she'd never hear her father's voice again or see their cottage near the sea. Tears flowed down her cheeks and dropped from her chin. She thought of the captain's sermon and did believe that God and time could heal her heartaches—the storm in her life—but for now, it seemed more than she could bear. She gripped the rail in front of her and felt so alone.

Nathan left the Hartmans' cabin and saw that Hannah's door was closed. He thought she had gone inside to rest, but as he walked toward his own cabin, he saw her standing under the Union Jack. He didn't know if he should go there or not. Since she had gone so far, perhaps she wanted to be alone, but he wanted to talk to her; besides, she stood in a dangerous place. If a large wave hit the *Monarch* just right, she could be tossed overboard.

He walked to where she stood and laid his hands on the rail beside hers.

"I thought you'd be resting," he said.

She turned her head away from him; her silence told him that something was wrong. He curled his finger under her chin and gently pulled her face toward his. It was wet with tears.

"Hannah . . . what's wrong?"

She bowed her head against his chest and sobbed silently. He put his arms around her and felt her trembling. "Talk to me, Hannah. Tell me why you're so sad."

After a moment, she stopped sobbing and lifted her head. He dried her face with his handkerchief. "Must you always catch me at a bad time?" she sniffed.

"Why are you crying?"

"I'll tell you later. You need to rest now and should not let me take more of your time." If she told him about her father, she would have to tell him she was indentured, and she couldn't tell him either.

Nathan remembered the message in her book. "Was he a wonderful man?" he asked.

She nodded her head.

"And you loved him?"

"Very much," she whispered.

She wasn't ready to tell him everything, but took his hand. "Thank you for holding me," she said. "I needed someone."

As she walked away, Nathan remembered why he had come. "Hannah," he called.

She stopped.

"This is a dangerous place to stand. If a large wave covered the bow, you could be washed overboard. Please don't come here again."

"I won't," she promised.

His heart sank as she walked away. She was in love with someone else. What had happened and could he make her forget?

Hannah went to her cabin and cried herself to sleep. She didn't go for the evening meal, but was up early the next morning for breakfast. She was alone in the dining hall until the Hartmans came in; Mary and Jenny ran to her table. "Will you read us another story?" they asked.

"Yes. Right after breakfast."

"Oh, goodie!" exclaimed Jenny.

Hannah felt better that morning, but she felt bad because she had cried in front of Nathan the day before. She wanted to tell him that, but he didn't come to the dining hall for breakfast, and she didn't see him on the deck when she read to the children. When he didn't show up for the noon meal, she began to ponder the questions he had asked. Did he avoid her because he thought she was in love with another man?

She was unaware that he'd watched her from high above, while she sat on the deck with the Hartman children around her. He felt discouraged when he thought of her being in love with someone else, but he did not avoid her.

He had risen at 5:00 A.M. that morning because there was much to be done after a day of rest. Every Monday he examined the rigging for signs of weakness. If any were found, new rigging was put up and then coated with tar. With it the ship's masts, sails, and spars were held in place and controlled. Slack would have to be pulled from loose rigging, and there were changes to be made in the sails. It was his job to determine what must be done and give the men their orders, but since they had been forced to sail short of a full crew, he worked as hard as any one of them. Every man respected him for it.

Nathan worked aloft all morning. Rather than stop and have

to climb back up later, he continued to work until the job was finished. It was past noon when he finally climbed down and went to the galley.

He'd found it difficult to do his work that morning because he couldn't stop thinking of Hannah, but there was so much to be done, and with such a small crew, they got further behind each day. Some jobs did not get done at all.

If Hannah was in love with someone, why had she left Ireland? Was it because things had not worked out, and did she now have second thoughts? So many questions ran through his mind and he had to know the answers.

He'd hoped to see her in the dining hall that evening and that they could go someplace and talk after the meal, but the captain sent a message that he needed him at the helm from 4:00 P.M. until 8:00 P.M. "Murray doesn't feel well," the message read, "and I need you to take over for him."

Before he left the mess hall, Nathan asked Jason to give Hannah a message. He then hurried to get cleaned up and took a nap, so he'd be alert for his duty at the wheel.

Jason forgot Nathan's message to Hannah, and that evening her eyes searched the dining hall for him. She ate a small amount of food and then left by the outside door. On the way to her cabin, she met Jason and he was reminded of the message.

"Oh, Hannah, Nathan asked me to tell you that he has duty at the wheel until eight o'clock." Then with a twinkle in his eyes, "You can spend time with me until then."

"Where is the wheel?"

"Awe man, I knew you were going to ask me that—the lucky mate! Wait a minute and you can take him some food."

While she waited for Jason, the Butlers came out of the dining hall, holding hands. She smiled and said, "Hello, I'm Hannah Thornton; I've wanted to meet you. Nathan told me about you."

"Nathan ought to know about us," said George. "He's known us all his life."

"Was he a neighbor of yours?"

Both seemed surprised at her question. Just as George opened his mouth to answer, Jason returned with the food. He hardly spoke to the Butlers and left so quickly that Hannah thought him impolite.

She asked him to stop by her room where she wrapped the last piece of pie that Sam had given her. She put it into the bag with the food and then followed him to the flight of stairs that was almost straight up and had a handrail on one side.

"Nathan's in the wheelhouse at the top," Jason pointed upward. "Can you climb the stairs with the food?" He put a bottle of tea that he'd held in his other hand into the bag.

Hannah hesitated. She was scared of the stairs and not sure if she should enter the room at the top. What would Nathan think of her being so bold? She looked at Jason who waited patiently for her to make a decision. "Will it be all right?" she queried. "Will the captain mind?"

"Not if you're with Nathan. Besides, you're taking him some food. The poor mate has to eat, hasn't he?"

Hannah feared height, and with the ship heeling back and forth, it would not be easy for her to climb the stairs. Her desire to see Nathan, however, was greater than her fear, so she took the sack in her left hand, and with her right hand on the handrail, she began to climb the steps gingerly.

She grasped the doorknob at the top with one hand and clutched the bag of food in her other. Jason still stood at the bottom of the steps; she looked down at him and nodded her head. He pretended to wipe sweat from his brow to let her know that he had been in great suspense, and then ran across the deck in order to make it to the mess hall before Sam closed it down.

Hannah stood alone on the small platform and almost panicked when she realized her dilemma. What if Nathan didn't want her here? After all, he was on duty. She still wondered if the room was off-limits to passengers, but she couldn't make it back down the stairs in the state she was in, and if she continued to stand on the platform, she was sure to be seasick. She opened the door and stepped inside the room.

By now, it was late in the evening, and the room was dark

except for a lamplight that shined on several mariners' instruments. It took a moment for her eyes to adjust to the dim light before she saw Nathan with his hands on the ship's wheel. He looked so tall and strong standing there and something stirred within her. His back was turned, and he looked out over the bow of the ship through a large window, while keeping an eye on a compass in the binnacle by the wheel.

He spoke without turning. "You feel better, Murray? I didn't expect you back this early." Murray had a cot in the wheel room and often rested there.

Hannah was silent, as she didn't know what to say. She stood very still and tried to calm her heart that beat much too fast.

When there was no answer from Murray, Nathan turned, and even in the dim light, she saw how surprised he was.

"Hannah! Is that really you, or do I have a vision and see an angel?" He seemed thrilled to see her.

"It's me, Nathan. Perhaps I . . . I shouldn't be here," she spoke slowly. Then more urgently, "I'll leave if you want me to, but first I must tell you something."

"Come tell me."

She crossed the room and handed him the cloth bag that contained the food and drink. He noticed that her hands shook.

"Jason sent you this."

"I'm glad he remembered me, but more than that, I'm glad you came." He set the bag on the table by the instruments and reached for her hand. "Hannah, your beauty takes my breath away."

She was quite frustrated and obsessed with telling him why she had come, so she blurted out all at once, "Nathan, I didn't climb those frightful stairs to talk about my beauty, but to tell you that there is no one else in my life. I know what you thought when I left you at the bow yesterday, and it's bothered me all day. When I didn't see you, I feared that you avoided me because of it. I must explain what I said."

He was relieved to know that she wasn't in love with someone else.

"No, Hannah, I wasn't avoiding you. I wanted to see you,

but I've worked since five o'clock this morning except for a short nap this afternoon." He explained why he was late for the noon meal. "I asked Jason to give you a message that I had duty at the wheel and couldn't see you this evening. Didn't he tell you?"

"Not until a few minutes ago. He said he forgot."

"I'm sorry."

"That's okay. Should I go?"

"No!"

"Will it bother you if I sit on the windowsill and talk to you?"

"Of course not; it'll be nice to have your company. It gets awfully lonesome up here. Tell me about yourself and why you were upset yesterday."

"First, let me help you with the food." She took it out of the bag and placed it in front of him and set the bottle of tea where he could reach it. She then took the pie out. "Sam really did bake me a pie and I saved you a slice of it."

"You're so special, Hannah."

"I got the pie because you're special to Sam."

"He's never baked me a pie."

Hannah laughed, then neither spoke as he ate the food. To break the quietness, she asked softly, "Am I special to you?"

"Yes . . . you are, and when I see you talk to Jeff Adams, I want to get my sword and cut out his liver to feed to the sharks."

"Nathan, that's an awful thing to say!"

"I know, and it's an awful way to feel, but does it tell you how special you are?"

"I don't want to be that special; Jeff is a nice person. I stopped him at the Sunday morning service to tell him that you had returned my book. He helped me look for it." She paused and then said softly, "He asked about us."

Nathan's eyes turned from the window to her face. "What did you tell him?"

"Well . . . that . . . ." She felt her face blush.

"That what?"

"That . . . that we care for each other."

He smiled. "You did?"

"Yes."

"Good; maybe he'll get to keep his liver."

"Nathan, don't talk like that."

"I'm sorry. I know it's no way to talk to a lady, and you know I don't mean it. I like Jeff—everybody does—but I don't like for him to talk to you. With his good looks and nice manners, I can see how any girl would fall for him."

"He's not as handsome as you are, and no one could treat me nicer than you have; besides, you found me on the dock, remember."

"Yes, I remember, and I won't mention his name again." Then muttering under his breath, "Until I catch him talking to you and then I'll get my sword and—"

"Nathan!"

"Sit down and tell me about yourself."

She settled on the windowsill with her back against the inside frame and circled her arms around her knees that were drawn in front of her. She was quiet for a moment, then said, "I don't know where to start. I suppose I should begin with my birth," her voice was sober. "That was the night my mother died."

"Oh, Hannah."

"I have no brothers or sisters," she continued. "I was the first child and Father never remarried. He said he could never love anyone else the way he did my mother.

"After giving up his job to stay at home and take care of me, he started a small business at home, making tables and other pieces of furniture. When I was just a baby, he would hitch the horse to the wagon that was loaded with his goods, and the two of us would go to the village of Midleton to sell what he had made. When I was older, he opened a shop in the village near a school, and I attended it each day, while he worked in the shop.

"I graduated from the school and attended college for a year. My education was very important to Father, because he was denied open schooling, while growing up. He received some schooling at home and, for a while, attended a hedge school that was taught in secret."

"Why didn't he go to a public school?" Nathan asked.

She hesitated before answering, "He was a Catholic and the British did not allow Catholic schools."

Nathan looked at her, and his lips parted, but his teeth came together and he said nothing.

"When my father was a young man, he went to Dublin to find work, and it was there that he met my mother. She was from County Fermanagh in the province of Ulster, but at the time, attended Trinity College in Dublin. Since Mother went there, Father sent me to Trinity, but I missed him awfully bad and knew he couldn't really afford the cost, so I came home after one year. Someday I'd like to return to college and complete my education.

"When I attended the school in Midleton, I looked forward to the ride home each evening with Father. He told me about different ones who came to the shop that day and would always ask me about my day at school. If I had a problem," she paused for a moment, "I would talk to him about it, and," her voice trembled, "he always made me feel better."

She really misses her father, Nathan thought.

"When we reached home, Father unhitched the horse and took care of him, while I fed and played with the other animals. We had a dog named Corky, after County Cork, and a cat named Sneaky. I named him Sneaky because he liked to sneak up behind me and jump on my leg."

Nathan smiled.

"He was a little, fluffy gray cat with a white streak under his neck. I miss him and Corky so much, but found a good home nearby for both of them. We kept a horse, a few sheep, and a cow and had a shed in the back for them to get under when the weather was bad. I hope to have animals again, someday, because they kept me from being lonely when growing up. Perhaps there will be some on the plantation in South Carolina.

"We lived in a stone house that had a thatched roof on a

ten-acre tract of land just east of the city of Cork. Father's
business left him little time to farm, but he planted a garden in
the spring, and I helped with its care.

"Almost every Saturday, Father went to the bog to cut turf
for our home. I usually stayed at home and cleaned, but
occasionally I went with him just for the ride. Every Sunday
morning, we returned to the village to worship with a small
congregation. Few Protestants lived in our area.

"Father was Catholic, but my mother was a Protestant. Their
parents were against the marriage, and when Father brought
Mother to Southern Ireland to live, my grandparents would have
nothing to do with her." She paused a moment before adding
sadly, "They never accepted me either.

"Since my mother's parents lived so far away, I have only
seen them twice in my life. I went to visit them, while attending
Trinity. They're wealthy and live in a very big house on a large
plantation. Grandfather and I rode over his land on fine horses,
and Grandmother was kind. She said my being there was like
having her daughter again. It was a wonderful time. I hope I'll
be able to see them again some day, but I fear that I won't, for
they are old in age. I'm thankful for the special time we had
together and shall remember it always.

"Through Mother's love and devotion, Father converted to
a Protestant and was baptized before I was born. With the help
of his friend, John Dudley, my parents were able to buy property.
Catholics were not allowed to purchase land."

Nathan now understood why her father disliked wealthy
British. He was from the mass of Irish Catholics who were of
Celtic stock or native Irish. Converted to Catholicism by St.
Patrick in the A. D. 400s, they hated being under the rule of the
British who had conquered Ireland during the Middle Ages.
But on the other hand, her mother—a Protestant—was of Anglo-
Norman stock . . . and they were the English conquerors.

"Father was good to me," said Hannah, "and we had a happy
life. His business prospered and made more than enough to
support the two of us. He bought me everything that I needed

and most things that I wanted. I wouldn't have traded his love for all the riches in the world."

She sighed and turned to face the window. "Almost three months ago, on Saturday, January 10, I left the house to take care of the animals. Father didn't feel well and had sat down in his chair to rest. When I returned and announced the birth of a new baby lamb," she paused and her speech became broken, "there was no response. My father was dead." Her head dropped forward to her knees.

"Come here, Hannah."

She stood and wiped tears from her eyes and then crossed the room to him. He circled one arm around her and pulled her close to him. Now he knew why she was alone on the dock the day she left Ireland, and he understood why she was sad.

"Why didn't you tell me about your father?"

"I wanted to, but I can't talk about him without crying, and I didn't want to do that in front of you. I'm sorry about yesterday, but it meant so much to feel your arms around me, while I was so homesick and filled with grief."

"I'm glad I saw you."

She returned to the windowsill. "The house seemed so empty, and I was so lonely," she continued, "I couldn't stay there. Father once told me that if anything happened to him, he wanted me to consider going to the United States. He said I could go to his friend, John Dudley, for help, and Mr. Dudley did help me settle my affairs. He found a buyer for our home and animals and even contacted Captain Barrington about passage across the ocean.

"With everything to do, there wasn't time to grieve, but since I've been on the ship, I've had more time to think. I became so homesick, yesterday, and missed Father so much. I thought of him when you asked if he was a wonderful man, and I loved him very much. He was the only one I had and now I feel so alone.

"The small book I dropped on the quarterdeck was the last present he gave me. I was upset when I thought I had lost it."

"Was his name Collin?"

"Yes. How did you know?"

"He wrote a message in the front of the book."

"Oh . . . yes. When I was a child, I called him Collin."

"I read the message before I went to bed the night after I picked the book up from the deck. I've been afraid that someone else is in love with you."

Someone else, she thought. Could it mean that he loved her? "No, Nathan . . . there is no one else."

"I'm glad."

"There is one other thing I should tell you." She sighed, then turned her face toward the window and was silent.

"What is it?" he cajoled. "You can tell me anything."

"Besides helping me with everything at home, Mr. Dudley told me about a plantation owner in South Carolina who needs a teacher for his children. 'The land owner,' he said, 'would pay for a teacher's voyage across the ocean if she would teach his children for five years.' I agreed to do this, so I'm indentured for that length of time."

"Did you sign papers before you left Ireland?" he quickly inquired.

"No, but I must sign them when I reach South Carolina."

Nathan knew that to be indentured meant you owed someone a debt, and you belonged to that person until the debt was paid. One had no more rights than a slave during the time that was agreed upon. This had worked out all right for some people, but he'd heard of cruel treatment to others. He didn't think that Hannah realized what she could be getting herself into, but he said nothing of it. Instead, he seemed to disregard it by saying, "Don't think of it right now."

"I've told you everything about myself, and I know nothing about you."

"It's almost time for someone to relieve me. May I wait until later?"

"Yes . . . of course." She turned back to the window and looked up at the stars. Would he have nothing to do with her now that he knew she was indentured?

Nathan feared what she thought, but after she had just revealed to him why her father felt the way he did and of her humble life and that she was indentured, how could he tell her who he was? He couldn't . . . not tonight.

"Hannah, come stand beside me."

She felt awkward and no longer knew what to say. "I must go," she muttered, and rose from the windowsill. But as she walked by him, he stepped from the wheel and locked his fingers with hers and then stepped back to the wheel.

"Please wait for me. I don't want you to go out into the darkness alone. You might fall down the steps."

"I climbed the steps alone."

"It wasn't dark then."

"I'm not afraid of the darkness."

"I know, but please don't leave me. Murray will be here soon." He lifted her hand to his lips.

"All right, I'll wait."

Nathan wanted to tell her about himself, she had told him everything, but what could he say without telling her who he was? They stood silently, looking out over the bow of the ship until Murray came.

He held her hand as they descended the steps and crossed the deck. Neither spoke until they stood by the rail outside her cabin. A bright moon gave light to the ship, the wind was still, and the water was calm.

He put his arms around her and pulled her close to him. "Hannah," he spoke softly, "nothing you could ever tell me would change the way I feel about you." He kissed her forehead and brushed his lips over her closed eyes, but when he tried to touch them to hers, she leaned her head forward. He lifted her face gently, and as his fingers entwined her hair, he kissed her forehead and cheeks, but again, she turned her lips from him.

"Why, Hannah? If you're not in love with someone else, why won't you give me your lips?"

"Oh, Nathan, I think you're wonderful, but both of us know

that things could never work out for us. If you kiss me . . . how can I ever forget you?"

"I love you, Hannah. I don't want you to forget me. I want you to love me."

"I do love you."

She didn't turn away again, and when their lips met, he kissed her with all the desire that had built up in him since he first saw her standing on the dock.

"Oh, Hannah," he breathed hard, "I've searched so long for someone like you. I won't let five years scare me off. Trust me to work things out."

He kissed her again. She held her arms around him and pressed her fingers into his back.

"Darling," he whispered, "you're not alone anymore."

CHAPTER 4

Right after breakfast the next morning, Hannah walked toward Captain Barrington's office. She wanted to find out if he knew anything about the plantation owner whom she would work for in South Carolina. She knocked lightly on his office door and heard him say, "Come in."

She pulled the heavy door open and stepped inside . . . to be very surprised. The captain was seated behind a desk that faced her, and Nathan sat on one corner of it with his back turned. He held papers in his hand that had her name stamped across the back of them in bold letters. More confusing to her was that he wore an officer's uniform, similar to the one the captain wore each day. She began to stammer; nothing she said made sense, so she backed through the door, muttering, "I'll come back when you're not busy."

When Nathan heard her voice, he jumped from the captain's desk. "Hannah," he called, but she was already out the door and it shut in front of her. She stood outside the doorway, trying to determine what went on. Nathan jerked the door open and asked, "What did you need?"

There was a bewildered expression on her face. "I . . . I came to talk to the . . ." She paused, and then, "Why were you talking to Captain Barrington about me?"

"I'm trying to help you. Please trust me."

She raised her hand to her heart. "When I told you everything about myself, I wasn't asking for your help. Did you think that I was? And did you tell the captain everything that I told you?"

"No, Hannah; I wouldn't do that. And I know you didn't ask for my help."

"Then why did you talk to the captain about me? And why do you have on an officer's uniform?"

"I'm the first mate. I need to wear my uniform sometimes to remind myself and the crew."

"Why didn't you tell me?"

"Because, right now, it doesn't mean anything. Usually, the first mate receives orders from the captain and relates them to the men to be carried out. I told you that we sailed short of a full crew. There's more to do than the men can take care of, so I help with the work.

"I talked to the captain about the fare for your passage on board the *Monarch*. He told me he received a letter from the lawyer, John Dudley, and that Dudley asked him to collect payment from Garrett Rey of Reybrook Plantation, near Charleston, South Carolina. You didn't sign a contract. So far as Rey knows, you're not even on this ship."

"The plantation owner is my only contact in the United States. If I don't have that, I won't have a job or a place to stay when I get there. Why do you want to take that from me?"

He took her hand and led her to the side of the captain's office. When under the stairs, away from all eyes on the ship, he put his arms around her and kissed her lightly. "Because," he answered, "I don't want you to belong to any man except me and only then of your own free will. I've heard of indentured servants receiving harsh treatment. I won't let that happen to you. I love you, Hannah, and I couldn't sleep last night after you told me you were indentured. That's why I came to the captain first thing this morning. He said you didn't have to pay for your passage. If you work for Mr. Rey, he'll have to pay you."

"I can't ask the captain to do that! I won't! I made a bargain with him and I must keep it!"

"That's why I asked him for you. He did it for me."

"But Nathan . . ." She was very uncertain about it.

"It's okay, Hannah. I also did it for another reason . . . a selfish one."

"What do you mean?"

"I don't want to wait five years to marry you. I know it's too soon for you to think about it, but I've thought of it, and before the *Monarch* drops anchor, I'm going to ask you to marry me, when I get back from the war. I hope it'll be over within a year."

"Oh, Nathan."

He touched his lips to hers, but just as he really began to taste them, she broke away from him abruptly and looked up into his face with wide eyes. "Since the *Monarch* has such a small crew," she said, "perhaps I can work to pay my way. I can't climb high in the sky, but there must be something I can do. If I don't stay busy, my days will become monotonous."

"No-o-o," he answered, and shook his head.

"But there must be something," she insisted. "You said that there is more work to be done than the crew can do."

"Hannah, stop worrying and let me take care of you."

"No! I can't do that, but I do have the money from the sale of my home in Ireland. I had hoped to keep it, in case I need it when I get to America, but if there is nothing I can do on the ship . . . Well, I must pay my way or work as an indentured servant."

"You don't have to do either; the fare has been cancelled."

"I won't let the captain do that."

"Why not?"

"My father said that when you have an agreement with someone, you should do everything possible to fulfill your part of the bargain. I don't mean to be contrary, but I must do what is right."

He gazed into her eyes until a sentimental smile spread over his face. "You put a lot of stock in what your father said, don't you?"

"Yes." Her voice was calm, but there was a resolute look on her face, and he realized she would not give in to him. It made him admire her even more.

"All right, Hannah. There are some jobs you can do. It will be a great help if you can take care of some of them. They're easy but time consuming. There are so many jobs that are too important to take men off of, and I hate to ask them to work on Sunday."

"May I start today?"

He laughed and nodded his head.

He showed her how to do some of the more pressing jobs that included running a spun-yarn winch and making rope-yarns. When the orientation was over, he dragged a large pile of old rigging to her outside door. "After repairing it," he said, "coil it up, and put it into the crate on the gun deck. We use it for chafing-gear and netting."

She caught on easily to the work and agreed she only needed time to complete it. The rope was threaded through her fingers until she recognized a weak spot. It was repaired as Nathan had showed her, then placed on a stack to be coiled up later.

She sat flat on the deck, but wished for a small stool or chair on which to sit; however, there was nothing in her room that would accommodate her need.

Near the middle of the morning, the Hartmans' door opened and Rachel brought her children outside. They circled around Hannah to see what she did.

"I'm helping the crew," she said, "for there is more work to be done than they can do."

"May we help?" Mary asked.

"If you'd like to. You may straighten and coil the pieces of rope that I've repaired."

Steven and Mary began at once to untangle the long pieces of rope. Each took an end of a segment, and they walked in opposite directions until it was stretched tight. They removed all the knots and coiled it up, and when a large stack had been repaired, they helped Hannah take it to the gun deck.

Jenny was too little to be of much help, but she brought Hannah her small stool to sit on. It was much more comfortable than the hard deck, and she could now see over the pile of rigging.

As Steven and Mary worked by her side, Jenny sat at Hannah's feet, and she told them a story about a man who had sailed the ocean in 1492. While she threaded the ropes through her fingers, she told about Christopher Columbus and how his discovery made it possible for them to go to America. Unaware that it was a lesson in history, the children found the story exciting.

Nathan worked in the captain's office after he left Hannah with the old rigging. He recorded information in the ship's log and then tackled the mountain of paper work on his desk. Later, he checked the crate where he'd told her to put the repaired rigging and could hardly believe how much work had been completed. He examined some of the ropes and saw that Hannah did an excellent job; no seaman could have done better.

By the end of the second week, Hannah had completed many of the jobs that Nathan was concerned about, but her muscles ached at night, and she lost more weight. The constant heeling of the *Monarch* kept her from getting hungry, and with being so busy, she often forgot to go for meals.

While she worked, she told the Hartman children more stories of famous people and of far away places. She taught Jenny how to count and to say the ABC's as her older siblings could. It gave her pleasure to share her knowledge with the children, and John and Rachel seemed grateful.

Mary grew tired of helping, but Steven worked such long hours that Hannah became concerned he worked too much for a boy his age.

"Oh, no," Rachel laughed when Hannah expressed her concern. "He likes to help you, and working has helped his self-confidence, but John and I worry that he bothers you."

"Not at all," Hannah assured her. "Steven is a great helper. He goes for things I need, he hands me things I can't reach, and when I finish, he helps me put the work away. I'm able to do much more when he's with me. I appreciate his help."

"I'm glad to hear that, Hannah, for he needs something to do. The girls entertain themselves in the cabin. They play with their dolls and with each other, but Steven is used to playing outdoors, and it's hard for him to stay cooped up in this small cabin all day. As long as I know he's with you, I don't worry. John thinks the experience will give him an opportunity to decide if he wants to be a seaman, someday."

Steven continued to spend time with Hannah. He wanted to learn about a seaman's life and of his daily tasks. As Nathan climbed the ladder to the crow's nest, one morning, he stretched his neck back and watched him climb all the way to the top.

"Would you like to do that," Hannah asked.

"Yes."

"Perhaps you can before we reach America."

A warm friendship developed between them. She told him about Ireland and of its rocky green hills and old castles and many rivers and bays. She talked about Corky and Sneaky and about going to school in the village and how she wanted to be a teacher.

"You are a teacher; you teach my sisters and me, and you make it easy to learn. I won't ever forget the people and places of which you have taught us."

"I'm glad, but I believe you learn because you have a desire to learn. You listen."

"I listen because you make it interesting."

"I suppose that would make a difference. I hope all my students will find my teaching as interesting as you have."

"I went to a large school in Liverpool," he said, "but it didn't have enough teachers. I hope schools in North Carolina have plenty of teachers."

"I'm sure they will," Hannah assured him.

She realized reading was difficult for him when he tried to read some of the words written on the side of a crate. "Steven," she asked, "would you like to learn to read better?"

"Yes, ma'am. I wish I could read everything."

"I'll see what I have in my trunk that will help."

After the evening meal that day, she returned to her cabin and opened her trunk. She found a chart that had all the letters of the alphabet and took it with her the next morning along with a book that was easy to read.

As the two of them worked, they talked about each letter and its sound and then thought of words that began with the same letter. Later, Steven sat beside her and read from the book. When he came to a word he didn't know, she pronounced it for him and explained its meaning. That night, he took the book to their cabin and read to Rachel.

———————

Up until now, the *Monarch's* crew paid little attention to Hannah except to notice how pretty she was with her long dark-red hair and fair complexion. Her smile could warm any heart, but she was shy and usually didn't speak unless spoken to first, and most seamen wouldn't speak to a passenger unless the passenger spoke to them.

With all the work that Hannah did, they began to think of her as one of the crew and not only spoke, but if time permitted, stopped to talk. They joked with Steven and he loved the attention.

Through a conversation with each, Hannah found that the three older and more experienced seamen on the *Monarch* had families in England. George Thomas had two children, age five and eight, and only made one or two voyages a year. He owned a small business in Liverpool, but needed the extra money he received from the voyages. Robert Moore, the ship's navigator, had four children and had worked for the captain almost ten years. Murray Mills, the oldest man of the crew, had worked for the Barringtons twenty-two years. Besides being an excellent pilot, he could do every job on the ship. Murray was a large burly man who had a kind heart, and Hannah felt comfortable talking to him.

"I quit once," he said, "because my wife was ill. She needed me at home to take care of our three daughters, but when she died and the girls got married, I got lonely, so I asked the captain for my old job back. He said 'yes' and seemed pleased when I returned to work."

"I'm sorry about your wife," said Hannah. "I know how lonely one can get if they live alone."

"You do?" Murray was surprised.

"Yes. I only had my father when growing up." She hushed, and Murray saw a tear trickle down her cheek. He took a handkerchief from his pocket and handed it to her.

"Did your father die?"

She nodded her head and took his handkerchief.

"I'm so sorry, Hannah."

"Thank you, Murray." She wiped the tears from her cheeks and then folded the handkerchief before handing it back to him.

The youngest member of the crew talked about home. Scott Hogan was homesick.

"Where are you from, Scott?" Hannah asked.

"A village near Liverpool. I sure miss my mom and dad and all my brothers and sisters."

"How many brothers and sisters?"

"Three brothers and two sisters. They're all older than me except one sister. Her name is Elizabeth, but we call her Beth. We were close when growing up, so I miss her the most."

"Why did you leave?" She feared she asked too many questions, but he didn't seem to mind, because he wanted to talk about home.

"I needed a job, and there was nothing to do in the village. I knew that merchant ships were always in need of hands, so I went to the waterfront and began to ask around. Someone told me to see Captain Barrington of the Barrington Shipping Company. I went to talk to him and liked him right off, so when he offered me a job, I took it. He's been more than fair to me, and I like working for his son."

"His son?" Hannah asked, without looking up. "I didn't know the captain had a son."

When Scott didn't answer, she looked up and saw a strange expression on his face. "You mean," he said, "you don't know that . . ." He stopped suddenly. "I've got to go, Hannah."

"Scott!" she called, but he left in a hurry. She wondered what came over him.

Stuart Anderson was a tall, thin boy. He was shy and found it difficult to talk to most people, but not to Hannah.

"I'm glad you talk to me, Stuart. I enjoy your company. Is there someone special you'd like to tell me about?"

"Yes, but I don't know if she'll wait for me."

"I'm sure she will. She could never find anyone nicer than you."

"Thank you, Hannah, but I'm not so sure. If she does wait for me, I'll ask her to marry me when I get back."

"I hope everything works out the way you want it to."

The seamen accepted Hannah as another crewmember. She did the jobs they didn't like to do and kept them from having to work on Sundays. She even offered to do small favors for them when she saw a need, such as a missing button or a torn place in their clothes. They trusted her and began to ask her advice on certain matters; she had gained their respect.

Mark Monroe and Jeff Adams were older than Scott and Stuart, and their company made Hannah a bit uneasy. She knew how it made Nathan feel for her to talk to Jeff, and she didn't want to upset him or cause trouble between the two. Jeff understood and had little to say to her, but Mark deliberately tried to make the situation worse. He stopped to talk often and stood too close and talked too loud. He noticed her uneasiness one morning, and asked, "What's the matter? Is Nathan coming?"

"Mark, will you please go?"

"Why? I'm not afraid of Nathan."

"You'll wish you had been," she retorted calmly, "when he cuts out your liver with his sword and feeds it to the sharks!"

"HANNAH, I can't believe you said that!"

Neither can I, she chuckled silently.

"I'm sorry, but I care for Nathan and don't want to upset him."

"All right, I'll leave. I want to keep my job . . . and my liver," he shuddered.

Hannah took a burden from Nathan's mind when she completed some of the work that had not been done. He found more for her to do, and she did it willingly.

The captain was pleased with her work, but Nathan was not pleased when he didn't see her very often. They missed each other at mealtime, and in the evening, she went to bed early in order to rise early the next morning. Determined, one day, to have the noon meal with her, Nathan looked for and found her in the mess hall, eating with the crew. He laughed as she seemed to be quite comfortable seated beside Murray.

That night he sat alone in the captain's office, recording information in the ship's log. He laid his pencil down a moment and rubbed his eyes as they felt strained after the long hours of close work under the oil lamp. He thought of Hannah and wanted to see her, but knew it was late, and he figured she had gone to bed long before now. He certainly would not disturb her. When his own eyes closed and he felt his head nod, he decided it was useless to try to do anything more, so he straightened the papers on the desk and left the office.

Jason patrolled the larboard on the late watch, and Nathan crossed the deck to talk.

"Do you see anything out there?" he asked.

"Only water."

"That's better than pirates or Frenchmen. I hope you don't see any of them. We don't have enough men to fight either, but I wouldn't give up the *Monarch* without a battle."

"I wouldn't want you to," answered Jason.

They leaned over the guardrail with their arms crossed on top of it, oblivious to familiar sounds around them. Another seaman paced back and forth on the starboard; the noise made by his boots on the wooden deck was escalated in the quietness. A night breeze rustled the *Monarch's* sails, and waves splashed against her hull. From toward the bow came the voices of a small group of off-duty seamen; occasionally one of them laughed.

Finally, Jason spoke again. "How is everything with you and Hannah?" he asked.

"I don't see her as much as I'd like to, now that she's working. I told her I was going to ask her to marry me, but I didn't intend to."

"Awe man! You don't ask a girl to marry you when you don't intend to marry her."

"Oh, I intend to marry her, but I hadn't intended to ask her."

"You don't know women very well!"

"Why do you say that?"

"She's not going to marry you unless you ask her to."

"JASON, I'm going to ask her, but I hadn't intended to ask her this soon." He explained that Hannah was indentured and how he'd talked to the captain about it. "First of all," he said, "I wanted to make sure she wasn't mistreated, but then I don't want to wait five years to marry her."

"Did you tell her your name?"

Nathan paused before answering, "No."

"Awe man! You asked Hannah to marry you, and she doesn't even know your name or who you are."

"I'll tell her, Jason! I will! I just said that I would ask her to marry me before we dropped anchor."

"And I suppose when the preacher asks, 'Do you, Hannah Thornton, take this man, Nathan Lee, to be your husband?' you'll have to say, 'Oh . . . uh . . . wait a minute preacher, make that name Nathan—'"

"Jason, will you cut it out?"

"Well, you need to tell Hannah who you are and accept the consequences. Maybe you shouldn't be in such a hurry to marry her."

"I **am** going to marry her if I get back from the war all right and she'll wait for me."

"What about the girls in Liverpool? You could marry any one of them . . . especially Gloria."

"What's that suppose to mean?"

"She's in love with you and waits for you."

"Who told you that?"

"Nobody. I just know."

Gloria Hesley was a girl that Nathan and Jason had known most of their lives. Her dad, Richard Hesley, owned factories in several major cities in England and shipped his goods to countries all over the world on Barrington ships. He was a shrewd and powerful businessman, but a faithful customer of the Barrington Shipping Company.

Gloria was a beautiful girl, and some people who did not know her well thought she had a pleasant personality, but Nathan remembered her as a selfish and vain person who was constantly scheming against those who did not go along with everything she wanted. She had inherited her father's arrogance instead of the humbleness of her mother who was a beloved friend of Martha Barrington.

He'd never had any special feelings for Gloria, but had escorted her to balls because her mother's friend had asked him to. He was shocked when Jason said that she was in love with him.

"That's absurd! I didn't make any commitment to Gloria. I certainly didn't ask her to wait for me. I've never been in love with her, and I don't believe she loves me. She could have most any man in Liverpool, so I can hardly believe she's waiting for me."

"When the two of you are in the same room, anyone can see that she's in love with you. Just in case things don't work out between you and Hannah . . . well . . . have you told her about Gloria?"

"NO! Why should I? I've never had any feelings for Gloria, so why upset Hannah about it? I won't have anything to do with her whether things work out between Hannah and me, or not."

"I'm telling you," Jason warned, "you'll find out about her feelings for you when you get home; just wait and see. You better think of what you're going to say to her."

Nathan didn't answer; he wished to end the conversation. He didn't intend to say anything to Gloria when he returned home or to go to the ballrooms where girls were dressed in gawky evening gowns, expecting to be escorted here and there. He'd never cared for it in the first place and had never met anyone he wanted to share his life with—until now.

He left Jason and was headed toward his cabin when he noticed a light in Hannah's window. It was late, but her lamp was turned up. Was she sick or having a bad night? He went to her outside door and knocked lightly. "Hannah . . . it's Nathan. Are you all right?" he asked in a low voice.

Her door opened, and she stood in the light with a white silk robe on that had tiny rosebuds down its lapel. Her hair fell over the front of her shoulders and curled up at its ends against the white robe. His heart began to race. No girl—certainly not Gloria—had ever made him feel this way.

"Yes, I'm all right," she said, "now that you're here."

She closed the door behind her and stepped out into the moonlight and into his arms. He felt her heart beating against his as he covered her lips with his own. A deep groan escaped her throat as they embraced each other. Neither wanted to let go.

"Darling," he whispered, "I've missed you so much. You're all I can think about, and I want to be with you every minute." He thought of Hannah's kindness and meekness compared to Gloria's selfishness and arrogance. "I love you, Gloria . . . Hannah. Hannah, I love you." He quickly repeated his words, then bit his lip and thought he would die, for in comparing Hannah to Gloria, he had accidentally called her Gloria. He tightened his arms around her for fear she would pull away from him.

Instead, she responded, "I love you, too, Nathan, and I want to be with you. I couldn't sleep tonight because I wanted to see you and to hear your voice. I feel protected and wonderful in your arms, and I'm so glad you came by."

Nathan buried his face in her hair and tried to shut out the voice of his friend that said, "You need to tell her who you are and accept the consequences."

"Hannah," he finally said, "I must tell you something."

"Not tonight, Nathan. Just hold me. It's late and I must go back in. We both have to get up so early."

"I want you to sleep late in the morning. You work too many hours, so take the day off tomorrow. I'll have someone bring breakfast to your room about nine o'clock. I'm concerned about all the weight you've lost. Don't argue with me."

"Aye, aye, Sir! You're the first mate! I agree that I don't need to skip meals, but I never get hungry, and if I force myself to eat, it makes me sick. I can eat only a little at a time."

When they parted, Nathan walked to his cabin. He was happy because Hannah loved him, but he was concerned about her inability to eat and her weight loss. And another fear escalated within him. Would Hannah love him no matter what, or had her father instilled a conviction in her that his love could not break?

Hannah went back to bed, but could not sleep. She had pretended not to hear when Nathan accidentally called her Gloria after saying, "I love you." He had wanted to talk about her, she thought, but she had desperately wanted him to hold her instead of talking about a girl from his past.

She didn't awake the next morning until someone knocked on her door. It was Lizzy with her breakfast, and Hannah insisted that she come in for a visit. "I hate to eat alone," she said.

Hannah ate at the table, while Lizzy sat on the side of the bed. She leaned backward with her arms behind her to give support to her large stomach. She appeared to be quite miserable. Hannah wished she could make her more comfortable.

"I'm glad to see you take a day off," Lizzy said. "You work too hard and you've lost too much weight. I wish I could give you some of mine." She laughed softly as she lifted one hand and rubbed her stomach carefully. "I've gained too much and should exercise more, but I'm afraid to walk on the deck for fear of falling. Michael didn't want me to make the trip now, but after Captain Barrington got him the job, and with our fear of a French invasion, we decided to come. Nathan made him feel better about it." Then to Hannah's surprise, Lizzy began to cry.

"This is our second child," she said. "We lost our first at birth. It was a boy and looked so much like Michael. If something happens to this baby . . . well, I don't know how we can stand it. We're very concerned about it."

Hannah laid down her fork and went to the side of the bed. She sat down beside Lizzy and put her arm around her. "You have reason to be worried," she said, "but I'm sure everything will be all right. Let's ask God to be with you." They bowed their heads and Hannah prayed, asking God to take care of Lizzy and her baby.

Lizzy felt better after Hannah prayed. She stayed a few minutes longer and then started to leave, but hesitated at the door. "Hannah," she said, "Nathan loves you so much."

"I love him too, Lizzy."

"I hope you can find it in your heart to always love him." She then left quickly, and Hannah wondered why she had said such a strange thing.

After Lizzy left, she dressed and departed her room for the deck. It was good to have leisure time; she walked slowly toward the bow with one hand on the guardrail. A thick haze covered the sky, and toward the west, dark clouds set heavy on the horizon.

She was surprised when a small piece of paper floated down from the sky. She tried to catch it, but the wind blew it out to sea. She looked up to see another one, but it too was blown away. She knew that someone had dropped the papers from aloft, and when another piece floated down, she managed to catch it. It was from a note pad that Nathan carried. A message on it read, "Hannah, I love you. Nathan." With the paper in her hand, she raised her arm high and waved to him and then folded the note and put it inside her pocket.

The swells were high that morning and hit the *Monarch* hard. She tilted far to one side and then the other, making it hard to walk on her deck. A sudden chill in the wind that swept across her bow caused Hannah to turn back to her cabin. She saw Nathan descending from among the sails and let go of the guardrail to cross the deck to him. She stumbled and fell just as she reached him. He caught her with his hands under her arms and attempted to swing her around in the air, but a forceful wave hit the *Monarch*. They both tumbled to the deck. Hannah laughed out loud as she tried to get up. It was a deep, wonderful laugh, and Nathan was thrilled to hear it; he'd never heard her laugh like that. Could his love help her get over her sadness and be happy again? He dared to hope so.

The wind gained strength, and Nathan felt sure they were in for rough weather. He'd watched the dark clouds roll in from the west and feared a storm would hit before noon. Even now the *Monarch* pitched hard, and her bow rose high above the water before it fell suddenly forward.

He helped Hannah across the deck and stood at her door, holding both her hands for a moment. He wished for a day, free of responsibilities, to spend with her, but it was no time to think of that. "You'll probably get seasick again," he warned. "Go to the galley and ask Sam to make a large container of gingerroot tea. You won't be the only one who will need it. As soon as it's made, drink some, and hopefully, it will ward off any sickness."

"It sounds like you're predicting a formidable storm."

"I never know how bad it will be, but we prepare for the worst and hope it doesn't come. I wish I could stay here with you, but I can't."

"I'll be all right, but I do wish I had a bit of earth from St. Kieran's grave."

"You wish what?"

"That I had a bit of dirt from St. Kieran's grave. It's supposed to bring tranquility to a storm at sea."

"Well, I wish you had some, too." He laughed and then muttered, "You Irish with your legends and folklore."

"Don't come outside," he said, "or open this outside door for anything. When you return from the galley, stay in your room—and pray."

"I will, Nathan, but I fear for you. Please be careful and let me hear from you as soon as you can."

"I promise to." He gave her hands a slight squeeze and left.

Hannah heard the voice of the captain. **"All hands on deck!**

All hands on deck! Prepare for approaching storm. Commence to take in sails."

Hannah ran down the hallway to the galley with one hand against the wall to keep from falling. Sam had already made gingerroot tea, but had trouble pouring it into containers.

"Let me help, Sam."

"Thanks, Hannah. I can use two extra hands."

He held a jar and Hannah filled it with the hot liquid. A lid was fastened on its top, then Sam wrapped it in a towel and gave it to her to deliver. She took the jar to the Butler's cabin and returned to the galley for another. Going to and fro, she made her way down one side of the hall and back up the other until all the passengers had a jar of the tea.

By now, she was very dizzy and fell against the wall as she entered the galley for her own tea. With her head leaned forward, she eased down to the floor. The intense heeling of the *Monarch* made her terribly sick, but she lifted her head and saw that Sam stood over her with a jar of the tea. He knelt beside her and lifted the warm liquid to her lips. She sipped it slowly.

As soon as Hannah was able to stand, Sam helped her to her cabin. She fell across the bed with her face in the pillow. The scriptures of when Jesus calmed the storm at sea came to her mind; she prayed He would calm this one. Within the hour, its full impact hit with a great gust of wind and a deluge of rain and hail.

The crew worked frantically to bring down the hoisted sails. Nathan tied down the square sail of the mainmast when the storm hit. It was all he could do to hold on against the force of the wind. He was concerned for everyone's safety, but confident that the *Monarch* would hold together. He knew her strength; she was built to weather the storms.

The storm raged for hours, but had become somewhat subdued when someone knocked loudly on Hannah's door. When she heard the panicky voice of Michael Sutterfield, a surge of fear went through her. There was only one reason why he would be at her door. She struggled to get up; everything seemed to spin around. When she finally managed to open the door, Michael stumbled in and almost fell to the floor.

"Hannah," he gasped, "the storm has scared Lizzy so badly, it brought on her labor. Will you stay with her, while I go for help?"

Where could he go for help? There was no doctor aboard. She gulped down the last of the gingerroot tea and made her way across the hall to the Sutterfields' cabin where Lizzy's condition made her forget her own sickness.

Lizzy was in dire pain. Michael took her hand, and she gripped it tightly and clenched her teeth to keep from crying out. Perspiration covered her face; her hair was damp and limp. Hannah lifted one corner of the bed sheet and gently blotted her face. She opened her eyes and whispered, "Thanks for coming."

"Yes, Lizzy; I'll stay as long as you need me."

After a moment, her pain subsided and she appeared to have dozed.

Michael turned to Hannah. "I've got to get Nathan," he declared.

Lizzy heard and held a firm grip on his hand. She begged him not to leave.

"I must go for help," he insisted. "Hannah will be here with you."

"No! Wait until the storm is over! I'll be all right."

But she soon shrieked with pain again. Michael was torn between staying with her and going for help.

"I'll go for Nathan," Hannah volunteered, although she didn't understand why. What could he do?

"No, Hannah! I won't let you go out in this storm! If something happened to you, Nathan would never forgive me."

"The baby will need a father, Michael. If something happened to you, I would never forgive myself. I know what it's like to grow up with only one parent." She wouldn't say it, but thought that if Lizzy died as her own mother did during childbirth, and Michael was killed in the storm, the baby would have neither parent. With no other words, she ran from the room, into the hallway.

The wind and rain struck her face when she opened the door to the outside. Although the hail no longer fell, and the wind had lost some of its stamina, the rain seemed to fall in solid sheets. She couldn't see anything until her eyes discerned the mast in the middle of the ship. She decided to try for that point and go from there. The cold wind almost took her breath away as she dashed from the doorway, but she staggered along until she reached the mast and flung both arms around it. The rain poured down upon her so hard that she realized she couldn't go on and that she couldn't go back. Her only hope was for someone to rescue her, but how long could she hold on? As her arms began to ache, a terrifying thought went through her mind. What if there was no one to rescue her? What if every man of the crew had been taken by the furious sea?

When the crew had done all they could do to secure the *Monarch,* most of them took refuge in the captain's office, but Nathan had climbed the steps to the helm to take the wheel from Murray, whose strength was depleted after battling the wind so long. Murray stumbled to his cot. He'd managed to keep the ship from capsizing, but had no idea where they were. It was impossible to hold a ship on course in such a storm.

After he'd rested awhile, Murray sat up and noticed something odd through the back window. He stood to get a closer look. "Nathan," he yelled, "there's someone on the deck! It must be one of the passengers!"

He took the wheel again as Nathan hurried to the back window and looked down. His heart leaped. "It's Hannah!" he cried, and ran toward the door.

He managed to get to her quickly and lifted her arms from around the mast. With his arms around her waist, he dragged her across the deck and inside the hallway. As he shut the door, she fell to the floor, retching and gagging.

Nathan dropped to his knees and pushed against her lungs

to force the water up. When she coughed, he turned her to one side and then repeated the procedure until she held up her hand to say that it was enough. He pulled her to a sitting position and sank to the floor beside her with his back against the wall and his hands on his knees. He breathed hard. Hannah could tell by the expression on his face that he was upset, but she was too exhausted to speak.

"What were you doing out there? I told you to stay in your room with the door shut!" He lashed out at her in an angry voice.

Before she could answer, they heard Lizzy cry out and both jumped to their feet. Hannah grasped the front of his dripping shirt. "It's Lizzy!" she cried. "She's having her baby!"

Nathan's head dropped forward. He groaned, "Not tonight, Lizzy . . . not tonight."

"Nathan, who's going to deliver her baby?" Hannah inquired frantically.

He saw she was near hysterical and gently laid his hands on her shoulders. "I am," he said.

"You!" She took a step backward and looked him in the face. "What do you know about delivering babies? Are you a doctor?"

"No, but when I attended navigational school, a medical school close by held classes on medical emergencies that could happen on a ship at sea. I took all of them, and one class was on delivering babies. I told Michael this before we left England; it helped him decide to come now, while a job waits for him." He then muttered under his breath, "I didn't really think I would have to; we were supposed to reach America before the baby came."

Lizzy cried out again. Nathan stood straight; he knew what to do and his leadership surfaced. "Listen, Hannah, I'm going to my cabin and change to dry clothes. I'll get my bag and be back in five minutes. After you change, go to the Hartmans' cabin to keep their children; Rachel and John will assist me. They know more about birthing babies than anyone on the ship."

Hannah gripped the front of his shirt. "Nathan, my mother died giving birth to me!"

"I know, sweetheart."

"Don't let Lizzy die!"

He took her hands and gently pulled them from his shirt. "I'll do everything I can," he replied, "but only God controls life and death. You know that. Now do as I said and ask Him to spare Lizzy's life."

"I will," was her feeble reply.

"Hey, she'll be okay," Nathan consoled. "I love you." His lips brushed her forehead.

She managed a weak smile and then opened the door to her room. By the time she reached the Hartmans' cabin, John and Rachel were ready to go. They had heard Lizzy's cries and Nathan knocked on their door as he went by.

Hannah sat on the bed with the children gathered around her. The wind still howled over the *Monarch*, and the rain poured, but the worst of the storm had passed. She felt warm and cozy in the cabin with Steven, Mary, and Jenny.

She knew they had not eaten; no one had during the storm. "We'll go to the galley," she said cheerfully, "and see what we can find. You will not go to bed hungry."

Sam was in the galley, preparing a late meal. He served Hannah and the children, and they took their food to a table in the dining hall. Just as they sat down, some of the men came to eat. Jason was among them. He came to their table, and Hannah inquired of him about the welfare of the crew.

"Every man has been accounted for," he informed her. "The captain made sure of that."

He pulled a chair up and began to help Mary with her potato, while Hannah helped Jenny. He'd heard about Lizzy having her baby and joked about her doctor.

After they finished eating, Hannah took the children back to their cabin and helped them get ready for bed. Steven was embarrassed and took his nightclothes to the water closet, but Jenny and Mary were pleased to have Hannah help them. As she buttoned Jenny's gown in the front, Jenny looked up at her and said, "I love you, Miss Hannah."

"I love you too, Jenny, and I love Mary." She gave both a hug.

When Steven returned, they all sat down on the same bed, and Hannah let them talk to her, one at a time. They each had stories they wanted to tell, and she listened to each one. They told her how scared they were during the storm and about their lives before they left England. They were sad about leaving family and friends, but were excited about going to the United States. "We're going to stay with Uncle Steven," said Mary. "He's daddy's brother and Steven is named after him. We'll stay with him in Wilmington, North Carolina until we can find a place of our own."

Hannah smiled when Jenny said suddenly, "Miss Hannah, Daddy said that Mr. Nathan loves you and wants to marry you."

"What else did your daddy say?"

"That Mr. Nathan should tell you who he is, so you won't be mad at him."

Hannah's eyes blinked as she leaned closer to Jenny. "What did he say?"

"That—"

"Shhh, Jenny," Steven interrupted her. "You're not supposed to tell everything."

"Oh," answered Jenny and yawned real big. She lay back with her eyes closed, and Hannah noticed that Mary was already asleep. Steven went to his own bed and pulled the cover over him.

"Good night, Steven."

"Good night, Hannah. Thanks for staying with us."

"You're welcome."

She tucked Mary and Jenny under the cover and then sat down at the foot of their bed and repeated Jenny's words to herself. "Mr. Nathan should tell you who he is, so you won't be mad at him." What did John Hartman mean? Did Nathan keep something from her, and was it why he refused to tell her anything about himself? She remembered Lizzy's words, "I hope you can find it in your heart to always love him." She did love

Nathan and knew how unbearable the voyage would have been without him. She felt sure he loved her, for he had done so much for her and, even tonight, had saved her life when he pulled her from the mast and helped her back inside. He was kind and considerate of others and a God-fearing person; they were all qualities of the man she had dreamed of marrying. But was Nathan not the Nathan Lee that he said he was? Was he not just a common seaman who, with all his goodness and hard work, had attained the rank of first mate?"

She curled up at the foot of the bed. Her body was tired, so she prayed for Lizzy and the baby and then tried to shut out all the jumbled thoughts in her mind. The next thing she knew, it was daylight outside, and the Hartmans had returned from the Sutterfields' cabin. Hannah jumped up; she couldn't wait to hear from Lizzy.

"It's a beautiful boy," said Rachel, "and he and his mother are fine." Her voice revealed her extreme tiredness. "No doctor anywhere could have done better than Nathan, and he gave God the glory for the miracle of childbirth. Hannah, he talked about you during the night; it's plain to see that he loves you."

She remembered Jenny's words and wanted to ask, "Well, who is this Nathan that loves me?" But she held her tongue. She wouldn't take her frustration out on the Hartmans; besides, the timing would be bad. Instead she said, "I'm thankful that all went well."

John and Rachel expressed their appreciation to her for taking care of their children.

"It was my pleasure. I'm glad you were able to assist Nathan."

She left by their outside door, but instead of going to her cabin, she circled her hands around a guardrail post and bowed her head against it. As streaks of sunlight brightened the eastern sky, she thanked God for everyone's safety after the storm and for His care of Lizzy and the baby. To end her prayer, she added, "And thank you, God, for Nathan, whomever he is. Amen."

She was reminded of another night when a baby was born, and there had not been a happy ending. She'd never really realized how awful that night was for her father until tonight. As much as she missed him, it gave her comfort to know that he and her mother were together again. She heard footsteps behind her and turned to see Nathan.

"What are you doing out here?" he asked. "I thought when the Hartmans left, you would come to see the baby. I waited there for you."

"I'm sorry; I didn't think Lizzy would want company so soon. I came here because I needed to talk to someone."

"Who?"

"God. I thanked Him for everyone's safety and for His care of Lizzy and the baby."

"I'm sorry I interrupted you."

"You didn't. I had finished my prayer and thought of the night that I was born."

He gently turned her to face him and stretched his arms across the top of her shoulders. With his fingers locked together behind her head, he leaned his head forward until his forehead touched hers. He drew a deep breath and released it slowly and then kissed her lightly on her lips. "What an awful night for your father. I know how terrible it would be for Michael if we had lost Lizzy and he was left with their tiny baby."

"That's what I thought of, and of how glad I am that my mother and father are together again." She put her arms around him, but pulled her face away and looked into his. She could tell by his eyes how totally exhausted he was. He couldn't take anything else. She reached up and pushed back a strand of his hair that had fallen over his forehead.

"Are you tired?" she asked, and smiled at him.

He chuckled. "I passed that point long ago."

"You must get some sleep."

"Hannah, I'm sorry I spoke so harshly to you last night and for the way I told you what to do. I had no right to do either. You're a real hero because you risked your life to come for me. I was angry at Michael for letting you until he explained what happened."

"If Michael had been killed in the storm and Lizzy had died during childbirth as my mother did, the baby would have had neither parent. I just couldn't let that happen."

"I know, but it scared me so badly when I saw what nearly happened to you. Now that I've found you, I don't know what I would do without you. I love you so much."

The placid waters that had raged so violently only hours before brought peace to Hannah like the calm after the storm. She felt its tranquility. As in the Holy Scriptures, God had, indeed, calmed the fury of the sea.

She looked into Nathan's face with questioning eyes, but spoke softly in his ear, "I love you, too, Nathan. You don't need to apologize to anyone after what you've been through. Everything is all right."

Nathan felt certain that Hannah did love him, but he sensed that everything was **not** all right.

CHAPTER 5

Rachel was right when she said the Sutterfield baby was a beautiful boy. Hannah saw an image of Michael in the tiny face that lay asleep on his mother's chest. His knees drawn beneath him made his diapered bottom higher than the rest of his body. A smile crossed Hannah's face, but when Lizzy announced that the baby's name was Michael Lee Sutterfield, she thought it strange they had given him Nathan's last name for a middle name.

"We shall never forget what you did for us," said Lizzy. "I prayed for the storm to end and never intended for you to go out in it. You could have been . . ." She shuddered.

"Don't think of it," said Hannah. "It didn't happen."

"We'll always be grateful to you," Lizzy insisted.

After her visit, Hannah left the Sutterfields' cabin for the deck. It was a beautiful day, and the crew displayed a good spirit in spite of all the work to be done. They were thankful to be alive. Some whistled a jolly tune as they hurried about, putting things in order. Captain Barrington had his sleeves rolled up and worked right along beside them.

It was near noon on the day after the storm. The main deck of the *Monarch* was in shambles, but nothing was broken that couldn't be fixed or replaced. Many sails needed mending, but most were salvageable. Part of the crew was scrubbing and swabbing, while others untangled rigging and hoisted sails.

Robert Moore and Murray bent their heads together over a chart on a table near the ship's wheel and pooled their maritime experiences to determine the *Monarch's* location. Her last known position was pinpointed on the map; with other instruments they estimated how far southeast the wind had taken them. They obtained a general idea of the area they were in, but not until the stars came out and Robert and Nathan took a reading of the sextant, would they know their exact location. Then Murray could steer the *Monarch* back on course.

Captain Barrington saw Hannah on the deck. "Will you come to my office?" he called to her. "I'd like to talk to you."

Hannah was surprised and looked around for Nathan. She hoped he would go with her, but then remembered that he was sleeping. With apprehension, she followed the captain to his office where he asked her to be seated in a chair beside his desk.

"Hannah," he began, "you came to my office to talk one day, but decided I was too busy. I try not to ever be too busy for anyone on my ship, especially if there is a problem. Please remember that, if you need to talk to someone before we reach South Carolina."

"I will, Sir, and thank you."

"The entire crew would join me in saying how much your work is appreciated," the captain continued. "Without it, repairs could not be made to the *Monarch*; it would be at least two days before the ship could sail again. We would be in a dangerous situation, should we come in sight of a French or pirate ship during the time. As it is, we'll be able to obtain full speed within a few hours.

"And I've heard of your good deeds from others. John Hartman and his wife are grateful for the educational instructions you have given their children. It's such a worthwhile way in which you occupy their time. You've kept up the morale of the crew by listening to them, and you did a heroic deed last night when you attempted to find Nathan in the storm. What I'm saying is that you have more than paid for your passage across the Atlantic and do not need to continue to work unless you want to."

"I like to stay busy, but it would be nice to have some time to spend with the new little passenger across the hall."

Captain Barrington laughed. "Only work when you want to," he insisted.

Hannah assumed she was dismissed and stood to leave. She thanked the captain again, but before she reached the door, he called her name as if he had one more thought.

"I have two sons and a daughter-in-law," he said. "I'm very proud of each of them and would be just as proud to have you for a daughter-in-law."

Hannah felt her face blush. Why did the wealthy captain say such a thing to a poor girl like her who, except for his own mercy, would be indentured for five years?

"Thank . . . thank you, Sir. I . . . I'm sure your son will marry a girl that you can be proud of."

"I hope so, Hannah. I hope so."

Back on the deck, she pondered the captain's last remark. Those around her noticed that something was wrong.

"Are you okay?" Jason asked. Had the captain told her who Nathan was?

"Yes," she nodded, but it was plain to see that she was disturbed about something. "I'm going to my cabin," she said. "I'll be back later."

Soon afterward, Nathan came from his room, but the men had gone back to work, and no one said a word about the incident.

"Has Hannah been here?" he asked Jason.

"Yes. She seemed upset when she left."

"What happened?"

"I'm not sure." Jason wasn't about to tell Nathan who had upset her.

When the captain left his office, he invited the men to a celebration party on Friday night. "To celebrate the birth of a child on the *Monarch*," he said, "and to show my appreciation for all your hard work." He sent Mrs. Barrington to invite the passengers.

When Hannah didn't show up in the dining hall for the noon meal, Nathan took food and a drink to her. He wanted to know what had happened that morning. When she opened the door, he walked by her and spread the meal on her table and then waited until she began to eat before asking, "Did someone say something that upset you this morning?"

As she chewed the food in her mouth, she determined her answer. Nathan was devoted to the captain. She feared if she told him what he had said, it would cause trouble between them.

She swallowed and answered, "No, I got tired and came to rest. I didn't mean to, but I went to sleep."

"Did you hear about the celebration planned for Friday night?"

"Yes, the captain's wife invited me."

"May I have the honor of escorting you there, my lady?"

She smiled. "Of course you may. I feel honored that you asked."

After Nathan left, she opened a trunk and took out her very best dress. Its pale shade of green complemented her red hair. The only problem was that it buttoned in the back, and she would have no one to button it.

Hannah worked most of the week since there was much to be done after the storm, but she decided to take Friday off. After all, the captain had said to work only when she wanted to. She slept later than usual that morning and was late getting to the dining hall.

After breakfast, she stopped at the Sutterfields' cabin, and Lizzy came to the door with Little Michael in her arms. He was crying. And from the distressed look on Lizzy's face, Hannah suspected he'd been crying for quite some time.

"May I hold him?" she asked.

Lizzy seemed near the point of tears. "I don't know what to do," she said. "He's cried for hours."

"Something must be wrong." Hannah tucked the baby under her right arm and gently rubbed his stomach with her left fingers. The pressure seemed to have made him feel better until she felt a rumble in his stomach. When he wrinkled his face and cried out, she was convinced that the trouble was stomach pains. She sat down with him on her knees and began to bounce him very carefully as she gently patted his back. After a moment, Little Michael burped, but she kept bouncing him until he burped again. It must have relieved his pain, for his tiny body relaxed and he closed his eyes. In a few seconds, he was fast asleep.

Lizzy and Michael were amazed. "How did you know what to do?" Lizzy asked.

"I felt the rumbling of his stomach. May I take him to my cabin, so you can get some rest?"

"That would be wonderful," Michael agreed. "Lizzy is exhausted, and she needs time to get ready for the party tonight."

"Take as long as you like; he'll probably sleep a long nap."

Hannah took the baby across the hall to her room and laid him in the middle of her bed. She lay down beside him and rubbed a finger across the tiny hand that was curled into a fist. She remembered Rachel saying that Nathan had given God glory for the miracle of childbirth the night Michael Lee was born. He truly was, she thought, a gift from God.

When it was time for the noon meal, Michael and Lizzy came for the baby, and Hannah accompanied the three of them to the dining hall. She held Little Michael, while Lizzy and Michael ate and then took her own food to her cabin and ate alone.

The evening was spent in her room, getting ready for the celebration. She cleansed her body, then fixed her hair differently. Her silver clasp was fastened at the top of her head; her long curls fell behind it. She gave careful attention to her face before she slipped the dress over her head and pulled it in place. It fit perfectly in spite of the weight she had lost; she'd been thinner when the dress was purchased.

She put her hands to her back and buttoned the dress from her waist up as far as she could reach. Then she raised her hands to her neck and buttoned downward. As she strained to reach the buttons at the middle of her back, someone knocked on her door. Oh, dear, she thought. Nathan was early and she wasn't ready.

She forgot her predicament, however, when she opened the door and saw how handsome he was in his officer's uniform. His hair had been cut and his sideburns trimmed, and both were combed back neatly. All her uncertainty about him was forgotten.

"Nathan, you look fantastic! I shall be the envy of every lady at the party."

"You'll be the only lady there that's not married. I'll be the envy of every man, but I won't be the only one that is single.

That scares me, because you're the most beautiful girl I've ever known, and you look absolutely stunning tonight."

"You say the sweetest things . . . to be an Englishman."

"And what's wrong with an Englishman?"

"Oh, nothing; you know I'm teasing, but I'll be a moment. I don't have on my shoes." She lifted her dress high enough for him to see her bare feet. He laughed and told her not to hurry.

He waited at the door, but as she knelt beside her trunk and rummaged through it, looking for the right shoes, he noticed two buttons that were not buttoned at the back of her dress. He walked into the room and the door closed behind him. As she slipped her feet into a pair of shoes, he asked, "May I help you with your buttons?"

"Oh, I forgot." She felt her face blush.

When the dress was buttoned, he turned her around and saw the pinkish color in her cheeks. "Hannah, don't be embarrassed with me. I thought you had gotten over that."

"I wanted everything to be perfect tonight." He noticed her frustration. "I'm sorry I wasn't ready," she said.

He pulled her to him gently and put his arms around her. "Things could never be more perfect for me than they are right now." His voice was deep and serious. "I like doing things for you, Hannah. I want to take care of you forever. Tell me you'll always love me, no matter what, for I can't bear to think of losing you."

"Why should you think of losing me? You know I love you."

"Please say that I won't."

"I don't want to lose you, either. If we'll always be truthful to each other, we'll always have each other."

Suddenly his lips were on hers. With a burning inside of him, he kissed her harder and harder. He breathed quick, shallow breaths, and she clung to him and kissed him with the same desire.

"I love you," he whispered, when at last, he forced his lips from hers. "You're right; we should always be truthful to each other." I must tell her, he thought. I must tell her who I am . . . tonight . . . before we part.

He placed her hand on his arm. "Art thou ready to attend the ball, my lady?"

"I'm quite ready, my knight."

They smiled at each other and departed her room, but when they came to his door, he asked her to wait, while he went in for something. In a moment, he returned with a mandolin made of exquisite wood. Hannah rubbed her hand across it gingerly and asked, "Can you play it?"

"A little."

"Nathan, is there anything you can't do?"

"Of course. Jason has a dulcimer. If he brings it, we'll have music and dancing."

"That would be wonderful."

The captain had asked Nathan to be the first one in the dining hall in order to greet early arrivals, but he had forgotten to tell Hannah, so a few people were there before them. He went to talk to those who had come early, while Hannah took a seat at a table.

Captain and Mrs. Barrington entered the room, and as usual, they were an attractive couple. The captain was dressed in his officer's uniform, and his wife wore a lovely dress made of rose-colored satin.

The Butlers arrived next and were also dressed quite fashionably. Mrs. Butler walked elegantly beside her husband with her small hand wrapped around his arm. He escorted her across the room proudly. Hannah wanted to know them better and went to talk. They seemed pleased that she did.

"You look beautiful tonight, dear," said Alice.

"Yes," her husband agreed. "It's plain to see how you swept Nathan off his feet."

"I don't know that I've swept Nathan off his feet," she said, "but he means a lot to me." She wanted to ask how they had known him for so long, but everyone else arrived all at once and their attention was diverted.

Most of the crew came in together. They stood apart from the passengers, but Hannah made an effort to speak to each of them; she felt comfortable in their company. Murray reminded her of her father, and the two of them had talked often. She knew his children by name and how much he missed them and their deceased mother. He gave her a hug and whispered in her ear, "You look lovely tonight."

The Hartmans were late, but when they arrived, the children looked adorable in their best clothes. Hannah told them so. Mary and Jenny beamed but Steven was embarrassed. His eyes were fixed on the floor, and he refused to look at her.

Hannah talked to his sisters, while she tried to think of something that would put him at ease. She knew he felt uncomfortable because he seldom dressed this way. "Steven," she said, "you look very nice. I hope I look nice enough to dance with you."

He lifted his eyes and drew a deep breath. "Oh, Hannah, you're beautiful!" After that, he forgot to be shy.

Michael and Lizzy sent a message by the Hartmans that they would bring the baby later for everyone to see.

Jason and Nathan began to play their musical instruments. The Butlers stood to dance and were joined by Captain and Mrs. Barrington. Mary and Jenny held hands and danced around and around, but Steven stood beside John until Hannah asked, "May I have this dance, Sir?" She suspected he didn't know what to do, but when she held out her arms, he came to her and circled one arm around her waist. She guided him across the dining hall floor.

They finished the dance and had started the next one, when Nathan laid down his mandolin and made his way toward them. As Jason played the dulcimer, he tapped Steven on the shoulder and asked politely, "May I have a turn with your partner?"

"Sure, Nathan," Steven replied, and ran to stand beside John.

Nathan took her in his arms, and she could feel all eyes upon them as he swept her across the floor. He was a wonderful dancer and she felt so comfortable in his arms. "I love you, my handsome prince," she whispered in his ear.

"And I love you, my beautiful princess."

"You play the mandolin very well."

"Thank you. You have captured the heart of everyone here."

"Why do you say that?"

"I've been watching, and they all love you, but not as much as I do. No one else could love you that much."

"One person here doesn't love me. She has hardly spoken to me."

"Who?"

"The captain's wife; I don't know her name."

"Her name is Martha and she loves you."

"How can you say that when she doesn't even know me?"

"She told me so, and she knows you. We talk about you everyday, and I've told her how wonderful you are."

Hannah was surprised, but when she opened her mouth in shock, Nathan leaned his head forward and kissed her right on the lips to keep her from saying anything more. She was embarrassed that he kissed her in front of everyone and sealed her lips together. He smiled and waited to see her face blush. He didn't have to wait long.

The tune ended, and Nathan went back to his mandolin, but Hannah danced with Scott and Murray and everyone else who was brave enough to ask her under his watchful eyes. When exhausted, she returned to her table.

Nathan came to the table and lifted one foot to an empty chair beside her. "I want to sing a song," he announced, "for someone very special to me." He rested the musical instrument on his knee and began to play an old English ballad about a young man who was going to war. In the words of the song, the young man asked his sweetheart to wait for him. Nathan looked into Hannah's eyes as he sang, and before he finished, tears fell down her face, as well as the face of every woman in the room, especially Martha Barrington's.

As soon as the song ended, Nathan stood on two feet, and to Hannah's delight, he played the Irish jig. The jig was a popular folk dance in Ireland, dating back to the sixteenth century, and she had heard the accordionist play it at many village parties. She quickly stood and lifted her hands to each side of her waist. Jason laid down his dulcimer and locked one arm through hers, and while everyone clapped, he kicked his legs as they kept in step with each other and the lively tune.

When the music stopped, everyone laughed and clapped harder for Jason and Hannah. They were still clapping when the Sutterfields arrived with the baby, and their attention was turned to him. He was wide-awake; his big blue eyes looked around at everyone. He seemed just as eager to see them as they were to see him. Lizzy had dressed him in a tiny, white baby dress with little white booties on his feet. Hannah thought he looked precious and could not take her eyes off him. She continued to admire him when everyone else turned to Captain Barrington, who stood to speak.

She heard the captain say, "The celebration tonight is held in honor of our youngest passenger. His name is Michael Lee Sutterfield, after his dad, Michael, and the young man who helped him enter this world, my son, Nathan Lee Barrington."

Hannah lifted her head and repeated the captain's words silently, thinking she must have heard him wrong. "My son . . . Nathan Lee Barrington . . ." She looked into Lizzy's face and saw that she watched her intensively. Then she realized that a hush had fallen over the crowd, and every eye was on her.

A jolt went through her body as the truth came with a sudden shock. She raised her hand to her heart when it began to beat erratically, causing pain in her chest. She breathed harder, but her lungs felt no air. I must get outside, she thought, but when she tried to stand, the floor seemed to move under her. She saw that someone ran toward her, then everything went black and she felt herself falling.

Before Nathan could reach her, Hannah fell to the floor and lay unconscious. He and the captain and Jason knelt beside her, while everyone else watched.

"I'm sorry, Nathan," said the captain. "I got carried away about the baby and forgot."

"This is my fault, Dad."

They both heard Jason mutter under his breath, "You can say that again, mate!" His and Nathan's eyes met for an instant. "Your battle is on," he muttered again.

Nathan said nothing, but gently lifted Hannah in his arms and hurried out of the room to the open air. He told the captain he would take care of her, meaning he didn't want any help.

As the breeze from the ocean touched her face, Hannah came to and realized she was in his arms. Then she remembered what had happened. Nathan was Captain Barrington's son. She recalled John Dudley's words that Captain Barrington owned a large shipping company in Liverpool. Nathan was of the wealthy British upper class that her father had hated. She sank again into semi-unconsciousness.

Nathan opened the door to her cabin and laid her on the bed. She gasped for air. He unbuttoned her dress to make it easier for her to breathe.

"Hannah, can you hear me? I'm going to my cabin to get my bag. There's some medicine in it that will help you."

Her eyes opened and tears trickled down her temples into her hairline. He leaned over her. She lifted one hand and slightly touched the front of his jacket with her fingertips. "Oh, Nathan," she groaned.

He held his hand to his forehead; her breathing was very irregular. "I've got to get you some medicine," he said. "I'll be right back."

When he left, she used all her strength to lift herself from the bed. She walked to the hall door and pushed the dead bolt in place and then crossed the room and did the same to her outside door. The top of her dress slipped over her shoulders and dropped to the floor. She stepped out of it and fell across the bed.

Nathan returned and grasped her doorknob, but the door would not open. He tried again, twisting it back and forth. Fear gripped him as he ran to her other door. When he found it locked, he knew what she had done. "Hannah," he pleaded, "please open the door. If you don't want to see me just take the medicine." When there was no response, he leaned his head against her door, and with his hand still on the doorknob, he called again, "Hannah, I love you." The only sound he heard in return was the ocean water lapping against the side of the *Monarch*. "I love you," he whispered to himself and clenched his teeth.

Hannah heard his plea for her to open the door. She had locked it because she couldn't think clearly enough to make a decision and would not talk to him until she could. Her chest hurt; to stop breathing would have been a relief, but Nathan's voice told her that someone wanted her to live. She struggled to breathe until near daylight when her frail body relaxed.

Captain Barrington and Jason tried to talk to Nathan, but he would not be consoled. There was no one with Hannah and he knew how alone she felt.

"I'm going to open her door," he said.

"No," answered the captain. "If Hannah locked her doors, she doesn't want to see anyone, and you must accept that."

"But I fear for her life!" Nathan argued. "She wasn't breathing normal, and I haven't heard a sound from her room since she locked the doors."

"You must consider her privacy."

"Dad, you don't understand. I have to see her! I have to talk to her!"

"You had over six weeks to talk to her. You should have told her who you are."

"I know that now. I didn't know it would be this hard for her."

Captain Barrington sighed. "Well, we can't do anything before tomorrow. If she doesn't respond to anyone by the evening meal, I'll open her door. She can't go longer than that without food and water. Ask Lizzy or Rachel to knock on her door; perhaps she'll talk to one of them."

Nathan went to his room and sat down on the side of his bed. His dad and Jason were right; he should have told Hannah who he was from the very beginning . . . certainly before she fell in love with him. He'd thought only of himself. Would she ever have anything to do with him again?

He dropped to his knees beside his bed and began to pray.

"Dear God, take care of Hannah. I lift her up to you, Lord, and ask that you provide her every need. Please heal her body and give her strength. Forgive me for not trusting you. You brought us together, but I tried to take matters in my own hands. I ask for her forgiveness and for a second chance. In Christ's name I pray. Amen."

Later that night, he heard a knock. Could it be Hannah? He jumped to his feet and opened the door, but it was Jason.

"I finished my watch and saw your light still on. Have you heard from Hannah?"

"No . . . not a word. She won't unlock her door and there's no answer when I call. It was a cruel way that she found out about me—in front of everyone—seeing that everybody knew but her. I was going to tell her right after the party, and if I could have held her in my arms and told her, it would have been easier for her. I would not have let her go until I made her understand. I know I could have. Hannah loves me and she must know how much I love her."

"You'll have to take her in your arms and make her understand."

"How can I do that with a locked door between us?"

"She'll come out. She has to eat."

"She doesn't care if she eats or not. You know how much weight she's lost. That's one reason I'm so worried about her. Jason . . . I'm afraid she'll die." Nathan bowed his head to his arms that were crossed on his knees. Jason had never seen him in such a state.

When it was time for the morning meal, Nathan went to the galley and asked Sam to fix Hannah a special breakfast.

"How is Hannah?" Sam asked.

"I don't know. She locked herself in her room."

"You can't let her do that!"

"What can I do, Sam? Tell me. I tried to get her to open the door." Sam saw how upset Nathan was and shook his head as he turned back to his work.

Nathan asked Lizzy to take the breakfast to Hannah, and Lizzy was happy to try, but her effort was to no avail. When she returned the food to Nathan's cabin, he became even more worried, so she stayed to talk.

"Nathan, I think Hannah will be all right," she said. "I know she's upset, and I can only imagine how she must feel right now, but she loves you. She needs time to think and you must be patient.

"I came close to telling her that you were Captain Barrington's son. Perhaps I should have. But it wasn't my place to. It was something that you needed to do, and I knew how it would make her feel if I did. I don't think she would have believed me because she trusted you. I hope this will be a lesson to you and you won't ever keep anything from the woman you love, again."

"I won't Lizzy."

It was a dreadful night for Hannah, but in the predawn hours, as Nathan prayed, a peace came over her, and she drifted into a deep sleep. Her body relaxed; her breathing became normal.

When Lizzy knocked lightly on her door the next morning, she was still asleep. Much later, she awoke and dressed, but could not leave her cabin. Why had no one on the ship told her who Nathan was? She could understand most of the crew not telling her since Nathan was their leader, but Scott and Murray were close friends. She really couldn't understand the Sutterfields or the Hartmans not telling her. They had talked with her so often, yet had kept his secret. She felt like a ninny.

Why had Nathan been attracted to her, a poor Irish girl, in the first place? Had he lied when he said he wanted to marry her? They had not discussed marriage. And he had told her nothing about his life or his plans for the future.

Perhaps he didn't love me at all, she thought, but found it hard to believe when she remembered how kind he had been and how much he had helped her. Her mind became jumbled with questions. She tried to shut them out. It didn't matter . . . the Nathan she knew no longer existed.

CHAPTER 6

Hannah lay across her bed the morning after she found out that Nathan was the Barringtons' son and thought of her home in Ireland. She longed to be there, away from everyone. There was a special place where she went when upset or had an important decision to make. She closed her eyes and pretended she was there. Green grass was all around her, and water splashed over rocks, while birds chirped in the clump of trees that provided shade.

Everything made sense to her now. She felt dense for not realizing who Nathan was. How easy it must have been for him to persuade his dad not to charge her for the voyage. And now she understood why the captain said that he'd be proud to have her for a daughter-in-law and why Nathan never introduced him or his wife to her. She recalled Lizzy's strange words and wondered if she had wanted to tell her who Nathan was. If for no other reason, she should have suspected who he was from the way he ran the ship, but she had trusted him so completely. Why had he deceived her from the day they met on the dock when he told her his name was Nathan Lee?

She tried to put him out of her mind and must have dozed, for she awoke suddenly when someone knocked on her door.

She rose from the bed and opened the door to see Steven with her book in one hand and a bag of food and bottle of tea in the other.

"Hello, Steven. Are you finished with the book?" She tried not to let her despair show.

"Yes, but that's not the only reason I came. May I talk to you?"

"Sure. Come in."

She turned and lifted her dress from the floor where she had dropped it the night before.

"You looked so pretty in that dress last night," said Steven. "I was glad you asked me to dance, but I didn't mind when Nathan took my place. The two of you looked perfect together."

"Steven, please don't talk about that."

"It scared us when you fainted, and everyone's worried about you, especially Nathan."

"Did Nathan ask you to come?"

"No. My mother did. Nathan wanted to open your door, but Captain Barrington wouldn't let him. The captain said if you didn't come out by the evening meal, he would open it because you couldn't go longer than that without food and water. He told Nathan to ask Lizzy and my mother to try to talk to you, but when you didn't come to the door for Lizzy this morning, Mother didn't think you would for her either. She said if you'd talk to anyone on the ship it'd be me. I'm glad you opened the door. I wish there was something I could do to make you feel better."

"You have made me feel better by telling me everything. I didn't hear Lizzy this morning, or I would have opened my door; I must have been sleeping. I'm glad you came. You're a good friend, and right now, I don't feel like I have many friends."

"My mother and daddy are your friends. They feel bad about what happened, but I guess you're mad at them for not telling you about Nathan."

"No, I'm not angry at your parents, or anyone. I just . . . well, I can't explain how I feel, but sometimes a person needs to be alone."

"I understand, but Mother said for you to try to eat the food and drink the liquid. Do you mind if I tell Nathan that I talked to you?"

"No. Tell him I'm all right. I went to sleep just before daylight, and when I awoke, I felt much better."

Steven left and Hannah shut her door, but she didn't lock it. She really did feel better after talking to him and was glad he'd come. She wasn't hungry, but knew she needed the food and ate all that he had brought.

Steven went straight to Nathan's cabin. When Nathan heard his knock, he hurried to the door and was disappointed to see a child, but tried not to let it show.

"Hi, Steven."

"I just talked to Hannah."

"You did? How is she?"

"She said to tell you she's all right."

"She did?" He was so relieved.

"Yes, she said she went to sleep just before daylight, and when she woke up, she felt better."

Nathan remembered that he had prayed for her just before daylight. God had heard his prayer, but would He give him a second chance? He thanked Steven for coming, and after he left, he thanked God that Hannah had sent a message that she was all right. He wanted to see her badly, but thought it best to leave her alone for now. He hoped she would talk to him before the day was over.

Hannah stayed in her room most of the day, but realized she couldn't stay there forever. When it was time for the evening meal, she washed her face and combed her hair and then held her head erect and opened her door to the outside. On her way to the dining hall, someone called her name and she turned to see Jason. He ran to catch her.

"Hannah . . . I'm glad to see you out of your room. How do you feel?"

"I'm all right."

"You've been through a rough time. I'm sorry."

She didn't answer, and both were silent as they walked along together.

She finally spoke. "How is he, Jason?" She couldn't say Nathan's name.

Jason shook his head before answering, "Awe man, Hannah, I've never seen him like this before. If I ever doubted that he loved you, I don't now. Will you talk to him?"

There was another pause as they lingered outside the door to the dining hall. Jason waited for an answer. Hannah leaned with her back to the guardrail and looked down at the deck.

"I wouldn't know what to say to Nathan Barrington."

"Awe Hannah, he's the same man you danced with at the party last night."

"Not to me," she responded sadly.

"I'm sorry; I should have told you he was Captain Barrington's son that first day we talked, and I realized that he hadn't. I thought he would, but he couldn't bring himself to after you told him how your father felt about wealthy British. He was afraid you wouldn't have anything to do with him. He wanted you to know him, but the longer he waited the harder it was. I see his worst fears have come to be, yet I understand how you feel. Maybe you'll feel better after you eat. Go sit down and I'll get your food."

"Thank you, Jason."

The Hartmans were already in the dining hall, and others came in, but no one spoke to Hannah. She was glad. Except for Steven, she thought of everyone on the *Monarch* as Nathan's friend. They had been loyal and kept his secret. She felt miserable.

Jason returned with two trays of food and set one of them before her. He placed his own tray at the other side of the table and sat down. "Nathan won't like it if he sees me here," he said, "but I won't leave you alone."

Just as he sat down, Nathan appeared in the doorway, and Hannah's heart skipped a beat. Their eyes met and held each other's for a few seconds. He was unshaven and bedraggled. When he started toward her, she stood up.

Nathan thought she intended to leave the room, and he didn't want her to miss another meal, but with only worry and frustration and no sleep the night before, his nerves were on edge. He raised his voice, **"Sit down and eat before you starve to death! I won't bother you, but I can't help who I am. I have nothing to do with ruling the Irish, and be it in my power, I would set them free."**

Jason jumped to his feet. **"Nathan!"** he cried.

Nathan turned to him angrily. "And **you** stay out of this!"
"Awe man!"

Nathan left the room quickly, and Hannah sank slowly to
her chair, but she couldn't eat. She felt everyone's eyes on her
and wanted desperately to be off the ship, away from them all.
She sat with her head bowed and wished that she had stopped
breathing the night before. Jason sat down beside her and took
her shaking hands in his.

"Hannah . . . Nathan didn't mean to do that," he defended
his friend. "You don't know what kind of night he had; it was
an awful time for him and he was so worried about you. He
thought you were going to leave, just now, and he couldn't
stand for you to miss another meal. You've got to eat something."

He put food on her fork and raised it to her mouth as
everyone in the room watched. They wanted to see her take it
and she did bite the food and began to chew, but it had no
taste.

When she had eaten all that she could, she left the dining
hall with Jason, and he walked with her to her cabin. They
walked in silence until they came to her door. Instead of going
inside, she went to the guardrail and looked toward the horizon
where the evening sun neared the water. Another day would
soon be over. She turned to Jason and asked, "How much longer
before we reach America?"

"Not long. We shouldn't be more than four days. I hope
you and Nathan can work things out before then."

"We can't work things out; we can't change who we are, but
I wasn't going to leave the dining hall when he came toward
me. I stood to meet him. I don't want to hurt your friend, Jason,
but he's not the person I love. I hope you can understand that."

Jason did understand; the same way he understood why
Nathan had not told her about himself and why he had acted
the way he did in the dining hall. He understood both of them
and couldn't stand to see either so broken hearted. When tears
slid down Hannah's cheeks, he handed her a handkerchief and
put his arms around her.

"He is the one you love, Hannah, and you've got to talk to him. You must know how much he cares for you."

"Yes, I know he cares, but my father would not have given his consent for me to marry him; besides, I wouldn't know how to live among the wealthy. I couldn't make him happy."

"He'd never been happier in his life after he met you until last night, but every time I talked to him, I insisted that he should tell you that he was the captain's son. So did others on the ship. We felt guilty for not telling you, but knew how much he loved you and of his fear of losing you. That's why we didn't; I guess we made a mistake. Everyone on this ship loves you, but we think a lot of Nathan, too. He's a good man, Hannah, and you won't ever find anyone else who loves you as much as he does."

"I know, Jason, I know," she groaned, "but when he returns to his real world with all its wealth and glitter, it will be different from on the ship. I won't fit in, and I don't think that I want to."

Jason sighed, but had nothing more to say. He understood.

The sun sank lower in the west and cast a long shadow behind Nathan as he stood at the corner of the cabins and watched his best friend hold the only girl he had ever loved. As difficult as it was for him, he was glad that Jason held Hannah, for if he could not, he wanted someone to comfort her. After watching them a moment, he went to his cabin and fell, tormented, across his bed. Since he had not slept for twenty-four hours, he sank into a restless sleep.

He dreamed the *Monarch* was in a fierce storm. The water covered her deck, and Hannah was washed overboard. He tried with all his strength, but could not reach her. Before she sank into the ocean, she looked at him with sad eyes, the way she had in the dining hall that evening. He screamed her name over and over until he felt someone shaking him.

"Nathan! Nathan! Wake up!" called the captain.

Nathan sat up. Perspiration ran down his face and he shook all over. He took a deep breath and dried his face with the sheet.

"Did you have a bad dream, son?"

"Yes, sir."

"Do you want to talk about it?"

"No, Dad."

Nathan fell back on his pillow. The dream had seemed so real, and he could still see Hannah's eyes. He went back to sleep to have the same dream occur again. This time, Martha Barrington heard her son and started to get out of bed, but the captain stopped her.

"No, Martha. Nathan has to fight this battle alone."

When Nathan awoke from the awful dream the second time, he got up and splashed cold water in his face and then sat down at his desk. He took out writing paper and a quill and began to write.

May 23, 1812

My darling Hannah,

I must write you this letter and will give it to you before I leave the ship. I'm getting off in New York City, as I believe you would want me to, but it's so hard to think that I'll never see you again. I want to tell you how happy you made me for a short time, and I'll always remember how wonderful I felt when I held you in my arms and kissed you. I love you, Hannah, more than anyone in the world, and I would give up everything that I own for you, for my life is nothing without you. I shall never forget you.

I didn't mean to deceive you. At first, I didn't think it would matter, and later, I wanted to tell you who I was but there never seemed to be the right time. For what it can mean, I was going to tell you after the celebration. You said in your room before we left that we must be truthful to each other, and I knew you were right, even if it meant I would lose you. I had hoped that you would love me . . . no matter what. I'm glad we had the special night, and I'll always remember dancing with you in my arms and hearing you whisper "I love you" in my ear.

I know that you did love me, and I would die a
thousand times for hurting you. Please forgive me. I
will love you forever.

Nathan

Hannah was unable to sleep and had tossed and turned in
her bed for several hours. Her pillow was drenched with tears.
She thought of Collin and of the way he felt about British
Aristocrats. He didn't know Nathan, she argued with herself;
besides, he was gone. She couldn't, however, put him out of
her mind, knowing that she should honor his wishes in death as
she would if he were alive. Could she live the way Nathan was
used to living? What would life be like with him? She knew he
loved her, but she was frightened of him now and felt inferior
to him and his family. But worse than that, if she married him,
would she be a traitor to her country and her father?

When she could no longer take the anguish, she got up and
dressed and then stepped out her door and into the night. The
wind swept across the *Monarch*, sending a chill through her. It
was after midnight, and Scott served guard duty on the mid-
watch. She tried to avoid him, but he saw her move in the
moonlight and called out, "Who goes there?"

"Hannah Thornton."

"Hannah, why are you out at this hour?"

"I can't sleep."

"Will you let me get Nathan for you?"

"No."

"Well, be careful, and let me know when you go back in."

"I will."

She walked to the other side of the ship and toward the bow,
forgetting that someone stood at the helm.

Nathan had finished the letter to her and read over it when
someone knocked loudly at his door. He heard Murray's voice,
"Nathan, Jason needs you at the helm. He said, 'on the double!'"

Thinking there was a serious problem, Nathan jumped to his feet and left with Murray, leaving the letter on his desk. Jason was at the wheel and when Nathan reached him, he pointed to the starboard bow. "Look there . . . by the guardrail."

He looked down at the moonlit deck and saw Hannah, then moved closer to the window and lifted one hand to the glass as if he tried to reach her. He watched her silently as he unconsciously bit the inside of his mouth. When she lifted a hand to her eyes, his heart felt wretched within him.

"Nathan, go talk to her," begged Jason.

"You know she won't talk to me. Why did you have me come here? Did you want to see my heart ripped out?"

"No, Nathan. I think she will talk to you. She told me that she wasn't going to leave when you started to her table in the dining hall."

"I don't know, Jason. You know I want to talk to her more than anything, but I told her I wouldn't bother her, and I'm afraid if I do, she'll lock herself in her room again and not eat."

"Well, if you won't go, I will, so take over here."

Jason was out the door before Nathan could answer, and his heart sank when it shut behind him. Perhaps he should have tried to talk to Hannah.

He watched from the window, as Jason knew he would, and saw him approach Hannah. At first, he couldn't believe what he saw, but the moon was bright, so he was not mistaken. Jason forced Hannah to him and tried to kiss her. She struggled to get away, but he held to her blouse until it tore. When Hannah screamed, Nathan cleared the floor in three steps and yelled for Murray, who was on his cot, to get the wheel. He made two giant steps on the stairs, then jumped to the deck. Hannah screamed again as he caught Jason by his collar and pulled him away from her. She fell backward, and Nathan's fist landed hard against Jason's cheek. He'd never hit anyone so hard before in his life. He pulled him from the deck to hit him again, but as he drew back his fist the second time, he saw Jason's hands go up and heard him say, "Awe man, that's enough. I know you'll throw me in the brig, but it'll be worth it if it gets you two back together."

"What are you saying?"

"Just go to Hannah and hurry before Scott helps her." Scott had heard Hannah scream and came running, but when he saw Nathan, he stood at a distance.

By the time Nathan reached her, she had managed to sit up; she shivered, and there was a dark spot on her back. He knelt beside her and pulled her torn blouse together. The dark spot became larger and it was warm; he realized it was blood. She was near the tool that was used to pull the ship's rigging tight, and at one end of it was a sharp piece of metal. Hannah had fallen backward across it.

Neither spoke as he took off his shirt and put it around her. He picked her up and was alarmed at how light she felt in his arms. One of her hands slid around his neck . . . she held her blouse with the other. He started to his own cabin, but before he could reach it, he felt blood on his arm. Inside, he sat her in the chair at his desk and then ran to the water closet for towels. When he pulled the torn blouse away from her back carefully, he saw an ugly wound that bled badly. He wiped as much of the blood as he could from her back, then spread a dry towel around her shoulders. She shivered hard.

"Hannah," he said, "I'm going next door to get my mother. I must uncover your back, and I need her to help me take care of the wound." He thought she would feel more comfortable with his mother there and started to leave, but stopped suddenly when he remembered what had happened the night before. He knelt beside the chair and looked up at her. "You won't lock me out, will you?"

"No," she spoke her first word.

He ran next door. "Mother, I need your help!"

Martha sat up in bed. "What's wrong?"

"Come to my room!"

"Give me a moment."

He ran back to his room, but when he stepped inside, he

stopped in his tracks. Hannah held the letter that he had written her. With everything that had happened, he'd forgotten it. What if she thought it had all been planned?

When she finished reading, she looked up with the letter still in her hand, and time stood still as they gazed into each other's eyes. A tear dropped from her face onto the paper and broke the silence. She crossed the room to him, and when he held out his arms, she collapsed in them just as his mother opened the door. Mrs. Barrington saw her limp body with blood all over it. "Nathan!" she gasped, "what happened?"

"She fell, Mother. Hurry, we must stop the bleeding! Get more towels and pull the cover back on my bed."

His mother did as he said, and when he laid Hannah on the towels, they heard a groan in her throat. To revive her more, he held smelling salts under her nose.

He dashed to the water closet for a bowl of water and a cloth, while Martha removed Hannah's blouse and everything above her waist. She pulled the bed sheet around her, leaving only her back exposed. Nathan wiped her face gently with the wet cloth, then sat down on the bed beside her and pulled her against him, so his mother could cleanse the blood from her back. He then examined the wound and saw that it wasn't as deep as he'd feared. The sharp metal had cut across her back and slashed a large piece of skin. It bled badly, yet this type of wound would heal faster than a deep wound. He felt her flinch when he lifted the skin to put an ointment under it. His hands began to shake; he worked as quickly as possible. By the time he finished, the blood had begun to clot. He hoped a tight bandage would stop it completely.

He placed the bandage over the wound, and Martha handed him a long strip of cloth to hold it in place. Hannah lifted her arms for him to put it around her, and being in such pain, she forgot the sheet. It fell from in front of her. Nathan quickly pulled it over her again, but he saw her cheeks turn a scarlet red.

Hannah was humiliated. It was bad enough to be at the mercy of these two wealthy British, and she had felt very uncomfortable in Nathan's bed with only a sheet wrapped around her from the waist up. Now this was more than she could stand. Perspiration popped out under her eyes, and a large lump rose in her throat. She was determined not to cry, but how long could she hold back?

Mrs. Barrington left the room to empty the bowl of bloody water, and Nathan opened his seaman's chest and took out a shirt. He sat down beside her with it in his hand.

"It's okay," he spoke in a low voice. "We know you didn't mean for it to happen. Let me help you put this on." He held the top of the shirt to her back, and she slipped one hand at a time through its sleeves, while holding the sheet with her other hand. Nathan buttoned the buttons over the sheet and pulled it out at the bottom when he had finished. She lifted her body, and he removed the towels from under her. She was exhausted.

"Nathan," she could hardly speak.

"What, baby?"

"I want to go to my room." She tried not to seem rude, for she didn't know what she would have done had he and Mrs. Barrington not helped her, but the lump in her throat grew larger. She felt herself falling to pieces and could not let it happen in front of them.

Nathan realized how desperate she was. "All right, darling, but please wait just a moment."

He quickly walked to the door of the water closet where Martha cleaned the wash bowl. "Mother," he said, "I'll do that later."

"But I'm almost finished."

"Mother, I'll do it later!" She recognized the urgency in his voice and left the room immediately.

He closed the door behind her and sat down beside Hannah. She looked into his eyes, and suddenly, instead of the wealthy British Aristocrat, she saw the young seaman she had fallen in love with. Her tears refused to wait longer, and she leaned her face against his chest and wept bitterly. He gathered her in his arms.

"Hannah," he groaned, "I'm so sorry. Please forgive me. I

love you so much." He held her to him and kissed the top of her head, but after she had cried for quite some time, he lifted her face and began to kiss it tenderly, tasting her salty tears.

"Does your back hurt?"

"Yes," she sobbed, "but not as much as my heart."

"I know, sweetheart."

"Why did Jason do what he did?"

"To get us back together. When he saw you on the deck, he sent Murray to get me. He wanted me to talk to you, but I had told you that I wouldn't bother you and was afraid that if I did, you would lock yourself in your room again and not eat. He left me at the wheel where he knew I'd be watching, and he knew what I'd do if he tried to kiss you. He didn't mean to tear your blouse or for you to get hurt.

"I hope you don't think that it was all planned or that I had anything to do with it. I had just finished the letter when Murray knocked on my door and said for me to come in a hurry. I thought something was wrong at the helm. With everything that happened, I forgot the letter, and when I saw you reading it, I was afraid you would think that I had left it there on purpose and that was why I brought you to my cabin."

"I don't think that."

"In a terrifying dream, tonight, I dreamed that you were washed overboard in a storm and I couldn't reach you. You looked at me with sad eyes, the way you did in the dining hall, and then disappeared in the water. I woke up screaming your name, and when I went back to sleep, I had the same dream again."

"How dreadful."

"I had the dreams because I was losing you, and there was nothing I could do about it. I wanted so badly to hold you in my arms when you were so upset last night, but I couldn't reach you. Oh, Hannah, you'll never know how awful it was for me." His voice broke and he had to stop talking.

"In the dining hall," he continued, "I thought you were going to walk away from me." He lifted his hand to his forehead and ran his fingers back and forth across it. "I'm sorry I yelled at you, and I'm sorry for what happened tonight. I know I've hurt you so much and at an awful time in your life. Can you ever forgive me?"

"Oh, Nathan."

"I don't want to leave the ship; I don't want to leave you, but I will if you want me to, and they can pick me up when the *Monarch* returns up the coast. I want to go to South Carolina with you to make sure you'll be all right on the plantation and return there for you after the war."

"You can't leave the *Monarch*; everyone on the ship depends on you. If one of us must leave, it has to be me. I can catch another ship from New York to South Carolina."

His eyes closed and his face grimaced. "Please tell me you won't do that."

"All right, I won't. Why didn't you tell me you were the captain's son?" She put her hands on his arms and pushed backward until her back was against the head of the bed.

He placed a pillow behind her back to make her more comfortable and then drew a deep breath before answering her question. "I didn't tell you the day I met you on the dock because I was afraid you would think I was being boastful. I wanted you to like me because I knew I would fall in love with you. I think I did that very moment. If I had told you my name was Barrington, you would have found out who I was. That's why I only told you my first and middle name. I didn't lie, but I knew you would think that Lee was my last name. After you told me that your father didn't like British Aristocrats, I was really afraid for you to find out that I was Charles Barrington's son. I thought if I could make you love me before you found out that you would still love me, no matter what. That was wrong and it was selfish of me; I thought only of myself. I'm real sorry you found out about me the way you did in front of everyone. I had intended to hold you in my arms and tell you and hoped I could make you understand. I didn't tell you because I love you and I wanted, so much, for you to love me."

"You were right about me loving you, no matter what."

"Then you do still love me?"

"Love isn't something you can turn on and off; it wouldn't hurt so much if you could. I still love the Nathan that you are to me, just a common seaman—someone like myself. Your family won't accept me, and my father would never have given his consent for me to marry you. I feel that I would be a traitor to him and my country if I did. I know you don't understand that. And you don't understand what I've been through since I found out who you are. I've argued with myself. My heart says it doesn't matter, but my head says it does."

"Hannah . . . not meaning any disrespect to him, but what your father thought about wealthy British is not true of my family. Not one of them will think less of you because you're from Ireland. Barrington ships dock often in Irish seaports, and we have many friends there. I wish I could talk to your father and make him understand that and tell him how much you mean to me, but I can't. I can't argue with a dead person!"

"That was a harsh thing to say." Her eyes filled with tears again.

"I'm sorry, Hannah. I just don't know any other way to say it. No, I can't understand you having to please your father when he's dead. Besides, he married a British. Why should he forbid you to?"

"My mother was Irish."

"Well, she had British parents, and from what you told me, they're quite wealthy."

Her eyes closed, and her body relaxed on the pillow behind her. Her strength was spent. She would not argue.

Nathan was distraught, and with his elbows on his knees, he leaned over and covered his face with his hands. Her silence was near unbearable for him until he felt her fingertips on his arm. He raised his head and looked into her eyes that now overflowed and spilled tears down her face.

"Do you want me to leave you alone?" His voice was filled with anguish.

"I don't know," her voice was weak. "I don't know what to do. I want to be angry, but I'm not, and I don't know how to stop loving you. I'm sorry you hurt; I don't want you to. I don't want you to feel the way I do."

"Darling," he took her hands in his, "you're tired and must rest; you'll feel better after you sleep. We'll talk about it tomorrow, and I know we can work things out. We have to, for I'll never stop loving you."

"Oh, Nathan."

"Hannah, if you could tell your father about me, what would you say?"

"That you were just a common seaman . . . until he got to know you."

He looked at her with disbelief in his eyes and chuckled quietly until they both laughed out loud. She felt better and said softly, "Tell me about yourself."

"You don't feel like listening tonight."

"Just one thing."

"I grew up in a large old house."

"How many rooms did it have?"

"Twenty-five."

"Twenty-five! I can't imagine a house that large."

"I want to take you there, and I want to build a house like that for us someday, only it will be new and more beautiful."

"I don't know why we would ever need a house that large. We'll never have that many children." She felt her face blush.

He laughed quietly. "Will you never stop being embarrassed with me? I want us to talk about children. The night Lizzy's baby was born and drew that first breath of air into his tiny lungs, I saw a miracle take place in my own hands. I decided that night that I wanted us to have lots of children."

"Rachel said you were wonderful that night and that no doctor could have done better. You should go back to school and become a doctor."

"No. God wants me to be a shipbuilder. He's instilled a dream in me to build the best ships on the seas and to sail them. I'll always be a seaman. Will you be waiting for me when I return from the sea?"

"Nathan, you must give me time."

"I will, darling, and you must get some rest."

"I'm going to my cabin."

"No! I need to change the bandage on your back, and what if the wound should start to bleed again? Stay here so I can watch it. I'll sit in the chair while you sleep."

"You can't rest in the chair. I'll be right across the hall if I need you, and the bandage will be all right until tomorrow. This way, we can sleep later in the morning and not have to explain to anyone why I was in your room. Maybe no one will ever know what Jason did, unless Scott or your mother tells."

"My mother doesn't know what happened. I'll think of something to tell her, and I'll ask Scott not to tell."

"You're good at that."

"At what?"

"Asking people not to tell."

He leaned his head and his mouth slightly twitched to one side, just the way it had the day she caught him watching her, while she was seasick. It was his way of admitting his guilt. She couldn't help but laugh.

He went with her across the dark hall and was the first to enter her room. He turned her lamp up and then waited by the door for her to pull the cover back on her bed. When finished with the cover, she walked to the door and lifted her hand to his cheek.

"Thank you for rescuing me tonight."

"You're welcome." He took her hands in his and lifted one of them to his lips. "Are you sure you'll be all right?"

"Yes, as long as you're nearby." She looked into his eyes and suddenly their arms went around each other. Their lips met and they held each other tightly.

"Nathan," she whispered, "you are my Nathan. No one else could make me feel the way you do when you kiss me. You're the person I love, whomever you are."

"Oh, Hannah, it's so wonderful to have you in my arms again. I don't ever want to let you go."

When they finally parted, Hannah went to bed and fell asleep immediately, but Nathan had someone else on his mind. He left her cabin in search of his friend.

Jason had been off duty for some time and had gone to his quarters and tried to sleep, but couldn't. He'd gotten up and dressed and walked back and forth in the moonlight when he saw Nathan come toward him. He didn't know whether to be glad or afraid.

"Jason, I know that what you did tonight wasn't easy for you. I know you did it for Hannah and me."

"Is Hannah okay? Is she upset with me? I didn't mean to tear her blouse or to scare her half to death. I had to do something to get you back together, and that was the only thing I could think of. I wouldn't have done it had there been time to think. It wasn't fair to her."

"No, it wasn't, but she's not upset with you. I explained to her why you did it, and I believe her wound will be all right."

"Wound! What wound?"

"When she fell backward, she hit the sharp end of the block. It's not a deep wound, but she lost a good bit of blood."

"Awe man! I didn't know that."

"I know you didn't intend for her to get hurt and so does she. I really think she'll be all right. My mother and I cleaned and dressed the cut with a healing ointment."

"Are things all right between the two of you now?"

Nathan sighed before answering. "I'm not sure, Jason. She still loves me, but feels that she must do what her father would have her to do. She asked me to give her time, and I understand that, but we don't have much time."

A glow appeared in the eastern sky; the sun would soon rise. Nathan put one arm across his friend's shoulder and said, "Come on, mate, let's get a few hours of sleep."

Jason breathed a sigh of relief.

CHAPTER 7

Hannah flinched from the pain in her back when she rose from her bed. She was reminded of the wound inflicted there the night before, but it was Sunday, and she would not let it keep her from the worship service.

She went to the dining hall early, because she refused to eat with other passengers, and returned to her cabin with a bag of food and a mug of hot tea. As she ate alone, she remembered the letter Nathan had written her. She had forgotten it the night before, but wanted it to keep.

When she finished eating the meal, she crossed the hall and knocked on his door. At first, there was no response, but as she was about to leave, the door opened. She had awakened him; he was unshaven and wore nothing above his waist. A gold chain hung around his neck, and something attached to it gleamed on his bare chest. She had never noticed it before and wondered if he wore it under his shirt.

He tried to smile, then leaned his cheek against the door facing. His eyes closed; he was more asleep than awake.

"Nathan, may I have my letter? I want to be sure I wasn't dreaming last night."

He didn't open his eyes, but muttered in a gruff voice, "You weren't dreaming."

She entered the room, and her eyes scanned his desk, but the letter wasn't there; she didn't see it anywhere. "What did you do with it?" she asked.

"I didn't do anything with it." One eye opened and he looked at her. "I'll find it later." He wanted to go back to bed.

"Please . . . I want it now. I'm afraid you'll forget and the letter will be lost."

He heaved a deep breath and lifted his head from the door facing. As he rubbed his eyes, he tried to think. "You had it in your hand when you fainted. I suppose it fell to the floor."

She knelt to her knees and saw it just under the bed where it had fallen when she dropped it. She crawled closer and reached for it.

"Hannah, get up from there before you tear open the wound on your back and get out of my room, so I can go back to bed."

"I got it!" she cried. "But you need to get dressed for the worship service."

"You sound like my mother." He grasped her arm as she started through the door. "How do you feel?" he asked.

"All right. I was able to eat breakfast this morning. My back hurts, but it will heal."

"It won't if you keep crawling around on the floor."

"I promise not to anymore, and I'm sorry I woke you. It was very inconsiderate of me. You've had such little sleep, but I thought you'd be up for the service. I just had to get my letter; I want to keep it forever."

"It's okay that you woke me. I'm glad you wanted the letter. I'll get you an envelope to put it in." He took one from his desk and put the letter in it before handing it back to her. "I'm thankful," he said, "I didn't have to give it to you the way I thought I would."

She stood on tiptoes and kissed his cheek and then darted out the door.

"I don't think I've slept all week," Nathan groaned as he fell across his bed.

Hannah arrived early for the worship service and took her usual seat on the back row. When the Hartmans entered the dining room, Mary and Jenny ran toward her. "May we sit with you, Miss Hannah," Mary asked.

"Of course," she agreed.

The two girls sat at one side of her and Steven at the other.

"Good morning, Steven."

"Good morning, Hannah. You look better than you did yesterday."

"That's because I feel better." She laughed at his lack of tactfulness.

"Did you make-up with Nathan?"

"Yes."

"I'm glad."

"So am I," she whispered, and smiled at him.

The congregation sang "We Gather Together" before Captain Barrington stood with his Bible in hand. Hannah was surprised when Nathan quietly walked in and sat down beside Steven. He laid his arm across the back of Steven's chair and gently rubbed his hand over the bandage on her back.

The captain's sermon that morning was on true happiness. He talked about salvation and how anyone could have it, and he said that to help others gave him a good feeling.

"To have real happiness," the captain brought out the last point of his sermon, "we must forgive others." And Hannah felt sure he talked to her. Forgiveness was something she struggled with. She had forgiven those who had hurt her in the past, yet there was bitterness in her heart toward Nathan, for deceiving her, and to everyone on the ship who kept his secret. Christ required her to forgive others, but why was it so hard to forgive the one she loved the most?

Nathan had asked her to forgive him, and she wanted to, but knew that to have bitterness in her heart was not true forgiveness. She bowed her head and asked God to take away the bitterness and to replace it with forgiveness and love, and as she prayed, she felt the Holy Spirit within her. He took away all of her unkind thoughts. When she lifted her head and looked out over the small group, she felt a deep love for each of them, especially Nathan. His wealth and power no longer frightened her. God had done what she could not.

The familiar lump rose in her throat and tears came to her eyes, but the service was almost over. She could not cry. She swallowed, but the lump grew larger, and her tears overflowed and trickled down her cheeks. She had nothing to catch them with and turned to Nathan just as everyone stood to sing the closing hymn. While they sang, he asked Steven to change places with him, and he took a handkerchief from his pocket. He handed it to Hannah and put his arm around her.

She quickly wiped the tears from her face and blew her nose quietly before the hymn was finished. The small congregation was dismissed. They turned and saw the two of them beside each other and Nathan had his arm around her. They were glad and many stopped to express their happiness for them. "I love you," Hannah said to each one and really meant it.

She noticed that Captain and Mrs. Barrington stood in the back and let everyone else talk first. When the line grew short, Nathan seemed nervous, but had a smile on his face as the Barringtons approached them. He held her hand and said, "Hannah, I want you to meet my mother and dad. They told me not to introduce you to them until I could say that, or they would tell you."

They hugged Hannah with their arms around her and Nathan at the same time. The captain had a big smile on his face, and Nathan was so happy. The only thing that overshadowed Hannah's happiness was the nagging thought of what Collin would have had to say about all of this.

The captain suggested they all go eat, but there was something that Nathan had to do. He asked the captain to get Hannah and him a tray and promised they'd be back. "Get five meals," he added, "and put five chairs at the table."

He took Hannah's hand and led her outside. "Jason isn't here," he said, "and had it not been for him, we wouldn't be together today. It's going to be tough for him to face you, after what he did, or to explain why his cheek is black. Will you go with me to talk to him?"

"Of course I will. I thought the same thing when he didn't show up for the service."

When they didn't find him in the little forecastle, they looked for him on the deck and found him at the guardrail near the place where Hannah had fallen. His arms were crossed on top of the rail, and he stared down at the water. He was surprised to see them. "Jason, we missed you at the service this morning," said Nathan.

"I missed being there, but . . . well, I just didn't go." He turned to Hannah. "How are you?" he asked.

"I'm fine, Jason. How is your cheek?"

He chuckled as he rubbed a hand across one side of his face. "It feels like it collided with an iron fist."

"I'm sorry I hit you so hard," said Nathan. "You may hit me if it'll make you feel better."

"I'll save it 'til I get angry at you."

Nathan didn't worry for Jason never got angry.

"Hannah, can you forgive me for what I did?" he asked. "Nathan said you hurt your back when you fell."

"It's all right, and I need to thank you instead of forgive you. What you did was for me; I just didn't know it at the time. Your friendship means a lot to Nathan and me."

"That's right," Nathan agreed.

"Awe man, it's sure good to see you two together again."

Nathan laughed and laid a hand on his shoulder. "Come on," he said, "let's go eat."

The three of them returned to the dining hall, where Captain Barrington and his wife had the table ready, and after everyone was seated, they bowed their heads, and the captain asked for a blessing of the food. As soon as Mrs. Barrington looked up, she noticed the dark spot on Jason's cheek.

"Jason, what happened to your cheek?"

Before Jason had time to be embarrassed, Nathan answered his mother. "He ran into a piece of iron," he said, "and it didn't move." They all laughed.

Hannah was quiet during the meal, but listened as everyone else talked. To include her in the conversation, Jason looked at her and said, "The Barringtons have been a second set of parents to me."

"That's right," said Martha. "He's like another son, and the

Williams think the same of Nathan and his brother. I don't know how I could have managed without them with Charles gone so much." She began to reminisce of when her sons were small and of the many ways in which the Williams had helped her. Just before the meal was over, however, she looked at Hannah, and without any warning, said, "Tell us about your family, dear."

Hannah was caught off guard and didn't know what to say. She couldn't talk about her father without crying, but didn't want to turn the happy occasion into a sad one. It wouldn't be fair to Nathan, but his mother waited for her to say something. She felt warmth in her face and began to stammer. "Ah—well . . ."

Nathan quickly spoke up. "Mother, I don't think Hannah wants to talk about them right now."

"Well, that's all right," said Martha, and she changed the subject.

Hannah closed her eyes and breathed a sigh of relief, but felt like a dunce. She had finished the meal long before everyone else, and her hands lay folded in her lap under the edge of the table. Nathan reached for them and caressed them gently. She gave him a forlorn look and the corner of her mouth twitched.

By now, other passengers had left the dining hall. Jason seemed to be himself again and asked to be excused. He said he had to get some sleep. Nathan also asked to be excused in order to sleep, explaining he had duty at the wheel from seven that evening until twelve o'clock that night.

He and Hannah left together, and as soon as they were outside, he turned to her. "I'm sorry, but my mother had no way of knowing about your parents."

"I know, but I should have been able to think of something to say. Your mother and dad will think I'm stupid, but I didn't want to spoil the special occasion for you."

"You don't have to explain anything to me, and they won't think you're stupid. They know you're intelligent."

"You really didn't tell the captain everything that I told you about my life."

"No, I didn't tell him anything except what I had to in order to protect you, and he already knew that. I couldn't let you be indentured. I'm thankful you hadn't signed papers, and don't sign any when you get to South Carolina. I plan to talk to the plantation owner and make sure everything is all right.

"Most indentured servants are required to sign a contract before they cross the ocean. Perhaps your friend, Dudley, contacted my dad because he knew he would not require it of you. If Dudley knows the person you'll be working for, there might not be a problem. Perhaps you'll be treated kindly, but if you're not, you won't have to stay. Even so, I don't plan for you to stay five years because I hope to be back in less than two. I love you, and I always want to take care of you. Do you believe me?"

"Yes."

"Do you want me to tell Mother and Dad that your parents are deceased, so you won't have to go through that again?"

Hannah bowed her head, but nodded it slowly. "I suppose you should."

"Will you come to the helm tonight and keep me company, at least part of the time?"

"Yes."

"There are so many things I've wanted to tell you, but couldn't."

"I want you to tell me everything about yourself."

"I'll tell you everything you want to hear and probably a lot that you don't want to hear."

"There could be nothing about you that I don't want to hear."

"Hannah . . . you're wonderful and I'm so lucky to have found you. I was so scared when I thought I had lost you."

"Were you?"

"Yes, I've never been that scared before." They stood at her door, and he bent his head and placed his lips on hers.

"Will I see you at the evening meal?" she asked.

"Yes, and we'll go to the helm from there. Please get some rest, so you won't fall asleep."

"I wouldn't do that."

Nathan went to his cabin and was asleep as soon as he laid his head on the pillow, but Hannah lingered outside. She placed her arms on the guardrail and looked far out to sea where the water met the sky. Nathan had said that he wanted to take care of her forever. Did he still plan to ask her to marry him before they dropped anchor? She had to make a decision.

The most important decision of her life was when she decided to accept Christ and to invite Him into her heart as her Lord and Savior. She would seek His help in making the second most important decision of her life.

Hannah dressed comfortably for the evening at the helm with Nathan. She chose a black dress with buttons down the front of it. White cuffs on its sleeves came to just below her elbows, and a white lace collar circled her neck. A silver clasp with black sets embedded in it held the top of her long hair back. She pulled part of it over the front of her shoulders and let it fall across her breast. With a pair of soft leather slippers on her feet, she was ready to go.

Nathan met her in the dining hall, and when they were finished with the meal, he returned both trays and picked up two bottles of tea from the galley. As they left for the helm, he held both bottles in one hand with the slender necks betwixt his fingers. With his arm at his side, the bottles swung lazily back and forth. He held Hannah's hand with his other hand, and they strolled across the deck. There was plenty of time.

They spotted dolphins swimming alongside the ship and stopped to watch. Suddenly one leaped into the air, followed by another, as though they played follow-the-leader. The second dolphin emitted a high-pitched whistle, and Hannah clapped her hands with excitement.

"What did he say?"

"Do you really want to know?"

"Yes," she laughed, thinking he would make up something. "The male whistles when he's romantically excited."

Her face blushed, and Nathan chuckled quietly. "You wanted to know," he muttered.

They reached the stairs, and she went first, but he was right behind her. Murray was glad to see them and said he would go to the galley, then get some sleep in the crew's quarters. While Nathan checked the ship's compass and other instruments, Hannah circled the room and looked out the windows. The sun had begun to set, but from the helm, she could see far out over the water. She yearned for the sight of land and thought how good it would be to feel the earth beneath her feet.

Sadness filled her heart, however, when she remembered that Nathan would return to Europe and to the war soon after they reached America. She crossed the room to sit on the windowsill where she had sat the night she told him about her life. With her knees drawn in front of her, she watched the British flag wave in the red glow that the sun cast as it sank beyond the water's edge. Nathan was proud of this flag, and if need be, would give his life to protect it.

Would the Irish ever rise against England? Her father would have. Her sadness deepened when she thought of her country and Nathan's country at war. She understood Collin's hatred for British Aristocrats, but yet, was treated so kindly by Nathan and his parents.

Nathan noticed the melancholy expression on her face and perceived that her thoughts were sad. "Are you sorry you came with me?" he asked.

"Oh, no. I'm glad you asked me. I'm waiting for you to tell me about yourself."

"As I told you," he began, "I grew up in a large old house. It's on a hill that overlooks the sea near Liverpool and was built in the late sixteen hundreds as the manor house of a large estate. The estate was broken up over the years, so my dad was able to acquire only two hundred acres of land when he purchased it. My parents moved there about the time I was born; it's the only home I've ever known. I understand how you must feel about leaving home. I know how hard it would be for me to leave Barrington Manor and never return."

Hannah looked at him to acknowledge what he had said, and her mouth twitched at one side.

"Sheep, cattle, and horses are raised on the land," he continued. "Hired servants care for them and grow food for them. I helped the servants when growing up and even now when possible.

"Dad went to sea at a young age and fought in the war between England and her American Colonies. England lost her colonies, but Dad gained recognition, and after the war, he came home and started a shipping business. It was small at first with just one old ship, but God blessed him and my mother. Their business grew and has now expanded to shipbuilding. I helped design the *Monarch* and it was built by our company."

"It's magnificent."

"Thank you."

"All my life, I wanted to be a seaman like my dad, and when I was small, I cried for him to take me to sea. I watched ships sail in and out of the harbor from my bedroom window and knew that one day I'd be on one of them.

"I have only one brother; he's three years older than me. He likes the sea, but is married and has a small son, so he stays home with his family and takes care of the business. I felt lost when he first married because we'd always been together; with Dad gone, we looked out for each other." He remembered that Hannah had no brother or sister and felt bad for her.

"A hired tutor came to live in our home when we were small, the way you will live on the plantation. Mr. Willoughby was a good teacher, and we were good students—most of the time. There were days when we didn't want to go to school and would run away from him. With so many places to hide in the old house, it was impossible for him to find us. After he returned to his classroom, we spent the rest of the day trying on medieval armor and fighting each other with old swords that we found on the third floor. Some days we spent hours practicing. When my brother and I stand back-to-back with a sword in hand, nobody can take us. We always got in trouble for running away from Mr. Willoughby, but when we showed Dad what we could do with the sword, he couldn't have been prouder.

"Jason's dad is a lawyer in Liverpool and has taken care of legal matters in our business for years. Jason and his older brother came to our home with him, many times. We played war and fought battles in the great hall and on the grounds. My brother and I taught them how to use the sword, and later when the four of us attended the same boarding school, we stayed together and no one bothered us."

Hannah was impressed and smiled at him.

"It was a Christian school and was where I met Jesus and trusted him as my Savior. One Sunday at our morning service, I went forth, confessing my faith in Him, and Jason did the same before the year was over.

"After graduation, my brother and I transferred to a navigational school, but Jason's parents insisted that he and his brother attend law school. His brother became a lawyer and works with their dad, but Jason dropped out of school because he's not sure he wants to be a lawyer. He loves sailing, but will be forced someday to make a decision of whether to return to school or keep working for our company. He's waiting for the war to end. If he's killed, he won't have to decide."

Hannah's head dropped forward, and she covered her face with her hands. Nathan realized what he'd said.

"I'm sorry, Hannah. I shouldn't have said that."

She stood and put her arms around him. "Nathan, I don't want you to go to war."

"I know, and I hate to leave you, but you heard me say that Jason and I have trusted the Lord, so if we die, we'll go to a better place. I'm not afraid. Please remember that if something happens to me."

She was silent. It's not that easy, she thought.

Nathan tried to make her feel better. "I'll be all right," he said. "I believe God will let me live through the war." They both knew he had no assurance, but when Hannah finally spoke again, she seemed to have put it out of her mind.

"Please tell me your brother's name and the names of his wife and son."

"My brother is James and his wife is Sandra. Their three-year-old son is Daniel Lee Barrington." He smiled and added, "After me, but we call him Dan." She could see that he was proud of his namesake.

"I wish I could meet them and Jason's family."

"I intend for you to as soon as the war is over. Speaking of Jason's family . . . his dad, David Williams, knows your friend, John Dudley. It was through him that Mr. Dudley arranged passage for you on the *Monarch*. Another passenger was booked to sail with us in the last vacant cabin, but he cancelled the day before Jason's dad received Dudley's letter. Because of his cancellation, my dad was able to write you that he could take on another passenger.

"I asked Jason to meet you on the dock and help you aboard, but for some reason, he couldn't. Had he gone, he would have claimed you for himself. There are so many reasons why things could have been different, and only God could have worked everything out. Don't you see, Hannah, He brought us together."

"Do you really think so?"

"Yes, I'm sure of it."

She stood behind him with her arms around his waist, and after a moment, she leaned her head against his back and yawned.

"You're sleepy." He pulled on her arm until she stood at his side.

"Yes."

"Did you take a nap?"

"No."

"Why not?"

"I had something else to do."

"What? Wash out your underwear?"

"No," she laughed. "I don't do that on Sunday."

"What did you do?"

"I can't tell you."

"Yes you can."

She hesitated before replying, "I spent the evening in prayer and searching the scriptures."

"All evening?"

"Yes."

"What bothered you?"

"Nathan, please."

Suddenly he knew. There was only one reason why she would spend the entire evening in Bible study and prayer. She had made a decision about him, and he felt the same fear that he had felt the night she locked her doors. He closed his eyes and his teeth clenched.

Hannah realized that he'd guessed what she had done. "I love you, Nathan," she said.

But not enough to marry me, he thought, and silently looked out over the wheel. Was it more important to her to do the will of her dead father than to make the two of them happy? He removed his arm from around her and ran his fingers through his hair.

"I love you," she said again.

The door opened and Jason entered. Nathan had asked him to come at ten o'clock in case Hannah wanted to go to her cabin; he didn't want her to go alone. He knew she was tired and sleepy and without looking at her, said, "Jason came to walk you to your cabin."

She looked at Jason and then back at him. "Do you want me to go?" she asked.

At first, he didn't answer, but then shook his head and muttered, "No."

"Then I'll wait until someone comes to relieve you."

"I'll take over for you, Nathan," Jason offered. He noticed all was not right between them.

"No, but thanks, Jason." While the two of them talked to

each other, Hannah returned to the windowsill and looked up at the stars.

Nathan had calmed down by the time Jason left. He was glad Hannah had stayed, and he asked her to return to his side.

"Will you tell me about your home in England," she asked, "that I might know what it was like when you grew up there?" He nodded his head, and she went to sit on the windowsill again.

He had not intended to tell her just how large and beautiful his home was, for fear of making her feel worse about their differences, but since she wanted him to, he would.

"You leave the main road out of Liverpool," he began, "and turn onto a narrow, winding road that leads uphill to our home. Trees line each side of the road, and in the summer they grow together over it to make a shade. Sheep and cattle graze in green meadows beyond the trees, and in the springtime, wildflowers bloom here and there."

"It sounds beautiful."

"It is. There's a wooden bridge over a stream, and just on the other side of it, the road curves sharply to the right, and then the house looms in front of you with the sea beyond it. When I've been away for a long time, I anticipate rounding the curve to see the most wonderful sight . . . my home."

Hannah turned her head toward the window and looked into the darkness. It would always be home to him, she thought, and he would always want to return there. She understood, because she missed the cottage that had been her home. She remembered how she felt when she went away to college and how happy she was to return. So it really wasn't the size of a house or where it was located, but that it was home. She decided that home could be anywhere, and she would find a new one in America.

When she turned away, Nathan stopped talking. She was lost in her own thoughts for a moment then realized what she had done and turned back to him. "Please go on."

"Are you sure?"

"Yes, I want you to describe all of it."

"Well, the yard covers a large area and is surrounded by an old brick wall where James and Jason and Jason's brother, Andrew, and I fought many battles. The enemy was the French, of course, and they were outside the wall, but we were inside it with the fort behind us. Perhaps Jason and I will be able to put fighting techniques that we made up to real use against the French."

Hannah realized that the pretend battles they had fought as children were fond memories for him.

"There's an opening in the brick wall for the road to pass through, and I suppose at one time there was a gate, but not since I can remember. Trees and plants surround the house, and across the back, a vine reaches to a balcony. When I was a child, I would climb out my bedroom window onto the balcony and then over the side of it and down the vine. I haven't done that in many years, and I'm not sure if it would still hold me up. I'd like to try, but the whole vine would probably fall to the ground with me." Hannah laughed.

"At the front of the home, a brick porch with tall pillars forms a half circle around double doors; a cover extends from the roof. Steps surround the porch, and the double doors open to a large entrance hall with walls of carved woodwork and mirrors. The floor is covered with marble that shines like glass."

Suddenly Nathan's voice changed, and his thoughts seemed to be far away as he described his home. Hannah realized he had been taken back to it.

"To the right of the entrance hall," he said, "is a ballroom large enough to accommodate two hundred people. Mother has decorated it with drapery and beautiful paintings from all over the world. I dream of dancing there with you."

"I suppose you've danced there with many lovely girls."

"No . . . I don't attend most of the balls that Mother and Dad give for friends and customers. I don't really care for them, for I'm not fond of dressing up and entertaining people that way, but you belong there. I can see how wonderful you would look in an evening gown that complements your beautiful hair. Every man would envy me."

"I would feel so out of place. It frightens me to think of it."

"I don't mean to frighten you, and I wouldn't let you feel out of place. You would be comfortable in my arms, and I would dance with you all night and not share you with anyone."

"Do you really want me to?"

"Yes."

"Then I want to. Now stop dreaming and finish describing the house."

"To the left of the entrance hall is a dining room where more than two hundred people may be seated. A large kitchen provides servants a place to prepare meals for a crowd of people. A great hall runs lengthwise through the house, and across it, a living area is furnished with chairs and divans. The library is there, next to my dad's office. Beyond the living area is a smaller kitchen where you'll find Marie cooking something good to eat."

"And who is Marie?"

"Our family cook. She can make an apple pie that will melt in your mouth."

"I'm sure I would love her."

"You would. She and her husband, Edgar, came to live at Barrington Manor when I was a baby, and I love her as much as my own mother. Edgar keeps the gardens around the home and helps out with other jobs. While growing up, James and I knew that when dad was away, we'd better do what he said, but we didn't mind, for Edgar took us fishing in the summertime.

"I forgot the music room. It's between the living area and the library."

"Please tell me about it."

"Well, there isn't much to tell. A grand piano stands near the center of the room and is surrounded by stacks of dusty old music books and sheet music. I think it was mostly all there when my parents bought the place. The door to the room has been shut, and no one goes there except a servant who cleans it occasionally. My mother wanted James and me to play, and Mr. Willoughby gave us lessons, but could never get us to practice. I like music, but I didn't like sitting on that piano stool for an hour."

Hannah smiled. "I would love the music room," she said.

"Do you play the piano?"

"Yes. The school I attended as a child encouraged their students to learn music. They taught me to sing and to play the piano, and I loved it. My father bought my mother a piano right after they were married, and I played it while growing up. I gave it to our church in the village, because I didn't think I could bring it with me. It was very hard for me to part with it.

"Father told me that my mother loved the piano, and that sometimes she would sit and play it for hours. When I was lonely and thought about her, I went near the piano and pretended she was sitting there playing. On the day that two men came from the church and loaded it onto a wagon, I felt an empty place in my heart and cried for a long time."

"I'll buy you another piano one day," Nathan promised.

"It could never be same. I would not be able to visualize my mother playing it as I did her own piano."

"Well, mother would be delighted for you to play her piano. She gave up on her sons long ago, and Sandra doesn't play.

"Two other rooms on the first floor of the house are large closets at each side of the entrance hall. Off the center of the great hall is a winding staircase that leads to the second floor. James and I slid down its banister every morning to see what Marie had fixed us for breakfast. My mother swore we would cause the stairs to fall one day, but they're still standing, and I have a feeling they will be for at least another hundred years.

"A set of double doors at the top of the stairs opens to a balcony that runs the length of the house, and many nights I climbed out my window onto it to listen to the surf and to think about my dad. They were lonely times for me. I sat with my back to the wall and drew my knees in front of me, and with my arms wrapped around my legs, I laid my head over and cried. You're the only one I've ever told this to."

"Oh, Nathan." She realized they had shared a common disappointment in life, and that his family's wealth had not compensated for his loneliness. She rose from the windowsill and put her arms around him.

"You missed your dad, didn't you?"

"Yes."

"Will you be gone from home the way he was?"

"No. There will be times when I must go, but I intend to be with my family and to spend time with my children as they grow up." He then muttered under his breath, "If I have any."

"You missed your dad the way I did my mother," she said, pretending not to have heard his last words.

"Yes."

She leaned forward to stretch her back.

"You're getting tired of listening."

"No. I want you to tell me everything."

"That's really all there is to tell about my home. There are bedrooms and water closets and a small office on the second floor. The third floor is filled with old armor, swords, and other weapons. . . . A place that catches discarded articles. Many things that Dad brings back from his voyages end up there. It's amusing to go through it."

"I would love to, and I'd love to see your room. It must have a magnificent view of the sea."

"It has. I wish I could turn the *Monarch* around and take you there right now, but I can't."

"I know you can't, darling . . . I know." She spoke in her kind, soft voice.

"Hannah, why has God brought us together at a time in our lives when things are so uncertain for both of us?"

"I don't know, but it's for a reason, and someday we'll look back and know the answer to your question."

Yes, he thought, if I live that long.

CHAPTER 8

At twelve, midnight, Jeff came to relieve Nathan of his duty at the helm. The two talked a minute before Jeff took the wheel. Hannah waited quietly, while Nathan checked the instruments.

"How you been, Hannah?" Jeff asked.

"I'm fine, Jeff; how are you?"

"I'm all right, but I seldom see you anymore."

"That's because you're so busy."

"I suppose so," he laughed.

Nathan listened to their conversation, and when finished with the instruments, he remarked, "That's right, Jeff. I've noticed how busy you stay."

"Well, I hope I don't go to sleep before daylight. It's going to be a long duty, and I wish I had someone like Hannah to keep me company. You're a lucky man."

"I know," Nathan agreed. He reached for Hannah's hand and asked if she was ready to go. They descended the steps slowly with him in front, and she held his hand tightly with one hand and the rail with her other. When he reached the deck, he turned, and she stepped from the last step into his arms. He couldn't wait another moment to hold her. Her lips felt wonderful against his.

"I don't need anyone to tell me how lucky I am," he groaned. "I already know."

"I love you, Nathan. You know I love you."

He wanted to ask her to marry him right then, but feared her answer would be no. True, he did know she loved him, but was afraid she would say, I love you, but I can't marry you. What was he going to do if she did?

He remembered Jason's question, "Do her feelings mean nothing to you?" Would it be as devastating to her if their relationship ended as it would be to him? He thought so and felt wretched. She had trusted him, but he had deceived her, and nothing he could do would make amends.

As they crossed the deck to her cabin, she looked up at the starry sky. "Nathan," she said, "look at all the stars. There are millions of them. Look! There's a shooting star!"

He caught a glimpse of it as it shot across the sky and disappeared.

"Did you see it?" she asked.

"Yes, but I would rather look at you than all the stars in the sky."

"Oh, Nathan." She knew he was still upset and wanted to take his mind off unpleasant thoughts. "The moon is so bright," she said. "It's beautiful and seems to be smiling at us."

"Your face is beautiful in its light." He did look up, however, and right above them was the Big Dipper. As all good seamen, he knew the stars like the palm of his hand, and using the Big Dipper as a guide, his eyes quickly followed a path to other constellations.

"Do you see the Big Dipper?" he asked.

"Yes."

He pointed to the star that pinpointed Regulus, and they found the head and body of Leo, the reclining lion. He described Orion from the winter sky and Pegasus from an autumn one. "And . . . and . . ." He couldn't think of the name of the queen that lives in the sky.

"Cassiopeia," she helped him.

"Uh . . . how did you know? You know all of the constellations, don't you?"

"Yes, but you brought back a wonderful memory of the time my father pointed them out to me. Nathan, you're so much like him."

She lifted her face to him; it was radiant in the moonlight. He leaned against a post of the guardrail and pulled her body against his. "I love you . . . I love you . . . I love you," he whispered between kisses.

"I love you, too," she responded and snuggled in his arms.

"Hannah . . . Hannah will you marry me?" He could hardly breathe.

"Yes, Nathan," she answered without hesitation. "If you're sure you want me to."

His breathing became harder. He couldn't believe her answer was yes and thought he had heard her wrong, but was afraid to ask again.

"Nathan?" she said his name questioningly.

"What?"

"Are you sure you want me to?"

"Yes, darling. I've never been surer of anything in my life. Suddenly, his knees felt weak and he leaned against her for support. She noticed the weight of his body and felt it trembling.

"Are you all right," she asked.

"No. I need to sit down."

"Come to my cabin." She helped him to the side of her bed; he sat down and fell backward with his eyes closed. She turned up her lamp and saw that his face was very pale.

"Nathan, what's wrong?"

"Give me a minute; it's not every day that I ask someone to marry me."

"Oh, Nathan." She laughed at him. He sat up and gave her a funny look that made her laugh even harder.

"I thought you were going to say no, since it took you all evening to make up your mind. Why did you put me through such agony?"

"I knew what you were thinking, but I couldn't say, 'I'm going to answer yes, if you ever ask me to marry you.'"

"You would have saved me from near heart failure if you had."

"I'm sorry. I shouldn't have told you what I did all evening. I knew I wanted to marry you, but I had to be sure that it was right with God and for both of us. I didn't want to tell you that I would marry you and then, later, have to tell you that I couldn't. God has given me peace about it."

"What about your father? Are you at peace about him, too?"

"No," she sighed, "not completely, but I know he would not deny us his blessings if he knew how much we love each other. He was a good man, Nathan, and I believe you two would have gotten along all right."

"I wish I could have known him."

"You will. I'll tell you about him for the rest of our lives."

"I want you to, and I want you to tell our children about him."

"There are other matters," she said, "that I'm concerned about, but if God in his infinite wisdom brought us together, he is great enough to take care of them."

"What are you concerned about?"

"Will all of your family accept me since I'm Irish? I know how much you care for them, and I never want to come between you and any one of them. I think it would be so wonderful to have a family."

"All of my family will love you." He wanted to add, you're part British through your mother, but was afraid she would think he was belittling her father.

"Where will we live?" she asked.

"I don't know, sweetheart, but I know I won't ask you to live any place where you're not happy."

"Or would I want you to."

"We'll talk about it and make plans when I get back from the war. Wherever we live, I know I want to spend the rest of my life with you. We have the same faith in God and that's what's important."

"I know, and I wouldn't want to live anywhere without you."

"Will you wait for me, darling?"

"Yes, you know I will."

"How long will you wait?"

"Until you return."

"What if I don't return?"

"Then I shall wait forever."

"Hannah . . . my precious Hannah."

"I pray that you will return to me."

"Only death can keep me away."

His fingers slipped beneath his collar, and he lifted a gold chain from around his neck and placed it around hers. "I don't have a ring to give you," he said, "but this is a representation of the Barrington coat of arms and its falcon crest in gold. It covered the shields carried by my forefathers when they rode into battle. Dad gave it to me before I left on my first voyage, and I've never taken it off. It's become a part of me. Will you wear it until I return with a ring?"

"Yes, darling. If you want me to."

"I do, and if something happens to me, I want you to have it forever."

"I'm honored that you trust me with something so special to you."

"You're special to me, and only God ranks over you in my life."

"He's the only one I could ever love more than you."

"We'll sight land day after tomorrow," he said. "I'll be busy until then, so if you don't see me, don't think that I'm avoiding you. I don't know what to expect, but remember that England is not on friendly terms with the United States right now. Dad thinks there will be no trouble, but we must be cautious."

"Nathan, I have a favor to ask of you."

"What is it?"

"Steven wants to climb to the crow's nest, and I told him that perhaps he could before we reach America. He's been a great help to me and has asked for nothing in return. Will you have time to climb there with him?"

Nathan was silent as he thought of what she had asked. Finally he answered, "I don't know, Hannah. That's a long way up, and you know what could happen if he fell. Maybe I can pay him in some other way."

"He doesn't want to be paid. He wants to climb to the crow's nest."

"I'll have to ask John about it. He's just a boy."

"He's more grown up than you think. How old were you the first time you climbed to the crow's nest?"

"That was different. My dad was the captain and was fully responsible for me. Steven is John's son, but my dad is still the captain, and I'll have to answer to both if Steven gets hurt. Worse than that, I'll have to live with myself."

"How old were you?"

"Ten."

"Steven is twelve and almost thirteen."

"All right—all right, Hannah! I said I would ask John. I owe Steven for letting me know that you were all right when you would talk to no one else."

"Thank you. It will mean so much to him. He loves the *Monarch* and I believe he'll be a seaman one day."

"You really think so?"

"Yes."

"I'll keep that in mind. I'll also be aware of how you can talk me into doing things."

"Well, I did kiss the Blarney Stone."

"You did **what**?"

She laughed and repeated, "I kissed the Blarney Stone. Haven't you heard of it and how that anyone who kisses it is supposed to acquire the power of persuasive speech?"

"No, I haven't."

"It's on the wall in the tower of Blarney Castle, near my home."

"So now you tell me after I asked you to marry me."

"Do you want to take back your proposal?"

"Not in a million years. But before I go, I need to change the bandage on your back and make sure the wound is healing. Would you feel better if my mother was here with you?"

"Oh, Nathan, we can't wake her at this hour. Won't it wait until morning?"

"I should have already changed it, and I won't have time in the morning."

"All right. Let me change into something that will make it easier for you to take care of it." She took her gown and robe from her trunk and went into the water closet to change, while Nathan went across the hall for his medical bag.

When she returned to the room, he had moved her chair near the lamp. She sat on the side of it and leaned forward with her robe draped over her back and the strap of her gown down the side of her arm. She held the front of her robe with one hand and pulled her hair to one side with the other.

He carefully removed the old bandage and examined the area around the wound. His hands were warm to her back, and their presence there caused a tingling sensation in her body. She tried to ignore it.

"It looks okay," he said. "It's not swollen or red. Does it hurt?"

"No, not any more. I seldom think of it."

"Good. I don't believe there is any infection. It appears to be healing." To make sure, he put more ointment on it and covered it with a new bandage.

Her skin was smooth and white under her gown, and it felt like silk to his hands. He rubbed them gently over the injured place and caressed her shoulders and the back of her neck. When they slid up her throat, she leaned her head backward, against him. His heart beat faster, and he had a strong desire to take her in his arms, but she had trusted him to help her, and he would not take advantage of her. Could it be possible that she felt the same way?

He carefully lifted the strap of her gown and the back of her robe to their proper place across her shoulders. "It should be all right now," he said, "but if it begins to hurt, let me know."

"I will, and thank you for taking care of it. I would do it myself if I could see it and reach it. I take so much of your time, but I don't think I could have survived this trip across the ocean without you. I've been a burden to you, and I can't understand why someone like you would love me."

Nathan sat down on the side of her bed, and she turned in the chair to face him. They gazed into each other's eyes an instant before she lowered hers to her hands folded in her lap.

He leaned forward and put his arms on his knees and locked his fingers together between them. He bowed his head a moment and closed his eyes and then looked at her and spoke in a solemn voice. "Hannah, I should take care of your back because it was my fault that you got hurt. I never have, and I never will think of you as a burden, so please don't say that again.

"As for why I love you, I could say it's because your beauty on the outside is only surpassed by your beauty on the inside. Perhaps I love you because you're sweet and warm-hearted, and to know you is to love you. I love your blushing face, for in it I see your shy humbleness. I could love you for your honesty and for being true to your word or bargain, even though you give so much and ask nothing in return. Perhaps it's because you're intelligent and want to teach others. I love you every time I hold you and kiss you; you make me feel so wonderful inside. If for no other reason, I love you because you love me, even after I hurt you. You understood and forgave me. Most of all, I love you because you're a wonderful person and the only girl I've ever met that I wanted to spend the rest of my life with."

"Nathan," she sighed lightly, "I can't be all of that."

"You are, my darling. They're all reasons why I love you, but I loved you the first time I saw you, and I knew nothing about you then. You looked so wonderful standing there with the wind blowing your hair, and when you spoke, your voice was so sweet and kind. I fell in love with you right then, but now that I know you, I love you even more."

"Oh, Nathan," she smiled, "you say the sweetest things . . . to be an Englishman."

"Uh . . . sweetheart," he laughed, "your sense of humor is not one of the reasons I love you. I've got to go."

They stood and walked to the door. She put her arms around him.

"Hannah," he asked, "do you think of me when you lie down at night?"

"Yes," she whispered, "every night."

"What do you think about me?"

"How wonderful you are and how much I love you."

"Is that all?" His lips played with her ear.

"No."

"What else?"

"I dream that you hold me and kiss me."

"Do you dream of me the way I dream of you?"

"Nathan . . . don't."

"Tell me, darling—please tell me you do."

"Yes," she finally confessed. "You know I do."

CHAPTER 9

Nathan left Hannah's cabin and returned to the helm. Duty at the wheel from midnight until four in the morning was the most difficult stint. He'd experienced the loneliness a seaman could feel during the time and knew how much it meant to have someone to talk to.

Jeff was surprised to see him, and at first, they talked of small matter, such as the bright moon and good weather, but Nathan had come to discuss more than heavenly bodies or the condition of the atmosphere.

"Jeff," he said, "I appreciate your hard work. You make a special effort to get things done. I talked to the captain about increasing your pay, and he agreed. He also said that with more experience and training, you could become a captain, that is, if you're interested."

"I'm interested, Nathan, but don't know what to tell you. I'm joining the King's Army soon as we return home. If we don't stop Napoleon's army, he'll find a way to cross the channel. Who knows what the future holds?"

"No one. It's hard to make plans when our country is at war, but the offer will still stand when the war is over. Jason and I enlisted. We leave for military duty the day after we return."

"What about Hannah? Will you marry her and take her back to England?"

"Not now. She promised to wait for me."

"Where?"

Nathan was slow to answer. He'd rather Jeff not know where Hannah would be waiting. "I'm not sure," he said and changed the subject. They talked more about the war and discussed the shipping business until Jeff heard Nathan's deep breathing and realized that he talked to himself. Nathan was asleep on Murray's cot, but it was good to have someone close by.

After Nathan left her cabin, Hannah sat on the side of her bed and thought of all that had happened that day. She lifted her hand and let her fingers touch the golden shield, the helmet, and falcon crest that made up the Barrington coat of arms. She was happy that Nathan had asked her to marry him and wished for someone to share her joy with. On special occasions in her past she had thought how wonderful it would be to have a mother to share them with. And when growing up, she told her father everything, but felt he didn't understand her feelings like a mother would. Tonight she had become engaged to be married and had neither parent to share her excitement with. She wished she could tell them about Nathan and of the happiness he'd brought her, but under the circumstances, perhaps it was best she couldn't. She went to bed and was soon asleep.

Stuart came to relieve Jeff at four o'clock the next morning, and Jeff woke Nathan before leaving the helm. Nathan sat up, but couldn't hold his eyes open. He asked Jeff to have the men meet in the mess hall before breakfast and told Stuart to wake him again at 5:45.

When Stuart woke him a second time, he hurried to his cabin and, within minutes, stood beside the captain, shaved and dressed in his uniform, waiting for the crew to assemble.

After everyone was seated, the captain spoke a few words and then turned the meeting over to Nathan.

"I want every man to be on alert as soon as we come within sight of land," Nathan briefed the men. "Report any ship sailing in our direction, no matter how small, and be ready to man your battle stations at all time. Have your rifles and gear ready.

"My position will be first cannon on starboard, and Jason will hold the same position at larboard." Mark and Jeff were stationed at the stern, and men were assigned to assist at each cannon. Sam was to be called out of the galley, if necessary, and Murray would stay at the wheel. "Passengers will be informed to stay in their cabins," said Nathan, "unless there is a battle, in which case, a rifle will be issued to the men." Before the meeting was adjourned, every man knew exactly what he was expected to do, should there be trouble.

"We're taking precaution," Nathan stated, "because the United States Navy and the British Royal Navy are not on friendly terms, but under no circumstances is anyone to fire a shot without an order from the captain. The *Monarch* is not a military ship," he reminded them. After the briefing, the men were dismissed to eat breakfast.

As he talked to the crew, Nathan saw Hannah pass by the mess hall door, and he assumed she was still in the dining hall. He went to join her with his own breakfast in hand, but found all three of the Hartman children seated at her table. John and Rachel ate alone. He realized he would never have a better chance to talk to them about the favor Hannah had asked of him. His eyes met hers and she smiled a beautiful smile. His gold chain with the Barrington coat of arms was around her neck, and at that moment, he would have done anything she could have asked of him.

John and Rachel were surprised when he came to their table. Rachel rose from her chair. "I'll get the children," she said. "I thought you had already eaten when Hannah asked them to sit with her."

So this was planned. He looked at Hannah through squinted eyes, but again, she smiled pleasantly at him, and he asked Rachel to be seated. He informed both parents of Steven's desire to climb to the crow's nest and then asked their permission to take him aloft. Rachel was hesitant, but John insisted it would be a great experience for Steven.

"Steven told Hannah that he wanted to climb to the nest," said Nathan, "and she asked me about it last night. She doesn't think he'll have any trouble, but in case he does, I'll be right behind him." When Rachel heard it was Hannah's idea, she agreed.

Nathan ate quickly and returned his tray to the galley. On his way out, ne stood behind Hannah with his hands on her shoulders, but spoke to Steven. "Steven, would you like to climb with me to the crow's nest this morning?"

Steven's eyes lit up. He jumped from his chair and answered, "Sure, Nathan!" It was a surprise, for Hannah had said nothing about it. She'd waited for John and Rachel to give their consent.

"Are you ready?"

"Soon as I return my tray." He hurried off with it in his hand.

"Are you happy now?" Nathan asked Hannah. "We'll do some training at first and don't watch, for it'll make him nervous." He then leaned forward and whispered in her ear, "You have never looked more beautiful to me than you do this morning . . . even if you are conniving against me."

She pretended to have no idea what he talked about, but said, "Thank you, Nathan," when he and Steven left together.

Nathan told Steven to take two steps up the rope ladder and then step back to the deck. "Go three steps up and back down," he said, "then four and so on until you get to the tenth rung. When you get that high, climb up and down until you really get the hang of it."

"All right," Steven agreed.

With these instructions, Nathan left him and went to the captain's office to record his briefing of the crew in the ship's log. He wanted to give Steven time to get used to the ladder, and after twenty minutes, he returned to find him going up and down it rapidly.

"Do you think you can make it to the top?" he asked.

"Yes," Steven nodded his head.

"Well, take off, mate, but don't get in too big a hurry and don't look down. I'm right behind you."

"Okay, Nathan."

Steven climbed slowly but steadily until he neared the top of the mast. He had not realized how high he would have to climb, and the higher he went, the farther out over the water the tall mast took him. From the deck, where he had watched the seamen scoot up and down the ladder, it had looked like such a simple thing to do, but from up here . . . well, it was scary.

"Do you want to climb down and try again later?" Nathan asked.

"No, I'm going to the top."

"Well, take it easy."

Steven's hands gripped the ropes, and he set his aim on the platform above him. With his face turned upward, he climbed until he was right under the crow's nest. Nathan instructed him to take hold of the rim around the nest and to pull himself through the open space. Steven did it slowly, just the way Nathan had said, and planted his feet on the boards that surrounded the mast.

He was nervous, but excited, and Nathan knew exactly how he felt. No seaman ever forgot the first time he scaled the crow's nest. The *Monarch* heeled gently in the cool early-morning breeze, and Steven walked around the nest with his eyes focused on the horizon. It was awesome.

He looked down at the deck that seemed far below. Hannah waved and then ran to get his family.

"She's the one to thank for this, Steven; she insisted you could do it. And she thinks you'll be a seaman someday. Have you thought about it?"

"Yes," Steven answered Nathan with only one word. His mind was elsewhere. "I'll miss Hannah when we leave the ship," he said.

"I know." Nathan laid a hand on his shoulder. "I'll miss her too when I leave her in South Carolina."

Descending the ladder, Steven found, was easier than ascending it. Nathan stepped from the nest first, but waited for him to get his feet on the ladder. They started down together and reached the deck without a mishap.

As they neared the foot of the ladder, Hannah became so excited she could hardly stand still, and her hands clapped when Steven's feet stepped onto the deck. He turned and ran toward her, and she met him with outstretched arms. Nathan stood with one hand on the ladder and watched her embrace him; she tousled his windblown hair, but looked over his shoulder at Nathan. He smiled at her, and when Steven ran to Rachel, she walked to where he stood.

"You gave him a memory that he'll never forget."

"You gave it to him and I told him so."

"We did it together."

Nathan returned to the ship's office, but couldn't keep his mind on the mount of paper work. He thought of what Steven had said about Hannah. How could he leave her in South Carolina? If he stayed in America, he would be wanted for desertion of the Royal Navy and most likely hanged if caught, and Hannah wasn't strong enough to make the return voyage across the ocean. She might die if she tried.

———————————

There was no use asking Steven to go to the gun deck, Hannah thought. She laughed as he went from one seaman to another, relating his daring accomplishment of scaling the great height to the crow's nest. His story grew with each telling, and the men's praise sent him to even greater heights.

She went to the gun deck alone. Sails that were torn during the storm had been hung there to dry and now lay heaped in a pile at the foot of the steps. She lifted the end of one and struggled to release it from the others. As she tugged and pulled, she heard a noise, but thought that it came from the upper deck and disregarded it.

When one sail was freed from the others, she sat down by her sewing bag and began to thread a large needle. She heard the noise again and realized it didn't come from the upper deck. She was not alone on the gun deck.

"Who's there?" she called out, but no one answered. Her first impulse was to drop the sail and run up the flight of steps to the main deck, but she decided not to let fear get the best of her and called again, "Who's there?" in a louder voice.

From the far end of the deck came a man's voice. "Is that you, Hannah?" It was Scott.

She picked up one corner of the sail and walked to the other end of the gun deck with the canvas trailing behind her. Scott's legs protruded from beneath a large cannon that he had cleaned and now swabbed with a solution that would keep it free of rust.

Hannah sat on the pile of canvas behind her and pulled the torn place to her lap. "You scared me half to death," she said.

"I'm sorry," laughed Scott. "I didn't mean to. I thought I heard somebody say something, but didn't know they talked to me."

She hadn't talked to Scott since she found out that Nathan was the captain's son and, at first, didn't know what to say. "Will you be glad when we get to New York City?" she tried to make conversation.

"Oh, I don't know. Is one port different from any other?" he answered her question with another as he slid out from under the cannon.

"I suppose not when you're in a foreign country."

Scott sat up and leaned his back against the cannon and watched as her hands mended the sail.

"You're pretty fast at that."

"I've sewed most of my life. I mended my father's clothes and my own, while growing up."

"Why didn't your mother do it?"

"She died when I was born."

Scott's brow wrinkled and his head slowly shook from side to side. "It must have been awfully hard growing up without a mother. I don't know how I could have made it without mine."

"If you've never had one, you don't realize how much you miss her."

"I guess not, but what about your dad? Who mends his clothes now?"

"My father died a short time before I left Ireland. I have no family, so I decided to go to America with hopes of finding one there."

"Why didn't you tell me about your parents? You listen to everyone else's misfortune."

"It's hard to talk about them."

"I can understand that."

"Why didn't you tell me that Nathan was Captain Barrington's son?" Hannah lowered her eyes and Scott realized she had spoken the words hastily.

He sat silently a moment, watching her push the needle back and forth through the canvas. When he spoke, he chose his words carefully, and she laid the sewing aside and looked into his face.

"I almost did tell you. I was shocked when I realized you didn't know and felt bad when you talked about him, after I found out. I wanted to tell you. I couldn't understand why Nathan kept it from you, but figured he had a reason. I suspected it was because he didn't want you to love him for his wealth, but then heard that it had something to do with your dad not liking wealthy British."

"I wouldn't have loved him for his wealth."

"I know that, but I didn't know if he did. Would you have loved him, had you known who he was?"

She sighed before answering, "Probably not."

"Then he did the right thing."

"How can you say that?"

"Because you two are meant for each other, and if that was the only way then he did what he had to. You don't know how difficult it was for him. He was afraid you would hate him when you found out."

"I could never hate him."

"Hannah, you could never hate anyone."

"I suppose not."

"I'll hate what Nathan will do to me if he finds me talking to you instead of finishing my work. I'll be in trouble for sure." He lay back and pushed his body under the cannon.

"Scott, are you still homesick?"

"Yes, but I'll probably leave again soon after I return. Captain

Barrington offered me a permanent job. He said I could live in Liverpool and work in the business if I would agree to sail when he really needed me. I could go home most weekends. It sounds like a good opportunity, and I like working for the Barringtons. If I found something that paid more, I wouldn't be treated as well."

"Then you really intend to keep working for Barrington Shipping?"

"Yes."

"I'm glad . . . and Scott . . ."

"Yea, Hannah."

"You're a good friend."

"Thanks. I'm glad to see you and Nathan getting along again. You deserve a good man, and I believe he'll treat you right. If he doesn't, you come looking for me."

"Oh, Scott," she smiled.

When the sail was mended, she folded it and put it away before going to the dining hall for the noon meal. She waited for Nathan, and when he didn't come, she suspected he didn't have time to eat, so she put two meals into a bag and crossed the deck to the captain's office.

"Hannah!" Nathan was surprised. "Thanks for the food; I'm starved!"

At the other side of the room, the captain laid down the quill he'd been writing with and stood up.

"Sir," said Hannah, "there are two meals in the bag."

"Oh, no, I need to get some exercise. I'll go eat with Martha."

Nathan cleared a place on his desk, and Hannah spread the food on it, but even as they ate, he calculated the figures on the papers.

"What are all those papers?"

"They go with the cargo that we carry and must be put in order. I'm sorry; I shouldn't work while you're here."

"I don't mind. I know it's my fault that you're behind on your work. I wish I could help you."

"You do help me."

"I mended a sail this morning. I'm glad I can work for my passage."

"You don't have to and I wish you wouldn't."

"I only work when I feel like it."

As soon as they finished eating, Hannah put the empty tea bottles back into the bag. "I must go," she said, "so you can finish your work."

He walked her to the door. "I'm glad you came and thanks again for the food."

"You're welcome."

The sun was directly overhead when Hannah crossed the deck on her way to the galley. It was a warm day.

Before he sat down again, Nathan took the work he'd finished to the ship's files. When he pulled the drawer out, he saw Hannah's papers at the very front of it, instead of where they should have been, under the T's. He remembered that he had removed them from the files the morning after she told him she was indentured and had dropped them on his dad's desk when she came to the office. Instead of returning the papers to their proper place, someone—probably his dad—had dropped them at the front of the file drawer. As he proceeded to file them, he noticed the date, May 19. A closer look revealed the words "date of birth" in front of the date. May 19, he thought; that's day after tomorrow. Hannah's birthday was the day after they would dock in New York Harbor. What perfect timing. He could buy gifts for her . . . unless the *Monarch* was attacked.

CHAPTER 10

Hannah returned the empty bottles to their proper place in the galley and left by the outside door. She met the Hartmans on their way to the dining hall, and Jenny asked, "Will you read us a story, Miss Hannah?"

"Later in the evening, Jenny. I need to do something else right now." With all the sails she had mended, Hannah's personal work had been left undone, and she needed to clean her room and wash clothes before they reached New York City. Jenny was disappointed, but Hannah felt she had to put her cabin in order. She entered her room and opened both doors to create a draft of fresh air before she began to clean.

Just as the Hartmans finished their meal, Michael and Lizzy came into the dining hall with the baby, and John stayed to hold Little Michael. Rachel took her children back to their cabin where the three of them got out a game and sat down on the floor to play. Like Hannah, Rachel opened both doors to let the breeze from the ocean blow through the cabin. While her children were busy with the game, she picked up a book and lay down to rest. She had not meant to, but the book was at a dull place, and she fell asleep.

Before long, Jenny became bored with the game, but with Rachel asleep and John still in the dining hall, there was no one for her to talk to. She would never have opened the door and left the cabin, but since both doors were already open, she walked out on the deck, alone.

While Nathan worked in the captain's office, he made plans for Hannah's birthday. According to her papers, she would be twenty years old, and he remembered how special his family had made his twentieth birthday. Hannah didn't have a family, but he would see that her birthday did not go by without a celebration, and he felt sure his mother and Sam would help.

Hannah was deep in her own thoughts and oblivious to noises around her that had become so familiar. She thought of her birthday and how sad it would be without her father; it would be her first one without him. She decided to put it out of her mind and not think of it at all. Perhaps she would be able to get off the ship that day, and it would help her forget.

She was excited that they were so near land, although New York was far from South Carolina. Nathan had said that it would probably be another month before the *Monarch* reached Charleston. She was thankful they would have more time together before he sailed back to England and to the war.

The Barringtons rested in their cabin as they did each day after the noon meal. Sam was in the galley, and most of the seamen were about their daily tasks. No one noticed Jenny beside the guardrail or saw her when she put her head between the bars and leaned out over the water. The large waves frightened her, and she moved away from the rail to the center of the ship where she saw the rope ladder that Steven had climbed to the crow's nest that morning. If her brother could climb it, she thought, so could she.

She lifted her hands to the ladder and stepped to its bottom rung. It was wide near the deck and steady, and at first, she had no trouble climbing it. With each step she went higher and higher, not realizing her danger. Suddenly a strong gust of wind blew the ladder back and forth, and Jenny looked down. When she saw only turbulent ocean water beneath her, she became frightened and quickly put one foot backward. In her haste, she placed her foot too near the edge of the rung, and the ladder flipped over. She held on when her small body fell beneath the ladder, and one leg slipped through a rung, but she could not pull herself back to the topside and hung high above the deck, dangling by her small arms and one leg.

Jenny cried out when the ladder flipped over, but no one heard her young voice. She cried louder, and since Hannah was in the first cabin with her doors open, she heard the unusual sound. That sounded like a child, she thought, and strained her ears to listen. She heard the cry again and ran outside, but saw no one on the deck and had turned to go back in when Jenny cried out a fourth time. Hannah determined the cry came from above and looked up and saw Jenny dangling near the crow's nest. "Oh, Dear God," she prayed and then screamed Nathan's name.

Nathan was so engrossed in his thoughts about her birthday that he didn't hear Hannah until she screamed the second time. "Now what," he muttered. But when he heard his name again, **"N-a-a-than,"** he recognized the panic in her voice and threw down his pencil and ran out of the office.

"What's wrong, Hannah!"

"Look!" She pointed to where Jenny hung high above the deck, and where each sway of the ship took her out over the ocean water.

"Oh, Lord!" Nathan gasped. As he ran to the foot of the ladder, he shouted, "Get a blanket and have four men make a net!" He quickly slipped off his shoes and began to climb.

Hannah ran to her cabin and jerked a blanket from her bed. By the time she returned several crewmembers had gathered under the ladder. Jeff quickly took the blanket and gave a corner to Mark and Scott. Robert Moore took the fourth corner, and they stretched it between them in hopes that they could catch Jenny if she fell on the deck.

John Hartman returned from the dining hall and noticed that Jenny was not in the cabin with the rest of his family. He woke Rachel. She jumped to her feet and looked around. "Where's Jenny?"

"I don't know," answered John. "I just came in. I thought you knew where she was."

Rachel ran out the door and down the hallway. At the end of the hall, she saw those who had gathered around the ladder and noticed that everyone looked upward. She suddenly gasped and her hand flew to her mouth.

John was right behind Rachel, and he put his arms around her, but never took his eyes off Jenny and Nathan. Rachel groaned and covered her face with her hands; she couldn't bear to look. Hannah laid a hand on her shoulder and spoke softly, "She'll be all right, Rachel. Nathan will get her down; you know he can."

Nathan had almost reached Jenny, and he now climbed slowly as not to jostle the ladder. Her small arms would be awfully tired, and he feared the least movement would cause her to fall. He spoke in a low voice as he approached her. "I'm here, Jenny; hold on, baby. I'll get you down." With his body flattened against the ladder to keep it from turning, he reached for her arm and grasped it firmly. With his other hand, he tried to lift her to the topside of the ladder, but she was in a hysterical state and would not cooperate. Both of her legs became entangled in the ropes, and Nathan realized he had to make her calm before she would trust him.

News about Jenny spread rapidly, and nearly everyone on the ship, including Captain Barrington and his wife, gathered under the ladder and watched in suspense as Nathan tried to pull her from underneath it.

Nathan talked to Jenny in a calm voice and told her exactly what he would do. He tried again to lift her from under the ropes, and this time, she let go and he was able to lift her to the topside, but it wasn't over yet. They were still far above the deck. He laid her against the ropes, to let her arms and legs rest, but talked to her as he planned how they would climb down.

"Jenny," he said, "I want you to put your arms around my neck and your legs around my waist; the way you do when you ride piggy-back on Daddy's back." Jenny did as he said, and he carefully began to descend the ladder with her on his chest, the way he had seen her on John's back.

Everyone began to breathe a little easier as Nathan neared the deck with Jenny. When he placed her safely in John's outstretched arms, Rachel threw her arms around him and would not let go. "How can we ever thank you?" she sobbed.

"You just did, Rachel."

"But we can never thank you enough."

"No, we can't," John agreed.

With Jenny and Nathan out of danger, Hannah suddenly felt drained of all energy and backed away from the crowd to sit on the bench near her cabin. Everyone else gathered around Nathan to praise him for the way he'd rescued Jenny. Hannah wanted to throw her arms around him, but it would have to wait. When Steven and Mary came to sit at each side of her, she put her arms around them and said a silent prayer of thankfulness.

The sun was halfway across the western sky by the time everyone calmed down enough to go back to work. Captain Barrington told the crew to take the rest of the day off. They all cheered, except Nathan. He had paper work to finish, and if the crew had an evening off, it would mean more for him to do later. He felt very discouraged as he turned back to the office.

"Nathan," called the captain, "where are you going?"

"Our papers must be in order before we can deliver our cargo." His voice revealed his disapproval to the captain.

"I'm still the captain of this ship," Captain Barrington reminded him.

"I know that." Nathan turned with his eyes fixed on the captain. "If I was," he retorted, "I would not have let the men off."

"Nathan, you work too hard," the captain said in a calm voice. "The lady, there," he nodded his head toward the bench where Hannah now sat alone, "looks somewhat distraught and could use your attention."

Nathan hadn't noticed Hannah on the bench and thought she had returned to her cabin. He looked at her and then back at his dad.

"You need time off," said the captain, "and you push the crew too hard. We don't want anyone to desert us when we reach New York City. The men should be rested and in good spirit in case we run into trouble. This is the best crew I ever had. I know I have you to thank for that because you work as hard as any one of them. Don't worry about getting everything done; that's my job. I've been dealing with the Americans for years, and they'll pay us whether our papers are in order or not. I still have the capability to take care of things on the *Monarch*."

Nathan gave him a sentimental smile and said, "I never thought that you didn't have."

"Enjoy your evening off. You deserve it. Your mother and I are proud of the way you handled a crisis."

The captain walked toward his office and left Nathan alone on the deck. Hannah had not been close enough to hear their conversation, but she could see that there was contention between them. She walked to where Nathan stood and took his hand. "What's wrong?" she asked.

"Nothing, sweetheart; nothing for you to worry your pretty head about. I need to talk to a couple of people, but I won't be long. Soon as I get back, may we go some place and be alone?"

"Yes. I want to tell you how wonderful you are."

"I don't need to hear any more of that; besides, had it not been for your quick action . . . Well, I'll be back in ten minutes and meet you at your cabin. I know a place where we can go."

Hannah returned to her room and Nathan went to talk to his mother. Martha Barrington promised that the two of them, with Sam's help, would make Hannah's birthday a very special day. "We can go shopping," she said. "I'll get ingredients that Sam will need to make a cake and—"

"Mother, I want to take her to eat at a restaurant that evening if all goes well."

"That's great! While you're gone, Sam and I will get everything ready. I'm sure I can call on Rachel for help if I need her." Nathan noticed a gleam in his mother's eyes. She loved a party.

"Thanks, Mother. I knew I could depend on you, and will you talk to Sam? Hannah's waiting for me. Dad gave the crew the evening off."

"I'm glad, but you're not one of the crew."

"Yes, I am. Dad just reminded me of it."

Hannah was ready to go when Nathan returned to her cabin. He led her down the hallway and beyond the galley to a small room that contained a round table and four comfortable chairs. A large window in the room gave a wide view of the ocean.

"I didn't know this room was here." Hannah was surprised.

"It's only used when merchants come aboard to bargain with my dad. If Sam's in a good mood," he smiled, "they're served a cup of tea."

He shut the door and pulled her to him. "Hannah, I've had such little time to spend with you." He kissed her tenderly. "I'm glad Dad insisted that I take the evening off, so we can have time together before we reach land."

"I love you, Nathan, but I didn't realize how much until I watched you on the ladder as you tried to lift Jenny to safety. I was so afraid that both of you would fall. You're so brave, and I'm so proud of you, but I was terrified. When you reached the deck safely, I suddenly felt terribly weak and had to sit down."

"I wondered why you left, but I understand. That's the way I felt the night I asked you to marry me. I was so afraid that you would say no, and when you said yes, I suddenly felt like a jellyfish."

"And I laughed at you. I'm so sorry."

"Well, since your answer was yes, I forgave you."

"Will you always forgive me? I know I shall need it often."

"How could I not when you forgave me for deceiving you?"

"We must always forgive each other," she said, "and that will make our marriage a happy one."

"Yes," he agreed.

It was a wonderful evening and one that neither of them would ever forget. They dreamed about the future and made plans. When it was time, Nathan went for their evening meal, and as they ate, they watched the sunlight fade and saw the moon rise over the water and the stars come out.

"Will you go with me to take a fix with the sextant?" he asked. "I need to pinpoint exactly where we are in order to know about what time we'll sight land tomorrow."

"Yes," she agreed, and while she waited on the deck for him, she noticed that extra men had been assigned guard duty to the night watch.

It was late when they returned to her cabin. Nathan turned her lamp up and was impressed with how fresh and clean everything looked. "I wish I had time to clean my room," he remarked. "It's an awful mess."

He held her a moment and whispered, "It was a wonderful evening."

"Yes," she agreed.

They kissed goodnight, and then she watched as he walked across the hall to his room. Before he went inside, he turned and waited until she closed her door. She leaned against it and a smile spread over her face as she thought, I finally know something I can do for him.

CHAPTER 11

"**L**and ho-o-o, land ho-o-o," boomed Scott's voice from the crow's nest. It was what Nathan had waited to hear since he posted him there early that morning. According to his reading of the sextant the night before, he felt sure they'd sight land before noon.

Hannah was the first passenger out of the cabins at Scott's announcement. She ran to the guardrail and leaned over it, but could barely make out a pale gray line far out on the horizon. Her heart leaped when she saw it.

Nathan laughed when she ran out of her room. He had thought she'd be the first one out. He walked up behind her and circled his arm under her neck. "There it is;" he said, "your new home—the United States of America."

"Oh, Nathan, I'm so excited."

"You have reason to be."

Soon, all the passengers were on the main deck, laughing and talking; it was a joyful time. Hannah mingled with the others until Steven and Mary and Jenny circled around her. Nathan leaned against the rail and watched her with the children and thought how it would hurt each of them when they had to part.

Most of the morning passed before the *Monarch* sailed close enough to see the skyline of New York City. They were still a long way from the city's harbor when Scott shouted, **"Sail ho-o-o."** It was a warning that sails had been sighted on the horizon. The captain lifted his glass and saw the stars and stripes of a United States flag and determined that an American Naval ship sailed toward them. He issued a command for the crew to man their battle stations.

The men sprang into action immediately and took only a few minutes to reach their posts. Scott descended the crow's nest and dashed to his assigned position. Nathan demanded that all passengers go to their cabins and lock their doors until further notice.

Hannah protested. "I want to stay with you," she said.

"No. There might be trouble."

"Please, Nathan," she begged, "let me go to the gun deck with you."

"I don't have time for this, Hannah!" Nathan was annoyed. "Now go to your cabin and lock the doors. I have to get to my post."

It was out of the question for her to accompany him to his battle station. He pulled her to her outside door and gently pushed her inside, but not until he heard the deadbolt fall into place, did he run for his post.

By the time he reached the gun deck, everyone else was in position. The three crewmen assigned to back him had run out his cannon. Directly across the deck, Jason stood calmly with three other crewmen.

The small crew stood bravely poised for battle and waited as the American warship drew near the *Monarch*. Nathan ventured to the end of his cannon and saw the large sails of a frigate, but it would not sail right alongside the *Monarch* as he had expected. This made him believe the Americans would not attack, but he stepped behind the cannon and prepared to fire, just in case.

Not until the ship dipped its colors of Stars and Stripes, did Nathan lift his hand and wave. Several American sailors waved back at him. With relief, he turned to put the men at ease, but his words were forgotten when he saw Hannah behind him.

The suspense had been more than she could stand, alone in her room, and although she understood that Nathan had ordered her to stay inside for her own safety, she felt compelled to be with him. She recalled their first evening together when he pretended to be shot and fell to the deck. With this in mind, she left her room and descended the steps to the gun deck and stood behind him. At first, no one noticed, and she watched in awe as the American ship sailed by.

When Jason realized that the ship would pass on their starboard side, he looked in that direction and saw Hannah. Awe man, he thought, for he knew if Nathan saw her, there would be a battle for sure. He got her attention and worded silently with his lips, "Go back to your room," but she ignored him and stood motionlessly as the ship made its way farther out to sea. There had been time to climb the steps before Nathan saw her, but she refused to go.

"How long have you been here?" his voice rang out, for the covered deck made it louder than he had intended. Everyone looked in her direction.

"I watched the ship sail by," she replied.

"Why didn't you stay in your room as you were ordered to do?" His hostile voice seemed even louder, and she felt blood rush to her face.

"I'm sorry, but I couldn't."

He clenched his teeth, and his eyes glared into hers, but when her cheeks began to blush, he turned back to the crew and informed them that they were dismissed, then walked to the open window and waited for them to leave.

Hannah leaned against the wall by the steps and held her head up as the crew passed by. Her arms were at her side, but her right hand held the tip of her left fingers. She appeared calm, and the men admired her for the way she stood up to Nathan, yet each feared for their relationship. Jason raised his eyebrows at her as if to say, I told you so. She blinked one eye to acknowledge his message and brought a smile to his lips. Scott held up his thumb and whispered "Good luck" as he walked by. Others made short comments, but most passed silently. Jeff lingered toward the back and was the last man to leave the gun deck.

"Come with us," he muttered.

"No." She shook her head.

"You're one of us and we're deserting you. He's awfully mad."

"I'll be all right," she whispered.

She didn't want Nathan to see that he talked to her. Jeff understood and reluctantly followed the others up the steps, but not before Nathan overheard the two of them talking, although he couldn't make out what either said.

When Jeff left, he turned toward her, but she had begun to climb the steps.

"Hannah, come back here," he called.

"No, Nathan. If you want to talk to me, I'll be in my cabin. And don't ever raise your voice at me in front of someone again." With this remark, she continued to climb the steps.

"Hannah!" Nathan called again, but she did not stop, and he didn't pursue after her.

He paced back and forth on the gun deck and then stopped and put his elbows on the rail and held his head between his hands. With his head bowed, he asked, "God, what am I doing wrong? First, my dad, and now Hannah, and even the seamen are against me."

He remembered how, as a child, he had gone to his mother when he had a serious problem. His dad was always at sea. He climbed the steps slowly and walked the hall to her door. It had been a long time since he had gone to her for advice. Had one of the crew defied his orders, he would have had him thrown in the brig for three days, but he couldn't do that to Hannah. He loved her.

He knocked on his mother's door. She opened it and greeted him cheerfully. "Come in, Nathan. I have some ideas about Hannah's party that I want to share with you."

Nathan walked by his mother quietly and slumped down on the side of her bed. She saw the disturbed look on his face.

"I don't think there's going to be a party."

"You said that tomorrow is Hannah's birthday."

"It is."

"Then why can't we have a party?"

Nathan relayed to his mother what Hannah had done; that she left her cabin after he explicitly told her not to and how she had stood behind him when the ship sailed by. "Had the Americans attacked," he said, "she might have been killed. If I had seen a cannon ball coming, I would have dropped to the deck, and it would have hit her." He leaned his head forward to his hands. "I couldn't have lived with that."

His mother sighed and sat down beside him. The only time she had seen him this upset was the night Hannah fainted and then locked herself in her room. "Nathan, it's hard to stand by and do nothing when you know the person you love is in danger."

"But, Mother, I didn't know she was there! If I had, I would have made her go back to her room!"

"I wasn't talking about Hannah, son. I was talking about you."

"Me! What do you mean?"

"I mean that Hannah worries about you just as much as you worry about her, and for her sake, you must acknowledge that. There were so many times when I wished I could be with your dad."

"But you were not with him; he would not have allowed it."

"I was with him today, Nathan. I stood beside him on the main deck, and he knew that we might be attacked. I watched as he dipped the Union Jack when the Americans passed by."

"Well, you're not making me feel any better. You **and** Hannah could have been killed."

"We all could have been and Hannah knew that. That's why she had to be with you. I know how it made me feel to be with your dad."

"Mother, do you think Hannah loves me as much as you love Dad?"

"Yes."

"What about when there are children? Will she put herself in danger then?"

"Did you ever know of me to put myself in danger when you and James were small?"

"No, you were always with us at Barrington Manor."

"And so will Hannah stay safely tucked away, while you go and fight your battles. She will protect herself in order to protect her little ones. But, Nathan, please don't leave them as much as your dad left us."

"I don't intend to. And Mum, I love you." He stood and had to lean a good bit forward to kiss her forehead.

"Oh, Nathan, it's been so long since you called me that."

"I know . . . too long. What were your ideas for the party?"

Nathan felt better when he left his mother's room, but still didn't know what to do. He walked the deck to the front of the ship's bow and stood under the British flag. It was the place where he had found Hannah crying the day she felt so alone and homesick. He closed his eyes and remembered that first time he had held her in his arms. There was the place where she had fallen and hurt her back, and he thought of how she had paid in more ways than one for his mistake. He thought of how much he loved her and of how miserable he was.

Finally, Nathan climbed aloft and began to furl sails in order to slow the *Monarch* before they entered the harbor. He tried not to think of Hannah or of what had happened, but he did, and he wondered what Jeff had said to her.

He missed the noon meal and worked until time for the evening meal. They would soon sail into the harbor, and he still worried that there might be trouble. The captain had raised his company flag, and Nathan decided to leave everything to him, for after all, he had said he was capable of taking care of matters on the *Monarch*. He knew his dad was, and under the circumstances, he wasn't; he couldn't think of anything but Hannah.

She wasn't in the dining hall, and he wondered if she had eaten since breakfast. Her appetite for food had been better, and she had even gained some of her weight back, but now he feared she would stop eating again. He sat at the table where they usually ate, but he ate alone. No one came to sit with him, and the men were silent when they passed by.

When he had finished eating, he went to the main deck where some of the passengers had gathered. The *Monarch* sailed slowly into the entrance of the harbor between Staten and Long Island. Small trees and scrubby shrubs grew on the islands; the grass was a dark green. It reminded him of Ireland, and he wished that Hannah was there to see it. He knew she wanted to be, for she had been so excited that morning when they came in sight of land. He wished he had not raised his voice at her, and he watched the guardrail by her door, but she didn't come outside.

They sailed farther inland and met ships from all over the world, headed out to sea. Their large frames were silhouetted against a red late-evening sky as they glided ghostly through the water.

With Murray at the wheel, they sailed past Governor's Island and slowly came upon the lower end of Manhattan Island. Murray guided the *Monarch* up the East River and brought it to a stop alongside a pier off Manhattan Island. She was secured with large ropes.

Hannah had stayed in her room all evening and tried to think of what her life would be like on the plantation. She wondered about the children that she would teach: how many were there, what were their names, and what were they like? She was anxious to get there and start a new life . . . perhaps without Nathan. Could she marry a man she feared?

As soon as it turned dark outside, she dressed for bed and took her mother's Bible from the desk. She got under the cover and tried to keep her mind on the scriptures, but her head nodded, and she was almost asleep when startled by a knock on the door.

"Who is it?" she called from the bed.

"It's me."

"I'm already in bed, Nathan."

"I have to talk to you."

"Just a moment." She stepped out of bed and slipped a long robe over her gown and then opened her door. Nathan noticed that she stood her full height with her shoulders back and her head high and was reminded of the first time he saw her. It was the day he fell in love with her; it seemed so long ago.

"Hannah . . . I won't say that I'm sorry."

"It doesn't matter."

"Was there a reason why you didn't stay in your cabin this morning?"

"Yes."

"Can you tell me why?"

"I'd rather not talk about it tonight, Nathan."

"Please, Hannah."

She sighed. "I was afraid you would be wounded or killed, and I wanted to be with you. I knew you'd be angry, and I had to prove to myself that I could stand up to you. I suppose I didn't do a good job of it."

"I think the crew thought you did an excellent job."

"I didn't mean to make you look bad in front of them. I'm sorry if I did."

"Why was it so important to you to stand up against me?"

"I won't fear the man that I marry."

"Don't you know that I would never harm you? I don't want you to fear me, but the danger around us."

"Do you?"

"Do I what?"

"Fear the danger around us?"

"Not for myself, but I do for you."

"Then you must give me that same right; the right to be concerned about the one I love."

"Hannah, I'm a man, and a man does what he has to do."

There was a pause as she gazed into his eyes, and then . . . , "So must a woman, Nathan." Her voice was soft, but she reached down and removed the gold chain from around her neck.

Nathan's eyes closed. His teeth clenched as she took two steps toward him and gently lifted his hand and placed the chain in it. He opened his eyes and whispered her name. Her head was still high, and she appeared quite stolid, but there was anguish in her face, and he knew her heart did break.

"I'm a poor Irish girl," she said, "but I won't live my life in fear of a wealthy Englishman."

"Hannah, I gave you this to keep."

"I can't accept it if you don't come with it."

"But I do. I want you to belong to me."

"I ask only to be your equal; a helpmate to support you. I want to be strong for you and to gain strength from you. I want to stand beside you and for you to be there when I need you. Would you want less a woman to bear your sons and daughters? You must make a decision about me, the way I had to you. I will not fear you, Nathan. I love you, but I won't live my life fearing you or your wealth and power. You best go now. I'm going back to bed." She expected to hear the door close behind him, but she didn't.

Thoughts whirled through Nathan's head as he watched her walk slowly back to the bed and pick up the Bible that she had read from. She placed a marker in it and returned it to the desk. Her shoulders now slumped and she no longer held her head so high. On her way back to the bed, she turned her lamp down, and all he could see was her silhouette in the darkness. She lifted one hand and wiped under her eyes with the tip of her fingers and then kneeled to her knees beside the bed, and with her elbows on the bed and her hands together, she bowed her head until it touched her fingertips.

Nathan knew if he left, he couldn't come back, but he had to do something quickly, and in his desperation, he prayed silently, "God in Heaven, what should I do?" And God gave him an answer.

He crossed the room and knelt beside her. Their arms touched, and in the darkness, he felt her hand search for his. As they locked their fingers together, she began to pray, "Oh Mighty God in Heaven, we ask your forgiveness of our sins and thank thee for all our blessings. Thank you for seeing each of us safely across the ocean, and I ask that you continue to bless everyone on the *Monarch*. We give you all honor and glory. Help us to understand . . ." Her voice trembled and she paused and then started over. "Help us to understand each . . ." She stopped again. A large lump in her throat made it hard for her to speak.

Nathan let go of her hand and put his arm around her shoulder. He continued the prayer. "Help us to understand each other and give us strength that we might each be strong for the other. Please protect our loved ones and direct us, oh Lord, in thou ways. In the name of Jesus, Amen."

Hannah's face fell forward to the bed, and she sobbed silently.

Nathan gently caressed her shoulders, but he didn't know what to say. Did she want him to go? He didn't think so.

"Hannah, please don't. I can't stand for you to cry when I know I've caused it." He pulled her from the floor to the side of the bed. "I love you and I can't let you go. That's the only decision I could ever make about you."

She tugged at the corner of the bed sheet and wiped her eyes. "I'm glad you didn't leave," she said. "I love you, too, and I realize you're over people and must tell them what to do, but you can't put me in a cage like a bird. I grew up being independent; my father allowed it. There will always be times when I must make decisions for myself, and I must give you an opportunity to back out of our engagement, if you can't accept that."

"I think God just answered a question that I asked Him today."

"What was it?"

"What am I doing wrong? It seems that everyone has turned against me: my dad, you, and even the crew. I mean well, but I'm burdened for everyone on the *Monarch*."

"I know."

"I've tried to carry this burden alone, and I should give it to God and trust Him to take care of all of us. I don't want anything bad to happen to you, but my mother made me realize that you feel the same way about me."

"Yes . . . I do."

He slipped the gold chain back around her neck and promised he would never back out of their engagement. His lips found hers and they held each other in the darkness.

"Darling," he whispered.

"Yes," she whispered back.

"I'm hungry. Will you go with me to the galley to see if we can find something to eat?" he continued to whisper. He wasn't really hungry but was afraid she was.

"If you'll wait outside for me to get dressed," she answered . . . still whispering.

CHAPTER 12

Later that night, Nathan and Hannah stood on the port side of the *Monarch* with New York City before them. Silence had settled over the city, but many lamp lights flickered in the darkness. The ship lay anchored for the first time since it left Cork Harbor, and the moaning of the ropes that held it against the pier made it seem as a giant beast that heaved under a heavy load.

Captain Barrington would see that cargo was unloaded the next morning, while Nathan and his mother went shopping. The captain asked Nathan to purchase something appropriate for him to give Hannah for her birthday.

Nathan could hardly wait to shop for Hannah, but found himself in a dilemmatic situation, as he didn't know how to tell her that he would take his mother without asking her to go. He wanted the party to be a surprise, yet knew how anxious she was to get off the ship and was afraid her feelings would be hurt. He didn't want anyone else to take her, and he certainly didn't want her to leave the ship alone.

Hannah was engrossed in her own thoughts, wondering if Nathan would be gone long enough for her to clean his cabin the next day. She hoped he would be and that he would leave his door unlocked, as she also wanted it to be a surprise. She had forgotten it was her birthday.

They turned to each other and began to speak at the same time, and then laughing, each offered to let the other go first.

"Will you leave the ship tomorrow?" Hannah asked.

"That's what I wanted to tell you," he replied. "My mother asked me to take her shopping in the morning." This was as near to the truth as he could say without spoiling the surprise.

"That's great!" she exclaimed. It would give her the time she needed to clean his room. She decided to take a chance on his door being unlocked. If it wasn't, she'd ask the captain to unlock it for her.

Nathan felt a twinge of disappointment. Not only did Hannah not ask to go with him, but she seemed elated that he'd be gone. At the same time, however, he was relieved, for he didn't know what he would have said if she had asked to go.

"Where can I find a large pail?" she asked.

"What will you do with it?"

"Wash clothes."

"I'll find one first thing in the morning and leave it by your door."

"Thank you."

"A restaurant near here serves good American food. Will you go there with me tomorrow?"

"What time?"

"Around four in the afternoon."

"Yes." That would give her plenty of time to finish in his room and get dressed. She really wanted to get off the ship, so it would be a good way to end the day.

They walked to her door, but he made no attempt to kiss her goodnight. He was quiet as he stood with her hand in his; she knew something bothered him.

"What's wrong?"

"I hate to bring it up after all we've been through today. I'm afraid it'll upset you."

"Tell me."

"I want to know what Jeff said to you as he left the gun deck this morning."

"He asked me to leave with the crew. You were so angry, and I suppose he was afraid you would hurt me. He felt like they were deserting me."

"Were you afraid I would hurt you?"

"I was afraid because I didn't know what you might do. I had never seen you so upset before."

"I'd never bring physical harm to you. Please believe that. I only get upset with you when you do something dangerous, and you had never done anything that dangerous before. Can't you understand that the reason I get upset is because I love you so much?"

"I told Jeff I'd be all right."

Nathan sighed. "He loves you, Hannah, and I don't know what to do about it. I suppose there is nothing I can do."

"He's never said anything out of the way to me; besides, I like to think that all the crew care about me."

"I didn't say that he cares about you, but that he loves you . . . the way I do. He won't ever say anything to you about it as long as I'm around."

"It makes me sad to think that. I've never done anything to make him love me."

"You don't have to. I fell in love with you the first time I saw you."

"How do you know he loves me? Did he tell you he did?"

"No. I just know." He put his arms around her and pulled her close to him.

"Nathan," she spoke his name softly.

"What, darling?"

"Does Gloria love you?"

She felt his body stiffen, and even in the darkness, she realized how shocked he was.

"How do you know about her?" he breathed. "Did Jason tell you?"

"No. You did when you accidentally called me by her name right after saying 'I love you.' I know you wanted to tell me about her the night you came to my door."

"No! That's not true! I was never going to tell you about her. There's nothing to tell; she means nothing to me."

"But right after you called me by her name, you said there was something you had to tell me. I was afraid you would say you still loved her, and I couldn't bear to hear it that night. I needed you so badly."

"Have you thought that all this time?"

"Yes."

"I didn't think you heard me when I accidentally said her name."

"I pretended not to."

He explained everything. "I had just talked to Jason, and he said that I had to tell you who I was. I was afraid you'd have nothing to do with me when you found out that I was a British Aristocrat, but Jason insisted that I should tell you and accept the consequences. He said I wasn't being fair to you and then he tried to make me feel better by saying that Gloria loved me. I have never loved Gloria or any girl except you, and I explained to Jason that I wouldn't have anything to do with her, no matter what happened between you and me. I thought of all this and of how selfish she is, compared to how sweet you are, when I got your names mixed up. I'm sorry and I hope it never happens again."

"Does she love you?" Hannah repeated her question.

Nathan sighed before he answered, "Jason thinks she does and he's usually right, but it doesn't matter; I love you. When I said I had to tell you something, that night, I meant to tell you who I was. I never intended to tell you about Gloria. I didn't see any reason to, because I've never had any special feelings for her at all."

"What is her last name?"

"Why do you want to know?"

"I don't know. I just do."

"Hesley."

"Nathan," she whispered, "I love you. I love you more than anyone else could ever love you."

"I could never love anyone else the way I love you." He pressed his lips hard against hers.

Right after Nathan and his mother left the ship the next

morning, Hannah sprang into action. She found the pail that he'd left by her door and took it across the hall to his room. His door was unlocked, so she went in and closed it behind her.

His cabin was awfully cluttered just as he had said. Dirty clothes were heaped on the floor and draped over the back of his chair. The bed covers were tumbled and hung from the side of the bed. Papers were scattered all over his desk, and some dirty dishes needed to be returned to the galley. She hurried down the corridor with them.

The bed was stripped of its sheets and washed first, so they'd have plenty of time to dry in order for her to make the bed. She stretched a rope back and forth from one partition to the other outside his door and hung the sheets where the wind and sun would dry them quickly. When all his clothes were washed and hung outside, she turned her attention elsewhere.

As quickly as possible, she cleaned the water closet until it shined and then went over all the furniture with a cloth that had a bit of oil on it. She cleaned the window inside and out. The room looked much better by ten o'clock, but she wanted to be completely finished before Nathan returned.

She swept the floor, and by this time the sheets were dry, and she brought them in and made the bed. When his underclothes felt dry, she folded them neatly and put them away in the seaman's chest at the foot of his bed. His shirts and pants were still damp.

Hannah worked until Nathan's room was spotless, but she had shuffled the papers on his desk, earlier, to dust beneath them, so while she waited for the rest of his clothes to dry, she began to arrange them in a more orderly manner. As she picked up each and stacked it neatly, one at a time, she noticed the name **Richard Hesley & Company** stamped in black letters on many of them. Hesley, she thought; that's Gloria's last name. Nathan had told her that just the night before. A closer look at the papers revealed that they were invoices for goods that had been shipped from several large cities in England. The company was owned by a man named Richard Hesley, and the amount of the figures on the papers was staggering. One didn't have to be too smart to see that Mr. Hesley was a very wealthy person, and that he did a lot of business with Barrington Shipping Company.

Hannah realized that Barrington Shipping would not want to lose Richard Hesley's business. Was he Gloria's father? If so, she sighed wearily, how wealthy she must be. Suddenly she felt guilty for prying through Nathan's things, and she quickly stacked them in order.

As soon as the rest of his clothes were dry, she brought them in and put them away in the seaman's chest. Before she left, she looked around the room and was pleased with her work. She was tired, but felt good in her heart. Nathan had helped her in so many ways, and it gave her pleasure to be able to do something for him.

Nathan and his mother had also hurried that morning. Mrs. Barrington had shopped in New York City many times and knew where to buy the latest fashions. She asked about styles worn in the South. The store clerk brought out several long dresses with full skirts and petticoats. He displayed bonnets that he claimed were popular in all the states. Mrs. Barrington picked out a dark green dress that had been made from an exquisite material. Its neckline was quite low, but there were yards of material in its full skirt. She chose a bonnet and a set of petticoats to go with it. Nathan asked to see other dresses.

"But, Nathan," said his mother, "these are top-of-the-line dresses and the most fashionable ones. Girls in Liverpool would love them."

"I know, Mother, but Hannah is not from Liverpool. She's from a small village in Ireland, and . . . well, I'm afraid she would feel uncomfortable in a dress like this. She dresses rather . . . rather . . . you know . . . plain and simple, and that's the way I like her. It's one thing that makes her special, unlike the girls in Liverpool, and I don't want to change her. But we'll buy her one dress like this in case she does like it."

"Well, all right," Martha agreed. The clerk returned with other dresses and Nathan picked one that he thought would be perfect for Hannah. He bought a second dress with a bonnet to match.

They left the dress shop and found a shoe store that sold ladies' bags and other accessories. The items purchased began to mount. Nathan had begun to wonder how he would get everything back to the ship, when a store clerk mentioned that they had trunks for sale. Hannah's three trunks were full; there would be no room in them for new clothes. He decided a new one would be an excellent gift to her from his dad, and he asked to look at them. He bought a large one, and when it was filled with the things they had purchased, he locked it and asked to have it delivered to the *Monarch.*

"That can be arranged for a small fee," said the clerk.

"Leave it with Captain Barrington," Nathan requested.

With this taken care of, Martha looked for a jewelry store.

"What do you have in mind?" Nathan asked.

"I'd rather not tell; it's something special. I do hope I can find it."

"So do I." He smiled at his mother.

They found the right place, but shopped apart from each other. Martha found exactly what she looked for, and Nathan also found something unique. It was a tiny, but beautiful, music box in the shape of a piano, and when he lifted its top, lovely piano music began to play. He remembered the story that Hannah had told him about her Mother's piano and thought she would like it, but he didn't want her to open the top and find the small compartment empty. Martha found him looking diligently at diamond rings.

"I thought you wanted to have a ring made in London," she said.

"I do, Mother, but Hannah doesn't have a ring at all. Perhaps just a small engagement ring would be nice." Since he had given her his coat of arms, he had not intended to give her a ring until he returned from the war. It would be hard for her to take it off, should something happen to him. He found one that would be suitable for her to wear forever.

"Yes," his mother agreed, "I think a ring from you would please Hannah."

"I'll take this one," he said to the clerk.

The morning was nearly gone, and they had not bought supplies for the cake or decorations for the party, but Nathan had noticed a bakeshop not far from the ship, and they stopped there on the way back. The shop had everything Sam would need to make a birthday cake, and Martha found decorations and gift-wrap with ribbons. As they left the shop, something caught Nathan's eye. It was a gift to be opened first.

The two returned to the *Monarch* with stacks of boxes and shopping bags. Jason saw them on the pier and hurried down the gangplank to take the armload of parcels from Mrs. Barrington.

"Oh, thank you, Jason; I must tell your mother what a gentleman you are when I return to Liverpool."

"You thought I would never make one, didn't you, Mrs. Barrington?"

"Well," she laughed, "I must admit there were times when I was quite dubious about you and Nathan."

"Hey, you two, leave me out of that conversation. I've always been a gentleman."

"Huh!" Jason snorted, and then disregarded his statement. "Did you buy yourself a new wardrobe?" he asked Mrs. Barrington.

"Oh, no! Most of this is for Hannah. Today is her birthday. We'll have a party after the evening meal, but it's a secret. Sam will make a cake, and he'll tell everyone they're invited when they come for the meal."

"A party! Awe man, I want to get her something!"

"You don't need to," Nathan said. "We have more than enough for her."

"But it's not from me," Jason insisted. He laid the boxes on Mrs. Barrington's bed and left in a hurry.

Hannah was excited about Nathan's plans for them that evening. She rested after cleaning his room and now it was time to get ready. She took clothes from her trunk and laid them across the bed. They all looked old and worn. She wished for something new to wear.

While Hannah sorted through her clothes, Nathan went to his room with boxes to wrap. He opened his door and walked inside, but began to back up quickly. He thought he was in the wrong room. Puzzled, he stood in front of the door and tried to figure things out. He saw that he was at the second door from the end of the cabins, and his room was the second room. But this wasn't his room . . . or at least . . . it wasn't the way he left it. He walked back to the door and stuck his head in slowly. The things on the desk were his, but were arranged in a neat order instead of scattered all over it. The desk had been cleaned and polished and so had all the other furniture. Where were the dirty clothes he'd left lying around? And who made up his bed? He peeped beneath the spread to see clean sheets, and when he opened the door to his water closet, he could hardly believe what he saw.

He stood in awe, wondering who had done this. His mother was with him, so it couldn't have been her. None of the crew would have done it, and his dad didn't know how. He lifted the top of his chest and found all his clothes, washed and folded neatly. Suddenly he remembered that Hannah had asked for a large pail. She had said she needed it to wash clothes, and he'd assumed her own. He remembered how impressed he was with her room after she cleaned it. Hannah! Of course! She had done it and had needed the pail to wash his sheets and clothes in. It was why she didn't ask to go with him and his mother, and why she seemed glad that he'd be gone. But how could she have done so much in such a short time? It was hard to believe.

He dropped the boxes on his bed and went across the hall. Her door was open, and she was on her knees by the trunk. She didn't see him, so he stood quietly in the doorway a moment and watched her. When he knocked, she looked up.

"Hello, Nathan. Did you just get back?" She didn't know if he'd been to his room or not.

"Hannah . . . how did you do so much in such a short time?"

She sat back on her feet and looked up at him. "Do you like your room?" she asked with a shy smile on her face.

He crossed the room and pulled her from the floor. "I love my room," he said, "and I love you." He put his arms around her and kissed her. "I thought I was in the wrong room. It looked terrible when I left and now it looks wonderful . . . and all my clothes are clean."

"I was glad to know of something I could do for you. You've done so much for me."

He saw how much it meant to her to be able to do something for him, and an uncertain feeling came over him. Would his gifts make her feel that her work had been insignificant? He feared that his mother and he had gone overboard and that Hannah would take it the wrong way. She might feel bad, as she could not buy gifts for him in return. He wanted her to have all the nice things that they had purchased for her, but not if it would make her unhappy. How would she accept them . . . if she accepted them at all? What should he do?

He decided not to wrap everything and not to take all the gifts to the party. He turned and noticed the clothes on her bed.

"Why are all your clothes on your bed?"

"I can't decide what to wear this afternoon. I wish I had something new, but I don't. Please help me decide."

"Do you really want something new to wear?"

"Yes, but I don't have, so—"

"Wait just a moment."

"Where are you going?"

He ran out the door and returned with two of the new dresses. One was the dress his mother had picked out, but the other was the one that he liked best. He brought the petticoats, a bonnet, and new shoes for her to wear with the dress of her choice.

"Where did you get all of this?" She was amazed.

"I bought them for you this morning. Please pick one to wear to the restaurant."

"I can't let you buy me clothes!"

"Why not?"

"It just wouldn't be proper."

"Hannah . . ." He looked so bewildered. "You cleaned my room. Can't I do something for you?"

"But—"

"You're going to be my wife, and it might be a long time before I get another chance to buy you something. Don't you like them?" His voice pleaded with her.

There was a pause while they gazed into each other's eyes, and then, "Yes—they're beautiful. I like this one the best; may I wear it tonight?" It was the one that he thought would be perfect for her.

Before he dressed for the evening, Nathan wrapped two small gifts and put one of them into his pocket to take with him. He still worried what Hannah would think when she saw all that they had bought for her. He went by his mother's cabin and left the other gift for her to take to the party. He told her how Hannah had cleaned his room.

"Oh, poor soul! You'll never find anyone that loves you more if she loves you enough to clean that room."

"Hey, Mum, it wasn't that bad."

"Yes, Nathan, it was." Martha Barrington laughed.

"I'm afraid we bought too much for her," he said, "and it'll make her feel that her work didn't mean so much. She did it with the labor of her hands and was happy to be able to do something for me. Mother, do you think I should give her everything now? I don't want to hurt her feelings."

"Nonsense," retorted Mrs. Barrington. "Girls love gifts, and she deserves everything we bought if she cleaned your room. Of course, you should give it to her now."

"I don't know, Mother. I hope it doesn't embarrass her or make her feel bad. Don't take the new trunk and other things to the party, but ask Dad to put them in her room after we leave. Here's the key."

"All right, if that's what you want. Now go and enjoy the evening."

It was a quaint old restaurant, nestled among the buildings on Pearl Street, not far from the waterfront. A brick walkway led to its entrance, and just inside, the candles of a large chandelier flickered in the dark room. The tables were made of mahogany, and under the candlelight, their reddish brown color resembled that of aged wine. A small fire that burned in an open fireplace made the room warm and cozy.

Nathan saw heads turn to get a second glimpse of Hannah as the headwaiter led them to a table. She looked beautiful in the new dress, but had chosen not to wear a bonnet, and her long red hair made her a striking figure. He would never tire of her company. When around others, she was shy and had little to say, but tonight they were alone, and she chatted about everything. She liked the restaurant and was excited to be there. The food was delicious, and for the first time since he had met her, she ate like she was hungry.

Finally she took the napkin from her lap and pressed it to her mouth. "I can't eat another bite," she confessed and laid the napkin beside her plate.

"Neither can I." Nathan laid down his fork and reached into his pocket for the small package. "Happy birthday, darling," he said, as he handed her the gift.

Her eyes grew large and her mouth opened in surprise. With everything else that day, she'd forgotten it was her birthday. Instead of a sad day, as she had thought earlier in the week, it had been a good day.

"How did you know?" she asked.

"I saw it on your papers. Someone left them in front of the files, and when I returned them to the right place, I noticed your date of birth. I'm glad I did."

"You've already given me presents."

"I hope you like this one best."

She quickly tore off the gift wrap and opened the small

box. She loved the small piano with its jewels embedded in pearl, but he couldn't wait for her to see what was inside.

"Oh, Nathan . . ." She breathed his name as she slowly opened the top of the tiny piano and heard the lovely tune begin to play. Tears filled her eyes when she saw the ring. He took it from the small compartment that was lined with green satin and placed it on the third finger of her left hand. It was a perfect fit.

"I'll always love you, Hannah. You made me the happiest man in the world the night you said you would marry me. I live for the day that you become my wife."

"I'll always love you, too, Nathan," she said softly, and then picked up the napkin to blot her eyes. "And I live for the day that you are my husband."

He put the small piano into its box and slipped it back into his pocket. "We better go," he said and reached for her hand. "I want to get you back to the ship before dark." He did want to get her back to the safety of the *Monarch,* but mostly, he didn't want them to be late for her party.

Four men on guard duty were the only people on the ship's main deck. "Let's go to the dining hall and see if we can find everybody," said Nathan. He didn't want Hannah to go to her room until after the party.

All the passengers and most of the crew waited for them in the dining hall and yelled, **"Happy Birthday, Hannah!"** as they walked in. Her hands flew to her face, showing everyone the ring on her finger.

The tables were decorated with Mrs. Barrington's decorations, and a large birthday cake set on the first table with three presents beside it. Nathan handed Hannah one of them.

"Will you open this first?" he asked.

As she took the gift, he noticed that her hands shook. "Are you all right?"

She managed a smile and nodded her head, although she was extremely tired. The excitement of the party made her heart flutter. Her quiet birthdays in the past had been celebrated with her father. She wished he was there.

Nathan saw that it was all too much for her. He took a knife from his pocket and cut the ribbon around the gift. She pulled the paper back and revealed a beautiful white book with a painting of children at play under a large oak tree on the front cover. The children were dressed in old-fashioned play clothes. Above the picture, the words "Guests of the Party" were written in gold letters. Inside, pages were decorated with small paintings, and there were lines for the guests to write on.

"Thank you, Nathan." Her voice was shaky. "It's beautiful and I shall keep it forever."

His mother had placed an ink quill and a bottle of ink beside the cake, and as the guests were served, each wrote a message to Hannah, some taking longer than others.

Nathan handed her a second gift. Jason had purchased a long-sleeved silk blouse for her. Its emerald-green color reminded her of home. Inside the package was a note that read, "To replace the one I tore. Love, Jason." She found his face in the crowd and worded "Thank you" with her lips.

Nathan saw one gift left on the table. It had to be the special one his mother had searched for. He had no idea what it was. It was another small package, and again, he cut the ribbon for Hannah. Inside the package was a small black box, and inside the box was a gold locket. Hannah gasped softly when she opened it and saw a picture of him.

It took awhile for her to calm down enough to eat some of the cake that Sam had made. She told him how delicious it was.

"I'm glad to see you happy, Hannah," he said.

"Oh, Sam, I am happy. I love Nathan."

"He sure loves you and I'm glad he found you."

"Thank you, Sam. He really did find me . . . on a dock in Ireland."

When the party began to break up, the Hartmans offered to stay and clean the dining hall. Nathan was glad because he knew Sam was tired. He was also concerned about Hannah. She had worked hard in his room that morning, and then there was the walk to the restaurant and back. He was apprehensive as to what her reaction would be to the gifts still to be found in her room. He wished they could wait until another day.

Before they left the dining hall, Mrs. Barrington helped Hannah gather her things. She tucked bits and pieces of decorations into the guest book for her to keep. "May we take the rest of the cake to your room?" she asked.

"Oh, no," replied Hannah. "Please leave it in the galley for everyone."

"All right, but I'll cut a large piece for you." She placed the cake on a plate and spread a napkin over it. She and the captain had both hands full when they left the dining hall with Nathan and Hannah.

All the way down the hall, Nathan feared what Hannah would think when she saw all the things in her room. She had given him her time and the labor of her hands; how would she accept what his money had bought?

He opened her door and held her hand as he turned up her lamp. His mother and dad entered the room and set the cake and gifts on her desk. When Hannah saw the new trunk filled with so many new things, she was overwhelmed and bowed her head against him.

"I'm sorry," he said, "if it's just too much."

She lifted her head. "You have all made me feel like . . . like . . ."

Nathan feared the worst, but asked, "Like what?"

"Like I have a family."

CHAPTER 13

By the end of the third day in New York Harbor, the *Monarch* floated higher in the water, because the ship had been emptied of much of its cargo. About two o'clock that afternoon, Scott Hogan, Stuart Anderson, and Billy Stevenson were sent to deliver a small amount of goods to a warehouse on Stone Street. It was the last to be delivered. Stuart and Billy returned two hours later, but Scott was not with them.

Hannah noticed that Nathan seemed upset when he entered the dining hall later that evening. She was already seated, but watched as he went through the line to receive his food. He spoke to no one, and there was a distressful look about his face. Even before he was seated, he said, "Scott didn't return to the ship this evening."

"Where do you think he is?" she asked.

"I suppose he deserted to an American ship."

Hannah's mouth flew open, and her eyes grew large. She looked at him in disbelief. "No, Nathan! Scott wouldn't have deserted." She remembered her conversation with him on the gun deck only days before.

"Well, he didn't return to the *Monarch* after he went with Stuart and Billy to deliver goods to Morgan's Warehouse. They both said that as they stacked goods in the warehouse, he just disappeared. They assumed he returned to the ship, but he didn't, and we plan to leave port tonight."

"Nathan, you can't leave him! I just know Scott would not have deserted the *Monarch*. He thinks too much of you and the captain, and he plans to work for your company in Liverpool. He told me that."

Nathan was silent, but studied Hannah's face as he ate. She knew Scott better than anyone else on the ship.

"You feel pretty sure about this, don't you?"

"Yes, I do. I just know that Scott didn't go to another ship. He's homesick and knows the *Monarch* will soon be on its way back to Liverpool. And he would not have deserted the rest of the crew."

"Do you have any idea where he is?"

"No, but I believe he's in trouble or he'd be here. Did he know you were to leave port tonight?"

"Yes."

"Then I'm afraid he's hurt or has been kidnapped."

"You could be right," said Nathan as he gulped down the rest of his tea. "I'll admit that Scott is the last man of the crew that I would expect to desert."

"What are you going to do?"

"I'm going to search Morgan's warehouse. I'll have to break into it, but if Scott's there, I'll find him."

"You're not going alone?"

"No. I'll ask Jason to go with me, and Stuart and Billy will want to go. They were both upset when they returned to the *Monarch* and Scott wasn't here. They wanted to go back and look for him, but I wouldn't let them. We'll wait until dark."

Hannah returned to her cabin and kneeled beside her bed. She asked God to protect Scott and those who would go to search for him, and then she went outside and waited beside the rail to see how many men left with Nathan.

When he left the dining hall, Nathan went straight to Captain Barrington and related to him what Hannah had said. The captain agreed to hold the ship in port, while someone went to search for Scott. "I'll send Robert Moore and George Thomas," he said. "They're familiar with the city."

"No," Nathan declared, "I'm going, and I'd rather have Jason with me than anyone else. He's better with the sword. I know Stuart and Billy will want to go, too; Scott's their friend."

"All right," the captain agreed, "but be sure to take your pistols along with your swords."

Nathan had returned to his cabin for a gun and his sword when Jeff Adams knocked on his door.

"Word is out among the crew," Jeff said, "that Scott didn't make it back to the ship, and you're going to look for him."

"That's right, Jeff. Come in; I need to talk to you."

"I'd like to go with you."

"I appreciate that and I'll tell Scott if we find him, but I need you to take charge of guarding the *Monarch.* I'd planned to ask you before we left. Since this has come up, we need to increase the number of men on guard duty. The captain still plans to leave port tonight and will need every man available to ready the ship for sailing. Will you take over for me?"

"If that's what you need me to do," Jeff responded.

"I knew I could depend on you, and . . . if . . . well, should there be trouble aboard the *Monarch,* would you be sure that Hannah . . . uh . . ."

"I'll protect her with my life, if it comes to that."

"Thanks, Jeff."

A few minutes later, Hannah leaned over the rail and saw four men walk down the gangplank and onto the pier. A gleam in the moonlight revealed the hilt of each man's sword, but she could not see the pistols that were tucked under their belts. Other gear that they carried included an unlit lantern, some ropes, and a crowbar for prying open the warehouse door. Hannah watched until they disappeared into the darkness.

She darted across the hall to tell Michael and Lizzy about Scott. Lizzy had just fed the baby and asked if she wanted to hold him. He was in a playful mood since he had just eaten, and his smiles and funny sounds helped to take her mind off Nathan and the small search party.

As Nathan and the three others neared Morgan's warehouse, they stepped into the shadow of another building and approached it with caution. They spotted two men in front of the old warehouse, and Nathan whispered to the others that they should split up and circle around to come in from each side of the building. Jason and Stuart were to take the right side and Billy and he, the left. "Let's each give the other plenty of time to get in position, and then we'll all four move in at the same time. Jason and I will go first."

Nathan and Billy advanced quietly to the left front corner of the warehouse as planned. While they waited for Jason and Stuart to reach the opposite corner of the building, they overheard the two men's conversation.

"We ought to get a good price for this swabbie. He's young and healthy," one said to the other.

"He ain't too healthy now with the knot on the back of his head. Nobody'll give us a plugged nickel for him if they think he's gonna die. You hit'im too hard. It's a pretty risky business, you know, and if we get caught, we ain't gonna only lose our jobs, but we'll go to jail."

"Think of the Americans them bloody Englishmen have kidnapped and taken on British ships."

"That's the only reason I 'greed to come in with you. I still say it's a risky business, and we'll be in a heap of trouble if we get caught. Ain't no telling what old man Morgan will do."

"Stop worrying and just hope that Jed and Willie find a ship that'll pay us before daylight."

Nathan heard enough to know that their plan was to shanghai a British—most likely Scott—to any foreign ship that would pay them. He had to find Scott and hoped he was still in the warehouse.

He stepped quietly from the corner of the building with his right hand at his sword's hilt. Billy was close behind him, and Jason and Stuart moved in from the opposite corner of the warehouse. Since the two men talked, they didn't notice anything until Nathan yelled for them to raise their arms into the air. Instead, both men drew swords from their sides, but found they were no match for Nathan and Jason. Within minutes, both men were penned against the front of the building. Stuart and Billy tied them up, while Nathan and Jason pried open the warehouse door.

Hannah left the Sutterfield's cabin and went to her own room. She paced back and forth, listening to the seamen shout to each other as they readied the *Monarch* for sailing. It was near midnight and she was filled with anguish. As soon as the noise died down on the deck, she opened her door and walked outside.

When she stepped across the deck to the guardrail, someone ran toward her and stopped near the rail. "Who goes there?" Jeff shouted. Hannah saw the barrel of a pistol, and it was pointed at her.

"Hannah Thornton," she responded quickly.

The gun dropped into a holster at Jeff's side, and he turned and gripped the top of the guardrail with both hands. She stepped closer. "Are you all right, Jeff?"

He reached out suddenly and grasped her arm and pulled her to him. She felt him trembling. "Nathan asked me to take care of you," he said, "and I pulled my gun on you."

"You didn't know it was me." She put her hands at his chest and gently pushed him away.

He let go of her arm as if he had come to his senses and realized he'd done something wrong. "I'm sorry, Hannah." He reached for the rail again and gripped it tightly. "They should be back by now; I'm afraid something went wrong. When I saw you move in the moonlight, I was afraid an enemy had gotten aboard. Why are you out so late?"

"I wait for them to return. I won't sleep until they do."

Jeff nodded his head. "You love Nathan a lot, don't you?"

"Yes."

"Do you think he'll marry you?"

"We plan to be married when he returns from the war."

"What if he doesn't come back?"

"I'll know he was killed or wasn't able to get back," she answered softly.

"How will you know that? You know how wealthy he is. He must know lots of wealthy girls in England."

"No, I don't know how wealthy he is."

"Didn't he tell you that he owns a third of the Barrington Shipping Company?"

"No."

"Well, he does, and they transport as many goods around the world as any shipping company of England and a lot more than most. In the last two years, they expanded the company and now build their own ships; Nathan attended a special school to learn how. When he returns from the war, he'll command one of their ships, unless he chooses to do otherwise. Hannah, I don't want to sound critical of Nathan, but do you really believe he'll come back for you? The ring he gave you makes me wonder."

She felt the ring on her finger. "What do you mean, Jeff?" she asked in her soft voice.

"The diamond is so small. He could have bought you one ten times that large."

"Why do you say these things to me?"

"Because I hate to see you waste your life waiting for him if he's going to marry a wealthy British girl."

Hannah was silent a moment. She thought of Gloria Hesley. Then she remembered Nathan's words, "He's in love with you, Hannah."

"I appreciate your concern, Jeff, but I believe he'll come back for me if he's able. And I like my ring. I wouldn't want a larger one now; I wouldn't feel right about it. I must trust Nathan because I love him."

"Then I hope he'll return for you. I wish for your happiness, always."

"Thank you and I wish the same for you."

"Please go back inside and don't come out again until they return. I'll let you know as soon as they do."

"All right," she agreed, but as she turned to go, they heard footsteps on the pier. She leaned over the rail and strained her eyes to see in the darkness. The silhouette of four men appeared, and when they came nearer, she saw that they carried a fifth man. As they approached the gangplank, Jeff called out, "Who goes there?"

To Hannah's ecstatic relief, she heard, "Nathan Barrington and rescue party."

Her feet flew across the deck to meet them, and when they stepped onto the quarterdeck, she ran to Nathan's side. He embraced her, but before their lips touched, he whispered, "You were right about Scott; I thank God you knew."

After the crew had prepared the *Monarch* for sailing, they had waited on the main deck for Nathan and the others. Some had discussed going to look for them. They now gathered around Scott and demanded to know what had happened.

Captain Barrington had worked in his office while he waited. He heard a commotion on the deck and came out to hear angry comments such as "Let's get whoever did this to Scott!" and "We'll hang him from the tallest building!" The captain gave an order to cast off immediately.

"Pull the gangplank," he demanded. "If anyone leaves the ship, he'll be left behind." The captain knelt beside Scott, and Stuart held a lantern up, so he could see the ugly gash on the back of his head. No one wanted the man who had done this to his youngest crewmember more than he did, but he feared what might happen if a group of angry British seamen caused a disturbance in New York Harbor. "Nathan," he commanded, "see me in my office as soon as you get Scott settled."

"Yes, sir."

The captain left and Hannah asked quietly, "Will Scott be all right?"

"I hope so," Nathan replied. "They hit him real hard. Will you help me examine the wound?"

"Yes, of course."

"Take him to my room," Nathan said to Stuart and Jason. "Billy, get a cot."

"Nathan, you won't have time to take care of him," Hannah insisted. "Take him to my room, and I'll sit with him the rest of the night."

"Are you sure?"

"Yes."

"Take him to Hannah's room," Nathan changed his command.

She quickly pulled the cover back on her bed and then ran to get a wet cloth to wipe blood from Scott's face. Jason looked at the bed and then at Nathan who shook his head slightly. Hannah returned to see the two still holding Scott. "Put him on the bed," she said, and Jason looked at Nathan again.

"We're waiting for Billy to bring a cot," he explained.

"I know, but put Scott on the bed."

"Well, where will you sleep?" Nathan had a perplexed look on his face.

"On the cot, Nathan!" Her face turned beet red.

"Oh," he muttered.

Jason and Stuart stifled a grin as they eyed each other.

Scott was conscious, but still dazed from the blow he'd received to his head. Hannah watched Nathan examine it, and the expression on his face told her that he didn't like what he saw. Scott's hair was a bloody mass, and a large bump had risen around the torn place in his scalp. Nathan cleaned as much of the blood as he could from the wound and put the same ointment on it that he had used on her back.

"Scott," he said, "you don't need to talk, but I want to know if you can hear me. Can you raise your left hand?"

Scott slowly raised his left hand.

"I'm going to ask you some questions. If the answer is yes, raise your right hand; if no, raise your left hand."

"Is your name Scott Hogan?" Scott raised his right hand. "Do you sail on the *Sea Breeze?*" He raised his left hand. "Does your head hurt?" It was the right hand again. "Are you homesick?" They saw a faint smile on his lips, and his right hand went up a little farther.

"I think you'll be all right in a few days," Nathan said.

He reminded Hannah that he had to report to the captain. "I'll come back," he said, "before I go to my cabin." She walked him to the door, and he took her hand and looked into her eyes. He breathed deeply and shook his head.

"What is it, Nathan?"

"I get sick at my stomach when I think we would have left Scott in the shape he's in and to the fate that awaited him. Some men had kidnapped him to sell to a foreign ship. He would have been forced to work on it, and after a period of time, they would have killed him. I'm so glad you knew that Scott didn't desert."

Hannah shuddered. "I'm thankful you listened to me and went to search for him," she said. "And I'm thankful you found him in time."

"I'll always listen to you from now on." He put his arms around her and showered her face with kisses. "Hannah," he moaned, but no words could express how he felt.

The captain waited to hear the whole story. Jason had told him that they found Scott in Morgan's warehouse, but he'd done business with Sam Morgan for years and couldn't believe that the man would do harm to anyone.

Nathan related to him about the two men in front of the warehouse and the conversation Billy and he overheard. "We took the two," he said, "then prized the front door of the warehouse open. Stuart and Billy showed me where Scott had disappeared. We found blood on the floor and decided that someone had hit him from behind and knocked him out. Whoever did it stepped in the blood, and we tracked it to the back of the building, but searched for two hours without finding a trace of Scott. After we moved every box and crate, I had decided that he wasn't in the warehouse, but then I noticed some blood on one of the crates and opened it to find him stuffed inside with his hands tied and his mouth gagged."

"What did you do with the two men?"

"We took them to the city police station and gave what information we had, including the names of Jed and Willie. They believed us when they saw the shape Scott was in. Two other British seamen had been reported missing, and they felt sure that this was the answer to their investigation. The two were put in jail, and policemen were sent to the warehouse to wait for Jed and Willie. The captain of the police department said he would question Sam Morgan, but didn't believe that he was involved in it and neither do I. They apologized that this happened in their city and thanked us for helping them solve the case."

"Good work," said the captain. "I'm proud of you."

"Thanks, Dad, but I didn't do it alone. Jason, Stuart, and Billy should be commended, and Jeff wanted to go with us, but I asked him to stay and take the responsibility of guarding the *Monarch* at a crucial time. I knew we could depend on him."

"Yes, Jeff's a good worker."

"Most of all, we have Hannah to thank. She refused to believe that Scott had deserted and convinced me to search for him."

Scott's condition took a turn for the worse, and before Nathan returned to Hannah's room, his body shivered so hard that his teeth chattered. Hannah put more cover on the bed and tucked it in around him. He seemed out of his head, and she was relieved when Nathan knocked on her door.

"He must have lost too much blood," he said.

"What are you going to do?"

"If he's not better by morning, I'll find a doctor."

"But you're a doctor."

"No, I'm not!" I took classes for medical emergencies when no doctor is available. I'm thankful for the training, but I'm a long way from being a doctor. Scott's condition is out of my hands."

Hannah laid her hand on Scott's brow. He opened his eyes, but didn't recognize her. His eyes looked feverish, and he began to toss and turn in the bed. He mumbled words incoherently, and at one point, seemed to be wrestling someone. Nathan was forced to hold him down.

"I'm glad he's not on the cot," he said. "You always know what's best."

"I thought he would rest better on the larger bed. I didn't think his condition would get this bad. I'm glad you're here with me."

"I won't leave, and I'm glad you're here, too."

About four o'clock in the morning, Scott began to sweat and was restless again. He sat up and looked around as if to see where he was and then fell back on the pillow. His fever went down, and he fell into a deep sleep.

Hannah suggested that Nathan go to his room, but he wouldn't leave. He feared what might happen if Scott woke up out of his head again.

When he refused to go, she took a blanket from the side of the bed, where it had been tossed when Scott began to sweat, and spread it and a pillow on the cot. "Please lie down," she said. "You must get some sleep. I'll wake you if I need you."

"What about you? You've been up all night, too."

"I can rest tomorrow, but you can't. Don't argue!" her voice demanded.

"Aye, aye, my lady!" He laughed, but stretched out on the cot with his head on the pillow, and in a few minutes, she heard him breathe deeply.

Hannah leaned over Scott and listened to his breathing. It seemed normal enough, so she wrapped a blanket around her and sat down on the floor with her back against the wall and her knees drawn in front of her. With her head bowed to her knees, she thanked God that Nathan and the others had returned safely, and she prayed for Scott's recovery.

She lifted her head and leaned it backward against the wall. The increased speed of the *Monarch* told her they had left New York Harbor for the open sea and were headed south . . . toward South Carolina. Her eyes turned to Nathan's face that was asleep on the pillow, and her head dropped to her knees again.

Nathan awoke that morning to find her curled up in the blanket, asleep on the floor. He lifted her and laid her on the cot before he dashed across the hall to shave and change clothes. By the time he returned, she and Scott were awake and she went to the galley for breakfast, while he examined Scott's head.

Scott's condition had improved with rest. His face was not so pale, and he could hold his head up without the help of pillows. The lump on top of his head, however, was large and had turned a dark blue.

Hannah returned with breakfast, and Nathan sat down on the cot to eat. He watched as she sat beside Scott and lifted food to his mouth with a fork. Scott reached for the fork and spoke his first words since Nathan had found him in the crate.

"I can feed myself, Hannah. Eat your own breakfast."

She looked at Nathan with a big smile on her face. He smiled back and scooted down on the cot to make room for her.

"How do you feel, Scott," he asked.

"Like I have a goose egg on top of my head. Where am I?"

"In Hannah's room. She offered to take care of you, for you do have a goose egg on your head with a crack in the middle of it. It doesn't look good, so you have to take it easy a few days. You were hit from behind with something heavy, and the men that did it intended to sell you to a foreign ship. You know the rest of the story. When you didn't come back from Morgan's warehouse with Billy and Stuart, I thought you'd deserted to an American ship, but Hannah convinced me that you didn't. She said you wouldn't have done that to the captain or me, and that you wouldn't have deserted the rest of the crew. I'm glad she knew."

"So am I," Scott muttered.

Dirty dishes were returned to the galley, Scott went to sleep, and Nathan was ready to go.

"I hate to leave," he said, "but I have to get paper work ready to deliver cargo in the next port. Please rest while he's sleeping."

"I will," she promised, "and if I need you, I'll send Steven."

"Good."

After Nathan left, Hannah pulled the cot closer to the bed and lay down, but just as her head touched the pillow, there was a knock at her door. It was Captain and Mrs. Barrington; they wanted to know how Scott was.

Hannah invited them in, and Mrs. Barrington sat down on the cot, but the captain leaned over Scott and looked at the gash on his head. It made him angry; he was glad that Nathan and the others had caught the men that did it.

"Hannah," he said, "I'm so thankful you knew that Scott had not deserted. Since so many men have, I didn't think of anything else."

"Be thankful that Nathan listened," she answered.

Before the Barringtons left, there was another knock on the door. It was Stuart and Billy and they wanted to know the condition of their friend. Hannah didn't have the heart not to ask them in.

After Stuart and Billy left, she lay down again, only to hear another knock at her door. It was Jason, and by now, Scott was awake.

"Hello, Jason."

"Hi, Hannah. Nathan asked me to come by and check on you and Scott."

"Scott just woke up and I need to go for his meal. Will you stay with him for a few minutes?"

"If you'll bring me one, too."

"All right."

The three of them ate together. Scott had little to say during the meal, but he ate most of his food. Hannah felt that something more than the lump on his head bothered him. After Jason left, she adjusted the pillow under his head and helped him get comfortable.

"Are you all right, Scott?"

"Yes; I'm okay."

"May I get you anything?"

"No. Why don't you take a nap? You must be exhausted."

"All right, if you're sure you're okay."

She had almost reached the cot when she heard his drowsy voice say, "Thanks, Hannah; thanks for everything."

She turned around, but Scott's eyes were closed, and he appeared to be asleep. "You're welcome, Scott." She wasn't sure if he heard her or not.

Hannah never got to take a nap, for company continued to come and go all evening. John Hartman and Steven came by, and several other crewmen came to the door to inquire about Scott's condition. Nathan returned at six o'clock and went for their evening meal. They had just finished eating when Billy and Stuart came; Scott had been asleep when they came earlier. Before they left, three other crewmen came. Hannah sat down on one of her trunks and leaned her back against the wall. Nathan saw her head nod; he knew she had trouble staying awake. She would not lie down on the cot with the other men there, and he realized it was a bad situation for her in her own room. He took her hand and led her outside.

"You didn't get any sleep today, did you?" He circled his arms around her.

"No," she sighed, "Scott had company all day."

"I'm sorry."

"Nathan."

"What, sweetheart?"

"Why did you ask Jeff to take care of me, while you were gone last night?" Her head rested on his shoulder.

"Because, with Scott missing, I was afraid there might be trouble on the *Monarch*, and I asked him to be in charge of the watch. Since I wouldn't be here and neither would Jason, I knew he could take care of you better than anyone else. He's smart and quick, and I can depend on him, but I didn't intend for him to tell you."

"He thinks you'll marry a wealthy British girl." Her words were slurred.

"Did he say that?"

"Uh-huh."

"You didn't believe him, did you?"

She didn't answer. Her body had relaxed against his, and she was asleep. Nathan lifted her in his arms and circled around the cabins to his outside door. He pulled the cover back on his bed and laid her on it and then removed her shoes and spread the cover over her. He knew she wouldn't hear, but he kissed her forehead and whispered, "I love you, and I'll never marry anyone else."

Before he left the room, he locked his outside door and turned up his lamp in case she awoke in the night. He left his door to the hallway unlocked and went back across the hall. As he entered Hannah's room, he spoke in a loud voice. "All right, men . . . back to your duty or to your quarters; Scott and I have to get some sleep." The men left quickly, but Nathan didn't shut the door. He pulled the cot in front of it, so he could see the door to his own room.

He was almost asleep when Scott said, "Nathan."

"Yea, Scott?"

"How can Hannah have so much love for everybody and see only the good in them?"

Nathan was so tired he could barely speak, but he managed to mumble, "Why don't you ask her?"

CHAPTER 14

The *Monarch* sailed into warmer waters along the eastern coastline of the United States. It was May 30, and the ship had been in and out of other seaports, but had spent only enough time in each to unload cargo. After what had happened to Scott in New York City, Captain Barrington took no chances. The men were forbidden to leave the ship alone, but in groups of at least four, and one of them had to be armed.

Scott's condition improved and the lump on his head began to shrink. He no longer needed help to get up and down, and the dizziness he'd experienced at first went away. Four days after the incident, Nathan came to Hannah's cabin, while she was gone for the noon meal. Scott sketched something on a scroll of paper, but when he took his hands from it, the paper rolled and he laid it aside. "I'm a lot better," he said, "and should go to my own bunk."

"Don't you like the way Hannah takes care of you?" Nathan asked.

"It's not that. I couldn't have better care, but I'm strong enough to take care of myself. I appreciate what both of you have done. I owe my life to you and I won't soon forget it."

"You would have done the same for me or anyone else on the *Monarch.* If you're ready to return to the little forecastle, I'll ask Jason to look out for you, and I'll be by to examine your head until it's completely healed. Don't return to work until you're sure you're up to it."

"Thanks, Nathan."

Later that day, Hannah helped Scott gather his things and put them into a pillowcase for him to take back to his own place in the crew's quarters. After everything was gathered, he sat down on the side of the bed and made no effort to leave. She pulled her chair closer and sat down beside him.

"Hannah . . . ," he leaned over with his arms crossed on his knees and looked down at the floor, "I don't know how to say how much I appreciate everything. I told Nathan, earlier, that I owed you and him for my life because I know where I'd be right now if it weren't for you two."

"Scott, only God gives you life. He allowed us to have the conversation on the gun deck when you shared your plans for the future and let me know that you would have never deserted the *Monarch*. And He gave Nathan love in his heart that made him go and search for you when he realized you could be in danger. Offer thanks to God and give Him the glory."

"Is it God that makes you love everybody and see only the good in them?"

"Yes. It's His love that lives in me."

"I don't understand that. Can you explain it to me?"

"Yes. Let me get my Bible."

She began by explaining God's Plan of Salvation for all mankind and read Romans 3:23 from her Bible, "For all have sinned, and come short of the glory of God." Then she turned to Romans 6:23, "For the wages of sin is death; but the gift of God is eternal life through Jesus Christ our Lord." She read from the first chapter of John and then explained that God came in the form of His own Son, Jesus, to pay for our sins by dying on the cross. "If you believe in Jesus," she said, "He will come to live in your heart and give you eternal life."

Scott listened to every word as Hannah read the verses from the Bible and explained them. He looked into her face and then back to the floor. She was quiet as he gave her message serious thought. Finally he spoke. "That's what Captain Barrington has tried to tell us on Sunday mornings, but I just didn't understand it 'til now. Someone had to hit me on the head to make me see the light."

Hannah smiled at him. "Maybe so, Scott. Sometimes it takes that for us to see the Light—the Light of Jesus."

"I think so, too, Hannah." She bowed her head as he prayed a prayer, asking Jesus into his heart.

Scott returned to the crew's quarters and Hannah walked out on the deck. She felt wonderful inside. Scott had accepted Christ as his Savior, and God had allowed her to lead him. She gave Him the glory.

It was a beautiful day. The blue ocean water sparkled as the *Monarch* glided through it. Gulls circled overhead and cried out their greetings as if to welcome the newcomers to their waters. A seaman whistled a pretty melody, and suddenly Hannah's heart seemed to overflow with happiness. She wanted to see Nathan and left the guardrail in search of him.

Jason and Stuart pulled slack from the rigging with the block and tackle. "Jason," she called, "who whistles that tune?"

"Don't you know?"

"No."

"Follow it and see."

The melody could be heard all over the main deck. It came from among the sails, and when she looked up, it suddenly stopped just as Nathan called out, "Hey, Hannah, grab a ratline and climb up." He was the whistler.

Ratlines were ropes that ran horizontally across the shroud of rigging and served as steps for going aloft. Nathan wasn't too high off the deck, but Hannah had never climbed more than the flight of stairs to the helm. That had been high enough for her, but she wanted to tell him how happy she was. She could scale the ratlines, she decided, but . . .

"I can't climb up in a dress."

"Change to pants."

"I don't have any."

"Go to my cabin and look in the bottom of my chest."

She ran to his cabin and dug to the bottom of his chest and found a pair of white seaman pants that were just a bit too large for her. She rolled the legs a couple of rolls and tucked her blouse in. On her way back she asked Jason for a piece of rope.

Jason cut one end from the rope in his hand. "You're not going to climb the ratlines, are you?"

"I'm going to try." She quickly worked the rope through the belt loops and tied it at her waist.

"Awe man! I've got to see this." He gave her a boost to the side of the ship.

With a tight grip on the rigging, she put one foot on the bottom line, being careful not to look down, but kept her eyes on Nathan until she was right beside him. He circled his hand around her arm.

"I can't believe you did it, but I'm afraid you'll fall; you better climb down."

"You won't get rid of me that easy, not after all the trouble I went to."

"I don't like you in pants."

"It was your idea."

"I know, but you belong in a dress."

"All right, I'll change, but I want to tell you how happy I am."

"Are you?"

"Yes."

"I'm glad. You made me happy the first time I saw you."

They leaned closer until their lips came together, and as the *Monarch* tilted far to her starboard side, they shared a blissful moment among the sails.

"I'll quit early today," he said, "and we'll have a special evening like our first one. Go change and look like a woman again."

"All right."

Hannah descended the ratlines slowly, and Jason was there to help plant her feet on the deck. Nathan began to whistle again, and her heart was lifted with the melody that drifted across the *Monarch* until it was caught up in the wind and taken out to sea.

She spent much time dressing for the evening. Nathan was overwhelmed with her beauty. "Can it be possible," he asked, "that you are more beautiful than when I first met you?"

"Nathan, please be yourself."

"I am being myself!" They laughed as they spoke the same words they had spoken on their first evening.

Sam had prepared a delicious meal, and tonight, Hannah was able to eat. They enjoyed each other's company and when finished eating, Nathan returned the trays to the galley and took her hand as they left the dining hall.

"Do you want to go to the gun deck?" he asked.

"If you'll promise not to fall down dying."

"I promise," he chuckled.

He opened the window in front of the cannon she had stood behind the day the American ship sailed by. They both thought of the incident, but dared not speak of it as not to mar the perfection of the evening. The window framed a giant painting with the ocean in the foreground and the shoreline in the distance. The soaring gulls and the cresting of the waves made the painting come alive.

"That's the state of Maryland," Nathan pointed toward the land. "We'll sail into the mouth of the Chesapeake Bay tonight and across it to Norfolk, Virginia, tomorrow. Norfolk was founded in 1682, and has been a busy seaport since its early days of trade with the West Indies. We pick up tar there that comes from the plantations of Virginia and North Carolina and use it to coat our rigging."

"How do you know so much about everything?"

"I don't know about everything, but I learned about seaports at the navigational school. If you're in the shipping business, it's important to know about them and what products you can buy there. That's the business I'm in, and it's the only one I know. I hope you can live with it after we're married. It's not an easy life for a wife, but it pays well, and I can buy anything you want."

"You're all I want."

"I know, sweetheart. I must tell you that I'll be forced to sail occasionally."

"I knew you were a seaman when I fell in love with you, but it will be hard each time you must go."

"I won't ever want to leave you."

He leaned against the barrel of the cannon with her in his arms. "I love you," he whispered in her ear, "and I could never love anyone else. I'll come back for you, Hannah; please wait for me."

"I will, Nathan, but my days shall be wretched until you return."

"I've tried to think of a way to help us keep in touch; something that will remind us of each other every day. Do you watch the sun go down in the evening?"

"Occasionally, after it's not so bright to look at."

"I like to watch it rise in the morning and then set in the evening. A seaman's time is divided into watches, and we have six four-hour watches in twenty-four hours with different names for them, such as morning watch and evening watch. One of my duties as first mate is to assign the members of the crew their watch duty, and I want to assign you one. I give you the watch of the sunset. Think of me as the sun sinks beyond the horizon each day, and I'll do the same. Wherever I am, I'll think of you."

"I'll think of you every evening," she said, "and say a prayer for you. It will be a special time of the day. I'm glad you thought of it."

They embraced each other tightly, and he kissed her for a long time. When he finally released her, they gazed toward the west and watched as the sun slowly sank out of sight.

"I better take you back to the main deck. It'll be dark here before long unless I light a lantern." He closed the window and then took her hand and led her back up the steps.

As they stood by the guardrail outside her door, Nathan reminded her that the Sutterfields would leave the *Monarch* at Norfolk. "The Butlers will also leave us," he said. "Their son lives near there."

"I'll miss all of them; especially Little Michael. Do you think I'll ever see him again?"

"We'll visit them on our wedding trip if you'd like to."

"Oh, I would! And can we go to Barrington Manor?"

"Yes, sweetheart. I hoped you would say that."

"It's been a wonderful day and I don't want it to end."

"Neither do I."

"Were you whistling today because you were happy?"

"Yes, and you made me even happier when you climbed up to see me. I didn't think you would do it."

"I couldn't have when I first came aboard, but I'm used to the ship now, and I've watched you climb the ropes so many times."

"I'll make a seaman out of you yet."

She laughed. "You whistled so beautifully. What was the name of the song?"

"I don't know. Just a tune I heard somewhere."

"You're so talented. I wish I could hear you sing again."

"Do you?"

"Yes."

"Well, maybe you can. Tomorrow is Sunday," he reminded her. "Will you be at the service?"

"Yes, I plan to be."

"Then I better let you go in. If I keep you out all night, you won't be able to get up that early. I love you, darling. Thanks for a wonderful evening."

"I love you too, Nathan."

Hannah rose early the next morning and dressed in a comfortable skirt and blouse that she could wear all day, for she thought it would be a busy day.

She opened her door to the shimmering waters of Chesapeake Bay and lingered at the rail a moment before going to the dining hall. Lack of the ocean's strong wind had slowed the *Monarch,* and after the rough waters of the North Atlantic, the bay seemed quite calm. Serenity filled the air.

Nathan didn't show up for breakfast, and Hannah thought that he would sleep as late as possible. She was amazed at how he could get to the worship service each Sunday morning at the exact moment the captain stood to begin. Since he wasn't there, she took her tray to the Sutterfields' table. It would be their last breakfast aboard the *Monarch*.

"I'm glad you joined us," said Lizzy. "I wanted a chance to tell you good-bye and to say how much we will miss you."

"I shall miss the three of you," Hannah responded. She laid down her fork and reached for Little Michael and held him close to her. He made a funny noise and wrinkled his nose and it made her laugh. She lifted him to her shoulder and took him to the galley to see Sam who made over him and fussed about how much he had grown. When she returned to the dining hall, the Hartmans were there, and she took the baby by their table. Mary held his tiny hand in hers, and Steven gently caressed the top of his foot with one finger.

He enjoyed the attention, not knowing that he might never see those who gave it, again. Hannah held her cheek to his and hugged him for a long time before she gave him back to Michael. "We'll see you at the service," said Lizzy, as they left the dining hall.

Since she had dressed for the worship service, Hannah stayed after the other passengers had left and helped Sam clean the tables. They talked as they prepared the dining hall for the service.

"I'll miss you when you leave the ship, Hannah."

"I'll miss you, too, Sam, but I hope to see you again after the war is over. Will you continue to work on the *Monarch*?"

"It's hard to say; no one knows what tomorrow will bring. Wherever I am, Nathan will know how to find me."

"You've done so much for me. The good meals, the special pie, and the beautiful birthday cake were all appreciated, but I would not have survived without your gingerroot tea."

Sam laughed as he recalled that first morning when Nathan came to get tea for her. "I knew you'd be sick," he said, "when I saw you eat all that breakfast, so I had it ready."

"You took care of me, even before I knew you."

"Well, I didn't want you to be sick, but Nathan was the one who really took care of you. He loves you, Hannah, and I wish the best in life for both of you."

"Thank you, Sam."

The dining hall tables were pushed against the wall, and the chairs were arranged in rows when people began to arrive for the service. Scott was the first one there.

"Good morning, Scott. How do you feel?" Hannah asked.

"I feel great. I plan to go back to work in the morning."

"I'm glad you're all right, but don't over do it on your first day back. Maybe you should only work the morning watch."

"We'll see."

Scott sat at the front of the room, and it wasn't long until Billy and Stuart sat beside him. Hannah had taken her usual seat on the back row when Jeff and Mark came in with Jason and Nathan. She was surprised to see Nathan there early and was really surprised when he said, "Let's sit on the front row this morning."

She felt more comfortable in her usual place, but at Nathan's request, made her way to the front. He sat beside her at the end of the row, and Jason sat at her other side.

Every chair was filled that morning, and some had to be brought from the mess hall. The captain stood with his Bible in hand, but before he began the service, he reminded everyone that the Sutterfields would leave the ship that afternoon. "I know each of you will want to say good-bye to them and to the Butlers," he said. "Alice and George will return to Liverpool with us after a visit with their son.

"Before I bring the message," the captain continued, "Nathan has agreed to sing this morning."

Hannah's mouth flew open in delight, and she quickly turned her head to see him smile at her. So this was why he was early and why he wanted her to sit on the front row. Nothing could have pleased her more.

He didn't say anything, but stood and began to sing "Amazing Grace," and as many times as she had heard the hymn, it had never sounded quite so wonderful before. As he sang its beautiful chorus, she was reminded of her mother and father, and tears came to her eyes. After he had sung the short verses, Nathan looked at her and whistled the tune softly, and she smiled at him as tears ran down her cheeks.

The captain's sermon that morning was on how to trust God for all needs and it was meant to bring comfort to those who would soon leave the safety of the *Monarch*. At the end, he gave an invitation to anyone who wanted to come forward and profess their faith in Jesus Christ. Scott stood and made his way to the front of the room. When Billy and Stuart followed him, Hannah was overjoyed.

After the noon meal, Nathan and Hannah helped the Butlers get ready for their departure. They also went to see Michael and Lizzy, and Hannah helped Lizzy pack their things, while Nathan talked to Michael. The baby was asleep, so the four of them had a quiet time together. When it was time to leave, Lizzy and Michael followed them to the door, and Lizzy looked at Nathan and said, "Thank you for the song that you sang today. I know you did it for us, as it was our last service, and we'll always remember it."

Nathan glanced at Hannah and then back at Lizzy. He didn't know what to say.

"Yes," Hannah spoke up. "He did it for you. Wasn't it beautiful?"

"Yes, and it shall always be a special memory we have of him."

It really was a busy day, just as Hannah had speculated. She watched tearfully when the Sutterfields departed down the gangplank. Little Michael's head bobbed over Michael's shoulder, and at the end of the plank, Lizzy raised his tiny hand and helped him wave good-bye.

The Butlers' son had been in town for some time, awaiting the arrival of the *Monarch*. There was a joyful reunion with his parents, and they all three anticipated more excitement at his home where Alice and George would meet their grandchildren for the first time.

The *Monarch* floated alongside the Norfolk dock. Her sails were furled and choppy water splashed against her hull. Hannah stood on the deck and watched the sun sink out of sight beyond the Virginia hills. Nathan finished some last minute paperwork and joined her by the guardrail. He'd not been alone with her all day, and he took her in his arms and spoke her name softly.

"Hannah."

"Huh-h-h?" Her lips nudged his.

"You know that I sang for you this morning, don't you?"

"Yes, and it was so special to me."

"Yet, you let the Sutterfields think that I did it for them."

"Oh, Nathan," she leaned her head back and looked into his face, "you couldn't disappoint Lizzy, and what did it hurt to give the two of them that special memory of you?"

"Nothing, darling, but it was a very unselfish thing that you did. And I suspect you had something to do with Scott and Billy and Stuart making a profession of faith."

"Perhaps God used me in a small way. I shared some scriptures with Scott when he asked me about God's love."

"I believe He used you in a greater way than you give yourself credit for."

She changed the subject by saying how much she would miss the Butlers and the Sutterfields.

"Nathan . . . it's been a bittersweet day."

"Yes," he agreed, "it has."

CHAPTER 15

The morning the *Monarch* left Norfolk, Virginia, a wall of dark clouds set heavy on the horizon toward the west. There was an intense stillness in the air that even the gulls seemed to respect. Their familiar cries were silenced as they glided through the sky with fully extended wingspans.

The hot, humid air caused sweat to run down the faces of the seamen as they worked diligently to prepare the *Monarch* for another storm. Many of them felt animosity toward the Americans as they left Norfolk behind. They had not forgotten what had happened to Scott in New York Harbor, and now, despite the captain and Nathan's effort to convince the proper authorities that the English people had demanded a revocation of the British Orders in Council, they were not allowed to unload any cargo in Norfolk. Unless they could dispose of it farther down the coast, they would be forced to take it back to England.

The American trade industry had profited by the neutrality of the United States as war raged between France and England. When both countries, however, turned to commercial warfare, the United States was pulled into the conflict and caught in between. The British Orders in Council prohibited any vessel from trading with ports in France or her allies and, later, blockaded ports in Europe that did not fly a British flag. Because of this, the United States refused to let British ships bring imports into their country.

By this time, France and England had retaliated back and forth with so many decrees and orders that it was almost impossible for Americans to trade with either country. In the past, England had held commercial supremacy on the high seas and British merchants disliked Americans growing rich at their expense.

The Barringtons wanted trade to resume between all three countries, for in spite of their shipping of goods all over the world, they had suffered a large decrease in profit. Nathan and the captain were equally disappointed in what had happened at Norfolk, and Nathan feared their problems would increase as they sailed farther south. Northerners of New England proved more sympathetic toward British merchants since the shipping business was a major industry there.

Hannah stood at the edge of the *Monarch's* covered walkway with John Hartman and Steven and watched as the dark clouds rolled in closer. Jagged flashes of lightening streaked across the sky and were followed by loud claps of thunder.

When all was snug aloft, the crew stood on the main deck and waited to see what would happen. Suddenly a hard gust of wind hit the side of the ship, and large drops of water began to splash here and there on its deck. The seamen darted for cover as the drops turned into a hard downpour.

"Do you think we're in for another bad storm like the one we had at sea?" Hannah asked John.

"No. Since the clouds are from the west, I believe they're just rain clouds."

John was right. The clouds only produced rain, in spite of all the lightening and thunder. There was no damaging wind as they had experienced at sea, and when the rain started, the dark clouds disappeared, but the rain kept up. After the initial downpour, it settled to a more steady rain that fell for four days and four nights.

The men carried out their duties as best they could. They waded through water that ran over the main deck and escaped through scuppers into the ocean. The sails were unfurled from around their yards, but the huge canvases hung motionlessly. A gloom prevailed over the *Monarch,* and there was little talk at mealtime; everyone seemed to be in a world of his or her own. Nathan tried to keep up the morale of the crew, and

Hannah didn't want to interfere, although their time for parting drew near, and she wanted to spend as much time with him as possible.

Her best prevention of depression was to stay busy, and in the early part of the afternoon, on the third day of rain, she left her cabin in search of something to do. She made her way to the galley and had hoped to find Sam there, but he had finished cleaning after the noon meal and had gone to his room to rest.

She decided to spend time at the winch, but heard men's voices as she descended the steps to the gun deck. A group had gathered around Nathan by an open window to tell jokes and tall tales. Jeff stood at the back and listened to the others. He saw Hannah come down the steps, but everyone else faced the window and didn't see her. Jeff watched as she stood on the bottom step a moment and then their eyes met. He looked at Nathan in the middle of the group and then back at her, but she laid her finger across her lips and shook her head, then quietly turned and went back up the steps.

Jeff realized she was lonely, and he wanted to talk to her, but couldn't. She belonged to Nathan. After she disappeared up the steps, he left the group and went to his own bunk in the little forecastle. He lay on his back with his hands behind his head and thought of Hannah. What if Nathan didn't make it back from the war, or what if he returned to England and forgot her? What would happen to her? He'd heard that she had no family or anyone to care for her . . . and he was in love with her.

Since Hannah could find nothing to do, she went back to her cabin and took out the book that Nathan had given her at the birthday party. She began to read what different ones had written in it. He had written on the first page, "To my precious Hannah, I'll always love you, and I want to share your birthdays for the rest of my life. You have brought me more happiness than I ever dreamed existed. Love, Nathan." She read the first words again. They were the same ones her father had written in her small book of scriptures. It meant a lot that he remembered.

Mrs. Barrington had written on the next page, "Dearest Hannah, you're a remarkable girl. Nathan's dad and I already think of you as part of our family. May your birthday be one that will give you fond memories for years to come. Love, Martha." The note from Lizzy read, "Happy Birthday, Hannah. You're a dear friend, and we shall never forget what you did the night Little Michael was born. We'll tell him of it when he's old enough to understand. We love you. Lizzy, Michael, and Little Michael."

Hannah read the words of a few others, and then she turned back to the first page and read again what Nathan had written. As she read, she lifted her hand to the chain around her neck and the golden figures that made up his family coat of arms. It was of more value to him than the gold it was made of, and he would not have given it to her had he not loved her.

She wished for something to give him; something with special meaning that he could take with him when they parted. She laid the book aside and crossed the room to her trunk that held memories of her past. She lifted its top and removed the wrap from some of the things inside, but found nothing that would be of much value to anyone, but herself, except the China dishes, and he certainly could not take a China cup to war.

She forgot everything around her as she dug deeper into the trunk. Objects that had belonged to her mother were of more value than anything of her own childhood. Her mother's parents of Northern Ireland were very wealthy, and her mother had grown up on their large plantation. She must have loved my father an awful lot, she thought, to give it all up for him.

She was so engrossed in her thoughts that she didn't hear Nathan walk up to her outside door and was startled when he knocked. She opened the door, and he saw the top raised on her trunk and all the things that lay on the floor around it.

"What are you doing?"

"Well," she sighed, "I looked for something that you could take with you when we part, but there is nothing here that is worthy of you. I wish I had something special to give you like you gave me your coat of arms."

"Just tell me I have your heart as you have mine. It's all I need to take with me."

"You know you have my heart, but I want to give you something you can touch."

"Well, what about this?" He reached down and picked up a lace-trimmed handkerchief with the words "Hannah Thornton" embroidered across one corner of it.

"My grandmother made it for me when I visited her in Northern Ireland."

"Then I suppose it means a great deal to you."

"Yes. Perhaps it is worthy. I believe she sewed each stitch with love. There are three of them, and I would be pleased for you to take one to carry in your pocket."

"Then it's settled." He carefully tucked the handkerchief into his pocket.

"Do you realize what time it is?" he asked. "If we don't go for the evening meal, Sam will have closed the galley. He has no mercy on anyone."

Hannah laughed. Sam always left food for latecomers, but Nathan rushed her because his stomach told him it was past time to eat. She quickly put the things back inside the trunk.

"Where did the evening go? I'm sorry; I didn't realize it was so late."

"That's okay. I went to the galley, earlier, to look for you, and Jeff said you came to the gun deck, while some of us were gathered there, but you wouldn't let him get my attention. Why wouldn't you?"

"I wanted something to do to keep from being heavyhearted. Sam was finished in the galley, so I decided to work at the winch, but didn't want to disturb you. I know the rain causes discontent among the crew, and they need you more than I."

"I'm afraid you're right."

On the fifth morning, the rain ceased. The sun rose bright, and the *Monarch* picked up speed when her sails dried out and billowed before the wind. The days passed quickly as there was much to be done after the rain. Ropes were found slack and had to be stretched taut, equipment was greased, rigging was tarred, and chafing gear was put on where needed. Who could ever say that a seaman was idle at sea? Surely not one who had spent time aboard a ship. Before the work was caught up, if ever it was, they sailed into a deep inlet that took them to the mouth of the Cape Fear River and Wilmington, North Carolina.

Hannah and Nathan stood with Mary and Jenny near the quarterdeck and watched as John's brother and his family moved everything from the Hartmans' room to a wagon that stood at the end of the gangplank. The young girls held to Hannah and cried when it came time to part. John had to pull them away in order for Rachel and Steven to tell her good-bye. He took them to the wagon, and Hannah heard them cry all the way down the gangplank. She laid her head on Rachel's shoulder and wept, but Steven stood aside and tried to hide his tears. Nathan lifted a hand to his shoulder.

"Hey, it's not like you'll never see Hannah again. Soon as I get back from the war, I'll bring her to see you. If you'd like to be a seaman, would you work for Barrington Shipping?"

"If I'm a seaman, I don't want to work for anyone else."

"That's great, and by the time you're old enough, England should be at peace with France and the United States, and commerce will thrive again as it did before the war." Nathan paused and then said, "Steven, if we don't come, you'll know that . . . well, that . . ."

Steven knew what he tried to say. "You've got to come back, Nathan." He shook his hand as one man would another and said, "I'll pray for you every day."

"Thanks, Steven. Try to get an education."

His talk with Nathan made it easier for Steven to say good-bye to Hannah. He put his arms around her awkwardly and whispered, "I won't forget you."

"I won't forget you either, Steven. Thanks for helping me earn my passage across the ocean." She yelled good-bye as he took off down the gangplank.

A team of horses pulled the wagon down the dock; Hannah

waved until they reached the far end of it. As she wiped a tear from her cheek, Nathan put his arm around her.

"That family would have adopted you," he said, "had they had a place of their own. I hope everything goes well for them, and it will. John will have a job and a home for them before I get back to England."

"I'll miss them," Hannah sniffed.

"I know, and they'll miss you. Listen, I have to go into town and find out if we can unload cargo here. Jason and Mark and Jeff will go with me, but we should be back by noon. Mother could use some help packing, and pack your own things, for we'll leave as soon as I get back." He had asked her to accompany him to the Barrington home in Wilmington where his mother would stay for the summer, or until the French army was defeated.

Hannah spent the rest of the morning with Martha Barrington, and the two of them packed all of her belongings. As she left Mrs. Barrington's room to pack a few things of her own, Martha said, "Hannah, you'll want to take a nice dress in case we have company, while you're there. Why don't you take the lovely dark-green one that Nathan gave you?"

"All right," Hannah replied. She didn't really expect to wear it, but to please Nathan's mother, she would take it.

It was way past noon before Nathan and the three others returned to the ship. They went straight to the captain's office and didn't come out for a long time. Hannah felt that something was wrong. She waited in her room, and when Nathan finally knocked on her door, he apologized that he had been so long, but he didn't explain why, and she didn't ask, for she would not pry into his business.

He'd rented a large surrey and a team of horses, and he took her bag and lifted it to the back seat of the surrey. Jason brought Mrs. Barrington's bags down the gangplank on a cart and when everything was loaded, Nathan helped Hannah to the front seat between his mother and him. They waved good-bye to Captain Barrington and others who had come to see Mrs. Barrington off. The captain thought it best he stay with the *Monarch*.

As they rode into the town of Wilmington, Nathan pointed out places of interest and related to Hannah a bit of the town's history. "It was settled in 1732," he stated, "and was named after the British official Spencer Compton, Earlof Wilmington." He pointed out the house that had served as the headquarters of the British general, Charles Cornwallis, during the American Revolution. "We lost the war, you know." He turned his head and smiled at her, but her lips were sealed, and his mouth slightly twitched to one side.

They passed many large homes that belonged to wealthy British, but at the edge of town, Nathan turned the horses onto a narrow road, and Hannah saw the largest and most beautiful one of all. It was nestled among trees near the edge of deep woods. She had never seen such a large or beautiful home. Was it the Barringtons' Home? It must be, she thought, and was astounded.

"This is it," Nathan said. "It's where Mother will live for awhile; perhaps until the war is over."

"It's beautiful! It's the most beautiful home I've ever seen," declared Hannah.

"Well, you haven't seen the Colonial South, yet. Many homes make this one look small. The home on the plantation where you'll live is probably larger than this."

Mrs. Barrington had had little to say on the way there, and since she was usually talkative, Hannah suspected she had second thoughts about leaving her family. She spoke suddenly as if the thought had just occurred to her. "Hannah, why don't you stay here until Nathan returns?"

Hannah was surprised and didn't know what to say. She looked at Nathan and he, too, seemed surprised.

"I . . . I don't know. I made a commitment to teach the children in South Carolina."

"You don't have to," Nathan reminded her. "You owe nothing to anyone and may stay here with Mother if you want to, but it's your decision to make."

"You'll have a couple of days to think of it," said Martha.

The horses pulled the surrey right up to the front of the mansion and an old man came out to meet them. A young lady about Hannah's age walked behind him.

The old man greeted them as he took the horses' reins and tied them to a post by the front steps. Nathan stepped from the surrey and reached for Hannah's hand, and when the horses' reins were secured, the old man offered Mrs. Barrington a hand.

Nathan looked at the young girl who stood quietly to one side. "Sally," he said, "I'd like for you to meet Lady Hannah Thornton, my fiancée."

The girl curtsied humbly and said, "I'm honored to meet you Lady Thornton."

Hannah was shocked. No one had ever called her Lady Thornton. Only the most distinguished ladies of Ireland were honored with that title, and she started to protest, but Nathan caught her eye and shook his head. Instead she said softly, "It's a pleasure to meet you, Sally."

Mrs. Barrington climbed the front steps, and Sally ran ahead to open the door. Hannah heard her ask, "Did you have a pleasant trip across the ocean, Lady Barrington?"

"Yes, Sally, but I'm very tired. I do hope to get a good hot bath tonight."

"Oh, yes, ma'am. Everything will be ready at the usual time."

Nathan helped the old man lift bags from the surrey, and then he turned to Hannah and said, "I want you to meet Henry Langford. He's worked here longer than I can remember and knows more about this place than any Barrington does."

Hannah took the old man's wrinkled hand. "I'm so very pleased to meet you, Mr. Langford."

"The pleasure is mine, Ma'am." He turned to Nathan. "Did I hear you say fiancée?"

"Yes, Henry, Lady Thornton and I plan to get married as soon as I return from the war."

"Well, blessings to you, my boy, but if I knew a girl that pretty, I wouldn't wait 'til the war was over to marry her. I'd be afraid some other man might capture her, while I was gone."

Nathan didn't know what to say, but he gave Hannah a melancholy smile. When her face blushed, he muttered under his breath, "Henry usually speaks his mind; you must disregard his words."

Both men lifted a bag in each hand and started for the front door. Sally returned to the surrey and offered to take Hannah's bag. When Hannah refused to let her have it, she lifted one much too heavy for her.

"Sally, let the men get those bags; they're too heavy for you, and I can carry my own. Will you call me Hannah?"

"Oh, no, ma'am! That would be disrespectful."

"How old are you?"

"Nineteen, but I'll be twenty in August. And I'm getting married in October after the crops are harvested."

"That's wonderful. I wish Nathan and I could get married that soon."

"Why can't you?"

"He enlisted in the Royal Navy before he met me and must return to England and the war."

"Aren't you going to marry him before he leaves?"

"No . . . we plan to marry as soon as he returns."

"Why don't you marry him now?"

"Well . . ." Hannah smiled meekly, "he didn't ask me to."

"Oh," Sally mumbled and closed the conversation.

The two girls climbed the steps to a wide porch that surrounded three sides of the home. Large white columns towered between the porch and its high ceiling. Sally set the bag down and opened the front door for Hannah, but instead of going inside with her, she returned to the surrey for the last bag.

Hannah was filled with awe as she entered the home. She breathed in a deep breath and released it slowly as her eyes viewed the splendid beauty around her. A marble floor looked like pearl, and a beautiful chandelier glittered overhead. Beyond the entrance, plush moss-green carpet covered the floor of a large room, and the steps of a wide staircase were covered with the same. Beautiful paintings had been hung in all the right places on gleaming white walls. Large green plants filled one corner of the room, and across the back wall, a brick fireplace had a two-foot-high hearth that formed a semicircle in front of it. The fireplace mantel and the staircase banisters were made of a fine wood that had been stained and highly polished.

A white vase on the mantel held a bouquet of fresh flowers and over the vase was a life-size painting of Captain and Mrs. Barrington. At each side of the flowers set small paintings of other family members. A picture of another, much larger, mansion hung in a conspicuous place on the wall. It stood on a hill with the sea beyond it, and Hannah saw that Barrington Manor was just as beautiful as Nathan had described it.

She had not grasped just how wealthy the Barringtons were until now. It was far more than she had imagined, and how could she, who had never known any home other than the small country cottage in Ireland, ever adapt to all of this. She felt she should be the servant instead of Sally. She was so taken in by it all that she didn't hear Nathan come down the stairs. As she stood and stared at the large painting, he walked up behind her and reached for her hand.

"That's Barrington Manor," he said.

"I know." A sharp pain pierced her heart as she turned and looked into his face and saw a very wealthy British Aristocrat instead of a common seaman.

She pulled her hand from his and ran out of the room and down the front steps. A swing hung from a branch of an oak tree in a corner of the yard, and she sat down in it and covered her face with her hands.

"Hannah!" Nathan called her name and ran after her, but he stopped when she sat down in the swing. He knew she needed time alone, so he sat down on the front steps to wait. This was his fault, he blamed himself. He had not prepared her for everything, and he certainly should not have left her to enter the house alone.

Hannah sat for quite some time and then dried her face with the bottom of her skirt and lifted her head. She saw Nathan on the porch steps and was thankful he had given her time to recover from the shock. The sun sank beyond the trees, and it reminded her of what he had asked her to do each day while he was gone. Had he not asked her to marry him before he left because he feared she could not adapt to his life-style?

When she rose from the swing and walked toward the porch, he came to meet her. They met in the middle of the yard, and he put his arms around her and held her close to him.

"I'm sorry, Hannah. I'm sorry I left you alone, and I should have prepared you for everything. I just forgot how different our lives have been."

"I'm sorry, too, Nathan, but I feel out of place here, and I don't want to be called Lady Thornton."

Nathan closed his eyes and sighed, but had no answer. He didn't know how to explain that to drop the title would create a problem between the servants and his mother.

"We won't have to live like this when we're married," he answered. "We'll go back to Ireland and live in your cottage near the sea with a dog and a cat." He smiled and caressed her cheek with his thumb.

"I sold my home in Ireland."

"We'll buy another one. You're tired, darling. You'll feel better in the morning and this place won't seem so bad."

"Oh, Nathan, it's a beautiful place, but I don't belong here."

"Yes you do; you're going to be my wife."

"But everything is so strange; I'm not accustomed to all of this."

"Darling . . . I want to give you everything I can afford to give you, but your happiness means more to me than anything else. We'll plan our home together, and we'll build it the way you want it and where you want it. You'll have plenty of time to think about it while I'm gone."

"Nathan . . ."

"What, sweetheart?"

"Did you not ask me to marry you before you leave because you were afraid that I could never adapt to your way of life?"

"No. That had nothing to do with it."

"Then you did think of us getting married now?"

"I've thought about us getting married every day since our first evening together."

He took her hand and led her back to the swing and they sat down.

"I wanted to explain why I didn't ask you to marry me before I leave, but didn't exactly know how since you're so easily embarrassed." He looked away, and she realized that what he was about to say was difficult for him.

"As captain of the ship, my dad could have preformed our marriage ceremony, and I wrestled with the thought nearly every night. But it's going to be awfully hard for me to leave you as it is, and I just couldn't if I thought that you . . . that you might be—"

"With child?" she whispered in his ear.

"Yes," he whispered back and buried his face in her hair. "Hannah," he groaned, "I don't think you realize how much I love you."

"I do, darling. I do now."

CHAPTER 16

Hannah did feel better the next morning, just as Nathan had said she would. She awoke early to a pleasant aroma of bacon frying. The room where she slept was at the end of the upstairs hallway and right over the kitchen. The smell rose through a narrow staircase.

She slipped on her robe and descended the narrow stairs quietly and entered the kitchen. A tall black lady stood in front of the stove and hummed a spiritual tune as she turned bacon in a skillet.

"Good morning," said Hannah.

The cook was apparently startled. She jumped and said rather loudly, "Lawd Child, what yo doing up s' early?"

"I smelled the bacon frying. Do you have a cup of hot tea?"

"I's gotta pot o' hot coffee ah perkin'."

"May I have a cup, and will you tell me your name?"

"Folks calls me Molly. It's shaut fo' Lamolly Mae Emmalou Kallieann Washington."

"Well, I'm glad I don't have to remember all of that," Hannah laughed. "Mine is Hannah."

"Lady Barrin'ton won't set fo me to calls yo dat. What yo las name?"

"I'm Hannah Thornton."

"Yesum, I's betta call yo Lady Thonton."

Hannah wrinkled her nose, but said nothing; she didn't want to get Molly in trouble. A small round table near a window in the room had three stools around it. She sat down on one of the stools, and Molly set a cup of steaming hot coffee in front of her.

"Now bes careful not to bun yo tongue, child."

Hannah smiled and thanked her. She liked the affectionate name "child," more than Lady Thornton.

She had never drank coffee, but knew that most Americans stopped drinking tea before the American Revolution because the British had placed a high tax on it. She recalled the story of "The Boston Tea Party" when a group of men from Boston dressed as Indians and went aboard an English merchant vessel and dumped all its tea into the harbor.

She gave the coffee a minute to cool and then found that its taste was strange, but it wasn't too bad. Molly began to hum again and went about her work, while Hannah sipped the coffee. Two fingers of her right hand were circled around the handle of the cup, and her left hand supported her chin. Both of her feet rested on the bottom rung of the stool.

She focused her attention on the view outside the window. A squirrel scurried up a tree and back down again with something in his mouth. Birds scratched the ground in their search for insects, and a small rabbit hopped out of the woods, but disappeared down a trail that led into them.

Nathan entered the kitchen dressed in a man's black silk robe. Hannah had never seen him in a robe. A low chuckle came from deep within her throat as her eyes moved from his face to his feet and back up again. The robe came to just below his knees, and a pair of black leather slippers covered his feet.

"What are you laughing at? If you can come downstairs in your robe, so can I. That coffee smells good; where did you get it?"

"Molly gave it to me. There's the pot on the stove."

"Why can't I get waited on like the guest?" Nathan grumbled. He poured himself a cup of the hot coffee, for Molly was now busy in the dining room.

Hannah laughed out loud.

"What's so funny?" He set his coffee on the table and sat down beside her.

"You. Where is my rugged seaman who sleeps in nothing above his waist and drinks his tea from a mug? You look like a

British Aristocrat that expects to be waited on. All you need is an English pipe."

"I take it you like me better the other way?"

"I do, Sir Barrington," she mocked.

"Your rugged seaman loves you." He leaned his face toward hers.

"I love him, too," she answered. The aroma from the coffee filled their nostrils as they leaned over the cups until their lips touched.

"Hannah," Nathan sighed, "be kind this morning. I have enough problems as it is."

"What's wrong?"

"My main concern is you. I want you to be happy, and I know how upset you were last night."

"Don't worry about me. You were right; I feel much better after a good night's rest. I was just so shocked when I realized how wealthy you are. I have nothing except my love."

"Your love has brought me more happiness than any amount of money could buy."

"You made me happy . . . at a time when I thought no one could, but tell me . . . what else are you worried about?"

"We have about a hundred thousand pounds worth of goods on the *Monarch* that we can't unload. I don't have time to take it to South America or Canada because I have to get back to England. It's merchandise that people need, but we can't go straight to the merchants, and town officials won't pay us a fair price for it."

"Don't they realize how much it cost to ship it across the ocean?"

"Sure they do, but they think we'll give it to them rather than take it back to England. Two town officials wanted two thousand pounds, each, to even discuss business with us."

"Did you pay it?"

"No! I won't do business with their kind. And I don't know if you should stay here; you might be safer on the plantation. I don't want to leave you or Mother here, although she has several friends that live here. Dad doesn't want to leave her, but if Napoleon finds a way to get his army across the English Channel, she won't be safe at Barrington Manor."

"I'm sorry, Nathan. You're so young to have such responsibilities. Why don't you let your dad worry about all of this?"

"He does, but he wants me to take over the *Monarch* when the war is over, so I need the experience."

"You mean . . . be its captain?"

"Yes."

Hannah looked down at her coffee and for a moment, said nothing. It would mean long periods of separation for the two of them. Nathan knew what she thought and realized that he had another problem.

"I thought you said we would talk about our life and make plans together when you returned."

"We will. Those plans were made before I met you, and they can be changed. I shouldn't tell you all this; I don't want to cause you to worry, but I want to share everything with you. I don't ever want to keep anything from you again."

She was glad he felt that way and was sorry she'd let her disappointment show. He had enough burdens without her adding to them.

"Well," she smiled, "I knew you were a seaman when I fell in love with you. And don't you consider my problems as yours?"

"Yes . . . but—"

"Then yours are mine. I can't take care of them the way you do mine, but I can ask God to."

"Will you, Hannah? Will you pray about everything?"

"Yes." She nodded her head.

When finished with the coffee, Hannah went back upstairs to dress for breakfast. Sally knocked on the door. "May I help you get dressed?" she asked.

"No," Hannah replied, "but I would like your company. Please come in."

The door opened slowly and Sally stepped inside the room. She stood beside the door with her head slightly bowed and held her hands in front of her.

"Are you ready for me to straighten your room, Lady Thornton?"

"Sally, when no one else is around, please call me Hannah. We're almost the same age, and I want to be your friend. Come sit on the bed and tell me about your fiancé, while I get dressed."

Hannah had put the servant girl at ease. She sat down on the side of the bed and seemed eager to talk about the boy she was going to marry.

"His name is Ethan."

"Ethan what?"

"Ethan Warren. He's twenty years old, and I think he's very handsome."

"I'm sure he is because you're a very pretty girl. You'll have beautiful children."

"Oh, thank you Lady Th . . . I mean Hannah. Ethan and I have known each other all our lives. I always liked him, and he did me, but we neither knew how much each of us really cared for the other until last year."

"I'm glad you found out." Hannah laughed, as she slipped a dress over her head.

"Me, too," said Sally. She stood and pulled the dress down over Hannah's body, and then she dropped to her knees and began to button the buttons near the bottom of the dress, while Hannah buttoned from the top.

"Did you and Ethan grow up in Wilmington?"

"Yes. My parents have a farm just out of town, and Ethan's family owns one near by. I stay here during the week and help take care of the house. I have a small room off the kitchen, next door to the Langfords. They're very nice to me."

"What about the Barringtons? How do they treat you?"

"Lady Barrington treats me kindly, and the captain pays me a generous salary. He provides a fund at a Bank in Wilmington, and Mr. Langford draws from it on the last Friday of the month to pay each of us that work here. I'm fortunate to have employment with kind people, so near home."

"How does Nathan treat you?"

Sally sat down on the bed again, and her eyes looked down at the floor. Hannah realized she was embarrassed and was sorry she had asked. In a quiet voice, Sally replied, "Nathan is one of the nicest men I've ever known. He always treats me very courteously, and I think you're so blessed to be engaged to him."

"Thank you, Sally. I'm sure I would feel the same about your Ethan."

"He's coming to take me to town this evening, if you want to meet him."

"I'd love to."

"Do you want to go to town with me? I'm going to look for a new dress to wear to a barn square dance at our farm on Saturday night."

"A barn square dance! That sounds like fun."

"Oh, it is. Everybody in my family comes and lots of neighbors. The older people gather in one group and young couples form another. When the fiddler begins to play, everyone grabs his partner and joins his group. It's fun to watch the little kids hold hands and dance around; they don't know the calls yet."

"I'd like to see them and I'd love the music."

"Why don't you come?"

"I'm not sure if I'll be here that long, but I will go to town with you. I'd like to see more of Wilmington."

"Good! Ethan will come for us early in the afternoon."

"I'll be ready."

Nathan and Mrs. Barrington had dressed and waited for Hannah in the dining room when she returned downstairs. Nathan stood and pulled a chair out next to his. His mother sat at the head of the table.

"I'm sorry I kept you waiting," Hannah apologized.

"That's all right, dear," said Mrs. Barrington. "I just told

Nathan that I sent Henry to invite some friends over this afternoon. I want them to meet you."

"Oh . . . I told Sally that I . . ."

Mrs. Barrington's eyes flashed her way, and the look on her face left no doubt in Hannah's mind that she had done something wrong. She didn't finish the sentence, but had said enough to show her disappointment. A young black girl served the breakfast, and Hannah picked up her fork and began to eat.

"Nathan, will you ask God to bless our food?" asked Mrs. Barrington. In her frustration, Hannah had forgotten the blessing and was terribly embarrassed. She laid down her fork and covered her eyes with her hand. How could a day that started so right be going so wrong?

After the blessing, Nathan turned to her and asked, "What did you tell Sally?"

She dared not say anything else and muttered to him under her breath, "Nothing."

"Tell me," he insisted.

"That I would go to town with her. Her fiancé will take her this afternoon to look for a new dress to wear to a barn dance that they will have on Saturday night. I thought it would be a chance to see more of the town, and I accepted her invitation without thinking. I should have consulted your mother first. I'm very sorry and will tell Sally that I can't go."

When Martha Barrington looked at her son with a disturbed look on her face, Hannah realized that she had put him in an awkward situation.

"It's not good to associate with the servants," he said. "It usually doesn't work out."

"I didn't know that; I'm very sorry," Hannah apologized again.

They all three ate quietly until Nathan blurted out, "What would it hurt for her to go to town with Sally?"

"Nathan," his mother answered sternly, "I told you I invited some guests over. I'll have Ella inform Sally that Lady Thornton will be unable to accompany her to town." Ella was the young black girl that served breakfast.

"But—"

"Sh-h-h," Hannah whispered. "It's all right." She'd caused discord between Nathan and his mother, and it was something she had hoped would never happen. She did wish, however, that she could tell Sally she would not be able to go, instead of sending her a cold message.

Mrs. Barrington finished her breakfast and asked to be excused. Nathan and Hannah were left alone, and Ella entered the dining room to see if they needed anything. "No," said Nathan, but Hannah was silent. She was afraid to speak to the servants at all.

Soon as Ella left the room, she turned to Nathan. "I feel terrible," she said. "Please don't let me cause trouble between you and your mother."

"Forget it, Hannah. Look, I'm going back to town this morning and try to talk to someone about the cargo. Will you be all right while I'm gone?"

"Yes."

"I hate to leave right now, but I better go, so I can get back before the bloody guests arrive."

"Nathan!"

Nathan returned to the business section of town and went to the law office of J. P. Taylor. After a lengthy conversation with the young lawyer, however, he was forced to ask, "Then there is nothing you can do?"

"I'm sorry, but my hands are tied. The merchants of town would be more than happy to take the goods off your hands and would pay you a fair price for them, but all imports must go through the proper channels, and Macon's Bill Number 2 won't let us accept imports from England at this time. Many people believe war is inevitable between your country and mine, and a few are trying to make a quick profit from it."

"I understand, Mr. Taylor, and I appreciate your time. How much do I owe you?"

"Call me James, and you don't owe me anything since I couldn't help you. Maybe next time we can do business together. If I were you, I'd contact the sheriff about the town officials who wanted a bribe before they'd talk to you."

"I would like to see him. Can you direct me to his office?"

The lawyer stood at his open door and gave Nathan directions to the sheriff's office. Neither he nor Nathan noticed the two men who stood outside his door and listened.

Nathan walked toward the sheriff's office, unaware that the men followed him. He'd not gone very far when they forced him off the walkway to a narrow space between two buildings. He recognized the two town officials who had demanded the bribe, and one of them held a musket to his head.

"Look Barrington," said the other man, "if you don't want your house at the edge of town to burn, you better board your ship and get out of here." He made it real clear that they didn't want him to talk to the sheriff.

There were two of them and they were armed. Since he was alone and unarmed, he had no choice but to listen to them. "I'll leave as soon as I can," he said.

The two let him go after they threatened him again with what they'd do if he said anything. He decided not to talk to the sheriff since his mother had come to stay at the house and would be alone, except for servants, but on the way home he did a lot of thinking. Later that day, James Taylor did talk to the sheriff, and he wondered why Nathan didn't go by his office.

Nathan returned to his parents' mansion and found Hannah in the swing under the oak tree. She had a book in her hands, but laid it aside and came to meet him.

"I pray you had a successful trip to town."

"No," he shook his head. "Let's go back to the swing and I'll tell you about it. I talked to a lawyer," he explained, "but there is nothing he can do because their law prohibits British imports right now. We were aware of this when we left Liverpool, but many have tried to get the law changed in both countries. It hurts American merchants as well as British.

"Hannah, I've made up my mind; I won't let you stay here, and I'm going to insist that Mother returns to England. I want you to come with us. The strife between the United States and England has grown stronger and some believe war will come soon. Do you think you're strong enough to make the return trip across the ocean?"

Hannah flinched at the thought of making the voyage again so soon. She slowly shook her head back and forth and answered, "I don't think so."

"Neither do I, but I won't leave you in this town." He told her about the threats from the two town officials. "I don't want to scare you," he said, "but to let you know what's going on. Please stay inside and don't leave the house without me."

"I won't."

"We'll leave tonight. I want to get you and Mother back to the safety of the *Monarch*."

"I'll be ready."

Mrs. Barrington stayed in her room most of the morning. She rested and then dressed for the small party with her wealthy British friends who owned homes in Wilmington and had come there to live until the war with France was over. She looked lovely when she met Hannah and Nathan for the noon meal, and she seemed to have forgotten what had happened at breakfast. "Hannah," she asked, "did you bring the pretty green dress with the full skirt?" Nathan heard, and he knew she referred to the one that she had picked out for Hannah.

"Yes. Would you like for me to wear it this afternoon?"

"I think it would be appropriate for the occasion."

"All right," Hannah agreed, and as soon as the meal was over, she hurried upstairs to change.

Nathan was dressed early and waited for her at the bottom of the staircase. He heard the soft swishing of petticoats as she descended the stairs gracefully. The color of the dress was so dark it appeared to be black and its yards of exquisite material glittered under the chandelier. It was beautiful, but as she stepped onto the floor, he saw that it was more revealing at the top than any of her other dresses. When she lowered her eyes and her cheeks turned a pinkish red, he realized that she felt uncomfortable in it. He smiled to give his approval, and it seemed to have made her feel better.

The guests began to arrive. A Lady Livingston came first with her daughter, Pamela. Pam, as she preferred to be called, was probably in her early twenties. She was short and overweight, but smiled a big smile.

The next guests to arrive were Lady Knottingham and her nephew, George Donaldson. George also appeared to be in his early twenties or Nathan's age. When Mrs. Barrington introduced him to Hannah, he reached for her hand and refused to let go. He bowed and kissed the back of it.

"Nathan, my friend, where did you find one so beautiful?" George asked, without taking his eyes off Hannah.

"On a dock in Ireland," Nathan replied, as he reached for Hannah's hand and took it from him. George attempted to start a conversation with her, but other guests arrived and she was called to meet them. It was a young lady with two small sons.

"Hi," said the younger son, with his head tilted way back in order to see Hannah's face. "My name's Luke. I didn't want to come and neither did my brother."

Hannah laughed at his honesty. Well, Luke, she thought, that makes three of us.

Several other guests arrived and were shown into the living room where Ella and Molly served coffee and tea with dainties. Nathan mingled among the guests and tried to speak to everyone. He felt almost as uncomfortable as Hannah because the guests were all ladies except George and the two small boys. The boys acted like brats, and Nathan had little respect for George. He was obnoxious, and everyone in town knew he lived off his uncle, while evading the King's Army.

For a moment, Hannah was lost to Nathan's sight, and his eyes searched the room. He wanted to be sure George had no time alone with her. He saw her at the far side of the room with Pam. Pam didn't seem to notice, but Hannah's attention was focused on something outside the window. He asked to be excused from the lady he conversed with to move closer to the window and saw a young man help Sally onto a wagon seat. A wistful look on Hannah's face revealed how badly she wanted to go with them. As the wagon rolled down the front lane, her mouth twitched slightly to one side, as if to dismiss her disappointment, and she turned her attention back to Pam.

Hannah found it difficult to stand for a long period of time, but she wanted to be her best for Nathan and his mother, so she smiled when she was expected to and was attentive to what everyone said to her in order to make the right comments.

As the evening was spent, the small boys became rowdy. They ran around her and pulled at her full skirt; she wondered if their mother had forgotten them. Pam was at her side constantly with the big smile plastered on her face. But worse than the boys' rowdiness and Pam's smile, were George's eyes. They followed her around the room and made her feel very uncomfortable.

When the pressure became too much, Hannah's head began to hurt and she felt faint. She hoped no one would notice as she backed away from the crowd and went to the corner of the room where the tall plants stood. With her head and shoulders against the wall, she rubbed her neck and had received a degree of relief when George took his opportunity. He suddenly appeared before her and lifted his hands to the wall over her shoulders and leaned his face close to hers. She was startled and tried to stand up straight, but his arms penned her against the wall. He breathed in her face, and his eyes were fixed on her revealing neckline.

"George, remove your arms!" she demanded.

"Why, Hannah?" he smirked. "I just want to talk to you."

"Please let me go!" Her heart beat faster, and her head began to throb as she pleaded with him. She didn't want to cause a scene, but feared she would faint. She was too weak to push him away, and his body blocked her view, preventing her from finding Nathan in the crowd.

She felt drops of perspiration on her face, and her legs were so shaky she could hardly stand when she heard Nathan's voice. "Hello, George! I see you like my Hannah!" George quickly removed his hands from over her shoulders, and Nathan saw the panic in her eyes. She stepped close to him and he felt her trembling.

"Oh, hello, Nathan," said George. "Yes, I find her quite charming."

"So I noticed," Nathan said, and then he calmly muttered under his breath, "but I'll run my sword through your guts if you ever get near her again." Only George and Hannah heard him, but George quickly found someone else to talk to.

"Nathan, my head ached, and I just wanted to let it rest against the wall a moment. I never thought about—"

"Come on," he said, "we're leaving." And without another word, he took her hand and led her from the room. On the way out, he informed his mother that she had a headache. As they climbed the stairs, he asked, "Do you need to lie down?"

"No, I feel better already."

"Hannah, I'm sorry you had to go through all that. I know the voyage left you weak, and Mother should have been more considerate. I would have told her that, but she had already sent Henry with invitations."

"I'm sure she didn't think. I'll be all right, but I couldn't have taken George another second. Thank you for rescuing me."

"He's a vile person and I meant what I said to him."

When they reached the top of the stairs, he took her in his arms. She leaned her head against his chest and he caressed her back. After she rested a moment, he put his hand under her chin and gently lifted her face upward.

"I love you, Hannah," he whispered, "more than anything." He slowly bent his head forward, and her eyes closed as his lips neared hers.

"You make me forget everything unpleasant when you kiss me," she spoke softly.

"I want you to forget this entire afternoon. Do you feel like going to town to see if we can find Sally and Ethan?"

"I would love to, but what about your mother?"

"We won't tell her. Now go change your clothes, and I'll be right back."

He went to his own room and also changed into something comfortable. Before he left the room, he opened a drawer in the chest by his bed and picked up a small pistol. He made sure it was loaded and then dropped it inside his vest pocket.

He and Hannah headed into town and met Sally and Ethan, who by now had finished with shopping and were on their way back. Ethan pulled his wagon over and tied the horses to a tree. Nathan did the same with the surrey, and after Sally introduced the two of them to Ethan, they all four squeezed onto the front seat of the surrey with Hannah and Sally in the middle.

Hannah loved the company of another girl her own age. She forgot her headache, and the four of them spent the rest of the evening together; they rode all over town, and it was late when they returned to the mansion. Just before Nathan turned the horses onto the narrow road that led to the house, five men rode past them. It was too dark for him to recognize any of them, but he wondered where they could be going, for the Barrington home was the last house on the road.

He and Hannah sat on the front porch steps and waited for Sally to say goodnight to Ethan. Nathan had not forgotten the five men on horseback, and he wondered if Ethan should leave. Suddenly he saw a light among the trees to the left of the house and was about to call Sally and Ethan to the porch when a shot rang out. The two ran across the yard as he and Hannah sprang to their feet. He hurried Sally and Hannah through the front door and told them to have everyone meet in the kitchen. He and Ethan then stood together on the front porch, and Nathan called out, "Who goes there?"

From beyond the trees where he had seen the light, came a man's voice. "We told you to get out of town, Barrington, but you didn't. We don't like British and we won't take your cargo.

Since it's taken you so long to leave, we're fining you four thousand dollars, and if you don't pay it right now, we'll burn the house."

"I told you I'd leave as soon as I could."

"Well, that's not fast enough, so give us the money or see your house in flames. And don't try anything; we have the place surrounded." Nathan saw the light in the woods get brighter and knew the men had a lantern from which they could light torches.

"You'll have to give me some time," he shouted.

"You have ten minutes."

He and Ethan stepped inside the house, and Nathan locked the door. "Do you have any guns?" asked Ethan.

"Yes, and plenty of ammunition, but the two of us can't hold them off, and what about the women?" They ran to the kitchen. Everyone had gathered there as Nathan had requested. "I wish there was a way to get out of the house without being seen," he said.

"There is!" Sally spoke up. "There's a secret door in the cellar. I found it when I stored some things there. It opens into a tunnel that comes out about two hundred yards from the house by a trail in the woods."

"Great! Hannah, can you find your way to the *Monarch*?"

"Ah . . . I . . . I don't think so . . . . Not in the dark."

"I can," said Sally. "And Mr. Langford knows the way to my home. He may take the others there, and Mom and Dad will take care of them until this is over."

"I'm not leaving," Henry insisted. "I'm staying here with Nathan and Ethan. This is the only home I have, and I'm going to help protect it."

"I won't leave Henry," said Mrs. Langford. "I can help by loading the guns."

Nathan looked at his mother and she shook her head. "You know I can shoot as well as anyone," she said. She didn't appear to be scared, so he would not waste time arguing with her.

Ella was so frightened, she trembled, but Molly stood tall as ever. "I ain't skerd of dem bandits. I's got de ole musket.

Come on, Ella; yo stays wit me, and da ain't nobody gonna harm yo."

The ten minutes were almost up, and Ethan and Nathan ran to get guns and ammunition. "Let's go, Hannah," said Sally. She held a lighted lantern, and they ran to the cellar where she moved some boxes and opened the door to the tunnel. It was dark inside, but she held the lantern up and motioned for Hannah to follow. The bricked passageway was narrow, but high enough for the girls to run through it. Sally unlocked the door to the outside before she blew out the lantern and left it at the end of the tunnel.

The moonlight shined through the open space in the trees and marked the trail in the woods that ended where the road began. As they neared the end of the trail, the two girls saw something move ahead and quickly stepped into the shadow of the trees. They listened and realized there were horses ahead and felt sure they belonged to the men who had come to rob the Barringtons. They had tied them at the end of the road, so no one would hear them approach the house. Sally had an idea.

"Can you ride?" she whispered.

"Yes." Hannah whispered her reply.

"Then come on."

The girls crept cautiously to the horses and untied two of them. Sally led them to a trail that was a shortcut around town, and as soon as they were out of hearing distance, they mounted the horses and slapped them across the rump. With Sally in the lead, the horses ran unrestrained down the path of moonlight, through the woods. Hannah held on with all her strength as branches slapped her in the face and scratched her arms. She felt no pain, for all she could think of was to get to the *Monarch* as quickly as possible.

Before long, they came out of the woods and slowed the horses to a gallop and then rode along the inlet until the black silhouette of the *Monarch* emerged from the darkness. Hannah jumped from the horse and quickly gave the reins to Sally and ran down the dock as fast as she could. As she approached the gangplank, Jason shouted, **"Who goes there?"**

"Jason," she yelled, "it's Hannah! Nathan's in trouble! He needs help . . . quick!" Jason flew down the gangplank to meet her.

"Some men," she gasped for breath, "with guns are demanding money—lots of money—and they said they would burn the house if they didn't get it. Nathan and some others are trying to hold them off."

Captain Barrington heard Hannah and began to shout orders. "Jason," he yelled, "run to the town's stable and get as many horses as you can. Some of you men get your rifles, and Murray, take charge of the *Monarch*. Wake those who are sleeping and be on guard until we return."

Within moments, the captain and seven seamen rode along the inlet behind Sally. She found the path of moonlight through the woods, and as she turned the horse onto the trail, she kicked him in the ribs to bring him to a fast speed. Hannah followed close behind with the captain and his seamen.

When they heard gunshots in the distance, Sally shouted that she would go for the sheriff, and the captain ordered Jason to ride with her. She knew the way and kept the horse at full speed until she pulled up in front of the office. The sheriff talked to a group of men across the street, but came running when he saw them. He figured something was up.

"I'm Sheriff Rosser," he said. "Is something wrong?"

"Yes, sir," replied Jason, "at the Barrington home on the outskirts of town. Some men are demanding money and have said that they'll burn the home if they don't get it; a small group inside the house is trying to hold them off." The young lawyer that Nathan had talked to that morning was with the sheriff. He mounted his horse and rode with them.

Meanwhile, as the captain led his seamen and Hannah up the path to the house, he saw five men with torches in their hands. He fired a shot into the air, and four of the men threw down their torches and ran, but one hurled his toward the home and it landed under the edge of the porch.

Scott jumped from his horse and snatched the blanket from

under the saddle. As the other seamen went after the five men, he ran across the yard and put out the fire.

Jason and Sally returned with Sheriff Rosser and the lawyer, and thanks to the seamen, the sheriff soon had all five men in custody. He was not surprised to find that they were town officials whom he'd suspected were taking advantage of the trouble with England to make a quick fortune. "You're going to jail," he said.

"And I'll see that you get prosecuted," added James Taylor.

Hannah jumped from the horse and ran across the yard to the house. She ran up the steps and to the front door. "Nathan," she called, as she beat on the door, and when Nathan opened it, she threw her arms around him.

"Hannah, what happened?"

"The sheriff is here and he has the men in custody. It's over, Nathan, it's over," she sobbed.

Before Sheriff Rosser left with his prisoners, he asked Captain Barrington to come to his office the next day in order to discuss the safety of the many British who lived in Wilmington. After he left, everyone gathered in the living room of the mansion, where Mrs. Barrington had entertained guests that afternoon. Although Ella was still a bit shaken, she helped Molly serve leftover snacks.

"I'm very grateful," said the captain, "to each of you. You kept our home from being destroyed, and you'll all be rewarded. Sally, what special thing may I do for you and Hannah for the brave deed you preformed?"

"You may attend our barn dance on Saturday night," Sally replied in a shy voice.

Hannah held her breath when Captain Barrington smiled and looked at his wife.

"We graciously accept your invitation, Sally," answered

Martha Barrington. Then to Hannah's great surprise, she added, "May we extend it to all the crew of the *Monarch*?"

"Oh, yes, ma'am," Sally replied. "The girls would be most delighted."

Everyone laughed.

Shortly after midnight, the captain and his seamen returned to the ship, and Ethan left for home. Nathan made Hannah and Sally sit at the same kitchen table that he and Hannah had drank coffee at that morning. He cleaned blood from the scratches on their faces and arms and examined the bruises they'd received from limbs. He put ointment on each scratch to keep down infection.

He listened as the girls relived their experience, and he laughed when Hannah told how they had taken the two horses that belonged to the bad men, but he said nothing. He didn't want to interrupt them. He perceived that more had taken place than just a brave deed. A memory had been made that would never be forgotten, and a friendship had developed that could never be broken.

When Sally went to her room, Hannah sat at the table alone. As Nathan put the medical things away, he thought of everything that had happened, and it scared him when he realized the danger that Sally and Hannah had been in. What if the men had kidnapped them? There had not been time, before hand, to think, but if they had not gone for help, all of them might have burned with the house.

"Nathan?" Hannah said his name questioningly.

"What?"

"Are you angry with me?"

"Angry! How could I be angry with you after what you did?"

"I don't know, but you haven't said more than two words to me since I returned."

"I'm sorry, Hannah, but I'm certainly not angry. When I think of what could have happened, it scares me. I haven't said much to anyone, but I do have a confession to make."

"What is it?"

"I knew you couldn't find your way to the *Monarch* when I asked you tonight."

"Then why did you ask?"

"Because I thought that Sally probably could, but I couldn't ask that of a servant. She did exactly what I hoped she would do, but I don't think she would have, had you not made friends with her. I hate to think what might have happened to all of us, had you not treated her so kindly."

"But, Nathan, she told me how kind you have been to her."

"I treat her courteously, as all servants should be treated, but it was your friendship that made her volunteer to go for help. Two Barringtons learned a lesson from you today."

He circled his arms around her. "Darling," he said, "I love you more than words can express, but I seldom have time alone with you."

All was quiet in the household; everyone else had gone to bed. "We're alone right now," she whispered.

"Yes," he groaned, as his lips savored hers. "We are, aren't we?"

CHAPTER 17

Shallow waves splashed against the windward side of the *Monarch* as her crew readied her for sailing on the morning of June 15. The sun bore down hot upon the ship, even in the early morning hours, and the southerly wind that swept across it brought little relief to those who worked tediously.

Most of the crew had attended Sally's barn dance the night before, while Murray and Sam kept vigilance over the *Monarch*. The young seamen had enjoyed the company of young ladies, and some even felt love-stricken as they climbed aloft that morning. Their hearts were not in their work, and the heat added to their weariness.

A crowded deck brought another hardship to the men. After the Sheriff of Wilmington had talked to Captain Barrington, he put out a warning to all British in the town that if war came between the two countries, he could not ensure their safety. The captain offered them passage back to England for only the cost of their provisions. Most agreed to leave but a few stayed behind.

Nathan moved to the crew's quarters, and the elderly of the group were given the more comfortable rooms that were vacated by him and those who had left the ship. Everyone else, regardless of their grumbling, was moved into the ship's actual forecastle where a hard bunk bed and a thin mattress were their only accommodations. Had the ship sailed from Liverpool with a full crew, there would not have been room for everyone.

Regardless of the overcrowded situation, Hannah was not asked to share her room. She had worked for her cabin, and Nathan was determined that no one would take her privacy from her. He knew how uncomfortable she felt around the wealthy British, and he wanted her to be able to escape their company at all time.

The heat made it almost impossible to remain in the forecastle or the cabins that morning, but when the *Monarch* sailed out of the inlet just before noon, a cooler breeze blew in from the ocean, and most of the passengers went back inside.

Hannah had never experienced such sweltering heat. Prevailing winds from the Atlantic had cooled Ireland in the summer and warmed it in the winter. Her cabin on the lee side deprived her of the breeze from the ocean that was relished by passengers on the windward side. Her long, thick hair added to her discomfort and brought beads of perspiration along her hairline. But in spite of the heat, she avoided the open deck and stayed in her cabin or close by her outside door. George Donaldson was aboard, and she feared what he might do if he caught her alone.

The first streaks of sunlight that morning found Nathan writing in the ship's log. He recorded everything that had happened during his absence from the *Monarch,* from the time he first talked to the town officials to what had happened at the home. He recorded the names of those who returned to England and their reason for leaving North Carolina.

Hannah skipped breakfast in order to sleep longer as it had been late when she and Nathan returned to the ship the night before. At noon, she took a small amount of food to her cabin and ate alone. When she returned to the galley for the evening meal, she found the dining room crowded with British passengers and decided to join Jason and Jeff at a table in the mess hall. She felt more at ease with them than with the new passengers, and both seemed pleased to have her company.

Nathan was bombarded with complaints when he entered the dining hall; he stopped to listen to each one. Hannah's eyes met his as she left the galley, and she smiled at him, but he didn't return her smile. Was he under too much pressure, or was he upset because she had eaten with Jason and Jeff?

She returned to her cabin and sponged her body with water, then changed into a dress that fit loosely about her. When the sun went down, she ventured outside to stand by the guardrail. The air was muggy. Sails hung limply from their yards as did her dress from her shoulders. Clouds formed overhead; she hoped it would rain.

With darkness, the rain did come. It came lightly at first, then harder, and Hannah settled in her bed with a book, but the constant rumbling of thunder made it difficult to concentrate on it. She laid the book aside and listened to the rain fall on top of her cabin. She thought of Nathan. Why had he not returned her smile in the dining hall? Suddenly there was a knock at her door. She jumped from the bed and hurried across the room.

"Who is it?"

She heard a deep guttural sound.

"Nathan, is that you?"

"Yes, Hannah." She recognized his voice, but it sounded differently.

She quickly opened her door and tried to put her arms around him, but he pushed her away. "Don't Hannah. I'm sick, and I don't want you to catch what I have, but I had to see you."

"Come in and sit down."

"No. I just came to tell you that you might not see me for a few days." His clothes were soaking wet.

"Please, Nathan," she begged. "I'll get you a towel and go for dry clothes." She took his hand and pulled him inside and made him sit down. His eyes were feverish, and his forehead was warm. She dried his head and face before she ran to the crew's quarters. When she knocked at the door, Scott answered.

"Hi, Hannah; you looking for Nathan?"

"No. He's in my room, but he's sick and I came to get dry clothes for him."

"Go back to your room," Scott said. "I'll find his clothes and bring them to you." He wouldn't let her enter the little forecastle.

She thanked him and returned down the hall.

Within a few minutes Scott brought the dry clothes, and

Hannah went to her water closet, while he took the wet clothes from Nathan and put the dry ones on him. Nathan began to shiver rigorously. He mumbled through clenched teeth, "Scott . . . help me to my bunk."

"I think you should stay here where Hannah can look after you. I'd like to help; you helped her take care of me." He pulled the cover back on Hannah's bed.

"No," Nathan argued.

"Do you think she'll stay away from you when she knows you're sick? Do you want her in the crew's quarters?"

"No—no."

"Then get in bed."

Hannah got more cover from her trunk and spread it over Nathan. His body shook hard until his fever began to rise. He sent Scott for his medical bag and two cots.

He took some medicine, but his fever continued to climb, and around 1:00 A.M., Hannah and Scott knew that it was dangerously high.

"I must let his parents know how ill he is," Hannah said.

"I think so too," Scott agreed. "I hate to wake them, but they have to know. I'll go knock on their door."

While Scott was gone, Hannah took Nathan's hand in hers and kneeled to the floor beside him. She prayed fervently for God to heal his body.

Captain and Mrs. Barrington came right away. The captain frowned when he laid his hand on Nathan's head. He looked at the medicine he had taken and then said to his wife, "Maybe this will help. There won't be a doctor until we reach Charleston."

Before daylight, Nathan became delirious. He talked out of his head and called Hannah's name several times. She answered each time, but he didn't seem to hear until she touched her lips against his ear and spoke directly into it. "I'm here, Nathan; I won't leave you." Then he seemed to have recognized her presence and fell into a deep sleep.

He was the only one in the room who slept. His parents and Scott and Hannah were still awake when they saw light through the window. His fever was extremely high, and at sunup, the captain sent Scott to fetch Murray. He had watched him care for other seamen when they were ill.

Murray came immediately. He ran his hands up and down Nathan's throat and behind his ears to check for swelling or bumps. He unbuttoned his shirt and examined his chest for any sign of rash, but found no reason for the fever.

"Do you think he could have contacted smallpox or typhoid fever in one of the ports?" the captain asked.

"Anything is possible, Sir, but I think it's highly unlikely since we didn't hear of an epidemic. He didn't eat at any of the ports and no one else on the ship is sick, so I'm guessing he has a bad case of the grippe."

He looked at the bottle of medicine and decided to give Nathan more of it. The captain and Scott held him up, while he poured it down him. He then asked Scott to get a bucket of cool water and for Mrs. Barrington to bring him several towels. With the captain's help, he removed Nathan's shirt and pants, and as soon as Scott and Mrs. Barrington returned, he wet the towels in the cool water and wrapped Nathan in them.

Hannah felt in the way—her small room was crowded—so she walked out by the guardrail and thought of what Murray had said. He didn't know, but Nathan had eaten in one of the ports. He'd taken her to the restaurant in New York City. The incubation period for smallpox was twelve days, and more time than that had elapsed, but the incubation for typhoid fever could be up to three weeks.

At first, the cool towels warmed quickly against Nathan's body, but Murray removed each, one at a time, and dipped it into the water before he wrapped it around him again. When he felt the time was right, he removed all the towels and dried Nathan from head to foot. His body was still hot, but he began to sweat and the fever came down.

About ten o'clock that morning, Nathan opened his eyes, but he lay listlessly upon the bed. His eyes moved around the room until he saw Hannah on a cot beside him. She was asleep, but her small hand lay on his arm. He lifted his other arm slowly and covered her hand with his own.

Word spread quickly that Nathan was ill. Jason took over for him and the captain, and with Murray and others taking turns at the wheel, they continued to sail south. Every seaman showed concern and doubled up on his watch, but there were problems with the new passengers. They complained constantly and wanted to turn north, toward England and cooler weather.

"Our destination is Charleston, South Carolina," said Jason to George Donaldson who demanded to know why they must continue to sail south. "We hope to unload the remainder of our cargo there, and that's where Hannah is going." Jason knew nothing of what had happened at Mrs. Barrington's party.

"Hannah!" snorted George. "You mean that Irish woman causes our suffering?"

"I didn't say that!" snapped Jason. He suddenly disliked George and refused to listen to his whining. He thought the captain should put him to work. If Hannah could work to pay for her voyage, he didn't understand why George couldn't.

Three days later, Nathan continued to run fever; his body ached and he felt pain in his head and back. The fever drained him of strength and he slept most of the time, but on the fourth day, Hannah noticed an improvement. He was awake more and he ate some food. It gave her hope that Murray's diagnosis was right.

Scott went back to work and the Barringtons went for the evening meal. Nathan and Hannah were left alone for the first time since he'd become ill. She stacked his dishes to be returned to the galley.

"Come sit by me," he said, "while we have a rare moment alone." She sat down on the side of the bed and he took both her hands in his. He looked into her eyes but was lost for words.

"Do you feel better?"

"Yes. I feel a lot better."

"I'm so glad," she said softly.

He tilted his head slightly backward and looked to the far

side of the room. Hannah suddenly remembered what had happened in the dining hall, the evening he got sick. She didn't want to bring it up, but was this why he didn't know what to say?

"Are you angry at me?"

"NO! Why do you think I'm angry? Do I look that way?"

"No," she sighed, "but you looked away as if you don't know what to say," then her words came quickly and all ran together. "You didn't return my smile in the dining hall, the evening you got sick. I was afraid it was because I sat with Jason and Jeff, but the dining hall was so crowded, and I didn't want to eat in my room, alone, so—"

"HANNAH, STOP IT!" He breathed heavily and rubbed his hand across his brow. "That doesn't bother me anymore. I think Jeff loves you, but I know you love me. I didn't return your smile because you were leaving, and I was disappointed. I didn't think I would see you again that day. I felt awful and wanted to let you know in case I didn't see you for several days."

He pulled her to him and spoke in a deep voice. "I don't know what to say because no words can express how I feel about you. I love you so much. I don't know how I got along before I found you, and I don't know how I'm going to make it when I have to leave you. I knew you were here with me, while I was so sick. I didn't know anything else, but I knew you were here, and that was what I needed to know.

"It's time for me to return to the crew's quarters. Will you help me?"

Reluctantly, she began to put his things that had collected there into a pillowcase. "Are you sure you're strong enough?" she asked.

"I think so. Scott will help me if I need him."

"He has helped so much. He said he wanted to repay you for what you did for him."

"You mean what you did for him?"

"What we both did."

She held his hand in one hand and carried the pillowcase in her other as they slowly walked to the crew's quarters at the far end of the hallway. When they passed the dining hall, Nathan noticed, out of the corner of his eye, someone seated at the far side under the dim light. He assumed it was one of the crew.

Howbeit, it was not one of the crew who sat and ate what Sam had left for those who worked late. It was George Donaldson, and he saw Hannah and Nathan go by. He figured Nathan's illness had left him weak, and that Hannah would be returning down the dark hallway—alone.

Hannah stood under the lamplight that glowed over the door to the quarters and looked up at Nathan with imploring eyes. Her lips were parted, and his lips burned for them, but he was still concerned that she would get his illness. Besides, he'd not shaved since he became ill and knew what his whiskers would do to her tender face. He lifted his hand to her throat, and she closed her eyes, but instead of her lips, he kissed the top of her head.

Disappointed, Hannah left to return to her room and Nathan went to his bunk. His strength was depleted. As he lay down, he heard someone cry out, but thought that one seaman had yelled at another and paid little attention.

George had waited for Hannah just inside the dining hall, and soon after Nathan closed the door to the little forecastle, he stepped out in front of her. She managed to cry out before he covered her mouth with his hand, but she couldn't free herself, and he dragged her down the steps to the dark gun deck. "To be nothing," he spoke crudely, "you act awfully high and mighty, but you won't act that way when I get through with you."

Meanwhile, Scott finished his watch and went by Hannah's cabin to see how Nathan was doing. He thought it was strange when no one answered his knock, and feeling that something was wrong, he opened the door slowly. "Hannah," he called, and when no one answered, he looked in and saw that the room was empty. He decided they had gone to the dining hall, but no one was there, either, so he went to the little forecastle and found Nathan lying on his bunk with his eyes closed.

"I wondered what happened to you," he said. "I came by Hannah's room and no one was there."

Nathan's eyes popped open. "No one was there?" he asked.

"No. I even opened the door and called Hannah's name, but she didn't answer."

"You didn't pass her in the hall?"

"No, and there's no one in the dining hall."

The figure that had sat in the dimly lit dining hall flashed before Nathan's face, and he remembered that someone had cried out. He jumped from the bed. "Scott!" he yelled, "I'm afraid George Donaldson has Hannah. Hurry! Get some lanterns and get every man on it. We must find her!" He yelled so loud that everyone in the quarters heard him, and every man jumped to his feet as Nathan reached for the sword that hung over his bunk.

Hannah struggled with George until her arms ached. He had dragged her to the floor of the gun deck, and his lips were pressed hard against hers as he tore at her clothes. He stopped suddenly when he heard a noise; there were several men on the steps with lanterns in their hands. He jumped to his feet and tried to run, but there was no way for him to escape.

Jason and Jeff went after him as Nathan ran to Hannah. He kneeled beside her and laid his sword on the deck and gathered her in his arms. She cried hysterically, but managed to say she was okay. They had found her in time. He lifted her and handed her to Scott who stood behind him. "Take her to her room, Scott, and stay with her until I get there." He bent over and picked up the sword.

Jason sent for Captain Barrington. He and Jeff held George with his hands behind his back and waited for the captain to arrive. Most of the crew gathered around them and wanted to take care of George in their own way. As soon as Scott disappeared up the stairs with Hannah, everyone heard Nathan's sword leave its sheath and they began to step aside. Not one of them had any doubt as to his intention.

Jason and Jeff began to back away with George to prevent Nathan from making a mistake, and both men were relieved to see Captain Barrington appear at the top of the steps. "Nathan!" the captain shouted, "put that sword away! You can't execute a man without a trial."

"I'm sorry, Dad, but I told him what I would do if he got near her again." As the men stepped aside, he walked toward George with the sword in front of him, and not one man attempted to stop him.

But Jason knew the British law, and that George was from a wealthy family who could afford lawyers. He felt sure that Nathan would go to prison, and there was a chance he would hang if he killed George without a trial. Just before Nathan ran the sword through his stomach, he stepped in front of him.

"Give me the sword, Nathan."

"No! Get out of my way!"

"I won't let you do this. We'll take George to the brig and turn him over to the police when we get back to Liverpool. My dad will prosecute him and try to get prison time for him. You heard the captain; you can't take the law in your own hands— not even for Hannah."

Nathan's weakness suddenly overpowered him, and to keep from falling, he stepped backward and sank to the steps. He dropped the sword and leaned his head over his knees. Captain Barrington sat down beside him, as Jason and Jeff hurried by with George.

Before he returned to Hannah's cabin, Nathan went to the quarters and showered. He shaved and brushed his teeth. Hannah was safe with Scott, and if he didn't get cleaned up now, he didn't know when he would have a chance to. As he dressed in clean clothes, he began to tremble and had to sit down on his bunk to button his shirt.

By the time he returned to her cabin, Hannah had fallen asleep; she was exhausted after her ordeal with George. Scott sat at the foot of her bed, but jumped up when Nathan came in.

He had cleansed her face with a washcloth and wiped blood from her lips.

"Thanks for taking care of her, Scott."

"Did you kill him?"

"No."

"I wish you had."

He started to leave, but Nathan stopped him, "Why don't you sleep here again tonight?" The two cots were still in Hannah's room.

"Do you need me, Nathan?"

"No . . . but . . ." He didn't think Hannah would want him to stay in her cabin when they were alone, but he wouldn't leave her.

"I'm going to the forecastle," said Scott. "I'll bring breakfast for both of you in the morning." He walked out the door and closed it behind him.

Nathan sat down on the cot beside Hannah and looked at her face that was asleep on the pillow. Her lips were swollen, and there were still traces of blood on them. A lump on her cheek had begun to turn blue as had other bruises on her face and arms, and he knew they were all over her frail body. Her hair, damp from perspiration, lay limply upon the pillow. He became sick at his stomach because he was partly to blame for what had happened. He should never have allowed her to walk the dark hall alone.

He remembered how beautiful she was the first time he saw her. He pictured her on the dock with the wind in her hair. Even from a distance, he had fallen in love with her—even before he could distinguish her silky white skin and beautiful blue eyes with long eyelashes. He remembered her first smile and her soft, sweet voice that had melted his heart.

The long voyage had already taken its toll and now this . . . . How could anyone do this to Hannah who was so sweet and had only love and kindness in her heart for everyone? Only an animal could.

He carefully brushed his thumb across the lump on her cheek; she stirred and opened her eyes. With her hand in his, he leaned over and let his lips gently touch her forehead. A low groan escaped her throat, and then her long eyelashes slowly fell over her eyes again.

With her hand still in his, he lay back on the cot and stretched out and closed his eyes. His body ached. He didn't know how long he slept, but was awakened by stressful sounds from Hannah, and he quickly jumped from the cot to the side of her bed. Her body trembled and her muscles jerked. He knew she was dreaming of what had happened, but when he tried to wake her, she fought him.

At first, he was very careful, as her body was so bruised, but the more he tried to wake her, the harder she fought. Finally, he had to grasp each of her arms and shake her. "Hannah! It's Nathan. Wake up, sweetheart; you're dreaming. Please wake up."

She opened her eyes. They were filled with terror until she realized who he was. Her head dropped to his chest, and he felt her intense breathing. "Oh, Nathan," her arms circled around him, "I'm so glad you're here. Please don't leave me."

"I won't, sweetheart." He spoke softly and caressed her hair tenderly. "It's over and he'll never touch you again."

She moaned deep in her throat and her eyes closed lazily as she snuggled her head against him, but suddenly her eyes opened wide, and she raised her head quickly and looked into his face.

"You didn't kill him, did you?"

"No. I tried to, but Jason stopped me. I would have had to kill him, too, and you know I couldn't do that. George is in the brig where he'll stay until we return to Liverpool and turn him over to the police."

She breathed a sigh of relief and said, "The court might have sent you to prison."

"I know. I suppose I'm glad Jason stopped me, but why would the court protect such an animal?"

He wasn't sure he was glad that Jason had stopped him, but he was sure that he had done it for his own good, and someday he would thank him for it, but not today. A faint light at the window revealed the breaking of the dawn.

By the time the *Monarch* sailed into Charleston Harbor, Nathan had gained most of his strength back, and the bruises on Hannah's face and arms had faded. Nathan met with the crew to let them know that he would be gone a few days and to thank them for everything they had done during his illness. The men had never seen him get emotional before, but he felt a big lump in his throat when he tried to say, "A ship never sailed with a better crew."

"I leave Jason in charge again," he said, "and know that all of you will give him your cooperation."

"No," Jason spoke up. "No you won't."

"Why not?" Nathan asked.

"I'm going with you."

"Who said you were?"

"Hannah asked me to go, so you won't have to return alone."

There was a dead silence in the room and every man waited to hear what Nathan would say. He stared at Jason until a smile spread over his face. "Then that's settled, I guess. Jeff, will you take over for me?" Every man laughed.

Cooler weather had come with the rain, but Hannah took her wide-brimmed hat from the peg on the wall where she had hung it the day she came aboard the *Monarch.* She would need it to protect her head from the South Carolina sun. With sadness in her heart, she looked all around the small room that had been her home for almost three months. Her things were packed in the four trunks, and while she waited for someone to take them to the wagon, she kneeled beside the bed that had just been made.

"Dear God," she prayed, "please be with me as I begin this new phase in my life. I pray for your guidance and for your protection. Thank you for a safe trip across the ocean, and be with those on the *Monarch* as it returns to England. Please be with Nathan in the war and bring him safely back to me. And Lord, if it be thy will, let him find a buyer for all the goods on the *Monarch*. I love you, Lord, and I praise your Holy Name. In the name of Jesus I pray. Amen."

After the prayer, Hannah sat on one of the trunks until Nathan knocked on her door. "Are you ready?" he asked.

"Yes, but it's hard to leave." She looked all around the room one last time. Two seamen lifted one of her trunks and started toward the door. Nathan took her hand, and the two of them followed behind the seamen. As they walked toward the quarterdeck, Hannah noticed a crowd had gathered near the gangplank.

"Why is everyone standing around the gangplank?" she asked.

"They have come to tell you good-bye; nearly everyone on the ship is here."

Tears came to her eyes. It was hard to leave the *Monarch*, and how could she tell everyone good-bye? When they approached the quarterdeck, the crew yelled, "We'll miss you, Hannah." Captain Barrington and Martha were among the others with Sam and Murray and everyone else. She hugged them all.

As usual, Jeff stood in the back, but she made her way to him and stood on tiptoes to kiss his cheek. "I love you, Hannah," he whispered.

"Oh, Jeff," she spoke his name softly.

Suddenly she heard a familiar sound and looked to see Scott and Jason push a cart across the deck. It was the same cart, with the same squeaking wheel, that Nathan had pushed down the dock in Ireland. "Hop on the cart, Ma'am," said Jason in a deep voice, "and we'll give you a ride down the gangplank." He had trouble keeping a straight face.

Hannah felt her cheeks burn, but plopped her hat on her head and jumped onto the cart with her legs stretched in front of her. Scott stepped aside for Nathan to take the front of the cart.

"I'll have no part of this," Nathan laughed.

Scott stepped back to the front of the cart, and everyone cheered as he and Jason gave Hannah a wild ride down the gangplank. She thought they had forgotten the incident.

CHAPTER 18

Charleston, South Carolina was a bustling, sophisticated city in 1812, with its excellent harbor being the hub of its activities. Piers jutted out into blue waters like fingers from the city's boardwalk. The tall masts of many ships that hugged the piers or lay anchored in the bay resembled a forest that had been stripped of its branches.

Founded in 1670, the city was originally named Charles Towne, to honor the King of England, Charles II, but was changed to Charleston in 1783, at the end of the American Revolution. Charles Towne began as a settlement a few miles inland on the western bank of the Ashley River, but ten years later the settlement moved to the peninsula that stretched out into the bay between the Ashley and Cooper Rivers.

Charleston was 142 years old when Hannah came to live near it. She sat on a wagon seat beside Nathan as two spirited horses pulled them down a street lined with palmetto trees. East Bay Street ran along the waterfront, past the Exchange Building that had been built by the British, while South Carolina was still a royal colony, to accommodate activities of the city's expanding shipping industry. After Construction of the building was completed in 1771, ships from all over the world sent their representatives there to bargain for rice and indigo.

Jason rode beside the wagon on a beautiful chestnut horse. He was a striking figure, being handsomely dressed with a sword buckled at his side. Its shining hilt rose and fell smoothly with each stride of the chestnut.

A lunch basket and a new British-made rifle lay under the wagon seat. Hannah's four trunks took up most of the space in the wagon's bed, but on top of them lay two seamen's bags with the drawstrings tied tight at the top. Nathan had heard of the famous hospitality of South Carolina's planters and hoped that he and Jason would be invited to spend a few days at Reybrook.

"Hannah," he said, as they approached the business area of town, "I need to stop at a bank. I don't mean to pry, but you said you had the money from the sale of your home. Would you like to deposit it for safe keeping?"

"Yes. I've been concerned about it and especially now that I don't know what to expect when I get to the plantation. I know you don't mean to pry; I appreciate your advice. Since my father died . . . well . . . I trust you; I trust you to give me sound advice. I also trust you to . . ." She wouldn't finish the sentence.

"To what?"

"Nothing."

"Tell me!"

"I don't want to upset you."

"You are if you don't tell me what you started to say."

She sighed. "I couldn't sleep last night and thought of what Jeff said; that you'll marry a wealthy girl in England." Her voice changed and she looked up at him. "I trust you to be faithful. It's just that I know you'll be gone a long time and will be so far away."

"I know how you feel." He laid his hand on hers.

"You do?"

"Yes. I have the same thoughts. I think of how long it will be, and I know you'll meet other men, while I'm gone. I'd rather die on the battlefield than return to find you married to someone else, but I trust you, too. I trust you to wait for me."

He pulled the horses to a stop in front of a bank. Jason dismounted and tied their reins to a hitching post, then volunteered to wait outside for the two of them to go in. Hannah carried her bag; it held the money from the sale of her home.

No one seemed to notice as they entered the bank. At the back of the room, two tellers were protected by bars that reached from the top of a counter to the room's ceiling. Two middle-aged ladies worked at small desks near a large front window. A row of chairs lined one side of the room, and across the room were two small offices.

"Why don't you have a seat, while I take care of some business?" said Nathan. "Then I'll ask someone about opening an account for you."

"All right," Hannah agreed. She sat down in one of the chairs against the wall.

Nathan read the name "Daniel Overteer" on an office door that was partially opened. When he walked toward it, someone said, "Come in." Hannah could see him as he sat in front of a man's desk and occasionally looked her way, but she couldn't hear what either of them said. Neither did she see the six hundred pounds in bank notes that Nathan placed on the bank officer's desk. After a short time, he stood and walked back across the room. "Mr. Overteer will open an account for you now," he said.

Most of the money Hannah had received from her father's estate was placed in the care of the Charleston City Bank. She was relieved to have it in a safe place. While they waited for a clerk to prepare a bankbook, Nathan asked Mr. Overteer if he knew of the Reybrook Plantation on the Cooper River.

"Yes," the banker answered. "Its owner, Garrett Rey, is a bank customer whom I've dealt with many times. The plantation is about five miles out of town, right on the river."

"Can you tell us anything about Mr. Rey?" Nathan asked.

The banker leaned back in his chair. "We don't ordinarily give out information about a customer, but I suppose it would be all right to tell you that he's an honest person who pays his debts. He's quiet and not one for joking or cutting up. His wife is friendly and quite charming; she comes in with him occasionally. Mr. Rey has great adoration and respect for her."

He took a piece of paper from his desk and drew Nathan a map. They were to follow East Bay Street to the edge of town and then take the road up the river. "You can't miss it," he said. "There's a large sign over the entrance to the plantation home."

Nathan thanked him, and when the clerk returned with the bankbook, he rose from the chair and took it. He glanced at the total amount that had been entered into the book before he tucked it into an inside pocket of his vest.

The sun was hot, but trees grew together over the road and gave it shade most of the time. Hannah removed her hat and laid it on the seat beside her. When Charleston was far behind them, Nathan reached inside his vest pocket for the small bankbook and handed it to her.

"You should keep this in a safe place," he said.

"I will." She opened the front cover to the first page and looked over the transaction that had been recorded there.

"Nathan, stop! We must go back to the bank. They made a mistake!" Instead of four hundred pounds that she expected to see, one thousand pounds had been entered into the bankbook. The total amount had been converted to nearly five thousand dollars. There was a distraught look on her face.

"Whoa!" Nathan pulled on the horses' reins. As Jason rode on ahead, he took the book from Hannah and looked at it. He determined it was right and placed it in her bag and then took both her hands in his.

"Hannah, no one made a mistake. I added to the amount you deposited."

Her mouth opened in surprise. "Why, Nathan?"

"I want to be sure you're taken care of. If you're mistreated on the plantation, or things just don't work out for you there, you won't have to stay. You can go to Charleston and find a place to live. The money should be enough for you to get by on until I return. If you leave the plantation, be sure to give the bank your new address, and I'll contact someone there to find you."

"Nathan, I can't let you do this! It's too much money! If I have to leave the plantation, I'll find a job in Charleston."

"I've already done it, and it'll help me not to worry about you as much. I want you to promise me you'll use the money if you need it. If you don't need it, we'll apply it to a home when I get back."

"Where?" she asked.

He laughed and circled his arms around her. "Wherever you want to live, sweetheart." He'd expected a greater argument.

As they traveled farther inland, giant cypress trees grew from the murky waters of a swamp at their right. To the left, oak and magnificent pine grew on higher ground where the land was mostly dry. When the sun was directly overhead, Nathan pulled the horses to the left side of the road under the shade. He tied the reins to a tree and reached for the lunch basket under the wagon seat. Hannah took a blanket from one of her trunks and spread it on the ground. The three of them sat upon it and ate the food that Sam had prepared.

At first, they ate silently. Hannah thought of the money that Nathan had put in the account for her. Although she hoped she wouldn't have to use it, it made her feel warm inside, because it told her how much he cared.

Nathan also thought of the money and was glad that Hannah had not put up too great a fuss. He had feared she would try to make him return to the bank and withdraw it. It seemed to have made her happy, he thought, when he told her they would apply it to a home when he returned, had it not been used. She hadn't promised him she would use it if she needed it, but he would insist that she did before they parted.

Jason felt awkward. He knew that Nathan would rather be alone with Hannah, and he wished he'd not told her he would accompany them. After all, he'd not seen any wild Indians around, but he knew that was not the reason Hannah wanted him to come. Nathan could take care of himself, but she knew how hard the trip back to the ship would be for him. Maybe his being there would help.

When finished eating, Nathan laid his head in Hannah's lap and looked up at the giant trees around them. "Jason," he said, "look at all these wonderful trees. Just think what great ships we could make from them, and the cypresses would make the tallest, straightest masts. Awe man, this is a shipbuilder's paradise."

Jason laughed at his friend for using the expression that he said so frequently. "Speak for yourself, Nathan. You're the shipbuilder; I'm a lawyer."

"Have you decided to finish law school?"

"There's no point in thinking about it until the war is over, but if I live through it, I probably will."

Hannah's eyes met Nathan's and he changed the subject.

The sun was still high when they reached the plantation. They saw the sign, just as Mr. Overteer had said. Two tall posts held it in place over the entrance to the home. **"REYBROOK PLANTATION"** was painted in large letters across its top, and near the bottom, in smaller letters, were the words, **"owner— Garrett Rey."**

Among the trees, a good ways off the road, was a large two-story home. The size of the trees and the weathered brick on the house revealed that it had stood for many years. Tall pillars towered across its front, and a wide porch lay beyond the pillars, upstairs and down. A swing hung from the lower ceiling.

Hannah was silent as she studied the home that seemed gigantic to her. The blank expression on her face made it hard for Nathan to know what she thought. He reached for her hand.

Three white children and one black child played under the trees in front of the home. When the wagon turned onto the narrow lane, the white children scampered up the front steps and ran across the porch and into the house.

Jason led the way on the chestnut, and by the time they reached the house, a man and woman stood on the porch. The man was dressed in a white shirt and black trousers. He had black hair, and his skin was tanned from the South Carolina sun. Nathan surmised him to be of French stock, but his wife was English. She was very pretty in a dress of cotton broadcloth, dyed the color of lilac. Its full skirt stood out slightly from her waist and hung to the floor. Her long light-brown hair was plaited in the back, and a white ribbon entwined among the braids held them against the back of her head. What a lovely couple, thought Hannah.

Jason tied the horses to a post near the front steps, and Nathan helped Hannah from the wagon. Both men unbuckled their swords and laid them under the wagon seat beside the rifle. The couple descended the steps, and when Nathan turned from the wagon, he and the plantation owner reached out a hand to each other.

"I'm Nathan Barrington, representing Barrington Shipping Company. This is my friend, Jason Williams, and my fiancée, Hannah Ruth Thornton."

Hannah was surprised that Nathan introduced her as his fiancée, and she didn't know that he even knew her middle name. He stood tall and spoke distinctly; she was proud of the way he presented himself to the plantation owner.

"I'm Garrett Rey," said the planter, "and this is my wife, Catherine. We're pleased to meet you. I assume you've come to collect a fee for a schoolteacher's voyage across the ocean. Where is she? I must have her signature on a contract before I can pay you."

Hannah started to speak, but Nathan shook his head for her to keep silent. He took her hand. "This is your teacher, Sir, but I've not come to collect a fee. May we sit down and talk?"

The man and his wife seemed confused and a bit shocked that Hannah was the teacher they had waited for.

"I thought you said that Miss Thornton is your fiancée."

"I did, Sir. If we could sit down and talk, I'll explain everything."

"Well, sure. All of you come in and have something to drink, and then we'll go to my office."

Catherine took Hannah's hand and smiled pleasantly as the two of them followed the men up the steps. "We're so glad you have finally arrived," she said. "The children have waited patiently, but we never expected to get someone so lovely or of such high quality. You must be exhausted after the voyage and the long ride from Charleston, but there will be plenty of time to rest. The children don't go to school during the summer, so I insist you do nothing for at least two weeks."

Her words were like music to Nathan's ears. He held the door open for the two ladies. "Yes," he remarked, "Hannah had a difficult trip. It would be nice if she could have some time to rest."

The front door opened into a foyer where the first thing to catch their eye was a large, old French-styled chandelier. Cobwebs around it revealed to the visitors that the candles had not been lighted in quite some time. Just beyond the foyer, a staircase extended from the second floor and curved to the left into a large room. French-styled windows were covered with heavy lace-trimmed curtains. Anyone could see that the lace had originally been white, but with age had turned a yellowish cream color. Little light filtered through the curtains, and the room was less than cheery, but it was filled with nice furniture and beautiful old tables.

To the right of the foyer was a small parlor. A settee stood in front of the only window in the room. There was a round French-styled table at each end of the settee; a lace cloth over each had also yellowed with age. Between the stairs and the parlor, a hallway led to other rooms.

Catherine invited the guests to have a seat in the spacious living area and then quickly sank into a chair. She breathed deeply and held her hand to her chest.

"Are you all right, dear?" her husband asked.

"Yes; I'll be fine."

"My wife has been ill," the plantation owner explained, "but she is better. We have tea that we keep for special occasions. I'll have Rosie make you some." He knew that British liked nothing better to drink.

Garrett Rey returned in a few minutes and took a seat near his wife. Soon afterward, a short, rather plump, black lady came with a tray that had five cups of hot tea on it. Catherine introduced her as Rosie, and Nathan told her what a fine cup of tea she made.

"Yasur, and hit takes uh Englishman to knows one."

Nathan smiled. "That's right, Rosie. I appreciate you making this for us."

"Yasur."

There was small talk among them as they sipped the tea. When finished, Garrett invited Nathan to his office. Catherine gathered the cups onto the tray and asked to be excused before she disappeared down the hallway.

Hannah and Jason were left alone in the living room. Jason leaned forward and let his arms rest on his legs with his fingers locked together between them. Hannah knew he was bored and really felt bad for him. She was about to say how sorry she was when they heard someone on the stairs.

"Mother! Mother! Where is Ben? He promised to take me to the Lambert plantation this . . ."

It was a young lady with golden blonde hair that bounced up and down as she descended the steps vivaciously. She was, undoubtedly, in a hurry, but stopped short when she saw the two of them. Jason slowly rose to an upright position, and Hannah saw his eyes open wide.

"I didn't know we had company," the girl spoke with a southern drawl. She stepped from the stairs, dressed in a lovely white dress made of thin cotton material. A wide band of lace trimmed the bottom of its skirt. It fit snugly around her thin waist and was cut low in the front where she was well developed. Her eyes were a dark blue; as blue as the sky of Ireland, thought Hannah, and long eyelashes fell across them when she blinked. She had a small nose that curved inward just a little at the top. Her lips were full with a touch of color on them and her cheeks were rosy. She was beautiful.

Jason quickly jumped to his feet and said, "Good evening, Ma'am."

Hannah saw the girl's eyes scan up and down him, and a lovely smile came to her face. She then frowned and asked, "Are you two . . . uh . . . together?"

"No, ma'am," Jason was quick to answer. He then looked

apologetically at Hannah and added, "Well . . . we are together, but not really. She's with Nathan and he's with your dad. We all just had a cup of tea, and your mother went to return the cups to the kitchen."

"Why wasn't I invited to tea?" She sounded annoyed.

"I don't know, Ma'am." Jason appeared annoyed, also, for her sake, Hannah determined.

She strutted around the staircase and down the hall, and Jason slowly sat back down. "Awe Man!" he muttered under his breath. "Maybe there is a reason for me coming after all."

The young girl and her mother soon returned from the kitchen. "Jason and Hannah," said Catherine, "this is our daughter, Charleen."

"It's a pleasure to meet you, Charleen," Jason responded.

"Yes, it is," added Hannah.

"Hannah is the new teacher we've waited for," Catherine explained to her daughter. The girl's pretty eyes rolled when her mother said "teacher," giving Hannah an uneasy feeling.

The evening wore on, and Nathan and Garrett still remained in Garrett's office. Hannah heard the planter raise his voice, and then all became quiet again. She was glad when Charleen volunteered to show Jason around the outside of the home; he would have been miserable in the living room with Catherine and her all evening.

She met her students one by one. A set of identical twin girls, named Emily and Emma, looked so much alike, she wasn't sure how she could tell them apart. They had the same golden blonde hair as their older sister, but unlike Charleen, both seemed pleased that their teacher had finally arrived.

The most energetic member of the family was a five-year-old named Otis. He ran in and out of the house constantly and was up and down the stairs. How could she keep him still long enough to teach him anything, Hannah worried? He had brown hair as his mother, but with a tint of red in it, and a patch of freckles was sprinkled across his nose. He was adorable, and Hannah loved him from the start.

"You've met all of our children," said Catherine, "except one son. He'll be home soon." Hannah noticed that there was quite an age difference between Charleen and her younger siblings, and she suspected the second son was between them. He would be a middle child.

Late in the evening the children were called in for supper, and Nathan and Garrett came from the office. Hannah noticed a pleased look on Nathan's face when he returned to the living room and sat down beside her. Catherine asked to be excused, after saying that Nathan and Jason would be expected to stay for the meal. She went to make sure everything was prepared properly. Garrett joined his wife in the kitchen, and a young black lady helped the children wash up. Hannah and Nathan had a moment alone.

"You seem pleased," she said.

"I'm very pleased. You'll have a room upstairs instead of in the servants' quarters, and besides your room and board, he agreed to pay you ten dollars a month. That's more than I expected." Hannah was elated, but knew she owed it all to him. Were it not for Nathan, she would be little more than the slaves that served in the household.

"Why did it take you so long to decide on that?" she asked.

"It didn't. We talked about everything, and he thinks he can take care of the cargo on the *Monarch*. That is, if we agree to take a load of cotton back to England. The warehouses in Charleston are filled with last year's crop and the plantation owners can't get it shipped. If it's not shipped by August, they'll have no place to put new crops.

"This will be wonderful if everything works out. All I had hoped for was to get rid of the cargo we're carrying. Not in my wildest dream did I expect to go home with a full load. The cotton will bring a high price in England because the textile mills are begging for it. Many have shut down since trade with the southern states has been cut off. Garrett is as excited as I am, and feels sure he can persuade the merchants in town to pay a good price for our goods, but the unloading and loading must be done after dark without city officials knowing. He'll go to Charleston with me in the morning to see if we can get everything set up. Hannah, I know you've prayed about this, and I feel like everything will work out."

"Yes, I have. Will you return tomorrow night?"

"It'll be late. We can't leave until the cotton is loaded. Garrett has extended an invitation for Jason and me to stay as long as possible. I like him, Hannah, and I feel a lot better about leaving you here." He looked around the room. "Where's Jason?"

"I don't know and I'm a bit concerned."

Nathan glanced at her with a worried look on his face. "How long has he been gone?"

"He left at least two hours ago with the Reys' teenage daughter. She's very pretty with blonde hair and a body that is well developed for her young age."

Nathan looked at her with an uncertain grin on his face, and then his eyes twinkled and he laughed out loud.

————————

Everyone was seated at a long rectangle-shaped table for the evening meal. Garrett sat at one end of the table with Catherine at his right and Otis to his left. Otis had to sit at the edge of his chair in order to reach his plate, but he didn't seem to mind because it gave him room to scoot back and forth.

Emily and Emma sat like little ladies across the table from each other, and next to them, also seated across from each other, were Jason and Charleen. Nathan sat beside Jason and Hannah beside Charleen. They had taken the last places at each side of the table and left only the chair at the end unoccupied. Heads were bowed and Catherine returned thanks for the food.

Rosie had just begun to serve the meal when the back door opened and someone came in, but he stopped at the dining-room door when he saw strangers at the table. He was the image of Garrett. The visitors did not need to be told that this was the other son.

His slender body stood nearly six feet tall. Beads of sweat ran down his handsome face, and his cheeks were red from the sun's rays. His black hair had been tousled by the wind and his hands were dirty. He looked tired and appeared to have been working very hard. Why . . . he is not a child . . . at all, thought Hannah.

"This is our son, Benjamin," said Garrett. "We call him Ben. He's our oldest and has been in the cotton field all day."

Nathan and Jason jumped to their feet and started toward the doorway where Ben stood. He stepped inside the room and wiped his hand on his pants leg—that was just as dusty—and held it out to them.

"I'm Nathan Barrington and I'm pleased to meet you, Ben."

"So am I. My name is Jason."

Hannah also stood, and as she reached out her hands to the new comer, Catherine said, "Ben, this is Miss Hannah Thornton, the new teacher we have waited for."

Ben sighed under his breath as though he was embarrassed at his appearance, but in a quiet voice said, "I'm glad to meet you, Miss Thornton. I'm glad to meet all of you, but please excuse me while I clean up a little."

The family resumed eating as though Ben's late entrance was a common thing. Rosie brought his plate and set it at the end of the table, but placed a cloth over it to keep the food warm. When he returned, his face and hands had been washed, his hair was combed, and he wore a different shirt. He took the empty seat at the end of the table, and Rosie sct a glass of milk by his plate.

"Thanks, Rosie. The food looks great."

"I's 'magine yo a hungry boy," Rosie responded to his compliment.

"Why did you stay so long, son?" Garrett asked. "I just asked you to see how things were going."

"Ole Ramey was sick, so I sent him to the house. I thought I should stay with the others. Dad, Ole Ramey is getting too old for the fields."

"I know, Son, but I've got no one to replace him with, except Nole, and he's needed around here. I don't know what to do."

"Well, we've got to do something."

"Please," Catherine spoke up, "let's not discuss our problems in front of guests."

"Sorry, Mom."

"That's quite all right, Mrs. Rey," Nathan replied to Catherine's plea. "I'd like to hear about the plantation. I worked on my dad's place when growing up and remember some of the problems we had."

"I bet you didn't use slave labor, did you?" asked Ben.

Not wanting to get into a discussion on slavery, Nathan quickly made a joke. "Well, I felt like one, myself!"

Everyone laughed.

Ben seemed eager to talk about the fields and said that he thought they would make a good cotton crop. "I just don't know where we'll put it," he added.

"Nathan thinks he can help us solve that problem," Garrett said. He explained about the cargo on the *Monarch.*

"Hey, it'd be great if you could take a load of cotton back to England."

"I'll take all we can get on the ship and be glad to get it. The textile mills in Liverpool will pay us a good price for it. They've not been able to get cotton since trade with the United States was cut off."

"You see, God will take care of our problems," Catherine reminded them.

Without the faith in God as his wife, Garrett said skeptically, "It won't be a final deal, dear, until the cotton is loaded on the ship."

Charleen was bored to death with the subject of cotton and reminded her brother of his promise. "You promised to take me to the Lamberts today, Ben."

"I'm sorry, Charleen, but some things are more important than you seeing your fellow."

Jason looked up from his plate at Ben and then at Charleen.

"I wanted to see his sister!" Charleen snapped at her brother.

"Yeah . . . sure!"

"All right, you two, stop your bickering," said Garrett. "Your brother is right, Charleen."

"Daddy, you always say that!"

Nathan looked across the table at Hannah with a twinkle in his eyes. He was amused at the teenagers' conversation, and Hannah knew that he suppressed a smile. She looked down at her plate as her own lips turned up at each corner.

Nathan and Jason left early the next morning with Garrett and Ben. The four of them were on their way to Charleston to talk to a group of merchants about the remaining goods on the *Monarch*. Garrett and Jason rode ahead of the wagon, but Ben had tied his black horse behind it and climbed upon the seat beside Nathan. Nathan was glad to have his company. They talked all the way and became well acquainted by the time they reached Charleston. It was the same with Garrett and Jason.

"Ben," Nathan said, at the outskirts of town, "may I ask a favor of you?"

"Sure. What is it?"

"Will you look after Hannah for me?"

Ben had not expected this at all. "Well . . . uh . . ." he hesitated.

"I'll make it worth your time when I get back."

"Oh, it's not that. It's just that . . . well, I don't know. What if she doesn't want me to look after her?"

"Don't let her know. Just be her friend and help her if she needs help. Don't let her do anything dangerous."

"All right, Nathan. I'll keep an eye on her. I reckon it's hard for you to leave her."

"It's the hardest thing I've ever had to do, but there's no other way. She's too weak to make the trip back to England, and if I don't get back . . . well, I have to, and she'll feel so alone when I leave."

"I'll see that she gets special attention. She and my mother will be good company for each other. Mom's been sick and gets depressed because she can't do all the things she used to. We'll keep Hannah so busy she won't have time to get lonesome, and you'll be back before she realizes you're gone. Don't worry; she'll be all right here."

"Thanks, Ben. I feel better about leaving her here since I've got to know you and your family. There's one other thing." He reached his hand into his pocket and came out with a key. "I put something in one of her trunks last night before I took it from the wagon, but I don't want her to find it until I'm gone. Will you keep this key and give it to her after I leave?"

"Sure. What's in the trunk?"

"I'll let it be a surprise to you, too. It's something she'll need your help with."

The four of them were almost to Charleston by the time Hannah awoke that morning. She sat up in bed and looked around her new room that seemed so large after the small one on the *Monarch*. It had been late, the evening before, when her things were brought from the wagon to the upstairs bedroom, and since she was so tired after the long day, she had fallen asleep quickly.

She dressed and descended a flight of narrow stairs and found Catherine in the kitchen with a cup of coffee in her hand. Catherine poured her a cup and the two women sat down for a quiet time together since the children were still asleep. Before long, however, they heard little feet on the stairs, and Otis ran to his mother's lap. He looked at Hannah with curious eyes.

"Good morning, Otis," she said. "Do you always get up this early?"

"Yes," Catherine answered for him with a flustered look on her face, "I'm afraid so." She ran her hand over a cowlick at the back of his head.

After the three of them had breakfast, Catherine showed her through the entire home. "Garrett's office and a downstairs washroom," she said, "are across the hall from the kitchen and dining room." The small parlor, the entrance, and the large room where they had sat the evening before were across the front of the house. An old piano stood in a far corner of the living room. Hannah had noticed it when she first entered the home, but said nothing about it. She lifted the cover from over its keys and ran her fingers across them to play the chorus of a pretty melody. Catherine's mouth opened in surprise. "You play the piano?"

"Yes. I love to play, and I'm delighted to see that you have one. I can teach the children about music. Do any of them play?"

"No, they have never had a music teacher."

"Well, they do now."

"Oh, Hannah, I've dreamed of the children playing this old piano. Garrett wanted to get rid of it. He says it just takes up space."

"Where did you get it?"

"It was here when Garrett inherited the plantation. This land was settled by his grandparents who came to the Carolina Colony in its early days. They were Huguenots and worked very hard as they drained the swamps and cleared the land. The lumber used to build the house was cut right here on the place.

"Hannah," Catherine continued, "we're not wealthy like most southern planters. Many own homes in Charleston and enjoy their days visiting and shopping or going to plays at the Dock Street Theatre during the summer months, while slaves work their plantations. We own only a few slaves, compared to most planters, and have a few indentured servants. Consequently, we aren't able to plant or harvest on a large scale as others who own many slaves. Not being able to sell last year's cotton crop, plus medical expenses, has made it a difficult year. If the shipping company buys our cotton, it will be an answer to prayer."

"I hope everything works out."

"So do I. I don't want to frighten you, but I'm very concerned. If the men are caught unloading the merchandise or loading the cotton onto a British ship, they could be arrested. The town merchants are also taking a risk if they buy the cargo."

"I know," Hannah said softly, "although it's products that people need."

"This is the guestroom," said Catherine, "and the only downstairs bedroom. Nathan and Jason slept here last night."

The cover was tumbled, but they had made an attempt to pull it over the pillows. Catherine began to take the cover off, and with Hannah at one side of the bed and her at the other, they made it neatly.

"I'm sorry you found the house so dusty," Catherine apologized. "Reneka usually cleans, but since my illness, she's had to take care of the children. It's a full time job to keep up with Otis." Reneka, Hannah thought, must be the young black lady.

"My teaching the children will give Reneka more time for cleaning."

"I don't know how you'll keep Otis still long enough to teach him."

"Well, we'll see. Surely something will hold his attention."

They continued their tour of the home by climbing the narrow staircase that Hannah had descended earlier. At the top she and Catherine had to stop a moment to catch their breaths, and Hannah realized that Catherine was as weak from her illness as she was from the voyage. What was her illness, and was she over it? She wanted to ask but thought it best not to.

Her bedroom was at the end of the hall, next to the stairs, and next door to it was the twin's room where Otis also slept. He had a small bed in one corner with a shelf over it that held some of his favorite things. There was an old bird nest with three pebbles in it and a slingshot plus a few other things he'd collected. The girls slept in a double bed at the other side of the room. They were still sleeping. Catherine leaned over to wake them.

Charleen's room was next and then Ben's. Ben's room was at the opposite end of the hall from Hannah's, and right across the hall from him was the large master bedroom that belonged to Catherine and Garrett.

The master bedroom was the most beautiful room in the house. Its furniture consisted of a large bed, a double dresser, and a chest that stood upright. Two small tables stood at each side of the bed. White ruffled curtains that matched the bedspread enhanced the windows, and lovely paintings hung on the walls.

"It's the most beautiful room I've ever seen," said Hannah.

"Thank you. I enjoy our room, and I can see the sun as it rises over the tree tops."

Hannah had not thought of it, but if Catherine could see the sunrise from her bedroom, it faced toward the east. That would mean the back of the house faced the west and would give a view of the sunset. This would make it easy for her to keep the watch of the sunset that Nathan had given her.

A small room at the far side of the staircase excited Hannah. Shelves covered three walls of the room, and the shelves were filled with books. "This is the library," said Catherine. "The books have been collected over the years by Garrett's parents and grandparents. Some are very old, but they have been taken good care of. There are many reference books, and we encourage you to use them in your studies. As I told you, Garrett's grandparents were Huguenots, and they wanted their children and grandchildren to obtain an education, so they started this library soon after the home was built. The library in Charleston was started in 1748 and is one of the best libraries in our state. If you can't find what you need here, you'll be able to find it there."

"I can't wait to browse through the books, but I want to see the rest of the house now."

"There is only one other room and it's your classroom. We chose this room to convert to a classroom because it's next to the library. I hope you like it and find it convenient."

"I love it, and it couldn't be more convenient with a library next door and my room right across the hall. It's far better than I expected."

"I do hope you like it here, Hannah, and will stay longer than the last teacher did. It bothers me when the children go long periods of time without being taught. I try to help them but have little education, myself, and Garrett is too busy."

"Catherine," Hannah asked, "did the last teacher have a room in your home, as you have given me?"

"No," Catherine admitted, "but the servants' quarters are right out back. She lived there with indentured workers and furnished her room quite nicely. I believe that's where she preferred to live. Nathan insisted that you have a room in the home, and Garrett wasn't sure if he was going to let you stay at all," she laughed. "He must love you an awful lot."

"Yes," Hannah answered softly, "I believe so."

As soon as the four men arrived in Charleston, they parted. Nathan and Ben returned the wagon to the livery stables and traded it for a horse. After finding out about his knowledge of the law, Garrett asked Jason to accompany him to a meeting with the town merchants.

Nathan and Ben left the stables and went to the *Monarch* to talk to Captain Barrington, and on boarding the ship, went straight to his office.

"Ben," said Nathan, "this is my dad, Captain Charles Barrington. And Dad, this is Ben Rey. His dad owns the plantation where Hannah will live."

The captain held out a hand to Ben and said how pleased he was to meet him.

The three of them sat down to talk, and Nathan informed the captain of Garrett's plan to rid the *Monarch* of her present cargo, so it could be loaded with cotton to be shipped back to England.

"That's good news," said the captain, "but we'll need more men if we do all that tonight."

"I think I can get some plantation owners who live in town to help," said Ben.

"We'll need all the help we can get." Before Ben left, Nathan took him to the galley.

As soon as Jason and Garrett boarded the *Monarch,* there was another meeting, and then the captain briefed his crew. He assigned guard duty to Murray and Sam, but everyone else on the ship, including himself, was to help unload their remaining cargo onto wagons that would be furnished by town merchants. "As soon as the ship is unloaded," said Captain Barrington, "we'll load it with cotton, but we must work quickly and quietly."

The merchants agreed to help with unloading and then loading the ship, and right at dark, Ben returned with several plantation owners. They were more than happy to help if it meant getting their cotton shipped.

The moon gave just enough light. Everything went smoothly until some of the cargo fell from one of the wagons and made a loud noise as it rolled down the pebble street. Every man held his breath when a light went out in the Exchange Building. Nathan whispered to the men around him, and they quickly followed him to the middle of the street. Just as three men walked out of the Exchange Building, they dragged the merchandise into the shadows. The three men talked calmly as they strolled down the street, but no one moved until they disappeared into the darkness and their voices could no longer be heard.

By the time the first gleam of the sun began to peep over the harbor that morning, most of the cotton had been loaded onto the *Monarch.* Of what was left, a few seamen loaded it, one bale at a time, and no one noticed.

Tired, but happy that all had gone well, Nathan and Jason left the *Monarch* with Garrett and Ben. They held their horses at a gallop until they reached the plantation. Catherine and Hannah had listened for the sound of horses; both ran outside when they heard them coming. Rosie served the men hot food, while they related to the women how everything had gone so well.

Later in the day, Nathan and Hannah walked across the grounds of the plantation. "Dad wanted to sail as soon as the

Monarch was loaded," he said, "but I had to come back; I had to tell you bye and hold you one more time." He took her in his arms. "You're a powerful lady, Hannah. You hold up a ship that is loaded to the helm, plus her crew and passengers."

"It's only your love that makes me powerful. If you stopped loving me, I would be nothing."

"I'll never stop loving you, darling. Never."

CHAPTER 19

The Reybrook Plantation home stood on top of a knoll that sloped gradually all the way down to the Cooper River. Large oak, pine, hickory nut, and chinquapin trees surrounded the home. To the left, where the land leveled out, a brook meandered through the woods at a lazy pace. Green ferns grew in the deep shade up and down its banks, and Spanish moss that hung from tree branches adorned its overhead.

Many years before, the brook had given the plantation its name. A Frenchman named John Reyeau settled the land, but over the years, he dropped the *eau* from his name to make it sound less French. In the early days of the colony, people on their way to Charles Towne stopped to let their horses drink from the brook that was fed from springs in the lowland. It became known as Rey's brook and later, the Reybrook Plantation.

Nathan and Hannah walked under the trees that surrounded the home. Their time for parting grew painfully near; he and Jason planned to leave early the next morning. He made her promise to use the money he had deposited in her name at the Charleston Bank, if she needed it for anything. "And, Hannah," he pleaded, "please take care of yourself."

"I will, and will you promise me the same?"

"Yes. I hope the war will end soon."

"Oh, Nathan, I pray that it will."

Hannah stopped suddenly; she thought she saw someone else amid the trees. Yes, there were two people near the brook, and they embraced each other. She realized it was Jason, and he held Charleen in his arms.

"Nathan," she whispered, "that's Jason and Charleen."

"I know."

"You must do something."

"Like what? Jason is a grown man."

"I know, and she is only a child!"

Nathan smiled at the couple entwined in each other's arms. He spoke slowly, "She doesn't look like a child to me." Hannah knew he referred to Charleen's well-formed figure.

"Ouch!" He suddenly yelled when he felt a sharp pain in the shin of his leg where Hannah had kicked him with the toe of her shoe. He hobbled a few steps before he could put all his weight on his leg as he ran after her. She was headed down the slope toward Jason and Charleen.

"Hannah, please!" He managed to catch her and grasped her arm. "Please let them be," he said. "Jason is going to war, remember, and what can it hurt for him to have this memory to take with him? I know she's young, but he'll bring her no harm, and it certainly doesn't appear that she wants to get away from him. Darling, you're suppose to be her teacher; not her nursemaid."

"But he's so much older than she."

"Not really. Ben told me his sister is sixteen and Jason is only twenty-one."

"I thought he was your age."

"He's a little younger but not quite a year. By the time we get back, she'll probably be all grown up, and their age differences won't be that important."

"Do you think he'll come back?"

"Knowing Jason, and from what I see right now . . . yes; I believe he will. He and Garrett got to know each other pretty well, yesterday, and Garrett was impressed with how much he knows about the law. They seem to like each other, so I don't foresee any problem there, but I do see a problem."

"What?"

"Because she's so young, he won't ask her to wait for him. It wouldn't be fair."

"No, it wouldn't."

"I love you, Hannah. I love you for the way you try to take care of everyone. I believe you'll get along fine here and fit right in with this family."

"I hope so . . . I do hope so."

There was excitement among everyone as they gathered around the table for the evening meal. Garrett and his family were happy because the planters had been paid for their cotton, and a warehouse had been emptied for new crops. Nathan was happy because the merchants had paid a fair price for the *Monarch's* cargo, and Barrington Shipping would gain a good profit from the cotton, in Liverpool.

Just as Garrett said that he couldn't believe how everything had gone so smoothly, there was a loud knock at the front door. A hush fell over the group as Reneka made her way down the hall to the door.

"Good evening, Ma'am," said a voice that Nathan and Jason recognized at once. They both rose to their feet and asked to be excused.

"Evening, Sir," answered Reneka.

"Is Nathan Barrington in the house? I have a message for him from the *Monarch.*"

"I'm here, Jeff," Nathan spoke up. "What's wrong?"

Hannah and the Rey family followed Nathan and Jason to the front entrance, and Garrett invited Jeff to come in. He stepped inside the door and let the screen close before he answered Nathan.

"The captain sent me to get you and Jason."

"Why?"

"He received a message that Congress of the United States declared war on Great Britain, June eighteenth. The news reached Charleston at noon today, and an hour later, a warning came from the commander of Federal troops stationed here that if the *Monarch* is still within the harbor at daybreak, it will be sunk."

There was a dead silence in the room as the shock of the news sank in. Even Otis was still. He realized that something was wrong.

Nathan was the first to recover. "Well," he said, "we better get her out to sea. We don't want all that cotton to get wet."

"I'll saddle your horses," Ben called as he ran toward the back door.

Nathan and Jason hurried to the guestroom to get their things, and Hannah followed them with a sick feeling in her stomach. Garrett invited Jeff to have a seat, giving Otis a chance to ask him all sorts of questions.

Things were quickly stuffed into Jason's and Nathan's bags and the drawstrings were tied at the top. Jason swung his over his shoulder and left the room first; Charleen waited for him in the hallway.

Nathan closed the door and Hannah leaned against it. She put her arms around him, and he lifted his hands to her neck and leaned his head forward until his forehead touched hers.

"There were so many things I planned to tell you at this time," he said, "but all I can think of is how much I love you. I hate to leave you, Hannah, especially in a country that is at war with England."

"I know, darling, but you must. I love you, too, and remember that I'll be waiting for you. Please take care and may God go with you."

"I put you in His hands until I return. I'll see your face in every sunset, and it will give me courage. Good-bye, sweetheart."

"Good-bye, my darling."

His lips covered hers, and he held them there until they heard Jason speak quietly through the door, "Nathan . . . we better go."

Everyone in the household, including Rosie and Reneka, came to the front porch to tell them good-bye. Ben stood at the bottom step and held the reins of the two horses from the livery stable. Nathan and Jason shook his hand and thanked him, while Jeff untied his own horse, and they all three mounted at the same time.

Nathan's eyes held Hannah's as he pulled the horse's reins to the right. The horse turned swiftly, but not before he read her lips that silently worded, "I love you," and he saw a tear run down both her cheeks.

She watched until the three of them rode out of sight and then listened until the sound of the galloping horses could no longer be heard. The silence pierced her ears and her body felt numb. The dreaded moment had finally come. It had come quickly and not at all as she had expected.

As soon as the three horsemen turned onto the main road, Nathan swatted his horse with the end of the reins and brought him to a run. Jason called to him, "Why such a hurry? We'll have plenty of time."

"I want to reach Charleston before the shops close," Nathan yelled back to him. "I need to buy a piano."

Jason and Jeff looked at each other. "A piano?" they queried. Had Nathan lost his mind?

As the sound of the horses disappeared, Hannah felt an arm around her shoulders and heard Catherine's kind voice say, "Come inside, dear, and sit down."

"I'd like a moment alone, if you don't mind."

"Of course; we understand. Just come in when you feel like it."

Everyone else went back inside the house, but Hannah walked to the far end of the porch and sat down. Her heart ached. She buried her face in her lap and let tears flow unrestrained.

After awhile, she heard footsteps on the porch and lifted her head to see Ben with a man's handkerchief in one hand and a glass of water in the other. He handed her the handkerchief and sat down beside her.

"He'll be back before you know it," he said cheerfully. "The war can't keep Nathan away from you for long."

Hannah smiled through her tears. She wiped her face with his handkerchief and blew her nose. He gave her the glass of water and she drank it. His presence made her feel somewhat better, and to her surprise, when she finished the water, he took her hand and pulled her from the porch. "Come on," he said, "you haven't seen much of our place yet."

Not more than a hundred yards behind the house, stood a small brick building that was rectangular in shape with a narrow porch across its front. "This is where the servants live," Ben said. "Three of them work to pay for their voyages across the ocean."

"The way I was suppose to?"

"Yeah," he nodded his head. "My dad had rather use indentured servants instead of slave labor."

"I understand that."

They crossed over the brook on a wooden bridge and followed a trail through the woods to where the land had been cleared. At the edge of the clearing, Hannah saw a small village of shacks with yards that were swept clean. Black children played around them. Every shack had a chimney, and two of them had a porch.

"We do own slaves," said Ben. He didn't seem happy about it.

Hannah gazed at the humble dwellings of only one or two rooms, but it was the children that held her attention. She imagined them gathered around her with an open book in her hands.

"Don't come here alone," Ben interrupted her thoughts.

"Why?"

"Just don't."

"But I could teach the children."

"No. It's not the way of the South."

They turned to face each other, but both were silent as his eyes gazed into hers.

"Promise me, Miss Thornton."

She slowly nodded her head, and when she spoke, she seemed to have dismissed the subject. "Will you call me Hannah?" she asked.

No trees grew beyond the shacks, but as far as the eye could see, long rows of cotton stretched across the land. Hannah raised her hand to shade her eyes from the sun that now neared the horizon and saw slaves trudge across the green field, each with a hoe swung over his shoulder as he made his way toward his own shack.

Back across the brook, Ben took another trail to a large barn that stood behind the servants' home. To Hannah's delight, she saw all kinds of animals in the barnyard, and as she walked among them, they seemed to be aware that she was their friend. She petted the long neck of a brown cow.

"Her name is Susie," said Ben.

"Hello, Susie." She spoke in a deep, but soft, voice.

The brown cow answered, "Moooo."

Ben laughed. "Nathan didn't tell me you talked to animals."

"He was afraid you wouldn't believe him."

He laughed again. "Where did you get such a way with them?"

"We had animals at my home in Ireland."

"I'd like to hear all about your home and about your family."

He knew he'd said the wrong thing when the smile on Hannah's face faded and sadness covered it.

"I'm sorry," he said, "I guess it's too soon for you to talk about either."

"Yes," she nodded her head and then changed the subject. "Who takes care of the animals?"

"Jim MacMillan. And come to think of it, he's from Ireland. He's one of the servants who agreed to work five years for his voyage across the ocean. He milks the cows and trains our horses, among other jobs. He's a nice fellow and I want you to meet him."

"I'd like to."

"I hope you like living here. I think you will when you get to know everybody."

"Thank you. I'm sure I will."

"I believe you'll get along fine with everyone except . . ." He stopped before he finished the sentence.

"Except who?"

"You'll find out. Would you like to meet Jim now? I see him in the corral."

Hannah noticed that the sun was right at the top of the trees; she wanted to be alone. "May I wait until tomorrow? I'd like to go to my room now."

"Sure. I'm sorry; you must be awfully tired after the trip across the ocean."

"It has left me a bit weak."

On entering the house, Hannah went straight to her room and raised the window. From the second floor, she could see over the trees. Leafy cotton stalks were silhouetted against the large red ball that sank slowly out of sight at the end of the long rows of cotton. As the last rays disappeared, she bowed her head and prayed, "Oh, Holy Father, please be with Nathan as he returns to the *Monarch*. Guide the ship through safe waters and be with everyone aboard. Give Nathan extra strength and encouragement for all the responsibilities he must bear, and please Lord, bring him back to me soon. In the name of Jesus I pray. Amen."

When she raised her head, twilight had begun to settle over the plantation; not a leaf stirred. She could see the animals in the barnyard as they settled down for the night. Woods hid the slaves' cabins, but smoke from their chimneys curled slowly in the sky as they prepared their evening meals. Hannah stood and surveyed it all. Never could she have imagined how the slaves, the indentured servants, the Rey family, and the plantation as a whole would become such a vital part of her life.

CHAPTER 20

Captain Barrington paced back and forth on the deck of the *Monarch*, stopping occasionally to peer into the darkness and listen for the sound of horses in the distance. It was past midnight. Jeff should have been back with Nathan and Jason long before now. The ship's sails had been hoisted for hours and its crew grew restless. They feared their mates were in trouble and wanted to search for them, but the captain had forbidden anyone to leave the *Monarch*. As time neared the dawn, however, he had second thoughts.

He heard footsteps behind him and turned to face his wife who refused to go to bed until she knew that her son and Jason and Jeff were safe. She took the captain's hand and asked, "Is there still no sign of them?"

"No, Martha, but I'm sure they'll be here any moment. Why don't you go to bed?"

"You know I can't sleep until they're back and we're out of this harbor. Perhaps you should try to get a message to the commander of Federal troops. If you explain the situation, surely he'll give us more time."

"I don't think so."

"You won't leave them, will you?"

"No. We won't sail until every man is aboard. I'm thankful we didn't leave you in Wilmington, but I would have fought my way back up the coast for you. I love you, Martha." He put his arms around her and leaned his head to kiss her cheek, but suddenly stopped. "Listen," he whispered. In the far distance, he heard something. It sounded like a team of horses pulling a wagon.

They stood still and listened until both were sure that it was horses. In the quietness of the night, they heard them come down the slope and onto the pier where the *Monarch* was moored.

"That must be them," said Martha. She leaned over the rail.

The wagon stopped at the end of the gangplank, just as the captain called out, "Nathan, is that you?"

"Yes, sir," Nathan replied, "and I need a couple of men to help load a piano."

Martha and the captain were as shocked over the piano as Jason and Jeff had been, but both were relieved to hear Nathan's voice, and there was no time for questions. Several seamen who had waited on the deck heard Nathan's request for help. They hurried down the gangplank and lifted the large piano out of the wagon, and then Jason and Jeff returned the wagon and team of horses to the stable.

"Prepare to cast off," yelled the captain, and lines were loosed from the pier. As soon as Jason and Jeff set foot on the quarterdeck, the plank was raised, and in the stillness of the night, the *Monarch* glided across the harbor, bound for the open sea, under the watchful eyes of Federal troops. Instead of north, up the American coastline, that would have been their usual route home, Robert was forced, as the ship's navigator, to plot their course due east toward Casablanca on the northwest coast of Africa.

The piano was taken to the crew's quarters, as it was less crowded there than any other place on the ship. Nathan anchored it against the wall and covered it with a tarp. It was one of the finest that money could buy, but everyone wondered why he took it back on the ship when he could have purchased one like it in England. His mother was especially puzzled because of all the years she had encouraged him to play the piano, and he would not.

The next morning, Captain Barrington got more than a little upset when Jeff relayed to him that the piano was the cause of their delay in getting back to the *Monarch* the night before. "The shop," he said, "where Nathan had seen it, was closed, and we had to find the owner and persuade him to come to town in the middle of the night. It wasn't easy, even when Nathan agreed to pay extra for the piano. Then a wagon had to be purchased from the stable. All of this took time, Sir."

"Who is the piano for?" the captain fumed. "If he bought it for Hannah, why does he take it to England? And where is Nathan now?"

"I don't think he bought it for Hannah. He's been in the crow's nest since sunup, because he doesn't want to talk to anyone. Maybe we should let him be; it's a bad time for him." Jeff tried to calm the captain.

"I suppose it is," Captain Barrington agreed. "If you see him, tell him I said to take the day off, but I'll expect him to be back at work tomorrow. This won't be an easy trip home. We were already overloaded with passengers and cargo, and now he has brought on a lot more weight. I can't understand it!"

"It must be important to him, Sir."

Nathan's hands gripped the mast in the middle of the crow's nest that early morning. He strained his eyes to get a glimpse of the South Carolina shoreline. The *Monarch* had made good time since it sailed from Charleston's harbor, but from up high he could still see the gray outline of the state far in the distance. He'd not slept during the few hours he lay in his bunk, but had tossed and turned until near daylight when he climbed to the nest.

He didn't want to face his dad or the passengers. His dad would bombard him with questions about the piano, and he had no intentions of explaining to anyone about it. It was too personal.

In the past, he'd been able to find a way for what was important, but he'd wanted to marry Hannah more than he had ever wanted anything in his life. There was no way to avoid the war. He didn't fear the French, but he didn't want to die, now that he had so much to live for.

He began to feel dizzy. He'd not regained his full strength after his illness, plus he was exhausted. He had to climb down, but first he bowed his head against the mast and asked God for strength, then he prayed for Hannah and a safe trip home.

Jeff kept an eye on the crow's nest until he saw Nathan on his way down the ladder.

"Captain said for you to take the day off," he informed him.

"That's good," Nathan muttered. He went to his bunk and fell asleep.

Scott made a sign for the door of the little forecastle that read, "Enter quietly—Nathan is sleeping."

He awoke in the middle of the evening and went to the galley. After he ate, he felt better, so he walked the deck to see the captain, who, by this time, had forgotten about being upset.

"How do you feel, son?"

"I'm all right, Dad. How are you and Mother?"

"We're fine, but you sure gave us a scare last night."

Nathan was silent as he looked at his dad and bit his bottom lip. He wanted to apologize, but didn't because his dad would expect him to explain about the piano. The captain paused and then changed the subject.

They discussed the danger they faced. Both knew the *Monarch* was overloaded and would be in trouble if caught in a storm. They agreed that if it came to it, some of the cotton would be thrown overboard. Now that the United States had declared war against England, the ship would be fair gain to any American Privateer. The owner of private-owned vessels would search the seas for such a prized bounty, and the *Monarch,* so heavy laden with cotton, would not be able to outrun them. Nathan and the captain decided to put more men on guard and to maintain a constant alert. After the evening meal, the captain briefed his crew and ordered each man to sleep with his rifle by his bed.

The next morning, Nathan tried to resume his normal duties, but all he could think of was Hannah and how difficult the first days of their separation would be for her. Would Ben help her as he had promised?

Every place on the *Monarch* reminded him of her. He saw her on the deck with the wind in her hair and in the shade of the sails with a book on her lap and the Hartman children around her. He remembered the day she stumbled across the deck and fell into his arms, and how she had laughed when they both fell. When he stood at the helm, he visualized her on the windowsill. He felt mental anguish and the passing of days brought little relief to his mind.

Late one evening as the sun sank beyond the water's edge, he knew she thought of him, and he yearned to see her face and to hear her voice. He lit a lantern and went to the bottom of the ship, into its hold, where no one ever went except to load or unload cargo. He hung the lantern over a nail and sat down on a bale of cotton with his back against another one and then bowed his head and cried.

He was taken to a deep pit of despair where his wealth brought him no consolation. He sank farther and farther into the depths of unhappiness until he seemed to hear Hannah whisper, "I love you, Nathan," and then again, "I love you."

Her voice lifted him out of the pit, and he rose and took the lantern from the nail and made his way back to the main deck. The sun had disappeared. Hannah had prayed for him, and he had heard her voice, although they were many miles apart.

From that day on, Nathan seemed more like himself. He rose early each morning and worked until dark, stopping only to eat and watch the sun go down. At the same time each evening one could find him at the stern with his face toward the west. When the sun disappeared out of sight, he bowed his head a moment and then returned to work.

Day after day, the hot July sun rose and set. Nathan and the crew worked with it bearing down upon them. The passengers complained and wanted to turn northeast for a cooler climate, but the captain was certain their provisions would not hold out long enough for that course, so the ship continued to sail due east toward Casablanca.

July turned into August. Since no ships had been sighted on

the horizon, the men became slack in guarding the *Monarch*. The hot weather continued, and although there was no storm, there was also no rain. When their water supply became critically low, the captain demanded that no baths be taken. Water was to be used only for drinking and cooking. Then the wind ceased to blow, and for days the *Monarch* drifted in doldrums . . . going no place. The nights were so hot that many slept on the main deck with only a pillow under their heads.

On one of those nights, Nathan lay on his back and looked up at the stars as he thought about Hannah. He was thankful she was not aboard the *Monarch,* but wondered what hardships she might have. He thought of the passengers they had left in America and how the war would affect them. Would Michael have to leave Lizzy and the baby to fight for the United States? What if he was killed? He tried to end his thoughts when they became too painful, but his mind continued to work and sleep would not come.

"Oh, no!" He sat up as he remembered the Butlers. They were to pick them up on the return trip. How would they get back to England? With everything that had happened and his mind so much on Hannah, he'd forgotten them and was sure the captain had, too. But they couldn't have returned for them even if they had remembered. The *Monarch* would have been taken for sure had they tried to enter the Norfolk Harbor. The Butlers were compelled to stay with their son until the war was over.

He heard Jason snore and was glad he could sleep. Did he dream of Charleen? He'd not mentioned her name. However, he hadn't really given him a chance to.

It made Nathan feel bad when he thought of what Jason had been through with Hannah and him and how he'd gotten the two of them back together when she seemed lost to him forever. He would be sure to ask about Charleen as soon as the opportunity came up.

At twilight that morning, he rose from the deck and went for the ship's sextant. He wanted to know exactly where they were since their water supply was so low and might not last until they reached Casablanca. With a good sextant, he could determine their location within a few degrees.

With information from the sextant in his hand, Nathan woke Robert and Murray. The three of them studied charts and maps until they determined that they were near the Madeira Islands, an archipelago about 700 miles off the coast of North Africa. According to Nathan's reading, they weren't more than twenty-five miles north of the islands, and with an adjustment of the sails, perhaps they would drift that far south.

Discovered by the Portuguese explorer, Joao Goncalves Zarco, in 1418, the islands were now occupied by British forces. They would be able to replenish their water supply there, as well as other provisions, without going as far as Casablanca. It would save a great deal of time plus they could then sail north, toward home and a cooler climate.

The crew was awakened early that morning; plans were relayed and carried out. The sails were set and Scott was posted at the crow's nest with the captain's glass. A breeze stirred and the sails billowed and word spread quickly among the passengers that the ship's course had been changed because islands were near by. Many of them watched the horizon, but it was Scott who announced the sighting of land. His voice bellowed over the main deck, **"Land ho-o-o! Land ho-o-o!"**

Cheers went up from the crew and the passengers, and many rushed to the rail. They held a hand over their eyes as they peered into the distance in order to get a glimpse of the land.

Murray sailed the *Monarch* around the western end of the small island of Madeira and into beautiful Funchal Bay, where warships that flew the Union Jack were a welcomed sight.

Beyond the city of Funchal were mountains covered with lush tropical forests. The island had a pleasant climate, being cooler in summer and warmer in winter. Craving the cooler weather, many of the British passengers went into the city and dined on fish, fruit, and fresh made bread that were served with famous Madeira wines.

The next morning, Nathan and Jason left the *Monarch* with

Jeff and Mark. The four of them ate breakfast together in the city, and then they visited the remains of sixteenth and seventeenth century forts and the fifteenth century Cathedral of Santa Clara where the tomb of Joao Goncalves Zarco lay. For awhile Nathan and Jason were separated from Jeff and Mark. Nathan took the opportunity to ask about Charleen.

"Do you miss Charleen?" he asked.

Jason was surprised. "I think about her," he said, "but I try not to."

"I'm glad you have her to think about. Why do you try not to?"

"She's so young and pretty and must have lots of fellows. What are my chances of her being single, if I went back to see her?"

"You are going back, aren't you? You'll never know unless you do, and from what I saw down by the brook, I would say your chances are pretty good."

Jason grinned. "Were you spying?"

"I didn't mean to be. Her dad likes you and that means a lot to a girl. If Hannah's dad was alive, we might never get married." He sighed because it was an unpleasant thought for him.

"You miss her a lot, don't you?"

"Sometimes, more than I can stand. I worry about her, but I believe I left her with a good family, and that makes me feel better. I'm thankful I had time to get to know them."

"So am I. Maybe I should go back to see Charleen. I did like her dad, but can you see me working a plantation the rest of my life?"

"No," Nathan shook his head and laughed, "I can't, but I'm sure the people of Charleston could use a good lawyer."

Early the next morning, provisions were loaded onto the ship and water barrels were filled with fresh water. Before noon, Funchal Bay was left behind and a stronger wind bore the *Monarch* northeast toward England. Everyone knew, however, they were still a long way from home and would be forced to pass through a dangerous area off the coast of France. No one needed to be reminded that England was at war with the country.

Instead of sailing along the European Coast, the captain ordered Murray to take the *Monarch* farther out to sea. "Since we now have plenty of provisions and water," he said, "I'd rather take longer to get home than be attacked by a French warship, while we carry such a heavy load." Murray agreed, and it was good news to Nathan. It meant they would have to sail around the southern tip of Ireland and right by Cork Harbor. He decided it was time to approach his dad.

He met both parents for the evening meal and played the part of a perfect gentleman by offering to get their food. He pulled his mother's chair from the table and waited for her to be seated. They knew he was a gentleman, but this was a bit too much, and both felt he needed a favor. He said nothing about it, however, until the meal was over and his dad was comfortable. He then casually mentioned that he needed to stop at Cork Harbor.

"That's impossible," the captain quickly replied, "when the crew is so anxious to get home, besides the weary passengers. How could I explain to them that you want to spend half a day in Cork?"

"Uh, Dad . . . make that three days."

"Three days! Nathan, are you out of your mind? You know I can't hold this crew for three days when we're so near home."

"Now, Charles," said Mrs. Barrington, "at least hear why he wants to stop." She and the captain waited silently for Nathan to explain why he asked for three days at such a crucial time. But Nathan looked at his mother and dad with sealed lips, and then a corner of his mouth twitched as he looked down at the floor and mumbled, "I can't tell you."

"Well then, the matter is closed," said the captain.

"All right," Nathan looked his dad straight in the eyes, "but I will go to Cork one way or the other. If you won't stop the *Monarch,* I'll catch another ship from Liverpool and run the risk of being arrested because I'm to report for military duty the day after I get back." He left the dining hall very disappointed.

Mrs. Barrington felt awful. Nathan seldom asked anything

of his dad. He'd worked so hard on the voyage and had arranged for the merchants of Charleston to take their cargo. His deal with the plantation owners would mean a good profit for the company. She knew something was very important for him to ask the crew to wait three days. Without a word to her husband, she left the room right behind her son.

The captain lifted his elbows to the table and covered his face with his hands. He hated discord with one of his sons, and why did his wife always side with them? Deep down, he knew the answer. She had never forgiven him for leaving them so much. Nathan was as good as any son could be, and after this trip, he deserved whatever he asked for, but how could he ask it of the crew who had served him faithfully, each doing the job of two men. Some had children they had not seen in six months, and he knew exactly how they felt.

When Sam finished in the galley, he poured the captain a cup of hot tea and joined him at the table.

"You have a problem, Sir?"

Captain Barrington lifted the tea to his lips. "Thank you, Sam. Yes, I have a problem."

"Is there anything I can do?"

"No."

"Sometimes it helps to talk."

"Nathan wants three days to spend near Cork Harbor. He won't say why, but it must be important to him. He's worked hard on the trip, and Martha is upset with me, but how can I tell the crew and the passengers that they must spend three days anchored in Cork Harbor when home is just across the Irish Sea?"

"Why don't you ask them, Captain?"

"Ask who, what?"

"Ask the men if they would wait for Nathan three days. I don't think any of them would say no. Your son is well liked by the crew, Captain Barrington. I wouldn't mind, but I don't have a family. The passengers certainly shouldn't mind after what you did for them."

"No, they shouldn't, but they would complain."

"Let them."

When the captain returned to his office, he thought of what Sam had said and knew the men probably would agree for Nathan to have the time, but he just hated to ask them. He had resumed his paper work when the office door flew open and a guard yelled, "Captain . . . Sir, there's a ship on the horizon! I can't tell what flag she flies!" Captain Barrington reached for his glass and followed the guard to the deck.

He held the glass to his eye and saw red, white, and blue stars and stripes flying at the ship's masthead. She was not a military ship, but a fast one and approached the *Monarch* at a remarkable speed. The crew began to assemble on the main deck and awaited their orders. Would the captain make a run for it or stand firm and fight? Minutes passed without a word, while the captain made a decision. He raised his glass a second time and then turned to the guard who had come for him.

"Have Nathan, Jason, Robert, and Murray meet me in my office . . . on the double!"

"Aye, aye, Sir."

The captain returned to his office, and the four men walked in behind him. Nathan stood at the back and kept quiet.

"Did you send for us, Captain?" asked Murray.

"Yes. An American schooner clipper approaches the *Monarch* at a fast speed. I'm certain she's a privateer and her captain is out for a bounty. They're sure to catch us, with our heavy load, so I won't make a run for it. I know the *Monarch* is well armed, but I don't want a battle because lives would be lost on both sides. Our new cannons are more powerful and have a longer firing range than the schooner's. If we could destroy one of her mast with a single firing of the cannon, there would be no chance that they could overtake us, but could rig a jury-mast and reach Ireland for repairs. Would this be asking the impossible, or is there someone on the ship who could accomplish such a task?"

The men were silent until Nathan spoke up. "I believe I can."

The hole was opened and a six-pounder, the cannon of

Nathan's choice, was pushed forward. Every member of the small crew manned his battle station, and other cannons were made ready for firing in case Nathan missed the schooner's mast. They knew he would have only one chance—one round of the cannon—before the enemy would open fire on the *Monarch* and there would be an all-out battle.

They were in good position since the *Monarch* was headed north; the American ship sailed due east toward her broadside. Every cannon on the gun deck's larboard side was aimed at the schooner, but she could be easily maneuvered. The *Monarch,* with her heavy load, could not be.

Nathan's timing was important. He couldn't fire before the schooner was within the cannon's range, but if he didn't fire the first shot, the whole plan would be blundered. It was a tense moment. When he determined the schooner was near enough, he took aim at the middle of her foremast. As the cannon rang out, every man held his breath.

The ship's foremast jolted. Her bow reared and then plunged suddenly forward. Was his hit in the right place; only the dead center would cut the mast in two? Nathan thought he had failed until he saw it toddle. It twisted to one side and then the other, being held by the ship's rigging. Then there was no doubt about it; the foremast would fall. It fell across the schooner's bow and dipped its topsail into the water.

The *Monarch's* crew jumped into the air. They cheered and slapped each other on the back, saying they knew Nathan could do it. He was, undoubtedly, their hero. The captain decided it would be a good time to ask for his three days in Cork Harbor.

The sun slowly sank out of sight on the twenty-eighth day of September, 1812, as the *Monarch* sailed into the entrance of Cork Harbor. It lacked three days being exactly six months since Nathan had met Hannah there on the dock. He watched the last rays of sun disappear as he reminisced of that memorable event and thought of how much had happened since that day.

He stood at the ship's bow and gazed at the green windswept hills with their maze of gray rock walls in the distance. The wind tousled his hair and held his collar tight against the back of his neck. He heard the surf strike with a powerful force. Hannah's Ireland, he thought, with her battered shorelines and old castles surrounded by green meadows that were grazed by fat, woolly sheep. Would she ever see it again? He felt sure his answer depended on whether or not he returned from the war. He said a prayer for her and asked for fair weather the next three days.

The sun was bright the next morning when Nathan lifted his seaman's bag with a bedroll in it over the side of the wagon that he had obtained from a nearby stable. He spread a tarp over the piano and tied it tightly around the bottom of each leg. Men of the crew had helped him load it, but all had returned to the ship except Jason who leaned against the wagon and watched him.

"You sure you don't want any company?"

"No, Jason, this is something I need to do alone, but thanks anyway. Just take care of things on the *Monarch,* and I'll be back in three days."

"If you're not, I'll come looking for you."

When he had secured the last leg of the piano, Nathan turned to him and held out his hand. "I know you will and thanks. It sure makes me feel good to have a friend like you."

He pulled himself up to the wagon seat and gently rapped the reins across the horses' rumps as he made a clicking sound in his cheek. He headed into the city of Cork where his first destination was the law office of John Dudley.

It was middle of the morning before he found Dudley's office, and then he had to wait until the lawyer finished a conversation with someone else. The small office was cluttered with an assortment of dusty books and papers. There were only two extra chairs in the room and both were covered with tattered material, but were by an open window from which Nathan could see the horses and wagon. As soon as the lawyer was free, he came around his desk and held out a hand.

"I'm John Dudley," he said, "and I'm sorry you had to wait. How may I help you?"

"My name is Nathan Barrington, and I'm here to talk about Hannah Thornton."

The lawyer scratched his head. "You mean Collin Thornton's daughter? She left for America several months ago. What did you say your name was?"

"Nathan Barrington."

"Barrington? Are you a son of Charles Barrington who owns Barrington Shipping Company?"

"Yes, sir, and I've asked Hannah Thornton to marry me."

Dudley raised his eyebrows, then sat down. He appeared to be quite shocked.

"Do you have a problem with that, Sir?"

"No—I don't, but Collin would if he was alive."

"So Hannah told me."

"Has she agreed to marry you?"

"Yes. We plan to be married as soon as the war is over, and I can get back to South Carolina."

Nathan told Dudley about meeting Hannah on the dock and of how he had fallen in love with her right away. He also told him about the problems they had when she found out who he was. Since no one else came into his office, he and the lawyer had a lengthy conversation about Hannah and her father. Dudley related to Nathan about growing up with Collin and why he felt the way he did.

"He was a bitter man," he said, "until he married Hannah's mother. When she died and left him with the baby, it seemed to have taken everything out of him and had it not been for his baby daughter, I believe he would have taken his own life. He devoted the rest of his life to her, and it would have been hard for Collin to let Hannah marry anyone. Maybe it's why the Lord took him when he did."

"I'd like directions to the place where Hannah grew up. I'm going to be near there and would like to see it."

"Oh . . . the Thornton place is for sale again . . . at a very good price. The couple who purchased it from Hannah decided it was too far out of town, so they moved back to Cork. The house is empty if you'd like to spend the night there. I'm sure the owner wouldn't mind and maybe you'll decide to buy it," the lawyer joked.

"I would like to spend the night there. And what amount do they want for it?" To Dudley's surprise, Nathan asked him to prepare a contract on the house and land and said he would give him an answer in three days.

Nathan felt good when he left the lawyer's office. He understood Collin Thornton better, and he had directions to Hannah's home. He had a house to stay in that night instead of under the stars where he had thought he would sleep. Before he left the city, he bought enough provisions to last three days, a pan for cooking, and a bucket for watering the horses.

He left Cork on the road to Midleton that was also the road to Hannah's home. It ran along beside the bay, and at first, he saw many wagons and carriages as it was a Saturday and people traveled to and from the city. Farther out of town, he saw fewer people and began to enjoy the scenery. At noon, he found a good spot that overlooked the bay and tied the horses' reins around a large rock and sat down in the shade of the wagon to eat.

As soon as he finished eating, he returned to the wagon and continued his journey. He wanted to reach Hannah's home before sundown. In his directions, John Dudley had informed him that there would be two houses close together, each to the left of the road, and then there was a hill. The lawyer had stated that he would be able to see Hannah's home from top of the hill. He became excited as he passed the two houses.

The tired horses plodded up the hill, and when they finally reached the top, Nathan recognized Hannah's home, for it was just as she had described it. He saw the cottage that was made of stone and had a thatched roof on its top. From the wagon seat, he could see the shed behind the house and the bay in the distance. A trail led toward the bay. There wasn't much difference in the appearance of this home from many of the others he'd passed along the way, but it was special. It was where Hannah grew up. He stopped the horses and gazed across the hillside to visualize her running and playing with a dog and a cat.

Nathan decided right then to buy the place and return there, one day, with Hannah. He wanted their children to run and play on the hillside, the way she had done, and he asked God to grant him this wish.

By the time he turned off the road in front of the house, darkness had begun to settle over the place. He pulled the wagon under the shed before he unhitched the horses and tied them to a post. The bit was taken from their mouths, so they could graze in the night and drink the water that he drew from the well. He found a stack of peat beside the house and took some inside and put it in the fireplace, and then he returned to the wagon for his seaman's bag. A chill in the night air caused him to take a light jacket from the bag and put it on. He felt to make sure that a small pistol he had put there was still in one pocket. With flint and steel from his other pocket, he kneeled in front of the fireplace and struck them together until the peat was lit.

Someone had left a small piece of candle on the mantle over the fireplace. Nathan held it to the fire and when the flame burned bright, he held it up in the dark room. The room was long in length, but not too wide. It must have served as a living area and a kitchen, he thought, since a half partition extended from one wall. He determined it was the room where Collin died.

Off the living area was a narrow hallway. There was a bedroom at each side of the hall and a water closet at the end of it. Nathan entered the room on the south side of the house, for Hannah had talked of watching the sun rise over the bay from her bedroom window. Being there made him feel closer to her. He pictured how it was with a bed against the wall and a table beside it. He pictured a lamp and things from her trunk on the table. With a curtain over the window and a rug on the floor it would be a very cozy room.

Excitement spread over him as he walked through the house. He would ask John Dudley to hire someone to keep the place up, but would let Hannah buy furnishings for it in Cork and fix it the way she liked. They would furnish it together on their wedding trip.

Back at the fireplace, he took out the pan he'd purchased to warm food in. After eating, he unrolled his bedroll and lay down by the fire. The flame had begun to die down, but inside the bedroll, he felt warm and comfortable, so it didn't take him long to go to sleep.

He didn't know how long he had slept, but fiery coals still smoldered in the fireplace when he was awakened by a noise. It was dark in the room; he couldn't see, but heard the back door open slowly.

He quickly sat up and reached for his pistol, but in the darkness, he fumbled with the jacket and couldn't get his hands on the gun. When he finally held it in his hand, he asked, "Who's there?" but no one answered.

He jumped to his feet and tried to open the front door, but it was locked, and he had no idea how to unlock it. He turned bravely with his back to the wall and asked again, this time in a louder voice, **"Who's there?"**

"Meow," said a small bundle of fur that rubbed against his legs and purred. With his heart nearly pounding right out of his chest, he bent his weak knees and let his back slide down the wall until he sat on the floor. He breathed a deep breath of relief and then reached for the little cat.

"Whew, little fellow, you sure gave me a big scare." When he was able to breathe normal again, he went back to the fire and put more peat on it and blew on the coals until a flame appeared. He lit the candle and walked across the room to fasten a dead bolt on the back door. He couldn't take another unexpected guest in the night.

The cat had settled on his haunches by the fire like he was right at home. Nathan bent over and picked him up before he had a seat on the bedroll. He rubbed his soft fur, and being able to see it better in the light of the flames, he was suddenly overwhelmed as he remembered Hannah's words, "He was a fluffy, little gray cat with a white streak under his neck." When the cat's head was gently lifted, a white streak was revealed under the neck.

"Sneaky!"

"Meow."

"Oh, Sneaky." Nathan cuddled him against his chest. "Do you miss Hannah?"

"Meow."

"So do I."

He lay back down with the little cat in his arms, and they both slept peacefully the rest of the night. The next morning, Sneaky woke him again by scratching on the back door. He wanted out. Before Nathan opened the door, he picked him up and rubbed him gently. He noticed how fat and clean he was.

"Someone is taking good care of you," he said. "I'll tell Hannah when I see her. She misses you, too, you know. I'll also tell her you really are a sneaky one . . . giving me such a scare in the night, but you can come around here anytime you want and scare the mice away. He opened the back door and watched as the little cat bounced off across the side of the hill, probably toward home.

Nathan drew water from the well and heated it over the fire in the fireplace and then shaved and put on clean clothes. It was Sunday and he planned to go to church. He heated some food and ate in a hurry because he didn't want to be late.

While the sun was still low in the sky, he turned the horses and wagon onto the road toward Midleton. He found it wasn't far and, even with having to ask directions to the church, was there before anyone else.

After the horses' reins were tied to a post out front, he entered a small rock building and stood still a moment and looked all around the room. A feeling of peace came over him. It was where Hannah and Collin Thornton had come for nearly twenty years, Sunday after Sunday, to worship God. He walked to the front of the church where an old piano stood at one side and took a seat on the bench. He ran his fingers across the keys. It had been so long since he'd played a piano, but the tune "Amazing Grace" came to his mind, and to his own surprise, he began to make the right notes. The words of the song escaped his lips, so he didn't hear the vicar enter. He was unaware of his presence until he heard him clap when the song ended.

"Oh, I'm sorry, Sir." Nathan jumped from the bench. "I just got here early and—"

"That's quite all right. It's a pleasure to have you join us this morning, Mr.—"

"Barrington; I'm Nathan Barrington."

The vicar had been curious as to what was under the tarp in the wagon out front. He recognized that Nathan was British and became concerned. Being in God's house, however, and having heard him sing "Amazing Grace," he didn't want to question his reason for being there and hoped that he had come to worship the Lord. He couldn't recall ever seeing him in their village before.

"It's a pleasure to meet you, Nathan. I'm Pastor Sean O'Quigley." He held out his hand.

"The honor is mine." Nathan took the vicar's hand. "I've come to worship, but for another reason, also."

"For what other reason?"

Nathan explained why he was there, and the vicar was relieved. "Would you like to talk to the congregation before or after the service?" he asked.

"I would rather wait until after. I don't want to interfere with God's worship service."

"I appreciate that." Pastor O'Quigley seemed pleased.

At the end of the service, the vicar announced to his small congregation, "We have a stranger among us today, and I hope each of you will extend a hand of welcome to him, but first, he has something he'd like to say. It concerns our beloved Hannah

who left us some time ago." He motioned for Nathan to come
to the front.

As Nathan walked down the aisle, heads turned to look at
him.

"I won't take much of your time," he began, and then quickly
relayed the story of falling in love with Hannah. He told them
how much her mother's piano had meant to her, and how as a
child, when she missed her mother, she would sit beside the
piano and visualize her playing it. "I offered to buy her a new
piano," he said, "but she insisted that it could never be the
same, so I have come to retrieve her mother's piano with a new
and much nicer one that I have purchased for you."

Before Nathan finished, ladies dabbed their eyes with
handkerchiefs, and the men had sad expressions on their faces.
He sat down and the vicar took over again. "Are we all in
agreement to let this young man take Hannah her mother's
piano?" Heads all over the sanctuary began to nod.

"If you agree, please stand," said the vicar, and to Nathan's
relief, everyone in the room stood.

Some of the men carried the old piano out to the wagon and
everyone gathered around it for the unveiling of the new one.
Nathan removed the tarp and heard many "ohs" and "ahs" from
the group. They were delighted.

As he climbed down from the wagon, he noticed a small
cemetery behind the church and asked if Hannah's father was
buried there.

"Yes," replied the vicar, "and her mother. I will show you
the graves."

While the men of the church unloaded the new piano and
then loaded the old one, Nathan walked with Pastor O'Quigley
to a shaded corner of the cemetery. A new gravestone stood at
one end of a heap of dirt that was not completely covered with
grass. Carved in the stone was the name, "Collin Patrick
Thornton." The dates were June 3, 1770-January 10, 1812.
Beside Collin's grave was the grave of Lillian Ruth Thornton.

"It was the saddest funeral," the vicar recalled. "Everyone

knew how alone Hannah was left and we tried to comfort her. Many church members invited her to stay with them, but she wouldn't, so I took her home after the funeral and left her there alone."

Nathan stood quietly beside the grave, and the vicar perceived that he would like some time to himself. "I'll wait for you at the wagon," he said.

A gentle wind stirred the leaves of a large tree that provided shade for the two graves. It was a peaceful place, but Nathan thought of the anguish that must have filled Hannah's heart as she stood by the grave with the small group of church members gathered around her. He remembered the sadness in her eyes the day he met her on the dock and the tear that had trickled down her cheek when she looked back for the last time. His heart ached.

Before he left the church, many expressed their love for Hannah and Collin and told him how much they were missed. He promised to bring her for a visit someday if God would permit it. Some invited him to stay and have the noon meal, but with a limited amount of time, he hoped to reach Cork before midnight, so after requesting prayers for Hannah and himself, he said good-bye.

He left Midleton with the old piano in the wagon and didn't stop until he reached Hannah's home. He was there only long enough to eat and to water the horses and let them rest. Before he left, he made sure the tarp was tied tightly over the piano because dark clouds had formed in the sky.

When it began to rain, Nathan stepped behind the wagon seat with the reins in his hands. He hunched down under the edge of the piano and pulled the tarp over him. The horses continued to plod down the road and didn't know that there was no one on the seat behind them.

Early the next morning, Nathan sat in the office of John Dudley and waited for him to finish the paper work that would permit him to buy the Thornton place. He signed papers for the lawyer to draw from his bank account in Liverpool and was asked his full name in order that it might be written on the deed.

"Put the name Hannah Ruth Thornton on the deed, and mail it to that name, c/o Reybrook Plantation, Charleston, South Carolina, United States of America."

The lawyer looked over the top of his glasses. "Are you sure?" he asked.

"Yes. If I'm killed in the war, Hannah will have the deed and will always know that she can come home. If I'm not killed, I plan for us to stop here on our way to England."

"I sure hope everything works out for you two," said the lawyer. He pushed his glasses up on his nose and continued to write.

So do I, thought Nathan, and then he asked Dudley about a caretaker for the place.

"I believe there would be many who would take care of it for the right to farm the land." When Nathan agreed, the lawyer assured him that he would find someone.

Before he left the office, Nathan asked Dudley for paper and quill that he might write Hannah a letter. He placed the letter in an envelope that Dudley gave him and paid the lawyer for his services and then shook his hand and thanked him for everything. It was late, but his work was not yet finished. He still had to make arrangements for the piano to be shipped to Hannah in South Carolina. He returned to the wagon and opened the top of the piano and tucked the letter inside.

Darkness had settled over the *Monarch* by the time he walked the gangplank and stepped onto her quarterdeck. Cheers went up all over the ship when the captain yelled, "Pull the plank and let's go home!"

CHAPTER 21

The *Monarch* sailed across the Irish Sea on her last leg of the journey home. Nathan was thankful there had been no casualties and for the profit the company would reap from the voyage, but he failed to share the excitement of others aboard. There was a feeling of emptiness within him, for he had left his heart in America.

He reached into his pocket for the lace-trimmed handkerchief Hannah had given him and let his fingertip trace over her name. When the sun's last rays disappeared at the water's edge, he went to his bunk, having no desire to celebrate with the others. At some time during the predawn hours, the *Monarch* sailed into Liverpool Bay.

Early the next morning, Nathan's brother came aboard the ship with a warm greeting and said that he would see that the cotton got unloaded. Nathan was free to go home. He went to the little forecastle for his gear and was ready to leave when Scott came to him with a rolled up paper tucked under his arm.

"Scott! I thought you'd be the first one off the ship."

Scott grinned. "I am anxious to get home," he said, "but I wanted to give you something before I left."

"What is it?" Nathan was in a hurry to leave.

As he took the paper from under his arm and unrolled it, Scott explained, "I've always liked to draw, and, whereas some seamen keep a journal . . . well . . . I sketch things." He stretched the long roll of paper lengthwise on Nathan's bunk, and Nathan was amazed.

Scott had recorded the entire journey with his sketches. And among the ocean scenes and landmarks were beautiful drawings of Hannah; the first one being of her on the cart when he and

Jason pushed her up the gangplank. He had captured the panic in her eyes when she reached for her hat. There was a picture of her at the winch and one of her with a book in her hands and the Hartman children gathered around her. He had put the wind in her hair as she walked across the deck and, again, as she stood by the guardrail. Nathan's favorite one was a close up of her face with a shy smile on her lips. It was so much like her. The many sketches included one of him rescuing Jenny from high above the deck. He'd recorded each harbor and sketched the skyline of every city from New York City to Charleston.

"Scott, this is great! When did you do it?"

"I worked on it in my bunk at night before I went to sleep. Each night I drew something that stood out in my mind from the day, and it helped me to relax and go to sleep without thinking about home so much."

"You're really talented. Have you ever thought of using this talent to design things—like ships? If instructed at the right school, there's no telling what you could do."

"No-o-o. Schools cost money, and that's something my family doesn't have much of."

"I wish you'd think about it. I'll show this to my dad and one of us will get back with you."

Nathan looked over the collage of pictures again. "I especially like this one," he said, and pointed to the close up of Hannah.

"I drew some small ones of her, if you'd like to see them."

"Well, sure."

"I'll get them." He turned back to his bunk.

"Uh . . . Scott . . ." Nathan wondered why he had sketched so many pictures of Hannah.

"Yea, Nathan."

"Why did you draw all the pictures of Hannah? Were you . . . uh . . . in love with her?"

Scott stopped. He didn't answer at first, but turned to face Nathan. Nathan saw that he was embarrassed and wished he hadn't asked.

"Sure, Nathan. Every man of the crew was. Didn't you know that?"

"No." Nathan shook his head and smiled sentimentally at him. "I just knew that she loved every one of you."

Scott chuckled and went for the other pictures.

"Thanks, Scott." Nathan chose another one of Hannah with a shy smile on her face. "I'll take this with me when I leave for military duty." He rolled up the larger picture. "And this will be put in a safe place at Barrington Manor. I want to keep it forever."

He held out a hand to Scott. "You're a good seaman," he said, "and thanks for everything. Should I not see you before I leave, I'll ask my dad to get back with you. I think after seeing your work, he'll agree to pay for you to go to school. I hope you'll stay with Barrington Shipping; the company needs every man it can get."

"I intend to, and thank you, Nathan. Thanks again for rescuing me in New York Harbor. I know where I'd be right now if you hadn't listened to Hannah and come looking for me."

"I'm thankful we found you in time."

Nathan put the rolled up paper of Scott's drawings in a leather case with other papers and left the little forecastle. With the case in one hand and his seaman's bag over his shoulder with the other, he crossed the main deck, but stopped at the quarterdeck and looked back. The *Monarch* was almost deserted. It had been a voyage he would never forget.

A maid met Nathan at the door of Barrington Manor and took his bag that was filled with dirty clothes to the laundry room. With the leather case still in his hand, he slipped into the kitchen and surprised Marie.

"Nathan!" she cried, and threw her chubby arms around him.

"Hello, Marie; I missed you." He returned her hug and gave her a kiss on top of her curly brown hair that had streaks of gray in it.

"Ah, you missed my apple pie, is what you missed. I'll bake you one today."

"Oh, no, Marie, please—no apple pie today."

"Are you sick?" She held her hand to his forehead.

"No," Nathan chuckled, "I'm just not hungry."

"You're either sick or in love," Marie insisted. "Which one is it?"

"How do you know me so well?"

"I just know how much you like my apple pie." She noticed the sadness about him and asked, "What's wrong, Nathan?"

"I am in love . . . with a beautiful girl. Oh, Marie, she's so wonderful, and I know you'll love her, too."

"Yes, Nathan, I will. Where is she? I want to meet her."

"She's in America."

"America!"

"I had no choice but to leave her there. It's a long story, Marie."

"I have nothing else to do. Sit down; I want to hear about her."

Nathan sat at the kitchen table and Marie poured him a cup of hot tea. She sat down with him and listened as he told her about Hannah from the time he met her on the dock until he had to leave her in South Carolina. Her eyes filled with tears several times, but she picked up her apron and wiped them away.

"Nathan, I'm so sorry. She must truly be a wonderful girl."

"She is, Marie. I love her more than anything in the world, and I live for the day when I can return to her. But tell me, how have you and Edgar been? Where is Edgar?"

"We're all right, and he's working in the gardens where he's been all week. He wanted them to look nice when you arrived home, although we didn't expect Lady Barrington to return with you. I suppose since the United States declared war against England, she would not have been safe there."

"No, but is it safe anywhere with Napoleon's army raging across Europe?"

Nathan climbed the staircase that he had slid down every morning as a child. He entered his room and laid the leather case on his bed and then opened it and took out the pictures that Scott had given him. He pinned the long collage on the wall by his bed and lay down to look at it. He thought about Hannah, then got up and crossed the room to his desk and wrote her a long letter . . . that he hoped she would never have to read.

When the letter was finished, he went to sleep and slept until a maid knocked on the door to let him know that the noon meal was ready. Marie had prepared a delicious meal, but he had no appetite and ate very little. After the meal, he dressed for a trip to Liverpool. He needed to talk to a lawyer.

Later, he entered the office of David Williams. Jason's dad stood from his desk and came to meet him. "Nathan! I didn't know you were back. How was the trip?"

"All right, Mr. Williams, but it's good to be home, if only for a short time. Have you not seen Jason?"

"No, I left home early this morning, and I guess he arrived after I left. How is he? Is he a good seaman?"

"He's fine, and an excellent seaman. You can be proud of him, Mr. Williams."

"Oh . . . I am . . . I am, but tell me, what brings you to my office so soon after returning from the sea? You must be tired."

"I'm all right, but something must be taken care of before I leave for military duty. I want to change my will."

The lawyer was surprised, but he didn't say anything for a moment. When he spoke, he chose his words carefully. "Nathan, are you sure you have given this careful consideration?"

"Yes, sir, I have." He offered no explanation.

"Very well, then, we'll proceed."

Nathan waited as the lawyer looked over his present will and then wrote something across the top of it. He dipped his quill into a bottle of ink and looked up. "What changes do you want to make?" he asked.

"In case of my death, I want three-fourths of all my fortune and worldly possessions to go to Hannah Ruth Thornton who resides on the Reybrook Plantation near Charleston, South

Carolina. You may write to Daniel Overteer at the Charleston
City Bank to transfer funds from my banks in Liverpool and
London to her account at the bank in Charleston. Also, in case
of my death, I want this letter to be sent to Hannah at the
Reybrook Plantation along with a letter from you that states the
amount to be transferred to her account. If she is no longer in
residence there, please contact Mr. Overteer. Be sure, somehow,
that she knows of the transactions that are made."

After he wrote all the information down, David Williams
looked at Nathan and said, "In case of your death, I will see
that this is taken care of in the proper way, but what about the
other one-fourth? Do you want to leave it to your parents?"

"No, Mr. Williams, my parents will never need anything
from me. You know that better than anyone."

"I know they will be well-off for as long as either can live."

"I want the remainder of my wealth to go to Marie
Willingham, a longtime cook for the Barrington family."

"Yes, I know Marie. She and Edgar make a fine couple."

"She's a friend that has been an inspiration in my life."

"All right, Nathan, I'll see that everything is taken care of,
but I have one more question."

"What is it, Mr. Williams?"

"Wasn't Hannah Thornton the Irish girl that I helped to
arrange passage for to America? Is she the daughter of Collin
Thornton who was a friend to John Dudley?"

"Yes—yes she is. Why do you ask?"

"Oh, no reason," the lawyer smiled. "We just never know
how things are going to work out."

"No, sir," Nathan smiled back at the lawyer. "We don't."

With the matter taken care of, Nathan felt better when he
mounted his horse outside Mr. Williams's office. Before he left
town, he stopped by a shop and bought a black picture frame
that he thought would be perfect for the sketch of Hannah.

Upon his arrival home, Mrs. Barrington informed him that
she had sent Edgar to invite a few friends of the family to a
small going away party for Jason and him that night.

"Mother, I wish you hadn't done that."

"Why, Nathan? They'll want to see both of you before you leave for the war. We can't deprive them of it."

"You know I'm in no mood for a party." It made him angry, but his mother didn't seem to notice. He started to his room and was halfway up the stairs when she called up to him.

"The Hesleys will be here."

Nathan stopped on the staircase. His eyes closed and his face grimaced when he remembered Jason's words concerning Gloria Hesley. "You'll find out about her feelings for you when you get home. You just wait and see. You'd better think of what you're going to say to her."

"Mother, you didn't invite Gloria, did you?"

"Of course, Nathan. The whole family would have been insulted had I not. You know how Richard Hesley is about his daughter, and we must not forget that he provides more business for Barrington Shipping Company than any other person."

"I won't be here!" Nathan yelled.

But, again, his mother didn't seem to notice that anything was wrong. "You must be," she answered calmly, "the party is for you."

He continued up the stairs and spent time in his room, getting things in order before he left. A maid had packed his seaman's bag with clean clothes and left it outside his door. He put more things into it before he returned downstairs to show Scott's drawings to his dad.

Later, as Nathan dressed for the party, he tried to think if he had taken care of everything. He and Jason would leave early the next morning. The most important thing had been to make sure that Hannah would be taken care of in case of his death, and he had written a letter to be sent to her along with one from his lawyer. He'd persuaded his dad to give Scott an opportunity to go to school in order to use his talent for designing ships. The picture of Hannah was framed and in his bag; on top of it lay her lace-trimmed handkerchief. He'd not forgotten anything, he thought, just as he heard a knock on his door. It was Jason.

"Jason! Come in. You look great."

"Thanks, Nathan. So do you. I brought my bag with me, so I can sleep here tonight. The maid put it in the room next door. If we arrive at the Royal Navy's headquarters together, chances are we'll get assigned to the same ship."

"I'm glad you thought of it; I do hope we stay together. Let's go downstairs and see what Marie has cooked for the guests. You know how good all those fancy little things taste."

There was no time, however, to sample Marie's goodies. The guests had already begun to arrive, and Nathan and Jason joined Captain and Mrs. Barrington near the front entrance. Nathan's brother, James, his wife, Sandra, and their son, Daniel Lee, arrived. Sandra looked lovely in a new dress that Lady Barrington had purchased for her in New York City.

"Sandra, you look beautiful tonight," said Nathan.

"Thank you, Nathan. We have missed all of you, and I'm sorry you and Jason must leave again so soon. We put you both in God's hands and shall pray for you daily." She spoke softly, the way Hannah did, Nathan realized.

He put an arm around his sister-in-law's shoulder and reached out his other hand to his brother. James held Nathan's three-year-old nephew, and the three of them laughed when the small child reached out his arms to him.

"Guess he hasn't forgotten you," said James.

Nathan took his nephew and held him high in the air. The child squealed with delight. When Jason held out his arms, the two of them tossed him back and forth until Jason's family arrived.

The Hesleys entered the room, and Jason quickly handed Dan to Nathan. "It would be to your advantage to hold him right now," he whispered. At first Nathan didn't understand, but then realized that as long as he held the child, he would not be expected to hug anyone. He held Dan with both arms and greeted the Hesleys.

After the arrival of many guests, Nathan muttered to his mother, "I thought you said a few friends." She only smiled in reply.

Sandra took Dan for some of Marie's goodies, and Nathan was free to mingle with the guests. Some spoke words of encouragement to him; others made comments about the war, such as, "I hope it'll soon be over." Many feared an invasion of French troops, although Napoleon's attempt to invade their soil had been unsuccessful in 1805. "The British," one man declared, "should not take for granted that he won't try again."

As the evening went by, Nathan avoided Gloria who, most of the time, was surrounded by men. He glanced her way, once, and found her eyes on him. She was beautiful, dressed in a black dress that fit tight around her waist. Its low cut left her shoulders bare and a large diamond sparkled at her neckline. A strand of her long blonde hair curled over one side of her shoulder and fell across her breast.

When some of the guests left, Gloria started across the room toward him, but Jason stepped in front of her and began to talk. He did it to give him an opportunity to escape, so he quickly slipped out a side door and into the great hall and then crossed the hallway and climbed the stairs to the upper balcony.

A full moon shined over the Irish Sea and spread light on the neatly trimmed gardens that surrounded Barrington Manor. Nathan stood at the edge of the balcony and listened to the surf and thought of Hannah. Suddenly he heard someone open the double doors behind him and turned to see Gloria in the moonlight. She closed the doors and leaned against them. He was trapped.

"How have you been, Gloria?"

"Dreadfully lonesome while you were gone. I missed you every day, Nathan. Why have you avoided me all evening?"

"I'll leave again early in the morning."

"Without a word to me? Why? You know how much I love you and how long I have waited."

"Gloria . . . I—"

Before he could tell her that he was engaged to another, she crossed the balcony and put her arms around his waist. She held her face up to his; it was beautiful in the moonlight. When he looked down at her, the dress seemed even lower in the front, and she leaned against his chest. She wore a perfume that could confuse any man's thinking. She was in his arms and she wanted him for her own. As her arms tightened around him, he slowly lowered his lips toward hers. He felt her hand move up his chest and under the edge of his shirt.

Suddenly, as though she was startled, her arms relaxed and she leaned slightly backward. "Nathan! Where is your family coat of arms?"

Hannah's face flashed before him, and he saw his coat of arms around her neck. He felt the same wonderful, proud feeling he had felt that first morning after he gave it to her, and he took his opportunity.

He forced Gloria's arms from around him, then grabbed the end of a vine that grew over the balcony railing and leaped over its side. "It's with the girl who has my heart," he called to Gloria as he scooted down the vine just the way he had as a child. The vine held firm, for over the years it had also grown larger and stronger.

Jason paced back and forth in the great hall. He'd seen Gloria climb the stairs and disappear through the balcony doors. He even thought of going to the balcony, when he saw Nathan on the vine, through a window, and ran outside to find him ripping off his evening jacket.

Nathan was glad to see him. "Come on," he said, "let's get out of here!"

They ran to the stables and saddled two horses and then rode swiftly down the narrow road. At the main road, they turned their mounts toward Liverpool and kept them at a fast speed until they were miles from Barrington Manor. When they pulled the horses to a slower pace, Jason began to laugh. He laughed so hard Nathan thought he would fall from the saddle. He could hardly talk, but managed to say, "I told you she waited for you." He then laughed even harder.

Nathan thought how ridiculous he must have looked as he scooted down the vine in his flight from Gloria, but he failed to see any humor in his predicament and refused to discuss it with Jason.

At dawn the two of them returned to Barrington Manor. They

tied the horses in front of the house and entered the mansion quietly. They were halfway up the stairs when Nathan noticed a light in the kitchen. He descended the steps a ways and saw that Marie sat at the kitchen table with her head down. He went to see why she was there and found a cold cup of tea beside her that told him she had been there for quite some time. When he laid his hand on her back and spoke her name softly, she awoke and sat up.

"Nathan, where have you been? I was so worried about you."

"Have you waited up all night for me?"

"Well, it was past midnight before all the guests left and I finished cleaning in the kitchen."

"Did you have to do everything?"

"Oh, no, the maids always help me cook when there are lots of guests and to clean afterward. Edgar is great help in the kitchen, also, and he stayed with me until all was finished. Lady Barrington said for both of us to take the day off today."

"I would think so. You must be exhausted."

"After you left last night, Gloria Hesley caused an awful scene. Captain and Lady Barrington were terribly embarrassed. I had to stay up and tell you about it."

"What did she do?"

"She ran into the ballroom screaming that you had insulted her. She called you names that I have never heard come from a lady's mouth."

"She's not a lady, Marie."

"She yelled at Richard Hesley and said that she never wanted him to do business with anyone in your family again. Poor Lady Hesley cried and apologized to your mother, but Mr. Hesley grabbed her arm and demanded that they leave immediately."

Nathan sighed and sat down beside Marie. "What did my dad say?" he asked.

"He didn't know what to say except that he would talk to you."

"They should not have been invited here. I tried to tell Mother that, but she insisted that Jason and I have a party before we leave."

"That's another reason I stayed up to talk to you."

"Why?"

"Because you will leave for the war this morning, and I had to tell you how much Edgar and I love you before you go."

"I already know that, Marie."

"You were just a baby when we came to work here, and we watched you grow to a man. I helped you learn to walk and to talk and many times I held you on my lap and fed you. When you got hurt, I gave you a cookie to help you forget the pain."

Big tears rolled down her cheeks, and Nathan put his arms around her shoulders.

"I'll be all right," he said. "Don't worry about me."

Marie was not finished.

"We never had children of our own, but you've blessed our lives as much as any son could have. We love James, too, but he was older and not so close to us."

"He knows you love him and he loves you and Edgar."

"Please, Nathan, stay alive and come home."

"I plan to stay alive, Marie, but I won't be home after the war. I'll return to Hannah as soon as possible, and it will be her choice as to where we live. But we'll be back to visit. I want to bring her to Barrington Manor on our wedding trip."

"I hope you can; I do want to meet her. Just let us know that you're all right. That's all I ask."

"I love you, Marie. If Hannah and I have children, will you and Edgar be their grandparents? Hannah's parents are deceased, and our children will need a cookie to take the hurt away."

Marie smiled through her tears. "Nathan, you say the sweetest things."

"To be an Englishman," he muttered under his breath.

"What?"

"Oh, nothing; I just thought of something."

"We would feel so blessed to be your children's grandparents."

"Then it's settled, and you must get some rest, my lady." He helped her from the chair and watched as she trudged down the great hall toward the servants' quarters. Her head was bowed and her shoulders slumped.

There was no time to sleep. Nathan woke Jason before he went to his room to write a note.

> Dear Mother and Dad,
> I'm sorry about what happened last night. Marie told me everything. I didn't wake you this morning because you were up most of the night. I'll write you a letter when possible. I love you both and thanks for everything. Give my love to James and family.
>
> Nathan

The note was left on a table outside his parents' bedroom as he and Jason left the house quietly with a seaman's bag swung over their shoulders.

Most of the day was over before they were officially sworn into the Royal Navy. Against Nathan's wish, but due to the navigational school he'd attended and his experience at sea, he was commissioned with the rank of a lieutenant. He and Jason were informed that after a short period of training, they'd be assigned to *HMS Squall*, a 40-gun British frigate. While pleased that they were assigned to the same ship, both were astounded when told that the *Squall* would soon leave for America.

"But I didn't enlist to fight the Americans!" Nathan protested. "I enlisted to fight the French!"

"Sorry, Barrington," said a young ensign. "The Royal Navy does not give you a choice."

CHAPTER 22

Hannah endured South Carolina's July and August heat, along with the state's ticks, chiggers, and mosquitoes, as gracefully as any lady could. The bite of all three bloodsucking pests left her with an intolerable itch, especially the tiny chigger that she could neither see nor touch, but could certainly recognize its presence. She kept a small bottle of coal oil handy for the critters that feasted upon her fair and delicate skin.

It seemed impossible that three months had passed since Nathan left. She thought of him on a Saturday morning as she walked by the brook, picking a bouquet of fall wildflowers that bloomed along its banks. The leaves had turned all sorts of vivid colors in the brisk October weather; some had fallen to the ground and crackled under her feet. Autumn in South Carolina was much more pleasant than summer.

She had completely recovered from her long journey across the ocean. Catherine had insisted she take time for convalescence until she regained her strength; therefore, she'd spent most of the first two weeks at Reybrook in her room, but not all of that time had been spent in complete rest. She had taken advantage of it to put her room in order and to work on five different educational plans after studying past school records.

Summer clothes had been taken from her trunk and hung in a beautiful old French armoire that stood in one corner of her room. Leaves were carved in the wood across the top of the armoire, and a mirror down one side of it let her see her body from head to toe. It was far better than the tiny mirror on the *Monarch,* but she longed to be on the ship with Nathan. She missed him terribly, and there had been moments of agony when she could do nothing but cry. It was easier now that she had regained her strength and was able to stay busy.

Hannah was pleased with her room and its location in the home. Its window provided a perfect view of the sunset, and the narrow staircase allowed her to exit the house without anyone knowing except Rosie who kept a close watch on the back door. With her classroom and the library right across the hall, it could not have been more convenient.

A comfortable bed, supported by four large posts, stood across the room from the armoire. Beside the bed, a heavy square-shaped table held a wash bowl and pitcher that had wild roses and green leaves painted on them. Smooth sheets on the bed smelled new as did the fluffy comforter that was also covered with wild roses. Handmade pillowcases with a wide lace trim around them held soft feather-filled pillows. A dresser that was made of the same wood as the bed had an oval-shaped mirror with a beveled edge. A small round table with two chairs had been moved to a corner of the room by the door. When her trunks were pulled in front of the table, she had created an isolated nook that served as a work area.

She had taken items from her trunk and set them on a linen cloth that covered the top of the dresser. A mirror with a matching comb and brush was put there along with the music box Collin had given her. A set of candlesticks was placed at one end of the dresser, and the guest book from her birthday party was put inside the top drawer with her mother's Bible. The golden locket that Nathan's mother had given her lay opened beside the music box.

She'd tried to open the new trunk that held the things Nathan and his mother had bought for her, but the top would not come up. It appeared to be locked and she didn't have a key. Perhaps Ben would help her open it later, she had thought, so the trunk was pushed against the wall and forgotten.

Time had passed quickly. June through September was the busiest time of the year on the plantation. Vegetables were gathered and preserved, cotton was picked and floated down the Cooper River to a gin in Charleston, and rice was harvested and threshed. Field hands had worked from early morning until dusk, but Ben and Garrett rose with the cock's crow six days a week and made sure that everything was done the way it should be.

Jim MacMillan worked in the hay field with slaves, helping them cut and store the hay for the animals to feed on during winter months. His work was not finished at the end of the day, as the animals still had to be taken care of. Two indentured sisters had worked in the large garden beyond their quarters and kept it weeded until the vegetables were ready to eat.

As mistress of the plantation home, Catherine Rey had kept everything organized. In a kindly manner, she had supervised the gathering of vegetables from the garden and made sure they were preserved correctly. There were nights when she had been so tired her husband had to help her up the stairs. He'd begged her to rest more, but was not there in the daylight hours when the many voices said, "Mis' Catherine, how's I's to do dis? Miss Catherine, please show me how this is done. Mis' Catherine, what I's gwinna do 'bout . . . ? Miss Catherine . . . Miss Catherine . . . Miss Catherine . . ."

After her own room had been cleaned and put in order, Hannah had begun to clean throughout the large home. She'd enlisted the help of the three young children and used it as a learning experience. She taught Emily and Emma how to dust the furniture by rubbing a cloth with a bit of oil on it back and forth across the wood gently. Otis had picked up trash and old leaves that had collected around the foundation of the home, and she had helped him pile it behind the barn for Nole to burn later.

By the time August faded into September, everyone was exhausted. Everyone—that is—except Charleen who had sat brooding most of the summer, complaining of the heat and of her lack of attention.

It had been a happy occasion the night Garrett announced to those gathered around the supper table that the cotton had been loaded onto a Portuguese ship that was bound for Europe. To his wife he had said, "We received a good price for it, and the money is in the Charleston City bank." Then he turned to his children, "It's time for you to go back to school." His comment brought frowns to their faces, but Hannah had been delighted.

To cheer everyone again, Garrett had announced, "We'll take a week off, and as soon as the weather cools, we'll have a barbecue."

"Oh, Daddy, can we invite the Lamberts?" Charleen had jumped from her seat and ran to put her arms around Garrett's neck.

"Yes, honey," he had agreed, "we'll invite everybody."

Hannah had become acquainted with almost everyone living on the plantation and had made friends with the two indentured sisters. Dolly and Julie Thomas had arrived at Reybrook a short time before her.

Both girls had worked hard in the large garden, but now that its vegetables had been preserved and potatoes dug and put in a dry place, they worked in the plantation home. Dolly laughed and talked as she worked, but Julie was quiet and withdrawn. The sisters were also different in appearance. Dolly was tall, and her broad shoulders made her seem stout and robust, but Julie was small. Her blonde hair was trimmed to shoulder length and combed neatly each day, whereas Dolly's mass of thick brown hair appeared unruly; a fact that didn't seem to bother her.

Daniel and Ruth Leander were an older Swedish couple who had come to the plantation in 1801, and had long since fulfilled their contract, but both liked living there and decided to stay when Garrett Rey offered them a small salary. Their presence in the servants' quarters helped relieve Garrett's and Catherine's minds as to the safety of young servant girls like Dolly and Julie.

Jim MacMillan had lived in the servants' quarters for two years. Hannah had come to know him well, as she went to the barn often to see the animals. She found Jim to be a talkative, witty Irishman who sang Irish songs as he worked around the barnyard. His friendly face with its ruddy complexion seemed to have a permanent smile affixed to it. No one could be around him long without having his spirits lifted.

Hannah was so engrossed in her thoughts that she didn't hear someone approach the brook. As she reached near the water's edge for a pretty flower, a voice startled her.

"Hannah! Don't get too close to the water!"

"Ben, you scared me. Why can't I get near the water?"

"An alligator might get you."

Her eyes grew large. "An alligator? No one told me."

"One swims upstream from the river occasionally. And you need to watch for snakes."

"Snakes?"

"Yeah . . . those long slimy things that slither through the grass. A water moccasin's bite will kill you."

"Don't scare me to death!"

"I'm sorry, but it's better to be scared now than dead later."

Hannah forced a nervous chuckle. "I suppose so."

"Don't you have snakes in Ireland?"

"No . . . I don't think so. I've never seen one."

"Well, you'll know one when you see it. Just don't get too close to it."

Hannah backed away from the water's edge. The flower there no longer seemed quite so pretty.

"Dad wants me to ride to the back side of the plantation," said Ben, "to make sure all the cotton was picked and everything's OK. Wonna go with me?"

"Ah . . . well . . . yeah. I mean yes."

Ben laughed. "You'll need to change," he said. "We'll be riding over rough ground."

"Change?"

"Yeah . . . your clothes. You can't ride there in a dress. Go change to pants, while I saddle the horses."

She felt the blood rush to her face. "I don't have any pants," she mumbled.

"Oh." He noticed the color of her cheeks. "What do you wear when it's freezing cold?"

"It doesn't get that cold in Ireland."

"It will in South Carolina and before too long. I'll see if I can find you a pair to wear today."

They climbed the stairs together, but she sat down on the top step and waited, while he went to his room. He returned with two pairs of denims that had faded after many laundries.

"See if these fit."

"I won't take your clothes." Her face blushed again.

"Why not? I can't wear them, and it'll be a long time before Otis grows into them." He held up a pair. "Put these on and meet me at the barn."

On the way to her room, she smiled at the thought of little Otis wearing his big brother's pants. As she pulled them over her hips and fastened them at the waist, she remembered the day she had worn Nathan's pants to climb the rigging of the *Monarch*. Ben's fit better and the length was just right. They weren't too large in the waist, but she thought they'd look nicer with something through the belt loops, so she laced a dark blue ribbon through them and made a bow in the front. She tucked in her blouse that had tiny blue and white checks and combed her hair, then tied it back with another blue ribbon. Before she left the room, she took a quick look in the mirror and realized that the blouse was the same one she had worn the first time she ate with Nathan. She reached for the gold locket on her dresser and gently brushed her fingertips across his lips and then touched them to her own. "I love you," she whispered.

By the time she reached the barn, Ben had one horse saddled. "How do they fit?" he asked.

"Perfectly." She held out her arms and twirled around.

"You sure look better in them than I did."

She smiled at him. "You're not as tall as Nathan," she said.

"What makes you think that?" He seemed offended.

"I had to roll the legs up when I wore his pants."

Ben cut his dark eyes at her. "Hannah, those would come halfway to my knees; besides, Nathan is older than I am."

"He's twenty-two. How old are you?"

"I'll be eighteen before Christmas."

"Then you still have growing to do."

He rolled his eyes, but said nothing. She'd never believe that he was as much a man as Nathan.

"Keep them," he said, "but you'll need new ones before cold weather because those are threadbare."

"Thank you for helping me, Ben."

Their eyes met. "You're welcome," he spoke in a low voice.

He handed her the saddled horse's reins. "Would you rather ride Bell," he asked, "or do you think you can handle Blaze?" He nodded his head toward a spirited horse that seemed to be having trouble standing still. The stall that restrained him appeared too small for the large black horse with a white streak down his face. He lifted his front feet from the barn floor and whinnied.

"No, I can't handle him. He's a beautiful horse, but I don't ride very well." She remembered how frightened she had been the night Sally and she rode the moonlit path and how she had clung to the horse with all her might.

"Don't worry. I wouldn't let you, anyway. That's Blaze and he's raring to go. It'll take a strong hand to hold him back."

Ben had a hard time getting the saddle on the big horse, but he wasn't afraid of him and in the end, he let him know who was boss. He tied his reins to a post and turned to help Hannah mount Bell. She lifted her foot to the stirrup, and he held her arm until she was seated in the saddle. He handed her the reins and asked, "Are you ready?"

"Yes." She made a clicking sound in her cheek.

Ben waited until she was out of the barn to mount the black horse, because he didn't want him to frighten the mare. "Calm down, Blaze," he said, but the horse kept pacing and he turned his head to and fro. When Ben failed to give slack in the reins, he made a swift turn in the barn and reared up on his hind legs.

With a tight grip on the reins, Ben let him go just enough to catch up with Bell.

"He wants to run," he said. "He hasn't been ridden much lately. There's a valley up ahead, and when we get there, I'm going to turn him loose." The horse reared into the air again, and Ben raised his voice. **"Whoa Blaze; settle down."**

Hannah made the mare go faster, and the horses galloped over the bridge and across the cotton field. Wind had scattered the dried cotton leaves and left only empty, brittle bolls that stuck out from shriveled brown stalks. Traces of dirty cotton with bits of crumbled dried leaves on it hung here and there from the empty bolls and made the field appear scraggly and ugly.

Beyond the cotton field, colorful leaves fell from deciduous trees that grew together over the trail. The horses' hooves trampled them on the ground. They came to the valley that Ben had spoken of, and the grass there was unusually green for October. Horses and cattle grazed on it.

"Will you wait here?" Ben asked. He still had trouble with the horse.

"Sure."

"If I let him run, maybe it'll wear him down."

Blaze felt slack in the reins and sprang forward. Ben let him go, and Hannah gasped with excitement, for she had never seen a horse run so fast. His legs blended together; she could not distinguish front ones from back ones. When Ben leaned slightly forward over the saddle, he and the horse appeared as one. He waved to her from the far side of the valley, and she lifted her hand and waved back. When they returned, the horse's black hide was shiny with sweat and some of the spunk had left him.

"I've never seen such a horse and rider," Hannah exclaimed. "You were both magnificent."

"Thanks." Ben petted Blaze's shiny neck. "He's a good horse," he said, "and maybe his manners will be better now." They both laughed and from then on rode side by side.

It was a long ride to the back cotton field, but when they reached it, they saw that all the cotton had been picked. The brown cotton stalks looked just as scraggly and ugly as the ones behind the barn. They rode to the backside of the field and stopped the horses on a ridge that overlooked a low marshy area that stretched to a line of timber in the distance.

"This is the rice fields," said Ben. "We plant in late April and harvest the rice in September. My dad grows it to make sure there will be plenty of food for everyone on the plantation, but before cotton, it was the main money crop in South Carolina and was known as Carolina gold. It thrives in the low land along the coast that's washed by the ocean tide. Do you see those trees in the distance?"

"Yes." Hannah nodded her head.

"They're on the border of our plantation."

"Oh, Ben," she realized the vastness of it, "how many acres are there?"

"My great-grandfather settled over a thousand acres, but some has been lost here and there as neighbors moved in. It's hard to keep up with it, exactly, but we try. That's another reason Dad has me to ride here occasionally; to make sure no one is living on it or running stock on it.

"There were three boys in his family, but both his brothers were killed in the revolution. Neither was married, so they joined up young, but my dad was just a child at the time. That's why he inherited all the land. He says it's too much for one family.

"My grandparents lived with us until they died. Grandma died when I was ten years old, but Grandpa just died last year. They're buried in the family cemetery near the house; I'll show you their graves when we get back. They never got over losing their sons, and both said their freedom came at too high a price. They hated the British."

"So did my father; especially wealthy ones."

"Then why you gonna marry one?"

He saw her mouth twitch slightly before she answered in a low voice, "Because I love him."

"That's good enough reason." He realized it was something hard for her to talk about and changed the subject because he wanted her to enjoy the day. "Are you hungry? I had Rosie pack us something to eat."

"Do you have enough?"

"Sure. I asked her to pack enough for both of us."

"How did you know I would come?"

"I didn't, but I hoped you would." He dismounted and took a blanket from behind his saddle and spread it on the ground.

"I'm glad you asked me. I've wanted a chance to tell you how proud I am of the progress you've made in school. Your marks are all good and I appreciate your hard work."

"The credit should go to my teacher."

"But you do the work and turn in all your assignments. Your writing could use some improvement. I plan for you to spend more time in that area."

"It could use a lot of improvement."

"I'm also very pleased with Emma and Emily's work and even little Otis has done his best. It's hard for him to sit still and his attention span is quite short, but he has learned the entire alphabet, and his counting is coming along."

"Otis is smart if you can get him to settle down."

"That will come with age."

Hannah sighed. "It's Charleen I'm concerned about. I just can't seem to find anything that will hold her interest."

"Have you tried boys?"

She chuckled. "They aren't in the category of school subjects, but perhaps it is her age. I must be patient."

"You are patient; more patient than any teacher we've ever had. I don't want to scare you, but Charleen is the reason our other teachers left. Had she not run them off, I would have finished school a year ago."

"Well, I don't intend to leave anytime soon, but I want all of my students to learn while I'm here."

"Don't worry about it." Ben dismissed the subject.

"Speaking of learning," said Hannah, "your mother told me that your great-grandparents were Huguenots. What does that mean?"

"Did you think it was something bad?"

"Well . . . no, but I don't know what the word "Huguenot" means. Even teachers must learn new words."

"I guess so. You probably don't know it because it's a French word. They were French Protestants who came to America to escape persecution."

"Then your parents are Protestants?"

"We all are."

"So am I. Where do you attend church and may we go tomorrow?"

"Hey, one question at a time, please, ma'am."

"I'm sorry."

"The nearest Protestant Church, or any church for that matter, is in Charleston, and as you know, a trip there and back takes the better part of a day. That's why we don't go during the busy season and not very often the rest of the year. We attend a Protestant Church and always go on Easter Sunday and at Christmas time if the weather's not too bad. We didn't go last Christmas because Mother was sick."

A scowl crossed Hannah's face and showed her disappointment. "My father and I went to church every Sunday in Ireland, and the captain held a Christian worship service each Sunday morning on the ship. I've missed not going since I've been here. Do you think we could start a Sunday morning service in your home?"

"Who would preach?"

"You."

"You're out of your mind!"

"Then your dad."

"Nope . . . I'm afraid not, and I don't know if he'll agree for you to have a service. If he does, you can preach."

"That would never do."

"Why not? You probably know the Bible more than any of us, unless it's my mother. She reads it a lot and is the one who led me to the Lord."

"I'm glad to hear that. Have you been baptized?"

"Not yet, but I know I'm saved through my faith in Jesus Christ. I want to be baptized."

"Then you will be. We'll just have to find a preacher and some water. Maybe someone will baptize you in the brook."

"Oh, no! Not the brook!"

Hannah had forgotten, but when Ben reminded her of the alligators and water moccasins, they both fell backward laughing.

When able to talk again, Ben asked, "Why can't you preach?"

"Because . . . I'm a girl."

"A very pretty one, but why is it a reason?"

"Preachers are supposed to be men; no one would listen to me. If your dad won't do it, then you'll just have to. We'll write your sermons in class; you admitted that you needed improvement in that subject."

"Hannah!"

"Please pray about it, Ben."

He didn't say anything for a moment, and she hoped that he thought about it. Finally, he nodded his head slowly.

With this promise, Hannah changed the subject. "You talk about your dad a lot," she said. "You learn more from him than you do anyone, don't you?"

"I guess so. He taught me how to plant and raise crops, but he doesn't know a thing about the ancient Greeks and Romans."

"He probably doesn't care, either," she laughed, "as long as he can grow a good cotton crop."

"That's right. He's anxious for me to go to college and learn improved ways of farming. He keeps saying, (Ben made his voice gruff) 'I'm gonna turn this plantation over to you one day.'"

Hannah laughed harder. "Is that what you want?" she asked.

"I don't know. I guess that would be the right thing to do, but . . . well, I don't know. We better head for home."

They mounted the horses and were back on the trail when Hannah remembered her trunk. "Ben," she asked, "do you think you could help me open one of my trunks? It seems to be locked, but I don't have a key to it."

Her trunk! He recalled Nathan's words, "I put something in

it that I don't want her to find until I'm gone." And he'd given him a key, but with the news of the war, he'd forgotten all about it. His hand reached to his forehead as he tried to remember what he had done with the key.

"Nathan gave me a key to the trunk," he said, "and asked me to give it to you after he left, but I forgot about it, and I don't remember what I did with it, but I'll find it. Why did you wait so long to ask me about it?"

"You were so busy during July and August, and then I forgot it. It's all right; I haven't needed anything out of it, but I wonder why he gave you the key instead of me."

"He put something in it that he didn't want you to find until he was gone. I asked him what it was, but he wouldn't tell me. He just said you would need help with it—whatever it is."

"What can it be?"

"I'll look for the key as soon as we get back. If I find it, we'll open the trunk after supper."

Ben and Hannah returned from the back land, but rode past the barn and house to the Rey family cemetery that was secluded by large oak and hickory trees that grew around it. A French wrought-iron fence surrounded the graves, and the letters R E Y had been forged in the ironwork across the top of its gate. Rust ate at the gate's black paint and it squeaked when Ben opened it.

He showed Hannah the graves of his great-grandparents, John and Eliza Rey, and then pointed out the graves of his grandparents. A solemn expression covered his face as he knelt and raked leaves from around their markers and pointed out the names and dates written on them.

"You loved them, didn't you?"

"Yes. They were good to me and taught me a lot about life. My grandpa taught me how to hunt and fish, but more than that, he taught me to have a strong faith in God, especially after Grandma died."

Hannah laid her hand on his shoulder. "I know how bad it hurts," she said. "I can't get over losing my father."

Ben rose from his knees. "When did he die?"

"Just before I left Ireland."

"I'm sorry. Did you leave your mother alone, or do you have brothers and sisters there?"

"No . . . I have no one. My mother died the night I was born, and I was their first child. My father never remarried, so we only had each other."

"I can't imagine what life would be like without my family."

"Well," she tried to smile, "you don't know what it's like if you've never had one. We better get back to the house; Rosie will have supper ready." The sun was low in the sky.

As they left the cemetery, Hannah noticed a large concrete angel in its front, left corner. It stood on a concrete pad and held a book with a ring of flowers around it. The angel's outspread wings came together in the back and touched the wrought-iron fence. Some vines had grown up on the outside of the fence and spread across the angel's wings and down the far side of them, making a secluded place underneath.

Ben waited for her to stop and look at the angel. "I like it too," he said. "Grandpa had it put here after Grandma died."

Back in the barn, Ben swung down from Blaze's back. "I'll take care of the horses if you want to go on to the house," he said.

"I'd like to stay and watch. I want to learn to do it myself."

"It's a man's job, Hannah, but you can watch if you want to."

He unfastened the two straps that held the saddle in place and pulled it from Blaze's back. It was lifted to a crosspiece between two posts, and then Ben removed the saddle blanket and folded it once before he laid it over the saddle. The bridle was pulled from the horse's face, and Ben gently removed the bit from his mouth, then gave him a pat on the neck. He made it look so easy and Hannah insisted that he let her try.

"All right, but be careful not to get under Bell's foot."

It took her awhile, but she finally got both cinch straps unfastened. She tried to lift the saddle, but it wouldn't budge, so she gave it a hard jerk and it frightened Bell and made her jump. When the horse jumped, the saddle fell from her back and knocked Hannah to the barn floor with it on top of her.

She couldn't see a thing with the saddle in her face, but could hear Ben laugh. He lifted it off her and pulled her to her feet. "I told you this was a man's job," he said.

"I got it off, didn't I?"

"Yeah, you did." He still laughed as he removed the blanket and bridle.

They walked across the barnyard together. Hannah stopped to pet Susie's neck and to say hello to her calf.

"Hello, Rosebud."

"Who named her?" Ben asked.

"I did. I've given them all names. The three lambs are Millie, Tillie, and Ellie." She pointed to each as she said their names.

"That won't do." A grin spread over Ben's face.

"Why not?"

"'Cause Ellie's a ram."

"Oh." Her face blushed. "I'll change it to Willie," she muttered.

Ben laughed and said, "Tell me all their names."

"The two pigs are Arnold and Abigail, and the other cow is Goldie. Sergeant is the gander and his mate is Sybil."

The rooster strutted around the corner of the barn with his cockscomb high in the air. "Did you name the rooster?" Ben asked.

"Yes. It was easy," she replied. "That's Beelzebub himself."

Ben laughed out loud. He knew the rooster had earned his name by waking her at dawn each morning.

Hannah glanced over the barnyard fence and saw that the sun was almost out of sight. "Why don't you go ahead, Ben? I'll be along in a moment."

"What's wrong?"

"Nothing. I'd just like a moment alone."

"Okay, but don't be long. Rosie can't stand to serve a cold meal."

As usual, Rosie had a good meal prepared. It consisted of hot cornbread with butter, mashed potatoes, black-eyed peas and ham. Hannah felt starved after the long ride with Ben and ate until she could not eat any more. She'd already gained back most of the weight she'd lost on the voyage, so her clothes were no longer too large. I must be careful with meals like this, she thought, or Nathan will find a plump lady when he returns.

All the Rey family sat around the supper table, and as usual, Otis squirmed in his chair. Catherine listened to the twins, and Hannah and Ben kept quiet, while Charleen complained about Reneka to Garrett. Garrett promised Charleen he'd talk to Reneka, and then he turned to Ben. "How did you find everything on the backland?" he asked.

"Everything was OK, Dad. Hannah rode with me, and we didn't see anyone or anything out of the ordinary. The cotton had been picked, and all the stock that I saw belonged to Reybrook. Blaze was awfully wild until I let him run it off. Hannah was impressed with the way he ran."

"Yes," Hannah agreed, "I think he could win any race." She remembered how her father and other men had raced their horses, just for fun, in Midleton.

"He's not a race horse, Hannah." There was a bit of sarcasm in Garrett's voice.

"But I didn't mean for mo . . . ." She stopped and was silent for the rest of the meal.

His dad had embarrassed her, and Ben tried to make her feel better by telling his family the names she had given the animals. When he told them the rooster's name, they all laughed, except Charleen.

"Hannah! Hannah! Hannah! That's all I ever hear anymore!" Charleen jumped from her chair and ran from the room.

Her outcry upset Hannah, and she lifted a napkin from her lap and placed it on the table by her plate. "May I please be excused?" she asked.

Catherine rose from her chair and followed Hannah out of the room. She called her name, and Hannah stopped at the foot of the stairs, but didn't turn around. Catherine walked behind her and laid a hand on her shoulder. "Please don't let Charleen upset you," she said. "It's her age, and . . . well, she was jealous that you and Ben had such an enjoyable day together."

"I'm all right, Catherine, but I'm sorry if I upset Charleen. Perhaps I should have meals in my room."

"I won't hear of that. As long as you live in this house, you'll be treated like family."

Hannah turned to face her. "You're so kind, Catherine."

"I'm glad you went with Ben today," she said. "I worry about him when he rides so far alone. Charleen would not have gone with him, had he asked her. I must talk to her about her selfishness."

"Please say no more about it. It would only make matters worse."

"All right; I won't this time."

It was dark when Hannah entered her room. She lit her lamp and then knelt beside her bed. "Dear God," she prayed, "please be with Charleen and help me to reach her as a friend. Forgive me, Lord, if I cause her unhappiness."

She had just sat down at her table to plan for the next school day when someone knocked on her door. It was Ben and he held a key up for her to see. "I found it in my top dresser drawer," he said. "I'm sorry I forgot about it."

Hannah reached for the key, but Ben held it higher. "I want to open it," he said.

"Okay." She pointed to the trunk.

He knelt beside it with one knee on the floor, and Hannah leaned over his shoulder. She couldn't wait to see what Nathan had left her. Ben turned the key in the keyhole and lifted the top of the trunk, but it was his eyes that lit up instead of hers when they saw what was inside. "Wow!" he exclaimed, as he lifted a shiny, new British-made rifle from the trunk. "Man, what I wouldn't give to own one of these! And there are cartridges to go with it."

"Well," Hannah sighed, "I don't know what in the world I'll do with it." She sat down at her table again. Ben saw how disappointed she was.

"Hannah, it's the best rifle money can buy," he stood and held the gun up to the light, "and with the war going on, you might need it." It was not the right thing to have said, he decided, from the look on her face. "I'll teach you how to use it," he tried again, "and you'll see the value of it." She was still disappointed. "I'd have to think an awful lot of a girl to leave her a gift like this." He knew he'd finally said the right thing when Hannah smiled.

"I know Nathan meant well, but I . . . I'm afraid of it."

"You won't be after I teach you how to shoot it. We'll take it to the riverbank and do some target practice. Hey, you can go hunting with me, and maybe you'll let me shoot it. I'm sure to get a deer with it."

"You may shoot it anytime you like."

When Ben laid the rifle back inside the trunk, he noticed an envelope tucked under the bag of cartridges. "There's something else," he exclaimed. "It's a letter from Nathan." He grinned and pretended to open the envelope. "You want me to read it, teacher?"

Hannah jumped from the chair and jerked the letter from his hand. "No," she answered. "And you may go now." She tore open the letter.

"Awe Hannah, let me read it."

"Will you please go," she laughed. She couldn't wait to read Nathan's letter . . . privately.

Ben was glad that something in the trunk had made her happy. He lowered its top and locked it again before he handed her the key. As he started to leave, he remembered something that he wanted to say.

"Hannah, don't let Charleen upset you. She only thinks of herself. We put up with her, but you shouldn't have to."

"Don't worry about it. I'm sure as she becomes more mature—"

"You never see anything bad in people, do you?" he interrupted her.

"I try not to."

She stood with Nathan's letter in her hand. Her face showed extreme anticipation of reading it. With his hand on the doorknob, he smiled at her. "Good night, Hannah."

"Good night, Ben."

As soon as he closed the door, Hannah took Nathan's letter from the envelope.

June 24, 1812

My sweetheart,

I don't know how long it will be before you open the trunk. Whether it's tomorrow, a month, or a year from now, I will love you. I will love you forever.

To leave you was the hardest thing I ever had to do in my life, but your promise to wait made it somewhat easier. I believe God will bring us together again. I know he did the first time, and would he have allowed us to meet only to cause either to suffer?

Ask Ben to teach you how to shoot the rifle. It's a good one. I hope you'll never need it, but if you do, I want you to know how to use it.

I love you, Hannah; I love you . . . I love you.

Nathan

CHAPTER 23

Beelzebub flew upon the barnyard gate and flapped his wings in the early morning breeze of October 23. As the rooster craned his long neck toward the heavens and sent forth his loud cock-a-doodle-do-o-o, Hannah sprang out of bed. It was the day of the barbecue.

Written invitations had been sent to other plantations and to friends in Charleston. The Rey family and their guests, plus all who lived and worked at Reybrook, would enjoy tender barbecued meats and fixings to go with them. It would be a day of feasting. Hannah dressed quickly and hurried downstairs.

Garrett and Catherine were already in the kitchen, overseeing preparation of the different meats to be roasted. Rosie and Reneka were cooking breakfast, and Hannah began to set the table in the dining room. Ben appeared in the doorway, holding his boots in one hand and looking sleepy-eyed. He sat down in a dining room chair, and as he pulled the boots over his heels, he thought how pretty Hannah looked in a tan-colored blouse with lace down the front of it. Its small round collar was also covered with lace and so were the sleeve cuffs that turned up just below her elbows. A dark brown skirt fit high over her slender waist, and its hem came slightly above her ankles.

"How did you manage to get up so early?" His voice was gruff.

"I'm excited about the barbecue," she replied. "Do you think lots of people will come?"

"Yeah." His mouth opened wide in a yawn. "They'll come; they always do."

The two of them ate breakfast with Catherine and Garrett, while Charleen and the three younger children slept. Garrett

341

talked about barbecues of the past when people came from all over the area, and Hannah became even more excited.

At sunup Ole Ramey and a slave called Big Bo came to the yard to dig a pit for the meat to be roasted over. Ole Ramey's five-year-old grandson, Sammy, sat nearby on the ground and watched them. Sammy's parents, Alicia and Nole, came early to help prepare the meats. Alicia was Ole Ramey's daughter, and like her father, was born and raised at Reybrook. She had helped with many barbecues and wanted her young son to learn how it was done.

Catherine turned the meats over to Alicia. A whole pig would be roasted along with a side of beef and some mutton. The aroma of a savory sauce drifted from the kitchen where Rosie tasted it to make sure it was just right before she gave it to Alicia to baste the meat with as it rotated slowly over hot coals of fire.

Hannah returned dirty dishes to the kitchen and cleaned the dining room table and then went outside and sat down beside Sammy.

"Hello, Sammy. I'm Hannah."

"Otis calls yo Mis Thonton."

"That's because I'm Otis's teacher."

"Wills yo teach me?"

Hannah was surprised at the young boy's request and didn't know how to answer. It was her nature to teach anyone who would listen, but did she have the right to tell this child she would be his teacher, while she was employed by Garrett Rey? How could she make a five-year-old boy understand that the answer would have to come from him?

She was concerned about Dolly and Julie Thomas and Jim MacMillan, who each had little education. Jim, raised in Ireland by Catholic parents, had been deprived as her father had been, and Dolly and Julie had poor parents in England who couldn't afford to send them to school. She feared that they wouldn't be able to get decent jobs when their contracts were fulfilled, and it would be easy for her to teach them to read and write and to work arithmetic.

Her first obligation, however, was to the Rey family. Garrett had been faithful to pay her the ten dollars each month to teach his children, but their school day ended at three o'clock in the afternoon. She would talk to him about evening classes for the servants and the slave children.

"I'm not sure, Sammy," she finally answered the little black boy. "I must speak to Mr. Rey about it."

By ten o'clock, people began to arrive, and Catherine and Garrett were kept busy greeting everyone. Most had brought a dish of food, and it was taken to a long row of tables that had been set up in the front yard. The weather was pleasant, so chairs were brought to the front porch where ladies gathered to talk of latest fashions or discuss summer plays they had attended at the Dock Street Theater in Charleston.

Charleen adorned the porch swing in a pretty dress made of heavy material. It had fall colors in it like the leaves that fell to the ground, and its long, full skirt stood out over ruffled petticoats. Her blonde hair had been combed back on top and was held with a dark-green velvet ribbon that brought out the same color in her dress. Long ringlets hung from a bow at the back of her head. *She really is a beautiful girl,* thought Hannah, and wished that her beauty could reach to her heart. She thought of Jason and how unhappy he would be, married to someone like Charleen. What if he and Nathan returned soon? Could she tell him of her selfishness?

Charleen suddenly sprang from the swing and ran down the front steps and across the lawn. A shiny two-seat carriage, pulled by a team of fine horses that were driven by a slave, ascended the hill toward the house. Before the horses came to a complete stop, a young man jumped from the back seat of the carriage, and with his hands at her waist, he picked Charleen up and swung her around in the air. It had to be the Lamberts.

"Oh, Frank!" Charleen shrieked.

An older gentleman stepped from the carriage and lifted his arm to a very well-dressed lady. A girl about Charleen's age stood on the carriage step and looked all around the yard. She seemed to be searching for someone.

Garrett and Ben crossed the yard to welcome the newly arrived guests. The girl on the step smiled at Ben and waited until he offered her his hand before she stepped down.

"Hello, Ben."

"Hi, Laci. You look nice."

"Thank you. I only came to see you."

"I find that hard to believe. Come on, I'll show you where everyone is." He took her to a corner of the yard where a group of young people had gathered, and to her disappointment, he left her there and returned to the pit.

Garrett escorted Laci's mother to the porch, and her father joined a group of planters who stood in the shade of the trees.

Hannah loved the excitement of the crowd. Most of the ladies wore fancy dresses and bonnets, but some had dressed in plainer clothing as Catherine and she had. Mrs. Lambert was, by far, the most exquisitely dressed.

From their nice carriage that was pulled by such fine horses and the way each of them was dressed, Hannah judged the Lamberts to be very wealthy.

Many people came; some from miles away, having left home before daylight. Others came from Charleston. The banker, Mr. Overteer, was there, and the reverend came with members of his church. The Reys' family doctor and a pharmacist brought their families.

Hannah played ring-around-the-roses with Emma and Emily and two other girls their age. They all giggled when she fell to the ground. Otis and Sammy made a London bridge and laughed when she stooped to her knees to crawl under it. The children ran off to play elsewhere, and she joined Catherine and other ladies on the porch. Catherine looped an arm through hers and introduced her to the others, saying how fortunate the Rey children were to have such a fine teacher. After she had met all the ladies, Hannah mingled among them with lemonade and tidbits of refreshments.

As last, Garrett rang the large plantation dinner bell. When a hush fell over the crowd, he called upon the Reverend Moore to ask a blessing of the food. Every head was bowed as the reverend thanked God for the abundant harvest that the planters had been blessed with that year. He prayed for those who were unable to be there because of sickness or some other misfortune, and he ended the prayer by asking God to bless the food that all were about to partake. Amens were heard throughout the crowd when the reverend finished.

A long line formed down each side of the tables, but there was plenty of food, so everyone enjoyed the company of the person next to him while waiting. Hannah remained on the porch with Dolly and Julie until the line shortened. She noticed how radiant Dolly's face became when Jim MacMillan joined them.

Julie spread a quilt upon the ground at the far side of the yard under the shade of an oak tree and then returned to stand in line with Dolly and Jim. When her plate was filled, she held it in one hand and something to drink in the other and went to sit upon the quilt, but Dolly and Jim went off to eat alone.

There was so much food that Hannah groaned, for everything looked delicious and she wanted to try it all. After filling her plate with as much as she possibly could and still expect to be thought of as a lady, she joined Julie on the quilt.

Slaves gathered on the back porch of the plantation home with their plates heaped high. After everyone else had been waited on, Ben served Ole Ramey and Big Bo and then Alicia and Nole, and they joined the others on the porch. Sammy had eaten with Otis, and the two boys now played down near the road.

After he'd helped himself, Ben looked around for Hannah's red hair that stood out in a crowd. As he approached the quilt where she and Julie sat, he asked, "May I join you?"

"Of course, Ben," Hannah replied, and she moved over to give him room to sit on the quilt. Julie nodded her head. She looked down at her food and ate silently, but Ben didn't seem to notice.

He hadn't been there long when Charleen came to join them with Frank and Laci. The three had been among the first to be served and were now finished with their meal. Laci sat down close beside Ben.

"Hello," Ben spoke. Hannah and Julie smiled, but both felt uncomfortable in the company of Charleen's friends who were dressed in the very best. Julie looked down at her faded skirt and blouse and her worn shoes. She was embarrassed and wanted to leave. Charleen made no attempt to introduce her friends to Hannah or Julie, as if they were unimportant. Ben stopped eating. "Frank and Laci," he said, "this is Hannah Thornton and Julie Thomas."

Frank flashed a big smile at Hannah and asked, "Where have you been hiding? At Reybrook, so Ben can keep you all to himself?" Ben saw Hannah's face blush and he noticed a toss of his sister's head. She was jealous.

"Hannah's engaged to be married," he mumbled.

"And who is the lucky man?" Frank refused to let the subject drop, and Charleen became more jealous.

Frank had directed his question to Hannah, and she opened her mouth to speak, but Ben quickly answered for her. "You don't know him."

"What a shame, as I'll not be able to arrange a duel for her hand."

Ben was annoyed at Frank's social conduct, but before he could say anything, his sister spoke up. "She's engaged to a British."

"Ah-h-h, so she's of our enemies."

"Well, I noticed you haven't enlisted to fight the British," said Ben.

"That's none of your business," Frank snapped.

"And it's none of your business whom Hannah's engaged to."

There was silence among them until Laci looked at Julie and asked, "Aren't you one of the servant girls?"

"Yes," Julie replied, and she stood to leave.

Ben reached for her hand and said, "Sit down, Julie; you were here first." He wasn't finished with his meal, but he set his plate to one side and looked at the three intruders. "Let's go for a walk down by the brook," he said. Charleen and Laci seemed delighted and each jumped to her feet. Laci wrapped her arm around Ben's, and the four of them left together.

Hannah and Julie were relieved; both knew why Ben had asked them to go. Hannah spread a napkin over his plate. She felt sorry for him, as he had not been able to enjoy his food after he'd worked all morning, but she and Julie continued to eat and to talk. They were surprised when Ben returned from the brook after being gone only a short time. He sat down on the quilt, picked up his plate, and began to eat without saying a word. There was blood on his right hand.

"Ben," said Hannah, "your hand is bleeding. Did you scratch it on something?"

"Na-a-a," he wiped the blood on the napkin she had covered his plate with. "It came from Frank's nose."

Hannah and Julie glanced at each other, but when Ben mumbled, "Somebody has to teach those Lamberts some manners," both girls laughed out loud.

The three enjoyed each other's company for the remainder of the meal, although Julie had little to say. Hannah left her alone with Ben and went for desserts. She returned with a pitcher of lemonade and a plate filled with cake, pie, and cookies.

When Ben finished eating, he lay back on the quilt and fell asleep. His fingers were locked together over his chest; they rose and fell as he breathed smoothly. His dark hair covered the top of his forehead and long black eyelashes rested on the upper part of his tanned cheeks.

Hannah leaned against the oak tree and closed her eyes a moment, but not wanting to seem rude to Julie, she opened them suddenly and saw that her eyes were fixed on Ben's face. "He's very handsome, isn't he?" she spoke softly.

Julie was embarrassed. She sighed deeply, but nodded her

head, then tilted it slightly backward and looked toward the
sky. There was a painful expression on her face.

Games were brought out and set up. Men tried to ring a
horseshoe over a stake in the ground, while ladies worked at hitting
a wooden ball through a series of hoops in a game of croquet.

Ben woke after a short nap and joined Garrett and other
plantation owners. He shook hands with Frank and apologized
to him. He's a southern gentleman, thought Laci, and will be a
perfect husband for me, one day.

In mingling with the guests, Ben talked to men from the
church where he and his family were members. He stopped to
chat with the Reverend Richard Moore.

"Ben," said the reverend, "I'd like to know how your mother
is doing. I know she was very ill for awhile and that it took her
a long time to recover. My wife and I spoke briefly with her on
our arrival, and she assured us that she was fine, but we want
to hear you or your dad say that she's all right."

"It's nice of you to ask, Pastor Richard. She seems to be all
right. She hasn't fainted lately and has regained most of her
strength. We appreciated the church's prayers for her."

"We shall continue to pray. Your mother is a very gracious,
Christian lady as I'm sure you're aware."

"Yes, sir, but thanks for saying it. By the way, I'd like for
you and Mrs. Moore to meet our new school teacher."

"We want to meet her." He darted off to find his wife.

"Hannah and Julie," said Ben, moments later, "I want you
to meet our pastor and his wife, the Reverend Richard Moore
and Mrs. Moore."

"Just call me Pastor Richard," said the reverend as he
extended a hand to both girls.

"And please call me Jane," added his wife.

Hannah was elated to meet them and was quick to ask their
opinion about establishing a church on the plantation.

"It would be a good thing," the reverend agreed, "but have
you spoken to Garrett about it? You'll need a place to meet,
and how will you provide for a pastor?"

"I'm hoping Ben will preach," Hannah replied. Ben had left them for other guests, and Julie picked up her quilt and went to help Rosie and Reneka clear the tables.

"He's just a boy," said the reverend.

"He's almost eighteen and more mature than most young men his age."

"Has he agreed to preach?"

"Not yet, but he agreed to pray about it."

The reverend seemed uncertain until his wife spoke up. She had no questions at all about the matter.

"I think it's wonderful that you want to start a church here," she said. "It's hard for the planters and their families to come all the way to Charleston to worship. If you have faith, God will provide a pastor and a place for you to meet. Isn't that true, Richard?"

"Well . . . yes, dear, of course." But the Reverend Moore was not quite as assuring as his wife, so Hannah changed the subject.

"Ben's mother led him to the Lord," she said, "and he wants to be baptized."

"We don't have a baptistery at the church, but we'll find a place. I'll talk to Ben about it."

"Thank you, Pastor Richard. I'm sure Catherine will be pleased."

"Will you come to Charleston soon?"

"I think so."

"Then I'll get some information together on how to start a church. Why don't you talk to Garrett, and we'll pray for Ben. God might use this young man in a mighty way."

Hannah walked across the lawn with the reverend and his wife to meet members of his congregation. When the pastor mentioned her desire to start a church at Reybrook, they promised to pray for her and some offered their assistance. Jane became excited. "Hannah," she said, "please come to see us every time you're in Charleston."

Suddenly the sun disappeared and dark clouds covered the sky. A strong gust of cold wind scattered leaves over the yard, and people began to hurry about, making preparations to leave.

Ladies scrambled for their dishes and quickly said good-bye. Hannah helped Dolly and Julie with the tables, while Reneka rounded up Otis and the twins to take inside. Ole Ramey and Big Bo came from the rear of the home and took what was left of the meat to the kitchen.

With the tables cleared, Hannah was about to go inside when someone walked up behind her and took her hand. Thinking it was Ben, she turned with a smile on her face, but it faded quickly when she looked into the eyes of Frank Lambert. She tried to free her hand, but he held to it.

"Please let go of my hand, Frank."

"I took a punch in the nose because I talked to you," he said, "and should get some reward for it. Will you come to our plantation next week and go riding with me? We raise beautiful horses."

"No, Frank, I can't do that. Ben told you I was engaged."

"So he did and to an enemy." There was sullenness in his voice.

Ben walked with Charleen to the Lambert's carriage. He held Mrs. Lambert's hand until she was settled on the front seat, and then he extended a hand to Laci. Suddenly he heard a loud voice in a deep Irish brogue.

"Let go o' me, Frank Lambert!"

Everyone who remained in the yard turned to see Hannah raise her right foot and give Frank a swift and powerful kick in the shin of his leg.

"Ouch," Frank yelled and limped away from her.

Ben kept a straight face. He was certain Frank's parents were embarrassed, and Laci became angry as her brother limped to the family carriage.

"Watch your step, Frank," Ben pretended to be helpful.

"Huh!" Frank retorted.

As soon as he was in the carriage, the driver turned the horses and they galloped down the hill and turned onto the main road. Only then did Ben bend over double, laughing, but Charleen lifted her chin and tossed her head in the other direction. She was furious.

She stormed past her parents and up the porch steps, and within seconds they heard the door to her room slam. Hannah stood quietly, not knowing what to say. She feared what Catherine and Garrett would think and was thankful that most of the guests had left before this happened.

"I'm afraid we'll hear more about this," Garrett said to his wife.

"It wasn't Hannah's fault," Catherine reminded him. "Frank should not have held her hand against her will."

"I know, but Charleen will have seen it differently."

"Garrett, I don't like Frank Lambert. He just isn't right for our Charleen."

"I agree, Catherine, but how can we tell her who is right or wrong for her?"

"I sure liked the young man who came with Nathan. I hope he comes back to see her."

"We can't think about that," said Garrett. "We're at war with England and he's on the wrong side."

"I know," Catherine sighed, "but he was such a nice young man."

He's on the wrong side. Garrett's words rang loud in Hannah's ears. If he thought that of Jason, he would think it of Nathan, and she realized that to the people around her, all British were enemies.

Catherine and Garrett climbed the front steps and disappeared through the door. Ben stood across the yard from Hannah and watched as she looked up at the sky. The wind blew strands of hair across her face and whipped her skirt against her legs. He heard a familiar sound and realized why Hannah looked upward. He lifted his own face and saw wild geese flying over in a perfect v-shape. He watched them for a moment and then crossed the yard to where she stood.

"We better go in," he said. "It's gonna rain. And wild-geese-going-south is a sure sign of cold weather. We need to go to Charleston soon to get you some warm clothes. I'm sure we'll need provisions for the kitchen with winter coming on, and maybe we can do some Christmas shopping."

Hannah nodded but bowed her head. Ben saw a tear on her cheek.

"I hope you didn't let someone like Frank Lambert upset you."

"No."

"Well, what's the matter?"

"Is it wrong," she asked, "to love an enemy?"

"No," he replied. "It's good to love an enemy."

"I do love him. I love Nathan."

"I know."

When more tears trickled down her face, he put his arms around her. She laid her cheek against him and sobbed silently. As raindrops began to fall, he felt her heart beating, and a twinge of pain went through his own.

CHAPTER 24

The first year into the War of 1812 brought little change for South Carolinians, and life went on much as it had in the past. When news reached them of bloody battles being waged in the Great Lakes, many realized it was a grim situation for the United States, but an occasional victory won on the high seas by some young and daring naval captain brought encouragement. Their own John C. Calhoun was a leader among the political "War Hawks" as they were called in Washington. The young "War Hawks" had convinced President Madison and Congress to declare war against England. The grounds—they said—were British impressment of American sailors and their arming of Indians against American settlers in the Northwest, but some believed that they had their eyes on Canada and were bound and determined to take it.

The war had come at a bad time for both countries. The British, long at war with France and heavily burdened with debts, took the United States' declaration of war against them as a stab in the back. After all, they fought Napoleon for all mankind.

The United States was totally unprepared for war. Thomas Jefferson, a man of simplicity, had been committed to keep the peace and spend little of the government's money, while he served as President before Madison; therefore, he did little to build a means of defense for his country. England held supreme power of the seas and maintained a large fleet of naval war ships, whereas the United States entered the war with a pitiful few.

Autumn turned to winter at Reybrook, and Hannah was thankful for warm clothing she'd purchased in Charleston. With Catherine's help, she was prepared for the cold north wind that blew in not long after the barbecue. Fires were lit in the large fireplaces throughout the home, and on most days, a small wood-burning heater kept her classroom warm and cozy. Nole replenished the woodbins daily and kept the fires burning until well into the night.

There was no fireplace in Hannah's room or any of the bedrooms except the master bedroom, but there was heat from the huge ones at both ends of the upstairs hallway. The house stayed fairly comfortable until the temperature dropped below freezing. On very cold nights, Emily and Emma snuggled together in order to keep warm. It was on such a night when something awoke Hannah from a deep sleep, and she realized that someone was at her door. She sat up in bed and called out "Who's there?" and heard the whimper of a small child and the pitter-patter of little feet on the floor. It had to be Otis.

He stood by her bed with a small blanket in his hands. "I'm cold, Miss Hannah" he said in a squeaky voice.

She quickly wrapped him in his blanket and tucked him underneath her warm cover and then cuddled him close to her until his small body stopped shivering. From that time on, Otis knew he had a warm place to sleep on cold nights.

When Reneka came to check on him the next morning and saw that he wasn't in his bed, she ran in and out of Charleen's and Ben's bedrooms and rapped on the door to Garrett and Catherine's room. "Miss Catherine," she called, "is Otis there?"

"No, Reneka; I'll be right out."

Ben was awakened by the commotion and realized that Otis was missing. He jumped from his bed and reached for his pants just as Garrett and Catherine ran from their room. He ran down the hall toward the narrow staircase and Reneka was halfway down the other, but Catherine darted into Hannah's room.

"Hannah!" she cried. "Have you seen . . . ?"

She stopped when she saw Otis's head on Hannah's pillow and that the two of them were asleep. Relieved, she tip-toed out of the room and announced that Otis was with Hannah. Reneka returned up the stairs, and the four of them gathered quietly at the foot of Hannah's bed to see Otis curled up in her arms.

Later, Hannah dressed Otis and held his hand as they descended the stairs and entered the dining room for breakfast. No one mentioned the incident until Ben came in. He tousled Otis's hair as he walked by his chair and said, "You gave us a scare this morning, little brother, until we found you in Hannah's bed." The smile on his face faded when Hannah's cheeks turned a pinkish red. He hadn't meant to embarrass her.

The wind whistled outside as Hannah and four of her students huddled around the wood-burning heater that morning. She had taken a blanket from the twins' bed and wrapped it around both girls' feet and legs. Otis's small blanket had been pulled from under the cover on her bed and put around him, while it was still warm. The three children sat at a small table that served as Otis's desk each day and had been pulled near the heater. Ben had pulled his desk near the heater, also, but Charleen had not come to class that morning.

Otis spent only half a day in class now that Hannah had decided—and Catherine agreed—it was torture to make him sit still for a longer period of time. Since it was a Friday and the weather was so bad, Hannah dismissed everyone early.

Ben lingered in the classroom. He pretended to read, but Hannah felt he had something on his mind, and when Emma and Emily left the room, she asked, "Did you have a question, Ben?"

"No, I just want to apologize if I embarrassed you at breakfast. I didn't mean to. It was nice of you to let Otis sleep with you on such a cold night. The little fellow has trouble keeping his cover over him, but if he bothers you—"

"Otis doesn't bother me. He doesn't bother me at all. He makes me feel needed, and I . . . I need that."

Ben studied Hannah's face. She seemed upset, and did she try to make him understand something? Something more than just the fact that Otis didn't bother her?

"We all need you, Hannah. You're the best teacher we ever

had, and you do a lot more than any of our other teachers did. You've been help to Mom, and she appreciates all the time you spend with Otis and the twins."

"Thank you, Ben. I wish Charleen liked me the way you do, but I can't seem to reach her. I want to be her friend, but more than that, I want her to have the education that your dad pays me to give her." She sighed and added, "I pray for her daily."

"Don't worry about Charleen. No one can change her."

"God can, Ben. God can change her. I must tell your dad that she skips classes and about her bad marks. He's agreed to meet with me in the morning, and I dread it."

"He won't be surprised. You want me to meet with you?"

"No, it's something I must do, and I plan to ask him about some other matters."

"What other matters?"

"I want to start a class for the servants and one for the slave children. I intend to ask his permission to establish a church on the plantation, and I want to buy my own horse."

Ben looked at her in amazement before she heard a chuckle deep in his throat. "Is that all?" he asked.

"Don't be facetious."

"Hannah, my dad doesn't like a lot of changes, especially all at once, and he won't allow you to teach the slave children."

"Why?"

"It's just not done in the South. I told you that when you came here. There's an unwritten law that southern planters don't educate their slaves. They're afraid if they do, they'll rise against them."

"I certainly don't want to cause a slave insurrection, but I can't believe that teaching a few children will make a difference."

"I guess it won't do no harm to ask, but when would you have time to do all of that?"

"I could teach the servants for a couple of hours at night, but the slave children must wait until next summer when you're out of school. It would be a good time, while their parents are busy in the fields."

"Well, good luck. I'll be around in case Dad gets violent."

Hannah tossed and turned in her bed that night, but at the exact time Garrett had agreed to meet with her, she stood beside his office door. She'd skipped breakfast, as this was her first parent-teacher meeting, and she was too nervous to eat.

"Good morning, Hannah," Garrett said politely as he opened the door to his office. "We missed you at breakfast."

"Thank you, Sir."

"Go by the kitchen when we're finished here, and Rosie will fix you something."

He pulled a chair to the side of his desk for her. "What did you want to discuss with me?" he asked.

Hannah sat down in the chair and looked him right in the eyes. She had decided, before hand, not to be intimidated by her students' father, even if he was her employer. "I'm concerned about Charleen's marks," she began. "She shows little interest in her school work and will not complete the assignments that I give her. Some days she doesn't even come to class. I can't justify giving her passing marks when she makes no effort to deserve them."

"I'll talk to her," Garrett replied. He dismissed the subject by asking, "Was there anything else that you wanted to talk about?"

"Yes, there are other matters that I wish to discuss with you, but I can't believe that you have dismissed one of such great importance so quickly."

Garrett raised his eyebrows at Hannah's retort. "I said I would talk to Charleen," he responded.

"What do you intend to do as a means of discipline?"

"Hannah, the way I discipline my daughter is of no concern of yours. Your job is to teach her."

Their eyes glared at each other. The conversation was not what she had expected. Perhaps she had expected too much.

"Very well, Sir."

"What else did you want to talk about?"

"I want to start a class for the servants and one for the slave children."

"Teaching the slaves is out of the question, and when would you have time to help the servants? I pay you to teach my children."

"I complete their classes by three o'clock each day."

"I expect the servants to work longer."

"I could help them at night, from six o'clock until eight o'clock."

Again their eyes glared at each other, but this time it was Garrett who gave in, at least about the servants.

"All right, do as you like at night," he agreed, "but leave my slaves alone."

Hannah was disappointed. She remembered Sammy's request, but would not push the matter further for the time being, but perhaps before summer . . .

"I talked to the Reverend Moore at the barbecue," she said, "about starting a church at Reybrook. He thought I should talk to you first."

"Well, I would hope so. Where do you intend to meet?"

"In your home."

"I won't hear of it!" Garrett raised his voice.

"I would think that you would be pleased to provide a place for worship of our Lord in such a large home." Without giving him time to answer, she asked, "May we meet in the servants' quarters . . . if it's all right with the servants?"

With more of a smirk on his face than a smile, he asked, "Are you going to preach?"

"No. Ben is."

Garrett laughed out loud. "Well, if you can get Ben Rey to preach, you may meet in the servants' quarters. There's a fireplace in the entrance; you may meet in front of it."

"Thank you. I need to ask one more thing."

"What is it?" He seemed irritated.

"I want to buy a horse of my own, and perhaps later, a carriage."

"What's wrong with Bell?"

"Nothing, Sir; she's a good horse, but she doesn't belong to me. I'd like to improve my riding skills on my own horse and saddle."

"A horse eats a lot of hay."

"I would ask that you deduct one dollar each month from my salary, for its keep."

"Do you have money to buy a horse?"

"Of course, or I would not have asked to buy one." The irritation was now in her voice.

Garrett's eyes glared at her again, but Hannah was exasperated and refused to look him in the face. She looked down at the floor and felt a strong desire to be out of his office and away from his presence.

"I'll think about it, Hannah." To her surprise, he spoke with more gentleness; perhaps he recognized her exasperation. Whatever the reason, she left the room without another word.

Ben was in the hall, and their eyes met, but neither spoke. He'd heard his dad raise his voice and saw the scornful look on Hannah's face as she hurried down the hallway and disappeared up the narrow staircase. Her door shut harder than usual. His dad remained in his office, and Ben was pulled between the two of them.

He went to the kitchen and asked Rosie to warm some of the leftover food from breakfast. When the food was ready, he put it on a tray with two cups of hot coffee and made his way to Hannah's room. He knocked lightly on her door, but there was no answer.

"Hannah," he called softly and opened the door slightly to see her sitting on the side of her bed with her head bowed. She didn't get up, but did acknowledge his presence.

"I'm here."

He opened the door wider and she saw the tray of food.

"I'm not hungry, Ben."

He ignored her remark and set the tray on her table, amid books and papers, and then placed a cup of coffee in her hands. She sighed and began to sip the coffee, while he stacked her school things on the floor and set a place for her to eat.

"Come eat something," he said in a cheerful voice. "It'll make you feel better." He sat down at the table with the other cup of coffee.

She realized he had gone to a lot of trouble to make her feel better. Only a good friend would do that, she thought, and made her way to the table. "Thank you, Ben. You're the best friend I've ever had."

At first, Ben kept quiet and drank his coffee. Like Nathan, he'd learned that it was hard for Hannah to talk when she was upset. Sometimes she needed to be alone, but he didn't think today was one of those times. The cold weather had kept her cooped up in the house too long and it would do her good to get out.

"It's warmed up some outside," he said. "If you want to, we'll take that new rifle down by the river, and I'll teach you how to shoot it. I'm dying to try it myself."

"All right, Ben," she answered slowly. "I do need to get out some today."

She was thankful that he said nothing about the meeting with his dad. Perhaps they would talk about it later after she had calmed down. When she finished eating, Ben took the dishes back to the kitchen.

She changed quickly to a pair of gray woolen slacks and slipped a red sweater over her head. She tied a plaid scarf around her neck and then pulled her black coat on over it. When she was ready to go, she opened the trunk and lifted the rifle along with the canvas bag that was filled with cartridges.

Ben returned to her door with a pair of old black boots in his hand. "These don't look too good," he said, "but I wish you'd put them on. They might keep you from getting a snake bite. They're some old ones of mine, but they're too small for me now. You may keep them if you want them."

She sat down at her table and pulled the boots on over her woolen stockings. They were a bit too large, but when she laced them tightly, they felt good on her feet. They felt warm.

"Are you ready?" he asked.

"Yes."

"There's a high place down by the river." He took the rifle from her. "Do you mind walking, or would you rather I saddle Blaze and Bell?"

"I'd rather walk."

By now the sun was high, and as Ben had said, the weather was much warmer than it had been for the last few days. It felt good to be outside in the sunshine after being in the small classroom all week. They walked down the hill to the road and up it a ways until they came to a trail that led to the riverbank. The trail was on higher ground, but to the right of them a swamp was filled with murky water out of which grew giant cypress trees.

The trees reminded Hannah that Nathan had said that the land was a shipbuilder's paradise. "Ben," she asked, "who owns this land by the river?"

"It's part of Reybrook. A little farther upstream is our dock where we load the cotton onto a barge that floats it downstream to the gin. I fish from the dock and usually catch a mess of catfish for Rosie to cook. Wanna go with me sometimes?"

"Sure." She laughed at his southern dialect.

"What you laughing at?"

"The way you talk."

"What about the way you talk?"

"I don't see anything funny about that."

"Of course not. Nobody from Ireland would."

She laughed, and he was glad. She seemed to have forgotten the unpleasant meeting with his dad, but he knew she would think of it again, later on.

Across the river was more marshland with cypresses that grew straight and tall. "Who does the land on that side of the river belong to?" She pointed to it.

Ben shrugged his shoulders. "I don't know. There's nothing but swampland from here to the Wando River. It would be of little use to anyone unless it was drained and the timber was cut. Why? You aiming to buy it?" He grinned, for he didn't think Hannah had any money except the small amount that his dad paid her each month.

"Are you being facetious, again?"

"No," he laughed, "but for what other reason would you want to know who the land belongs to?"

"I'm interested in the timber for building ships," she replied. "Do you think someone could buy it at a reasonable price?"

He realized that Hannah really did want to buy the swampland. "Yes," he answered, "I think someone could buy it at a very reasonable price. A banker in Charleston named Daniel Overteer could probably find out about it. I'll be glad to introduce you to him." She'd reminded him of how wealthy the person she was engaged to was.

"I already know him."

Hannah noticed a change in Ben's voice. It seemed too serious and almost hostile. He didn't speak at all as he looked for medium-sized rocks and placed them about a foot apart on an old log. When ten of them were lined up on the log, he loaded the rifle and raised it to his cheek. He shot three times, and three of the rocks were gone. He handed it to Hannah and she took it cautiously.

"Don't be afraid of a gun unless somebody points it at you," he said. "It's a useful tool, and you don't know what some men would give to own this one."

"I know you're right and I want to learn to use it."

He stood behind her and positioned the rifle against her shoulder. "Did you meet him at the barbecue?" he asked.

"Who?"

"Daniel Overteer."

"No. I met him at the bank in Charleston." She offered no explanation.

With his cheek against her hair, he put his arm around her and held her hand in his, and they lifted the barrel of the gun together. He told her how to take aim by lining up the front sight and the rear sight with one of the rocks on the log. He then showed her how to place the first finger of her right hand on the trigger. Her hands were shaky, but he tried to steady the rifle and told her to squeeze the trigger gently. Just as the gun went off, he noticed her eyes were closed tightly. She missed the target.

"Hannah! You gotta keep your eyes open."

"I'm sorry."

"Let's try again."

It took the third try before Hannah was able to fire the rifle without closing her eyes, and even then, she missed the target several more times. Each time, however, it became easier for her until she was able to hold the rifle steady. They were both thrilled when the first rock exploded into tiny pieces.

"Hey, you hit it!" Ben was as proud as she was when she accomplished the task he had set out to teach her to do. As a teacher, she knew how he felt.

"Thank you, Ben. You have taught me something that I might never have learned without your help. You're the teacher today and a very good one."

"I couldn't have taught you, had you not put some effort into it."

"I know. Can you understand how frustrating it is to try to teach someone something when they put forth no effort to learn it?"

He knew Hannah referred to Charleen and that she thought of the meeting with his dad. He hadn't intended to say anything about it, but since she had brought it up . . . He sat down on the log and removed the rocks to make room for her to sit beside him. Neither of them saw the snake that had emerged from the swamp and lay basking in the sun near the trail.

"Yeah, I do understand," he said, "and I've tried to talk to Charleen, but she won't listen. My dad understands, too. He knows you're a good teacher and that Charleen is missing an excellent opportunity, but he just doesn't know what to do about it. He and Charleen have always been close, the way Mom and I are, and because of this, it's hard for him to discipline her. I think he feels sorry for her, being the age she is and having no young people to associate with. The only boy she knows is Frank Lambert."

"She knows Jason Williams."

"Yes, and she really liked him, but doesn't believe he'll ever come back. I think if she knew he would, she'd be content to wait for him."

"The way I wait for Nathan?"

He nodded his head and turned to look at her. "You love him a lot, don't you?"

"Yes."

"What will you do if he never comes back?"

"I don't know; I don't like to think about it."

"You could stay here."

"I don't think so. I believe your dad will be glad when he is rid of me."

"Hannah, my dad's not so bad. You just don't understand him or plantation life. The planter is responsible for the welfare of everyone on his plantation, and he must consider every aspect of something before making a decision. Dad talks things over with Mom."

"Well, I believe that a church would be a good thing for everyone here."

"Did he say you couldn't start one?"

"Not exactly, but he said we couldn't meet in your home. He laughed and said that if I could get you to preach that we could meet in the entrance of the servants' quarters. He only gave his permission because he doesn't believe you will preach. You will, won't you, Ben?"

Ben looked down at the ground and was silent; he knew Hannah waited for an answer, and after a moment, he drew in a deep breath and let it out slowly before he spoke. "To preach God's word would be an awesome responsibility," he said. "It's not for just anyone. I ask myself how I would know what God wanted me to say, and what if I didn't get the facts just right; yet something inside of me won't let me say no."

"You're not just anyone, Ben. You're good and honest and have love in your heart. If we study God's word and pray, He'll give you a message."

"I have prayed about it and wrestled with it, and if that's the only way my dad will let you meet, I'll try, but you'll have to help me."

"I will. We'll read the Bible together, and I'll help you write your sermons. It'll be good practice in reading, and you'll learn new words to improve your writing."

"Maybe it will help."

"Ben, I'm glad you helped me understand Charleen, and I'll try to do more things that she is interested in. I'll visit the public schools in Charleston to see if there are special activities that she can take part in, and we'll go to the public library and places where she can meet other students her age. It would be a good thing for both of you, and perhaps we can have something for everyone, here on the plantation."

"Sounds like a lot of extra work for you."

"It will be worth it if I can get Charleen interested in school."

"If your arms are rested, let's see if you can shoot this rifle without my help." He stood up and put the rocks back on the log.

Hannah raised the gun and took careful aim. She hit five out of seven rocks, but wasn't satisfied with that. She leaned the gun against a tree and went closer to the riverbank to look for more rocks. There was one just the right size in the leaves by the trail, but when she reached for it, something jumped from the leaves and darted at her hand. She screamed and Ben was filled with terror. He grabbed the rifle and quickly raised it to his cheek as a poisonous water moccasin slithered toward the river.

He knew there was no cure for its deadly venom, and one's only chance was to make a cut, where bitten, and try to get the blood out before it spread to the rest of the body. He shot the snake's head off and then threw the rifle to the ground and grabbed Hannah's arm.

"Where did it bite you?" he yelled. His other hand reached into his pocket for a knife.

"It didn't," she said.

"Where?" When he saw no place on her hand or arm, he took her other hand, for panic overpowered him and kept him from hearing.

Hannah pulled both her hands back. "The snake didn't bite me, Ben. I'm okay." His face was as white as a ghost, and his hands shook like leaves on a windy day.

"Ben," she said louder, "I'm okay."

When he understood that the snake had not bitten her, he pulled her close to him, and she felt his body trembling.

"Oh, Hannah," he groaned in her ear. "Oh, Hannah." It was all he could say as he held her head to his chest, and then his arms went around her.

She let him hold her for a moment, as he seemed compelled to do so. He breathed hard and pressed his cheek against her head. She tried to escape his arms, but he continued to hold her until he heard her soft voice say, "Ben, please." Only then did he let go.

"I'm sorry I screamed and scared you, but the snake did try to bite me, and it frightened me so badly—"

"You did what any girl would have done. Just be careful where you put your hands from now on."

Ben managed to calm down, but Hannah thought there was something different about him. She picked up the bag of cartridges and put it over her shoulder. "We better go," she said.

He lifted the rifle from where he had thrown it. There was little talk between them on the way home, and that night when the family gathered around the table, Hannah kept silent when he related to them how close she had come to being bitten by the poisonous snake. Catherine was horrified, but Charleen chuckled to herself. Since Hannah was so afraid of snakes, she thought of what she could do to get even with her for the lecture she had taken that afternoon. She'd show Hannah that to tell her dad about her bad marks was not a safe thing for her to do.

That night Hannah lay in bed and thought of all that had happened that day. The meeting with Garrett had been a great disappointment, but all was not lost. Through it and her conversation with Ben, she had gained a greater understanding of Garrett and Charleen.

Perhaps the servants' quarters would be a better place for the church to meet; she tried to be optimistic. It was between the big house and the slave quarters, and the slaves might attend the service, whereas they would never come to the big house. And as for owning her own horse, she would give up the idea. It had been selfish of her to think of it.

She turned to her side, but before she fell asleep, she saw the tall and straight cypress trees that grew out of the marshland. Did she dare to spend the money that Nathan had left for her, so he could have the timber to build ships with when he returned from the war? She would think of it tomorrow, she decided, and her eyes closed.

Three doors down the hall, Ben lay on his back with his hands under his head and thought of how close the snake had come to biting Hannah. After the way he felt when he thought she had been bitten, there was no denying it anymore. He was in love with her. He closed his eyes and relived the incident, but in his dream, instead of trying to escape him, Hannah circled her arms around him and he lowered his lips to hers.

CHAPTER 25

It was almost Christmas. Hannah stood at her bedroom window and watched snowflakes fall from the sky. She looked beyond the leafless woods to the cotton fields where new fallen snow covered the ground. It was the time of day when she usually watched the sun sink, but a thick layer of clouds prevented it from shining. The dismal weather, however, did not keep her from thinking of Nathan. She longed to see him.

It was the kind of evening when she liked to curl up in bed with a book to read, but instead, she put on her coat and wrapped a woolen scarf over her head. With books and papers in her arms, she left the house by the back door and walked gingerly across the frozen ground to the servants' quarters.

A fire burned in the large fireplace at one end of the long entrance room, and she stood near it a moment. This was where she met with three students each day, Monday through Friday, from 6 P.M. until 8 P.M. Sometimes they continued until 9 o'clock. All three students were usually seated around a table that stood in front of the fireplace when she arrived, but she had come early tonight, as she hoped to leave early. She took off her coat and scarf and hung them on a peg by the door, then picked up a twig that had fallen to the hearth, but still burned on one end, and lit a lamp that stood in the middle of the table.

It was the same table that she sat at each Sunday morning and taught a Bible study before Ben preached. While she waited, she thought of that first Sunday when only a few had gathered to worship. Everyone on the plantation had been invited, but only nine showed up that cold November morning.

Catherine had come with the twins and Otis, but to her disappointment, neither Garrett nor Charleen came with them.

Rosie and Reneka had come together, and just as Ben stood to preach, Julie stepped from her room and sat down beside Reneka.

Ben had done an excellent job of preaching his first sermon, although it lasted only fifteen minutes. He had not been nervous in front of the small congregation, and after the service, Catherine let him know how proud she was.

"I wish your dad had come," she said.

"Maybe he will next Sunday," Ben was hopeful.

As of yet, however, neither Garrett nor Charleen had attended a service, but those who came that first Sunday returned the next, plus the Leanders and Dolly and Jim. Hannah hoped that by spring everyone on the plantation would attend each service. Being so engrossed in her thoughts, she was startled when Julie opened her door.

"Hannah! We didn't know you were here. Have you waited long?" She hurried to tell Jim and Dolly.

When the three were seated around the table, Hannah began to read from a small book that was easy to read. She read a couple of paragraphs and then let her students read from the book until it was finished. They each wrote a short summary of the story.

Arithmetic was taught during the last thirty minutes of each class. Addition and subtraction had come easy for each of them, but Dolly and Jim had trouble with multiplication and division. Hannah was amazed at how quickly Julie caught on to everything. She was bright and eager to learn; it was a joy to teach her.

Hannah gazed into the fire and watched it burn down as they worked the problem she had given them. It was eight o'clock, and she was anxious to leave because she felt uneasy about walking home alone in the snow.

"Julie, will you please stand," she asked, "and explain the problem?"

While Julie explained the problem correctly, the door suddenly flew open, and to everyone's surprise, Ben stepped through it and shut it quickly behind him. They all turned their heads to look at him and he smiled awkwardly as if he didn't know what to say. Hannah crossed the room and asked quietly, "Is something wrong, Ben?"

"No," he whispered. "I came to walk you to the house."

"Please give me a moment."

She returned to the table and asked Julie to continue.

"Uh . . . well . . . I . . ." Julie could no longer think, and she gave Hannah a dreadful look. Dolly picked up where she had left off and explained the problem. As soon as Dolly finished, Hannah dismissed the class, and Julie went straight to her room. She usually gathered the books and papers for her, but tonight, Dolly did it.

Hannah was puzzled at Julie's behavior and wanted to talk to her, but she would not keep Ben waiting. He took her books and papers and they left together. Before they stepped from the porch into the snow, he linked his arm through hers.

"I'm glad you came, Ben. I was afraid to walk home in the snow, alone, but I'm sorry you had to come out on such a cold night."

"I didn't have to. I was afraid you might slip and fall on the frozen ground. I worry about you every night and never go to sleep until I hear you come in. It's not safe for you to be out alone after dark."

"It's such a short distance, but I don't want you to worry. If it will make you feel better, I'll ask Jim to walk me to the back door."

"It would. I would come for you every night, but I don't know what time to come. You never get home at the same time."

The snow had stopped falling, but a thin layer of it on the ground made the night almost as light as day. Hannah walked close beside Ben, for the temperature was well below freezing, and a cold wind chilled her to the bones. He stopped suddenly. "Shhh," he whispered.

She looked in time to see a tall figure jump from the back porch and dart across the yard toward the barn. As they stood motionlessly, the back door opened and revealed a dim light for an instant and then closed again. Two people had left the porch quickly when they saw the two of them on the trail.

Ben tightened his grip on Hannah's arm and hurried her to the back door and inside the house. Not until the door was locked did they stop to catch their breaths. They climbed the dark stairway at the end of the hall and found that a fire still burned in the hall fireplace. It gave light and some warmth in Hannah's room. While she hung her coat and scarf in the armoire, Ben laid the books on her table and lit her lamp.

"Ben, who ran across the back yard?"

"Big Bo, and I hate to think what he might have done to you, had you been alone. I might have found you lying on the trail with your throat slit." It was a harsh thing to say, but he wanted to impress on her the danger of being out alone at night.

"Big Bo is always on the prowl," he said, "and some say that he never sleeps. He hunts at night for rabbits and coons, and if he catches something, he starts a fire and cooks it right then. Most planters wouldn't allow slaves to roam about at night, but Dad says he does no harm."

Her hair gleamed in the soft light of the flickering lamp. The tip of her nose was red from the cold, and her eyes were wide with fear. Her lips were parted; she looked like a frightened child. Ben wanted to take her in his arms and tell her that everything was all right, but he couldn't. He couldn't forget that she belonged to Nathan. He lifted his hand and gently rubbed the back of his fingers up and down her cheek. "I better go," he said. "Please talk to Jim tomorrow."

"I will," Hannah promised. "Thanks for coming for me." She seemed anxious for him to leave.

Hannah was cold and exhausted, and as soon as Ben left, she quickly undressed and slipped a warm flannel gown over her head. Before she blew out the lamp, she pulled the cover back on her bed . . . . A terrifying scream escaped her lips when a long black snake slithered across the white sheet. She dropped the cover and tried to run, but couldn't. Like in a bad dream, she could neither move nor make a sound. As consciousness left her, she fell to the floor and her head hit hard against it.

Everyone in the household heard Hannah scream. They froze for a second, but then realized that it came from her room and sprang into action. Everyone—except Charleen—who sat in the middle of her bed . . . smirking.

Ben reached Hannah first and found her collapsed on the floor. Catherine and Garrett were close behind him and all three knelt beside her.

"Ben, what happened?" Garrett demanded to know.

"I don't know! I just left her a few minutes ago, and she was fine." He lifted her head and felt a large lump on the back of it. "Mom," he said, "feel of this."

Catherine's hand gently touched the back of Hannah's head. "Oh, Garrett," she moaned, "this is bad. What could have happened?"

Otis and the twins peered through the doorway, but were held back by Reneka. Rosie ran across the hall to the washroom and quickly returned with a wet cloth. Hannah stirred when Catherine wiped her face with it.

"Hannah," Catherine spoke affectionately, "can you tell us what happened?" She folded the cloth and held it to the lump on the back of her head. Hannah groaned, but she didn't speak.

Ben and Garrett stood and began to look around. Ben noticed that the cover on Hannah's bed was pulled back, and it had not been when he left her room. Suddenly the cover moved.

"Dad, look!"

Garrett nodded his head; he had seen it too, and both felt sure they knew what was underneath the cover. Ben stepped to the window and opened it, while Garrett went to the fireplace for a fire-poker. With one at each side of the bed, they slowly pulled the cover back until they saw the tip end of the snake. Aiming at what he thought was its head, Garrett raised the heavy poker and whopped it hard, but he didn't kill it, and it wiggled out from under the cover.

"It's a king snake!" shouted Ben. And since it wasn't poisonous, he grabbed it at the back of its head and slung it far out the window. The cold air helped Hannah regain consciousness and she sat up, but felt an awful pain in her head. Ben closed the window and knelt beside her.

Garrett and Catherine took everything off the bed to make sure there were no more snakes. Garrett lifted the lamp from Hannah's table and looked under her bed and under everything else in the room.

The bed was made with fresh sheets, and as Ben lifted Hannah from the floor, he assured her the snake was gone.

Her head hurt badly, but she lay back on the pillow and listened as Ben and Garrett talked.

"Do you have any idea how that snake got into Hannah's bed?" Garrett asked.

"Yes, sir. I know exactly how it got there. Who didn't bother to come see what happened?"

"If you mean Charleen, she's scared to death of snakes and wouldn't touch one."

"She didn't have to. Big Bo—"

"Shhh." Hannah made a faint sound.

"What about Big Bo?" Garrett demanded to know.

Ben looked from his dad to Hannah and saw a slight shake of her head.

"Well . . . I don't know," he said. "Maybe Charleen didn't do it." But he knew that she did and that Big Bo had captured the snake for her.

Garrett left the room, and also felt, deep down, that Charleen had something to do with the snake being in Hannah's bed, but she would never own up to it and how could he accuse her if he had no proof. What if he was wrong? But what if he was right? This was a very serious thing, and if Charleen had anything at all to do with it . . .

Hannah lay on her side, for she felt an awful pain at the back of her head. She was suddenly overcome with drowsiness and wanted everyone to leave her room, but she heard Ben say,

"Mom, why don't you go to bed? I'll sit with Hannah awhile longer to make sure she'll be all right."

"What would I do without you, Ben? You're so good. We raised all of you the same way; how could one have turned out to be so . . . so . . . ?" Her voice cracked and she covered her face with her hands.

"Come on, Mom. Let me help you to your room." Ben's voice was so kind.

Before she left, Catherine leaned over and caressed Hannah's cheek. "I'm so sorry," she moaned.

Tears glittered on her face and Hannah reached for her hand. "I'm all right," she whispered.

Catherine leaned on Ben's arm as she walked slowly down the hallway. Her shoulders were stooped and there was an awful ache in her heart. Garrett sat on the side of their bed; he took her in his arms and Ben slipped quietly out the door.

He returned to Hannah's room and found her asleep. He listened to her breathing, and as far as he could tell, it was normal; her chest rose and fell steadily. He carefully rubbed his hand over the back of her head, and then he sat down at the foot of her bed to think. There was no doubt in his mind that it had been Charleen at the back door with Big Bo. Big Bo would do anything for money, but he wondered what he had put the snake in to deliver it. His dad was right; Charleen would never touch one.

Since Hannah was asleep, he took her lamp and walked the hall to his sister's room. Her door was partially opened, and he heard her breathing deeply, so he tiptoed into the room and lifted the side of her bed cover. Just under the edge of the bed, where she barely had time to toss it, was a thick burlap sack. Chicken feed came in it, and there were plenty of them lying around the barn. He pulled it from underneath the bed and took it to Hannah's room and stuffed it behind her armoire.

He now had the evidence he needed to convince his dad that Charleen was guilty of putting the snake in Hannah's bed. But why did Hannah not want him to tell? For the time being, he would abide by her wish and hold his tongue. Perhaps she was afraid of what Charleen might do next.

The fires went out at each end of the hallway, and the house became very quiet. Everyone was asleep, except Ben, and when his head began to nod, he thought he might as well go to bed. Hannah seemed to be all right. He was about to leave when she stirred and he heard her groan.

Hannah opened her eyes, and between her and the lamp on the table, she saw the silhouette of a figure at the foot of her bed. Everything seemed foggy and she wasn't sure where she was. Who was the person at the foot of her bed? When she was a little girl, she remembered, her father would sit there when she was sick. If she was very sick, he would sit there all night long.

"Father?" she questioned.

Ben thought she was not completely awake, but she tried to determine in her confused mind, where she was and who was in her room. Was she on the *Monarch?* Was this Nathan?

"Nathan?" She was so confused about everything. "Nathan, why are you in my room?"

"Hannah . . . I'm Ben. You fainted and hit your head on the floor. We were afraid to leave you."

"Oh, Nathan, you always take care of me. I love you."

Ben realized she wasn't thinking straight. She thought he was Nathan and didn't hear a word he said. What should he do?

"Please hold me, Nathan," she pleaded.

He sat down beside her and put his arms around her. Her lips found his and he kissed her, gently at first, but as her lips became more demanding, he kissed her harder, and for a blissful moment he let himself forget what had happened and kissed her with all the love that he had in his heart for her. He pressed his body against her and was enthralled in the sweetness of her lips until she withdrew from him. A faint groan escaped her throat, and she laid her head on his shoulder and went back to sleep. He held her a moment longer, not wanting to let her go, but when he felt the gentle rising and falling of her breasts on his chest, he carefully laid her back on the pillow.

He returned to the foot of her bed and leaned over with his elbows on his knees and ran his fingers through his hair. His heart beat rapidly. He clasped his hands together to make a fist, and his face flinched with pain as he pressed his forehead hard against it.

Hannah loved Nathan and would marry him if he returned for her. If he didn't return, she'd be heartbroken and might never get over him. He wished he'd not promised him he would take care of Hannah, because he no longer did it—for Nathan.

Hannah's mind was clear when she awoke the next morning, and she thought she had dreamed that she saw Nathan and kissed him in the night. Catherine insisted that she stay in bed a couple of days, but with so much to do, she was up on the second morning and back in the classroom. The incident was not mentioned and Charleen gloated, as she thought no one had suspected that she put the snake in Hannah's bed, but she wondered what had happened to the burlap sack that she'd tossed under her bed hastily.

Ben told Hannah about the sack. "I want to show it to Dad," he said, "and I think we should tell him that we saw Big Bo at the back door just moments before you found the snake in your bed."

"I don't think it would do any good, Ben, and might tend to make matters worse." Hannah remembered how quickly Garrett had dismissed the subject of Charleen's bad marks. She looked at Ben and quoted a scripture. "But I say unto you which hear, Love your enemies, do good to them which hate you. Bless them that curse you, and pray for them which despitefully use you." (Luke 6:27-28).

"Even when they put a snake in your bed?"

"Yes, Ben. Even when they put a snake in my bed."

Hannah gave her students a week off from their lessons to enjoy the holidays, and it gave her time to help clean and prepare the plantation home for the festivities. Ben and Garrett cut down a six foot tall pine on the plantation and set it up in the living room. Hannah helped the twins and Otis make paper decorations for it, and Charleen and Catherine got out store-bought ornaments. That evening when the family gathered in the living room, Ben lifted Emily to the very top of the tree with an angel in her hand.

Ben had grown taller in the six months Hannah had been at Reybrook. He was now as tall as Nathan. He seemed more mature than his eighteen years, and tonight he looked especially handsome in a long-sleeved plaid shirt and black pants. The top button of his shirt was unbuttoned and his sleeves were rolled a couple of turns.

Hannah's attention was diverted from the Rey family when she noticed Julie at the end of the hallway. Julie's head peeped around the staircase banister and she watched as Ben lifted Emily to the top of the tree. She had spent the day in the kitchen, helping Rosie with Christmas baking, and was ready to return to the servants' quarters.

The angel was set in place. The Christmas tree had been made complete and it was beautiful. Ben lowered Emily to the floor, and Hannah turned back to Julie, but she was gone. Hannah heard the back door shut and decided to follow Julie to her room in the servants' quarters. She found her lying across her bed, weeping as though her heart was broken. She crossed the room and sat beside her. Julie was startled; she'd not realized that Hannah followed her. She sat up quickly and wiped her eyes with her fingertips.

"Julie, what's wrong?"

"Nothing." She pretended to be all right.

"Come now, one doesn't weep tears like this over nothing. Tell me."

"I'm fine, really," Julie insisted.

But Hannah knew that something was wrong. "All right," she said, "if you won't tell me, I'll have to guess. I think you're in love with Ben."

"Oh, no, Miss Hannah!"

"Julie-e-e . . ."

Julie hid her face in her hands and began to weep again. She spoke between sobs, "Please . . . Miss Hannah . . . you must not tell . . . anyone."

"Why?" Hannah asked cheerfully. "I think it's wonderful that you're in love with Ben. I think he needs to know."

"Oh, please promise me that you'll never tell him. It's not proper that I should love him, for I'm just a servant girl and he's the plantation owner's son. I shall die if he finds out."

"Julie, I was on my way to Reybrook as an indentured servant, when I met Nathan, and he let me work on his father's ship to pay for my passage across the ocean." The two girls had a long conversation about all that they had in common. Suddenly Hannah realized it was almost dark outside.

"I must go." She jumped to her feet.

"Why?" asked Julie.

"Ben doesn't like for me to be out after dark."

"Good-bye, Hannah," Julie muttered. A pain pierced her heart.

Hannah ran down the trail and up the back porch steps. She closed the door and leaned against it to catch her breath just as Ben came down the hallway.

"What's wrong?" he asked.

"Nothing."

"Where you been? I thought you were upstairs." He walked past her and into the kitchen.

"I've been talking to Julie."

"What about?" he called from the kitchen.

Hannah didn't answer and hoped he wouldn't ask again. He walked out of the kitchen with a glass of milk in one hand and a handful of cookies in the other.

"Well," he said, and offered her one of the cookies.

"Well, what?" She reached for the cookie.

"What did you talk to Julie about?"

She looked into his dark eyes as she raised the cookie to her mouth. "I can't tell you," she said.

"Okay." Ben shrugged his shoulders as though it was of no concern to him.

Hannah bought Christmas gifts for everyone. They were wrapped with pretty ribbons around them and were ready to be placed under the tree. She'd spent most of the money that Garrett had paid her, but the Reys had taken care of her every need, and she saw Christmas as a chance to do something for each of them. It made her feel like part of the family.

For Otis, she had purchased a set of large and colorful building blocks with numbers on one side and letters on another. For Emily and Emma were two small slate boards with chalk and eraser for each. She spent more on Charleen, hoping to win her friendship, and bought her a new bonnet and muff that matched; each was made of a soft furry material in a light brown color.

It was hard to decide on something for Catherine. She wanted something special, because Catherine was special, yet she wanted something personal. She decided on a blue silk dress with tiny white flowers and a white lace collar. She hoped Catherine would like it.

She'd noticed that Ben and Garrett needed new belts and had purchased leather ones for both. Each belt had a plain small buckle, and she knew it would be fine for Garrett, but when she found a large silver one with a horse's head on it, she bought it for Ben and wrapped it in a special box. The gift would not be put under the tree; she would hold it until after he opened the belt.

She spent more on the Rey family, but didn't forget the servants and slaves. For Dolly and Julie, Rosie and Reneka, new shoes with warm knee socks were wrapped. Jim got new denims, and she thought the Leanders would appreciate a new blanket.

Alicia and Nole and Ole Ramey also got blankets for their beds, but Sammy would receive buildings blocks; the same as

Otis. For other slave families, Hannah prepared a basket of food to be delivered Christmas morning.

She rose early on Christmas Eve to help Catherine with last minute preparations.

"Hannah," said Catherine, "I don't know how I got everything done before you came to Reybrook. You're so much help with the children and the housework. It gives me time to rest. Garrett thinks I should make the servants and slaves do more. He doesn't realize that cooking for everyone is a full time job for Rosie. And Reneka does her best; I can't ask more of her."

"I think you do a marvelous job of running such a large household, Catherine. I have never known one in charge to be as patient and kind to others as you are. You're like the mother or sister that I always wanted but never had."

"You're like a dear sister to me, Hannah. With all my family so far away in Virginia, I seldom see any of them, but I don't mean to complain. I've never regretted that I married Garrett. He's a wonderful husband. I thank God for him and my children and for the good life we've had at Reybrook. I know Garrett must seem harsh to you at times, and he's not as close to the Lord as I would like for him to be, but . . . well . . . I must not speak of his faults but of his good qualities. It's been a bad year and he's under a lot of pressure."

"I understand. I hope, someday, to have a home and a family."

"I'm sure you will."

The house had been cleaned, and the gifts were all wrapped and placed under the Christmas tree; everything was in order. At noon, the Rey family gathered around the table. Ben was the first to ask to be excused and Hannah noticed that he left the house by the back door. She followed him to the barn and saw that he had a bridle on Blaze. He led him from his stall and placed a blanket over his back and then lifted a saddle to it.

"Ben," she asked, "may I go riding with you?"

"Not this time, Hannah."

"Please. I have nothing to do, and I don't want to sit in my room all evening."

"It's too cold and you might get sick."

"I can change by the time you saddle two horses and with my coat and woolen scarf—"

"You can't go, Hannah." Ben was firm.

"Why not?" she persisted.

"I'm going to the Lambert's plantation. It's a long way and I'll let Blaze run. You can't keep up on Bell, and even if you could, it'll be dark before I get back."

Hannah was very disappointed. It was obvious that Ben was going to see Laci, and he would probably take her a Christmas gift. She didn't want him to see her. Laci wasn't right for Ben; she wanted him to notice Julie. This was the only reason she felt the way she did . . . yes . . . of course it was.

She watched as he lifted his foot to the stirrup and swung into the saddle, then made a clicking sound in his cheek. Blaze whinnied and lifted his front legs into the air. The horse and rider were soon at the bottom of the hill, and when Ben turned Blaze onto the main road and gave him the reins, they quickly disappeared out of sight.

Ben pulled his hat low over his forehead, as Blaze ran against the wind. His face was cold, but his heart warmed as he thought of the disappointment he had seen in Hannah's eyes when he told her where he planned to go. She had, no doubt, thought he intended to see Laci. But why would she care? Could it be possible that she was jealous?

The sun was in the middle of the western sky when he turned off the main road into a passageway through giant oak trees. The Lambert's large southern mansion was framed at the far end of the trees. Near the front steps, Ben dismounted and tied Blaze's reins around a post. He climbed the wide steps to the porch, and with some apprehension, he lifted the knocker on the front door. An elderly butler opened the door.

"Mista Ben, hit sho ben a lon time. Com'n, com'n."

Laci's heart leaped when, from her upstairs bedroom, she heard Ben's name and then his voice.

"Hello, Tom. I've come for the horse that my dad bought from Mr. Lambert when they met in Charleston last week. He said we could come for it at any time."

Tom offered him a seat before he left the room to find the plantation owner, but Ben preferred to stand. He was in a hurry. He had hoped to avoid seeing her, but Laci came down the wide staircase that ended near the front door where he stood. She was dressed in a red velvet dress, and starched petticoats made its skirt stand out around her. Her dark brown hair was held back with a red ribbon and ringlets of curls adorned her shoulders. She walked gracefully and her voice was enticing.

"Hi, Ben. It's been so long since you have been to see me."

He didn't know that he had ever been to see her, but their paths did cross occasionally. "Hello, Laci. I stay pretty busy with school and helping my dad on the plantation."

"Oh, I suspect that new school teacher keeps you real busy."

He would ignore her sarcastic remark, and have nothing to do with her. He turned to look out the window, but she stepped from the foot of the staircase and laid her hand on his arm.

"You will stay for supper tonight, won't you?"

"I want to get back to be with my family on Christmas Eve."

"And her!" she snapped.

"Her?"

"You know very well that I speak of that redheaded servant who lives in your home."

Ben felt anger swell inside of him. "Hannah is not a servant," he spoke abruptly.

Laci's eyes flashed, and he was glad to see Mr. Lambert walk through the door.

"So you've come for the horse, aye, Ben?"

"Yes, sir, Mr. Lambert. I'd like to get it and be on my way." His and Laci's eyes met a last time, but neither spoke to the other.

"They're in the stables. Let's go pick you out one."

Franklin Lambert II had come to South Carolina from England when he was quite young. His father had been a wealthy British gentleman who brought his wealth and fine horses with him to the new land.

Beyond the stables, Ben saw long rows of slave cabins. Franklin owned more slaves than any other plantation owner on the Cooper River. He planted nearly a thousand acres of cotton each year, plus rice and indigo. He also bred horses of the finest breed and Garrett had paid the wealthy plantation owner for one of them.

Ben picked out a young mare that seemed gentle enough, yet had plenty of spunk, and Franklin told a stable boy to saddle the horse.

"She's a jumper," the plantation owner called to Ben as he let the horse gallop around the tracks near the stables. After circling the tracks a couple of times, he guided her to the middle of them where several white obstacles were set up, and she cleared them all with a first rate performance. Ben felt her strong power beneath him, yet she was easy to handle.

"I like this one, Mr. Lambert. She'll do just fine."

"You're a good judge of horses, Ben, and she's all yours. Do you need a saddle for her?"

"No, sir. Dad bought a new saddle and bridle in Charleston the same day he paid you for the horse. Ben pulled the saddle from the mare's back and gave it to the stable boy before he led the reddish-brown colored horse to the post in front of the home. He exchanged her bridle for the new one he had brought and then turned to Franklin. "I sure thank you, Sir, and I hope all of you have a good Christmas." He mounted Blaze, holding the mare's reins in his hand, and with her trailing along beside, he rode back through the passageway of oaks toward the Cooper River that was framed at the end of it.

Laci stood at the window and watched as he rode off. When her father entered the house, she asked, "Daddy, what would the law do to someone who had anything to do with the British right now?"

"Laci, we're all British."

"But I mean someone in the British Royal Navy."

The mare kept up without any trouble when Ben speeded Blaze to a fast gait. It had taken longer than he'd hoped, but his mother had promised that his family would not eat the Christmas Eve meal without him.

As Ben rode toward home, two men sorted out last minute Christmas mail at a United States Post Office in Charleston. Among the mail was a letter for Hannah Thornton, postmarked Liverpool, England.

"Look at this, Jake. It's a letter from England to a Hannah Thornton at the Reybrook Plantation."

"Hannah Thornton," Jake pulled at his chin and repeated the name. "Where have I heard that before? Oh," he remembered, "that's who the old piano in the back room belongs to. It arrived over two weeks ago, from Ireland. They delivered it here from the ship, and I told them we would see that it got to the right person. I'm headed out that way as soon as we close. If you'll help me load it, I'll deliver Miss Thornton her letter and old piano."

"All right and here's a stack of mail for the Reys."

Hannah spent the evening in her room; she read her Bible and prayed for Nathan's safety and for him to have a happy Christmas. From her bedroom window, she watched smoke rise lazily from the chimneys of the slaves' cabins. It reminded her of home.

It was to be a special night for the Rey family, and out of need for something to do, she decided to dress special. With Reneka's help, she filled the tub in the washroom with warm water. Reneka laid out a towel and washcloth and then gently scrubbed her back. She poured the warm water over it and it felt wonderful.

Hannah wondered about Reneka. She was a kind and gentle

person. Unlike Rosie, she was quiet and seldom spoke unless spoken to first. When she did speak, it wasn't in the dialect that most black people spoke. Hannah was curious, but afraid to ask. She laid her head back in the tub, and Reneka washed her hair and used a pitcher of fresh warm water to rinse it.

"Thank you, Reneka."

"You're welcome."

She decided to wear the dark green dress that Mrs. Barrington had picked out for her. Among her things was a gold-colored ribbon for her hair that would go beautifully with the dress, and it matched the gold chain around her neck. Nathan's chain was usually hidden beneath her blouse, the way he had worn it under his shirt, but tonight the Barrington family coat of arms would be seen at her bare throat.

By the time her bath was completed, darkness had settled over the plantation, and as she pulled the dress over her head, she heard someone ride up the front lane. Could Ben be back? She had not expected him to return home so early, but had thought that he would stay with Laci until late into the night.

With a touch of color, her face was beautiful, and as she combed her hair back and tied the ribbon in it, she heard him bounce up the stairs on the other side of her wall. His footsteps stopped at her door and there was a knock. She stood in front of the dresser and called "Come in." She would not let him see her disappointment, but took in a deep breath and with her chin up, she stood tall and turned to face him.

He opened the door and his face glowed with excitement, but the expression suddenly changed when he saw her. For a moment he was speechless; she felt his eyes move up and down her. He had never seen her dressed like this.

"Hannah . . . ," he breathed her name, "you . . . you're beautiful."

"Thank you, Ben. I didn't expect you back so soon."

Was it a caustic statement? "I'm sorry I couldn't take you with me," he said. "I'll take you riding tomorrow."

"Why did you go?" She knew it was none of her business but asked anyway.

Ben's eyes were fixed on the little sunk in place between her breasts. His heart began to race as she crossed the room to him. He was so taken in by her appearance that he didn't hear her question.

"Ben!"

"What?" He spoke louder than he intended.

"Why did you go?" she asked again.

"I can't tell you."

That settles it, she decided. He went to see Laci and probably took her something very expensive for Christmas. The corner of her mouth twitched.

"Will you give me time to get cleaned up," he asked, "and let me escort you to the dining room? I won't be long?"

"Of course."

In a short time, Ben returned. He wore his black trousers with a dark green pullover sweater that matched her dress perfectly. His black hair was combed neatly. He was very handsome.

When Hannah stepped out into the brightly lighted hallway, he beheld the gold chain around her neck. He heaved a weak sigh, then forced a smile and held out his arm to her. She wrapped her hand around it and they descended the winding staircase together.

Catherine greeted them at the foot of the stairs. "You look wonderful tonight, Hannah. Where did you find such a beautiful dress?"

"Mrs. Barrington found it in New York City."

Catherine noticed the golden British coat of arms around her neck, but didn't comment on it. She also noticed that Hannah's hand was wrapped around her son's arm and how pleased he was for it to be there. It was all somewhat disturbing to her.

The meal was wonderful, and afterward, the family gathered in the living room where a fire crackled in the huge fireplace.

Rosie served hot apple cider and Ben went to the kitchen for a platter of Christmas cookies.

"Rosie, your cookies are so good, I could eat a whole platter of them."

"Dem ain't mine. Miz Julie done bakes dem, and yo almos done eats a platter of'um, Mistr Ben." She spoke in a jolly voice.

"Well, whoever made them, they sure are good."

Hannah uncovered the keys on the Reys' old piano and ran her fingers up and down them. She sat down on its bench and began to play a soft tune. The twins and Otis ran to join her; she lifted Otis to her lap as Emily and Emma climbed on the bench at each side of her. Within minutes, she had all three of them singing a lively Christmas carol. Catherine and Garrett were amazed. They left the divan to stand in front of the piano.

Ben gulped down the last of his milk and cookies before he took Charleen's hand and pulled her to the piano. With the Rey family gathered around her, Hannah began to play some well-known Christmas hymns, and they all began to sing. She played until everyone was tired of singing. As she rose from the bench, she noticed an ornament had fallen from the tree and bent over to pick it up.

"Let me," begged Otis. "Let me put it on the tree, Miss Hannah."

She handed Otis the bright red Christmas ball and stooped to help him find a place for it. She was in this position when an unexpected knock came at the front door. The room became quiet. Who would be calling on Christmas Eve?

Garrett and Catherine made their way to the door, but Hannah thought it was of no concern of hers and turned her attention back to Otis and the red Christmas ball. She heard Garrett speak with another man, but could not make out what either said. However, just as she and Otis found a perfect place for the ornament, she distinctly heard the name Nathan Barrington.

She rose slowly from the stooped position and turned toward the door. The stranger had left, but Catherine and Garrett stood near each other with their heads bowed together.

"Dear God," she prayed. Had the stranger brought a message of Nathan's death? She suddenly felt sick and her body broke out in a cold sweat. She began to tremble and feared she would faint.

Ben had also heard Nathan's name, and when he saw the expression on Hannah's face, he hurried to her side. He helped her to the nearest chair and then darted across the room to find out what had happened.

He saw that his mother shuffled through a stack of mail, while his dad looked on. "Dad," he asked, "did something happen to Nathan?"

"No, son, he sent something to Hannah from Ireland. A man from the post office in Charleston has delivered it and this mail. We need to help him unload it; get a lantern."

"Just a minute." Ben ran back across the room where Hannah sat with her face in her hands. He knelt to his knees in front of her. "Hannah, it's not what you're thinking. He's okay."

"Are you sure?" She lifted her face and wiped tears from her cheeks with the back of her hand.

"Yeah. A man from the post office in Charleston has delivered something for you from Nathan. That's why he said his name."

"Oh." She was so relieved, but the incident left her weak and she trembled for quite awhile.

When the others realized what had happened, they gathered around Hannah to console her. Otis climbed in her lap and patted her cheeks, although he didn't really understand. Emily and Emma stood behind her and caressed her shoulders. Even Charleen seemed sympathetic and Catherine apologized for not thinking.

"Come on, Ben," Garrett coaxed, "the man's waiting, and I expect Hannah would like to see what Nathan sent her."

Catherine handed Hannah a letter, and in its top left hand corner was a seal of the same coat of arms that hung around her neck. It helped her forget what had happened.

Outside, Garrett introduced Ben to the man named Jake. He

was in the back of the wagon, removing ropes he'd used to tie the piano down.

"What is this?" Garret asked. He fumbled with one corner of the cover and tried to see what was underneath it.

"It's an old piano," Jake replied.

"Well, isn't that just what we need?" Garrett muttered sarcastically. "Another old piano to go with the one we got."

Ben was puzzled. If Nathan was so wealthy, why had he sent Hannah an old piano for Christmas? "Did you get any papers with it?" he asked Jake. He wanted to know when the piano was shipped. Maybe it wasn't meant to be a Christmas gift.

"Got one," Jake replied. "Have it right here in my shirt pocket." Ben held the lantern near the paper, and Jake read, "Shipped from Cork, Ireland on October 1, 1812, by a Swedish shipping company. They delivered it to the post office on December 8."

The first day of October, Ben thought. That would have been when the *Monarch* was on its way back to England. Nathan must have stopped at Cork and had it shipped. Hannah was from near Cork. Was there something special about the old piano?

"Let's be careful with it," he said. The three men lifted it over the back of the wagon and into the living room.

By now Hannah had recovered from the shock she'd experienced. Ben watched her face as Jake lifted the dusty cover from over the old piano. She blinked her eyes and stepped closer to it with her head tilted slightly to one side. Suddenly she gasped and her mouth flew open wide. A groan of pleasure escaped her lips, and Ben knew he had been right.

She ran her fingers over its keys to make sure it would still play. "It's my mother's piano," she explained in a shaky voice. "It meant so much to me as I grew up, but I never expected to see it again." She turned to Jake, "Was there a letter, a note, or anything with it?"

"None that I ever saw, Ma'am. All I got was this here paper, saying who shipped it and where from. I need your signature at the bottom of it." He handed her the paper and a pencil. "I'll tear off that part and you can keep the rest."

As she signed the invoice, Jake began to look over the piano carefully. "Sometimes people tie a note to the merchandise," he said. "I've seen'em stuck in all sorts of places." "The top," Hannah remembered. "The top will lift up." Jake pulled on one end and Ben the other, and the top of the piano was lifted. Tucked inside was an envelope. Hannah's heart skipped a beat as Jake carefully pulled it out and handed it to her.

"Please excuse me," she said. And Ben watched as she ran all the way up the staircase with the two letters in her hand. Catherine saw his face flinch when they heard the door to her room close.

Not too long afterward, the large fire in the fireplace was allowed to burn down until there was only a bed of glowing embers. Lamps were blown out and the Rey family ascended the stairs. The house became quiet, but Ben could not fall asleep. Moonlight shined through his window, and he lay on his back, looking up at the ceiling. He recalled Hannah's reaction when she thought something had happened to Nathan, and he thought of how much trouble Nathan must have gone to in order to regain her mother's piano.

He finally closed his eyes, but opened them suddenly when he heard the far off sound of Christmas music being played softly on an old piano. He slipped out of bed and tiptoed to the top of the stairs where he stood in the shadows and looked down. Hannah sat at her mother's piano; a candle's flame illuminated her face. She still wore the pretty dress, and Nathan's gold chain was at her throat. Her long red hair shined under the light of the candle.

She was beautiful, but looked so lonely. Ben could only imagine what filled her mind. The piano had belonged to a mother she never knew, her father was dead, and only God knew the whereabouts of the man she loved. He yearned to go to her, but he didn't. He returned to bed and left Hannah with her memories.

CHAPTER 26

As soon as the door to her room was closed, Hannah tore open Nathan's letter.

October 1, 1812

My darling Hannah,

I'm at the law office of your friend, John Dudley, and must write this in a hurry. There's so much to be done before the day is over. Before I left Charleston, I purchased a new piano for your church in Midleton, and the congregation was more than happy to give me your mother's piano. I'll put this letter in the top of it before it's shipped.

I also bought your home place today as it was for sale again. You should receive a deed for it, if you have not already. Dudley will arrange for a caretaker, and we'll go there on our wedding trip.

I love you, Hannah, and hope all is well with you. I'll report for duty as soon as we return to Liverpool and probably shouldn't write to you as the authorities there might question you getting mail from someone in the Royal Navy. They might cause trouble for you. Please write to my parents at 3214 North Hampton Road, Liverpool, England, and I'll hear from you through them.

I spent the night at your home last night, and Sneaky came to see me. He looks great and said to tell you that he misses you. So do I, sweetheart.

All my love,
Nathan

Hannah read Nathan's letter a second time. She even read the paragraph about her home in Ireland a third time. It seemed she'd been gone forever, but she thought of it often, and it made her happy to know that she could return there. How wonderful it would be to return with Nathan. She finally laid his letter aside and opened the one from his mother.

October 15, 1812

Dearest Hannah,

I pray this finds you in good health and well recovered from your voyage to America. The course we were forced to take home brought near unbearable heat and misery for everyone aboard the *Monarch*. Our water supply ran short and Charles was forced to ration it. Then it was discovered that we were near the Madeira Islands and were able to replenish our provisions and water enough to reach Liverpool.

It was agony for Nathan to leave you in the United States, but he was thankful you did not have to endure the hardships we went through on the return trip. I received one letter from him before he left England in which he stated that he would return to America. He doesn't want to fight the Americans, but I believe he will be safer there than in Europe. I pray for his safe return to you, Hannah, and I know that you pray for him daily. May both wars end soon.

I hope you're being treated well on the plantation. Nathan seemed to think that he left you in the hands of a good family. He loves you, Hannah, so very much.

You're better off in America because we suffer hard times in England. Everyone is weary from so many years of war, and many grieve the loss of a loved one or live in fear of losing a family member. We're heavily taxed in order to pay war debts, and now with the conflict in America, there seems to be no end to it all.

Our company has suffered great loss at the hands of

American Privateers. They have taken many of our ships, and should the war not be over soon, I fear we shall have no company at all. Men under our employment have been killed and each death weighs heavily on Charles's heart. Other shipping companies are experiencing the same misfortune. Forgive me; I should not worry you with our problems. I'm sure you face enough of your own each day.

Please take care of yourself, Hannah, and write if you can.

Love,
Charles and Martha Barrington

Hannah was glad to hear that Nathan was in America; the war news from Europe was very frightening, but news of battles fought on and around the Great Lakes also reported many casualties on both sides. When Garrett and Ben talked of Washington's "War Hawks" and of their desire to take Canada, she couldn't help but feel animosity toward the young politicians.

She didn't return to be with the Rey family, as she thought they might like some time without her company on Christmas Eve. Garrett was far from being elated about her mother's old piano in the living room. She wished it could be brought to her room, but knew it was too heavy to be lifted up the stairs. She put the two letters in the top drawer of her dresser and sat down to think of Nathan.

After the house became quiet, she rose and held a candle to the flame in her lamp. When it was lighted, she set it in a small metal candleholder and placed her first finger in its handle and held it up in front of her. It was dark in the house, but the candle gave off enough light for her to see where she walked. With it in one hand and her other hand on the banister, she descended the stairs and set the candleholder on top of her mother's piano. She ran her fingers over the keys lightly, and when a deluge of memories came to her mind, she forgot the time and played far longer than she had intended.

As Hannah played her mother's old piano in the stillness of the night, she had no way of knowing that far away in Northern Ireland, she was the topic of two people's conversation.

"But Lady Kelley, you have seen your granddaughter only twice in her life. It's hard for me to believe that you would leave your entire estate to her. What has she done that entitles her to such an inheritance? In order that you might change your will, I'm compelled to remind you that I have served you faithfully all these years."

"Indeed you have, Barney, but I would remind you that you have been paid a substantial salary for your services."

The lawyer and financial advisor to the wealthy Lady Mary Kelley sighed and then muttered, "I cannot deny that."

"My granddaughter was denied all the luxuries of life that I could have given her. Since my daughter's death came at her birth, I chose to have nothing to do with her, yet when she had the opportunity, she visited her dear grandfather and me and brought much joy to our home. I found that we had missed a wonderful blessing in life."

"Yes, ma'am."

"Since all of my family except this one granddaughter has preceded me in death, I shall leave everything I own to her, including my fortune in money, land, and houses. This home and everything in it is to be left to my only heir, Hannah Ruth Thornton."

"And where shall I find Miss Hannah Ruth Thornton?" the lawyer asked reluctantly.

"You must contact John Dudley, my son-in-law's lawyer in Cork, to whom I have already sent a copy of my will and the worth of my estate."

"You do not trust me after all these years?"

"I trust you for as long as I live, Barney, but the doctor has said that my death will come within a short time, and no, I do not trust you in death."

In the predawn hours of Christmas morning, the wealthy Lady Mary Kelley died quietly in her sleep, leaving Hannah all of her earthly possessions.

Ben was up and dressed early the next morning. He had intended to wrap a gift for Hannah, but now he didn't know what to do. He opened the top drawer to his dresser and took out a small box, and with it in his hand, he sat down on the side of his bed and opened it.

"What do you have, Ben?" Catherine asked from where she stood at his doorway.

He quickly closed the box, but not before his mother got a glimpse of what was inside.

"Is it a silver necklace?"

"Yes, ma'am."

"Who is it for?"

"I bought it for Hannah, but I don't think I should give it to her."

"Why not? I think it would be appropriate to give her a gift."

"I should have gotten her something else. I forgot that she wears Nathan's gold chain."

"May I see it?"

He lifted the top of the box again and handed it to Catherine.

She sat quietly for a moment and looked at the expensive piece of jewelry. "It's beautiful," she said. A silver heart-shaped locket had three small diamonds down one side of it. "You must have spent a good bit of your savings. Ben . . . are you in love with Hannah?"

Ben paused before he nodded his head and answered in a low voice, "Yeah, Mom . . . I am."

"Son, lots of boys your age fall in love with their teachers who are much older than them."

"Hannah is not much older than I am. She's only twenty and I'm eighteen."

"Well, I feel it's a passing thing, and you'll forget her when the right girl comes along. I just wish that you and Charleen could be with more people your own age. Hannah," Catherine reminded him, "is engaged to someone else."

"I know," Ben sighed. He was relieved that Catherine knew of his love for Hannah; he had told no one else, but he didn't need to be reminded that she would marry another. He returned the top to the small box and dropped it into his shirt pocket.

The twins and Otis scooted down the stairs that morning to see what was under the Christmas tree. When Hannah heard their squeals of delight all the way up to her room, she jumped out of bed and reached for her robe. She didn't want to miss the excitement and ran out her door and down the hallway without so much as combing her hair.

Catherine sat on the divan with a cup of coffee in her hands. She smiled at Hannah and moved down to make room for her. Garrett stood near the Christmas tree and laughed as his children discovered all the toys that had been put there. There were baby dolls for Emily and Emma and a doll cradle for each, but Otis found wooden soldiers and a wagon.

Ben and Charleen came down the stairs together; neither was as excited as Hannah. Finding Santa Claus under the Rey family Christmas tree was nothing new to them. Charleen sat down on the divan with Hannah and Catherine, while Ben went to stand by Garrett.

"Look, Ben!" Otis's voice squeaked with excitement.

Ben squatted down beside him. "What did you get, little brother?"

"Look at all the soldiers! They can beat the British!"

Ben smiled halfheartedly at his younger brother and glanced up at Hannah. He hoped she'd not heard Otis's remark, but figured she did when he saw her eyes closed.

"Yeah . . . well, let's don't talk about the British, today, Otis." Ben lifted his small body and sat him in the wagon. "Let's see

how fast this thing will go." He began to run around the room
with Otis in the wagon behind him, and Otis loved it. The faster
Ben ran, the harder he laughed. Ben was glad to see Hannah
laugh at the two of them.

She left the divan to sit on the floor beside Emma and Emily.
To their delight, she took one of the dolls and cradled it in her
arms and rocked it back and forth. She carefully handed it back
to Emma and put her finger to her lips. "Shhh, don't wake her."
Both girls giggled.

Reneka came to announce that breakfast was ready, but the
three children could not be coaxed from the living room.
Hannah didn't want to eat with her hair all tumbled about her
head and said that she would get something later.

Back in her room, she dressed comfortably in a pair of tweed
pants that were lined with a soft material and had the colors of
brown, beige, and red in them. She pulled a red sweater over
her head and let Nathan's gold chain hang down the front of it.
Instead of tying her hair back with a ribbon, she anchored it at
each side of her head with a set of small brown combs. After
applying a touch of color to her face, she was happy with her
appearance and hurried down the stairs.

She and the family came together in the living room again.
Rosie and Reneka were summoned from the kitchen and all
the adults had a seat except Charleen, who gathered Emma
and Emily and Otis around her. Hannah sat on the divan between
Catherine and Ben and held the wrapped box that contained
Ben's silver belt buckle. She was happy to be with the family
and could hardly wait for them to open the gifts she had
purchased for them.

Charleen called out the name on each gift then handed it to
one of the children to take to that person. The first gift was for
Catherine and the second one for Garrett. Charleen put her
own gifts to one side and before long, they began to mound.
There were gifts for Reneka and Rosie and several for Ben and,
of course, more for the children, but not one gift was brought
to Hannah. At first she didn't notice, as she watched others

open their gifts. Each one made a fuss over what she had gotten
them and Catherine got tears in her eyes when she saw the
dress. Otis and the twins seemed pleased and even Charleen
thanked her with a hug. Ben and Garrett both said they could
sure use a new belt, and then Ben could stand it no longer. He
jumped from his seat and left the room.

Hannah was disappointed when the last present was given
out and there had been none for her. She told herself that it was
better to give than to receive and tried to hide her disappointment.
It wasn't so much, however, that she wanted a gift, but that she
wanted to be a part of the family. Perhaps the Reys didn't want
her to be a part of them, she thought, and fought back tears.

Catherine and Garrett watched the front door, but Hannah
stood to return to her room, for she wanted no one to notice her
disappointment. She heard Ben run up the front steps and
everyone, including Reneka and Rosie, stood.

"Hannah, will you come outside a moment?" asked Catherine.

Confused, she followed Garrett and Catherine to the porch
and saw a horse tied to the handrail at the bottom of the steps.
It was a beautiful horse, the color of chestnuts with a white star
on its face, and on its back was a new leather saddle. She
wondered who the horse belonged to; there was no company
in the house. She was shocked when Garrett untied the reins
and handed them to her.

"Merry Christmas, Hannah," everyone said together.

"What . . . what are you saying?"

"That this is your Christmas present from all of us," replied
Garrett. "Sorry we couldn't wrap it and put it under the tree, but
you do still want your own horse, don't you?"

"Yes," she breathed. "Oh, yes."

She gasped and felt her face grow warm when she realized
that the horse was a gift to her from all of them. Both hands
flew to her cheeks; she found it hard to believe. The horse was
far more beautiful than one she had ever dreamed of owning,
and with a new saddle and bridle. She was too emotional to
speak as she looked around at the family . . . at her family.

"You deserve it, Hannah," said Catherine. "You do far more than you're paid to do. We love you, dear."

"And you spent everything that I did pay you on all of us," Garrett acknowledged. "We appreciate the education you're giving our children and the extra time you spend with the little ones." Hannah was surprised to hear these words from Garrett; she had felt sure that he didn't like her.

"Thank you, Mr. Rey. Thank you all."

One at a time, the family went back inside until only Ben and she were left on the porch. Ben smiled when tears of happiness trickled down both sides of her face. "I told you my dad wasn't so bad," he said.

"Yes, you did."

He reached to his back pocket for a handkerchief and wiped the tears from her face. "What do you think of your horse?" he asked.

"He's the most beautiful horse I've ever seen," she sniffed.

"It's not a he; it's a she. It's a gentle mare for a gentle lady, but she's a lot more horse than old Bell, and it'll take some time for you to get used to her. I asked Jim about giving you riding lessons before you ride her alone. I hope you'll wait."

"Yes, of course I will."

"If you'd like to mount her, I'll lead her around the front yard."

"I'd love to," but as she reached for the saddle, she realized that she still held the silver belt buckle in her hand.

"Oh, I forgot . . . this is for you." She handed him the small gift.

"You've already given me a gift."

"This goes with it. I held it because I wanted you to open the other one first."

"Hannah . . ." He untied the ribbon around the second gift, and his eyes lit up when he saw the belt buckle, but then he sighed and looked across the front yard and didn't know what to say.

"You don't like it?"

"Yes, I like it! I've wanted one like it for a long time," he seemed angry, "but I know how much you paid for it."

"You do a lot for me. You're a special friend and I wanted to give you something special."

He felt anguish in his heart and wanted so badly to take her in his arms, but knew she wouldn't allow it. "Get on the horse," he muttered. He wanted her to hurry before he did something stupid.

With one foot in the stirrup, Hannah stepped up to the saddle, and Ben led the mare among the trees. She felt the power of her muscles beneath her and realized that it was indeed a fine horse. She was gentle, as Ben had said, but Hannah agreed that she was not used to such power and that she did need help to learn how to control it.

They returned to the porch. "If you'd like to," Ben suggested, "we'll ride to the valley after dinner."

"I would like to. Will you go with me now to deliver gifts to others on the plantation?"

"My mother will. She takes gifts to everyone." He had to get away from her, so he could think. After he returned the horse to the barn, he went to his room and lay across his bed with the silver heart in his hand.

Jim hitched Bell to the family carriage and brought it to the front of the house, and he and Garrett loaded Catherine's and Hannah's gifts for others on the plantation. When the last one was loaded, Garrett held Catherine's arm, and she stepped to the front seat of the carriage and took the reins. With Hannah seated beside her, the two ladies set off to deliver their gifts.

The servants' gifts were put under a small Christmas tree that stood in the corner of their entrance. A wonderful aroma came from Mrs. Leander's kitchen; she dried her hands on a pretty apron as she came from there to thank them for the gifts. Julie came out of her room to help. She pulled two chairs near the fire and invited Catherine and Hannah to warm before they left.

She was dressed neatly in a light blue sweater and dark blue denims. Her short blonde hair was feathered around her face that had a touch of color on it. She was very courteous and spoke in a quiet voice. When back in the carriage, Catherine commented on her thoughtfulness.

"Yes," Hannah agreed. "Julie is always thoughtful of others, and she's doing so well in the class."

"It's a kind thing that you do, Hannah," Catherine commended her, "teaching the servants without pay."

"Oh, but I am paid; not in money, but in rewards and blessings. I'm rewarded each time I hear one of them read or see the correct answer to a problem they have worked. And I receive a blessing each time I see how proud they are of their accomplishments. I'll be paid for years to come if I receive letters that I've taught them to write."

"Yes," Catherine nodded her head, "you will."

Some slaves came to meet Catherine, and they appeared to have anticipated her arrival. There were greetings such as "Moaning, Miz Catherine," and "How's yo chillins doing?"

"Good morning," Catherine returned their greetings. "My children are all fine, thank you."

She and Hannah began to pass out the baskets of food and fruit and were thanked by each of them. When all had disappeared back inside, Catherine pulled the carriage to the front steps of Ole Ramey's cabin, for he had not been among the others. She climbed the rickety steps and knocked on the old man's door to hear a weak voice say, "Com'n."

As they entered the cabin, the two ladies saw the old man seated in a rocking chair by the fireplace. His back was stooped and his eyes gazed into the fire, but they lit up and a smile came to his face when he saw Catherine. "Laud, Miz Catherine, I thought that bes Alicia ah com'in in. She say she's qwinna com to g't me when dinner's redy."

"Good morning, Ramey. How are you this morning?"

"I's ah doin pooly dis moaning, Miz Catherine. Cant get up'n'down too good no mo."

"How would you like to come live in the big house, where I can keep an eye on you? On days that you feel like it, you can help Rosie in the kitchen or do a few odd jobs around the house. If you don't feel like doing anything, you can rest."

"I's speck Mr. Garrett qwinna needs me 'n de fields, comes next summa."

"Well, I expect Mr. Garrett will just have to find someone else to take your place in the fields. Now you have Alicia pack your things, and I'll send Mr. Jim over in the wagon to get you one day next week." She gave him the basket of food. "I brought you some food and Miss Hannah brought you a nice warm blanket."

Ole Ramey smiled a big smile and tried to get up, but Catherine placed her hand on his shoulder. "No need for you to get up, Ramey. Here, let us spread this blanket over your legs."

"Yesum, Miz Catherine. I's sho thank yo, and hits a mity fine blanket." As they left his cabin, Hannah looked back and saw the old man rub his hand over the blanket carefully.

Nole had come out to meet Catherine, but she stopped the carriage in front of his and Alicia's cabin to deliver Hannah's gifts. Alicia came to the door with a disturbed look on her face. "I's sho glad to sees yo, Mis Catherine."

"Is something wrong, Alicia?"

"Hit's Sammy. He's ben sick'n de nite and run'n plenty fevor. I's ben werd 'bout him."

Catherine went to the side of a bed that stood in one corner of the shack. She leaned over and placed her hand on Sammy's head. "He does have a fever," she agreed with Alicia. "I don't think it's too high, but I'll send Ben with some medicine. If he's not better in the morning, we'll take him to Charleston to see the doctor, so don't worry. Maybe this present from Hannah will perk him up."

Sammy sat up, and a smile spread over his face when he saw the colorful blocks. They really did seem to make him feel better.

Bell lumbered slowly down the trail through the woods toward home. The trail was covered with leaves, but they no longer crackled beneath the wheels of the carriage as they had done in early fall. The rain and snow had made them soggy, and they lay flat, heaped on top of each other. As they came out of the woods and passed the servants' quarters, Ben saw them from his upstairs window and met them at the back porch. He helped his mother from the carriage and up the porch steps. He knew she'd be tired after her visit to the slave quarters. "Are you all right, Mom?" he asked.

"I'll be fine after I rest awhile. I want you to take a bottle of medicine to Alicia before you put the carriage away. Sammy is sick. And I want you to help Jim move Ole Ramey to the house, next week, so we can keep an eye on him."

"All right, Mom. I'll see that he's taken care of. Ah . . . where we gonna put him?"

"We'll have to clean out the storage room beyond the kitchen and fix him a bed there. He'll have the heat from the kitchen, and Rosie and Reneka can help keep an eye on him or hear if he calls in the night."

Catherine crossed the back porch and opened the door, but then stopped.

"Ben," she called.

"Yes, ma'am?"

"Julie is a very nice girl. Maybe you should pay more attention to her." Before Ben could answer, his mother stepped through the door and closed it behind her.

He quickly looked at Hannah, who was as surprised as he was. The perplexity on his face brought a smile to her lips, but she ran up the back steps and across the porch.

"Hannah!" he yelled.

"Yes, Ben?"

"What did Mom mean by that?"

"I'm not sure," she answered naively. "Perhaps she just wants you to look at her." She darted through the door and closed it quickly and then leaned against it. "Yea," she whispered with her fist in the air.

Catherine went upstairs and rested until Rosie announced that the Christmas dinner was ready to be served. She looked lovely when Garrett escorted her into the dining room. Charleen came down the stairs in a new dress that her parents had given her for Christmas. She was very pretty and Hannah thought what a shame it was that there was no young man to see her. She understood why Garrett felt sorry for his daughter.

Otis brought two toy soldiers to the table and was more content to play with them than to eat, but the twins laid their dolls aside and seemed eager to eat the delicious food that Rosie had prepared.

When everyone was seated, Catherine asked Ben to ask a blessing of the food. Ben looked at his dad, and not until Garrett nodded, did he bow his head and began to pray. "Oh, Lord God in heaven, we thank you for the special gift of your Son that you gave to all mankind. As we celebrate His birthday, we thank you for His willingness to die for us that we might live forever. And thank you for this food of which we are about to partake. We ask you to bless it for the nourishment of our bodies. In the name of Jesus we pray, Amen." Hannah thought it was a beautiful prayer and smiled at Ben when he looked her way for approval.

Food was passed around the table and plates were heaped high, but while everyone else laughed and talked, Hannah sat quietly and thought of Christmases in Ireland with only her father. She missed him. And she thought of the empty place at the Barringtons' home. Would Nathan have anything special for Christmas; would he even have enough to eat? Suddenly all the wonderful food didn't taste so good.

Ben noticed how quiet she was and that she ate very little. He knew her thoughts were sad, so as soon as he finished eating, he asked, "You ready to go riding?"

The barn smelled of hay. Hannah sneezed, while she waited for Ben to saddle the horses. She intended to learn how to saddle her own horse and would ask Jim's help. Ben insisted on doing everything for her, but she wanted to be independent and was determined that she would be.

As they mounted the horses and left the barn, Ben held a tight rein on Blaze. The mare could keep up, but Hannah might lose control of her. They rode side by side until they reached the rim of the valley.

"Remember the first time we came here?" Hannah asked as they dismounted.

"Yeah. The day Blaze acted so crazy, and I couldn't do anything with him."

"I thought you handled him well. I'll always remember how magnificent the two of you were as you circled the floor of the valley. I want to learn to ride like that."

"I don't know, Hannah . . . . I grew up riding horses, whereas you didn't. They've always been a part of my life on the plantation."

"I know, and I know I can't learn over night, but in time . . ."

"Well, when you set your mind to do something, there's no stopping you, but I hope you'll be careful. Get to know your horse and find out what she will and won't do. Have you decided what to name her?"

"No." She turned to pet the mare's face. "Look," she said, "there's a white star on her face."

"Yeah, I noticed it."

"Do you think I should name her Star?"

"That's how Blaze got his name."

"Then it's settled; her name is Star."

Ben tied both horses' reins to a tree. "Come on," he said, "let's walk down the valley a ways. I need to talk to you."

"About what?"

He didn't say anything for a moment, like he didn't know how to start, and then he asked, "How does a person know if God wants him to do something?"

She stopped and looked in his face, but didn't know how to answer. Tears came to her eyes.

"Now don't go gettin' emotional with me right now. I need your help."

She smiled through her tears, but all she could say was, "Oh, Ben."

"I feel something . . . like a tug at my heart, and it won't go away. Dad's got his head set on me going to college and learning how to be a better cotton planter, but I'm afraid God's got other plans for me. I think He wants me to keep on preaching. I've struggled with it ever since we started the service on Sunday mornings. You got me into this, so you gotta help me with it."

Hannah wanted to laugh, but didn't dare. She saw how desperate Ben was. He loved the Lord, but had not learned to trust Him in all things. She chose her words carefully.

"If God is calling you to preach, He'll work everything out for you. I don't know what it's like because He hasn't called me in that way. You must wait upon Him, and He'll give you an answer in His time. Meanwhile, you should study His word and pray."

"Well . . . yeah, I'm doing that, but meanwhile, what do I tell my dad?"

Hannah heaved a big sigh. Knowing Garrett, she understood Ben's plight. "Leave him to God," she said. "Trust Him and give it time."

"All right, but that's not all." He turned to face her. "We haven't been affected by the war much, here in the South, but it'll come and when it does, I'll have to enlist."

She looked away and refused to acknowledge what he said.

"Are you listening to me, Hannah?"

"No. I don't want to talk about that."

"We have to talk about it."

"No!"

"I want you to understand that I know how much you love Nathan. I don't want to fight against his country, but I won't have a choice. I'll be expected to join the state militia or the United States regulars."

"I won't think of you and Nathan fighting against each other; you both mean so much to me. I pray for the war to end before it comes to that."

"So do I, but news in Charleston is that the Duke of Wellington and England's allies are gaining ground on the peninsula. If they stop Napoleon's army and put an end to the war in Europe, the British will then come at the United States like a bunch of stirred up hornets. Every man may be called on to defend our freedom."

"Stop it, Ben!" She covered her ears with her hands.

"I'm sorry, Hannah, but I want you to understand."

"Please . . . let's go back."

Just as they reached the rim of the valley, one of Hannah's combs dropped from her hair to the ground. When Ben bent over to pick it up, a small box fell from his shirt pocket. The box came open, spilling the silver heart-shaped locket on the ground. Hannah reached for it and held the beautiful piece of jewelry betwixt her fingers. "Was she not at home?" she asked.

"What?"

"Was she not at home?"

"What are you talking about? Was who not at home?"

"Laci. Didn't you buy her this for Christmas? And is that why you returned so early last night after you went to see her?"

"I didn't go to see Laci. I don't intend to ever go see her."

"You said you were going to the Lambert's Plantation."

"I did, but I didn't go to see Laci."

"What did you go for?"

"Your horse."

Suddenly it all came to her. "That's why you wouldn't let me go."

"Yeah."

"Oh, Ben . . . I'm sorry. I thought you went to take Laci a Christmas present. I didn't expect you to return until late into the night."

"Did that bother you?"

"Well . . . I . . . I just don't think she's right for you."

"I won't argue that, but it didn't answer my question." He lifted her chin with his finger and forced her to look at him. "Just a little . . . maybe . . . huh?" His eyes questioned hers.

Her mouth slowly curved into a smile as her head nodded up and down. "Who did you buy the necklace for?" she asked.

"I bought it for a pretty lady, but . . . ," he lifted Nathan's gold chain from the front of her sweater, "she already has something to wear around her neck."

He took the necklace from her and put it back inside the box, then dropped it into his shirt pocket. As he untied the horses' reins, he smiled and said, "Come on, pretty lady, let's get home before Otis eats all of Rosie's Christmas cookies."

"Oh, Ben," she laughed.

CHAPTER 27

A young seaman's body hung from a makeshift scaffold with a noose around its neck and dangled back and forth as the British frigate heeled from one side to the other. It had hung on the main deck of the ship for two days and served as a deterrent to all seamen aboard against desertion of the British Navy. On the morning of the third day, it was cut down and buried at sea. The date was April 19, 1813.

Nathan watched the burial with a hollow pit in his stomach, with eyes that were sunken in his head, and with a tremendous ache in his heart. It was a man of his own age—a good man—who had rather chance death than face the miserable wretchedness that seamen experienced on the British naval vessel. Some said that it was hell afloat. While Nathan believed that nothing on this earth was as bad as the eternal hell, he did agree that it was one of the worst possible situations that a man could be called upon to serve in.

Officers aboard *H.M.S. Cannon* were onerous and showed only arrogance toward the enlisted men. And Nathan, while holding the rank of a lieutenant, was expected to behave in the same manner. He felt little respect for the officers' offensive sense of superiority and hated their pompous attitudes. He was reprimanded for befriending low-ranking seamen and shared the companionship of no one except Jason.

For the enlisted, the ship's food consisted mostly of dry sea biscuits and water. If one was lucky, he got a biscuit without worms, but all the seamen's water was a greenish color and tiny shapes floated in it. Officers ate better, but Nathan refused to join them. He ate in the mess hall with men under him, although he was required to sit apart from them. Had it not been for Jason, who had been promoted to an officer, and his memory of Hannah, he didn't know how he could have stood it.

"Will I ever see her pretty face again, Jason?" he asked. The two of them stood on the main deck of the ship at starboard side and watched the last rays of sun sink beyond the water's edge.

Jason gave him a sympathetic glance, but had no answer for his friend. After seeing the body hang on the deck for two days, he had doubts that either of them would get off the ship alive. The way Nathan hated the arrogance of other officers, Jason feared he would do something to bring punishment upon himself. If so, he would be compelled to defend him and was sure that each of them would be flogged to death.

"At least you have her to help keep your mind off more unpleasant thoughts," he finally answered.

"I worry about her."

"I'm sure she's better off than either of us," Jason retorted bitterly.

"I hope so."

"I felt safer fighting with the Canadians and their Indian allies than I do on this ship. We were treated with respect and the food was edible."

"But we're not being shot at by the enemy," Nathan reminded him.

"Oh, no . . . we're just hung by our own superior officers," Jason muttered under his breath for fear of one of them hearing him.

"He deserted to the enemy, Jason, and any military leader would have done the same. It's a part of war."

"He tried to survive, and I fear we won't."

"We will survive! We must! I have to return to Hannah and you're going with me."

A cool wind blew across the ship as darkness settled over the rough waters of the North Atlantic. They sailed south, not more than ten miles off the coast of New York. The frigate was to become a link in a chain of British ships that would form a blockade along the Atlantic seaboard of the United States; a blockade that would bring near devastation to the cotton growers of South Carolina.

Aboard the ship, was an ensign named William Tally. An ensign was the lowest-ranking commissioned officer in the navy, but he was an officer, and Tally didn't let the enlisted men forget it. He harassed them every chance he had and forced them to perform unnecessary duties in order to show his authority. He tried to impress higher-ranking officers with his intimidation of the lower-rank.

The men hated Ensign Tally and called him "Bully Billy" behind his back. Nathan had as little to do with him as possible and thought the name fit perfectly.

On the morning of April 20, sails were sighted on the horizon. The captain raised his glass and saw red, white, and blue colors of the Union Jack flying above the ship's top sail. It was a supply ship out of Liverpool, and along with supplies, she brought a bag of mail. There were letters from home for Nathan and Jason.

They found a quiet place and sat down to read. Nathan saw the seal of his family coat of arms and recognized his mother's handwriting, but when he opened the envelope, he was surprised to find not only a letter from his mother, but another envelope. It was from America. Before he read his mother's letter, he opened the second envelope, and his hands began to shake when he saw two letters from Hannah. One was to his mother, but the other was to him. He quickly read the one to his mother first, saving the best until last.

January 2, 1813

Dear Lady Barrington,

I was thankful to receive a letter from you with news of Nathan. I, too, believe that Canada is a safer place for him to be. News from the war on the peninsula is very bad. I pray for him daily and for both wars to end.

As for myself, I am well and have regained my strength. The family with whom I reside has treated me kindly and makes me feel as one of their own. When I left Ireland, I had no family at all and now I have two. God has blessed in so many ways.

I love to teach and would like to obtain a higher education someday. I hear there is a very fine college in Charleston, but it is too far to go each day; besides, there is no time.

I pray that all is well with you and Captain Barrington and hope that you will write again in the near future. I have enclosed a letter for Nathan and ask that you send it the next time you write to him.

With love,

Hannah

Nathan smiled as he carefully folded the letter and then unfolded the second one. To know that Hannah was well and happy made him happy. He began to read the second letter.

January 2, 1813

My darling Nathan,

I pray this letter will reach your hands and that it will find you safe and well. My health has never been better, but my heart is lonely without you. I miss you every day and I pray for your safe return.

My days are busy, for which I am thankful; it helps the time to pass quickly. I look at your picture as the sun sinks at the close of each day and say a prayer for your safe return. I love you, Nathan. I love you so much and continue to wait for you. I know you love me, or you would not have done all the wonderful things that you did for me.

A man from the Charleston Post Office delivered my mother's piano on Christmas Eve, and I can't tell you how much it meant to see it again. I asked that it be moved to the servants' quarters, as we now have a church service there each Sunday morning. I play a hymn, or two, for the small congregation. Ben preaches a short sermon and is doing an excellent job.

I was elated to find your letter in the top of the piano. It was so good to hear from you and from Sneaky. It will be wonderful to return to my home with you; I wish my father could be there to meet you.

The Rey family treats me kindly and takes care of all my needs. Ben is a good friend, and I would adopt Otis and the twins. Catherine is the mother I never had and a sister and aunt, all in one. She's a wonderful person.

If Jason is with you, tell him that Charleen is just as beautiful, if not more so, as when he left her. At first, it was very difficult to be her teacher, but now that I understand her better, I see her as a challenge instead of a burden. I strive to find things that will hold her interest.

I love you, darling, and I shall love you forever.

Hannah

By the time Nathan finished Hannah's letter, his eyes were filled with tears. Jason saw him wipe them away with his hand, and assuming he'd read a letter from his mother, he said, "I'm so sorry about your dad."

"What about my dad?"

Jason was stunned when he realized that Nathan had not received the tragic news about his dad of which his own mother had written him.

"Didn't you get a letter from home?"

"Yes, but there were two letters from Hannah enclosed in it, and I read those first. What happened to my dad?"

Jason sat down beside him. "Read your mother's letter," he spoke in a soft voice.

Nathan quickly unfolded his mother's letter and began to read. When Jason saw his back slump forward, he laid a hand on his shoulder.

March 1, 1813

Dear Nathan,

It's with great sorrow that I must write you such tragic news. At 3:04 in the afternoon of February 16, your dad departed from this world, and we laid his body to rest in the family cemetery on the morning of February 20. His last words were of you and James, and he asked me to tell you both how much he loved you.

The Lord has been gracious and given me extra strength to help me through such a sorrowful time. Our friends have been loving and kind and have taken care of all my needs. And, of course, James, Sandra, and Little Dan come often, and we grieve together. It gives me such heartache that I must send this message in a letter, and you will have none of your family with you. I pray that Jason is there and that he may be of comfort to you. I know he is like a brother. His family has given their steadfast support.

Our ships have been taken by American Privateers, and with the loss of each one, your dad grew weaker. Many seamen under our employment are missing; he didn't know if they were alive or dead. I have heard since his death that the Americans are holding many as prisoners, to be released when the war is over. The *Monarch* was taken with Murray, Sam, and Robert aboard.

Scott is in London at the school where your dad had arranged for him to go. I'll be sure that he is able to complete his studies and hope that another shipping company can use his talent, as James has dissolved the Barrington Company. With only two ships left and no one to man them, he had no choice. Jeff and Mark enlisted in the Royal Navy.

Jason's dad was a great help to James in taking care of legal matters concerning the company. He also referred him to a bank in Liverpool that has given him employment. He and Sandra reside there for the time being; however, more bad news is that the Duke of Wellington is calling for volunteers of every able-bodied man to fight Napoleon's army. James has made preparation to go, and when he leaves, Sandra and Dan will stay at Barrington Manor.

I feel so alone here without any of my family and have given some thought to selling the large home. I don't believe Sandra will be happy here, but would like a smaller place near the city. I shall not, however, make this decision hastily and will do nothing until I hear from you. My greatest concern in the matter is the kind people who have served us faithfully for so many years. What would become of them?

I pray daily for your safety and for the war to end.

I love you my son,
Mother

Nathan folded the letter slowly and handed it to Jason. His head fell forward and he felt numb. He would never see his dad again and there was a chance he would never see his brother again. By now, he fought against the greatest army of the times. And if his mother sold Barrington Manor, he could never go home again. He was devastated.

That night was the longest and darkest night of his life. He tossed and turned and thought of all the things he had intended to do with his dad; now time with him was no more. As a child, he'd yearned for him to return from the sea, but when his dad had needed him, he had been the one at sea. Life could be cruel; he wept silent tears. He thought of his mother, alone in the large house, and of how much Dan would miss his granddad. It was a stab to his heart when he realized that his own children would never know him. With Hannah's father dead and now his . . . He thought of Edgar and Marie.

Nathan gave up on sleeping. He turned up his lamp and reached beneath his pillow for Hannah's letter. It had brought him such joy the first time he read it, but how quickly that joy had been snatched from him. He read her letter a second time and could hear her voice; it brought him comfort.

The captain demanded that the deck of the British frigate be scrubbed and swabbed every morning at daybreak, and then there was duty for each man until sundown. Under his feared whip, no man stood idle. They were allowed three short breaks a day for the pitiful meals they were served. They climbed the ratlines with tar buckets and covered the rigging with the hot tar. The sun glared down on them, day after day, and they suffered by night with bodies that were burned by the sun and the wind. They grew weary under the harsh conditions of the British tar, as so they were called.

To relieve their pain, Nathan gave out everything he had in his medical bag, and they begged for more. He gave words of encouragement, such as, "The war can't last forever," and he pleaded for them not to desert, because he knew if they did, their fates would most likely be at the end of a rope.

The frigate continued to sail south until it reached its destination and took its place in a line of British ships. Its anchor was dropped no more that ten nautical miles from the entrance of Charleston Harbor. The captain had received orders to stop any ship that tried to leave or enter the harbor.

Two weeks later, Nathan and Jason stood on the *Cannon's* deck at sunset. "She watches the sun less than twenty miles from here," said Nathan. "I'm so close, yet might as well be a thousand miles away. If I could get a boat into the water, I could be there and back before sunrise."

"Don't even think of it!" Jason shuddered.

"Don't worry. If I thought I could make it without being missed, I would have already. But there must be a way," he sighed, and not many days hence, found there was.

It was a dark night, and the captain sent three men on a reconnaissance with orders to search out and report any sign of military activities within the harbor and surrounding area. As bad as Nathan wished to go ashore, he wanted nothing to do with the captain's scouting party.

The next morning the party returned and reported a fire they had seen in the woods during the night. For fear of being captured, they had not investigated the fire, but assumed it was a campfire that a lone sentry kept ablaze for a military unit. The captain was familiar with the large plantations up and down the Ashley and Cooper Rivers, and he determined that one of the plantation owners permitted the state militia to camp and train on his land. If so, he concluded, there was a chance that the plantation home was used as a headquarters. He had been ordered not to take his ship within the harbor, but if a small group of men could go in and destroy a military headquarters . . . well, a report of such would look good on his record.

The next day, the captain called a meeting of his officers and related to them the information from the reconnaissance. "I need a volunteer," he said, "to take a small unit of men up the Cooper River with orders to find the plantation home and destroy it, should there be a military headquarters based there." William Tally's hand shot up in the air immediately.

"I'll go, Sir," he said, hoping to gain favor with the captain by being the first to volunteer. I'll order the home to be burned, he thought, whether it's an enemy headquarters or not. I'll say that it was, and the captain will be pleased. I'll be a hero.

The captain looked Tally's way and nodded, but continued his briefing. He used a pointer to point out places on the map in front of him. "The plantation," he said, "where the campfire was spotted is five or six miles up the river." He pushed the end of the pointer up the Cooper and stopped exactly where Reybrook was. Nathan and Jason quickly looked at each other.

As soon as the captain finished speaking, Nathan rose from his seat. "Sir," he said, "my dad did own the Barrington Shipping Company of Liverpool, and I've sailed into Charleston Harbor with him. I'm familiar with the area and will take a small unit of men up the Cooper if you'll permit me to pick my men."

"Permission granted, Lieutenant Barrington, but take Ensign Tally with you since he was the first to volunteer. Pick your men, have them dressed in full uniform, and be ready to depart as soon as the sun goes down."

"Yes, sir."

Nathan was disappointed that he was forced to take the ensign. He and Jason decided on seven good men they could trust in case something unexpected happened at Reybrook. Both knew the risk they were taking. If the captain found out they were acquainted with the family who lived at the plantation home . . . well, they couldn't think about that, for there was no way either of them would allow Tally to take his pick of British soldiers to Reybrook.

Tally was equally disappointed because Nathan ranked over him. He would not be in charge of the men and would not get credit for the mission's success. There was no point in him going unless . . . things worked out his way. He'd think of something; besides, it would make him look bad if he backed out now.

Near sundown, *H.M.S. Cannon* sailed closer to the harbor. A long-boat with muffled oars was launched, and ten men, each armed with a sword and a rifle, were lowered over the side of the ship and into the boat. Nathan and Jason sat at its bow, but Ensign Tally sat at the rear and planned an evil scheme. Should Nathan get killed, the command would fall to him; it would also give him a reason to destroy the home.

By the time they neared land, the night was pitch-black. They circled around Sullivan's Island where William Moultrie and his 600 militiamen constructed a fort from palmetto trees and defended Charleston against British attack during the American Revolution. Moultrie became a hero in South Carolina: the fort was named after him, he was promoted to a major general, and later served as governor of the state.

Nathan and his men headed straight across the harbor toward the wide mouth of the Cooper River. They avoided the city by clinging to the river's north bank. Silhouettes of giant trees with Spanish moss that hung scraggly from their limbs and moved about in the soft night breeze gave the men an eerie feeling. Frogs croaked in the marshland along the river's edge, and there was an occasional splash in the water when a fish leaped above its surface.

The silent oars of the long-boat dipped in and out of the water steadily until they reached the point where the Wando River met the Cooper. They kept to the left and glided up the Cooper till Nathan felt sure they were on Reybrook land.

Suddenly they all saw a fire with flames that leaped into the night air. The men lifted the oars from the water and strained their eyes to get a glimpse of someone near the fire, but saw no one and began to row again. As soon as they were out of sight of the fire, Nathan looked for higher ground.

Farther upstream, he made out the outline of a bank on each side of the river. It was the terrain he'd looked for and ordered his men to row toward the left bank. As soon as the boat hit land, he jumped over its side and tied it to a tree that grew at the water's edge. They crossed the marsh on higher ground and soon reached the entrance to Reybrook Plantation. Nathan divided his men into two groups; instead of up the front lane, he and Jason led them through the woods along each side of it.

"When we reach the house," he instructed them, "I want each of you to remain in the yard, while Jason and I go to the front door. I'll tell whoever comes to the door that we have the house surrounded, then demand that we be allowed to search the inside of it."

He called each man by his last name and gave him a direct order. "Tally, I want you, Edwards, Burns, Hart and Hampton to follow Williams and me inside the house." He didn't expect to find anyone other than those who lived there, but he wanted Tally to see that there was no one else there. "Jeffers and Cole . . . I want you on the porch, and Miller . . . remain in the yard. Have your rifles ready, but don't fire until I give the order, or it's absolutely necessary."

Nathan and Jason climbed the steps of the plantation home and Nathan knocked loudly on the front door. He heard someone on the stairs. A lamp was lit in the front room, and then Garrett opened the door.

Nathan spoke low enough that none of the men behind him could hear. "It's Nathan Barrington," he said, "but you must pretend that you don't know me. Don't call Jason or me by name. We have orders to search your home for signs of military activity, but if you'll cooperate, I'll see that no one gets hurt. Garrett, I don't like this any more than you do, but my captain was going to send someone, and anyone else might have destroyed your home or killed somebody."

"Well . . . well, come in." Garrett backed away from the door as Ben came down the stairs. Nathan waited for Garrett to give him the message before motioning for his men to come forward.

Garrett and Ben had no choice but to trust Nathan. Even if they could get their hands on a gun, they had no idea how many men were outside. When five more soldiers entered the house, with rifles ready to fire, Garrett felt helpless and hoped that Nathan would not allow any of them upstairs where Catherine and his children slept.

Nathan's knock on the front door had awakened Hannah. She lay still and listened. When she heard men's voices downstairs, she decided to get up and investigate. Her new black silk robe that she had purchased in Charleston lay across the foot of her bed. She reached for it in the darkness and felt her way to the door. On her way down the hall, she closed the door to the children's room.

From top of the stairs, she counted seven British Redcoats in the living room, and four of them held a gun on Ben and Garrett. At first sight of the British soldiers, she was filled with fear and didn't know whether to run or stand still. She thought of the gun in her trunk, but feared they would shoot Garrett and Ben if they saw her with it.

Suddenly anger overpowered her fear. The British had no right to invade the Reys' home; they had done nothing. To hold them at gunpoint was inexcusable. She took three steps down the stairs, but stopped when one of the soldiers started up them.

With her left hand on the banister, she stood tall and was ready to look him in the face and tell him what she thought.

Nathan's heart skipped a beat when he saw her at the top of the stairs, but he had to do something quickly before she recognized him or Jason. He pulled the brim of his hat low over his eyes and started up the staircase with his chin down. He dared not look up until he stood right before her. "Shhh," he whispered. "I can't let the others find out that you know me. Don't say my name or Jason's."

Hannah was so shocked she couldn't say anything. Her mouth flew open, but all she could do was gasp. When he was sure she understood what was taking place, Nathan smiled and whispered, "I love you, sweetheart. You're so beautiful."

"Oh, Nathan," she worded with her lips, "I love you." It was torture not to fall into his arms.

In a low voice, he explained why they were there, and then asked, "Are there any American soldiers in the house?"

"No," she whispered.

"Is anyone here, other than the Rey family and Rosie and Reneka?"

"Just Ole Ramey who now sleeps in a room beyond the kitchen."

"Does Garrett permit the militia to camp and train on his land?"

"No."

"We saw a fire down the river."

"One of the slaves prowls around at night, looking for wild game. Ben said that he starts a fire to cook his prey. This was probably what you saw."

"Thanks, sweetheart, but I've got to make it look good. Stay here while I search upstairs."

"Please don't wake the children."

"I won't."

"Williams," Nathan called in a quiet voice, "come with me."

Jason climbed the stairs, but stopped when he reached Hannah. He tipped his hat and said, "Good evening, Ma'am," then paused long enough to whisper, "Where is she?"

"To the right, then first door on the left."

As soon as Nathan and Jason disappeared into the upstairs darkness, Ensign Tally began to climb the stairs. He hoped to hear gunshots and wanted to make sure Nathan was a victim. Hannah stood still as he approached her. Her slender body was covered only by a thin gown and the silk robe. Her dark red hair was tousled about her head. The ensign was captivated by her beauty.

"Well," he spoke, "what a treasure I have found! I've heard of the South's lovely women, but never expected to find one with such rare beauty tonight." He lifted his hand to her face.

Hannah shrank from his touch and pressed her back against the banister as he rubbed his hand up and down her face. She became nauseated when his hand slid down her throat and under her collar. Suddenly he lifted Nathan's gold chain with the Barrington coat of arms from under her robe. It burned against the back of her neck as he pulled it closer to his eyes. When he realized it was pure gold, his greed became stronger than his desire for a beautiful woman. There wasn't enough light to read the Barrington name, but Hannah knew it could be identified as Nathan's. She was filled with anguish.

Meanwhile, Nathan lit the lamp in her room and held it up to make sure there was no one there. He searched that end of the hallway, going in and out of each room except the children's room.

At the other end of the hallway, Jason found Charleen's room. A ray of moonlight through her window spotlighted her face asleep on her pillow. He stood by the bed a moment, listening to her breathe, but hated to wake her and had turned to leave the room when she stirred in her sleep. Her deep breathing stopped, and he feared she knew that someone was in the room. Suddenly she sprang up in bed. He quickly covered her mouth with his hand and pressed his lips to her ear.

"Charleen . . . it's Jason Williams. Please don't scream." He removed his hand from her mouth and explained about the fire in the woods and why they were there.

"That crazy Big Bo . . . he'll get us all killed! You scared me to death!"

"I'm sorry. I didn't mean to. I just had to see you." He sat down beside her and laid his rifle on the floor at his feet.

Her arms went around his neck and he leaned his head forward. Their lips had almost touched when—**wham**—something crashed against the floor downstairs. Jason grabbed his rifle and ran from the room.

As Ensign Tally had climbed the staircase, Ben looked at his dad, but Garrett shook his head slightly. Ben didn't like for Nathan and Jason to search the upstairs where his mother and brother and sisters were sleeping. He felt, however, that they could be trusted, but when Tally started up the stairs, he slid forward to the edge of the divan. He watched every move Tally made, and when he put his hand at Hannah's throat, it was more than he could stand.

He sprang from the divan and reached the bottom of the stairs before the four soldiers could stop him. They knocked him to the floor, and two of them held his arms behind him, while another held a gun at his head. The fourth soldier knelt beside him, then leaned over and whispered, "He'll kill you; let the lieutenant take care of him."

Nathan and Jason reached the head of the stairs at the same time. "Tally!" Nathan yelled. "Take your hands off that lady!"

Ensign Tally smirked. "You may have the lady, Barrington, but I shall have what's around her neck." The ensign proceeded to lift the gold chain from Hannah's neck, but his hand froze when he heard Nathan's sword leave its sheath.

"We're not here to rob ladies, Ensign Tally, and you have five seconds to remove your hand from her neck, or I shall remove it from your body." The two glared into each other's face for what seemed an eternity to Hannah.

"All right! All right, Barrington!" the ensign replied angrily. He released the chain and the piece of gold fell to Hannah's chest. She breathed a silent sigh of relief and slumped to the stairs with her hand at her heart. The ensign slouched down the stairs with Jason right behind him.

Nathan knelt beside Hannah. "Are you all right, Ma'am?"

"Yes, but would you be so kind as to help me to my room?"

"Sure, ma'am."

When Jason left her room, Charleen dressed quickly in a pretty red dress with a full petticoat under it and ran a comb through her hair. She stood at the top of the stairs and watched as Nathan helped Hannah to her feet. She took three steps down the stairs and whispered, "I'll entertain the soldiers to give you some time."

Inside her room, Hannah quickly closed her door and melted into Nathan's arms. He entwined his fingers through her hair and kissed her all over her face, while pressing his body against hers. "Darling," he groaned, and then their lips found each other's.

His lips felt so wonderful against hers and she savored every second of his kiss. She clung to him, and everything was shut out of her mind except him. It was a blissful moment.

"I love you . . . I love you," he whispered. "I miss you so much, and I've thought about you every day since I've been gone."

"I've missed you just as much. Oh, Nathan, I can't believe you're here."

"I can't stay, sweetheart. We have to be out of the harbor before daylight."

"Then you must go now."

"Not yet, darling, not yet."

Charleen bounced down the staircase, just the way she had done the first time Jason saw her. Her blonde curls sprang up and down and there was a big smile on her face.

"Why, good evening, gentlemen!" She spoke louder than usual and with an extra long drawl in her voice. "Didge yawl come for tea? I do declare, I would ah had my mame whip you up a meal, had I known you's a comin'." She sashayed among the British soldiers with her petticoat swishing briskly beneath her full skirt. The men knew they were being mocked, but they didn't mind, because she smiled and flirted with them. They enjoyed it; it had been a long time since they'd seen a pretty girl. And Charleen loved the attention. She laid her hand on one man's arm and gently pinched another one's cheek. She lifted her hand to Jason's face, "Well, aren't you just the most handsome thing I've ever seen in my whole life."

Jason put his hand over hers and held it firmly. "What are you doing?" he muttered under his breath.

She pretended to give him a hug and whispered in his ear, "I'm giving them time together."

The British soldiers relaxed and even Ensign Tally smiled. Garrett and Ben were amazed at how Charleen held their attention, but how long could she keep it? What kept Nathan, Garrett fretted? Ben knew who detained him.

It seemed forever to him before Nathan appeared at the top of the stairs and quickly descended them. His sword was buckled at his left side, and he carried a rifle in his right hand. He appeared stoic for the pain he must have felt. Their eyes met, but when Nathan spoke, it was to Garrett.

"I must search the downstairs, Sir, before we leave."

Garrett gestured with his hand for him to do what he had to. Charleen suddenly ran down the hall, and one of the soldiers raised his rifle and yelled for her to halt, but Nathan stepped in front of him. "Williams," he yelled, "don't let her get away."

Jason ran toward the back door that Charleen had disappeared through. She waited for him on the porch.

Nathan hurried through each room, although he knew there was no one there. As he left the kitchen, he quietly opened the back door and mumbled, "Jason, let's go."

He had told Hannah to stay in her room, as he feared there might be trouble, but when he returned to the living room, she was there, dressed in a pretty dress.

Nathan held his hand out to Garrett. "I find no sign of any military activity in your household, Sir, and will report as such to my commander. My men and I shall be on our way, and I'm sorry for any inconvenience we have caused you." Garrett returned his handshake.

"In order to insure the safety of my men," Nathan announced, "I ask this lady to accompany me to the front yard." He took

Hannah's arm, and once they were outside, he ordered his men to head for the boat.

He turned to Hannah in the darkness and put his arms around her. "Will you ever obey my command, my lady?"

"I'm sorry, Sir, but I had to see you one more time."

"Good-bye, sweetheart. You looked so wonderful tonight . . . even more beautiful than I remembered. I probably won't see you again until the war is over, but I'll be back. I love you, Hannah; I'll always love you."

"I love you, my darling, and I'll be waiting when the war is over."

He kissed her once more, then waited for her to run across the yard and through the front door. Just as he turned to catch up with his men—**WHAM**—he felt a hard blow at the back of his head. His knees buckled beneath him and everything went black.

In the dark of the night, large hands reached down and unbuckled Nathan's sword from around his waist and picked up his rifle that had fallen to the ground. His body was then dragged from the yard.

The men took their places within the boat and listened for Nathan behind them, but heard only the croaking of frogs and a whip-poor-will somewhere in the woods. They waited and listened and then waited longer; each knowing that every minute counted and what would happen if they were caught within the harbor at daylight.

As soon as the British soldiers left his home, Garrett ran upstairs. He hurried to the children's room and saw that all three slept soundly as though nothing had happened. He found that Catherine had also slept through the whole ordeal, but when he bent over and kissed her lightly, she awoke.

"Why are you up, Garrett?"

"I went to check on the children." He saw no use in alarming her.

"Thank you," she muttered and went back to sleep.

Ben still sat on the divan. He leaned forward with his arms across his knees and waited for Hannah to enter the house before he locked the door. As Charleen climbed the stairs, he raised his head and asked, "Why did you entertain the soldiers the way you did?"

"To give Nathan and Hannah a few minutes together."

"I thought you hated her?"

"I do. I did it for Nathan because he's Jason's friend."

"Why do you hate her?"

"Because she's my teacher. Why do you love her?"

Ben sat up straight and looked at his sister. "Who said I did?"

"No one. It was written all over your face, while they were upstairs together."

Ben's eyes held hers until she smiled a fake smile and then disappeared up the stairs. He leaned forward again with his hands together and didn't look up when Hannah came in, as he expected her to run happily up the stairs. Instead, she sat down beside him and began to cry.

Ben raised his head and turned toward her. "What's the matter?" he asked.

"He didn't want to come here like this," she sobbed, "but if he hadn't, Ensign Tally, who tried to take his chain from my neck, would have been in charge and brought his choice of soldiers. They might have burned your home or even killed all of us."

"Did he tell you that?"

"Yes, but you don't believe him, do you?"

Ben sighed. "What difference does it make what I believe?"

"It makes a difference to me." She wept softly.

When he could no longer stand to hear her cry, Ben lifted his hand to her back and caressed it gently. He realized that she thought he was upset because Nathan had brought the enemy into their home, and he could tell her no differently.

They both jumped to their feet when someone rapped loudly on the door.

"Who's there?" Ben yelled, as he reached for the lock.

"It's Jason. Nathan didn't make it back to the boat. Did he return to the house?"

Ben unlocked the door and opened it. "No," he replied.

"If I don't find him in a hurry, Ensign Tally will leave us, and we'll both hang for desertion."

Hannah gasped and began to tremble. "What could have happened to him?" she asked.

"Maybe he got lost in the woods," Ben suggested.

"I called him as I backtracked, and he didn't answer. I don't think he could have gotten that far off the trail."

Ben was quiet a moment as thoughts ran through his head. "I know what might have happened," he said. "Hannah, wait here, while Jason and I look for him."

"No! I'm coming with you!"

"Well, there's no time to argue. I'll get a lantern." He ran to the kitchen and took one from the wall. When it was lit, he headed for the back door with Jason and Hannah behind him. The three of them ran down the back trail to the slave quarters and saw a dim light in the window of one shack.

Ben ran up its steps and burst through the door. Big Bo sat on the side of his bed. Ben's eyes searched the room, but he saw no sign of Nathan or anything to make him believe he had been there until he noticed Big Bo's foot slide backward to push something farther under the bed. He grabbed the large man and pulled him to his feet, and while Jason held his rifle on him, Ben reached under the bed and came out with Nathan's sword and gun.

He quickly pulled the hammer back on Nathan's rifle and jammed it under Big Bo's chin. "All right, Bo, what did you do with him?"

"I's left 'em down by de crek, Mistr Ben. I's thought dem redcoats wus yo 'nemy."

"Not this one, Bo; take us to him." He lowered the rifle.

"Yassur, I's shows yo 'ere he bezs."

They found Nathan on the ground near the brook. He was conscious, but stunned from the blow to his head and had no idea where he was. Jason and Hannah knelt beside him, while Ben held the lantern to the back of his head. He saw an ugly gash, and blood ran down the back of his neck. He took a handkerchief from his pocket and wiped the blood.

"If you can come back to the house," he said, "Mom will clean this wound and put some medicine on it."

"Thanks, Ben, but there isn't time. I'll get it taken care of on the ship, but I need your help to get back to the river. I don't think I can walk too straight."

"Hannah," Ben asked, "can you go ahead of us and carry the lantern?"

"Yes."

Ben and Jason helped Nathan to his feet, and Nathan lifted an arm to both their shoulders. Jason buckled his sword around his waist, and then he and Ben held a rifle in their free hands as they carried him to the river.

When they came near the boat, the men heard them and some ran to help. They held Ensign Tally at gunpoint. "He ordered us to leave," one of them told Nathan.

Nathan shook Ben's hand. "Thanks," he said. "I'm sorry about everything tonight." He was careful not to call him by name.

"You're welcome. I guess we're all forced to do things we don't want to sometimes."

Jason untied the rope that held the boat to the tree and Nathan turned to Hannah. "I'll be all right," he whispered. There was a moment of silence and Ben knew that he kissed her.

"Good-bye, Ma'am. I hope we meet again someday."

"So do I, Sir."

The men helped Nathan aboard, and Jason shoved the longboat from the riverbank. As its oars dipped into the water, Hannah and Ben heard one of the men say, "We were not going to leave without you, Lieutenant."

"Thanks, Burns," Nathan replied. "Thanks to all of you."

The men rowed the boat swiftly through the water near the bank of the river. When out of hearing distance, one of them spoke up. "Sir," he said, "that pretty lady must have been that young man's wife."

"Why do you say that, Hampton?" Nathan asked.

"'Cause when Tally put his hands on her, it took all four of us to hold him back. He's sure in love with her."

CHAPTER 28

The month of May brought hot weather to Reybrook and a new plague of flesh biting insects along with the hustle and bustle of the busy season. Hannah released her students early in the month; all with passing marks, for even Charleen had made a greater effort toward the end of the school year. The servants' class was also put on hold until school started back in the fall.

The summer break, however, brought little rest. The heat made Catherine weak and Hannah assumed many of her household duties. She made sure that vegetables from the garden were taken care of properly and that seeds were saved for the next planting. Before long, everyone came to her for advice about the many chores to be done. She rose at the crack of dawn each morning and worked until dark, overseeing the home.

Though the hot weather brought Catherine weakness, it seemed to have restored Ole Ramey's health. As each day grew warmer, his frail, stooped body seemed to grow stronger. He helped Rosie in the kitchen and Reneka with the children; both had cared for him through the winter months. When Sammy and Otis played beneath the oak trees in front of the house or wondered down by the brook, Ramey was usually close by, keeping an eye on them. Sometimes he sat both boys on his knees and told them stories.

After vegetables were gathered and preserved, there was less to be done in the hot kitchen, but the temperature continued to rise, and on the first day of July, it was a sweltering 103 degrees. Hannah suffered more than anyone since she was not accustomed to the hot weather. She considered having her long, thick hair cut short, as it added to her discomfort, and even asked Reneka if she would cut it.

"Oh, no, Miss Hannah. I'll trim it, but I won't cut it short."

"Why not?"

"It's too pretty. Everybody would be mad at me if I cut it. Come to the porch and I'll trim and braid it for you."

The porch was shaded, and a breeze blew across it occasionally, giving some relief from the heat. Hannah sat still and listened to Reneka talk as she worked with her hair.

"I learned to braid my misses hair when I was just a little girl."

"Tell me about her, Reneka."

"Well, my mammy died when I was little more than a year old, and the misses come and took me to the big house to live. A house slave with a boy 'bout my age took care of me. Her boy's name was Ollie. The misses was an old woman and her children were grown, so she say it be good to have me and Ollie around. She taught us how to talk and how to count and to write our names. She read to us and even taught us how to read some of the words in the books."

"How did you come to live at Reybrook?"

"The misses died, and since her husband already be dead, her children took over the plantation. By this time, Ollie and me know that we love each other and want to get married one day, but the misses' children said their mother done spoiled us and we weren't fit for nothing. They took us to the slave market in Charleston, and Mr. Rey just happened to be there, looking for a house slave to help Miss Catherine."

"What happened to Ollie?"

"I don't know, Miss Hannah." Her voice was sad.

"Do you still love him?"

"Oh, yes, I love him very much, and I pray for the good Lord to bring us together again."

"Well, you keep praying, Reneka, and I'll ask around about him." She understood now why Reneka was different from the other slaves.

"Thank you, Miss Hannah." She tied a blue ribbon around the end of the large braid that hung down Hannah's back and made a pretty bow and then held a mirror up for her to see. Hannah liked it, regardless of how it looked, because her neck and shoulders felt wonderful.

That evening when the sun sank, Hannah prayed for Nathan and for Reneka and Ollie. She thought of the money in her account at the Charleston City Bank. Was there enough to buy a slave and timberland? She didn't think so.

When Catherine's health worsened, Hannah spent hours with her. She bathed her face and arms with a cool cloth and read to her. She tended to all her needs and kept her room clean. Sometimes the two of them would just talk.

Garrett and Ben were busy overseeing the cotton crop, but Garrett had his meals upstairs with Catherine and spent as much time with her as possible. Ben went to her room every night and sat at the foot of her bed and talked, but Charleen seldom darkened her door.

As Hannah read to Catherine one evening, Garrett came with a tray that held his and his wife's supper, and Hannah laid the book aside. "I didn't realize it was so late," she commented.

"It must be a good book." Garrett looked at his wife and smiled.

"It's a wonderful book." She returned his smile.

He set the tray of food beside the bed and walked to the door with Hannah. "I appreciate all the time you spend with Catherine," he said.

"I love Catherine and wish I could spend more time with her."

"She loves you, too, Hannah, and said you were better to her than her own daugh—," he stopped, but Hannah understood. She looked down at the floor and closed the door softly.

Garrett sent Ben for Doctor Holmes, and Hannah sat quietly at Catherine's bedside as he examined her. He listened to her breathe with his stethoscope and then had her watch his finger as he moved it back and forth in front of her eyes.

Before he left, the doctor shook his head and told Garrett

there was nothing he could do. "She's suffering," he said, "from a disease that I'm familiar with, but can do little about. There's no cure for it, but this medicine will help her rest." He gave Garrett a bottle of pills. "I believe she'll get better," the doctor was optimistic.

Hannah prayed for Catherine as she worked during the day. At night she knelt to her knees and prayed for long periods of time. She asked God to restore her health, and Catherine did get better.

With so much to be done, little attention was given to the home. It became very cluttered. Hannah didn't want Catherine to see it that way, should she be able to leave her room, so with Emma and Emily's help, she began to clean. They dusted and polished the old French furniture, while Otis picked up his toys and returned them to their proper place. Hannah then turned her attention to the floors.

She was on her hands and knees, scrubbing, when the front door opened, but she thought it was one of the children and paid no attention. Someone started up the stairs and then stopped. She glanced up to see Ben look down at her; their eyes met, but neither spoke.

She had seen very little of him since the night Nathan had come with the British soldiers. He'd missed the last days of class. She felt he was angry and that he avoided her because Nathan had invaded and searched his home. She'd hoped he would understand why Nathan had come and how much worse it might have been, had he not.

Hannah knew nothing of the torment going on inside of Ben. He'd realized the night Nathan came that there was no chance of her ever loving him, and that he had to get over his love for her. But this wasn't the only thing that bothered him. The tug at his heart had become stronger, and he couldn't put God off much longer. But how could he surrender to preach the gospel when the legislature of South Carolina had put out a call for all young men to take up arms and be ready to defend their state against the British?

He worried how his dad would take the news that God wanted him to preach and what it would do to his mother if he joined the militia. Today, on top of everything else, he'd noticed that the green leaves on the cotton plants had begun to curl up and turn brown. If rain didn't come soon, there would be no cotton crop to harvest. How could he tell his dad? How could he tell him anything when he was already in agony over his mother's illness?

Hannah sat back on her feet when Ben came down the stairs and sat down beside her.

"Hannah . . . you don't have to do this."

"I know, but I want the house to look nice if your mother comes downstairs, and everyone else is so busy."

"Not everyone." He looked up the stairs toward Charleen's room.

The long braid of hair had fallen to one side of Hannah's shoulders, and perspiration trickled down her face. Ben pulled his knees up and crossed his arms on top of them. He heaved a deep sigh and his head leaned forward to his arms.

"What's wrong, Ben?"

"Everything."

"Tell me."

"I shouldn't worry you."

"Please talk to me, Ben."

"I can't, Hannah . . . not any more." He raised his head and looked deep into her eyes, hoping she would understand.

But she didn't understand. Ben was her best friend, and she was deeply hurt when he said he could no longer talk to her. She was certain that he felt the way he did because she was in love with a British. Without saying anything more, Ben rose and climbed the stairs, and she leaned forward to continue scrubbing with tears in her eyes.

There was no break in the heat, but Hannah didn't let it keep her from working. With Reneka's help, she took curtains from all the downstairs windows and washed and ironed them. Ole Ramey washed the windows before the clean ones were put back in place. The yellowed curtains that had hung for so long over the large windows in the living room came to shreds when they were washed. Hannah threw them out and decided to make a trip to Charleston for new material. She asked Julie to go with her.

"I'd like to go," Julie replied, "if it's all right with Mr. Rey."

That night before she retired to her room, Hannah asked of Garrett his permission for the two of them to make the trip to Charleston the next morning in order to purchase material for new curtains.

"I don't mind," he answered, "but who will go with you?"

"No one."

"I'll go," Ben said, somewhat reluctantly.

"No!" Hannah refused his offer. "We won't go if we must have someone go with us."

"It's not safe for you girls to go off to Charleston alone," Garrett insisted.

"I'm not a girl, Mr. Rey," Hannah referred to her adulthood. "I'll take my rifle, and I can't see any danger so long as we get back before dark."

"She's pretty good with that rifle," Ben commented.

"Well," Garrett concluded, "we do need new curtains, and Catherine would be awfully pleased, but if you're not back before dark, I'm sending Ben to look for you." Hannah threw Ben a grateful glance before she ran up the stairs.

Early the next morning, Jim hitched Star to the Reys' family carriage and brought it to the front steps of the home. Hannah and Julie were dressed and ready to go; both were excited. Hannah laid her rifle within reach under the seat and stepped up into the carriage and took the reins. Julie climbed up beside her from the other side.

Star pulled the carriage along at a comfortable speed, while the two girls enjoyed each other's company. As they discussed the Sunday morning worship service, Julie began to reminisce of a small church her family had attended in England.

"There was a piano in the sanctuary," she said, "and the

vicar encouraged me to come during the week and play it. He said I had an ear for music. I hope you don't mind, but I've been practicing on your piano."

"I don't mind at all, and I'm glad to know you can play. Will you play for the service on Sunday morning?"

"I don't know how Ben would feel about that. I can't play as well as you."

"I don't think Ben would mind."

"All right . . . if you don't think it would upset him."

"Miss Hannah . . ." Julie hesitated as though she wasn't sure she should say what was on her mind.

"What?" Hannah questioned.

"I feel like God wants me to do something special for him, but I'm not sure what it is. It's like . . . well, I can't explain it. It's a feeling that won't go away."

"Is it like a tug at your heart?"

"Yes. How did you know?"

Hannah smiled as she remembered Ben's words.

"Julie, do you think God could be calling you to be a pastor's wife?"

"Perhaps, but I don't even know a pastor, except the one I met at the barbecue last fall, and he already has a wife." They both laughed.

"Well, you must be patient and wait upon the Lord. If He's calling you to do something special, He'll surely show you what it is."

"I know, but I want to be prepared for whatever God has for me to do. It's why I want to learn to play the piano better, and I'm so thankful you've taught me to read, so I can study the Bible."

"Why don't you talk to Ben about it after he preaches Sunday morning?"

"You know I can't talk to Ben."

"Please, Julie; if he could just get to know you—"

"No, Miss Hannah. I won't make a fool of myself."

Julie refused to discuss the matter any further, because she knew that Ben was in love with Hannah, but that Hannah didn't know it. She wished that Hannah didn't know that she loved Ben.

They made a safe trip to Charleston and back, and both had agreed on a light green material with white flowers on it for the curtains and white lace panels to go behind them. The material was thin enough that light from the outside would filter through it and make the room more cheerful. Hannah was eager to get started on the curtains and sat up late that night, cutting the material.

As she worked, she thought of Julie. Why had Ben not noticed her? She was very pretty and the right age for him. Since both had revealed to her that God had called them for a special service, there was no doubt in her mind that they were meant for each other. But she also knew that God in his infinite wisdom didn't need her feeble mind to help carry out His plan, so she decided to leave it to Him. When her head began to nod, she laid the material aside.

She lit a candle before she blew out the downstairs lamp and held it up to light her way. As she passed the children's room, she thought she heard a noise. She stopped . . . yes . . . there it was again. She pushed their door open slowly and heard a whimper; it came from Otis's side of the room. The palm of her hand on his forehead told her that his body temperature was extremely high. She had to do something quickly. But what? It was past midnight and everyone else in the household was asleep. She hated to wake Catherine, as she was so ill, but she had to let someone in the family know. She decided to wake Ben.

With the candle in her hand, she hurried down the hall to his room, but hesitated at his door. She'd never been in Ben's room. What would he think if she came in the middle of the night? But there was no time to worry about that now. She knocked lightly on his door, but he didn't answer.

She pushed the door open and saw his bed by an open window. He lay on his stomach with his face toward the window, and his body was bathed in the moonlight that shined through it. The sheet had been tossed to the foot of his bed; he wore only his undershorts. She heard him breathe deep breaths and felt a sudden impulse to run from the room, but she had to let someone know about Otis.

"Ben," she called his name softly, but there was no response. He was in a deep sleep. She laid her hand on his shoulder and shook him lightly as she called his name again. Suddenly his deep breathing stopped and his head shot up from the pillow.

"Hannah . . . ?"

"Yes, it's me."

"What's wrong?" He thought of his mother.

"It's Otis. He's real sick, Ben. What should I do?"

Ben sat up and reached for the sheet at the foot of his bed. He rubbed his eyes and tried to make them stay open. "I'll see about him," he yawned. "Go back to bed."

She became frustrated at his lack of concern.

"Ben, you don't understand!" her voice rose slightly. "His fever is way too high and we must do something quickly!"

The urgency in her voice made him realize that a critical situation was at hand.

"Hand me my pants."

She reached for his pants that were draped over the foot of his bed and threw them at him and then ran from the room. By the time she returned to Otis, his breathing was irregular and his pulse beat much too fast.

Ben was right behind her, and he realized that Otis could go into a convulsion or even die if they didn't get his fever down, but he didn't know what to do. His mother took care of the sick.

Hannah recalled the night on the *Monarch* when Nathan's fever went too high and what Murray did to bring it down. There was no time to wake anyone else.

"Ben . . . I know something that might help. Hurry and go for a bucket of cool water, while I get some towels."

Ben ran down the steps three at a time and quickly pumped a bucket of fresh water. When noise in the kitchen woke Reneka, she realized something was wrong. She grabbed her robe and followed him to the children's room where Hannah dipped a large towel into the bucket of water. Ben lifted Otis and she wrapped him in the wet towel. Reneka soaked another towel as Hannah worked with Otis, and the three of them didn't stop until his small body was completely covered with the cool towels. As they began to feel warm, Hannah removed them, one at a time, and handed each to Reneka to dip into the water again before she put it around Otis.

Otis cried and tried to pull the wet towels from his head and body, but Ben knelt at one side of the bed and held his hands. Hannah spoke soft loving words to him, and he responded to her voice. When he tried to reach for her hand, Ben let go and Hannah took one of his small hands and held it to her lips. It felt cooler.

Reneka returned downstairs with the bucket of water and wet towels. The crisis was over but Otis was still very ill. Hannah asked Ben to take him to her bed, because his was drenched. She placed her sheet over him and his body began to sweat and the fever came down more. He breathed easier and his pulse slowed down.

Hannah sat down at the foot of her bed and ran her hand across her brow. Ben noticed she was completely dressed, and he realized that she'd never gone to bed. He laid his hand on her shoulder and felt her trembling. "Do you still want to be in this family?" he asked jokingly.

"You are my family."

A sober expression came to his face and he muttered, "I don't think of you as family, Hannah." He tried to tell her that he loved her, but she thought he meant that he didn't want her to be in his family.

She stood and crossed the room to the window and looked out at the night sky. She would not let him see her cry. Perhaps she should leave Reybrook, since he felt the way he did, but how could she leave with Catherine sick and now Otis . . . ?

Ben thought she walked away from him because she didn't want to hear of his love, and he didn't realize how deeply he had hurt her. He left her room and returned to his own where he lay on his bed and thought of her until Beelzebub crowed. As soon as it was daylight, he went across the hall to wake his dad.

"Dad, Otis was awfully sick in the night with a high fever." He related to Garrett how Hannah had gotten his fever down and that she had been up all night.

"You better ride to Charleston and see if you can get the doctor out here," said Garrett.

And as the sun brought full light to the day, Ben gave Blaze free reins and didn't pull back on them until he rode into the city. He and the horse were drenched with sweat, but he rode straight to the doctor's office.

The doctor was busy as usual. His white jacket was dirty and crumpled and it looked as if it had been slept in; however, his red eyes did not appear to have had sleep in quite some time. His hair had not been combed and he needed a shave. Ben had never seen their family doctor look so scraggly. Something had to be wrong.

The doctor peered at Ben over the top of his glasses. "Is your mother worse, Ben Rey?" he asked.

"No, sir. Mother is better, but my little brother is awfully sick and Daddy sent me to get you."

The doctor shook his head. "Can't go," he said, "but I'll send some medicine. I know what's wrong with him." He asked Ben some questions, while he wrote out a prescription. "Is he running a high fever?"

"Yes, sir. It went real high last night. Our teacher wrapped him in cool wet towels until it began to come down."

The doctor looked over his glasses again. "You mean Miss Hannah?"

"Yes, sir. She'd seen somebody do that on the ship when she came across the ocean from Ireland."

"You Reys are fortunate to have someone like Miss Hannah at the plantation. I wish I had her for a nurse right now. Half the kids in Charleston are sick, and I've had little sleep for a week. It's the worst epidemic of malaria I've seen in a long time. How many people live at Reybrook?"

"Uh . . . you mean in our house?"

"No, I mean on the plantation."

Ben was puzzled, but tried to count in his head.

"There's eleven in my home and five at the servants' quarters," he hesitated to think how many slaves there were, "and twenty slaves, counting all the children."

"That's thirty-six. Are you sure that's all?"

"Yes, sir."

"This will be enough quinine for everyone. I want you to make sure that everybody on the plantation takes it as soon as possible. Five people have died in the city, so it's important that you get this to everyone as soon as you can. Do you hear me, Ben?"

"Yes, sir, Dr. Holmes. I'll get back as fast as Blaze can run, and I sure thank you." Ben ran out of the doctor's office . . . and right into the banker, Daniel Overteer.

"Oh, I'm sorry, Mr. Overteer."

"Ben Rey! I'm glad I ran into you—or you ran into me," he laughed. "Does Hannah Thornton still live at Reybrook?"

"Yes, sir."

"Tell her she needs to come see me at the bank as soon as she can."

"Do you want me to tell her why?"

"No, just tell her I need to see her right away."

"Okay, Mr. Overteer," Ben called to him. "I'm in a hurry to get medicine to my little brother, but I'll give Hannah your message." He stuck the prescription into his pocket and untied Blaze's reins.

"Be sure that you do," yelled the banker as Blaze lifted his front legs into the air and then took off running.

Ben leaned forward and patted his horse on the neck. "You can make it, Blaze—you've got to."

He raced to the drugstore where his family had done business for years, but it was out of quinine, and he didn't know if another one would let him have that much medicine on the credit. He took out his moneybag and looked inside.

"You don't have enough money, Ben?" asked the druggist.

"No, sir. I didn't know I'd be buying this much medicine."

"I'll send a note for any druggist in town to let you have it. I know that Garrett Rey pays his debts."

"Thank you, Sir."

But the note was of little use, for no drugstore in town had quinine. At the last one that Ben knew of, its druggist was sympathetic and told him of yet another one that was way across town near the waterfront. He had no choice but to try to find it.

Ben knew that quinine came from the bark of the cinchona tree that grew in the South American jungles, but he didn't understand; they'd always been able to get quinine before. He thought the drugstores were out because of the epidemic until he remembered the British blockade that prevented other ships from entering or leaving the harbor, and he realized that there was an epidemic in the city because the drugstores couldn't get quinine. The war had come to South Carolina.

He feared the trip across town would be a waste of time, but kept riding and prayed that by some strange miracle, the drugstore would have the quinine. It was late in the day by the time he found the drugstore. He could hardly believe it when its druggist said he had enough quinine to fill the prescription. "I just got it this morning," he said. "A blockade-runner slipped through the British line last night." God had given Ben the miracle he asked for.

The druggist divided the medicine into smaller bags and put directions in each bag. It would make it easier for Ben when he got home. Ben gave him all the money that he had and the note. "My dad," he said, "will make sure you get the rest of your money next time one of us comes to town."

"I'm not worried. I don't know the man who wrote this note, but I'll let you have it anyway. I hope everyone gets the medicine in time, but be sure you give it to your little brother first."

"I will, Sir, and thanks." Ben ran out of the drugstore with the bundle of medicine in his hands.

The news of Otis's illness had spread rapidly at Reybrook and brought a dismal atmosphere to the plantation. Prayers were offered up for him, and everyone waited to hear what the doctor would say. The large home was quiet without his cheerful laughter and other noises that a five year old makes. Emily and Emma would not go outside to play, but stuck close beside Reneka and asked her questions about their younger brother. Garrett refused to let them see Otis, because he feared that his young son had the dreaded disease of smallpox or diphtheria. Even Catherine was forbidden to enter Hannah's room.

"But I must see him," she argued with her husband. "What if he should die?"

"He won't die, Catherine. He's better and is asleep right now. I know you want to see him, but please wait until Dr. Holmes says it's okay. Hannah has already been exposed to whatever he has. She's agreed to stay with him and is doing everything for him that can be done."

Garrett sighed and walked to the window of their bedroom. He pulled the curtain back and looked down at the front lane. "Ben should be back with the doctor by now," he said. "I wonder what's keeping them."

Several hours later, Ben had still not returned and it was almost dark outside. Hannah stood by her open window and listened as a whip-poor-will began his night song. Smoke curled over the servants' quarters from Mrs. Leander's kitchen stove as she prepared the evening meal for those who lived there. Jim walked the trail from the barn toward home. Life must go on for others, Hannah thought, even when a small boy's hangs in the balance.

Otis's body had been afflicted with fever and chills throughout the day. Hannah tried to keep him cool when his fever shot up and wrapped him when he shivered. For the moment, he slept, and she knew that she should rest while she had the chance, but she couldn't. She was too worried about him and about Ben. Something had happened to Ben or he would be back by now, and no matter how much he had hurt her, she still cared for him. The house was quiet. She listened, hoping to hear him ride up the front lane, but instead, she heard a knock at the back door.

Dolly and Julie had come to inquire of Otis's condition, and Garrett invited them in. "Otis seems to be resting better," he said, "but he's still awfully sick. Ben didn't come back with the doctor, and I was about to leave to go look for him. You came at a good time; I need your help."

"What can we do, Mr. Rey?" asked Julie.

"I hate to ask it of you, as Otis may have a contagious disease, but I need someone to sit with him, while I'm gone. Hannah has stayed with him all night and all day; she has to get some sleep. I'm afraid if my wife gets another illness—"

"I'll be glad to sit with him," Julie offered.

"So will I," added Dolly.

"Dolly, I wish you would stay with Catherine until I get back. She's worried sick about Otis, and now we don't know what's happened to Ben."

"Of course I will, Mr. Rey."

Garrett walked with Julie to Hannah's room. He knocked lightly on the door and heard her weary voice say, "Come in."

She stood near the lamp and its flame revealed her haggard face; her clothes were wrinkled and her hair was tumbled. The room had an odor of illness about it. It was cluttered with half-filled glasses and a tray of food that had been brought, but not eaten.

"Hannah, you're exhausted. Julie has agreed to sit with Otis, while you sleep. I'm going to look for Ben, and I'm taking Star, for next to Blaze, she's the fastest horse on the place."

"I'm glad you're taking her, but what shall we do if you don't come back?"

"If I'm not back by early morning, and neither is Ben, I want you to have Jim ride to Charleston and tell the sheriff. If I don't make it back, I want you to take charge of the plantation."

"But, Mr. Rey, Catherine is mistress of the home."

"With her illness and with Otis sick and Ben missing . . .

well, if I don't come back, Catherine won't be able to make a decision about anything."

"What about Charleen?"

"Hannah, I need you to take over for me." He seemed annoyed.

There was a pause and then, "All right, Mr. Rey, I'll do the best I can."

Garrett was soon on the road to Charleston, running Star as fast as she could go. He'd only ridden about a mile, however, when he saw someone's shadow on the road. "Ben," he called.

"Yes, sir, Dad, it's me." Both were relieved to hear the other's voice.

Garrett jumped from Star's back. "Ben, what happened?"

"It's a long story," he answered in a tired voice. "Blaze is tied to a tree, not far down the road; he couldn't go any farther. Let's get this medicine to Otis, and I'll tell you on the way."

When they arrived at the house, Garrett tied Star out front, and Ben ran up the steps with the quinine. As soon as he could divide the medicine, Garrett and Ole Ramey left for the slave quarters. Ben mixed a dose of it in a small amount of water and held it in one hand and a glass of fresh water in the other as he climbed the stairs to Hannah's room. He tapped on the door with the toe of his boot and heard a soft voice say, "Come in."

He pushed the door open with his foot, and in the dim lamplight, he saw someone leaning over Otis. She bathed his face with a cloth.

"Hannah . . . ," he spoke softly, and was shocked when Julie Thomas turned around.

"Oh . . . ah . . . I'm sorry. I thought you were—"

"She's sleeping." Julie nodded her head to where Hannah lay at the other side of Otis. "Mr. Rey asked me to stay. Should I go now?"

"Ah—no, Julie. I appreciate you sitting with Otis. Will you help me give him this medicine?"

"Yes."

Ben set the fresh water on the floor as Julie carefully lifted

Otis's head from the pillow. Ben coaxed him to open his mouth enough to get the medicine in it, and then he quickly gave him the fresh water to drink. Otis swallowed it all down, but the quinine was bitter and he began to cry.

Julie lifted him to her lap and gently rocked him back and forth. "I wish I had a rocking chair," she said.

"I'll get you one after I give everyone a dose of medicine."

"I'm not sick."

"Everyone has to take it. It's the doctor's orders, so don't argue." He left the room, but soon returned and explained about the epidemic. "That's why Dr. Holmes said everybody on the plantation has to take the quinine."

"Have you taken yours?"

"Not yet, but I will." He watched as Julie turned the glass up, and it was as if he saw her for the first time. Her blonde hair curled around her pretty face. She held her head backward and when the liquid was consumed, she shuddered and her slender body shook.

"Ugh! No wonder Otis cried," she commented. Ben laughed quietly.

He went to the other side of the bed, where Hannah lay sleeping, and knelt beside her. Julie noticed how saddened he was by her appearance. She pretended to be busy with Otis and not to see when he lifted her hand to his lips.

"Hannah," he spoke her name tenderly. She opened her eyes.

"Ben, you're back."

"Yes, and I need you to take this medicine."

"Your dad?"

"He's okay."

"Oh, thank the Lord. Ben, what happened?"

"Please, Hannah, take the medicine. I have to give it to everyone in the house before they go to bed. I want you to go back to sleep, and I'll tell you everything tomorrow."

"All right." She swallowed the quinine and gagged. "Ben! What was that?"

"I'll tell you in the morning when you must take another dose."

"Oh, no!"

Finally, after everyone else, Rosie was the last one in the house, except Ben, who had not taken the medicine, and he knew she was going to be difficult. He found her working in the kitchen.

"Nawsur, Mistr Ben, I's ain't qwinna take nutin."

"Come on, Rosie, the doctor said everybody. Why won't you take it?"

"'Cause, I's knows how it tase."

"You gotta take it."

"Why yo say dat?"

"If you die the rest of us will starve to death."

"Huh! Mistr Ben, the ways yo eat, I's spect yo gonna get sumpin if yo has to fix hit yoself."

"Well, I'd starve for sure if I had to eat my own cooking."

Rosie laughed, but she didn't take the quinine.

"Come on," Ben cajoled, "I've still gotta go to the servants' quarters and back down the road to get my horse. You're gonna cause me to be up all night. It doesn't taste as bad as it used to. Look, I'll show you; it's not bad at all." He turned up the glass that held the medicine and swallowed it down without so much as a flinch and then smiled pleasantly at her. "See, I told you," he said, and fixed her another dose.

Rosie eyed Ben suspiciously, but turned the glass up and swallowed the liquid down quickly. He was sure her black face turned red, and smoke must have come out her mouth when she yelled at him.

"Mistr Ben, yo done tricked me fo sho!"

He ran from the kitchen, spitting and sputtering from the awful taste in his mouth. At least I got one dose down her, he thought.

He took the medicine to the Leanders and Jim and then returned to the house and climbed the stairs with a small rocking chair. He tapped quietly on Hannah's door with the toe of his boot, and Julie opened it.

"You remembered."

"I'm sorry I was so long. Rosie refused to take her medicine, and I thought I was gonna have to pour it down her."

Julie smiled. "How did you get her to take it?"

When he told her how he'd tricked Rosie, she chuckled deep in her throat.

For some reason—she wasn't sure why—her heart didn't beat as fast as it usually did when she was around Ben. She'd never thought she could talk to him, but tonight was different. She felt calm.

He set the rocking chair beside the bed and then leaned over to feel Otis's forehead.

"He has fever," he said, "but not as high as last night. Maybe the medicine will keep it down."

"I hope so," Julie whispered.

"Do you mind staying for another hour?" I left my horse tied to a tree about a mile down the road, and I have to go back for him."

"No. I'd planned to stay all night."

"That would be great. I'm awfully tired and could sure use some sleep."

"You must be exhausted."

"Yeah—I am, but I need to give Otis more of the quinine about one o'clock. If I don't wake up, will you knock on my door?"

"Yes."

"Thanks, Julie."

Within twenty-four hours, Otis was much better and went back to the children's room. Everyone was relieved that he didn't have a more serious and contagious disease that could have spread over the whole plantation. It seemed that Ben had gotten the quinine in time, as no one else had come down with malaria, but the sickness spread more among children, and the next night, after all the Rey family was asleep, a knock came at Hannah's door. It was Reneka.

"Miss Hannah," she called. Hannah's first thought was that Otis was sick again.

"Yes, Reneka, what is it?" She sat up in bed.

"Nole be at the back door and say his Sammy has a high fever. I done told Alicia how you got Otis's fever down and they ask if you'll come?"

"Yes, Reneka." Hannah jumped from the bed and reached for her clothes. "Will you pump a bucket of cool water and get some towels, while I get dressed? We must hurry."

Within minutes, she hurried down the narrow staircase and ran down the hallway. Reneka was at the back door with towels, and Nole held the bucket of water she'd pumped. "Miss Hannah," she said, "I'd go with you, but if one of the children needed me and Mr. Rey found I was gone . . . well, he'd be upset."

"There's no need for you to go." Hannah knew that Reneka was afraid of Garrett; all the slaves were.

She was out the back door and across the porch, when Ben's words came to her mind. "Don't come here alone," he had said of the slave quarters.

She hesitated a moment, but remembered how long it had taken her to wake him the night Otis was sick. If she was too late, the fever might affect Sammy's mind—or worse. Besides, Nole was with her.

Alicia opened the door as soon as she heard them on the porch. Sammy lay on one of two beds in the front room of the two-room shack. Hannah touched her hand to his forehead, and just as Otis, he burned with fever. She quickly dipped a towel in the cool water.

Several hours passed before the fever came down. Hannah inquired of Alicia if she had given the quinine properly.

"I's don't knows how to read dem directions, Mis Hannah, but I's done like Mr. Rey says to."

"I'm sure you did fine, Alicia. I suppose it hasn't had time to take effect."

About 4:00 A.M., Sammy went to sleep and was breathing much easier, so Alicia insisted Hannah get some rest. Nole offered to walk her back to the house.

"That won't be necessary, Nole. I'll be all right."

A bright moon shined overhead when she left with the bucket of wet towels. She wasn't afraid since she could see all around her, but when she entered the woods, it was dark, and she heard noises among the trees. The shadow of their limbs danced mysteriously on the trail. She tried to convince herself that there was nothing to fear—it was only the wind—but as the noises became louder and louder, her fear grew stronger and stronger . . . . Just as she had an impulse to run as fast as she could, a twig snapped behind her and she turned quickly to see a tall figure pass through a patch of moonlight.

Her heart leaped and began to beat rapidly. She couldn't outrun Big Bo; her only chance was to hide. She slowly backed off the trail and into the edge of the woods where she stood motionlessly. The silhouette of a large figure moved down the trail and stopped no more than ten feet from her.

"Miz Hannah," came Big Bo's voice, "I's not qwine to hurt yo. I's knows what yo here fo and I's gwine to make sho yo git back to de big house. I's don't mean to sker yo."

Breathing somewhat easier, but still scared, Hannah left her hiding place. Big Bo walked on the opposite side of the trail from her, and they didn't talk until they came to the back door. Hannah felt much safer now, and said, "Thank you, Big Bo. I appreciate you walking with me."

"I's 'preciate how yo treat all de slaves, Miz, and I's sho sorry 'bout hittin' yo man. I's didn't knows who he wuz."

"I know."

Hannah had determined that Big Bo was a self-appointed leader of the slaves, and that he knew more of what went on among them than any of the others.

"Big Bo," she asked, "have you ever heard of a slave named Ollie?"

"Nawum. I's not heard of 'im."

"Well, if you ever do, will you let me know?"

"Yesum."

Big Bo had already started down the trail when Hannah realized she'd missed a wonderful opportunity.

"Big Bo," she called.

"Yesum?"

"Will you come to our church service on Sunday morning?"

The large man thought for a moment before he replied, "I's be there, Miz Hannah." She was elated.

At the breakfast table, Hannah tried to hold her head up and to keep her eyes open, but had trouble doing both. Ben saw her head nod a couple of times, and thought she had probably worked on the curtains until late. He was about to mention them when Reneka came with coffee.

Reneka leaned forward to pour Hannah's coffee and said in her ear, "Sammy is better this morning."

"Sh-sh!" Hannah whispered quickly, but Ben had heard, and he realized what had taken place during the night and why Hannah had trouble staying awake. His eyes peered at her.

Hannah perceived that he knew her secret. She turned her attention to her plate, but glanced back at him and saw that his eyes were still on her. His teeth were slightly clenched; he appeared to be angry. After eating a small amount of food, she asked to be excused.

Ben laid down his fork and rose to follow her from the table, but Garrett said, "Ben, I need to talk to you before you get off this morning." Ben sat back down, and Hannah glanced over her shoulder at him as she went through the dining-room door. Their eyes met.

She hurried upstairs to her classroom, hoping to avoid him until much later, but it wasn't long before she heard him knock on her door across the hall. When she didn't open it, he knocked louder.

In a deep voice, he said, "Hannah, I need to talk to you."

She wanted no argument with Ben, but decided he wasn't going away until she talked to him, so she rose from her desk and walked to the door of the classroom. With her arms folded in front of her, she leaned against the door facing right behind him.

"I'm here, Ben."

He whirled around and glared into her eyes.

"You went to the slave quarters alone last night . . . didn't you?"

"Yes. A child's life was in danger."

Ben shouted irately at her. "I told you to never go there alone. I can't believe you went in the middle of the night! Why didn't you wake me to go with you?"

"There wasn't time. I'm not a slave, Ben Rey. I can go and come as I please."

In a softer voice, he said, "I know that, and I know now why Nathan asked me to not let you do anything dangerous. How can I keep my promise to him when you sneak out of the house in the middle of the night?"

His words made Hannah's face blush. She stood up straight as her arms dropped to her side. "I didn't sneak out of the house, and what do you mean, keep your promise to Nathan?"

"Nothing," he muttered. He was not to have told her, but out of fear of what could have happened . . . He turned to leave.

"Ben!" she yelled, "tell me!"

He stopped, but didn't turn around. "He asked me to look after you while he was gone."

"Is that all?"

"No."

"What else did he ask of you?"

"That I be your friend and help you when you need help."

"And how much did he agree to pay you?" her voice trembled.

Ben turned to face her.

"Hannah . . . you don't think that—"

"How much?" she demanded to know.

He sighed and muttered under his breath, "He said he would make it worth my time when he returned."

Hannah's eyes filled with tears. "So that's why you don't want me to go out of the house at night. If something happened to me, you wouldn't get your reward."

Ben would never forget the expression on her face as tears spilled from her eyes and ran down her cheeks. She crossed the hall to her room and closed the door. He heard her fall across the bed and felt worse than he'd ever felt in his life. He raised his hand to knock on her door, but then lowered it. What was the use? What could he say?

CHAPTER 29

Hannah listened for Ben's knock at her door, but heard only his footsteps disappear down the hall. After crying for quite some time, she washed her face and dressed for riding, but didn't bother to look in the mirror because her appearance didn't matter. She had to get out of the house and the sooner the better. Without even taking time to close the door, she ran from her room and down the narrow stairs and out the back way.

The sun beamed from high above the horizon. Its hot rays would make it another scorching day. Birds chirped in the trees around the home, but as Hannah ran from the porch, a blue jay's shrill cry sent forth a loud warning. The birds hushed and eyed her suspiciously with heads cocked to one side, but then decided she brought no danger and resumed their chirping.

Jim had finished taking care of the animals, so there was no one to see when she cornered Star in the barnyard and pulled a bridle over her head. She led her into the barn and quickly threw the saddle over her back and yanked the cinch straps tight, then climbed into the saddle and gave her a sharp rap with the end of the reins.

At the barn door, Hannah pulled the reins to the left and took the trail that led to the back country. She hoped that putting miles between her and the home would help unleash the frustration inside of her. With Star at a full gallop, her hooves came down hard on the wooden bridge that crossed the brook and scared up a covey of quail that fed near its edge. A large black crow sounded an alarm to his flock from top of a tall pine tree. He then met them in the air, and they flew off over the woods with a loud caw . . . caw . . . caw that could be heard for miles in the still morning air.

The horse and rider crossed the cotton field and rode the trail to the rim of the valley. Cows and horses grazed on grass that was now a yellowish-brown color instead of bright green as it had been in the spring. Hannah stopped to reminisce of the first time she had come there with Ben. She saw him again as he circled the valley on Blaze, but when the memory brought an ache to her heart, she put it out of her mind and turned Star back to the trail.

It was past noon when she came to the back cotton field. Several slaves chopped grass from around cotton stalks that had withered leaves which drooped downward toward the parched earth. Each man stopped his labor and leaned on his hoe to watch her ride by at a distance. Beyond the cotton field, she brought Star to a halt along the ridge and looked out over the vast lowland that stretched between her and the line of timber in the distance. Could she make it there and back home before dark?

Star showed her impatience by letting her head drop forward, then spring upward. With the expert horsemanship that Jim had taught her, Hannah turned the animal north and held on as the sure-footed beast made her way along the top of the ridge. The slaves watched in amazement as Hannah disappeared out of sight with a trail of dust behind her.

Ben worked the rest of the morning, helping Jim clear a plot of ground at the far side of the barn for a better place to train the horses. It was what his dad had talked to him about at the breakfast table that morning. He had trouble keeping his mind on the work; all he could think about was what had happened between Hannah and him. Jim noticed how quiet he was.

"You feel all right, Ben?"

"Yeah, Jim, I'm OK."

"You're not coming down with malaria, are you?"

"No—I'm fine."

"There's something I've wanted to talk to you about," said Jim, "and I guess I won't get a better chance than now."

"What's on your mind?"

"My contract will be fulfilled in less than a year, and at that time, Dolly and I want to get married."

"That's great, Jim, but I didn't know you loved Dolly."

"Oh, I do. She's a fine girl and a hard worker."

"Yes, she is," Ben agreed.

"I want to get a job and pay off hers and Julie's contract or else work on the plantation until they have fulfilled them."

"It's good of you to be concerned about Dolly's sister and want them to stay together."

"Neither of us could leave Julie behind, but I don't know if she'll stay with us."

"Why wouldn't she?"

"She feels like God wants her to do something special for Him, and since Miss Hannah has taught us to read and write, she wants to get more education and prepare herself for whatever God has in mind for her. She hopes to get a job in Charleston and work during the day and go to school at night. Julie has a mind of her own, you know."

"No . . . I didn't know that." Ben stopped his work and looked at Jim. "What does God want her to do?"

"Well, it's real frustrating to her because she's not sure."

Ben was silent and thought about the tugging at his own heart until Jim spoke again.

"I know I need to talk to your dad about the contracts, but we want you to do the service."

"The service?" Ben asked.

"You know . . . the wedding service. Will you help us recite our vows?"

"Oh—well—ah . . ." Ben was overwhelmed and didn't know what to say. Finally, "You need an ordained minister for that, Jim, and I'm not one."

"How do you get ordained?"

"I don't know. I think a church has to do it. I guess I could ask Hannah."

"Well, find out about it, will you? We both think you're a fine preacher, and Dolly has her heart set on you doing the service."

"I—I'll try. The next time I go to Charleston, I'll go by and talk to the Reverend Moore. I'm glad you gave me plenty of time to find out about it. Is it about time for dinner?"

After he washed up, Ben entered the dining room. Rosie had dinner on the table, and Charleen and their three younger siblings were already eating, but Hannah wasn't at the table. He walked the hall and climbed the stairs by her room, because he couldn't eat until he apologized to her. He would tell her that he could never accept pay for anything he'd done for her, and it certainly wasn't why he didn't want her to be out at night. He would let her know how disappointed he was that she would say such a thing. Her door was open, but he stood in the hall and said, "Hannah, may I talk to you?"

When she didn't answer, he peeped inside the room and saw that no one was there. He went across the hall to her classroom and then looked in the library. After he'd searched the entire upstairs, he looked for her downstairs and discovered that she was not in the house.

He returned to the dining room, but couldn't enjoy the meal. When he finished eating, he asked Rosie to fix Hannah a plate. He took it and a drink to her room and set it on the table. Before he left, he found a piece of paper and scrawled the words, "I'm sorry. Ben," and tucked one end of it under the edge of the plate.

On his way back to work, Ben noticed a cloudy overcast in the eastern sky. The hot air was still and humid, like before a hurricane. They could sure use the rain, he thought, but a hurricane could bring flood and destruction.

Jim returned and the two resumed their work, but Ben began to worry.

"Jim, did you see Hannah this morning?"

"No. Is she missing?"

"Oh, she's around. Little Sammy is sick. I think I'll go see if she went there to help. I'll be back in a little while."

"All right, Ben."

Alicia came to the door when Ben knocked on it lightly. She looked tired.

"Did yo come to see 'bout my Sammy, Mistr Ben?"

"I knew he was sick, Alicia. How is he?"

"He's betta, but sho been sick and feverish. I's sho glad Mis Hannah comes las night fo 'is fever wuz so high, I's skered. She done be sent by de good Lawd and I's sho glad Reneka done told me she knowed what to do."

"I'm glad Hannah could help. Has she been here today?"

"Nawsur. She says she bez back today, but I's not seen'er."

"Well, if she comes by, will you tell her I'm looking for her?"

"I's hope Mis Hannah bez alright, Mistr Ben."

"I'm sure she is, Alicia, and you take good care of Sammy."

Ben was really worried after Alicia told him that Hannah had promised to return today. The overcast now covered the entire sky, and the clouds in the east were a strange color. Fear came over him; he had to find Hannah. He went down by the brook where he had seen her many times and to the high place by the river where he had taken her to shoot the rifle. He walked through the woods and called her name, but his only reply was a low rumbling of thunder.

It was late when he returned to the house, and slaves came in from the back cotton field. Two mules lumbered along the trail, pulling a wagon with four large wheels that made it set high off the ground. Just before they entered the barn, Big Bo jumped from the back of the wagon and met Ben coming up the front lane.

"Mistr Ben," he said, "we seed Miz Hannah ride by de back cotton field on dat hoss of huzs."

"The back cotton field! You mean in the back country?"

"Yassur. Hit wuz hur alright. She bez ridin' dat hoss fast as he can go, and she don't stop at de ridge. She head down hit lak she'd be lookin fo a place to get down to de lowlands. I speck she headed cross dem."

Ben became terrified at the news from Big Bo. From the looks of the sky, a hurricane was just off the coast, and it would flood the back country lowland. Hannah didn't know that, and she couldn't have realized how far it was across the rice fields. Once the rain started, Star wouldn't be able to make it back across. It was his fault she'd run away, and if something happened to her, he would never forgive himself. And what would he tell Nathan?

The slaves unharnessed the mules and left in a hurry in order to get home before the storm hit. A flash of lightning that lit up the barn was followed by a loud clap of thunder.

Ben threw his saddle across Blaze's back and jerked its cinches tight under his stomach. He had one foot in the stirrup when he heard a horse running. Star ran into the barn so fast she could hardly stop, just as a deluge of rain began to fall. Ben lowered his foot from the stirrup as Hannah swung down from her saddle. He'd never been so glad to see anyone in his whole life. He felt relief and anger at the same time.

"Where you been, Hannah?" he tried to sound calm.

"I rode to the back country," she muttered. Her hands reached to unfasten the saddle straps.

"You might of told someone." She noticed the anger in his voice and didn't answer.

He tied Blaze's reins to the saddle post and reached to take her saddle from Star's back. Hannah held the reins until he removed the saddle, and then she pulled the bridle from her horse's face. Together, they put the saddle and bridle in the proper place, and their eyes met.

"I didn't know anyone cared," she finally answered him.

Her words pierced his heart as if a sharp sword had been thrust into it. He leaned forward and gripped the front and back of her saddle and clenched his teeth. Blaze demanded attention by whinnying and lifting his front legs; he wanted to go with the mare. The wind howled over the barn and the rain poured down upon it. Ben's heart raged with the fury of his horse and the storm, and he could not hold back any longer.

He ran across the barn to where Hannah stood near its open door, not two feet from where the rain poured down. He grasped her arm and forced her to turn and face him and then raised his voice above the storm. "I care, Hannah! I care a lot more than you want to hear about!"

"You're hurting my arm."

"Well, you're hurting my heart! I looked for you all evening, and I was frantic when Big Bo told me you might have crossed the rice field. Why did you put me through this?"

"I'm sorry!" she yelled back at him. "I didn't mean to put you through anything. I just wanted to get away from you. I know you're angry, because you were held at gunpoint, but it had to be. I explained why Nathan came, but you won't believe me."

Ben was surprised at her words. "I believe you," he said, but she didn't hear him.

"You stopped having anything to do with me and won't even talk to me. I know it's because Nathan is of your enemies, but I've missed you, Ben." Tears streamed down her face.

He tried to speak. "Hannah—"

"Then the night Otis was so sick, you said you didn't want me to be part of your family."

"I didn't say that!"

"Well, you said you didn't think of me as family."

"But I didn't mean—"

"I care so much for you, and it hurt so badly to find out that you'd been my friend because you would be paid for it and that you worried about me for fear that you wouldn't get your money."

"That's not true!" Ben grasped both her arms and shook her lightly. "Will you listen to me? You don't understand at all. I would never take money for anything I did for you, certainly not for being your friend. How can you accuse me of that? I stopped taking care of you for Nathan long ago. I'm in love with you, Hannah, and I want to take care of you. I worry about you because I love you so much, but I realized that you would never be mine the night Nathan came. That's why I tried to stay away and why I can't talk to you the way I did; if you only knew what I've been through. I don't think of you as family because of the way I love you, and I tried to tell you that the night Otis was sick. I loved you so much that night," his voice trembled, "but when you walked away from me, I thought it was because you didn't want to hear about my love. Oh, Hannah, I love you so much. I want you to be in my family; I want you to be my wife." He pulled her to him, and as a loud clap of thunder boomed in the sky, his lips covered hers.

Hannah felt sheltered from the storm in Ben's strong arms. Her eyes closed as her arms went around him. His lips felt wonderful against hers; she basked in the warmth of his kiss. His arms tightened around her and he breathed hard. When she withdrew her lips, he let his move gently down her neck until they came to the gold chain that held Nathan's family coat of arms. His hand reached for it.

"Take it off," he whispered in her ear. "Take his chain from around your neck and his ring from your finger. You don't belong to him."

Nathan's face flashed before her. She saw his smile and the twinkle in his eyes, and she remembered the night he'd placed the gold chain around her neck. His voice came to her as if he stood right beside her. "Will you wear it until I return with a ring?" It was the night she'd pledged her love to him and said she would marry him. She had promised to wait.

"No . . . no, Ben! No! I do belong to him." She held to the chain and tried to free herself. "Please let me go," she pleaded.

Slowly, Ben removed his arms from around her. He could not hold her against her will.

"Oh, Ben, I'm so sorry," she groaned. "I didn't know. I'm so sorry for what I said." Her hand raised and almost touched his cheek, but then it closed slowly into a fist and dropped to her side. She turned and ran out of the barn and into the storm.

"Hannah!" Ben called. "Wait." But she disappeared into the darkness.

Blaze made a loud noise and tried to rear up again. Ben had to set him free before he pulled the saddle post from the barn floor.

Hannah caught a flicker of light from Rosie's kitchen as she ran through the blinding storm. The kitchen meant warmth and safety, but it was time for the Rey family to have their evening meal, and she would not enter the back door and have them stare at her. She didn't belong with the family tonight; she didn't belong anywhere. Ben would soon come behind her, so she left the trail and ran forward, groping in the darkness.

The wind blew giant tree limbs about as if they were twigs. There was no place to get out of the storm, but Hannah kept going until she ran into the wrought-iron fence that surrounded the Rey family cemetery. She grasped the ironwork with both hands and hung her head over its top. Her long, tangled mass of hair covered her face as water ran down her and filled her boots.

She reached and pulled strands of hair from before her eyes, just as a streak of lightning lit up the heavens and revealed the concrete angel that stood in the corner of the cemetery. While holding to the iron fence, Hannah worked her way to the gate and raised its latch. When inside the cemetery, another bolt of lightning lit up the space under the angel's large outspread wings. A thick layer of vines had kept the space dry. She crawled beneath the vines and sat on a slab of concrete that served as the angel's obelisk.

Her body shivered with coldness and she felt wretched inside. With her legs pulled up in front of her, she folded her arms across her knees and buried her face in them. The storm continued to rage with jagged streaks of lightning and loud claps of thunder, but she had found a haven under the angel's wings.

She thought of Ben. How could she have been so wrong about him? She blamed herself for what had happened and was so sorry for what she had put him through. Dear Ben . . . he meant so much, but she loved Nathan. "Oh God," she prayed, "forgive me for what I have done to both of them." She was racked with guilt.

She would have to leave Reybrook; it would not be fair to

Ben for her to stay. But where would she go, and what would she do? In desperation, she cried out, "Oh, Nathan, I need you!"

The *Cannon* had taken shelter from the storm in an inlet just south of the city. After its crew had furled her sails, they were allowed to go below to ride out the storm. Nathan had retired to the officers' quarters to get a few hours of rest, and despite the raging weather, he had fallen into a deep sleep. Suddenly he sat straight up; someone had called his name. He got up and woke Jason.

Jason sat up and opened his eyes. He yawned and ran his fingers through his hair. "What's wrong?" he asked.

"Hannah's in trouble."

"How do you know?"

"I just know. I was asleep, but I heard someone call my name. I know it was her."

"Well, what can we do? We sure can't leave the ship in this storm."

"We can ask God to help her, and I know He will hear us because the scriptures say, 'For where two or three are gathered together in my name, there am I in the midst of them.'" Matthew 18:20.

"Awe man." Jason lay back and closed his eyes.

"Jason!"

"I'm coming! I'm coming!" He jumped from his bed.

After he'd set Blaze free, Ben stood at the barn door for a long time. He peered into the darkness and wondered what Hannah would think. Would she hate him or fear him? At least they understood each other. He didn't want to cause her more heartache and decided it was time for him to leave home. He would join the military.

By the time he left the barn, the wind and rain had let up some and he walked slowly down the trail to the back door of the house. He went to his room and changed to dry clothes before he returned downstairs to the dining room. Rosie had cleared the supper table of dirty dishes, but left the food on it. She still worked in the kitchen.

Garrett came to return his and Catherine's dishes from upstairs and sat down to talk to Ben, while he ate.

"Why were you so late getting in, son?"

"I did some things in the barn. How is Mother?" he asked, hoping to change the subject.

"She seems to feel better. She ate most of her food tonight."

"I'm glad to hear that."

There was a pause and Ben took his chance. "Dad, I think it's time for me to join the South Carolina Militia or the United States Regulars. The British won't be satisfied with blockading our coast, forever, and when they attack, we need a strong defense."

"I know, son, but don't leave me now. Your mother is still sick, and I need you to help me get the crops gathered if there's anything to gather after this storm. I hope enough cotton survives that I won't have to see Daniel Overteer about a loan."

"Daniel Overteer!" Ben almost choked on his food.

"Yeah . . . the man at the bank. You know Mr. Overteer."

"Yes, I know him, and I ran into him when I left Dr. Holmes's office with the prescription for the quinine. He asked me to tell Hannah to come see him as soon as possible, but with all the trouble I had, I forgot about it." He put his elbows on the table and held his head in his hands.

"Well, go tell her right now if she hasn't gone to bed, but she can't go tomorrow. The road will be too muddy."

Ben became nauseated when he realized what he had to do. He shouldn't let another day go by without telling Hannah, but how could he face her tonight after what had happened? He put down his fork because he couldn't eat another bite.

Hannah's door was open, but the room was dark. Ben

knocked lightly, but she didn't answer. He assumed she was asleep and wouldn't wake her . . . not after the kind of day she'd had. He was halfway down the hall when he remembered that Hannah closed her door before going to bed except in very cold weather.

He went to his room and returned with a lighted candle. He knocked again and called her name, but no sound whatsoever came from the room.

"Hannah," he called, "I hate to bother you, but I have to tell you something." When she still didn't answer, he held the candle up and peeped inside her room. There was no one there. The tray of food and the note he'd left on her table at noon was just as he had left it. It had not been touched.

Ben ran to the kitchen. "Rosie, did Miss Hannah come in about an hour ago?"

"Nawsur, Mistr Ben, I ain't seed Mis Hannah since breakfas. Where'd she be alday?"

"Rosie, are you sure?" he yelled at her.

"Yassur, I's sho!" she raised her voice back at him. "Da ain't nobody come in dat do 'cept yoself, and dats fo sho!"

Ben wanted her to be wrong, but he knew there was no going or coming through the back door that Rosie didn't know about.

Garrett came to the kitchen to see what all the yelling was about. "What's wrong, Ben?"

"Hannah didn't come in; she's out in the storm!"

"That's not Rosie's fault."

"I'm sorry, Rosie."

"Yassur."

"It's not like Hannah to stay out at night," said Garrett. "Are you sure she isn't upstairs in her room?"

"Yes."

"Did you find her this evening?"

"Yes, Dad."

"What happened?"

"Dad, Hannah is out in the storm; I don't have time to answer a lot of questions." He took a lantern from the kitchen wall, and when Rosie brought a light from the stove, she noticed his hands shook so, he could hardly light it.

"I'll go with you," said Garrett.

"No . . . I'll find her."

As he left the kitchen, Ben heard Rosie mumble, "Well, da ain't nobody come in dat do and dats fo sho."

He ran to the barn, hoping Hannah had returned there. When he didn't find her, he ran all the way to the slave quarters, thinking she might have gone there to see about Sammy, but Nole came to the door and shook his head. As he came back by the servants' house, he saw a light in Julie's window. Perhaps Hannah had gone there to talk since Julie was her friend. He went inside and knocked lightly on her door.

"Who is it?"

"It's Ben. Is Hannah here?"

The door opened and Julie stood tying the sash of her robe. "No," she replied. "Is Hannah still missing?"

Ben held his hand to his head; he didn't know what to say, and he didn't know where else to look. He was scared.

"I don't know where she is, but I've got to find her. I saw your light and thought she might have come here to talk. She rode from the back country right at dark, and I thought she went to the house, but she's not there. Rosie said she never came in."

"You mean . . . she was out in the storm?"

"Yes. I'm sorry I bothered you; will you pray that I find her?"

"I'll do more than that! I'm getting Jim and Dolly and we'll help you look for her." She ran next door to her sister's room and then to Jim's. Within a few minutes, the three of them were dressed and held lighted lanterns in their hands.

"Dolly and I will search around the house," Julie said to Ben. "You and Jim circle back to the barn, and make sure she's not asleep on the hay." Seeing the state Ben was in, she took command of the search.

They all four called to Hannah, but she didn't hear. She had planned to stay only a short time when she crawled beneath the angel's wings and had not meant to cause trouble for anyone. Howbeit, with being up most of the night before, she had leaned against the angel's back and fell asleep.

Julie and Dolly searched around the house and peeped under the edge of it. They looked on the back porch and the front porch, but found no sign of Hannah. They huddled together and walked through the rain and mud to the cemetery. Dolly held her lantern over its fence and said, "There's no one here." But Julie circled around to the gate and noticed that its latch had been lifted. She went inside the cemetery and held her lantern up to the angel.

"Dolly! She's here! Hurry—get Ben and Jim!" The two came running, and they all four stood by the angel and looked at Hannah asleep under its wings.

Ben handed his lantern to Julie and knelt on his knees to lift her.

"Let me, Ben," said Jim. "Let me get her."

Did Jim realize what went on between Hannah and him? Did he suspect why she'd had such strange behavior that day? Ben had a feeling they all did. He stepped out of the way and Jim lifted her in his arms. He took his lantern from Julie, and the two of them followed behind when Jim and Dolly rushed ahead with Hannah.

"I would never have thought to look there," he said. "I'm thankful you did."

"I'm thankful you came to my door."

"I thought she might be with you because she thinks a lot of you."

"Hannah has helped me so much; I shall always be indebted to her."

"She helps everybody."

"I know . . . oops!" Julie's foot slipped in the mud, and she almost fell, but Ben caught her.

"Are you okay?"

"Yes."

"Let me hold your arm until we get to the porch."

Julie's heart beat faster; she was afraid to speak for fear he would notice. When they reached the back porch, she stopped at its edge.

"Won't you come in?"

"No. I . . . I'm cold and I want to go change."

"Then I'll walk with you."

"No . . . you don't need to. I know you want to see Hannah. I hope she's all right."

"Thanks for helping me find her."

"I wonder why she went so far from home and why she stayed out in the storm."

"I upset her this morning. I was angry because she went to the slave quarters alone during the night."

"You're in love with her, aren't you?" She had asked without thinking, but added quickly, "I'm sorry; I shouldn't have asked that."

"It's okay," he muttered. "Yes, I am, and I told her I was tonight, but it only upset her more." He sighed softly. "She loves Nathan and will never love me."

"I'm sorry, Ben. I know how it hurts to love someone and know that they'll never love you. Do you think Hannah will leave Reybrook?"

"No, I won't let her. I'm leaving."

"Where will you go?"

"I'm joining the military to fight the British."

Julie drew in a quick breath. "Oh, Ben!"

"What?"

"Nothing. I have to go."

"Wait; I'll walk with you." He tried to help her down the steps, but she pulled away from him and dashed into the rain.

"Julie, wait!" He caught up with her and forced her to turn and face him.

"Let me go!"

"What's wrong? What did I say?"

She didn't answer. Her heart beat rapidly. He put his hands at each side of her head and pulled it against his chest to keep the rain out of her face. And with his lips at her ear, he spoke softly, "Do you not want me to leave?"

She shook her head.

"Why?"

Again, she would not answer, but her previous words came to him. "Julie . . . who are you in love with?"

"Oh, Ben," she groaned.

"Tell me," he whispered in her ear.

"Don't you know?"

"Is it me?"

He felt her head nod up and down and realized that she hurt the same way he did.

CHAPTER 30

The summer storm was over by midnight, but rain continued to fall all night. Ben tossed and turned in his bed, thinking how complicated things were. He loved Hannah, but she loved Nathan, and Julie loved him.

Before morning, his mind was made up. He'd tell Julie he had no choice but to join the military. His dad wouldn't like it, but if he stayed, it would be difficult for Hannah. For her sake, he must go, and he'd tell her first thing that morning when he gave her the message from Mr. Overteer.

By the time Beelzebub announced the new day, he was up and dressed, but was surprised to see a light in Hannah's room as he walked by it on his way to the kitchen for a cup of coffee. He expected her to sleep late after everything that had happened the night before. He poured two cups of the steaming hot coffee and returned to her room with a cup in each hand.

"Hannah," he called, and tapped on her door with the toe of his boot.

"Yes?"

"I brought you a cup of coffee."

"Set it on my table, please."

He entered the room and saw her crouched over one of her trunks. The drawers of the armoire were pulled out, and a lot of things were stacked on her bed.

"What are you doing?"

"I'm packing."

"Why?"

"I'm leaving Reybrook."

"No!"

"Yes, Ben; it will be best for both of us. I'm sorry. I'm sorry about everything."

"You're not going anywhere, so come drink your coffee, while it's hot."

They both sat down at her table and she took a sip of the hot coffee. It felt good to her sore throat.

"I shall miss Rosie's coffee."

"I'm the one who's leaving, Hannah."

"No! I won't stay here and make you leave your home."

"You're not making me leave. I've decided to join our state's militia. It's time for me to go."

She'd dreaded hearing these words from Ben.

"You're leaving because of me, and I won't permit it. Your family needs you. Besides . . . ," she hesitated.

"Besides what?"

"I can't stand the thought of you and Nathan fighting against each other."

"We're not, but our countries are at war and we each owe our loyalty. I doubt our paths will cross. I hope not under the circumstances."

"I won't let you go," Hannah argued. "I asked Jim, last night, if he would help me move to Charleston. He said he would and Dolly said she would help."

"What about their class? If Dad finds another teacher for us, she won't teach anyone else."

Hannah looked down at the floor and mumbled, "I must go."

"Why? And what will you do?"

"I'll find a job, maybe a teaching job, and I'll be all right. I have some money in the Charleston Bank. Some of it is from the sale of my home in Ireland, and Nathan added to it in case I need it. I don't want you to worry about me at all."

"I will worry about you. How can I keep from it? Hannah, I promise that what happened last night, will never happen again. I didn't intend for it to happen, but I just couldn't stand for you to think that I didn't care when I care so much."

"That's not why I'm leaving, Ben."

"Then why?"

"It won't be fair to you if I stay. You shouldn't be made to feel the way you do in your own home, and I should have realized how you felt and left before now. I'm so sorry that I misunderstood you and for the misery I put you through. Please forgive me for what I said yesterday?"

"Will you stop it? What happened wasn't your fault. You did nothing to cause it. I knew you loved Nathan; everyone knows it. You've not tried to keep it a secret. I just couldn't help falling in love with you, and I realized how much I loved you the day I thought the snake had bitten you."

"Please, Ben—don't." Tears filled her eyes.

"Let's go eat breakfast," he said. "Maybe you'll change your mind about leaving."

There was chaos in the dining room that morning. Rosie hurried back and forth from the kitchen, filling everyone's plate with pancakes, and Reneka was right behind her with coffee and milk. Since Catherine was better, Garrett had breakfast with his children. He and Charleen talked. Emily and Emma giggled at faces they made in their round pancakes, and Otis was busy pouring too much syrup on his.

Rosie stacked pancakes high on Ben's plate because he liked them so well, but Garrett noticed that he wasn't eating. "What's wrong, Ben?" He raised his voice over all the noise.

"Hannah's leaving," Ben shouted from the other end of the table, and every movement in the room suddenly stopped. It became so quiet that one could have heard a pin, should it have dropped to the floor, and every eye turned to Hannah.

Garrett's fork stopped in midair with a mouthful of pancakes on it, and Rosie's mouth opened wide as she cut her eyes toward Hannah. Otis was the first to move. He ran to Hannah's lap and patted her cheeks with sticky fingers. "I won't have nobody to sleep with when it's cold," he said, "and nobody to read me stories. Don't go, Miss Hannah."

Emma and Emily began to cry. "We won't have a teacher," they said.

"Your daddy will find you a new teacher," Hannah spoke kindly to them.

"We don't want a new teacher," they cried harder. "We want you."

Garrett recovered from the initial shock and put the pancakes into his mouth, then pointed his fork toward Hannah, "You can't leave us now," he said. "Where would I find another teacher, and who would take care of the sick? Catherine will be awfully disappointed if you don't finish the curtains. If it's more money you want, see me in my office, but don't leave."

For once, Charleen agreed with her family. "Hannah, you can't leave now. Since you have the house so clean, I asked Daddy if we could have a party, and he said we could if you'd plan it. Please, Hannah, it would be so much fun."

Tears ran down Reneka's cheeks, and Hannah remembered her promise to help find Ollie. Reneka's sad eyes told her that she was the young slave girl's only hope of finding the one she loved.

Rosie was more positive than the others. "We ain't gwinna let yo leave, honey child. Nawsur, we ain't gwinna." She shook her head back and forth and mumbled all the way to the kitchen.

"It don't do no good to argue with her," said Ben. He had a smile on his face as he picked up what was left of the syrup after Otis finished with it and poured it over his stack of pancakes.

Hannah remained silent until all the Reys left the table except Ben. He swallowed the last of his pancakes with a glass of milk and then wiped the white mustache from his upper lip with a napkin. He rose from his chair and stood behind her. With his hands on her shoulders, he leaned forward and spoke in her ear, "Who's needed around here?"

As she heaved a sigh, he said, "I have a message for you from Daniel Overteer. He wants to see you at the bank in Charleston as soon as possible, but we can't go today because the road will be too muddy. I'll be around to take you later in the week."

Hannah turned quickly and looked up at him with
questioning eyes. "No," he smiled, "I'm not leaving either."

Three days passed before the road to Charleston was fit to
travel. Ben saddled Blaze and Star early on a Saturday morning
and led them to the front steps where he mounted Blaze and
waited for Hannah. The sun was bright, but the storm had
brought cooler weather, and he thought it would be a good day
for them to make the trip to see Daniel Overteer.

Upstairs in her room, Hannah fretted over how to dress for
the trip to town. She hated to wear pants, especially to see the
banker, but felt she had no choice since she'd be riding Star
most of the day.

With haste, her fingers pushed buttons through holes down
the front of a long-sleeved white blouse. As she tied a navy-
blue silk scarf around her neck, she coughed and felt pain deep
in her chest. Her sore throat was worse and she had trouble
getting a deep breath, but hoped that spending a day in the
sunshine would make all her ailments go away.

She pulled on a pair of denims and ran a leather belt through
the loops, then rolled the sleeves of her blouse a couple of
times before she thrust her feet into a pair of soft leather riding
boots. Her face and hair had been tended to, but she adjusted
the blue ribbon that was tied in a bow at the back of her head.
When a quick glance in the mirror gave her satisfaction about
her appearance, she grabbed the canvas bag she'd put a few
things into the night before and ran from the room with it over
her shoulder.

"I'm sorry you had to wait," she apologized to Ben as she
swung into the saddle.

Ben noticed the hoarseness in her voice. "That's okay," he
said. "I haven't been here long. Do you feel all right?"

"I have a cold, but I think a day out will be good for it."

"You sure you feel like going?"

"Yes." She smiled at him.

Ben returned her smile. He'd been his old self since the two of them understood each other. Hannah looked forward to the ride to Charleston with him and gave Star a rap across the rump with the end of her reins as they left the front lane and turned onto the main road.

It was a beautiful June morning; the rain had made everything green. Pretty wild flowers bloomed along the road, and the fragrant smell of the yellow jasmine filled the air. Its climbing vine ran along the ditch and up the side of trees with small colorful flowers clinging to it.

A buzzard soared lazily, high above them in a bright blue sky. Now and then the shrill cry of a blue jay came from somewhere in the woods, and a rabbit scampered across the road in front of them. They pulled their horses to a stop and watched a whitetail deer feed beside the road until the wind gave him a wisp of their scent. He lifted his stately head and looked at them before he bounced off into the swamp between the road and the river.

Hannah saw branches in the road that had been torn from trees during the storm. She was reminded of the cotton crop and asked, "How did the cotton weather the storm?"

"Some stalks were broken, but most survived and has perked up after the rain. I think we'll harvest a good crop, if . . . ah . . ." He stopped.

Hannah turned her head toward his. "If what?" she asked.

"Nothing."

"Tell me."

"If we can get it shipped."

"You mean through the blockade?"

"Yeah . . . I'm sorry. I didn't mean to bring that up."

"It's okay."

"Maybe everything will work out."

"I hope so."

As they rode into town, Ben said he had other stops to make. "If you'd like to do some shopping," he said, "we can meet at the restaurant on the corner of Calhoun and Meeting Street. It's getting near dinner time."

Hannah smiled. Ben never forgot when it was time to eat. "Where are you going?" she asked.

"Dad told me to stop by the feed store for a sack of chicken feed. And after we eat, I need to go by the post office and to see Pastor Richard."

"All right," said Hannah. "I would like to buy something for your mother, and then I'll meet you at the restaurant."

A slight smile crossed Ben's lips. "I'll take Star with me," he said.

Hannah walked down the street to a lady's shop where she had seen gowns and robes displayed in a front window. While browsing, she noticed a sign in a back corner of the shop that read, **YOUR WEDDING NIGHT.** She wanted to look but dared not. However, when a saleslady saw her look longingly at the sign, she said, "Come, let me show you some things."

"Oh, no, I shouldn't."

"Are you getting married?"

"Yes . . . but I don't know when."

The lady looked at her strangely.

"My fiancé is away in the war," she said, but didn't tell her he was British.

"I'm sorry. Perhaps you would like to look anyway."

"I suppose it wouldn't hurt."

But it did hurt when she saw beautiful nightgowns with matching robes and frilly underwear and wished right away that she hadn't come to the corner. She wouldn't buy anything, for if Nathan didn't return, it'd always remind her of the night that never was. The saleslady held up a beautiful white silk gown that was cut low at the neckline and had thin straps at the top. A robe that matched had a belt made the same as the thin straps; soft ruffles trimmed its edge near the floor.

"It's beautiful," Hannah breathed.

"Are you sure you wouldn't like to take it?" The saleslady tried to coax Hannah into buying it.

"No, ma'am," she answered. "It would hurt to see it, should he not return."

"I understand, and I'm very sorry. May I help you with anything else?"

"Yes. I'd like something for a dear lady who is ill."

"May I ask who?"

"Catherine Rey. Do you know her?"

"Yes! Mrs. Rey shops here often. I've heard that she's ill. How is she?"

"She's better. I'll take this set." It was a lovely pink gown with a bed jacket that matched. Hannah hoped Catherine would like it. After it was wrapped, she tucked it under her arm and set out to find the restaurant, but before she reached it, she began to cough. She coughed so hard it made her feel faint. After resting on a bench in front of a store, however, she felt better and continued her walk to the restaurant.

Blaze and Star were out front. A sack of chicken feed was tied behind Blaze's saddle. Ben waited inside at a table that had two large glasses of water on it, and Hannah quickly drank some of it. She felt faint again, but said nothing of it.

Ben ordered for both of them, and while waiting, he explained why he wanted to see the preacher.

"Jim and Dolly are getting married," he said. "They want me to do their wedding service."

"That's wonderful!"

"I don't know what to do."

"You're going to the right person to find out."

"Did you know they were getting married?"

"Yes. Julie told me, but I didn't know they wanted you to do the service."

"You know more about what goes on at the plantation than I do."

Hannah smiled. "Weddings are for women to talk about, I suppose."

"Yeah . . . and for men to dream of."

Their eyes met and her smile faded.

"I'm sorry," he muttered.

"That's okay."

It seemed that everything he said was wrong. To change the subject, he asked, "Did you tell Julie that I feel God calling me to preach?"

"No. I didn't tell anyone."

"Did you know that she feels like He wants her to do something special for Him?"

"Yes. How did you find out? Did she tell you?"

"No. Jim did. I guess you know that she's in love with me, too, don't you?"

"Yes," Hannah looked down at the table, "I've known since last Christmas that Julie loves you."

"Why didn't you tell me?"

"She made me promise not to."

He sat across the table with his eyes fastened on her, but she refused to look at him. Why was it hard for her to talk about him and Julie? She had hoped they would find each other.

"You're a remarkable girl, Hannah."

"If God meant the two of you for each other, He doesn't need me to work things out. He'll let you know without my help."

"I wonder why she made you promise not to tell me."

"She feels inferior to you, because she's an indentured servant and you're a plantation owner's son."

"That doesn't matter."

"I understand how she feels. I felt the same way."

"You're not indentured."

"I was until I met Nathan."

"Do you think God has called Julie to be a preacher's wife?"

"I don't know, Ben. Why don't you ask her?"

He smiled, but didn't answer.

Their food was served and it was very good. After eating, Hannah felt somewhat better, but as they climbed the steps to the post office, she put a hand to her chest and began to cough. She felt dizzy again and held to the steps' handrail.

"You all right?" Ben asked.

"Yes."

"It doesn't sound like it. Maybe you ought to go see Dr. Holmes before we leave town."

"I'll be all right. I just have a cold from being in the storm. Let's hurry and get the mail; I'm anxious to go to the bank."

"Don't forget that I need to see our pastor."

"I haven't; if we don't hurry, the bank will be closed."

Jake recognized them as they entered the post office. He looked at Hannah and asked, "You been playing that piano that come all the way from Ireland?"

"Yes. I'm glad you delivered it all the way to the plantation."

"It was my pleasure, Ma'am."

"Is there any mail for Reybrook?" Ben asked.

"Sure is and lots of it."

Jake went to the back and came out with a stack of envelopes that he handed to Ben.

"Thanks, Jake."

Ben and Hannah sat down on the post office steps to take a quick look at the mail. There were business letters to Garrett and a letter to Catherine from someone in her family. He handed an envelope to Hannah from John Dudley in Ireland, and she opened it carefully. Inside was a letter, along with a legal document.

"What's that?" Ben was curious.

"It's a deed." He noted excitement in her voice.

"To what?"

"My home in Ireland. I sold it before I left, but when I became homesick, I wished that I hadn't. Nathan didn't know that, but he bought it back for me when he went there to take a new piano to my church in Midleton so he could retrieve my mother's old one."

Ben chuckled. "It must be nice to be able to do all of that. Here's three more letters for you."

"Yes," she agreed, and took the letters.

She was delighted to see a letter from Rachel Hartman, one

from Sally and Ethan, and one from Mrs. Barrington. There was a letter to Ben from a college he had written, requesting information, and another—to his surprise—from Laci Lambert.

They put the mail in the saddlebags and left for the preacher's house where Pastor Richard and his wife greeted them graciously. They all had a glass of lemonade before the preacher and Ben went into his study. Hannah and Jane visited in the parlor.

"How is the church at Reybrook doing?" Jane wanted to know.

"It's coming along," she informed the pastor's wife. "All the Reys attend except Garrett and Charleen, and all five of the servants are there every Sunday. Three house slaves and another slave family come regularly. I have a promise from a leader among the slaves that he will come this Sunday; I'm excited about it." She told Jane about Big Bo.

"Oh, Hannah, God is truly at work there."

"Yes, I believe so. Ben preaches a wonderful sermon each Sunday, and Julie, the young servant girl you met at the barbecue last fall, plays the piano for the congregation. I teach a Bible class before Ben preaches."

"It will be an example for others to follow. Would you be willing to help start churches at other plantations?"

"Ah . . . well . . . I suppose I could."

"I just can't wait to tell Richard."

Since they were rushed for time, Ben got right to the point with his pastor and shared with him how he felt God calling him to the ministry. The pastor set a date for his baptism and a time for his ordination. He loaned Ben a book for weddings and one for funerals and a book on sermons. It was a world of information to Ben, and he left with peace in his heart because he felt it was what God wanted him to do.

He and Hannah apologized that they could not stay longer as they said good-bye and departed for the bank. Hannah's head had begun to hurt; she was anxious to start home.

She'd not been to the bank since the day she went there with

Nathan. As soon as she entered through the door, the memory of that visit came to her mind so vividly. She heard his voice ask her to wait in a chair, while he talked to the banker. He'd wanted to talk privately because he knew she would not have agreed for him to put the money in her account. She looked around for Mr. Overteer; why did he want to see her?

He came from behind the bank's counter. "Well, Ben," he held out his hand, "you did bring Miss Thornton to see me. Why don't you have a seat out here, while I talk to her?"

Ben started to sit down, but Hannah spoke up. "I'd like for Ben to come to your office with me if that's all right."

"Sure. It's a private matter, but if you want him there, that's fine."

They followed the banker to his office, and he asked them to have a seat in two chairs that faced his desk. He turned to a cabinet behind him and took a folder from it.

Hannah was nervous. Ben figured it had something to do with Nathan and reached for her hand when the banker began, "I'm very sorry to have to inform you—of your grandmother's death. She passed away in the early hours of December 25, 1812."

Hannah drew in a quick breath and then groaned, "Ohhh."

Without giving her a chance to get emotional, the banker continued. "The Lady Mary Kelley, being ninety years of age, outlived all of her immediate family and has left her complete estate to her one and only surviving granddaughter, Hannah Ruth Thornton."

Hannah's eyes opened wide. Her mother's parents had been quite wealthy, but not being able to have had a relationship with them, she had not expected to inherit any of their estate. She was shocked at what the banker said and found it hard to believe.

"The estimate of Mary Kelley's estate being," Mr. Overteer read from the will, "not less than three million dollars, but not more than three and a half million, including money, property of two thousand acres, tenant houses, investments, the estate mansion and all of its contents."

Hannah was speechless and feared she would faint. "I can't believe it," she whispered.

Mr. Overteer handed her the papers. "It's all there," he said, "in your grandmother's will, signed by her attorney, Barney Reeves. You're a very wealthy lady, Miss Hannah Ruth Thornton."

She was in no condition to read anything and gave the papers to Ben. His eyes scanned them; he saw her name and the amount of the figures. As far as he could tell, it was a legal document that stated Hannah Thornton had inherited a great amount of wealth. He handed the papers back to her, nodded his head, and gave her a big smile.

"A bank draft was enclosed with the will," said the banker, "and I have made out a new bank book with your correct balance. You may destroy the other one. I have also taken the liberty to enclose one hundred dollars in cash, which you will find in your book. The amount of two million, one hundred six thousand, nine hundred ten dollars and forty-two cents has been added to your balance of four thousand, nine hundred twenty-seven dollars and forty-three cents."

Ben took the bank book and quickly added the two figures together and saw that the balance was correct. He counted the hundred dollars before he placed the book with the money in Hannah's hand. She was thankful for his help. With the throbbing in her head and her mind being so disturbed over her grandmother, plus the shock of it all, it was very difficult to think.

"What are you going to do with all that money?" Mr. Overteer joked with her.

"Buy timberland and a slave named Ollie."

The banker nodded. "You can buy a lot of timber and a lot of slaves with that much money. Oh, I almost forgot." He reached for a paper on his desk. "An overseer has been arranged for your home and property in Northern Ireland, and proceeds from the estate will be sent to this bank and deposited into your account. You may contact the attorney, Barney Reeves, for any information. The attorney requested a letter from you to let him know that you received the information in the will and the money. This is his address, and if I can be of further help to you, Miss Thornton, I'm at your service."

"Thank you, Sir. I really would like to buy land, if you should hear of any for sale at a reasonable price."

"What kind of land do you want? Property in the country or the city; land to resell or to hold?"

"I want land with good timber on it that's suitable for building ships, wherever it's located. Pine, oak, and cypress can all be used."

"There are thousands of acres of swampland around here that anyone could buy for very little per acre. Most of it has timber on it, especially cypress. I'll be glad to go with you to look at some of it if you want me to."

"I do, but not today. Perhaps one day next week." Her voice was very hoarse.

"When you're ready, just come by the bank, and we'll go together."

"All right. And if you hear of anyone who owns a slave named Ollie, will you tell them that I'm looking for him? I'm willing to pay a top price."

"I've never heard of him, but I'll begin to ask the plantation owners that I deal with about him."

"I'd certainly appreciate it, and good-bye, Mr. Overteer."

"Good-bye, Miss Thornton; good-bye, Ben. Both of you drop by anytime we can be of help to you."

By the time they left the bank, Hannah felt so weak her hands shook. Her head and chest hurt and she wished she was home in bed.

"Do you want to go anywhere else?" Ben asked. "Maybe you'd like to do more shopping, now that you have so much money."

"No, Ben, I need to get home."

"You're sick, aren't you?"

"I don't feel well."

"Did you take all the quinine I gave you?"

"Yes."

"Then you should go by to see the doctor before we leave town."

She didn't feel like going any other place, but wanted to get home as fast as possible. "I'll be all right," she said.

"Hannah, it could save me another trip to town."

She took Star's reins in her hand, but instead of mounting, she leaned her head against the horse's side. Ben was right; she had to make a decision. Her sore throat had worsened, and a pain in her chest made it hard to breathe. She realized that her illness was more than just a cold.

Besides feeling so badly, Hannah grieved for her grandmother. Although she had only seen her twice in her life and could barely remember one of those visits, she had loved her. She thought of the little tea pot that was packed away in her trunk and how it had come to be there.

Ben mounted Blaze and waited for Hannah. When she didn't get in the saddle, he dismounted and circled around Blaze and Star to where she stood with her head against Star's side.

"Come on, Hannah," he took her arm, "let me help you to the saddle."

But instead of getting on the horse, she turned and bowed her head against his chest. She needed someone to hold her.

"I didn't know that my grandmother loved me so much. I wish I could have been with her. Oh, Ben, she had to die alone." Tears trickled down her cheeks, but she wiped them away with her hand. "I dreamed of going to see her, but now it's too late, and she'll never know how much I cared."

Ben put his arms around her. "I'm sorry about your grandmother," he said, "but she must have known you cared, or she wouldn't have left you everything she owned. She must have known that you cared very much, and she's not alone anymore." In trying to console her, he realized how sick she was. "Please, Hannah," he said, "get on the horse. We're going to see the doctor."

Dr. Holmes looked in Hannah's throat and listened to her breathe. He asked her lots of questions to determine his diagnosis before he went to the back of his office for medicine. With it in his hand, he went to talk to Ben.

"Does she have malaria?" Ben asked.

"No," the doctor replied. "I believe she has pneumonia and needs complete rest. This medicine will make her sleep. Give her one in the morning and one at night. She'll run a fever for several days, so be sure she drinks plenty of liquids. Now remember, and you tell Garrett, she is not to do anything but rest; she is not to get out of bed. I'll be out that way on Thursday to check on her."

"Yes, sir, Dr. Holmes; I will and thanks." He got out his moneybag, but the doctor held up his hand.

"Hannah has already paid for her visit," he said. Ben had forgotten how wealthy she was.

"Are you in a carriage?" the doctor asked.

"No. We rode our horses to town."

"Then hitch them to mine. Hannah's in no condition to ride. I'll ride my horse when I come on Thursday and pick it up."

Ben hitched Star and Blaze to the doctor's carriage and helped Hannah to the front seat beside him. He made her as comfortable as he could, but it was a long ride to Reybrook and before they reached home, she was very ill.

She leaned against him, and he thought she was asleep, but when the carriage turned off the main road, she sat up. "Ben," she said, "please don't tell anyone about the inheritance."

"Why?" He was excited for her and wanted to tell everybody.

"I don't know. I just don't want to tell anyone. They might think that . . . that—"

"You're bragging?"

"Yes."

"You're too humble, but I won't say anything if you don't want me to."

Garrett saw them ride up the front lane and came to the porch to meet them.

"What's wrong, Ben? Isn't that Dr. Holmes's carriage?"

"Yes, sir. He loaned it to us because Hannah's too sick to ride. The doctor said she has pneumonia and is to have complete rest. He's coming to see her on Thursday and will get his carriage then."

"Well, let's get her inside and upstairs to her room."

Ben picked Hannah up and handed her to Garrett who lifted her down from the carriage.

"I can walk, Mr. Rey. Please put me down."

"Are you sure?"

"Yes."

"Then I'll take the doctor's carriage to the barn."

Ben helped Hannah up the stairs and to the door of her room, but he would not go inside.

"I'll get someone to help you," he said, and went to look for Reneka, but she was busy giving the twins a bath. Rosie was cleaning the kitchen, and his mother was still upstairs in her room. He thought of Julie, but could he ask her? She'd helped him find Hannah in the storm, but he didn't know then that she was in love with him. Hannah would need help all week and there was no one else, so he walked the trail to the servants' quarters.

Julie and Mrs. Leander were in the kitchen when he arrived; both ladies seemed surprised to see him. "What do you need, Ben," Julie asked in a quiet voice.

"I need to ask a favor of you."

She took off her apron and followed him to the front porch. "What do you want me to do?"

"Hannah's ill. The doctor said she has pneumonia and needs complete rest, but there's no one in the household to take care of her. I know it would be asking too much of you and if you'd rather not—"

"Of course, I'll take care of Hannah. How could I refuse after all she's done for me? I'll get a few things together and be there as soon as possible."

"Thanks, Julie."

Julie found Hannah lying across her bed, still dressed in the clothes she had worn to Charleston. A comfortable gown was found for her. But not until Ben came to administer the medicine the doctor had given him, did Julie realize how sick Hannah was. The fever was so high she could hold nothing on her stomach, and the medicine, along with the water she had drank, came back up.

Julie changed the sheet on her bed and cleaned the floor, then brought a basin in case she threw up again. Ben stayed, for he was worried about Hannah, and he wouldn't leave Julie alone, with her being so sick.

Around midnight, the fever went so high that Hannah became delirious. She tried to sit up, but Ben wouldn't let her.

"You can't get up," he said.

"Nathan?"

"No, I'm not Nathan." He remembered the other time she had thought that and what had happened. He couldn't let it happen again, not in front of Julie, but Hannah held to both his arms and would not let go. He looked around for Julie, hoping she would know what to do, but discovered that she was not in the room. She had left quietly.

"Nathan, I love you."

"Nathan's not here, darling," Ben held her in his arms, "but he'll be back. He'll come for you."

Her body burned with fever and he was so afraid. Why had Julie left him at such a crucial time? Suddenly the door opened, and she came in with a bucket of water in one hand and towels in the other. She had heard how Hannah had brought Otis's and Sammy's fever down.

She wrapped a cool, wet towel across Hannah's shoulders before she forced her hands from Ben's arms and gently laid her back on the pillow. She worked quickly, but talked kindly to Hannah as she covered her with the wet towels.

Ben got another pill and held Hannah's head up. Julie put the medicine in her mouth and lifted a glass of water to her lips, and Hannah swallowed it with a bit of the water. She lay still as the cool towels soothed her body, and the medicine did not come up, but her fever did come down. Ben took the bucket and wet towels to the kitchen, while Julie helped her change to a dry gown and to the other side of the bed. By the time Ben returned, she was asleep.

"I think she'll sleep now," Julie said. "Why don't you go to bed?"

He was so grateful for her willingness to help and wanted to tell her so. "Julie—"

"Please go rest, Ben," she interrupted him and let him know that she didn't want to talk. "I'll get a blanket and pillow and sleep on the floor beside Hannah."

"I'll get them for you."

After Ben left, Julie spread the blanket on the floor, and she laid her head on the pillow, but she didn't sleep. She kept a close vigil on Hannah throughout the night and held her hand to her head often to make sure the high fever had not returned . . . and she prayed.

The next morning was Sunday. Hannah awoke and insisted that she must get ready for church.

"But, Hannah," Julie argued, "you're very ill and should not get up. I don't believe Ben will have church today. He got very little sleep last night."

"Oh, we must have church!" Hannah put her feet over the side of the bed and tried to stand, but she was too dizzy.

"Please, Miss Hannah . . . you're not able to get up. If you'll lie down, I'll tell Ben that you want him to have the service."

"I must go; someone special is coming."

"Who?"

"You'll see." She lay back on the pillow and Julie ran to wake Ben.

"Ben!" she knocked loudly on his door.

He opened it quickly. "What is it?"

"Hannah insists that she's going to church. She said someone special is coming."

"I'll talk to her."

As Ben entered her room, Hannah leaned forward to tie her shoes.

"Hannah, stop that and get back in bed." Ben spoke firmly.

"I have to go to church."

"You're not to get out of bed and that's the doctor's orders."

"But, Ben—"

"No. We'll have church but you won't be there."

"Will you tell him why I'm not there?"

"And who is he?"

"Big Bo. He said he would come today."

"When did you talk to Big Bo?"

"The night I went to the slave quarters. He walked me back to the house. Ben, he's not a bad person. Do you know what this could mean since he's a leader among the slaves?"

"Yes, Hannah, I know. Now please lie down." He shook his head as he thought of what could have happened. Julie brought her a glass of water with more of the medicine and smiled at Ben as he rolled his eyes at what Hannah had done.

"Do you feel like playing the piano this morning?" he asked.

"Yes."

"I'll ask Reneka to stay with her."

The church service began at the regular time. Dolly taught the Bible class, but Big Bo wasn't there. After the music, Ben stood to preach, thinking Big Bo had let Hannah down, but the door began to open slowly, and the tall black man stuck his head in. He looked around with uncertainty until Rosie moved down a seat and motioned for him to sit by her. He took off his old hat and tucked it under his arm as he sat down.

Ben had prepared a different sermon for that morning, but when Big Bo came in, he changed and told once again of how Jesus had died on the cross so that everyone could be forgiven for everything they had ever done, or ever would do, wrong. He preached this simple message in words that any child could understand, hoping that Big Bo would come forth when he gave the invitation and make a profession of his faith in Jesus Christ. However, at the end of the sermon, when Julie began to play softly, Emily and Emma made their way to where Ben stood and Big Bo slipped quietly out the door.

Catherine was elated to hear that the twins had confessed to others their faith in Jesus. She insisted they come to her, and she gave each a hug and had them sit on her bed and share their experiences.

When Hannah's condition worsened, Julie worked around the clock taking care of her. She bathed her face and arms with a cool cloth and did everything possible to make her comfortable. Ben was needed in the cotton field by day, but he came each evening and stayed until late into the night. Since Hannah could keep no solid food down, Rosie made chicken broth, and Julie spoon-fed it to her. Catherine said it had a healing effect.

On Wednesday of that week Hannah became so ill that Julie feared she wouldn't live through the night. Late that evening, she took her hand and knelt beside her bed and began to pray fervently. The room was dark when Ben entered quietly and thought that there was no one with Hannah. He couldn't see Julie at the far side of the bed, but when he walked closer, he heard a sound like someone whispering. As his eyes adjusted to the dark room, he saw her on her knees, and he took Hannah's other hand and knelt to his knees at the opposite side of the bed. Before long, he felt a slight squeeze to his hand. Julie's head rose at the same time as his, and he knew she had felt it too. Hannah was awake.

He sat on the side of her bed and spoke softly. "How do you feel?"

"Not very well, Ben. Will you do something for me?"

"Anything you ask."

Julie walked to the open window and looked up at the night sky. A whip-poor-will's song drowned out the conversation behind her. She had put her own feelings about Ben aside, and all that mattered was for Hannah to get well.

"Please write down what I tell you," Hannah said to Ben, "and I shall sign it. Should I die, I want you to buy the timberland for Nathan, and try to find Ollie for Reneka."

"You're not going to die, Hannah. I won't let you."

"Oh, Ben, only God controls life and death." She spoke Nathan's words from the night Little Michael was born on the *Monarch*.

"After you have bought many acres of timberland and the slave, please divide the rest of my inheritance between the church, yourself and Julie, Dolly and Jim, and Rosie and Reneka."

"Hannah—"

"Sh-h-h . . . promise me, Ben."

"All right . . . I promise," he answered reluctantly.

"And please tell Nathan how much I loved him. Tell him that I wanted, so badly, to be here when he returned."

"You will be, Hannah." But she didn't hear him because she'd slipped away again. He buried his face beside hers and cried.

Hannah was near death for the next two days. The doctor came on Thursday, but there was nothing he could do.

"She's in the hands of God," he said. "Only He can restore her health at this point, but continue to care for her and get as much liquid down her as possible. Talk or read to her as if she listens. Sometimes this helps to bring one out of a coma."

That night Catherine and Garrett came to Hannah's room, and Garrett bowed his head while Catherine prayed over her. Otis and the twins were allowed to see her, and Otis patted her cheeks, but Emma and Emily cried when Hannah did not wake up. They knew that something was terribly wrong. Rosie and Reneka came together and held to each other for support. Dolly and Jim came, and Dolly insisted that she stay with Hannah that night, so Julie could rest.

Julie gathered her things to leave.

"I'll walk with you," Ben said.

"You don't need to."

"Yes, I do; I need to talk to someone."

They left the room together and descended the narrow stairs. "I appreciate everything you've done," he said. "You've gone far beyond the call of Christian duty to help Hannah. I don't know as I could take care of Nathan the way you've taken care of Hannah."

"You don't know him the way I know her. Good night, Ben. Thank you for walking with me."

"Don't go in, Julie. I need to talk to someone, and you're the only person who understands how I feel. I need your help."

Julie sighed. "I'm sorry, Ben. I'm sorry that you hurt so badly, but I didn't take care of Hannah just because it was my Christian duty. I love her too, and I don't want her to die any more than you do."

"I know, and I know it's my fault she's so sick. I caused her to stay out in the storm. If she dies, how can I tell Nathan that when he returns? He asked me to look after her. Oh, Julie, I'm so scared. I love her, but I want her to live for Nathan. He loves her and she loves him."

"You must not blame yourself for her illness. She wouldn't want you to."

"No, but I do."

"Ben, I'm quite exhausted."

"I know and I'm sorry for keeping you." They said good-night, and Ben returned to his room to write down Hannah's request. He didn't know if she'd be able to sign it or not.

Before Catherine left Hannah's room that night, she asked Dolly to let her know of any change.

"Please come, Dolly, and knock on our door. Whether the news is good or bad, I want to know."

"I will, Miss Catherine."

Dolly talked to Hannah throughout the night, just as though they carried on a conversation. Hannah lay motionlessly with her head on the pillow, while Dolly talked about her and Jim's wedding plans. She talked about everything she could think of, hoping something would bring Hannah out of her deep sleep.

When Beelzebub crowed at daylight, she picked up the sheet to straighten it. "I bet you could kill that rooster," she said, "for waking you this morning."

"No, Dolly," came Hannah's feeble voice, "nothing ever sounded so good."

Dolly dropped the sheet and sprang to her side.

"Hannah—oh, Miss Hannah!"

Hannah raised her hand to Dolly's cheek and asked, "Do you think you could get Rosie to make me a cup of coffee?"

"You bet I can!" Dolly ran from the room.

Beelzebub had awakened Ben, too, and he jumped out of bed when he heard Dolly run down the hall. He grabbed his pants, as he thought she would come for him. His heart pounded, and he dreaded to hear what she had to say. He opened his door just as Dolly knocked on his parents' door. He stood in the darkness and listened.

"Miss Catherine!" Dolly called.

Ben heard his dad open the door. "Is she gone?" he asked sadly.

"No, Mr. Rey. She's awake and wants a cup of Rosie's coffee. She seems to be all right."

"Thank God," Ben heard his dad say.

He closed his door quietly and leaned against it. "Yes . . . thank you, God," he whispered, and then walked to his dresser and tore up the paper he had written before he went to bed.

CHAPTER 31

When two countries are at war and one of them blockades the other, it cuts off important ports of that country to the rest of the world, helping to defeat such country by cutting off needed material and supplies. A blockade also prevents exports that are vital to the country's economy from leaving its ports.

The export of cotton was very important to southern planters along the coastal waters of South Carolina. The large profit it brought them, when shipped to the textile mills of Europe, made it their chief money crop. By autumn of 1813, Great Britain held a tight blockade along South Carolina's coastline, making it a high risk for blockade-runners to ship anything out of Charleston's harbor.

Garrett's cotton lay in a warehouse; Ben had been justified in his concern to get it shipped. There would be no barbecue that fall, and Charleen begged to have just a small party.

"I'm sorry, honey," was the same answer Garrett gave his daughter everyday at suppertime. "There just isn't enough money right now. Winter provisions have to be bought, and end-of-year taxes must be paid along with salaries and other debts I owe. There will be no money for Christmas unless a blockade-runner gets our cotton through."

Not accustomed to being told no, Charleen ran from the dining room in tears every evening, leaving Garrett and Catherine somewhat distraught.

Finally Hannah could stand it no longer. "I'll teach without pay this month, Mr. Rey, and I'll be glad to help with a party. It would be a good thing for each young person on the plantation. May Julie, Dolly, and Jim come as guests?"

Before Garrett could answer, Catherine spoke up. "Of course

they may. It's wonderful of you to offer to go without pay for a whole month just so Charleen can have a party, isn't it Garrett?"

"Yeah," Garrett's response was more of a guttural sound in his throat than a word.

"Are you sure you can get by without the money?" Catherine asked.

A grin spread across Ben's face, but vanished quickly when Hannah's eyes sent him a message. "Yes, ma'am, Catherine," she said, "I'll be fine."

Charleen was elated and started to her room at once to compile a list. "Frank and Laci Lambert would be first on the guest list," she insisted, and it was Hannah who was forced to suppress a smile when she saw Ben's face grimace. She was reminded of the letter he'd received from Laci.

Several evenings as she watched the sun disappear over the horizon from her bedroom window, she saw Ben walk the trail to the servants' quarters to spend time with Julie. She knew that her illness had brought them together and was convinced that God had allowed it for that reason, yet didn't understand the prick to her heart each time she saw him walk that way.

She and Ben remained at the table after everyone else left. Rosie put the food away, and the two of them stacked the dishes near the dishpan. While she wiped the table clean, Ben sat back down.

"How do you feel?" he asked.

"Okay."

"I hope you'll go by Dr. Holmes's office next time you're in Charleston. I'm afraid you're not over the pneumonia."

"All right . . . if you think I should. I suppose I'll be going soon to get things for the party."

"I'm glad you want to include Julie, but I don't think she'll come. She won't have proper clothes to wear and will feel out of place."

"I'll talk to her."

"I wish you would."

"I'll have to think of something for entertainment. We'll play games and it would be nice to have music. I'll play the piano. Does anyone else play an instrument?"

"Jim plays the harmonica and Mom has a dulcimer . . . if you can get her to play it."

"Perhaps I can talk her into it," Hannah smiled.

There was a pause in their conversation, as Hannah thought about Laci and Frank. Without thinking she asked, "What did Laci Lambert say in her letter?"

"Hannah!" Ben was embarrassed. "Did I ask you what Nathan said in his letter . . . after you wouldn't let me read it?"

"No—but . . . ah . . . I just . . . I'm sorry." She felt her face blush. It was a stupid thing to have asked and certainly none of her business.

Ben laughed when her face began to blush. To make her feel better, he asked, "What did Nathan's mother say in her letter?"

All of the mail that she'd received at the post office, the day she and Ben went there, lay on her dresser for several days, as she had been too ill to read. She remembered the day Julie handed her the letters and helped her sit up with pillows behind her back.

Sally had written how wonderful it was being married to Ethan and how excited they were that she expected their first child. Rachel wrote about her children and related that Steven was almost as tall as John. They were all three in school and everyone was well. John had gotten a job soon after their arrival and everything was fine. The letter made Hannah yearn to see them.

"Hannah." Ben's quiet voice brought her back.

"Oh, I'm sorry, Ben. I thought of the mail I received."

"I asked you a question."

"Mrs. Barrington said that Captain Barrington died." A smile faded from Ben's lips.

"I'm sorry to hear that."

"Yes . . . so was I. Nathan loved his dad so much. I can imagine how hard it was for his mother to send him the terrible news in a letter."

"I can imagine how hard it was for Nathan to receive it in a letter. I met the captain the day I went aboard the *Monarch* with him. He seemed to be a good man and treated me awfully nice."

"He was a good man, Ben, and since my father is dead, I had thought that . . . well . . . it is of no use to think about that."

"You would have been close to him?"

"Yes. I felt closer to him than I did Nathan's mother."

"Did you have a problem with her?"

"Not really, but sometimes I felt a little uncomfortable around her. I know she didn't mean to make me feel that way. It's just that I was raised so differently from Nathan. He understands that, but I'm afraid she doesn't."

"Maybe there won't be a problem after you're married."

"I hope not. I'll do everything I can to get along with her."

"You do everything you can to get along with everyone."

She mumbled, "Thank you," and rose from the chair. "I must go to my room; I have a stack of papers to grade."

"I'll walk upstairs with you."

They climbed the stairs together and Ben went to his room, but Hannah stopped by her classroom for the papers to be graded. When she entered her room, she noticed an envelope on her table that had not been there before. She picked it up and smiled when she saw that it was addressed to Mr. Ben Rey. It was the letter from Laci.

June 10, 1813

Dearest Ben,

I'm so sorry for my behavior on the day that I last saw you. It seems it was so long ago, but I think of you every day. I do hope you will come back to see me again soon.

My father really likes you, Ben, and said he would be pleased to have you for a son-in-law. And my brother has forgiven you for hitting him in the nose.

I'm even sorry for what I said about your teacher whom you were so quick to defend. Does she still live

in your home, or has her British fiancé returned for
her? I hope he has, so you might have more time for me.

I love you,

Laci

Hannah was astonished at Laci's boldness. She'd practically
proposed marriage to Ben. And what had she said against her
that made Ben feel it necessary to defend her. Did she know
that Ben loved her?

No wonder he made such a face when Charleen announced
that she would invite Laci and her brother to the party. If he and
Julie were together, would Laci cause a scene? An uneasy feeling
came over her.

The very next week, invitations to the party were sent out,
and Laci was elated when she received one for herself and her
brother. She erroneously believed that since she had written
the letter to Ben, he had really planned the party for her sake.
She would buy the most beautiful dress that could be found in
all of Charleston, for after all . . . she would be the guest of
honor.

It was the day that had been set for the party and everything
was ready. Hannah had spent hours going over every detail
with Charleen. Besides the Lamberts, invitations had been sent
to several students from Charleston and a couple of young
people they had met at the city library. Dr. Holmes's son was
among those to receive an invitation, and a Miss Anna Overteer
was the banker's daughter. Three young people from other
plantations had also been invited.

The trip to Charleston for party goods gave Hannah a chance
to purchase new dresses for Julie and Dolly. She'd even bought
a new suit for Jim who promised to bring his harmonica. She
also bought a new dress for Catherine, in hopes she'd be able

to come downstairs, but decided it best not to ask her to play the dulcimer. It was more important for her to mingle with the young people.

Catherine loved the new soft-blue dress. "It's beautiful," she commented. "I wanted a new one for the party so badly, but didn't think we could afford it right now. I didn't feel like making the trip to Charleston if we could have. I love the color and shall wear a blue ribbon in my hair."

"You'll look lovely," Hannah remarked.

For herself, Hannah purchased nothing new. The party would give her an opportunity to wear the dress that Nathan liked; the one she had worn the night he took her to the restaurant in New York City. It was Charleen's party, and she wanted nothing to draw attention to herself.

Since everything was ready that morning, Hannah took a child's book from her classroom shelf and looked for Otis. He needed help with his weekly reading lesson. She found him pushing a make-believe wagon along the edge of the front porch.

"Otis," she called to him, "bring your wagon and sit with me." Just as the two of them sat down on the porch with their legs dangling over its edge, Sammy peeped around the side of the house.

"Come here, Sammy," Hannah lifted her hand and motioned to him. "Come and listen, while I read a story." And unaware of any harm that she did, Hannah pointed a finger to the words as they were read aloud. Sammy watched her finger as he listened, and being the smart little boy that he was, the figures on the paper began to make sense.

Before the story was completed, Charleen summoned Hannah from within the house. She laid the book down and went inside, planning to return soon. But Sammy and Otis couldn't wait to find out how the story ended, so they picked up the book and began to figure the words out together. When the story was finished, they laid the book aside and began to push two make-believe wagons along the edge of the porch.

Hannah became busy within the house and the book was forgotten.

Right after the noon meal, Hannah and the Rey family went upstairs to dress for the party. It was almost time for guests to arrive. Catherine helped Charleen with a beautiful emerald-green dress that had small satin bows down its front. Its puff sleeves stood up just right, and a v-shaped neckline fit nicely over her breast. She looked fantastic with a green satin bow at the back of her blonde curls.

Hannah dressed quickly and returned downstairs. She wanted someone posted at the front door to welcome the guests, and Reneka and Rosie were busy in the kitchen, preparing food to be served. Punch and lemonade and good things to eat, such as homemade cookies, candies, and pies awaited the guests at one end of a table in the living room; ham and cheese, sliced in small pieces, and breads from Rosie's oven were at the other end of the table.

Although she desired no attention, Hannah looked lovely. She wore the pretty bonnet that came with her dress, and its dark lavender color enhanced the dress's color. A ruffled ribbon circled the front edge of the bonnet and was tied in a bow under her chin.

Catherine was beautiful as she descended the stairs on her husband's arm. Garrett wore a dark blue suit that looked marvelous with his wife's new dress, and the starched ruffles on his white shirt stood out perfectly. They were a handsome couple.

"You both look wonderful," said Hannah.

"Thank you, dear. It's such a pretty dress, and I could not have picked one that I liked better. But I wish you had not spent so much."

"Think nothing of it," Hannah insisted. "Be happy and enjoy the party."

"Oh, I will, and I don't think I've ever seen Charleen so excited. The living room has never looked this nice before, and I appreciate all the work you put into the beautiful curtains.

I always felt bad about the old ones when company came. You do so much for all of us, Hannah; I don't know how we ever got along without you."

"Thank you, Catherine. You're like family to me and I need a family."

"You'll always be part of our family."

As Catherine and Hannah talked, the first carriage arrived, bringing Miss Anna Overteer and her dashing young escort. Miss Overteer and the young man were invited in with great to-do. Soon afterward, several guests from Charleston arrived together, and Julie came with Dolly and Jim.

Dolly and Jim looked nice, but it was plain to see that the way they looked was not the most important thing in the world to either of them. Julie, on the other hand, had gone to a great deal of trouble to be beautiful—and beautiful she was. Her dress was made from a fine cloth and its fall colors were very becoming to her. She wore a pale yellow ribbon in her hair. Hannah was astonished at how she walked elegantly across the room and appeared older than her seventeen years. She had noticed what a pretty face Julie had and that her body was formed with a very flattering figure, but she'd never seen her dressed up and neither had anyone else at Reybrook. A set of silver rings that she had loaned her dangled from her ears, but her throat was bare.

The Lambert's fine family carriage, driven by a slave, pulled into the yard and stopped in front of the steps. Frank stepped from the carriage and lifted a hand to his sister. He was dressed in an expensive suit with a gray silk vest over a white shirt. The dark suit with his dark hair made his white teeth very noticeable, making him even more handsome when he smiled.

Without a doubt, Laci was dressed in the most beautiful red dress in all of Charleston. She was a striking figure, but was very disappointed that there was no one to take her hand except her brother when she stepped from the carriage. Since many guests had arrived before them, no one noticed when the Lambert siblings climbed the steps to the front porch.

There was no one on the porch to greet Frank and Laci except little Sammy who had come to play. He sat reading the book that had been left there that morning as he waited patiently for Otis to come out. When Laci realized that Sammy read words from the book, she lifted her eyebrows and looked down at the little black boy. "Who taught you to read?" she asked.

With a shy grin on his face, Sammy looked up at Laci and replied proudly, "Miss Hannah."

Frank's knock brought Catherine and Garrett hurrying to the front door with apologies. The two were invited in and escorted cordially to the refreshment table. "I'm so glad I wrote to Ben," Laci remarked to Catherine, "for he's thought of a wonderful way to bring the two of us together."

Catherine had no idea what Laci meant, but Hannah overheard her comment and realized that she thought the party had been planned by Ben, so the two of them could be together. Before she could warn Ben, Charleen appeared at the top of the staircase, and all heads turned to see her. She looked more beautiful than anyone had ever seen her before and was escorted by her brother who wore a black suit and white shirt with a black tie. He was as handsome as she was beautiful. Hannah stepped backward against the wall as Charleen made her debut.

At the foot of the stairs the guests closed in around Ben and Charleen, but Ben slipped through them and made his way to the punch bowl. As Charleen greeted her guests, his eyes scanned the room. He saw Dolly and Jim, but not Julie. Who, he wondered, was the pretty blonde that stood apart from everyone else?

When the guests began to mingle, Hannah made an attempt to warn Ben, but before she could reach him, Laci circled her hand around his arm. Hannah saw the distraught look on Julie's face. Matters became worse when Frank Lambert and two other young men circled around Julie and left Charleen standing alone. Hannah's hand went to her forehead in despair. How could everything go so wrong?

Nothing was as it was meant to be; Dolly and Jim were the only ones who seemed to enjoy the party. Dolly's friendliness, however, soon put all the young girls at ease, and they began to talk to the young men.

Ben noticed that more men gathered around the pretty blonde. He thought Frank stood much too close. Even with Laci clinging to his arm, the girl glanced his way several times as if to ask for his help. For a fleeting moment he thought he recognized her—there was something about her—then he looked away quickly. He didn't want her to see him staring.

Why had Julie not come? He'd ask Hannah to see about her, but first, he had to get Laci off his arm. He escorted her to the punch bowl and poured her a glass of the bright red punch and then handed her a small plate of cookies. While she stood with the punch in one hand and the cookies in the other, someone walked by and spoke. She turned her head and Ben took his chance. He darted across the room where Hannah was engaged in a conversation with a group of students from Charleston. She was relieved to see him, without Laci, and quickly asked to be excused.

"Ben, Laci thinks that you planned the party," she informed him, "so the two of you could be together."

"That doesn't surprise me," he muttered, "but what can I do? Will you go see what's keeping Julie, and while you're there, take off that silly bonnet?" He reached and pulled one end of the ribbon to untie the bow at the side of her face.

"Julie is here. What's wrong with my bonnet?"

"I can't see your hair." He lifted it from her head.

"Please go see about Julie and take this with you."

"Julie is here," Hannah repeated. She nodded her head toward her as she took the bonnet.

Ben looked in the direction she had indicated, but he saw only the elegant lady that was now completely surrounded by young men. "Where?" he asked.

"There . . . with the yellow ribbon in her hair."

Ben looked again, and this time his eyes lit up and he gasped quietly. He knew there had been something about the girl, but he would never have guessed that this beautiful lady was Julie. He was speechless.

A pleasant smile spread over Hannah's face. "I wouldn't have recognized her either," she said, "had I not seen her come in with Dolly and Jim."

"She's beautiful!" Ben breathed.

"Yes, she is, but very uncomfortable at the moment."

"I don't know how you can think that with all the attention she's getting."

Hannah noted a bit of envy in his voice. "Hurry," she said, "and rescue her from Frank Lambert."

"Gladly!"

She laid her bonnet on a table in the parlor and made her way to the piano. Jim came to stand behind her with his harmonica, and as the two of them made music, Catherine mingled among the young people. Everyone could see that it brought her a great deal of pleasure, and it was good for Charleen and Ben.

Hannah observed the young faces as her fingers ran up and down the piano's keyboard. Charleen, now thoroughly disgusted with Frank, talked with David Holmes. Ben pulled Julie from the ring of young men and held his hand at her arm to let others know she was with him. As he guided her to the table of food, Laci watched them with an evil look in her eyes.

Before long, Ben ran up the stairs, but soon returned and led Julie to the front door and out onto the porch. When they returned to the living room, they held hands, and Julie wore a silver heart-shaped necklace around her neck.

The necklace looked beautiful at Julie's throat, and Hannah was happy for her, but felt a prick to her heart at seeing it there. It was the special gift that Ben had purchased for her that first Christmas. When he looked her way for approval, she lowered her eyes to the piano keys in order to hide her feelings.

Laci was filled with jealousy and hate, and she had no

intentions of hiding her feelings. Her face turned as red as the dress she wore when she saw the necklace around Julie's neck and knew, as everyone else in the room did, that Ben had put it there.

Things were not in her or Frank's favor. Charleen gave Frank a cold shoulder, while she enjoyed the company of David Holmes, but David left her side for a moment, and Laci took the chance to talk to her friend.

"Who is the girl with Ben?" she asked.

"She's the servant girl, Julie Thomas. Hannah insisted that she be invited to the party and even bought her new clothes to wear. She bought clothes for her sister and for another indentured servant and a new dress for my mother. I don't know where she gets so much money."

"I should have known that Hannah had something to do with this!"

"What do you mean?" Charleen asked. She was grateful to Hannah for her party and had even begun to like her, but should she take her side against her best friend? No, she decided, she would not.

"Ben's in love with Hannah," she said, "but she loves the British naval officer who came to our home one night. His men held Ben and Daddy at gunpoint, while he searched the house."

Laci's mouth opened wide. "You don't mean it!"

"Yes, I do."

"Do you think Hannah gave them valuable information?"

"No-o-o," said Charleen, but then thought of how exciting it sounded. "Well, I don't know . . . she could have." She knew in her heart that it wasn't true.

"That's probably where she gets all the money. You know—the pay off for information. She's also taught your slaves to read, and I'm sure she hopes they'll rebel and help the British."

"How do you know that?"

"I heard a slave boy read words from a book on the front porch when Frank and I arrived. I asked him who taught him how to read, and he said, 'Miss Hannah.'"

"My daddy doesn't know that."

"He's about to find out."

"What are you going to do?"

"Tell my daddy."

An uneasy feeling came over Charleen, but she brushed it off. She would let nothing spoil her party. As the evening passed, other guests had a wonderful time. Some played games, but everyone in the room stopped what they did and began to clap when Hannah played the Irish jig with Jim backing her on his harmonica. As they gathered around them, the young men stood in the back, allowing the ladies to stand near the piano.

While Ben was not at her side, but everyone was close enough to hear, Laci decided it was a good chance to embarrass Julie and send her crying from the room. "Excuse me," she said suddenly in a loud voice, "aren't you the servant girl that I met at the barbecue, last fall?"

Just as Laci had hoped, everyone heard her mean comment. When Julie's face blushed, they felt sorry for her, but no one said anything for fear of making matters worse. Everything became very quiet.

Suddenly Hannah jumped from the piano bench and rushed to take Julie's hand. "Yes," she answered Laci. "Julie is a servant of God. Come, Julie, and play for us the way you do for our church service each Sunday morning."

Julie played an old familiar hymn, and the guests moved in closer around her and began to sing. For the remainder of the evening, no one wanted to have anything to do with Laci. She and Frank were the very first of the guests to leave.

Just before dark, the last of the guests left and Hannah sank into a chair. Dolly and Jim went to their quarters to change, but both promised to return and help clean. Ben left with Julie, and Catherine went upstairs to rest.

Hannah was pleased with the way things had gone. Although the party had an unfavorable beginning, everything had ended perfectly. Charleen had finally seen what Frank Lambert was and no longer wanted to have anything to do with him, and it was very obvious that Ben did not care for Laci.

She ran upstairs and changed to a comfortable pair of denims and a short-sleeved blouse. By the time she returned to the living room, Dolly and Jim were busy taking down decorations. Charleen came to help, and when Ben and Julie returned, the six of them soon had the living room in order again.

Later that night, Charleen lay in her bed and thought of what she had said to Laci, and she began to feel bad about it. Had it not been for Hannah, her daddy would never have agreed for her to have the party. And besides everything that she had done, Hannah would miss a month's salary. For the first time in her life, she felt guilty, and when she heard Ben climb the stairs, she opened her door and waited for him.

"Charleen . . . I thought you'd be in bed asleep by now."

"May I talk to you, Ben?"

"Sure. That's what big brothers are for. Come to my room."

Once inside his room, Ben closed his door and then turned to Charleen and asked, "Do you have a problem?"

Charleen shrugged one shoulder. "Where does Hannah get so much money that she can go without pay for a whole month and can afford to buy new clothes for everyone?"

Ben didn't think he had the right to discuss Hannah's finances with anyone, and she had asked him not to tell about her inheritance. "Why do you want to know?" he asked.

The guilt ate at Charleen, so she suddenly blurted out, "Do the British pay her to give them information?"

Ben's mouth opened in shock. He couldn't believe that his sister would ask such a question after what Hannah had just done for her.

"No! You know better than that!"

"Then where does she get so much money?"

"That's none of your business. Where did you get such an idea?"

"From Laci. And she knows that Hannah taught the slaves to read."

Again, Ben was shocked at the accusation Charleen made against Hannah. "Hannah hasn't taught any slaves to read," he defended her.

"Laci said that Sammy was on the front porch when she and Frank arrived for the party, and she heard him read words from a book. She asked him who taught him how to read and he said, 'Miss Hannah.'"

"What else did you and Laci discuss about Hannah?" Ben raised his voice at Charleen. He was furious. "How can you be so mean to someone who has done nothing but love you? Really, Charleen . . . this is worse than putting a snake in her bed. I can't understand how you can be so evil!"

Charleen began to cry. Ben had never talked to her in such a way. She was sorry for what she'd done, but didn't know how to say it. She ran from his room and slammed the door.

Ben paced back and forth, trying to think what to do. It was because of him that Laci was angry, but she would take her revenge on Hannah. When would she make her move and what would she do? Should he warn Hannah? He didn't want to upset her, but what if they came for her during the night? Most Plantation owners didn't take too kindly to anyone who tried to educate slaves, and if they thought that person was a traitor . . . well, he shuddered to think what they might do.

Laci would tell her daddy that Hannah had given information to the British and that she had taught slaves to read. Would his dad believe that? What would he do to Hannah if he did? Ben felt sure he'd believe Charleen over Hannah.

He decided not to say anything until morning. Hannah wouldn't sleep all night if he did. He tossed and turned in his bed and was afraid to go to sleep. Several times, he imagined he heard riders ride up the front lane. He finally dozed, only to have a bad dream.

The next morning was Sunday, but Ben was afraid for Hannah to leave the house. He spread the word that there would be no church service. Hannah was already dressed for church, so when she heard that Ben had cancelled the service, she knocked on his door.

"Are you sick, Ben?" she asked. And without giving him a chance to answer, "We can have a service without you. I'll lead Bible study and Julie can—"

"I'm not sick, Hannah."

"Then why did you cancel the worship service?"

"Come in and sit down. I've gotta talk to you." He told her everything that Charleen and Laci had accused her of doing. "I know you didn't give information to the British," he said, "but did you teach Sammy how to read?"

Her eyes stared into his. "No," she answered. Her head shook back and forth.

"Laci told Charleen that Sammy was on the front porch when she and Frank arrived for the party, and that he read words from a book. She asked him who taught him how and he said that you did. Where did he get the book?"

"I took a book to the porch yesterday to help Otis read his lesson for the week. When Sammy came to play, I invited him to listen to the story. As I read, I pointed to the words with my finger, and . . . ohhh . . ." Hannah lifted her hand to her cheek.

"What?"

"Oh, Ben, he saw the words just once and remembered them. He must be very intelligent. Think what he could do if—"

"Hannah! You seem to have forgotten the matter at hand. Now tell me exactly what happened."

"Well . . . like I said, I pointed to the words, but I never thought about Sammy remembering them. Charleen called me, and I laid the book down, thinking I would come back in a few minutes, but I became busy inside the house and never went back to the porch. The book was left there; I'm sure it was the one Sammy had when Frank and Laci arrived."

"You don't realize the danger you're in."

"I've done nothing wrong."

"I know, but Laci will convince her father that you have, and he has a lot of influence over other planters."

"What will they do to me?"

"Nothing, if I can stop them."

"What will they try to do?"

"I don't know," he replied. Hannah felt sure he lied.

When Catherine received word that there would be no worship service, she demanded to know why. On hearing the trouble that Hannah was in, she insisted that Garrett must be told. He questioned Hannah and Charleen before making a decision.

"Ben," he said, "ride to Charleston and get the sheriff in case there's trouble."

"I'm not going anywhere, Dad, unless Hannah goes with me."

"Well, that's not a bad idea. She could stay with the pastor and his wife a few days until this is over. Tell her to pack a bag."

"No, Ben! I won't go!" Hannah was dead set against the idea. "If I've caused trouble," she stated firmly, "I'll stay and face whoever has accused me. I certainly will not go where there is safety and leave everyone here in danger."

"You haven't caused anything, Hannah, but I'll tell Dad you won't go."

Jim volunteered to go for the sheriff; Ben insisted he ride Blaze. "Hurry, Jim," he said. "Every minute could count." The two of them saddled the horse, and Ben gave Blaze a hard slap across the rump to send him out of the barn.

The news of Hannah's plight spread rapidly over the plantation, and Julie heard that Jim had gone for the sheriff because Ben refused to leave her. Why would Laci take her anger out on Hannah when Ben was with her at the party? Was it because she knew that Hannah was the one Ben really loved? Regardless of the reason, she went to the side of her bed and kneeled in prayer for Hannah.

Ole Ramey and Big Bo rallied the adult male slaves and told them to get any weapon they could find and meet behind the barn. Mr. Leander got out his old gun and wiped it clean of dust, then loaded it and stood it by the front door of the servants' quarters. While Julie prayed, Dolly loaded a small pistol their father had given her before they left England. She slipped it inside the pocket of her skirt and went to the big house.

Everyone was concerned about Hannah, but felt scorn for Charleen who sat alone in her bedroom, thinking selfish thoughts. Why did everyone always take up for Hannah? Perhaps she had given information to the British, for after all, she went to Charleston often and could meet with anyone there. Her daddy would believe her. He was the one person she could count on.

About four o'clock in the afternoon, Ben heard horses on the road in front of the house. The unwelcome company had arrived. He ran down the hall and knocked on Hannah's door. As soon as she opened it, he walked past her to the trunk where she kept the British rifle.

"I need to borrow this," he said. "We have company."

Hannah put her hand on his arm. "Ben, surely they'll listen if I explain that I've done nothing wrong."

"If any explaining is done, I'll do it. You stay in this room."

"I can't do that," she mumbled as Ben ran down the hall with the rifle. She followed him to the top of the stairs and heard horses in the front yard. She eased down the steps until she could see the men on horseback. There were six of them.

Garrett stepped out the front door with a rifle in his hands and yelled, "Don't come any closer, men!" Ben stood beside him, holding the new rifle. Hannah heard a commotion below and peeped over the banister to see Ole Ramey and Rosie run from the kitchen toward the front door. Ole Ramey had a shotgun and Rosie carried an old musket that was longer than she was tall. Both of them ran right out on the porch and Rosie peered around Ben with the long barrel of the musket pointed right at the men on horseback. Hannah was afraid she would let the thing go off and kill someone for sure.

As the men had ridden up to the house, Catherine and Reneka had hurried Otis and the twins to Catherine and Garrett's bedroom and locked the door. Suddenly the door opened and

Otis shot out of the room with a toy pistol in his hand that Ben had whittled for him from the limb of an oak tree. He made it halfway down the stairs before Reneka managed to catch up with him. She caught him by the back of his suspenders, but he jerked them loose from his breeches and left her on the stairs with two straps in her hands. Hannah nearly laughed out loud as Reneka took out after him again and caught him just before he darted out the door. Had it not been for his breeches falling down around his feet, she never would have caught him.

After Otis was returned to her side, Catherine stood at the window and looked down. She saw Franklin Lambert with his son, Frank, and four other men. There was fear in her heart and she prayed for Jim to return with the sheriff.

"Garrett, we don't want no trouble with you," yelled Franklin, "but we don't like traitors." He dismounted his horse.

"Who you calling a traitor?" Garrett shouted back at Franklin.

"Your school teacher, Hannah Thornton, and we've come to get her. Your own daughter told my Laci that Miss Thornton gave important information to the British and received pay for it. And if that's not enough, she taught your slaves to read . . . so they could help the British, no doubt."

"Not a word of it is true," Garrett rebuked his neighbor's accusations. "If you'll come in and sit down, we can get this misunderstanding straightened out."

"There is no misunderstanding, Garrett, and I came here to get the troublemaker. We aim to teach her a lesson." Frank pulled out a long black bullwhip. "We intend to give her a whipping before we put her on a ship to Ireland. We're sending her back where she came from with a message to others like her who plan to come here." When Hannah heard his British accent, she was reminded of her father's hatred for wealthy British . . . and Franklin Lambert was certainly wealthy.

The others dismounted with their guns and started toward the porch, but stopped when Ben fired Hannah's rifle over their heads. The slaves heard the shot and ran from behind the barn with large machetes, pitchforks, and clubs. Mr. Leander stepped from around the side of the house, and he stepped out far enough that the men would be sure to see that he had a gun. Dolly eased down the hall from the back door and stood just inside the front door with her hand curled around the small pistol in her pocket.

Hannah trembled. If it came to a shootout, many would be killed. She could stop it all by giving herself over to them, and she began to descend the stairs slowly. "Dear Lord," she prayed, "give me courage."

The men looked around and took stock of their situation. They counted the guns pointed at them and eyed those who inched closer. The one in the lead was a giant, and he held a pitchfork that was just as large. Not one of them wanted to tangle with Big Bo.

Ben stepped forward. "I want to tell you," he yelled, "that the girl you want is engaged to the Englishman who paid you a good price for your cotton and kept it from rotting in a Charleston warehouse. He took a risk to do that, and he took another risk for this family when our home might have been destroyed, so we'll do everything we can to protect her. She knows no information to give to the British and wouldn't do such a thing if she did."

"Where does she get so much money to spend on people?" Franklin insisted on knowing.

"She's a faithful employee and my dad pays her well, plus she has money from the sale of her home in Ireland."

"Well, maybe she's not collaborating with the British, but we know that she's taught slaves to read."

Again, Ben made an attempt to explain what had happened, but Garrett interrupted him. "Franklin, do I tell you what you can or can't do on your plantation?"

"No, but—"

"Then don't come telling me what I can or can't do."

"You know it's the unwritten law of the South that we don't educate slaves," Franklin argued.

"From now on, the law must be written for me to abide by it, and don't try to force me to obey one that's not." You could tell by the tone of his voice that Garrett was angry. "I'm sorry for the trouble my daughter caused," he said, "and she'll be punished for it, so why don't you men get back on your horses and ride away from here before the sheriff arrives? I sent for him this morning." As he spoke, the sound of running horses could be heard in the distance.

Three of the men jumped on their horses and left in a hurry. Franklin and Frank and one other plantation owner took a look at the angry slaves and the number of guns that were pointed at them and decided they would do the same.

Big Bo was so angry, he ran at them with the pitchfork, and when Frank tried to hit him with the bullwhip, he caught the end of it and jerked him off his horse and began to beat him with the wooden end of the whip. Frank jumped on his horse so fast that he fell right over the other side of him. His horse reared in the air and then took off down the hill and left him lying at the feet of Big Bo. Bo cracked the whip across his back before he rolled a couple of turns in the dirt and managed to get to his feet. He fled down the hill so fast that he almost caught up with his horse.

The sheriff was at the bottom of the hill, and Frank was as glad to see him as anybody for fear that Big Bo would pursue after him with the whip. The sheriff made the three men halt.

"What's the trouble here?" he asked Franklin.

"No trouble, Sheriff—no trouble at all; just some false information that my daughter brought home."

The sheriff was angry for having ridden so far. "If I have to come back out here, Franklin Lambert, I'm taking somebody to jail, and if you cause any more trouble, it'll be you."

"Yes, sir," Franklin mumbled under his breath.

Relieved and filled with gratitude for all who had come to her defense, Hannah heaved a big sigh as she sank down on the stairs. Rosie and Ole Ramey came inside to put their guns away, but Ben and Garrett remained outside, talking to the sheriff. Dolly unloaded her pistol and put it back into her pocket before Reneka and Catherine brought the children downstairs.

"Dolly," Hannah asked, "where is Julie?"

Dolly answered just as Ben came in the door, "She and Mrs. Leander are on their knees, praying for your protection."

Tears came to Hannah's eyes. "Will you please go tell them that God has answered their prayers?" she said. "I would go, but I must let Charleen know that I have forgiven her."

Ben looked at Hannah in amazement and wondered how she could think of forgiveness. He shook his head back and forth, but spoke to Dolly. "I'll go tell them," he said. "Thanks for your help."

Hannah turned to run up the stairs just as Garrett entered the house.

"Hannah!"

"Yes, Mr. Rey." She stopped on the steps.

"I told you to leave my slaves alone!"

"But—"

"Your stubbornness is gonna get you killed one of these days."

"Yes, sir," she replied, and continued up the stairs.

CHAPTER 32

By spring of 1814, Charlestonians felt the strong squeeze enforced upon them by the British blockade that had lined their eastern seaboard for a year. Many provisions, such as sugar from South Louisiana and coffee from Central and South America, were no longer found on their pantry shelves. Clothes from Europe, made of silk and other fine materials, could not be bought. Blockade runners earned high bounties if successful in getting through the line of British ships, but few were willing to take the risk, for although the stakes were high, the consequences could be fatal.

The Political War Hawks' dream to annex Canada had vanished. For almost two years the United States tried to conquer this vast territory, but failed. In doing so, they lost their own Northwest Territory to the British, but through the command of men like Oliver Hazard Perry and William Henry Harrison, they were able to regain it. Several Canadian towns were burned, but the British soon retaliated by burning the public buildings in the city of Washington. Dr. William Thornton persuaded them to leave the Patent Office.

It had been a harsh winter at Reybrook, and Christmas had not seemed like Christmas at all. Without sugar, Rosie was unable to bake cookies or any other sweets, and without money from the cotton crop, Garrett and Catherine were unable to buy gifts. Had it not been for Hannah, there would have been none under the tree.

Hannah stood at her bedroom window and thought of hard times over the past months. Ben had kept meat on everyone's table with the rifle Nathan had left. There was an abundance of wild game in the woods, and once he had his aim on a deer, he seldom missed. She now understood the value of the gun and why Nathan had left it.

Sadly, she recalled the morning Rosie entered the dining room with tears streaming down her face. She had raised her apron to her eyes and announced that Ole Ramey had died in his sleep during the night. She would never forget the bitter cold morning of January 21, when everyone on the plantation huddled around Ramey's coffin as Ben said the last words over him. He was buried beside his wife and among others of his own race, just outside the family cemetery. She had stood with an arm around Alicia, while Nole tried to comfort little Sammy. Garrett held Otis who cried just as hard as Sammy, for Ole Ramey had been grandpa to him, too.

Silence lingered over the plantation for many days after the funeral, as everyone mourned the death of the faithful slave. Jim didn't sing Irish tunes around the barn, and no one heard Rosie hum a melody in the kitchen. Ole Ramey had lived on Reybrook land all his life, and the plantation would not be the same without him.

The long winter passed and spring brought renewed hope to Reybrook. Green grass sprang up for the stock, the trees put out new leaves, and wild flowers bloomed along the brook. It was planting time.

On a Saturday morning, Hannah took a bouquet of wildflowers from her desk in one hand and Otis's hand in the other. Together they walked the trail to the cemetery. Otis laid the flowers on the new grave and then ran to sit under the angel's wings, while Hannah pulled a few weeds that had sprung up there.

On the way back to the house, Otis ran ahead of Hannah. She smiled as she watched him skip along the trail with his mop of hair bouncing up and down. It made him happy to put flowers on Ramey's grave, and he hurried up the steps of the plantation home and through the door to tell Catherine about it.

Hannah sat down on the front steps and listened to the birds. Her spirit was lifted when Jim began to sing loudly. He worked at building a rail fence around the place he and Ben had cleared. Emily and Emma came outside and began to chase each other up and down the porch. Their gleeful laughter lifted Hannah's spirit higher.

Her blissfulness ended, however, when she entered the house. Garrett called from the downstairs hallway, "Hannah, may I see you in my office?"

"Of course, Mr. Rey." She entered the office and was told to be seated. From the expression on Garrett's face, she knew something was wrong.

"I'll get right to the point," he said. "There's no use in him-hawing around about it. I'm going to have to let you go."

"Let me go? You mean . . . I'm fired?"

"No-o-o, you're certainly not fired. You've been the best teacher my children have had."

"Then what, Sir?"

"Well—I just can't . . . I have no money to pay you, and I can't ask you to stay and work for nothing when I know you can find a job somewhere else. I talked to a man at the post office, and he said one of the public schools on this side of town needs a teacher. There are furnished living quarters at the rear of the school."

"You don't have to pay me, Mr. Rey. You provide a place for me to live and food to eat . . . that is more than enough. I surely can't leave before the end of May when my students have completed their present grades."

"I'm afraid the job will be filled by then. You should go to town on Monday and talk to the school board. Ben will go with you. Hannah, I'm sorry about this, and it's not a spur of the minute thing; I've given it a lot of thought and don't know what else to do. I can't even pay the taxes on Reybrook and might lose the plantation if I can't get a loan. If I thought things would get better . . . well, they won't until the war is over, and it won't do no good to think about it. I don't even know if I should plant a cotton crop this spring. The warehouses in Charleston are filled with last year's crop."

Hannah rose from her chair, but then sat back down again. "I can pay the taxes, Mr. Rey."

Garrett leaned back and looked at her dubiously. "Where would you get so much money?" he asked.

"I've not wanted to say anything about it, and I asked Ben not to tell, but the day we went to see Mr. Overteer, he informed me of my grandmother's death and of her will in which she left me her entire estate. She was a very wealthy land owner in the province of Ulster in Northern Ireland, and I now have more money than I can ever spend, so please let me pay the taxes for you."

Garrett's eyes peered at Hannah as if he didn't know whether to believe her or not.

"It's true, Mr. Rey. If you don't believe me, I have a bank book I will show you."

"That won't be necessary." He leaned forward again. "I believe you, but I won't take any money from you."

"But, Sir—"

"There's no use arguing."

Hannah sighed and rose from the chair, but before she left the room, she turned to Garrett once more. "If you change your mind, will you let me know?"

"I won't change my mind."

Garrett sat quietly in his chair after Hannah left his office. To inform her that she must leave Reybrook had not been an easy thing for him to do, but he thought he had no other choice. He had no money to pay her, but had promised Nathan Barrington that he would. What would Nathan do if he came back and found her working for nothing? It was a relief to know that she had enough money to take care of herself.

Hannah went to her room and sat down to think. Her first concern was for her students. They had almost completed their present grades; she would have to work something out, especially for Ben. It was his last year and she needed to send a letter to the state capitol, along with his test scores, to request a high school diploma for him. Why had he said nothing of his dad's decision to terminate her position? Perhaps he'd not wanted to mention it until Garrett talked to her, but if he had, it might have come a little easier.

She stayed in her room the rest of the morning and tried to determine how she could condense her lessons to make sure her students would be ready for the next grade. They had worked too hard to not get credit for the year.

When time for the noon meal, she returned downstairs, for she didn't want the Rey family to think she was angry. Ben was seated at the table; he spoke to her as if nothing was wrong. She managed a smile, but when Rosie began to fill her plate, she said quietly, "Just a little, Rosie. I'm not very hungry."

"Yo sik, honey child?" Rosie asked.

"No."

Ben looked her way, but said nothing as the rest of his family were seated and began to eat. Hannah's feelings were hurt. At least, she thought, someone might say they would miss her. Then Garrett spoke up.

"Ben, I want you to go to Charleston with Hannah on Monday. She needs to talk to the school board about a teacher's job at one of the public schools."

"What you talking about, Dad?"

"I had to let her go. I can't pay her."

Ben's mouth opened wide, but it was Catherine who spoke first.

"Garrett! You can't do that! Hannah is like family."

"You think I wanted to, Catherine? I had no choice. If Nathan Barrington comes back here and finds her working for nothing after I promised to pay her a fair salary . . . well, he won't like it."

"So you'll just throw her out!" Ben was irate.

"No, I'm not throwing her out. I'm trying to help her find another job." He told them about the public school. "It has living quarters at the rear of it, and we can stop by to see about her when we go to town."

"Garrett," said Catherine, "there must be another way."

"Well, I don't know what it is," he mumbled.

Charleen listened to every word that was said. When Garrett had punished her by not letting her out of her room for a week after she got Hannah in such trouble with neighboring planters, it was Hannah who had stood by her. She'd not only brought her meals, but had stayed to talk, while she ate. And at night, she had sat up late, helping her with schoolwork, so she wouldn't get so far behind. She had not understood why, but Hannah had been friendly when no one else would speak to her. She rose from the table and left the room quietly.

When the children realized that Hannah would leave, they began to cry. Hannah felt awkward; she had caused contention between Garrett and his family. And he really didn't have money to pay her.

"I'll be all right," she said to each of them as she rose from her chair to follow Charleen from the room. She slipped out the back door and walked down the hill to the brook. From the wooden bridge, she watched water run lazily under the Spanish moss and listened to a frog that croaked downstream someplace. Spring wildflowers, clothed in their brilliant colors, danced in a gentle breeze up and down each bank. She had come to love the natural beauty of the land. It would not be easy to leave Reybrook or the family she had claimed for her own. Life had dealt her another disappointment, but she would trust God to take care of her.

Being so engrossed in her thoughts, she didn't hear Ben as he walked up behind her and was startled when he laid a hand on her shoulder.

"I'm sorry; I didn't mean to scare you. Hannah, I know Dad has no money to pay you, but he can't just send you away. If you could work for awhile without pay—"

"I offered to work without pay, Ben. I even offered to pay the taxes on Reybrook, but he won't allow me to do either. Perhaps it's time for me to go. We both knew I couldn't stay forever."

"I hoped you could stay until Nathan comes for you, but . . ."

"What, Ben?"

"I don't want to be here when he takes you away."

"Why?"

He heaved a sigh, and then in a deep voice, "You know why."

"Don't you care for Julie?"

"Yes," he nodded, "I care for her, but I love you."

"I understand."

"How could you?"

"Because I care for you and for Nathan."

"Do you love me, Hannah?"

"Oh, Ben, how could I not love you after all you have done for me, but I love Nathan, too, and I could never be unfaithful to him?"

"I know, but I'm glad you love me."

Since they understood each other, she no longer feared for him to hold her. She bowed her head against his chest, and he circled his arms around her and pulled her close to him. When her arms slid around his waist, he kissed her gently, then they held each other and rocked back and forth with the trees that swayed in the wind above them, and for a moment . . . time stood still.

Hannah managed to hide her nervousness as she sat before three men and two women who made up the board of the Charleston Public Schools. She answered their questions confidently as they interrogated her about her own education and past experience.

When one of the ladies noticed the ring on her finger, she asked, "Are you engaged to be married?"

"Yes, ma'am . . . to Nathan Barrington; he's away, fighting in the war." She dared not tell them that Nathan was British.

"I hope he returns safely," replied the lady.

"Thank you, Ma'am."

After all their questions were answered, the board

members voted unanimously to hire her and wanted to know the earliest date she could begin. She hated to ask but felt she must. "Would it be possible for me to have another month in order to finish my classes at Reybrook and get moved in?"

They were disappointed, but after conversing with each other, all five members agreed it would be all right. "In order to give you that much time," one gentleman spoke up, "we can't start your salary until September, but you may go ahead and move in and, perhaps, find work in the city for three months."

"That will be fine, and I appreciate you giving me a chance. I shall do my very best."

They gave Hannah a key and directions to the building. Ben waited in the carriage outside the school board's office, and she relayed the directions to him. The small school had a fresh coat of red paint. A rope by the front door was attached to a bell in a bell tower above. Some shrub in need of trimming grew in front of the school, and two large trees provided shade for the school ground.

Hannah sat in the carriage and looked all around her, but Ben climbed down and walked to the front steps. He pulled the rope that hung from the bell tower, and the little bell made a loud, clear ring. To their surprise, three children ran from behind the school and gathered around Ben.

A little girl with curly red hair and large blue eyes tilted her head way back and looked up at him. "You gonna be our new teacher?" she asked.

"No, sweetheart." Ben squatted down beside her. "The new teacher is a very beautiful lady. Come on," he said to all three of them, "and I'll introduce you to her."

Hannah jumped from the carriage and the children formed a semicircle in front of her. "Oh-o-o, she is beautiful!" said the little curly-headed girl.

"Uh-huh!" her older brother agreed. The two had to be siblings because they looked so much alike. His hair was sandy red and freckles covered his nose.

Hannah held out her hands. "I'm Miss Thornton," she said, "now tell me your names."

"I'm Joel Cole, and this here is my little sister, Janie. Her real name is Jane Marie, but we call her Janie." He then turned to the boy beside him who looked to be about his age. "This is my friend, Billy Ruebald. He lives with his grandma, way down at the end of the street." Joel lifted a finger and pointed that way. Billy's eyes looked down at the ground, and the big toe of his bare foot pushed a small mound of dirt together.

"Well, Billy Ruebald and Joel and Janie Cole, it's a mighty fine pleasure to meet you, and I look forward to having you in my class this fall. This is my friend, Ben Rey," she turned to Ben, "and he's been a student of mine for almost two years."

"That's right," Ben said, "and she's the best teacher in the world." He held out his hand to the two boys and patted the top of Janie's head.

Joel and Janie talked to Hannah before they ran off to play, but she wasn't able to get a word out of Billy. She tried to get him to say something, but he just looked at her and grinned. She wondered why he was so shy and why he had to live with his grandma.

The month of May was so busy that Hannah had little time to think. She finished educational plans for the present grade of each of her students, and toward the end of the month, gave Ben a state-required test. She was delighted to put a score of ninety-seven on it.

She announced his score that evening when his family was gathered around the dining table. Garrett's face lit up with a big smile, but tears came to Catherine's eyes.

"Ben," said Garrett, "you're ready to take those business classes and to study improved farming methods at college. We'll talk to Daniel Overteer about a school loan next time we're in Charleston."

Ben looked at Hannah. She was the only one he had told that God wanted him to preach. She realized what was on his mind and nodded her head.

"Dad."

"Yeah, son?"

"I'm not going to take business classes at college or learn new ways of farming."

"What do you mean?"

"I'm going to take religious classes; I'm going to be a preacher."

"A preacher!" Garrett's face turned red and he almost choked on his food.

"Yes, sir."

"I suppose this is Hannah's doings?" Garrett shouted.

"No, sir, Dad," Ben answered him calmly. "This is God's doings."

Tears overflowed from Catherine's eyes. She rose from her chair and came to the end of the table where Ben sat. He stood up, but had to bend over for his mother to put her arms around his neck. He was so tall now and towered over her frail body. He said, "I love you, Mom," when she kissed his cheek.

"Don't worry," Catherine whispered, "he'll be all right." Ben smiled and squeezed her hand.

Catherine's gesture seemed to have made everyone at the table feel better except Garrett. He finished his meal in silence. His shoulders slumped forward, and before the meal was over, Ben was really worried about him. Perhaps the shock had been too much.

As her last days at Reybrook went by, Hannah felt Garrett's indignation toward her. He blamed her for Ben's decision to be a preacher, but what bothered her more than that was the way he treated Ben. Ben was closer to his mother—they understood each other—but he loved his dad and wanted to please him.

Hannah prayed daily for both of them. She prayed that Ben would not let his dad's reaction keep him from answering God's call to preach, but at the same time, she tried to understand Garrett. He worked hard for his family and had looked forward to the day when Ben could take over some of his responsibilities. She knew Ben was miserable and wanted to console him, but since that day by the brook, they had both tried to keep their emotional feelings from each other, and she wanted to do nothing that would make it harder for him.

The last day of school came, and that night, Hannah began to pack. Since Catherine's health was better and with Garrett feeling the way he did toward her, she felt she should leave right away. But she had not forgotten the unpaid taxes on the plantation and wanted to talk to him about them again before she left.

She stayed up late that night, for Jim and Dolly would come early the next morning to help her move, and she wanted to have everything ready. Her trunks were full, but many things were left. She'd not realized how much she had acquired since she'd been at Reybrook.

She lifted a bird nest that Otis had found under the oaks out front from the windowsill. The wind had blown it from the tree long after the baby birds were gone. She stood with it cupped in her hands, remembering the joy in his face when he held it up to her. Suddenly she was startled by a knock at her door. She thought everyone in the household was asleep except her. She opened the door and Ben held up her rifle.

"I just cleaned it," he said. "That's why I'm so late bringing it to you." It was shiny and looked like new.

"Ben, why don't you keep it? I have no use for it."

"No, I want you to have it with you. I'm glad you know how to use it, since you'll be . . . well . . . I'm just thankful you have it. It's a fine rifle so take care of it."

"I will. I understand the value of it now, just as you said I would."

"I'm glad. Are you all packed?"

"I have a few things left." She smiled and held up the bird nest.

"I'll throw that away." He reached to take it from her.

"Oh, no!" She quickly drew it to her. "I could never throw it away."

"It's just an old bird nest."

"I know," her voice changed, "but Otis . . ." A lump rose to her throat and she found it hard to speak. "Otis . . . brought it to me."

Ben had meant to bring her the gun and leave, but his arms reached out to her.

"No . . . I'm all right," she sniffed, and pushed him away. "I must be strong."

He sighed heavily. "Then I'll see you early in the morning."

"Why, Ben?"

"I'm going with you—to help you move."

"You don't have to. Jim and Dolly are—"

"You don't want me to go?"

"I—I didn't mean that, but I didn't think you'd want to go. I was afraid that . . . well . . ."

"That what?"

"It would be hard for you."

"It will be hard for me. That's why I asked Julie to come with me. We both want to help you move, but if you had rather we didn't—"

"Oh, no! I'd like for you to come. Both of you."

"Then I'll see you in the morning."

"Goodnight, Ben."

Beelzebub crowed loud and long the next morning, and as Hannah slowly crawled out of bed, she couldn't help but think that one thing she wasn't going to miss about Reybrook was that blasted rooster.

She tiptoed downstairs to get a cup of hot chicory that was Rosie's substitute for coffee. As she left the kitchen, she saw Garrett go into his office and decided it would be her last chance to talk with him about the unpaid taxes. With the cup in one hand, she knocked lightly on his door with the other.

"Come in."

She entered the room and said, "Good morning, Mr. Rey."

He more or less grunted back at her and did not offer her a seat, but asked, "What do you want?"

"I want to pay the taxes on Reybrook, and I'd appreciate it if—"

"I don't need anything from you, Miss Thornton!"

"Garrett, please . . ."

"Is that all you came for?"

Suddenly Hannah felt her face grow warm, but it wasn't caused by shyness. She was angry.

"No!" she shouted at Garrett, "that is not all I came for! I want to tell you that I don't think I deserve to be treated the way you have treated me during my last days at Reybrook. And worse than that, is the way you have treated Ben. It's disgraceful; how can you be that way to your own son?"

"Miss Thornton—"

But she refused to be interrupted again. "What kind of man are you that you would let your family suffer, just because you're too proud to accept my help?"

Hannah yelled so loudly, she awoke Ben. His eyes popped open, and he raised his head from the pillow and listened. Was that Hannah shouting? Across the hall, Catherine also awoke and wondered what on earth was going on, but it was Otis who bounced out of bed and ran to his daddy's rescue. He pushed his way into Garrett's office and took Hannah by the hand. She would not yell in front of Otis, but allowed him to pull her from the room.

He led her up the stairs, and by the time they reached the top, Ben and Catherine were in the hall. Catherine tied the sash to her robe, and Ben buckled his belt without a shirt on. Hannah looked their way and they saw fire in her eyes. Ben raised his eyebrows at his mother and shrugged one shoulder before he returned to his room. He leaned against his closed door, and a smile spread over his face as he thought of how Hannah had unleashed her Irish vehemence on his dad.

Otis left her at her bedroom door and went back to his room. She closed the door and sat down on the side of her bed to think of what she had done. She was sorry for the way she'd talked to Garrett, even if he did have it coming. Was she angry because he had dismissed her employment? No, she thought, she was angry for the way he had treated her, or was it for the way he had treated Ben? Whatever it was, he had been unfair. She'd worked hard at Reybrook and did her job as well as anyone could have. With this in mind, she finished packing.

Downstairs in his office, Garrett laid his head on his desk. Hannah had reason to be angry because he'd taken his frustration out on her. She was the best employee he ever had, and it wasn't her fault that everything had gone wrong. How would they manage without her? And if she really had more money than she could spend and she wanted to help . . . should he let her . . . ?

Later that morning, Jim pulled a wagon and a team of horses up to the front steps. He and Ben loaded Hannah's things, but Garrett didn't come to help. After everything was loaded, and they were ready to leave, Catherine and Charleen brought Otis and the twins out to say good-bye. Rosie and Reneka came with them, but Garrett still didn't come. Hannah hated to leave with him so angry at her. If he would only come to the door, she would apologize.

Garrett stood at his and Catherine's bedroom window and watched as his family said good-bye to Hannah. He saw Otis and the twins hide their faces in Catherine's long skirt. Hannah embraced Charleen after all the mean things she'd done to her. She hugged Rosie and Reneka, and after she had said good-bye to everyone, he saw her look up at the window where he stood.

"Tell Mr. Rey good-bye for me, Catherine."

"I will."

"And tell him . . . tell him I'm sorry for everything I said this morning."

"All right, dear."

"I love you, Catherine; I'll always love you." The two women embraced each other for a long time.

"I love you, Hannah. We all love you, and remember that you'll always be part of our family, no matter where you are."

"Yes, Catherine, I'll remember."

"Lawd, Mis Hannah, we sho gwinna mis yo." Rosie groaned and dabbed her eyes with the tail of her apron.

"Oh, Rosie . . ." was all Hannah could say. She clenched her teeth and held back tears until Jim helped her to the back seat of the wagon beside Julie. He climbed to the front seat with Dolly and took the reins in his hand. Ben pulled himself up to the other side of Julie, and when Jim made a clicking sound in his cheek, the horses started down the lane. Hannah looked back and saw that Otis and the twins still clutched Catherine's skirt. Charleen had an arm around her mother and both waved. Hannah lifted her hand and then turned her face forward with a mental picture in her mind that would remain there for the rest of her life.

Tears trickled down her cheeks, for she had nothing to catch them with until Ben handed her a handkerchief. She bowed her head to her lap and cried silently. When the tears ceased, she sat up and saw Ben with his arms folded across his knees; his head rested on them. She wadded his handkerchief and threw it at him and he raised his head.

"What are you squalling about?" she asked. "You're not leaving home." As she had hoped they would, everyone laughed.

CHAPTER 33

News had not reached Charleston that Europe's Fifth Coalition had united against the forces of Napoleon Bonaparte, and as of April, his military officers had refused to fight. It was Napoleon's downfall, and his defeat released thousands of the Duke of Wellington's battle-hardened troops. The British could now go after the Americans with full stamina.

Until this point in the war, the United States had been the aggressor, striving to take the British colony of Canada, and with the war in Europe, the British could only hold their ground. Now the tide had turned, and Americans would soon find themselves fighting for their independence—a second time—against the most powerful nation in the world, when it would seem that only the hand of God could preserve their freedom.

When the small party from Reybrook rolled onto the school ground, word spread quickly around the neighborhood that the new school teacher had arrived. A group of mothers came to welcome her, each bringing an item for her pantry or a household necessity such as oil for the lamp. To Hannah's delight, one mother had sewed new curtains to cover the windows of the small dwelling place. The ladies brought dinner and stayed to clean the school's living quarters.

Ben and Jim surveyed the fenced area beyond the school where a previous teacher had kept a horse. The fence needed to be mended and a new gate would have to be put up, but there was a shed large enough to put a buggy under and still have room for a horse to get in out of the weather. If Star was with her, Ben thought, maybe Hannah wouldn't feel so alone.

Hannah was a bit apprehensive about her first night to be completely alone since she'd left Ireland, but by the time everyone left, she was very tired. She went to bed and slept soundly. The next morning, she awoke to the rumbling of thunder and the pleasant sound of soft rain falling on a tin roof. She was tempted to turn over and go back to sleep, but there was much to be done in her new home, so she rose early.

She pumped water into a wash basin, then cupped her hands together and splashed it on her face. With her eyes closed and her face dripping, she reached for a small towel that a lady of the neighborhood had hung by the pump. She dressed in a comfortable skirt and a long-sleeved blouse and tied a blue bandana over her head.

She rolled up her sleeves and decided to tackle the stove first thing that morning, for after all, she would have to eat. She'd watched Rosie start fires in the kitchen stove at Reybrook, and it seemed easy enough. Howbeit, when she opened the small door to put wood in, black soot fell to the floor, and she had nothing to sweep it up with. She dropped to her hands and knees and attempted to brush it together, only to spread it more. With her nose just a few inches above the black powdery material, she sneezed, and the fine particles went everywhere, especially to the front of her white blouse. A hand that was covered with the soot touched her nose impulsively and left a black streak down the middle of her face.

Just as she rose from the floor to return to the wash basin, someone knocked on the door. A lady of the neighborhood stood on her doorstep, holding an umbrella over her head with one hand and a flour sack with the other.

The lady laughed when Hannah opened the door. "Good morning," she said, "I'm Rebecca Cole."

Hannah's face blushed. "Yes, you came yesterday. Please come in, but excuse my mess and give me a moment to wash up."

"Thought you might have trouble with that old stove." Rebecca followed Hannah to the kitchen and laid the flour sack on the table. "That's why I brought you some breakfast. It's just a couple of buttered biscuits filled with blackberry jam and a slice of bacon. I brought a jar of chicory and two cups, so I could have a cup, while you eat your breakfast, that is, if you don't mind."

"I would love for you to."

Rebecca poured two cups of the chicory, then sat down at Hannah's kitchen table. As the spring rain continued to fall, she sipped the warm cup of liquid and talked, while Hannah ate the breakfast she had brought her.

"The biscuits are delicious," said Hannah. She insisted Rebecca give her the recipe.

"I don't have a recipe," Rebecca confessed. "I've made biscuits most of my life. My mother taught me how, but I don't think she has one, either; she learned from Grandma. I'll show you how to make them, but first, we have to do something about this stove."

She rolled up her sleeves and took a wooden bucket from under the pump and began to rake all the soot from the stove into it with a stick of stove wood. She showed Hannah an easier way to start a fire and soon had a good one going. The heat felt good since the rain had brought a cool spell in the weather.

"Your real problem," Rebecca stated as she rinsed her hands, "will be getting enough wood to burn."

"Why is that a problem?"

"Because there's no forest in the city," she laughed. "We have to depend on those who own land in the country."

"If someone brought a wagon load of it to town, would it sell easily?"

"Yes. I'd buy half of it myself. Do you know someone who has wood for sell?"

"Perhaps. I know someone who needs the money if he's willing to cut timber on his land." She thought of the large woods around Reybrook.

Before she left, Rebecca insisted that Hannah come to her house for supper. "We live in the first house past the school yard," she said, "so you won't have far to walk. You will come, won't you, and meet my family?"

"I'll be happy to come, and thank you, Rebecca; thank you for everything."

As soon as her neighbor darted off across the school ground in the rain, Hannah cleared the table and put more wood in the stove. She was thankful the last teacher had left a good bit of it stacked against the back wall. With breakfast out of the way, she set about putting her new home in order.

The living room was the largest room and ran the width of the school. It was rectangular in shape and had a door to the kitchen, one to the classroom, and one to the outside. The outside door was at one end of the room and a fireplace was opposite it. Beyond the living area was the kitchen with a back door, and off the kitchen, a small bedroom also served as a washroom.

The living room furniture consisted of a divan and a rocking chair. The rocker had been placed near the fireplace and a small square table beside it had an oil lamp on it. The neighborhood mothers had left everything clean, including some shelves that covered the wall by the fireplace.

Hannah brought wood from the kitchen to the fireplace and built a fire large enough to take the morning chill out of the room. The place reminded her of the cottage in Ireland. It seemed like home.

At her request, Ben and Jim had put the trunk that was filled with memorabilia against the wall in the living room to provide another place to sit. She opened it that morning with excitement because each item within held a special memory for her.

The first thing to be lifted from the trunk was a very old China doll that had belonged to her mother. It was a beautiful doll, when new, and before she left Ireland, it had adorned her bed for as many years as she could remember.

"Oh, me Lady Miranda," Hannah groaned, "your dress is ragged and faded. I shall make you a new one, and you'll be very beautiful again, the way you were when my mother played with you. How I wish you could talk and tell me about her." Miranda smiled at Hannah with the *Mona Lisa* smile that had been plastered on her face so many years before. Hannah cuddled the doll in her arms a moment before she put her on the shelf.

Next to Lady Miranda, she put her own, less expensive doll that her father had bought for her when she was very small. "And you, me Lady Lucy, shall have a new dress, too," she said.

After the dolls, Hannah took seven small stuffed animals from the trunk. Each of them had been made by a lady of their Midleton congregation from brightly colored material. She reminisced of Miss McGillion with fond thoughts, for the lady had been as near to a mother as she had known when growing up. She suspected that Miss McGillion had wanted to marry her father. She had no family of her own and had often brought the two of them good things to eat. On seven of these visits, she had brought a small stuffed animal that Hannah cherished and could never part with. When the last one was put on the shelf, she vowed she would go to see Miss McGillion and have a long talk with her, should she ever return to the village of Midleton.

As Hannah emptied the trunk, she placed her favorite things in the middle of the third shelf. The music box Collin had given her, his watch, her mother's Bible, and the teapot that had belonged to her grandmother were all put beside each other. She picked up the two lace-trimmed handkerchiefs that her grandmother had made and remembered the rainy day on the *Monarch* when she had given Nathan a third one to take to war. She held one of the handkerchiefs against her cheek and whispered, "Oh, Nathan, will you ever return?" She opened the locket that Mrs. Barrington had given her and looked at his picture for a long time, remembering the softness of his touch, the twinkle in his eyes, his wonderful smile . . . . Without the locket it would be hard to remember how he looked. She closed it slowly and laid it on the lace-trimmed handkerchiefs beside the tiny piano that had held her ring, and then she touched her fingers to her cheek and wiped a tear that had trickled down it.

The teapot had an unusual handle, a lovely spout, and small

blue flowers painted over white China. Hannah remembered vividly the time she had sat with her grandmother by a fire in the fireplace and listened to her tell of growing up in England. A maid had come, bringing tea and dainties, and the teapot had attracted her attention. She commented on how unusual, but beautiful, it was. Later, as she packed to leave, her grandmother had brought a small box and placed it in her hands. "I want you to have this," she had said. "It's been in the family for many years, and perhaps you will pass it on to my great grandchild someday."

"I will, Grandmother. And I shall always remember you and Grandfather and how kindly you treated me."

"We shall remember you, Hannah. Your visit has been like a visit from our dear daughter. You're so much like her."

"Thank you, and thank you for the gift."

When she returned to her room at college, she opened the package and found the teapot inside along with a note. "Dearest Hannah," the note read, "I'm glad you liked the old family teapot and that you commented on it. I tried to think of a gift that would have special meaning to you and I believe this will. Please remember your grandfather and me when you look at it. I love you. Grandmother." Hannah had dropped the note inside the teapot and it was still there.

Collin's grandfather had given him an old spyglass and a compass that was contained in a metal case. One could hardly see through the spyglass, and the compass no longer worked, but she was glad she'd kept both. The ancient nautical equipment was placed on a higher shelf, and beside it, Hannah set a small sketch of Collin.

Her things on the shelves made her new residence seem more like home. She would be all right there until Nathan came. God had opened a door for her, but she would miss the Rey family. She thought of her empty room at Reybrook with the rain falling outside its window; she thought of the empty classroom . . . and she thought of Ben . . . .

Hannah carefully unpacked the set of China dishes that had

been a wedding gift to her mother and father. A handle was missing from a cup, but she dug through the wrappings until she found it and dropped it into the cup to be glued back later. She felt fortunate that nothing else was broken. As she put the dishes away in the kitchen cupboard, she dreamed of serving Nathan a meal on them.

After the dishes were all put away, she returned to the living room and came across the book that Nathan had given her the night of the birthday party. She let the pages pass through her fingers slowly and realized that she'd not read what everyone had written. More wood was brought from the kitchen and put on the fire before she settled in the rocking chair with the book on her lap. She read again what Nathan had written and then turned a few pages over.

A smile came to her lips as she read, "Dearest Hannah, you're a beautiful flower that never withers. May your life be filled with the joy that you bring to others. Love, Murray."

"Hannah, thanks for listening. Scott Hogan."

She read what several others had written, and then turned to the very back where Jeff Adams was always found, and a note from him said, "Dear Hannah, I love you. I've loved you since that first morning when I saw you on the deck at daybreak. The wind blew your beautiful hair over one side of your shoulder and it whipped your dress around your legs. I can still see you standing there. Nathan is the luckiest man alive. Jeff."

Hannah touched her hand to her face with shock. Nathan had been right, but it was hard to believe that Jeff had written of his love for her in the book. It made her sad to think that she never acknowledged to him of what he'd revealed to her. There was no worthy excuse for not having read the entire book, but the party had lasted until late, and she had been exhausted after cleaning Nathan's room that morning and then walking to the restaurant that afternoon. The book had been put away in her trunk and forgotten.

Jeff's message helped to explain what he had said to her the night Nathan left him in charge of guarding the *Monarch*. He'd asked if she thought Nathan would return to her after the war, and she knew now that he assumed she had read the message from him. He'd implied that Nathan would return to England and marry a wealthy girl; a girl like Gloria Hesley, she thought, and for a moment, she was filled with fear. Did Jeff know something that he didn't tell her?

Hannah read what everyone had written in the book, then laid it on the table beside the rocking chair. She glanced at the clock and realized it was time to get ready for her first visit with a neighbor.

The rain stopped during the night, so the sky was clear when Hannah awoke early the next morning. She was up and dressed by the time the sun peeped over the horizon in front of the school, as she was used to Beelzebub waking her at dawn.

She had better luck with the stove that morning and soon had breakfast cooking from the box of provisions Rosie had packed for her. After the table was cleared, she went out back to look at the fenced-in area and realized she could keep Star there if the fence was repaired and a new gate was put up. She'd ask about a handyman for hire.

There would be plenty of grass for grazing through the summer months, but come that winter she'd have to buy hay. Perhaps Garrett would sell her enough for Star, she thought, and then another idea came to her head. Why couldn't he grow hay to sell to others in town? It wouldn't bring as much money as cotton, but would provide some cash to help them get by until the war was over.

Alongside the schoolhouse someone had made a feeble attempt to grow flowers. More weeds grew there than anything, but Hannah saw a few perennials among them. Some daffodils had already bloomed, and a hydrangea had green leaves on it. Rocks that lined the flowerbed kept rainwater from draining, but when she removed a large one at its lower end, the water ran swiftly from it. She'd buy flower seeds to plant as soon as the soil dried.

Shrubs across the front of the school called for a pair of shears, and a yard rake was needed to rake last winter's leaves from around the building. Back inside, she began to make a list of things she would need, including items for the kitchen.

Rebecca had told her of a neighborhood store that sold groceries and household needs. "Miller's has everything," she had said, so with money in her pocket, Hannah set out to find the store. It wasn't far from the school. The building had weathered with age and was in dire need of paint; the name "Miller's General Store" written across the top of it could barely be read. Hannah climbed five short steps and crossed a porch made of wooden planks. A screen door squeaked when she opened it. The store was dark inside, and at first, she could see very little, as two small windows on each side of the front door let in the only light from outside. As she stood still, letting her eyes adjust to the darkness, a man's voice came from back of the store.

"May I help you?"

"Yes, I need to purchase some groceries and household items. She could now make out a man and a woman in the back, and as her vision became clear again, she saw that the woman smiled.

"You the new school teacher?" she asked.

"Yes, ma'am."

"May we help you find something?"

"I need many things, but I have no way to carry them. I'll have to make several trips."

"We keep a wagon hitched up out back for deliveries. Our son tends to that, and we usually charge a little extra, but since this is your first visit—"

"Oh, I'll be happy to pay extra," said Hannah, and she began to read from her list. Besides groceries, she needed a coffeepot, a broom and dustpan, towels and washcloths, and tools for yard work. Her face blushed when she asked, "Do you have an extra large washtub?" She needed it to wash her clothes . . . and for bathing.

"Yes," replied the lady, "we have them in three different sizes." She pointed toward the back wall.

Hannah picked a large one, and the man took it from the wall. She began to fill it with provisions and needed items. After finding everything on her list, plus a few more things, she stopped to talk.

"I'm Hannah Thornton," she said, "of County Cork, Ireland. I came to Charleston two years ago to work on the Reybrook Plantation up the Cooper River. Do you know the Rey family?"

"Can't say as I do," the lady shook her head. "We're Henry and Maggie Miller, and our son, Jed, makes deliveries. He'll attend your school in the fall, so we're glad to get to know you."

"Thank you. I'm pleased to meet you and I'll be glad to meet Jed. Is he your only child?"

"Goodness no! We got five, but Jed is the oldest. He's fifteen and will be in the eighth grade this fall. Jennifer is thirteen and Laura is ten; Billy is eight and Bobby, six. Bobby starts to school this year, and," her brow wrinkled, "I hope he won't give you trouble. It's awfully hard for him to sit still."

"That makes him normal for a six-year-old boy, and I'm sure it won't be a problem." Maggie looked relieved and gave her a smile.

After Henry added up the cost of her purchases, he went out back to fetch his son and the wagon, while she paid his wife. Jed drove the team of horses and wagon to the front steps and helped his dad load everything. Henry introduced the two of them, then helped Hannah to the wagon seat. Jed laughed when she began to give directions to the school.

"Oh," she felt silly. "I suppose you know the way quite well."

"Yes, ma'am," Jed nodded, but said nothing else.

"Will you be glad to return to school in the fall?" She made another attempt to get him to talk.

"No, ma'am," he replied.

Hannah decided he was a boy of few words, and she guessed that was normal at the age of fifteen.

When they arrived at the school, Jed helped her unload everything, and she paid him the delivery fee, plus a small amount for himself. "May I hire you to take me to the bank tomorrow and to one other place?" she asked.

"I'll have to ask Pa. He keeps the wagon ready in case somebody needs something delivered, but I think I can take you if we go early."

"The bank doesn't open until nine o'clock. Would that be early enough?"

"I'll ask and if I can, I'll be here before that time. If I don't come, you'll know why."

"Yes, I understand."

By the time everything was put away, Hannah was tired. She ate a small amount of food, then lay down to rest, but before she dozed, she thought of everyone at Reybrook. Rosie would be in the kitchen and Catherine was upstairs. The children were, most likely, outside at play, and Ben worked somewhere on the plantation. Did anyone miss her?

At 8:30 the next morning, Jed came in the wagon. Hannah saw him coming and met him in front of the school.

"Good morning, Jed. Was everything all right with your pa?"

"Yes, ma'am. He said I could make deliveries when I get back."

"I'll try to hurry."

"No need to."

They arrived at the bank just as it opened, and Hannah went inside to find Mr. Overteer, while Jed waited for her in the wagon. The banker saw Hannah and came to meet her.

"Good morning, Miss Thornton. It's a pleasure to see you. I have good news, so come to my office."

"Good news, Sir?" Hannah took a seat in front of his desk.

"Yes, I've found a slave named Ollie."

"Oh, Mr. Overteer, that's wonderful news!"

."The owner isn't sure he's willing to let him go, but—"

"I'll give whatever he demands if he's the Ollie I'm looking for. A girl from Reybrook must go with me to see him."

"All right. I'll give you directions to the plantation. It's up the Ashley River a good ways." He took a piece of paper and began to draw a map.

"Mr. Overteer . . . I'm afraid it won't be so simple for me to go."

"Why?"

"I don't live at Reybrook anymore."

"You don't?" The banker raised his eyebrows.

"No, sir, and I won't have a way."

"What happened?"

As quickly as possible, Hannah told him everything that had happened in the last month. He laid his pencil on the desk and leaned back in his chair.

"I knew Garrett was having a hard time; most planters are since they can't get their cotton to market. He came in yesterday to borrow money, but I would never have thought that he'd let you go. Where do you live?"

"One reason I came to see you is to give you my new address. Nathan said that if I was not at Reybrook when he returned, he would come to you to find my place of residence." The banker wrote down her new address.

"I'm glad you got on with the school district, but you don't have to work, you know."

"Yes, I know, but I need something to keep me busy until Nathan returns, and I like to teach."

"I understand. Reybrook's loss will certainly be the town's gain."

"Thank you, Mr. Overteer, but back to Ollie—"

"We'll take my carriage. There are three hundred acres of swampland that anyone could buy, on up the Cooper, past Reybrook. I want you to look at it, and we can pick the girl up on the way back. She can spend the night with you, and we'll make the trip to the other plantation the next day. There's more land for sale in that direction; we'll stop to look at it if you're interested."

"I am interested."

"Then it's settled, and I'll notify the bank that I'll be out of my office the next two days."

"Thank you, Sir, but there's one other thing. You said that Mr. Rey came in to borrow money. Did the bank loan it to him?"

"I'm sorry, Hannah. I can't give out that information. I shouldn't have said anything about it at all."

"I'm sorry for asking, but he needs the money for the taxes on Reybrook and might lose the plantation if he doesn't get it."

"That's right."

"I want to pay the taxes."

The banker lowered his chair to the floor and looked Hannah in the eye. "He owes four hundred dollars," he said.

"I know. Will you make out a bank draft for the entire amount and direct me to the tax office?"

"You mean you would do this after he fired you?"

"He didn't fire me, Mr. Overteer. He couldn't pay me and wanted me to take a job where I would be paid. Mr. Rey was more than fair to me, while I was employed at Reybrook. The Reys are like family and I want to help them."

"Did you ask Garrett about it?"

"Yes."

"What did he say?"

"He said, 'No.'"

The banker laughed and began to write out a bank draft for four hundred dollars on Hannah's account.

"Garrett won't like it," he said, as he handed it to her.

"I know, but he'll get over it."

Jed and Hannah stopped by the tax office, then were on their way home when they passed a small shop with a sign that read, "Fabrics and Sewing Notions."

"Jed, do you have time for me to buy some material?"

"Yes, ma'am."

Hannah jumped from the wagon before it came to a complete stop and ran inside. She quickly decided on three kinds of material, some lace, and a package of tiny pearl buttons. While the saleslady cut the right amount of material, she picked a color of thread for each kind and was back in the wagon in less than ten minutes.

"Thanks for waiting, Jed."

"You're welcome."

Jed really was a quiet person, so Hannah was surprised when he asked, "What you gonna make?"

"New dresses for my dolls."

"You're a little old to be playing with dolls."

She laughed, but made no effort to explain. He wouldn't understand.

Early the next morning, Hannah sat beside Mr. Overteer as two horses pulled his carriage down the road toward Reybrook. She had mixed feelings about returning there so soon after leaving. It was like going home, but Otis and Emily and Emma would be upset when she couldn't stay.

She felt anxiety when the horses turned off the road onto the lane, and the feeling escalated as she crossed the front porch and knocked lightly on the door. Her anxiety, however, subsided when Reneka opened the door.

Reneka threw up her hands. "Oh, Miss Hannah, I was afraid I'd never see you again."

"Reneka, don't tell anyone I'm here; I can't stay and Otis and the twins will get upset."

"Can't you stay for dinner?"

"No. Mr. Overteer and I are on our way up the river to look at some land to buy, but listen carefully. Mr. Overteer has found a slave named Ollie." Reneka's mouth opened wide. "Now before you get excited, we must be sure that he's your Ollie. We'll be back here by middle of the afternoon, and I want you to go to Charleston with me. Mr. Overteer has agreed to take us to the other plantation tomorrow. Talk to Mr. Rey and try to be ready to go when we come back; pack a bedroll."

"I will, Miss Hannah."

Reneka stood at the door until Mr. Overteer's carriage turned onto the main road. She then ran to the kitchen to tell Rosie her exciting news.

Garrett came out of his office. "What's all the excitement about?" he asked.

"Oh, Mr. Rey, Mr. Overteer has found a slave named Ollie, and Miss Hannah wants me to go with her, so she can take me there tomorrow, to see if it be my Ollie."

"How do you know that?"

"She just told me, Sir. She and Mr. Overteer be on their way up the river. She say something 'bout looking at some land to buy."

"Hannah was here?"

"Yes, sir, but she say she couldn't stay and there weren't no use in getting Otis and the girls upset. She'll be back by about middle of the evening and wants me to be ready to go. May I, Mr. Rey?"

"I don't mind," he answered, "but what does Miss Hannah aim to do if this is the right Ollie?"

"She gonna buy him, Sir."

"What does she intend to do with him?"

"I don't know."

"Well, you better find out."

"Yes, sir."

Up the river, Hannah shaded her eyes with her hand and looked into the swampland. She saw tall and straight cypress trees, and on higher ground, pines towered to the sky. Oaks and other hardwood grew along the edge of the swamp.

"There's a lot of good timber here, Hannah, and you can get it for fifty cents an acre."

"Then I shall buy it. Can you get me a deed?"

"Yes. I'll take care of the paper work in my office. You and the owner must sign the papers, and the bank will charge you five dollars."

"I didn't expect to get it done free."

When they returned to Reybrook, Garrett came out to meet them and insisted they come in. He wanted to talk to Hannah.

"Have a seat, Hannah." But she refused to sit down in his office, as she had not forgotten their last words to each other.

"I shouldn't keep Mr. Overteer waiting."

"What do you intend to do with Ollie?" he asked.

"To buy him and set him free."

"Do you know how much that will cost you?"

"At least five hundred dollars."

Garrett nodded his head. "And what good will it do if Reneka's not free?"

Hannah looked into his eyes a moment, and then the corner of her mouth twitched, and she looked down at the floor, but said nothing. He'd asked her the same question she'd asked herself, but had no answer for. Her silence told him so.

"Would you buy Reneka's freedom for four hundred dollars?"

He'd answered the question she had asked Mr. Overteer. The bank didn't give him a loan. Garrett was in a bind, but he saw a way out . . . . He saw a way to keep his plantation.

If he knew the taxes were already paid, he'd never give up Reneka. But if she didn't tell him . . . well . . . she'd think about that later. Garrett would have the four hundred dollars that he needed, and Reneka and Ollie could be together again.

"Yes," she replied. "If Ollie is the one I'm looking for, I'll have Mr. Overteer transfer four hundred dollars from my account to yours."

"All right."

"They'll need a place to live."

"They may stay here until they decide what to do."

"Will Ben help them say their wedding vows?"

"You'll have to ask him."

"Where is he?"

"He and Julie went riding on Blaze and Star."

Hannah glared into Garrett's eyes. Had his words brought him as much pleasure as they did her pain?

"Hannah . . ."

"What?"

"Does that upset you?"

"Of course not," she lied. Ben must not know how it made her feel that someone else had taken her place so quickly. After all, it was what she'd hoped for; she wanted Ben to find happiness with someone else. She left Garrett's office and called softly, "Come Reneka, we must go."

Mr. Overteer rose from his chair and shook hands with Garrett and then followed Hannah to his carriage where she was already seated on the front seat. Reneka climbed to the back seat behind her. Garrett stood on the porch and watched the horses turn the carriage around as he thought of the agreement he'd made with Hannah . . . and how it upset her when he told her where Ben was.

When Ben returned home, Garrett told him about Hannah's visit and how upset she got.

"What did you say to her?"

"That you and Julie were riding Blaze and Star."

Ben sighed. "I wish you hadn't told her," he muttered.

"Why should she care?"

"Because . . ." Ben stopped; he didn't want to explain to his dad. The times that Hannah and he had spent riding Blaze and Star were special memories for him and now he knew they were for her, too. He would share them with no one. From the very beginning, he'd known it was a mistake to take Julie riding. In the first place, she'd had no riding lessons and could hardly handle Star. He'd only asked her to go because Star needed to be ridden. Every time he'd looked at her, he saw Hannah's face and was sure it made her feel uncomfortable.

He went to his room to think of Hannah and even thought of riding to Charleston to see her . . . but he couldn't. He had to let her go. He'd finish the gate for the fenced area behind the school and ask Jim to take it and the post to repair the fence. He'd send Star and her saddle, and perhaps this would make Hannah feel better. He was glad Reneka was with her for the night.

The next day, there was no doubt in Hannah's mind that Ollie was the right person when she saw the look on Reneka's face. A transaction was made and four people left the plantation on the Ashley River instead of three. Reneka and Ollie rode beside each other on the back seat of Mr. Overteer's carriage.

They stopped to look at more timberland before they reached Charleston, and again, Hannah agreed to buy.

"Mr. Overteer," she asked, as they rode toward home, "What will I do with the land if Nathan doesn't return?"

"You can hold it a few years, then sell it for a good profit."

"It's swampland. Would anyone else want it?"

"Yes. Our city is growing, so there's a demand for lumber and fire wood. Swamps can be drained, leaving rich farmland. I believe you're making a good investment."

"Well," Hannah sighed, "I hope you're right."

Daniel offered to take Ollie and Reneka on to Reybrook, but Hannah didn't want to return there and asked to be let off at the school. Before she climbed down from the carriage, she informed Reneka and Ollie of their freedom. Both cried tears of joy.

As the horses pulled the carriage away, Hannah heard a noise behind the school and went to investigate. A man dug a hole by the fence. He reached down for a post and set one end of it in the hole, and she realized he mended the fence. He turned enough for her to recognize him.

"Jim!"

Jim waved. "I'm glad you're home; I need your help."

"What are you doing?"

"Ben sent me to repair the fence. He built a gate and it fits perfectly." He nodded his head in that direction. When Hannah looked toward the gate, she saw Star tied to the side of the shed and ran to pet her. It was so good to see her, and it would certainly be nice to have a way to go.

"Her saddle is under the shed," Jim yelled across the fenced area. "I brought extra posts and fixed a place to hang it."

"Thank you, Jim. What can I do to help?"

"Hold this post straight until I get some dirt around it."

When Jim finished with the repairs, Hannah asked, "Won't you come in and let me fix your supper?"

"I better get back. Mrs. Leander always leaves something on the table if I'm not around at meal time."

"Then let me pay you for repairing the fence."

"Oh, no. Ben would be upset if I did."

"How is he, Jim? How is everyone?"

"They're all right. Ben misses you; everybody can see that. Dolly is fine and is making plans for the wedding."

"And Julie?"

"Well, you know how Julie lives in a world of her own. She misses you too—we all do—but she seems to be happier since Ben . . ." He stopped and looked awkwardly at Hannah.

"It's all right, Jim," she said in her soft voice. "I'm glad for both of them. I had hoped they would find each other. I believe it's God's will."

"It seems that way since both of 'em want to serve Him the way they do."

"Reneka and Ollie want to get married. Will you ask Ben if he'll talk to them and perform a marriage service for them?"

"Sure will, and I better get going. That sun is sinking awfully fast." The two of them picked up his tools to take to the wagon.

Hannah watched as Jim turned the horses onto the road. She waved as he headed toward home. The large red sun was almost out of sight when she bowed her head reverently. "Oh, God," she prayed, "thank you for friends like Jim and Dolly, and forgive me, Lord, for being selfish about someone else riding my horse with Ben. Help me get over the way I feel. I love Nathan, Lord, and pray that you'll keep him safe. In the name of Jesus, I pray, Amen."

As she watched the sunlight disappear, she thought of Ben and Julie. She would let go of her feelings for Ben; he and all of Reybrook would become a memory. God had opened another door for her and she must close that one.

Not in her wildest dream could Hannah have imagined how God was yet to mingle her life among the Reys.

CHAPTER 34

The sun was barely up the next morning when Hannah stepped out her back door with the leftovers from her breakfast and a canteen of water in a cotton flour sack. Birds began to chirp as she threw the saddle over Star's back and pulled the cinch straps tight. Excitement stirred within her when she lifted her foot to the stirrup and swung into the saddle.

She tied the end of the flour sack around the saddle horn and leaned over to give Star a pat on the neck. "It's sure good to ride you again," she talked to the mare. Star recognized her voice and lifted her legs high as she pranced across the school ground, but when they came to the road, Hannah pulled her rein toward the harbor and she speeded to a gallop.

A few town merchants had just opened their shops when Hannah rode down the main street of Charleston. They stopped to stare at the strange lady with the long red hair on a horse that was the color of chestnuts. Some watched until she was out of sight.

By the time the horse and rider reached the far end of the peninsula, the sun had climbed well over the horizon. Its rays stretched across the bay and generated a sea of glimmering hue. Hannah pulled Star to a halt and gazed out over the vast body of water.

She remembered the day the *Monarch* had sailed into the harbor. Ships from all over the world had lain anchored in the bay or hugged the piers that jutted out into the water. On that day, an array of colorful flags crowned the masthead of large frigates, schooners, brigs, and small one mast sloops, but the port's busy activities were now quelled by the British blockade. Only two small schooners were anchored nearby. Hannah suspected they were privateers that belonged to brave blockade-runners.

She backtracked and rode a ferry across the wide Cooper. From the ferry landing, she took a road that circled the bay on higher ground, and the city was soon left behind. It was a beautiful day, and she hated to turn back, but decided she must when she noticed how high the sun had climbed.

She brought Star to a halt, then pulled hard on her left rein. As the horse turned, a small sign at the far side of the road caught her attention. It read, **LAND FOR SALE**, and appeared to have been there for quite some time. The paint had faded and it leaned to one side. An arrow at the bottom of it pointed inland where sand ate into the grass at the foot of a hill.

Hannah hesitated to leave the road, but decided to risk it and turned her horse inland. She felt Star's muscles straining to climb the high bank with its drifts of sand. At the top of the hill, she looked back, and the beautiful harbor stretched before her as far as she could see.

She dismounted and looked all around. A strong wind blew off the Atlantic Ocean and large billowing clouds floated low in the sky. Suddenly a strange thing happened. Nathan's face appeared among the clouds and he called to her. "H-A-N-N-A-H." It was as though his voice was carried in the wind, and she heard it a second time. "H-A-N-N-A-H."

"Nathan!" she called back, but the sound of her own voice seemed to have made it all disappear. She gripped Star's reins and looked all around her, thinking there had been another voice that only sounded like Nathan's, but she saw no one. There was nothing in sight except a few trees that were scattered over the windswept terrain, and the only sound was the crashing of the Atlantic Ocean's powerful surf against the South Carolina shoreline.

The place seemed familiar to Hannah, like she had been there before, and then she remembered the dream she'd had on the *Monarch*. It was the night after the first time that she and Nathan had spent time together, when he had told her that he must go to war. It all came back to her, although it had happened so long before. In the dream she had stood on a hill that overlooked a vast body of water. She had seen his face in the clouds, and she distinctly remembered that he called her name.

There must be something special about this place, she thought, and it's for sale. As her eyes surveyed the land around her, she recalled how Nathan had described Barrington Manor. He had said, "It's high on a hill that overlooks the sea, and I could hear the surf at night when I climbed out my bedroom window onto the balcony."

Thoughts raced through her mind. Could this place look like Nathan's home in England? She lifted her hand to shade her eyes and looked in the other direction to see green hills that reminded her of Ireland. Should she buy the land, so she and Nathan could build a home there someday? She wanted to think yes, but would he live in a country that had declared war against his own country?

She tied Star's reins around a tree and took the sack of food and water from the saddle horn. While eating, she made a decision to buy the land.

With the canteen of water back in the sack and over the saddle horn, she mounted Star and was headed down the hill when a covey of quails flew up in front of the horse. Star raised her front legs high into the air. It happened so quickly and unexpectedly. Hannah fell from the saddle to the ground with one leg twisted beneath her.

The frightened horse ran until she disappeared over a hill. When Hannah tried to stand, a sharp pain shot through her knee, and she fell back to the ground. Would Star come back? She didn't think so, and the horse couldn't return to the school or go home to Reybrook because they had taken the ferry across the Cooper.

When Hannah's injured knee began to swell beneath her pants leg, she realized the seriousness of her dilemma, but tried not to panic. She wasn't that far from town and there were bound to be some houses near by. Sooner or later, someone would ride down the road and she would yell for help. She lay back, and in order to get her mind off her predicament, tried to think of other matters.

She thought of Reneka and Ollie and how happy they must be on their first day of freedom. It had come at a great expense to her, but she'd learned early in life that helping others was the key to real happiness; besides, the money had been given to her.

She was thankful that Garrett had agreed to . . . Oh, no! She suddenly remembered her promise to Garrett. With being so excited to have Star again, she'd forgotten all about the four hundred dollars. What would Garrett think when he rode all the way to Charleston and found no money in his account? He'd be furious!

Garrett and Ben did make the trip to Charleston that morning. It was urgent that the taxes be paid on Reybrook as soon as possible. When Garrett checked his bank balance and found no money in the account, he was upset, but somewhat baffled because he'd never known Hannah not to keep her word.

"Maybe she hasn't had time to get to the bank this morning," said Ben. "Let's sit down and wait for her." But after they had waited for quite awhile, both felt sure that Hannah wasn't coming. Garrett decided to pay her a visit and Ben had no choice but to go with him.

When they arrived at the school, Garrett knocked on her front door, but it didn't open, so he went to the back door. Ben walked to the fenced area to look at the gate Jim had put up and saw that Star and her saddle were gone. He returned to Hannah's back door to tell his dad there was no use knocking.

"She's not here."

"How do you know?"

"Star is gone and so is the saddle. She must have gone riding and forgot about the money or else something happened and she couldn't get back."

Ben turned the knob on the back door and it opened. They went inside and waited until it began to get dark. Ben felt sure that something had happened to Hannah, but had no idea where to look for her.

Finally Garrett could wait no longer. "I have to go," he said. "Your mother will be worried. You stay here, and if Hannah doesn't come home tonight, we'll begin a search for her in the morning."

Garrett left, but Ben couldn't sit down and do nothing. He went to the house nearest the school to inquire if anyone there knew of Hannah's whereabouts. Rebecca Cole came to the door and recognized him as one of the men who had helped Hannah move.

"No," she shook her head slowly, "I haven't seen Hannah all day, but come in, and I'll ask my family if they have seen her."

The little curly-headed girl that Ben had talked to in the school yard ran across the room and hid behind her mother's skirt. When her eyes peeped around the side of it, he smiled at her. He followed Rebecca into the kitchen where her husband and two young sons had just finished their supper.

"Have any of you seen Hannah today or have any idea where she is?"

"I saw her, Mom," the older boy spoke up. "When I went out to burn the trash this morning, I saw her leave on a horse."

"Do you know what time it was, and did you see which direction she went?" Ben asked.

"It was early . . . right at sunup. She rode toward the harbor."

"You didn't see her return?"

"Nope. I don't think she did."

"Ben, this is my husband, Neal, and our sons, Joel and Justin. And this is," Rebecca placed her hand on the top of her small daughter's head, "our daughter, Janie."

Neal stood and shook Ben's hand.

"I've met Joel and Janie."

"That's right," Joel spoke up. "Me and Janie was playing

behind the school with Billy Ruebald when he rung the school bell. Him and the new teacher had come to see the school."

"Well," said Neal, "the rest of us are pleased to meet you. I'll be glad to go with you to look for Hannah, but it seems to me her horse would have come home if something had happened to her."

"The mare would probably have returned to our plantation, up the Cooper a ways, but I believe someone would have come to let me know if it had. I think I'll ask some of the other neighbors if any of them have seen her."

"I'll go with you since I know them. If no luck, we'll ride over and ask the sheriff if anything unusual happened in town today." He reached for his hat and said, "Justin, saddle Boots for me."

"Yes, sir, Dad."

Ben and Neal went to the house at the other side of the school and to the one across the street, but no one at either place had seen Hannah all day, so they mounted their horses and rode to the sheriff's office. It wasn't far, but by now, it was late. The sheriff recognized both of them. "What's wrong?" he asked.

"The new schoolteacher is missing," Neal replied. "She left on her horse early this morning and hasn't returned. Did anything out of the ordinary happen around town today?"

"No," the sheriff shook his head, "not that I know of.... Wait a minute! Was her horse a big reddish brown mare with a white star on her face?"

"Yes, sir, it was," Ben quickly replied.

"Come around to the back of the office."

They walked with the sheriff to the back of the building, and Ben saw Star tied to a post.

"That's Hannah's horse! How did it get here?"

"A plantation owner from across the Cooper brought her in just before dark. He was on his way into town when he saw the horse on his place. Since it was bridled and saddled, he figured it had gotten away from someone. I intended to send a couple of men out there to look around, first thing in the morning, but I didn't think about it being a woman. I'll get some men and go right now."

"You got two, right here," said Neal.

"Good. I'll get my deputy and some lanterns. We'll search the area where the horse was found."

On the hill where she had fallen, Hannah burrowed her body in the tall grass that shielded her from the wind off the Atlantic. She looked up at the clear night sky and found all the constellations that could be seen on a summer night. The outer rim of the Big Dipper pointed to Polaris, and from there, her eyes traveled across the sky to Cassiopeia. She recalled the night she stood with Nathan on the moonlit deck of the *Monarch* and helped him remember the lady's name. It was the same night he asked her to marry him.

"Nathan," she whispered his name. "Will I ever see you again?" Her hand touched his gold chain.

As she lay on the ground with the darkness around her, she relived their short time together from the moment he first spoke to her on the dock in Cork Harbor until that dreadful day when he rode away from Reybrook. She remembered their first kiss and how wonderful and exciting it was, and she recalled the night they prayed together after she had almost ended their relationship.

Hannah was cold and hungry, but she was not afraid. She had prayed for God's deliverance from her perilous situation and had faith that He would. Not a soul on earth knew where she was, and it could be days before anyone missed her, but God had given her peace. She didn't understand it, but accepted it. Perhaps her leg would be better the next morning and she'd be able to walk. If not, God would provide another way.

In the quiet stillness of the night, she listened to the sound of the surf and thought of how Nathan had listened to the sea at night when he was quite young. They would build a house, she dreamed, right here on this hill when he returned and would listen to the surf together. She began to visualize the home; a wide porch would face the harbor. It would not be such a large home as Barrington Manor or Reybrook, but large enough for several children. As she created the house within her mind, she dreamed of living there with her husband . . . her children . . . in her own home.

"Oh, Nathan," she whispered, "I love you—I love you." And she realized that it really was him she loved. Ben would always hold a special place in her heart, but Nathan was the one she wanted to spend her life with. She was glad she'd left Reybrook. Her hand clutched the gold chain around her neck as her eyes closed.

She'd almost drifted off to sleep when suddenly her eyes opened wide. She had heard something. It was people and they called her name.

The next morning, Dr. Holmes fussed at Hannah just like a father would his daughter as he examined her swollen knee.

"You had no business riding so far out of town, alone."

"I know, Dr. Holmes," she fully agreed with him, "and I'm very sorry for all the trouble I caused."

"Well, you should be! Kept the sheriff up all night and Ben, here, hasn't had a wink of sleep, besides the scare you gave him."

"I'm sorry, Ben," she apologized for the third time.

"What if that man hadn't found your horse? You'd still be out there, miles from nowhere," the doctor fretted.

"Yes, sir. You're right, Dr. Holmes, but it was only three miles, and it won't happen again, I promise."

Ben relished every word that the doctor said to her, but he smiled when Hannah rolled her eyes at him to let him know that she thought the old man was going a bit too far with his lecture. He helped her down from his bench when the doctor was finished, and back at the school, he propped her leg up with books and a pillow. "The doctor said you had to stay off it at least a week," he said.

"I heard the old kook," she muttered.

"Hannah," Ben laughed, "he's not a kook; he's a good doctor."

"Well, he needs to mind his own business."

"You are his business and he cares about you."

"I know, Ben," she finally admitted. "I know he cares and I know he's right. It was a stupid thing that I did. I'm thankful that you and your dad came . . . oh . . . ," she remembered. "You came to pay the taxes, and I haven't transferred the money from my account. I'm so sorry, but when I saw Star the evening before, all I could think about was going for a ride. I'll go right now and take care of it."

"No, you won't!" He reminded her of what the doctor had said. "The taxes will have to wait another week."

"The taxes have been paid," she mumbled.

"What?"

"The taxes have already been paid," she spoke more distinctly.

"What do you mean?"

"I paid them. With all the money I inherited, you know I couldn't let your family lose Reybrook."

They gazed into each other's eyes a moment, but neither spoke. He sat down beside her on the divan and leaned forward with his arms on his knees.

He stared at the floor and asked, "When did you pay them?"

"The third day after I moved here."

"Did you walk to the bank and the tax office?"

"No. The man who owns Miller's Store let his son take me in a wagon that is used to deliver groceries."

"You went to a lot of trouble."

"Not really."

"Why didn't you tell my dad, the day you came to Reybrook?"

"I knew if I told him that the taxes had been paid, he would not agree to give up Reneka, and I wanted so much for Ollie and her to be free."

Ben sat up straight and nodded his head; he understood. She hoped that Garrett would.

"Then you don't need to transfer any money," Ben said.

"Oh, yes, I do! I told your dad that I would put four hundred dollars in his account, and I'm going to the bank to do it right now."

"Hannah, you can't walk!"

"Then I shall hop. Are you going to help me or not?"

Reluctantly, Ben helped her into the saddle and hoped that Dr. Holmes wouldn't see them. At the bank, Hannah had four hundred dollars transferred from her account to Garrett's account, and on the way home she told Ben about the need for stove wood within the city and put the idea of raising hay to sell in his head.

"I can't understand you wanting to help us after Dad let you go the way he did. I'm still bitter at him about it."

"Please don't be. He thought he did what was best for me."

Ben helped her from Star's back and to the divan, where he put the books and pillow under her bandaged leg again. "I have to go," he said, "and meet Dad before he gets all the way to town, but I'll be back later today and bring Reneka to help you. She shouldn't mind after what you did for her. I'll come in the wagon and get provisions for the kitchen, now that we have money. Rosie says her flour barrel is "Sho gettin' lo!" He made Hannah laugh.

Ben walked to the door and opened it, but then stopped and closed it again. With his hand still on the door knob, he leaned his head against the door, and it was obvious that something bothered him.

"What's wrong, Ben?"

He didn't look up, but replied, "Dad said it upset you when he told you that Julie and I went for a ride on Blaze and Star."

She had not wanted him to know, but she couldn't lie to Ben. "Yes, it hurt that someone had taken my place so quickly, but it was very selfish of me, and I wish he had not told you."

Ben lifted his head and looked across the room at her. "No one," he said, "can take your place in my heart."

"You'll always have a special place in mine, Ben."

He turned to open the door again just as someone knocked on it. It was Rebecca and she had brought Hannah something to eat.

"Come in, Rebecca. I was just leaving," Ben said. But Rebecca didn't hear him because there was something strong on her mind.

"Have you heard the news?" she asked.

"What news?" Ben inquired.

"Napoleon has been defeated, and the Duke of Wellington sends thousands of his troops to America. We're about to be faced with a lot more than a blockade."

The news devastated Hannah. She and Ben looked into each other's eyes and neither heard what else Rebecca had to say. When she was finished, Ben opened the door. "I have to go," he mumbled, and left quickly.

CHAPTER 35

News of Napoleon's defeat spread like wildfire. Everyone in Charleston talked about it. Town merchants began to board up shops to protect them from bombardment. Fear filled the heart of everyone in the nation, for the freedom that they so highly cherished was now seriously threatened after only 38 years of independence.

Many from Charleston remembered the day of June 28, 1776, when the British attacked their city in the war for independence. Six hundred militiamen under the command of Colonel William Moultrie had successfully repelled a British naval attack. And again in 1779, they had been successful in defending the city, but on May 12, 1780, after a six-week siege, Charleston had fallen to the British and was held until December 14, 1782.

Reneka came, as Ben had said she would, to help Hannah. She pampered her by waiting on her hand and foot and refused to let her get out of bed except when absolutely necessary. With all the attention that Reneka gave her, what Hannah enjoyed the most was when she pulled up a chair or sat on the side of her bed, and the two engaged in a long conversation. They talked until late into the night and each enjoyed the company of the other.

"It's so wonderful to have you here, Reneka. I like having my own place, but have to admit that I get lonesome, especially at night. I lived alone after my father died and had no one to talk to except my animals. I was very lonely and came to America with hopes of finding a family here. I thought I had," her voice became sad, "but sometimes things just can't work out the way we want them to."

"Miss Hannah," Reneka took her hand, "you did find a family, and they each love you as much as they do anyone else in the family. The next day after you left Reybrook was just awful."

"What happened?"

"Miss Catherine had cried so much until Mr. Rey yelled at her and say he can't stand it no more. Then Mr. Ben and Mr. Rey got into it, and Mr. Ben threatened to leave home and take his mama and the three little ones with him. He would have, too, had Miss Catherine not done made herself sick again."

"Oh, Reneka."

"Otis cried himself to sleep the night after you left and Emma and Emily refused to eat. Miss Catherine couldn't stand for you to be alone, and she begged Mr. Rey to come get you, but he say you done got another job and don't want to come back. He say it wouldn't be fair to ask you to when you be making good money soon as school started, and he couldn't pay you one cent.

"I heard a noise late that night and slipped out of my bed to see where it come from, and I see Mr. Garrett in his office with his head down on his desk. I ask him if he be sick and he sat up and shook his head. 'No, Reneka,' he say, 'I just don't know what to do 'bout everything.' Miss Hannah, I never seen a sadder man in all my life."

"Oh, dear," groaned Hannah.

"Now, Mr. Ben come home today and say he gonna join the state militia, for the Redcoats be ah comin', and he say they'll attack Charleston. He told what happened to you and blamed Mr. Rey for it, but Mr. Rey say he ain't had nothing to do with you going off by yoself."

"Please, Reneka, don't tell me anymore. Just tell me how happy you are to be with Ollie again."

"Oh, Miss Hannah, it's like he done come back from the dead 'cause I didn't never expect to see him again. Mr. Rey let him sleep in Ole Ramey's bed and he's been talking to Ollie 'bout taking Ramey's place in the fields. He say he can't pay us right now, but if we stay 'til the blockade ends, he'll pay us a small salary, and we can build a cabin on the plantation."

"Now that's wonderful news! Have you talked to Ben about a wedding?"

"Yes, but me and Ollie want a little time to get to know each other again. We set a date, but now Mr. Ben will be gone, and I don't know when we can get married. Miss Dolly be upset, too, but hopes Mr. Ben will be back by the date that she and Mr. Jim have set."

"Poor Ben," thought Hannah. She shook her head back and forth. "How is Charleen doing?" she asked.

"She stay in her room mostly, but do seem to be growing up some. Since you been gone, she do more 'round the house and spends time with Otis and the girls. She take all three to the swing on the front porch and read them a story yesterday evening."

"I'm so glad to hear that. I know there is good in Charleen, but she must see it for herself."

"Well, up 'til now, there ain't nobody else seen nothing no good 'bout her."

"Jason did. I don't think she was that way with him, and I believe he'll come back to see her someday if he can."

"Yes, ma'am."

"Reneka, I just can't tell you how much it means to have you here."

A tear trickled down Reneka's cheek, "Miss Hannah, I don't know how to thank you for what you done for Ollie and me. Through you, God done answered my prayers."

"There is something you can do for me, Reneka."

"What that be?"

"Seeing how God answered your prayer that seemed impossible, I ask that you pray for Nathan and Jason's safe return and for Ben's safety. Pray for the war to end."

"I will, Miss Hannah. I'll pray for it every day."

The next morning, Hannah refused to have breakfast in bed, but insisted that her leg was much better, and in spite of Reneka's strong objection, she hobbled to the kitchen table.

They had just finished breakfast when they heard a knock at the front door. It was Mr. Overteer, and he'd come to inquire of Hannah's condition and to offer his service for any need she might have. He was invited in and seated at the kitchen table, and Reneka placed a cup of hot chicory in front of him.

"I'm glad you came by, Mr. Overteer. I need to talk to you."

"What about?"

"The land where I fell from my horse. There was a small "for sale" sign and that's why I had left the road and was on the grassy hill when the birds flew up in front of Star."

"Was it on the high road about three miles out of town?"

"Yes. Do you know the place?"

"I do, and I knew it was for sale, but there isn't much timber on that land."

"I know, but I want to buy it."

"It belongs to the man who found your horse and brought her to the sheriff. He owns a large plantation, but like everyone else, is behind on taxes and wants to sell part of his land to pay them. He'll sell at a bargain price because he's desperate."

"How many acres does he need to sell?"

"Two hundred."

That's perfect, thought Hannah. "Can you make a deal for it?" she asked.

"I'll ride out there this morning. Do you think you'll be able to meet him in my office tomorrow afternoon?"

"Yes, I'll be there."

The next evening, Reneka helped Hannah put the saddle on Star and then watched as she rode off toward the bank. On the way there, Hannah thought of the home she'd visualized in her mind. She was sorry that the planter couldn't pay his taxes, but his misfortune was her blessing.

Mr. Overteer greeted her on her arrival at the bank and invited her to his office where a man and a lady were seated.

"Hannah, this is Joseph and Susan Johnson."

"I'm pleased to meet you," she said. "I'm Hannah Thornton from County Cork, Ireland."

Mr. Johnson stood up. "It's a pleasure to meet you, Miss Thornton, and when I was a boy, my home was across the Irish Sea from yours. We came to America when I was nine years old; my father cleared the land where we live."

"What town are you from, Mr. Johnson."

"Liverpool."

She could hardly believe it, but didn't say anything about Nathan. That could wait.

"Our home is just over the next hill from where you had the accident," said Mrs. Johnson. "You were so close, yet lay there nearly all night. It must have been awful."

"It was frightening to think that no one knew where I was. I'm thankful your husband took my horse to the sheriff."

"Mr. Johnson had joined the search party," the banker mentioned.

"I shall always be indebted to you."

"Not at all, Miss Thornton; not at all. We're grateful to you for making it possible for us to keep our plantation."

"Will the road from Charleston border my land?" Hannah inquired.

"Yes, and it continues on to the next town, north of here."

"That's good."

After a price was agreed upon, Hannah signed a bank draft for Mr. Overteer to withdraw that amount from her account. In return, Joseph and Susan Johnson signed over two hundred acres of their land to her. A bank clerk wrote out a deed and put it in a large envelope before he gave it to Hannah. She rose and shook hands with the people she had done business with, and after a few words, started to leave. At the office door, however, she turned and asked, "Do you have children?"

"Yes," replied Mrs. Johnson. "We have three girls and two boys, ranging from age three to fifteen."

Hannah smiled. You'll make a wonderful neighbor, she thought, as she left the office. Mr. Johnson stepped ahead of her and opened the door.

Hannah took it easy for the next two days. Her time, however, was not wasted. She filled out papers to be sent to the state capitol for Ben's high school diploma and put them in an addressed envelope. Reneka mailed them at a small post office, not far from the school.

According to a roll book left by the preceding teacher, Hannah realized she would have a few students in each grade when school started in the fall, and she began to work on an educational plan for all twelve grades. Her new job would be much more difficult than her class of five students.

After she had worked for several hours on the educational plans, she put them away and took out her sewing box and the new material she had purchased. It was all taken to the kitchen table, and while Reneka made a fresh pot of chicory, Hannah began to cut out the new dress she had promised Miranda.

She liked the way the material cut; it was sturdy, yet thin enough to make an elegant dress for the doll. After she'd cut every piece she would need, she carefully folded the material that was left and placed it in the sewing box. As the evening was spent, the small dress began to take shape.

Hannah made beautiful stitches with her fingers. She knew just how to handle the material to make it stand up or lay down smoothly where it should. The dress had a small round collar onto which she sewed a tiny lace trim. There were little puff sleeves that stood up nicely when she gathered the ends of them and sewed a thin band around each. Reneka watched the creation of the doll dress with awe and was amazed at Hannah's talent.

"Miss Hannah, who taught you to sew like that?" she asked.

"No one ever taught me. It just came with time after I had sewed for so many years. I found my mother's sewing box when I was a child and began to sew for my father and myself. At first, I sewed up rips and split seams, but later, I learned to make clothes. My grandmother was a seamstress; perhaps I inherited some of her talent."

Hannah showed Reneka the lace-trimmed handkerchiefs that her grandmother had made, and Reneka admired them.

"Would you like to keep one?" Hannah asked.

"Oh, yes. I'd like one to keep forever, to remember the wonderful lady who gave Ollie and me our freedom."

"You know, Reneka, it was the lady who made these that really gave you your freedom."

"How that be so, Miss Hannah?"

"When my grandmother died, she left me all of her possessions, making it possible for me to help you."

"Then the handkerchief will remind me of two people." Hannah smiled as Reneka carefully ran her fingers over the lace.

When the evening light faded, Reneka lit a lamp and set it in the middle of the table. Its soft glow let Hannah continue to sew on Miranda's dress until late into the night. She gathered the skirt at the waist and stitched it to the bodice. The tiny pearl buttons were sewed down the front of the dress to add attractiveness, but at its back, they held the sides together. At eleven o'clock, Reneka went to bed and was soon asleep, but Hannah remained by the lamplight since she was so near finished with the dress. She turned up the edge of the gathered skirt and stitched a hem in it and then held the finished dress up to the light. It was beautiful. "Miranda," she said, "tomorrow I shall make you a bonnet, and you will be the best dressed doll in all of Charleston."

Hannah dressed Miranda in the new dress before she put everything back into her sewing box. With the doll in one hand and the lamp in the other, she went into the living room to put the doll on the shelf. As she bent over to set the lamp on the table by the rocking chair, she heard a horse running fast in the distance and wondered who would be out so late. It was now after midnight.

She set Miranda on the shelf and arranged her dress and had reached for the lamp again when she heard the night rider's horse turn from the main road and run all the way up to her door. Almost instantly, someone knocked loudly. Having no idea who it could be, she eased toward the bedroom for the rifle under her bed. The knock came again and this time harder.

"Hannah! Wake up!" It was a familiar voice. Something was wrong; she ran to open the door.

"Ben, what's wrong?"

"It's Mother. She's real sick . . . . Dad and I brought her to Dr. Holmes. Hannah . . ." He could hardly talk.

"Come in, Ben, and sit down."

Seated on her divan, he tried again. "Dr. Holmes told my dad and me . . . ," tears came in his eyes, "that Mama is going to die. He doesn't think she'll live until daybreak."

"Oh, Ben," Hannah breathed his name and sat down beside him. Her heart began to race. Not Catherine . . . oh Lord . . . not Catherine.

"Mama's asking for you, Hannah, and Dad sent me to get you. I know it's late, but will you come?"

"Of course, I will. Let me tell Reneka and I'll be ready." Moments later, she asked, "Do I need to saddle Star?"

"No . . . there isn't time. I'll ride behind you on Blaze. Mama's at the city hospital and it's not too far." Hannah insisted, however, that she ride behind the saddle. She couldn't handle Blaze the way Ben did and would slow them down. She circled her arms around him and held on tightly.

At the hospital, they dismounted quickly, and ran hand-in-hand up the hospital steps and down a long corridor until they came to Catherine's room. Ben opened the door. Garrett stood at the foot of her bed. Dr. Holmes was bent over her with a stethoscope, and a younger doctor stood at the other side of her bed with a nurse beside him. Catherine lay with her head on a pillow; her eyes were closed.

Ben waited in the hall to talk to the doctor, but Hannah entered the room and laid her hand on Garrett's arm. He covered it with his own and whispered, "Thank you for coming." She nodded her head.

Dr. Holmes took Catherine's hand and spoke softly, "Catherine, Hannah is here." Catherine opened her eyes, and both doctors and the nurse left the room, leaving the three of them alone.

Hannah stepped to the side of the bed and took Catherine's hand. Garrett moved to the window and looked out into the darkness.

"Hannah," Catherine could barely speak. "Our dear Hannah; I'm so glad you came."

"I love you, Catherine."

"I know; you have so much love for everyone. But please listen to me, Hannah. My time is very near. I shall be with the Heavenly Father before long, but it's my family that I'm concerned about, and that's why I've asked for you. Will you please return to Reybrook and take care of them? They will need you. The children love you so much, and I know you love them."

Hannah's job, her new home, new friends, and the students she was anxious to meet, all flashed through her mind. She didn't want to return to the plantation to live, but this was Catherine—the most wonderful lady she had ever known—and it was her dying request. There could only be one answer. She looked up at Garrett and he nodded his head.

"Yes, Catherine. I'll do anything you ask, and I do love the children. I love each of you, and I promise to do everything I can for your family, just as if they were my very own for as long as they need me." She felt a faint squeeze to her hand; Catherine was satisfied with the promise. Her eyes closed and did not open again.

At 6:23 A.M., just as the sun peeped over Charleston Harbor, Catherine went to be with her beloved Heavenly Father . . . but the sun continued to rise on the worst day of Hannah's life. She remembered the terrible agony she had felt when Collin died, but had only her own grief to deal with. Now she was left with the six members of Catherine's family who would feel that same grief. "Oh, God," she prayed silently, "give me strength, and give me words that will bring comfort."

She waited at the hospital with Ben and Garrett until a funeral home came to take Catherine's body. The three of them then returned to her place for Reneka and for things she would need until everything could be moved back to Reybrook. Garret wanted her there when he told Otis and the twins of their mother's death.

Reneka wept bitterly when Hannah gave her the news, and although she knew she must hurry, Hannah took a moment to put her arms around her friend and then made her sit down at the kitchen table, while she packed a few clothes. Ben saddled Star and brought her to the front door, and when Hannah was ready, he tied her bag and Reneka's behind Blaze. Reneka climbed on Star behind Hannah, and the four of them started the long and solemn trip to Reybrook.

As soon as they rode up to the home, Charleen came out to meet them to inquire about her mother's condition. Ben dismounted and put his arms around her, while Garrett kneeled on the porch with his three youngest children. Hannah stood close behind Garrett, and Reneka went inside to tell Rosie. When Garrett stood, he lifted Otis in his arms. Emily and Emma ran to Hannah; she kneeled and gathered them to her, and they buried their faces on her shoulders.

The rest of the day was like an awful dream for Hannah, but one from which she knew she would never awake. She went to inform the servants and the slaves of Catherine's death and had never witnessed such heartbreak before. She had known that Catherine was loved by all who knew her, but she had not realized how much.

Jim and Nole were sent with a message to tell others, and by night fall, people had begun to come in order to pay their respects to Garrett and his children. They brought food and wept tears with them. Hannah greeted the visitors at the door and took the food and then ushered them to the living room. She was kind and understanding to those who wanted to talk for a long period of time, relating to her of some good deed Catherine had bestowed upon them. When possible, she helped in the kitchen, for poor Rosie was in an awful state.

It was late by the time everyone left, and Hannah's injured leg ached, but her body felt numb as she climbed the stairs to the room she had occupied for two years. She crossed the room to the window and looked out into the darkness. The sun had gone down long before . . . and she had forgotten her watch of the sunset.

The next morning, the funeral home brought the coffin that held Catherine's body and placed it on a bier at one side of the small parlor. Hannah stood aside and wept silently as Catherine's family gathered around it. Emily and Emma clung to Garrett and Ben held Otis. It was Charleen who turned to Hannah, but there were no tears in her eyes.

On the third morning, Hannah rose early and dressed for the funeral. She went to Charleen's room and found her sitting on the side of her bed, staring at the floor; it seemed she couldn't function. Hannah chose a dark blue dress for her and slipped it over her head. She buttoned the dress and combed her hair and lifted her feet into a pair of shoes. To others in the family, Charleen appeared to be quite stolid, but Hannah recognized that out of all of Catherine's children, she was having the hardest time dealing with her mother's death.

Julie had been at Ben's side, and she walked with him to the cemetery. Hannah walked behind them and was amazed at how many people had gathered for the funeral. Pastor Richard stood at the head of the coffin and many of his church members stood behind him.

Other plantation owners, including Franklin Lambert, were there with their families. Even Frank had come, but Laci did not. Mr. Overteer, Dr. Holmes, and many others from Charleston, crowded inside the small cemetery. An aunt and uncle of Catherine's had heard and come from a long way off.

Garrett stood near the coffin with Charleen beside him; her arm was linked through his. Ben held Otis and Julie stood at his side. Hannah stood beside Charleen and held Emily's hand in one hand and Emma's in the other. Dolly, Jim, and the Leanders supported Catherine's family by standing close behind them.

Every slave on the plantation huddled together just beyond

the cemetery's wrought-iron fence. They could be heard moaning and weeping as Pastor Richard preached a short service; he had words of encouragement for Catherine's family, assuring them of her salvation, and closed by earnestly pleading for the lost to accept Jesus as their Savior.

Right after the funeral, Garrett and Charleen walked back up the hill and took the children with them, but Ben stayed and mingled with the crowd. He thanked them for coming and invited them to stay for dinner. A few accepted his invitation, but most soon left. Hannah talked with Pastor Richard and Jane, and Mr. Overteer wanted her to meet his wife.

Dr. Holmes noticed that Hannah limped badly, and he suspected she was in a lot of pain, but he waited until most of the people had left before he confronted her about it.

"How is your leg, Hannah?" he asked.

"It hurts, Dr. Holmes, but it'll be all right. I'll rest tomorrow."

"I want to examine it while I'm here."

"All right. I would appreciate it; the bandage feels awfully tight. If you can come to the house, we'll go to my room."

They walked up the hill together and made their way through the crowd of people that were on the porch and in the home. Ben had also noticed how badly Hannah limped. He watched as she and the doctor climbed the stairs.

Hannah sat on the side of her bed, next to the window for more light, and lifted her dress above her knee. The doctor kneeled in front of her, and with a small tool from his pocket, he cut the bandage loose. Her kneecap was a dark color and very swollen. She flinched with pain when he pressed against it.

"Hannah, you have to get off this leg and keep it elevated for at least an hour." He reached into his pocket again and brought out a small bottle of pills. "You've been on it too much," he said, "and the blood is not circulating properly. I want you to take one of these and lie down."

"But, Dr. Holmes, dinner must be served."

"I'm sorry, Hannah. Someone else will have to take care of that. If you don't take care of your leg, you're going to have very serious problems," the doctor spoke firmly. He frightened Hannah, which was exactly what he intended to do.

With no more argument, she lay back on the pillow, and the doctor lifted her legs to the bed and then placed a pillow under her injured leg. He handed her the bottle of pills and went for a glass of water.

Ben stopped him at the foot of the stairs. "How is Hannah?" he asked.

The doctor shook his head. "She's been on her leg too much, and I've ordered her to lie down for at least an hour. I gave her something to help her rest and have come for a glass of water."

"I'll get it for her. You fix yourself a plate."

"All right, Ben, but be sure she takes the medicine. Tell her to keep it and take two a day for as long as they last."

"All right, Dr. Holmes."

Ben climbed the stairs with the water and knocked on Hannah's door.

"Come in," she called.

She was surprised to see him; they had barely spoken to each other the last three days. He sat down on the side of the bed and held up the water. She took the bottle of pills from under her pillow and put one in her mouth, and with the water, swallowed it down. Ben set the glass on the table beside her bed. He didn't speak; there was no need to. His face expressed his feelings.

"I'm all right, Ben. You must return downstairs. Julie will miss you, and she'll be upset if she finds you here. I'm glad you have her support."

"I'll bring you something to eat."

"I can't eat now. I'll get something later."

He stood and walked to her door, but before he left, he turned and spoke in a low voice, "Thank you for being here, Hannah, but I wish you'd stay off your leg the rest of the day." She nodded her head slowly as her eyes closed. Ben lingered at the door a moment longer and gazed at her face asleep on the pillow.

The medicine that Dr. Holmes had given Hannah made her sleep much longer than she intended. She arose to a dark room, but lit a candle and tiptoed to the children's room and found them sleeping soundly. The house was quiet except for the muffled voices of Rosie and Reneka who talked softly at the small table in the kitchen. She thought the Rey family had all gone to bed until she crept down the stairs and found Garrett seated on the divan. He was bent forward with his elbows across his knees, and he stared at the floor.

When Hannah sat down beside him, he sat up straight and sighed deeply. "She loved you so much, Hannah, and I curse the day that I sent you away from her. I know it hastened her death."

"You must not say that, Sir. She would not want you to."

"No . . . she would have no one think badly of me, and you're so much like her."

"Oh, no, Mr. Rey," Hannah disagreed. "Miss Catherine's virtues far outshined mine."

CHAPTER 36

Hannah's injured leg felt better after a night's rest. She had taken more of the medicine that Dr. Holmes had given her, and when she awoke the morning after Catherine's funeral, the dark color of her knee had begun to fade, and the swelling had decreased. She felt little physical pain as she walked the trail to the cemetery, but her mental pain was agonizing.

She hated the merry melody that the birds sang and wanted them to fly away and sing some other place. They only added to her wretchedness. She lifted the latch on the wrought-iron gate and entered the cemetery to see the mound of fresh dirt over the new grave. Flowers that had been brought from the yards of some who attended the funeral were now withered.

Hannah knelt to her knees beside the grave and bowed her head. Her soul was filled with despair and she wept bitterly. She tried to pray, but could not, and in her desperation, she lifted her face to the sky and cried out, "Why, God? Why must you take those that I love the most? You took my mother and my father and now one who had filled my mother's place. Will you take Nathan and Ben, also? Catherine loved you so much, Lord. Why did she have to leave her children . . . her husband . . . and others who loved her?"

Suddenly her strength left her, and she felt only hopelessness. It was God she had always turned to in sorrow and without Him . . . there was no hope. She covered her tear-streaked face with her hands and leaned forward until they touched the surface of the grave and her long hair lay in a heap on its fresh dirt.

In her agony, Hannah was unaware of anyone's presence until she felt someone's arms lift her from the grave. Ben pulled her close to him and she leaned her face against his chest.

"Shhh, don't cry," he muttered soft words and caressed her back and then lifted her chin and gently brushed hair from her face. "You must not blame God for Mama's death," he said. "She wouldn't want you to. It wasn't His will for her to die or your mother or father, and it won't be His will for Nathan or me to die." Ben realized that for three days she had consoled everyone at Reybrook, but no one had heeded to her own hurting.

"I know you loved Mama. You'll miss her as much as any of us, but we all must remember that she's gone to a wonderful place, and she won't be sick anymore. She'll be with Grandma and Grandpa and even your own—"

"Mother and father," she finished the sentence.

"Yes," he nodded. A smile came to her lips. Ben reached to his back pocket for a handkerchief.

"I have not thought of that."

"Mama wouldn't want you to be angry at God, but to praise Him in all things."

"I know; God forgive me." Her head bowed to his chest again and he felt her sobbing.

He held her close to him and brushed bits of dirt from her hair. When her crying ceased, he sighed and said, "Hannah . . ."

"What?"

"I have to go. I'm leaving this morning to join the militia."

"Must you go so soon? Your dad will need you."

"I know, but I have no choice. I'll have little time to train as it is; the British won't be long in reaching our shores. I hate to burden you with anything else, but . . . well, it's Julie."

"What, Ben?"

"When I told her last night that I'd be leaving this morning, she got awfully upset. Will you talk to her?"

Hannah remembered how she had felt the day Nathan left and how much it had meant when Ben came to talk, but she had been among strangers and Julie knew everyone on the plantation. She even had a sister, so why should Ben ask this of her?

"I'm sorry." Ben took her silence to mean that she didn't want to. "I shouldn't have asked," he said. "You have enough on you as it is."

"It's not that, Ben. It's just that . . . well, I don't understand why you want me to talk to Julie when she has a sister whom I'm sure she is much closer to, and—"

"No—it's hard for her to talk to Dolly; they're different. She likes to talk to you because you understand her."

"All right; I'll try to help."

"Thanks."

"Ben?"

"Yes?"

"Is this what Nathan asked of you when he had to leave me?"

"Well, he wanted someone to look after you . . . someone you could turn to for help." He smiled sentimentally. "He didn't intend for me to fall in love with you."

"Do you still love me?"

"I'll always love you."

"What will you do if you come face to face with him?"

Ben heaved a deep sigh and shook his head back and forth. "God only knows," he answered. "I hope I would do nothing."

"I shall pray that he would do the same."

"Don't think of it; just be strong. Be strong for my family . . . for Julie . . . and for you."

"I will, Ben, and may God go with you."

There was a look of helplessness on Garrett's face as he watched his oldest son ride away. How much more, Hannah wondered, could he take? After the blockade, Catherine's death, and now Ben leaving for the war, was the worst yet to come?

Otis and the twins tugged at her skirt as they wiped tears from their eyes with it. Ben was their hero, and she did her best to comfort them. Charleen kept her eyes on him until he was out of sight, and Rosie cried as if it was her own son leaving for the war. Julie stood apart from the family; she cried silently and Hannah wanted to go to her, but she had her hands full with the three children. She was glad to see Dolly put an arm around her, and when the two of them left with Jim, she turned to take the children into the house. They had started up the front steps when Garrett called to her.

"Hannah."

"Yes, Mr. Rey?"

"I need to talk to you. Will you sit here on the steps a moment?" Reneka took the children with her, and when everyone had left the front yard, Garrett sat down beside her.

"Ben told me you paid the taxes on Reybrook," he began, "so I intended to give back the money you put into my account."

"No, Mr. Rey." Hannah shook her head.

"Let me finish, please. I don't know what I would have done without it the last few days, as I had to pay the hospital and funeral expenses. I was able to pay Dr. Holmes, also, although he would have waited."

"Mr. Rey, I owed you four hundred dollars for Reneka's freedom. It was the agreement that we made. As for the taxes . . . well . . . I paid them because . . ." She stopped and Garrett turned his head to look at her.

"Because why?"

She didn't want to make him feel worse than he already did, so she looked across the front yard and remained silent.

"Hannah," Garrett asked again, "why did you pay the taxes on Reybrook?"

"It's home to me, too," she mumbled. "It's the only home I have."

"And I sent you away." His face grimaced.

"You didn't understand, but thought you did what was best for me."

"I know now that I made a mistake, but I had promised Nathan I would pay you and I couldn't. I acted rashly because I wanted you to talk to the school board before they hired someone else."

"Please put it out of your mind."

"I still can't pay you, Hannah, and I know that come September, you'll have a good job in Charleston. I would think that you wouldn't want to come back here to live, and no one will blame you if you don't."

"Mr. Rey, I promised Catherine . . . ."

"I know. I heard you, but we can get along all right without you."

"You don't want me to stay, do you?" She had thought that the matter was settled, but realized that it wasn't with the plantation owner.

Garrett placed his elbows on his knees and leaned forward to cover his face with his hands. He breathed heavily and nodded his head. "Yes, Hannah, I want you to stay. We need you, but I won't hold you to your promise."

She then realized that Garrett had meant to give her a way out, and it was true . . . she didn't want to move back to Reybrook. She wasn't sure how she could stand it without Ben or Catherine. But the younger children needed someone to fill their mother's place, and Charleen needed her, perhaps even more.

She thought of the small living quarters with all her things and how she wanted to wait there for Nathan. She thought of Rebecca Cole and her family and of Jed Miller and Billy Ruebald. She would never know why little Billy had to live with grandparents or why he was so shy. And how could she tell the school board? Then she remembered Catherine's plea in her last words, "Will you return to Reybrook and take care of my family?" She thought of Ben's request, "Be strong for my family . . . for Julie . . ." No . . . she couldn't leave them. If she did, Catherine's and Ben's words would haunt her forever.

"I shall stay. I shall stay for as long as I'm needed."

Garrett seemed relieved. "Well," he said, "we'll move you back home. I'll have Jim and Ollie hitch a team to the wagon first thing in the morning. Maybe Dolly and Julie will go and help you pack."

"I'm sure Reneka would like to go if Ollie goes."

"Yes," Garrett agreed.

"But I don't want to leave Julie. Ben asked me to talk to her."

"Oh, no, Julie must not be left."

"Who will watch Otis and the girls? May we take them with us? I had hoped they could see my place and the school."

Garrett looked at her and smiled. "Then they will. We'll all go! Rosie needs a day out of the kitchen, so we'll pack some food and have a picnic."

"Oh, Mr. Rey, it would be a good thing for everyone!"

Early the next morning, two wagons were driven to the front of the home and Rosie and Reneka loaded two baskets of food. Hannah helped the twins and Otis get ready to go, and Otis was so excited that it was difficult for him to be still long enough for her to dress him and comb his hair. When she finally let go of him, he ran down the stairs, and Rosie lifted him to the back of the wagon.

Hannah went to Charleen's room and found her sitting on the side of her bed . . . still in her nightgown.

"Charleen, dear, they're waiting for us."

"I'm not going." Her voice trembled.

"Please, Charleen, the children are excited, but we can't leave you here alone. Your daddy would not hear of it."

"I won't leave Mother." Her words didn't come at too great a shock to Hannah. She had noticed Charleen's strange behavior from the time she'd received the news of her mother's death. They had to talk, and they had to talk right now, no matter what.

"Charleen," she sat down beside her, "your mother will not be left, but she has gone on before us to a wonderful place. She didn't want to leave you, and she can't come back, but one day you can go to be with her. She's not here, Charleen. Your mother is in heaven with Jesus."

Charleen placed her hand over her mouth and looked up at the ceiling, and for the first time, Hannah saw tears in her eyes.

"I don't understand about heaven and Jesus," she said. "Mother tried to tell me, but I wouldn't listen."

Scriptures about heaven came to Hannah's mind and she began to quote them. She spoke to Charleen of the everlasting life. "For God so loved the world, that he gave his only begotten Son, that whosoever believeth in him should not perish, but have everlasting life." John 3:16. "Charleen, your mother has been living the everlasting life for a long time and her life will never end."

Charleen's head fell to Hannah's lap and she began to sob. "All I know is that she's in a deep, cold grave."

"No, dear, she's not there. Only her earthly body that was sick for so long is there. She now has a new body and is not sick anymore. We'll read about it in the Bible tonight, but everyone is waiting for us now. Won't you come and help me move back to Reybrook?"

As Charleen wept in Hannah's lap, her door opened slowly and Hannah looked up to see Garrett peep through it. She held up her hand for him not to interrupt, and he closed the door softly and descended the stairs. He seemed pleased when the two of them soon followed him.

The wagons rolled down the hill, leaving only the slaves and the Leanders behind. Garrett had given the slaves a day off and left Mr. Leander in charge. Charleen sat on the wagon seat between Hannah and Garrett, and Reneka and Ollie rode in the back with Rosie and the children. Julie, Dolly, and Jim came in the wagon behind them.

They didn't stop until they reached the school, where Rosie spread a quilt in the shade of a tree, and while Otis and the twins ran to play on the school ground, she began to unpack the food. As Hannah watched the children, she imagined that many ran and played around the building or were seated under the trees with a lunchbox. After a moment, she heaved a sigh and dismissed her thoughts.

She dreaded informing school officials that she could not fulfill her position as a teacher, but it was a matter that must be tended to, while in Charleston, and as soon as Garrett finished eating, she told him of her desire to have the distasteful task behind her.

"All right, Hannah. I'll take you there, while the others begin to pack."

"Charleen," Hannah asked, "would you like to come with us?" She hoped that she would.

"Yes," Charleen seemed glad she had asked.

At the school office, while Garrett and Charleen waited for her in the wagon, Hannah expressed her regrets to school officials that she would not be able to fill the teacher's position as she had agreed. She took a moment to explain why.

"We're sorry it didn't work out, Miss Thornton, but we understand . . . under the circumstances. Perhaps there will be another opening in the future."

Hannah thanked them and was relieved to leave the office. As soon as they returned to the school, she paid Rebecca Cole a visit. By the time she entered her small living quarters, the kitchen cupboard was bare, and Reneka was carefully packing things from the living room shelves. She picked up Miranda to put her in the trunk.

"Let me hold her, Reneka. I don't want her new dress to get squashed."

While Jim and Ollie loaded her trunks onto the wagons, Hannah clutched Miranda in her arms and looked all around. With an ache in her heart, she thought of Nathan returning there for her. The dream must be forgotten. She took one last look and closed the door slowly.

Hannah climbed up beside Charleen on the wagon seat. As they waited for Garrett to make sure everything was secure on the wagons, Charleen asked, "Where did you get the doll?"

"It was my mother's. I made her a new dress. Do you like it?"

"It's beautiful. May I hold her?"

"Sure."

Charleen carefully touched her fingertips to the doll's soft hair. "How old were you," she asked, "when your mother gave it to you?" Garrett climbed up to the wagon seat beside her and took the reins in his hands. He listened as they continued the conversation.

"Actually, my father gave it to me."

"Your father? Why didn't your mother?"

"She died."

"How old were you?"

Hannah felt her and Garrett's eyes on her face. She looked down at her hands that were cupped together in her lap before she answered softly, "Only a few hours. She died the night I was born."

"Oh, Hannah . . . the doll must be very precious to you." Charleen handed it to her gingerly.

"Yes . . . Miranda means a great deal to me."

Back at Reybrook, Hannah tried to forget herself, so that she might fulfill her promise to Ben and Catherine. This was easy since it was the busy time of year. She took over Catherine's household duties and cared for the sick. With Rosie's help, she made sure that food was preserved correctly. She saw that the home was kept clean and that the family laundry was done properly. She mothered Otis and the twins and even Charleen when she would let her. Before the summer was over, everyone came to her for advice. "Mis Hannah, what we gwinna do 'bout dis, or what we gwinna do 'bout dat? Miss Hannah, please tell me what should be done about . . . Miss Hannah . . . Miss Hannah . . ."

With Ben gone, the church did not meet, but at night after the children were in bed, Hannah and Julie shared quiet times together. They read the Bible and had prayer for Ben and Nathan. They prayed for Garrett and all his family and for Julie's family in England. They prayed for everyone who lived on Reybrook soil and for many in Charleston. When time permitted, the two girls engaged in long conversations.

Garrett didn't plant a cotton crop that spring, but the ringing of axes and felling of trees could be heard in the woods daily from early morning until dusk. Wood was split, then cut into small pieces that would fit into any stove. It was hauled by the wagonloads to Charleston where each load sold quickly and people begged for more.

When July turned to August, hay that had grown in the cotton fields was cut and floated down the Cooper River to the city. The wood and hay brought enough cash to buy winter provisions, with some left over.

There was news that a British naval fleet had sailed into the Chesapeake Bay, and people feared it was only a matter of time until it reached Charleston. Hannah prayed fervently for Nathan and Ben, wondering where each was.

As soon as the busy season slowed down, she and Julie decided to start the Sunday morning worship service again. Both girls were elated when Jim agreed to preach a short sermon. Julie accepted responsibility for the music and Hannah would plan the Bible study.

That first Sunday, Hannah was overjoyed when Charleen came with Otis and the twins. After hours of Bible study with Charleen, Hannah felt sure she was ready to profess her faith in Jesus Christ, but she would not pressure her. It had to be her decision.

It was Garrett that Hannah was the most concerned about now. The busy season had been good for him, as it left him little time to think of Catherine. He'd moved into the downstairs guestroom the night after her funeral, and Hannah had heard him leave in the middle of the night, several different nights, and not return until a long time later. She knew that he went to Catherine's grave and her heart cried for him.

Now that his workload was less, he stayed out late at night. Charleen worried about him, and Otis cried when he didn't come home. One night Hannah waited up for him, hoping they could talk. It was near daylight before she heard him ride up the front lane. She tiptoed downstairs, but Garrett never came in.

After she had waited for quite awhile, Hannah left the house and walked to the cemetery. In the moonlight, she saw Garrett beside Catherine's grave. He sat on the ground with his knees pulled up in front of him. He had his arms wrapped around his knees, and he talked to her as though she sat right beside him.

"You would never have thought it, darling, but next to me, Charleen misses you more than anyone. You always thought it was just me that she loved, but she loved you an awful lot, and it's been so hard for her since you've been gone. I wonder if Ben cares as much for me. I haven't heard from him, but there has been no fighting in our area, so guess he's all right. Hannah is good to Otis and the girls, just as you knew she would be, and she and Charleen have become friends. She spends as much time as possible with all of them."

Hannah listened to Garrett awhile and then went back up the hill without him knowing she had been there. She had no right, she decided, to interfere with something he had to do. Beelzebub crowed as she entered the house, and a ray of light came from the kitchen. She heard Rosie's coffeepot perking and decided to have a cup of chicory before she went to her room. She had just poured it and sat down at the kitchen table when she heard Garrett come in. She thought he'd go straight to the guestroom, but he also came for a cup of chicory and sat down at the table.

"Why you up so early?" he asked.

"I couldn't sleep for worrying about you. Are you all right?"

"No . . . . I miss Catherine so bad that I ask myself what is there to live for."

"You have five children that love you very much, Mr. Rey. That's what you have to live for. Otis cries when you don't come home at night. Your children miss their mother, so they need you more than ever. Everyone on the plantation needs you. You have a responsibility and a lot to live for."

Garrett drank the hot liquid from his cup silently until Hannah was finished. He then stood and looked down at her before he left the room. "That was my answer, too," he said.

People gathered each day around the Charleston newspaper office to hear of any news about the war. On September 10, the paper's headline read, **"BRITISH ATTACK WASHINGTON D.C.—PUBLIC BUILDINGS BURNED!"** "The attack," the story read, "was by way of Bladensburg, Maryland, where on August 24, many Americans died while trying to defend our capitol city. Most town people evacuated before British soldiers arrived, but the city's beloved Dr. Beanes was taken prisoner and is being held aboard the British ship, *Tonnant*. Our First Lady, Dolly Madison, managed to escape with important papers and a painting of George Washington."

Many Charlestonians gathered that night in the streets and in people's homes to discuss what to do if Charleston was attacked. The militia stepped up its training and put out a call for more volunteers.

Garrett came home early with the news. Hannah and Charleen were eating the evening meal with Otis and the twins when he entered the dining room and sat down at the head of the table.

"The British burned our capitol city, Miss Thornton." He said it as if he blamed her with the whole ordeal. Hannah was silent, but her heart began to race with fear. She assumed there had been an awful battle and that many soldiers were killed on both sides. She could no longer eat and asked to be excused. As she stood from the table, Garrett asked sarcastically, "Who are you concerned about . . . ? Your Nathan or my Ben?" She was surprised when Charleen spoke up in her defense.

"Daddy," she raised her voice, "must you torment Hannah?"

"Well, my dear daughter, she's in love with an enemy."

"You didn't call Nathan an enemy when he bought your cotton and took it to Europe," Charleen responded quickly. Garrett had no further comments.

Hannah walked to the far end of the front porch where she had sat and cried the day Nathan left, and where Ben had come with words of encouragement and a glass of water. Her heart ached and the cooing of mourning doves magnified her agony.

She left the porch and walked the trail to the cemetery, but instead of entering through the gate, she grasped the top of the fence with both hands and looked over it to Catherine's grave. "Oh, Catherine," she groaned, "if only my body lay there instead of yours."

She felt a hand on her shoulder and turned quickly to see Garrett standing behind her. "I've said that same thing a thousand times," he avowed. Hannah kept silent; she had come to the cemetery to escape his company.

"Hannah, I'm sorry for my rudeness. I don't know why I always take my frustration out on you. Can you forgive me?"

"Yes, Mr. Rey." She spoke in a quiet voice.

"Will you call me Garrett?"

"If you want me to."

"I do."

"Were many people killed in the battle?"

"No. Only sixty-four British were killed and twenty-six Americans. The British were probably new arrivals from the war in Europe. I doubt that Nathan was among them."

"And Ben?"

"I believe our state militia will keep all volunteers from this area at home to defend Charleston Harbor and the city. No, I don't think Ben was there."

Come September, more war news was that the British fleet under the command of Admiral Cochrane had bombarded Fort McHenry at Baltimore. The fort had been retained, and for this the people of Charleston cheered. They didn't know that the British Admiral had withdrawn his forces from Baltimore with his aim on a greater fortune elsewhere.

Among the war stories was an inspiring poem written by a young lawyer, Francis Scott Key. After the night's bombardment of Fort McHenry, Key had caught a glimpse of the United States flag still waving over the fort. He and a man named John Skinner had stood with Washington's Dr. Beanes, shortly after the two men had successfully negotiated the release of the doctor from the hands of the British. A few weeks later, the poem became known as "The Star Spangled Banner."

Hannah began fall classes in September, and among her students sat a proud new one. Garrett had given his permission for Sammy to take a seat beside Otis each morning. Together, the two boys learned to read and write and to work arithmetic problems. After school, two evenings a week, there were piano lessons for Charleen and Emma and Emily. Otis and Sammy showed no desire to learn to play, and she would not torture either by making them sit still for a longer period of time. Classes were held for the servants three nights a week and on Saturday mornings.

Hannah worked long hours with her students and often burned the midnight oil to plan for the next day. On one of those nights, she sat at her desk, but had almost finished her work when she heard footsteps on the stairs. She knew it was Garrett; everyone else was asleep, but he had just come in. He came down the hall and stood at her classroom door with a large envelope in his hand. With being tired and irritable and quite fed up with his late hours, she snapped at him. "Where have you been, Garrett?"

He laughed quietly and mumbled under his breath, "Such little respect that I get from my household employee, but when she works without pay, I suppose that's what I should expect."

"I'm sorry, Garrett." Hannah laid down her pencil and rubbed her eyes. "I'm sorry. It's just that the children worry so when you don't come home before they go to bed."

"I'm the one who should be sorry." He sat down in Ben's desk and leaned his head forward until it rested on top of it. "But there are not so many memories of her at the town taverns as here at home."

Hannah put her work aside and rose from her desk. "Garrett," she said, "why don't you come to our worship service this Sunday? I believe it helps Charleen cope with her mother's death, and I think it would help you. Catherine would like for you to come."

"I don't know, Hannah," his voice was muffled as his head still lay on the desktop. "I'll think about it." He raised his head and wiped tears from his eyes. "Oh, I forgot. This is for you." He handed her the large envelope.

She became excited when she saw the return address from the state capitol. It was Ben's diploma. She pulled the certificate from the envelope carefully, and it was beautiful. She held it down for Garrett to see, but his only comment was, "Catherine would have been so proud."

"Yes," Hannah sadly agreed, "she would have been. Come Garrett, you must get to bed." She helped him to the top of the stairs and watched as he descended them slowly. After that night, Garrett didn't go to the town taverns, but he was home every evening with his children and made trips to Charleston only when necessary.

Hannah was amazed at the progress Charleen now made in school. It was like she wanted to make up the time she had wasted. Arithmetic and science were her favorite subjects, especially botany, and in order to obtain extra points for her marks, she had completed on her own, an experiment with plants. Hannah became excited when she read the report Charleen had written on the experiment. She read it a second time, for Charleen had explained in explicit details how different plants thrived or died under certain conditions; it was exactly what Garrett wanted Ben to study. God had answered her prayer. Ben could be a preacher and Garrett could grow a better cotton crop. She couldn't wait to tell him of Charleen's interest, but first, she would talk to her about it.

In class the next morning, Hannah gave her four young students enough work to keep them busy, while she talked to Charleen. First, she told her how impressed she was with her report and handed it to her with an excellent mark on it.

"Charleen, have you talked to your daddy about your interest in the study of plants?"

"No."

"It's what he wanted Ben to study in college, so he could learn better farming methods."

"I know."

"Then why haven't you told him?"

Charleen looked down at the floor. "I'd love to study plants in college, but Daddy won't have enough money to send Ben and me. He's always spoken of Ben going, and if God has called him to preach, then he must go, so he can prepare for what God wants him to do. I'm afraid if I say anything to Daddy about it, he'll send me to college instead of Ben, with feeling the way he does about Ben being a preacher."

Hannah was overwhelmed. What an unselfish concern Charleen had for her brother. God was surely working in her life. Reneka's words came to Hannah's mind. "Up 'til now, ain't nobody seen no good in her." Well, she could tell Reneka that things were different now. There was lots of good in Charleen, but it had taken her mother's death for her to see it for herself.

"You're probably right, Charleen; this is very considerate of you. We'll keep your interest our secret for the time being, but I shall not forget and we'll work something out. The entire South could benefit from your studies. I'll write a letter to the state government to see if any grants are available, and if you keep up the good work, I'll send reports to the proper places in order to obtain scholarships for you. You have another year in school and that will give us plenty of time."

"Thank you, Hannah." Charleen was excited when she returned to her desk. She worked even harder after their talk and offered to help Hannah in various ways, such as grading papers for the younger students. Hannah gladly let her.

The real surprise came on a Saturday morning in October as Hannah taught the servants' class. Charleen came to tell her that Mr. Overteer had come and that he waited to see her.

"I'm very sorry," Hannah apologized to her students.

Charleen looked at the arithmetic problems. "I know how to do this," she said. "Would you like for me to finish the lesson?"

Her students all nodded their heads, and Hannah handed her the book.

"Good morning, Mr. Overteer. What brings you to Reybrook on a Saturday morning?"

"I have exciting news, Hannah, and it couldn't wait!"

"Tell me!"

"An investment company of Charleston owns five thousand acres of good timberland. It's farther inland and has no swamps on it, but the company fears that the British will confiscate it and have decided to sell ... at a very low price. It's a good opportunity if you're willing to invest that much money."

Garrett stepped from his office. "How much money, Daniel, and what if the British do take it?" He surprised Hannah and caused her some embarrassment.

"Five thousand dollars, Garrett, and that's a risk she'll have to take."

"That's an awful lot of money, Hannah, and what will you do with five thousand acres of trees? You can't plant anything on it." Her face blushed and he realized he'd embarrassed her.

"I'm sorry," he muttered. "I'll leave you two alone."

"Ah ... Garrett ... wait .... I appreciate your concern, but I want to buy the land, and I trust Mr. Overteer to give me sound advice."

"And who am I to intrude? Where is the land, Daniel?"

"Well, that's the only problem. It's twenty miles up the Cooper and I want Hannah to look at it."

"You won't get there until after dark and where will you stay?"

"I said it was a problem, Garrett; there is no place to stay. We'll have to take a wagon and bedrolls. Perhaps another lady in the household will accompany Miss Thornton. They may sleep in the wagon, and I'll sleep under it."

Garrett looked from the banker to Hannah and their eyes met. He stared at her face a moment and then said, "I'll go with you. Get your rifle and a bedroll; I'll tell Jim to hitch a team to the wagon."

"Garrett, we can't leave Charleen and the children."

"I'll ask Jim if he and Dolly and Julie will stay the night. Jim can have Ben's room and Dolly and Julie can share yours."

"All right, I'll tell Otis and the girls and be ready in a few minutes."

Mr. Overteer sat down to wait. Garrett went by the kitchen on his way to the barn and had Rosie to pack food and cooking utensils.

Hannah ran up the stairs and changed from her dress to a pair of comfortable black pants and a long-sleeved white blouse. The night air would be cold, she thought, as she took a black vest from the armoire and slipped it on over the white blouse. She quickly rolled a bedroll and was halfway down the stairs when she remembered the rifle.

She left her room a second time, loaded down with gear, and heard Charleen on the back stairs. She waited for her.

"How did everything go?"

"OK. Everyone finished the assignment. Here are their papers."

"Thanks, Charleen. Will you tell the girls and Otis that I'm going with Mr. Overteer to look at some land for sale? Your dad is going with us, but Jim and Dolly and Julie will stay here tonight. Is that all right?"

"Sure, but why is Daddy going?"

"Ah . . . I don't know."

"Guess he wants to see the land," Charleen answered her own question. "When will you be back?"

"Late tomorrow evening . . . hopefully before dark."

"Well, be careful."

"We will. Thanks again, Charleen, for everything."

"You're welcome."

Hannah laid the papers on the table in her room, and this time, she hurried all the way down the stairs. Garrett and Mr. Overteer waited for her on the wagon seat. She threw the bedroll into the back of the wagon, but lifted the rifle and ammunition over its side carefully. Since Garrett held the reins, Mr. Overteer stepped down to assist her to the seat.

She sat between the two men and tried to catch her breath, but as the horses started down the front lane, she suddenly developed a case of the nerves. There had not been time before hand to think of the journey she was about to embark upon. Would it be proper for a lady to accompany two men so far into the wilds? After considering the age difference, she decided it would be all right.

The horses pulled the wagon along at a good pace, and Hannah, having caught her breath, listened silently to Garrett and Mr. Overteer discuss the war. It reminded her of how she used to sit quietly when Collin and a friend discussed a similar subject. Garrett was like Collin in some ways, and Daniel Overteer was a lot like John Dudley. She began to reminisce of the two and didn't hear Garrett when he spoke to her.

"Hannah, I said you're awfully quiet. What are you thinking about?"

"Oh . . . I'm sorry, Mr. Rey."

Not until he turned his head and frowned at her did she realize she'd called him Mr. Rey.

"Garrett," she muttered. "I thought of how I used to listen to my father and his friend talk about the British."

"Do we remind you of your father and his friend?" asked Daniel.

"A bit," she replied, and the two men chuckled.

They traveled inland along the Cooper River until the sun was directly overhead. Mr. Overteer took the reins, and Garrett reached under the wagon seat for a flour sack that Rosie had filled with bread and slices of ham. They ate as the horses pulled the wagon down the wagon trail.

They rolled along all evening. As the sun disappeared beyond the tall trees that surrounded them, Hannah bowed her head and said a silent prayer for Nathan. She was very tired and hoped to reach their destination soon. Her fanny was numb; she swore she would sit on her pillow for the return trip.

A moon rose behind them and the team of horses continued down the trail that led deeper into the forest. "It can't be much farther," Mr. Overteer finally said. "There's a sign where the land begins, and we'll stop there for the night." Before long, they saw the sign, and the wagon was pulled to the side of the trail.

Garrett unhitched the team of horses and took care of them, while Daniel lit two lanterns. He set one lantern at the back of the wagon and took the other one to look for firewood. When he had gathered a large stack, he raked leaves and pine straw from the ground and laid the wood within the circle. He reached into his pocket for two pieces of flint and attempted to start a fire, but after many tries, was unable to get a flame going.

It was more than two hours past Garrett's regular mealtime, and his stomach told him so. With flint from his own pocket, he knelt beside Daniel and picked up a handful of dry leaves. He stuck the leaves under the wood, and when he struck his flint together, the sparks set them on fire.

"I'm glad you came," said Daniel, and the three of them laughed.

Garrett warmed the food that Rosie had packed, while Hannah took utensils from the flour sack. By the time the food was ready, the three of them were half starved, so it tasted good.

As soon as he finished eating, Daniel spread his blanket under the wagon, and before long, Hannah and Garrett heard him snore.

"Not very sociable, is he?" Garrett commented.

Hannah smiled. "I'm sure Mr. Overteer is very tired," she said. "It was nice of him to bring me so far."

"But to go to sleep and leave you in the wilderness alone?" Garrett spoke irritably. "I was afraid he would. Why don't you get out your bedroll? I'll finish here and watch the fire until it burns down."

"Thank you, Garrett."

Hannah unrolled her bedroll and wrapped the blanket around her before she lay down and put her head on the pillow. The floor of the wagon was hard and cold and the blanket was thin; she wished she had brought two. She dozed, but awoke shivering in the cold night air. The fire had burned down, and she could only see a bed of coals smoldering in the dark. She assumed that Garrett and Daniel were asleep under the wagon.

She dozed a second time, but something other than the coldness awoke her. There had been a noise; she wasn't sure what. She lay still and listened. It wasn't long before she heard it again, and it sent shivers down her spine. It was a cat . . . a big cat. She was too scared to move and lay very still until in the moonlight she saw Garrett reach over the side of the wagon and pick up the rifle.

She sat up and whispered, "Garrett."

"Yeah . . . I heard it, but it's not too close . . . yet. Go back to sleep. He loaded the rifle and put more wood on the fire and then sat down at the back of the wagon with the gun across his knees.

Hannah lay down, but she was too cold to sleep. The flames of the fire now leaped into the air. She wrapped the blanket around her tightly and crawled toward the back of the wagon.

"Where you going?" Garrett asked.

"To the fire. I'm cold."

"Not with that cat on the prowl. I don't want you between it and me if I have to shoot in a hurry. Come here." He reached under the wagon for his blanket and pillow.

She scooted to his side with her blanket still wrapped around her. He placed his pillow behind his back, but spread his blanket over her and tucked it under her feet. He put one arm around her and pulled her close to him, and through her thin blanket, she felt the warmth of his body.

"Garrett," she spoke quietly.

"What?"

"Is this why you came? To take care of me?"

"Yes. I knew Daniel Overteer couldn't take care of himself in the wilds, much less a woman like you."

"What do you mean . . . a woman like me?"

"You're soft, Hannah, the way Catherine was. You're gentle and the kind of woman that needs a man to take care of her.

Ben knew that. He's in love with you." Hannah was silent. She would not discuss Ben's love with his dad. "Hannah, I said Ben's in love with you."

"How do you know that? Did he tell you?"

"No. Catherine did, and I didn't have to be too smart to see it the night Nathan came. If Ben could have made it to the top of the stairs, he would have killed that man that had his hands on you. Do you love him?"

Why would Garrett force her to talk of Ben? He waited for an answer; she sighed lightly and replied, "Yes . . . I love Ben, but not the way I love Nathan. It's Nathan I want to marry. I know he's your enemy, but he's good and kind and it's not his choice to be anyone's enemy.

"I feel bad that Ben loves me, but at the same time it makes me feel warm inside. I feel guilty that I let him fall in love with me, but he was my best friend, and I didn't realize that it could happen. He loves Julie, too, and she'll make him a good wife, for she loves him very much and feels called of God the same as he. It would have been best for Ben and me if I had not returned to Reybrook, but we do what we must."

"I don't think he'll ever love anyone else the way he loves you."

"Garrett . . . please."

Neither spoke for a long time. Her body became warm, but she still snuggled close to him with her head on his chest. He laid the rifle at his side and put both arms around her.

She felt safe in Garrett's arms. He gently rubbed his cheek against the top of her head, and she was almost asleep when he broke the silence.

"Hannah."

"Huh-h-h?"

"Why do you want to buy all this land?"

"For Nathan," she replied drowsily. "He needs timber to build ships."

"I should have thought of that. Does he know?"

"No."

There was another pause, and then, "What will you do if he never returns for you?"

"I don't know," her voice was almost a whisper.

It was the last that she remembered and didn't know when he picked her up and gently laid her head on her pillow beneath the wagon seat. She didn't know that he wrapped his blanket around her tightly, and she didn't feel his lips softly brush her cheek. She didn't know anything until at daybreak when— **BANG**—the gun went off, and she jumped to her feet to see a dead mountain lion lying near the wagon.

CHAPTER 37

By mid October of 1814, men aboard *H.M.S. Cannon* were nearly out of their wits. Most had toughened under rigid treatment, but it was the ship's day after day monotonous schedule that drove them to insanity. News of the burning of Washington was received with cheers, and many expressed a desire to have been there, but Lieutenant Barrington failed to find pleasure in the report.

He wasn't sure why, but the ship's captain had promoted him to a lieutenant commander. The captain had spoken of his knowledge of sailing and his leadership ability. It certainly wasn't for his popularity with other officers aboard, especially Ensign Tally.

In a written account of the mission to Reybrook, Nathan reported Tally's desire to leave his injured superior officer behind and of his attempt to rob a civilian lady of the jewelry around her neck. When every man involved upheld the report, Ensign Tally was reprimanded and told that he was an embarrassment to the British Navy.

On October 30, a large British warship from Halifax pulled alongside the *Cannon*. It was on its way to join an assembling of British ships in Negril Bay at the western tip of Jamaica, and its captain was in dire need of more men. At his request, the *Cannon's* captain agreed for ten men to transfer from his ship.

Nathan and Jason responded quickly. The warship was, most likely, bound for action, but each saw it as a chance to get off the *Cannon*. Not only did the captain honor their request for transfer, but allowed Nathan to pick eight more men from a list of volunteers.

On the morning of November 19, the warship sailed into

the already crowded Negril Bay, and within a week, more than fifty vessels had gathered from British dominions all over the world. Nathan determined that something big was in the making, but he didn't know how big until it was announced that the purpose of the armada was to take the city of New Orleans. If the British could succeed in taking the city, they would divide the United States by controlling access to the Mississippi River. It would be a splendid prize for the peace table. There was no doubt about it, with New Orleans in hand, Great Britain could name her own terms.

By now, both countries wanted peace, and Ghent, Belgium had been agreed upon by the two powers as a place for negotiations. The first meeting had already been held on August 8, with little being accomplished.

Under the British blockade, New Orleans's lack of exportation left her large warehouses filled with cotton, sugar, tobacco, and other products. Top rank among the British military saw it as an abundant wealth that would fatten their pockets, and it lay for the taking in a city that had little, if any, fortification. New Orleans, however, was not as vulnerable as one might think, for although her location was indeed strategic, it was also, as the British were soon to find out, her best means of defense.

"Will New Orleans be as easy to take as our superiors would have us think?" Jason asked Nathan. The two were alone in the small room they shared in the officers' quarters.

"Don't count on it," Nathan replied.

"Why?"

"The city is more than a hundred miles up the Mississippi River, and even if we could get through the mouth of the river, we could never make it that far upstream. It has so many twists and turns, and for a ways, even flows north. I've seen no galleys in this armada.

"New Orleans is surrounded by a treacherous terrain of swamps and marshlands that are filled with alligators and snakes. Before we can take the city, our superiors must figure out a way to get to it. No, I don't believe it will be an easy gain . . . if a gain at all."

The British fleet sailed from Negril Bay toward New Orleans on November 26. Four days before, a man named Andrew Jackson had left Mobile, Alabama, and was also on his way to New Orleans. Jackson was a major general in the United States Federal Army and had been ordered to New Orleans to defend the city against the British.

Jackson's parents were from Northern Ireland, but his father died a few days before he was born. Raised in the backwoods along the North and South Carolina border, Andrew learned at an early age to be tough. His toughness earned him the name "Old Hickory" by troops under him who swore he was as tough as the wood from the hickory nut tree.

Two weeks before Jackson left Mobile, the South Carolina Militia found out that the British had bypassed Charleston and gathered at Negril Bay to take New Orleans. It was a great relief to the residents of Charleston that their city had been passed up by the bulk of the British Navy for a greater prize elsewhere. Word spread throughout the land that the big battle would be fought in New Orleans and everyone awaited news from that city, for the fate of their country depended on the outcome of the battle. New Orleans was a long way from Charleston, and perhaps they wouldn't get there in time, but a regiment of volunteers from the South Carolina Militia rode southwest. Benjamin Rey was among them.

Sprawling between Lake Pontchartrain and the Mississippi River, the city of New Orleans had been established in 1718, by the French explorer, Jean Baptiste Le Moyne, sieur de Bienville. It came under Spanish rule in 1763, but was returned to France in 1800, and sold by Napoleon in 1803, to the United States as part of the Louisiana Purchase. Napoleon needed money to finance his wars in Europe.

Made up of many cultures, but predominantly French, the people of New Orleans were of a suspicious lot. They had had no say in becoming a part of the United States and weren't sure what they thought of it. And they didn't know about this man, Andrew Jackson, whom the Federal Government had sent to defend their city.

Mostly, they had little use for those who came down the river from the North, and Jackson was from the North with Tennessee being his home. He didn't appear to be much of a general at their first sight of him when he rode into their town on December 1, 1814.

Jackson was tired and sick, and his least concern was what the people of New Orleans thought of him. On his arrival, he began to work toward bringing an army together, and before the day of the big battle, his force of 5,000 was made up of regular troops, Creoles, blacks, and yes . . . even pirates. The notorious Jean Lafitte and his brother, Pierre, offered their service to him, and against the will of some prominent city leaders, Jackson accepted.

Spirits were high on the impressive British fleet as it wended across the Gulf of Mexico. The last battle, most thought, before the United States would be back in the hands of Great Britain. Nathan wasn't so sure, but excitement ran through his blood as he prepared to fight. His training and experience had been on the seas, instead of infantry, but he knew that nearly everyone able to walk would be expected to go, and only a small crew would be left to man the fleet. His gear was ready and his rifle was clean; if it came to it, he was ready to die.

"Jason," he said, "if I don't make it and you do, will you take the message to Hannah? I want her to know as soon as possible, for she's waited so long already."

Jason hesitated before he answered. To take such news to Hannah was the worst thing he'd ever been asked to do.

"Yes, Nathan. I'll tell her and do everything I can for her. If you make it and I don't, tell Charleen how much I thought about her and that I wanted to come back to see her."

"I will," Nathan promised.

The British fleet had been delayed at Negril Bay, as they awaited their commander-in-chief's arrival, and had been forced to sail without him. They were held up again when a strong wind scattered the ships. Nathan felt uneasy about it all. Did God want them to retreat before the battle began?

They reassembled and arrived December 10, at Lake Borgne, east of New Orleans. The lake was no more than a lagoon and too shallow for large ships to pass through. After American gunboats were knocked out, they floated across the lake in small boats.

Nathan and Jason traveled in an advance force that came ashore at Isle aux Pois. A cold rain fell and the wind had a sharp edge. The land was soggy and boggy, and being laden with heavy gear, they sank farther into it with each step, but after several days, they reached a plantation named Villeré. The owner's young son escaped them and ran to inform Jackson of their arrival. There was a skirmish that very night, but the big battle would be yet to come.

It seemed there was no dry land for men to place artillery. They were far from their base and had to work at night in the wet and cold as not to be seen. They were hungry and had had little sleep. Their enthusiasm faded and they became discouraged; some men cursed.

"Lieutenant Barrington . . . Sir, how can we fight in this place when we can barely walk?" a soldier complained to Nathan.

"We'll find a way," Nathan answered.

How could he expect his men to fight in such a dreadful place, especially when they were cold and hungry?

Their commander-in-chief, Major General Sir Edward Packenham, was now on the scene, but there was some disagreement between him and other superior officers as to how the battle should be fought.

Meanwhile, the Americans were building their line of defense along the Rodriguez Canal, out of everything they could get their hands on. Dirt from the canal and bales of cotton from the warehouses were used to form a wall for protection against British artillery. The battlefield stretched before them with the Mississippi River to their right and a swamp to their left.

The first day of January brought a show of artillery from both sides with each army finding its method of defense to be a failure. Packenham called a retreat, and the battle was put off a second time.

On the night of January 7, Nathan and Jason were huddled in a tent with other men in their unit. It was a cold night, but adrenaline ran high in their bodies; the big battle would begin at dawn. They joked with each other and laughed quietly, but everyone hushed when a major walked up. "Is Lieutenant Nathan Barrington here?" he asked.

"Yes, sir," Nathan quickly responded.

"Are you a doctor, Lieutenant?"

"No, sir."

"Your record states that you've had training in the medical field."

"Yes, sir, but I'm not a doctor. I attended medical classes in order to know what to do when certain emergencies arise on a ship at sea and there is no doctor aboard."

"He can deliver a baby," Jason quietly informed the major and brought snickering from others in the tent.

The major ignored Jason. "Can you stop a wound from bleeding," he asked Nathan, "and do an amputee?"

Nathan hesitated before answering, although he distinctly remembered how each was done. He had never performed an amputee and had hoped he would never have to.

"Yes, sir," he replied. "I've had training in both."

"Then we need you to stay behind and assist the doctors."

"If it's all the same to you, Sir, I'd rather go with my men."

"You'll be able to help your men more at the field hospital than on the battlefield."

"Sure, Nathan," Jason mumbled under his breath, "I'd rather have you cut off my leg than anyone I know." Again, he brought a chuckle from several of the men, but neither Nathan nor the major was one of them.

"All right, Sir," Nathan agreed. He suspected the officer had not come to give him a choice, and just before dawn, he joined a group of doctors and their staff at the field hospital that was located near the British headquarters. The doctor in charge was a high-ranking officer, and Nathan was assigned to his command. Just before the battle began, the two discussed the extent of his medical training, and as they became acquainted, each acquired a liking for the other.

Just before daybreak, the British fired a rocket that signaled the beginning of the battle. Things went bad for them from the start. In the darkness of the night before, Colonel William Thornton and his men were sent across the river to overtake a battery of guns. At the firing of the rocket, Thornton's men were to open fire on the Americans, but instead the guns were aimed at the British. Colonel Thornton and his men had drifted far downstream in the swift current of the Mississippi River and couldn't make it back in time.

British soldiers began to fall from the cannon fire, but Americans' rifles were silent until those behind the Rodriguez Canal were sure their guns would reach its target. When ordered to open fire, Redcoats fell everywhere. Major General John Keane, commander of an advance column, was the first British officer to fall. His wound was so bad that he was taken from the field. A short time later, Major General Samuel Gibbs was killed and then Packenham fell. The commander-in-chief's last order was for Major General John Lambert to continue the battle, but the British were being slaughtered, and Lambert ordered a retreat.

The battle had been short, but when cannon smoke cleared the air, more than 3,000 British lay dead, dying, or wounded, whereas only a few Americans were dead.

The wounded British soldiers were brought to their field hospital much faster than doctors could take care of them, and orderlies laid them all around it. Nathan was commanded to walk among them and tell the orderlies which soldiers were in the worst condition that they might be brought in first.

It was a dreadful sight. Bloody men lay all over the ground. Some had already departed from this world, while others were more dead than alive. The mouth and eyes of the dead gaped open and there was no one to close them. Nathan felt guilty that he had not fought in the battle, but at the same time, thankful he'd been spared.

Men moaned and cried for help everywhere in the sea of misery, and he had nothing with which to stop their suffering. And how could he determine who was worse off than the other, but he went about pointing to one after another that was missing an arm or a leg and was bleeding badly? The orderlies with their stretchers had difficulty keeping up with him until he dropped to his knees beside one of the wounded.

The soldier's blonde hair had caught Nathan's attention. He then recognized the face that was smeared with blood. It was Jeff Adams, and he had a hole in his stomach large enough to put a man's fist in.

"Jeff, it's Nathan!" He pulled a handkerchief from his back pocket and wiped blood from across Jeff's eyes. "Get a doctor!" he yelled to an orderly.

"I'll try, Sir."

"Jeff, can you hear me?" Jeff's head nodded and he tried to speak.

"Don't talk. The doctor is coming. We'll take care of you."

But when Nathan realized that Jeff really wanted to say something, he lifted his head to his knees.

"Is that you, Nathan?" Jeff's voice was barely above a whisper.

"Yes, Jeff. It's Nathan Barrington from the *Monarch*."

"Hannah," Jeff whispered her name. "Will you return to Charleston for Hannah?"

"Yes—soon as the war is over."

"Will you tell her I loved her?"

"If you want me to, but you never tried to take her from me."

"I couldn't have. She told me she loved you, and that she knew you'd be back for her if you were able. I saw her on the deck at daybreak the morning after she came aboard. The wind blew her hair to one side of her face, and it whipped her dress around her legs. She was so beautiful." There was a far away look in Jeff's eyes and Nathan knew he dreamed of that morning on the Monarch.

With his last bit of strength, Jeff reached and grasped Nathan's coat. "I hope you make it," he said. "I hope you make it back to her."

"I will, Jeff, but please stop talking; you're making the bleeding worse."

Jeff's body suddenly relaxed in Nathan's arms, and his head fell to one side. Nathan felt for a pulse, but there wasn't one; Jeff was no longer in pain. The doctor never came, and Nathan knew it would not have made a difference if he had.

"Oh, Jeff," Nathan groaned in agony as he brushed his hand over Jeff's eyes. He held him to his chest for a long moment and then reached into his pocket and brought out the lace-trimmed handkerchief with the name, Hannah Thornton, embroidered on it. He spread it over Jeff's face and clipped one corner of it to a twig of his blonde hair with a clamp from his belt.

Two men took his body from Nathan's arms and laid it with the dead. Nathan rose from the ground and pointed to one man after another. "This one . . . that one . . . and this one."

As soon as General Lambert issued the order to retreat, the British began to withdraw. Nathan looked across the battlefield and saw American soldiers cross their line of defense. Some picked up guns and swords, but others had come to help the wounded British. He admired those who tried to help, and as he watched, he noticed in particular, one young man that kneeled to the ground and lifted his canteen to the lips of a fallen British. His hair was dark and he looked like . . . could it be . . . ? Nathan walked farther across the battlefield and shaded his eyes with his hand. Yes . . . it was Ben Rey!

Ben rose from the ground and began to back away when

Nathan ran toward him. "Ben," Nathan yelled, and Ben recognized him.

"Nathan! Are you all right?"

"Yes, I had to work at the hospital."

"I was afraid I'd find you here on the field. I'm glad you're okay."

"Thanks, Ben. How is Hannah?"

"She was okay when I left home. She waits for you."

"Tell her that—"

"Nathan," one of the wounded called faintly from the field, and Nathan's attention was distracted.

"I better go," Ben said, and with his canteen in hand, he ran back across the line.

The voice called again from the battlefield, and this time, Nathan recognized it and began to search frantically for his friend. He found him on the ground with a piece of shrapnel protruding from his chest. The wound bled badly.

"Jason!" Nathan dropped to his knees beside him. He tried to lift him, but the pain was more than he could stand, so he lowered him back to the ground. There was no orderly in sight, and even if there had been, a doctor would never come that far from the hospital. The shrapnel had to be removed, and he would not let Jason die without doing something.

He quickly lifted a knife from his pocket and then took a flask of whiskey from the back pocket of a dead soldier and poured some of it over the knife blade. He poured the rest of it down Jason and told him to hold on.

Jason passed out as Nathan probed for the bottom of the metal fragment and lifted it carefully from his chest. He stripped to his waist in the cold wind and jerked off his undershirt. With the bloody knife, he ripped strips of cloth and then folded what was left of the undershirt and placed it over the wound. He tied the strips together until they were long enough to go around Jason's body, then stretched the long strip over the folded cloth and tied it tightly at his side. He hoped it would stop the bleeding.

He ran all the way to the field hospital with Jason in his

arms, but found chaos there. Medics shouted orders as they worked to prepare the wounded for retreat. Nathan pleaded for the doctor in command to take a look at his friend, and with haste, the doctor pulled the bandage to one side and looked at the wound.

"You did a good job, Lieutenant, considering what you had to work with, but he's probably lost a lot of blood and one lung may be punctured. If it is, he won't make it back to England, but should be in a hospital right now."

"Sir, can you give me permission to stay behind, so I can try to get him to a hospital?"

The doctor was surprised. He looked at Nathan and then back at Jason who was still out from the whiskey. "How long have you known this man?" he asked.

"All my life, Sir. We've always been best friends."

With no more questions, the doctor took a note pad and pencil from his pocket and began to write. When finished, he handed Nathan a signed, written permission for him to stay behind in order to render medical aid to a British soldier.

"You know the danger, Lieutenant; you risk your life, but for a good cause. I hope you get him to a hospital. If I were you, the first thing I'd do is get both of you out of those red coats."

"Thank you, Sir." The note was folded quickly and stuck deep into his pocket. He removed Jason's coat and wrapped him in a blanket and then took off his own red coat and ripped a hole in another blanket to put over his head like a Spanish poncho. With a small white flag in one hand, he lifted Jason in his arms and started toward the enemy line.

Andrew Jackson hated the British, so it was to Nathan's luck that the general had returned to his headquarters at the Macarté house, just behind the Rodriguez Canal. An officer at the American line of defense lifted his spyglass and realized immediately what this young soldier was doing. He lowered the glass and shouted, "Hold your fire, men!" The officer liked the bravery in this young man who had stayed behind to save a friend at the risk of his own life. He ordered a wagon brought up and told the driver to take the two of them to the New Orleans Hospital. After all . . . the battle was over.

The streets of New Orleans were jammed with people, but when the crowd saw the wagon carrying a wounded soldier, they quickly stepped aside, and had no idea that the wounded one was a British.

When they arrived at the hospital, Nathan spoke slowly so that his British accent would not be so conspicuous. Two nurses hurried forth, and he simply stated, "My friend was wounded in the battle. An officer told me to bring him here." Jason was taken to a hospital room and a doctor was summoned.

It was a long time before the doctor came, but when he finally arrived, he was friendly and apologized for being so long. The young doctor was tall and thin, and a mass of wavy, black hair made his head seem large for the rest of his body. His complexion was dark, but he wasn't French as one might expect in a predominantly French populated city. He was Spanish.

"I'm Dr. Ramirez. I'll take a look at your friend." To Nathan, his words all seemed to run together.

"Thank you, Doctor. I'm Nathan Barrington."

The doctor held out a hand. "You and your friend be British, *Si?*"

And Nathan realized he'd fooled no one. He and Jason had been permitted to stay, only through the mercy of hospital employees.

He hesitated before replying, "Yes—*Si.*"

"You may stay as long as your friend is critical. When he is better, you'll be asked to leave."

Nathan nodded his head. "That's fair enough," he agreed.

Dr. Ramirez gave Jason a thorough examination, starting with his eyes. While Nathan held a candle near his face, the doctor opened each of Jason's eyes and looked deep into them. He bent over him for a long time and held a stethoscope at one place and then another, only to move it back to the first spot. He did this back and forth over Jason's chest several times before he peeped under the bandage that Nathan had made with his undershirt.

"What caused the wound?" he asked.

"Shrapnel was embedded in his chest," Nathan replied.

"Who removed it?"

"I did."

"On the battlefield?"

"Yes . . . after the battle was over. I couldn't get a doctor and had to do something. He's my best friend."

"Well, he's fortunate to have such a brave friend." The young doctor was impressed.

"He'd do the same for me."

"I am sure, and your battlefield surgery will probably save his life, but as you can see, he's far from being out of trouble. His recovery will be long in coming, but with the right medicine and plenty of rest . . . well, we will see. He'll not be able to travel for months. Where will you stay, once you leave the hospital?"

"I'll have to find a place."

"I will help you."

"Thank you."

"Once the intoxication wears off, your friend will be in much pain." He held up a bottle of medicine. "Give him a teaspoon of this when be begins to come to and then one three times a day."

"All right and thanks again." Nathan held out his hand to the doctor.

"*De nada*," said the doctor, meaning you're welcome. "A nurse will come soon to administer medicine and a clean bandage to the wound. She'll see that both of you get something to eat, and I'll come by tomorrow. What is your friend's name?" he asked. "I must make a report."

"Jason—Jason Williams."

A hospital orderly brought food and a cot to the room for Nathan and a bowl of broth with a glass of milk for Jason. Nathan was very hungry, but before he ate, he spoon-fed the

broth to Jason and managed to get all of it down him. He then
let Jason rest and ate his own food, but after he'd finished eating,
he spoon-fed Jason the milk and didn't spill a single drop of it.

It was dark outside by the time the nurse came with a clean
bandage and medicine for the wound. As she applied both, she
nodded her head at Nathan but did not speak. She felt Jason's
pulse and listened to his breathing with a stethoscope.

Nathan stood to one side and watched the nurse. Her
complexion and hair was dark; she was definitely French. She
had a pretty face and her slender body was a medium height.
Her work seemed important to her, but she appeared tired and
leaned against the bed rail as she held a thermometer in Jason's
mouth. When it had been there long enough, she removed it
and turned toward the lamplight. She talked to Nathan, but kept
her eyes on Jason.

"He's very ill," she spoke English fluently, "and since you're
British, the nurses are afraid to come. Dr. Ramirez asked me to
come by after I got off work; it's why I'm so late."

"I don't blame the others under the circumstances, but I'm
glad you came. I'll pay you for off-duty time."

"I didn't come for money."

"I didn't mean to imply that you did. I'm Nathan Barrington;
may I ask your name?"

"Joséphine LeFleu. People call me Josey."

"It's a pleasure to meet you, Josey."

She nodded her head. "I'll come tomorrow before I go on
duty."

"It's dark out," Nathan stated, "and men may be drunk as
there is celebration in the streets. Will someone come for you?"

She seemed surprised that he had concern for her, and he
thought she almost smiled. "I'm not afraid," she said. "I walk
home alone every night. I carry a pistol."

Nathan bit his bottom lip as her eyes held his a moment,
and then he lifted both hands from the sides of his body. "That's
good," he said. "Just don't use it on me." She was unable to
suppress her smile a second time.

The next weeks were critical ones for Jason, and Nathan found his own mental capacity stretched from one day to the next with hope or hopelessness. At one point, he committed his friend to God, but stayed by his bedside day and night, applying all of his medical knowledge to Jason's care. Dr. Ramirez was deeply impressed.

"I've never seen one so dedicated to a friend," he remarked.

"He'd do all he could for me."

"Sí, I am sure."

Through conversation, Dr. Ramirez perceived that Nathan and Jason were not ordinary soldiers who swore and spit and drank too much. Nathan had to be intelligent to have learned so much in the medical field, and he displayed a great knowledge of geography and of the sea.

Likewise, Nathan discovered the doctor was a master in his field. He credited his friend's life to God and then to Dr. Ramirez's great knowledge and ability. Surely God had led him to the best and he was very thankful. The doctor was not only intelligent, but showed genuine concern for his patient. No one else, Nathan thought, would have felt such compassion for an enemy. It was plain to see that his life was committed to saving the lives of others, no matter what nationality they were. He and the doctor became good friends.

"Why don't you go back to school and acquire a license to practice medicine?" he asked Nathan. "We're in need of good doctors here at the hospital, and I'll make sure you're accepted on our staff."

Nathan smiled. "Thanks for the offer, but I'm a seaman and have other plans for my life."

"Sí, I thought as much. Josey studies to be a doctor, but it's very hard for her, as she has no money and must work in order to pay for living expenses and her education. The hospital works with her since she has agreed to stay on here after she obtains her license. To take care of Jason is good experience for her."

"I offered to pay her, but she refused it."

"She's very proud."

"She's been good with Jason and a great help to me. She bought clothes for me and other necessities."

"*Sí*, she will make an excellent doctor."

It was usually late when Josey came, and since Nathan had come to trust her, he was often asleep, but tonight he would wait for her. How hard it must be, he thought, to work a full time job and go to school. He understood now why she always seemed to be tired. He turned the lamp up when she entered the room.

"Are you unable to sleep tonight?" she asked.

"I stayed awake to talk to you." She stood at the opposite side of the bed from him and held a thermometer in Jason's mouth.

"Jason's health has improved." She squinted to read the thermometer. "He still has a slight fever, but it decreases each day." They were both silent as she held her stethoscope to his chest. "The rattle in his chest is not as loud as at first. That tells me his lung has healed."

"That's all good news, Josey, but I stayed awake to talk about you."

She looked at him with wide eyes. "Me! What do you want to know about me?"

"Dr. Ramirez said that you study to be a doctor. I admire you for working so hard to achieve a goal that will enable you to relieve others of suffering."

"Thank you, Lieutenant Barrington. I appreciate your encouragement, but I'm afraid the doctor talks too much."

"I'm glad he told me. Will you call me Nathan?"

She looked at him as if she was uncertain about his request. After a pause, however, she smiled and answered, "Yes."

"You've been a great help, Josey. I don't know what I would have done without you. How much longer do you have to go to school?"

"I hope to finish in two years."

"I wish I could help."

A low, hoarse chuckle came from deep within her throat. "I'm afraid you're in no position to help anyone right now."

His mouth twitched and he nodded his head. "That's true," he agreed.

He wanted to tell her he was wealthy, and although he trusted her, he didn't know if he should tell her that. If the wrong person found out, he could be held for ransom. No, he decided, no one in New Orleans should know how wealthy he was; besides, he wasn't sure himself anymore.

Perhaps the Bank of England had put a hold on his money until all debts of the company were cleared. He trusted Jason's dad to do everything he could to protect his fortune, but could he transfer funds to him at this time? He doubted it and decided it best not to speak of the matter to Josey.

Up until now, Nathan's only concern had been Jason's health, but since his condition had improved, he began to take stock of his situation. He had paid for hospital care weekly. It had cost a great deal, and there would be the expense of a place to live when Jason was able to leave the hospital. His financial situation looked bleak, but there was nothing he could do except put it in the hands of God.

A few days later, Nathan and Jason heard a commotion outside the window, and workers within the hospital seemed extremely happy. Nathan looked out and saw men shake each other's hands and slap one another on the back. Women cried, while children danced in the street. Only one thing would bring such a celebration. The war had ended.

News of peace between England and the United States had finally reached New Orleans. The Treaty of Ghent had been signed on December 24, 1814; two weeks before the Battle of New Orleans was fought. With a heavy heart Nathan thought of the British soldiers who had died in vain.

Another two weeks passed before Jason was able to leave the hospital, and then he was far from being able to travel. With Josey's help, Nathan moved him to an old tenement house in the French Quarters of town. Josey lived in two rooms across the hall.

Now that the war was over, Nathan thought it would be safe

to write letters. He gave Josey money to purchase writing paper and envelopes for him. That night he wrote four letters with the first one being to the British Naval Department of Defense, seeking his and Jason's release from the Royal Navy. He enclosed the note that had given him permission to stay behind. The second letter was written to his mother, and a third one to Jason's parents informed them of his condition. The last letter was to Hannah. He explained why he was still in New Orleans and promised to come for her as soon as Jason was able to travel. He asked Josey to mail the letters.

On her way to school the next morning, Josey mailed three of the letters, but kept the one addressed to Miss Hannah Thornton. She put the letter into her bag, and that night when she returned home, she opened it and read it. She had acquired romantic feelings for Nathan and wanted to know why he had written to a girl in South Carolina. Now that he lived right across the hall, she hoped she could persuade him not to leave New Orleans. After she read Hannah's letter, she pulled a box from underneath her bed and dropped the letter into it and then pushed the box back to its place.

Jason was able to get up and down by himself and could walk for a short distance. He was still very weak, however, and would be unable to defend himself should someone try to harm him.

"Now that I'm able to walk," he insisted to Nathan, "you may leave. I know how anxious you are to return for Hannah."

"I'm not leaving New Orleans without you, Jason. Hannah will wait; I wrote her a letter."

CHAPTER 38

News of the victory at New Orleans and the Treaty of Ghent brought a time of celebration throughout the land. Although the treaty had been signed before the battle was fought, it gave Americans something to be proud about and would go down in history as one of their greatest battles. Andrew Jackson emerged a hero at a time when the country needed a hero. The people of New Orleans cheered him and held a parade in his honor.

British ships left the United States coastline, and her seaports were opened to the world again. In the South, it meant the shipment of cotton. People resumed their way of life with renewed confidence in their government; its military had withstood attacks from the most powerful nation in the world. It was a glorious time.

Ben returned to his home state and was officially dismissed from the South Carolina Militia with honor. As he left the state headquarters, someone called his name.

"Hey, Rey, let's go to Charleston and celebrate with the rest of 'em!"

"Sorry, Parker," Ben replied, "I'm going home. I have good news for a pretty lady and it can't wait."

He mounted Blaze and turned him toward Reybrook as thoughts of Hannah raced through his mind. It was right at dusk when he rode into the yard, and a few minutes later, he walked through the front door. "Is anyone home?" he yelled. Hannah graded papers, upstairs in her room, when she heard him.

No one returning from the war could have received a better welcome from his family. In the time it took Hannah to descend the stairs, they had gathered around him. She stood aside to let them greet him first. He looked wonderful, she thought, and smiled to see Emma and Emily so happy. Otis literally climbed his body until Ben lifted him into the air. Charleen threw her arms around him and Garrett shook his hand.

Rosie ran from the kitchen, wiping tears from her eyes with the tail of her apron. Ben gave her a big hug. "I sure missed your cooking," he said. "I hated that military food."

"Oh, Mistr Ben, Mistr Ben," Rosie groaned, "I's sho glad to sees yo!"

Ben turned his eyes toward Hannah. As always, he thought, she let others be first. He held out his arms to her just as the back door flew open and Julie ran down the hall.

"Ben!" she exclaimed, "Jim said he saw you ride up the lane."

Ben's family left to give him a moment alone with Julie. As the smile faded from Hannah's face, she eased backward behind the stairs and then circled around them and climbed the far side. At the top, she looked down at the two of them entwined in each other's arms. Ben looked up at her from over Julie's shoulder and their eyes met.

Hannah returned downstairs for supper, but Ben wasn't there. She assumed he and Julie had gone someplace to be alone. She listened as his family chatted happily about his homecoming and smiled occasionally when one of them looked her way.

Garrett noticed how quiet Hannah was and that she ate hardly any food. He'd seen a change come over her since the war ended; he figured she worried about Nathan. The Charleston newspaper had reported that nearly three thousand British were either killed, wounded, or missing after the Battle of New Orleans, and he realized there was a good chance that Nathan was among them.

Charleen asked to be excused, and when Reneka came for the children, Hannah and Garrett sat alone at opposite ends of the table. Garrett watched as she lifted the last of her food to her mouth and chewed it slowly as though it had no taste. She took a napkin from her lap and laid it beside her plate and then rose from her chair.

"Hannah."

"Yes?"

"Will you go to the cemetery with me?"

"If you want me to."

"I do."

"I'll get my coat and hat."

She returned to her room for a heavy coat and pulled a woolen hat down over her ears. Her shoe laces were tied tightly above the calf of her legs.

Garrett met her at the front door; he wore a long coat with a woolen scarf about his neck. He held the door open and took her hand as they descended the steps.

A large yellow moon had begun to rise over the treetops. Directly above them were the three brilliant stars that made up Orion's belt. The mighty night hunter held dominion over the winter sky.

The squeak in the cemetery's iron gate broke the quietness of the brisk night air. Garrett let go of Hannah's hand and stood aside for her to enter first, but she lingered behind him as he walked to Catherine's grave and began to speak.

"Ben came home today, darling. He looks good, although he's lost a few pounds. He told Rosie he missed her cooking, but didn't show up for supper. He went all the way to Louisiana to help win a great battle. You'd be so proud of him, Catherine. He's . . . he's," his voice quivered, "everything you could want in a son."

When Garrett made a fist and covered his mouth, Hannah stepped to his side and linked her arm through his.

"I miss her, Hannah. I miss her so much."

"I know. And you miss her most when one of your children does something you want her to know about."

"Yes; you understand. I don't know how we could have gotten through this without you. You always know what to say."

"I understand grief. I still miss my father and now . . ." She stopped.

"You're worried about Nathan?"

"Yes; I'm scared. I'm afraid he was killed in the battle at New Orleans. So many British soldiers were."

Garrett took her hands. "I'll take care of you," he said. "You've done so much for us. You'll always have a home here; Catherine would have wanted that."

"Thank you, Garrett, but I really shouldn't stay much longer. With Catherine gone . . . well, people will talk. I promised her I would stay for as long as you needed me. Now that Ben is back, perhaps Julie will take my place."

"No one can take your place."

"You must give her a chance," her own voice began to fail. He put his arms around her. "Oh, Garrett . . . I don't know what to do." She laid her head on his shoulder and they cried.

They returned up the hill with their arms linked together and found Ben waiting for them in the living room. He was bent over the fireplace, putting wood on the fire when they entered the house. "Where have you two been?" he asked cheerfully.

"It's good to have you home, Ben," said Hannah. Her voice wasn't right.

"It's good to be back. Will you sit by the fire with me? I have something to tell you."

"Not tonight, please." She fought to hold back more tears until she was upstairs in her room.

"It can't wait. Please sit down with me." He reached for her hand.

Garrett was halfway up the stairs, but he stopped. "Hannah said not tonight, Ben. She's tired; let go of her."

Ben was surprised. He looked toward his dad and then back at Hannah. "What's going on?" he muttered.

"Nothing. We'll talk tomorrow."

Ben let go of her hand. His eyes peered into hers a moment before he turned and walked swiftly toward the front door and disappeared through it without a coat on. When the door slammed, Garrett continued up the stairs to the children's room.

Hannah waited for Ben to return inside. When he didn't, she worried, for he would freeze without a coat. She saw his on the divan where he had tossed it and picked it up to take to him. He stood in the moonlight at the far end of the porch.

"Ben, you'll freeze out here without a coat." She tried to give it to him, but he refused to take it.

"Why should you care if you won't even talk to me?" he snapped at her angrily.

"Why should I talk to you when your lips are still warm from her kisses?" She lashed back at him, but flinched the moment the words escaped her lips.

"You're jealous!" he shouted at her. "You don't want me, but you want to hold on to me just in case Nathan doesn't come back."

"No, Ben, no!" She didn't want to hear his words, but knew they were true. She loved Nathan and wanted him to come for her, but if he didn't and she had lost Ben, too, what would she do? It was unfair to Ben and to Julie. She was so sorry for what she had said.

"I thought you wanted me to love Julie!"

"I did."

"Well, what happened? Did you get worried that Nathan might not come back? He is coming back, so where does that leave me except in the cold?" He grasped her arms and began to shake her. "I can take it, Hannah." He shook her harder. "Do you hear me?"

"Ben, please stop!"

"I can take it from you," he ignored her plea, "because that's how much I care about you!"

He shook her so hard her knees buckled beneath her, and she fell to them, sobbing. Ben dropped to his knees beside her.

"Hannah, you got me so confused, I don't know what to do. Julie loves me, and I don't want to hurt her, but if I thought I had a chance . . ." He put his arms around her and spoke softly,

"I know you love Nathan and he loves you. He loves you so much, and he's coming back. I saw him after the battle and he was fine. I couldn't wait to tell you, but I didn't want it to be like this."

"Oh, Ben, are you sure it was him?"

"Yes . . . I talked to him."

"What did he say?"

"That he had to work in their field hospital."

"Is that all?"

"No. He asked about you and started to give me a message for you, but a wounded soldier called his name, and he turned to him. I wanted to wait, but I was afraid. It was awful; so many British lay dead or dying. I'd gone there to look for him, and if I had found him wounded, I would have helped him, but had he been dead . . . well, I wanted to know."

"Ben, I'm so sorry for what I said, but I wanted to feel your arms around me just once when you came home. I felt so alone while you were gone."

"I know," his voice was soft.

"Please forgive me."

"You know I will. Let's go inside; I'm freezing!"

Hannah was too excited to sleep that night after hearing that Nathan was alive. When would he come? Would he be forced to return to England with his ship, or would the British Navy release him in America? It could be tomorrow or the next day, or it could be longer. She was happy just to know he was alive.

Nathan would want them to be married as soon as he returned. I must go to Charleston, she thought, to purchase a wedding dress and clothes for a wedding trip. And the next day, Garrett said he would leave early the next morning for a trip to the city if she wanted to go with him. He had business to take care of, now that the blockade had ended.

There was little talk between them as the carriage rolled along the road that morning. While Garrett wondered if his cotton had been shipped, Hannah was deep in her own thoughts. Before he dropped her off in front of the shops, they agreed to meet at the restaurant where she had eaten with Ben.

She hurried from one shop to another, purchasing pretty dresses and bonnets, skirts and blouses, and pants and sweaters. She bought new shoes and new ribbons and clasps for her hair. At THE LADIES' SHOP, she purchased frilly undergarments and nightgowns. She was surprised to find the white silk gown and robe; it had been so long since she first saw it. Perhaps it was another like the first set, but no matter, it was beautiful, and she had to have it for her wedding night.

By noon, she was loaded down with shopping bags and boxes and had not yet been to a bridal shop, but knew of one near the restaurant where she would meet Garrett. She hurried that way and was filled with awe when she entered the shop. There were many beautiful wedding dresses. How could she decide on one? After spending much time looking, she picked three to try on, and a saleslady led her to a back room. The one she liked most needed a tuck here and there, but was promised that alterations could be made within an hour.

It was near the time she'd agreed to meet Garrett, so she paid for the dress and then hurried down the street and was nearly out of breath by the time she reached the restaurant. Garrett had arrived early; he laughed when she came through the door loaded down with all her parcels. He jumped to his feet and pulled out a chair for her. The two of them stacked her boxes and bags on the floor beside her.

"I went ahead and ordered," he remarked. "I hope you like it."

"I'm sure I will; I'm starved."

"Did you find everything you needed?"

"Yes, and more. I left something to be picked up in an hour. Do you mind if I return for it?"

"Not at all." He reached into his vest pocket and brought

out a small bundle wrapped in brown paper. "This is yours," he said.

"What is it?"

"The money I owe you."

"You don't owe me any money."

"Yes, I do. I owe you four hundred dollars for the taxes you paid on Reybrook and sixty dollars in back pay for teaching my children. You'll find it all there. My cotton was shipped and I got paid for it."

She picked up the small bundle and laid it on the table in front of him. "I won't take it," she said. "Not a dime of it."

"Hannah!"

"Please, Garrett. I told you why I paid the taxes on Reybrook, and I came back because I made a promise to Catherine and Ben. You didn't ask me to come back to work and even told me you couldn't pay me if I did."

She didn't need the money and knew that Garrett did. He had salaries to pay, his children needed clothing and shoes, and Ben needed funds for college. However, she knew how important it was to Garrett that his debts be paid. That was the first thing she'd learned about him.

The money lay on the table until they were ready to leave. Before he paid for their meal, Garrett picked it up and put it back into his vest pocket. They left the restaurant with all her boxes and bags and returned to the bridal shop. The wedding dress had been packed in a large box, and when it was added to the other parcels, the back of the carriage was filled.

When on the road toward home, Garrett asked, "What's in all those packages?"

"Enough clothes for a long trip. Nathan promised to take me to his home in England, and we'll visit my home in Ireland. It'll be so wonderful to return there with him." Garrett noted the excitement in her voice. He turned his head and smiled at her.

"What's in the big box?" he asked.

"My wedding dress."

"Oh."

He asked no more questions, but before they reached home, he pulled the horses and wagon to the side of the road and took out the bundle of money. Hannah had thought that he would.

"Garrett," she said, "I won't take the money, but I'll make a deal with you."

He chuckled and asked, "What kind of deal?"

"Our congregation has outgrown our meeting place; we need a building. I think people would come from other plantations if there was a church building."

"What did you have in mind?"

"I'd like to buy a plot of land from you. You may keep the money for the land, and I'll hire someone to construct a building."

"How much land and where?"

"Five acres on the road at the far side of the cemetery."

"That would be eighty dollars an acre. Nobody pays that much for land."

"I won't take the money."

He sighed and stared into her eyes. "You're the most stubborn woman I've ever known!"

"Does that mean you'll sell me the land?"

"I don't know as I want a church building in my front yard."

"It won't be in your front yard," she argued. "It'll be by the road at the far side of the cemetery. With the trees between there and the house, you won't be able to see it."

"How long have you thought about this?"

"A long time. Catherine would have liked it, and if Ben studies to be a preacher . . . well, he and Julie could build a house close by, and he could preach on Sundays and help you on the plantation during the week."

Garrett laughed. "Have you talked to Ben about that?"

"No." She sighed and looked down at her hands. "I've seen very little of Ben since he's been back. He spends most of his spare time with Julie."

"I've noticed that. Does it bother you?"

"I miss him, but I want him to be happy."

"I'll talk to him about the church and tell him what you

said. I'll have to think about selling the land, but I'll let you know soon."

"All right."

Her eyes looked up into his. He'd never noticed how blue they were. Her lips were slightly parted and he leaned his head forward.

"Your eyes are as blue as a summer sky," he spoke softly. Their lips almost touched before he remembered her wedding dress in the back of the carriage. He lifted his head and made a clicking sound to the horses and didn't speak again until they reached home. Hannah felt that something had happened, but she wasn't sure what.

Everyone at Reybrook noticed the change in Hannah. They had never seen her so happy before. She and Charleen talked until late at night, both thinking that Jason would come with Nathan.

"Do you really believe he'll come, Hannah?"

"Yes," Hannah reassured her, but she remembered how many British had been reported dead or wounded on the battlefield in New Orleans. She didn't tell Charleen and neither did Ben. If Jason had died, Nathan would have to bring her the awful news.

When winter turned to spring . . . and then summer, Nathan still had not come and Hannah's happiness faded to apprehension. Even if he had returned to England with his ship, he would have had time to get back to South Carolina. What, she wondered, was keeping him?

One night as she lay in her bed thinking of him, she recalled Jeff Adams's words. "You know how wealthy he is," Jeff had said. "He must know lots of wealthy girls. Do you really believe he'll come back for you? The ring he gave you makes me wonder."

Hannah thought of how small the diamond was in the ring

that Nathan had given her. She ran her fingertips over the Barrington coat of arms. Did it really mean that much to him? She began to have doubts.

As more days went by and there was no word from Nathan, Hannah wondered if his love for her had faded. He was older now and might see things differently. England was his home and America was so far away.

By the middle of May, she began to lose all hope that Nathan would return, but she still sat on the front porch in the late evenings and strained her ears to hear a rider coming. She no longer watched the sun go down, but continued to pray for him. Her new clothes were packed away in the armoire, and the box that held her wedding dress was put under the bed. That night she cried herself to sleep.

During the day, Hannah was so busy that there wasn't time to think of Nathan. She pushed her students, including the servants, to get more work done before school was out for the summer, and she spent many hours making plans for the church. Garrett had agreed to sell five acres of his land.

A carpenter was hired and lumber was bought. The church building began to go up, and it was hard to tell who was the most excited, Hannah or Ben. She ordered pews for the inside and wrote notes to other plantations about the new church.

With everything else that had to be done, Hannah found time to write a letter to the State Department of Education, requesting information on grants available for the study of cotton and other plants. She wrote letters to colleges, recommending Charleen for scholarships. When she asked Ben to mail them, she told him of Charleen's decision not to seek a higher education until she was sure he could study to be a preacher. Ben found it hard to believe.

Every night Hannah tossed and turned in her bed, wondering why Nathan had not come. She drenched her pillow with tears. On one of those nights she was unable to sleep at all and knew it would be a long day when Beelzebub crowed at dawn.

She almost fell asleep that morning as she listened to Emma

and Emily read and was cross with Otis when he couldn't sit still. He'd done nothing wrong; she felt bad and let all the students leave earlier than usual. After they left, she tried to grade papers, but her head nodded, so she put them aside and went to the church to see what progress had been made that day.

She was surprised to see all that had been done. The roof was completed and front steps were in place. Since several people on the plantation helped the carpenter, the building was being built much faster than Hannah expected. Jim spent his free time there; Nole and Ollie helped out when possible. Ben rose at daybreak each morning to work on the plantation, but he spent some time almost every evening at the church. The front of the building had been completed and Hannah found him there when she arrived that afternoon.

He had painted the front of the church white and now painted something over the door. She walked to where she could see and was filled with anger when she read the words, "The Hannah Thornton Church." With no sleep the night before, she was unable to suppress her anger. Ben had no right, she thought, to make that decision.

He saw her and waved. "How do you like it?" he yelled from the ladder. He was proud of his work.

"I don't!" she shouted back, letting her anger show.

Ben climbed down and stood back from the building. "I don't see anything wrong with it," he said. "I didn't misspell any words."

"That's not the right name!"

"When you and Nathan get married, it can be changed to Hannah Barrington." He had erroneously thought that this was why she was upset. His words were like a spear that pierced her heart and she stared at him in disbelief.

"How can you make a joke?" Her face turned scarlet red. "You know Nathan isn't coming back."

"No, I don't know that! I know something has held him up, but he'll come. I wasn't joking."

Hannah's heart beat much too fast and her head began to spin. She feared she would faint, and without saying more, she turned and started toward the house.

"Hannah!" Ben called to her, but she didn't stop. He couldn't leave the open paint bucket or the ladder in the way of other workers and was forced to return to them. He closed the bucket and put it and the ladder away and started to the house, hoping to see her along the way.

It wasn't like her to get angry so quickly, he thought. It wasn't like her to get angry at all. He'd never seen her that way at anyone except his dad. He climbed the hill, but didn't find her along the way, and she was not at the house.

Garrett was in his office. "Have you seen Hannah?" Ben asked.

"No, she probably went to the church."

"She did, but she didn't stay long. She got upset because she didn't like the name I painted over the front door."

"What name?"

"The Hannah Thornton Church."

"Well, it should be named after her."

"I guess she doesn't think so. I promised Julie I'd eat with them. Will you be sure Hannah comes in?"

"I'll go look for her now."

Hannah had walked in the woods beyond the cemetery until she calmed down. She felt bad for the way she'd talked to Ben and would be sure to apologize. It had been an awful day.

On her way to the house, she passed by the cemetery and saw weeds on Catherine's grave. She left the gate open when she entered through it and knelt beside the grave to pull the weeds. With her mind so much on what had happened, she didn't notice Garrett walk through the gate.

"Hello, sweetheart," he said affectionately, hoping to make her feel better.

Hannah's heart skipped a beat. No one but Nathan had ever called her that. She sprang to her feet . . . to see Garrett behind her.

"Don't call me that!" she yelled.

The expression on her face told Garrett what he'd done. "I'm sorry, Hannah. I didn't know that was what he called you. If I had, I would have never—"

"I know." She tried to swallow the lump in her throat. "I'm sorry I yelled at you, but for a second I thought he had come. Oh, Garrett . . . for a short second . . ." The lump grew larger and she couldn't speak.

Garrett took her hand. "He'll be back," he consoled. "Ben talked to him and he was okay. He asked how you were. Something has kept him, and he has no way to let you know."

"He could have written me a letter, but I've had no word from him. I—I'm afraid he married someone else," she began to sob, "and I don't know what to do."

"You don't have to do anything; you'll always have a home here."

"I can't stay forever. I would have left already," she sniffed, "but I thought he would come for me. I'll stay until the building is completed; I don't want to leave before then."

"Hannah . . . I don't want you to leave until you have someone to take care of you."

"I'll be all right."

"Ben said there was a problem with the name he painted over the church door. He thinks it should be named after you since you paid for the land and the building. I agree with him. It can be changed later if—"

"Don't you think I should be able to decide on a name for it?"

"Well—yes. What do you want to name it?"

"The Catherine Rey Chapel."

Garrett was speechless and tears came to his eyes.

"I want the building to be in memory of Catherine. No other name will do."

"Hannah . . . you're a wonderful person."

"No, Garrett. Catherine was a wonderful person, and the church must be named after her. Will you please ask Ben to change it; it's very important to me."

"Yes," he replied.

As soon as they returned to the house, Hannah went to her room and fell across her bed and went to sleep. The next morning a tray of cold food set on her table with a note that read, "Ben agreed to change the name." It was signed by Garrett.

The church building was completed by the middle of June. So many on the plantation had volunteered their time, making its cost much less than Hannah had anticipated. It was painted white with blue shutters, and "Catherine Rey Chapel" was painted over the front door, also in blue. Everyone at Reybrook was pleased with the name.

Hannah could hardly wait for the congregation to meet in the new building. Big Bo and Ollie moved her mother's piano to the front of the sanctuary; she picked out several hymns to play. Another notice had been sent to other plantations with the date and time of the first meeting. Pastor Richard even announced the completion of the Catherine Rey Chapel to his congregation, for it was much closer for several members.

Big Bo picked up trash around the new building and burned it, Ben spent hours preparing a special sermon, and Jim prepared a lesson to teach to the men's Sunday-school class. Dolly studied for the women's class, and Julie planned a Bible story for the children. Everyone on the plantation was excited about the first meeting in the church house . . . except Garrett.

Garrett had never come to worship with the congregation, and he still resented the fact that Ben would be a preacher. If he could only hear him preach, Hannah thought. What would prompt him to come? God gave her an idea; she ran down the hall to share it with Charleen.

"Charleen," she burst into her room without knocking, "do you think you could play some simple music for the worship service on Sunday?"

"I suppose, if I could practice beforehand. What do you want me to play?"

Hannah named a couple of children's songs that she had taught Otis and the twins to sing.

"I think I could play those, but they're children's songs."

"I know. Your daddy might come to church if we told him that Otis and the girls would sing in front of the congregation and that you would play the piano for them."

"You know, Hannah, you could be right. It's worth a try. While you're here, do you mind if I ask you some questions?"

"Of course not."

"I've really listened to Ben's sermons, and I want to go to heaven to be with Mother when I die, but there are some things I don't understand. Will you help me with them?"

Hannah was overjoyed. "Let me get my Bible," she said. The two of them talked far into the night, and after many questions with answers found in the scriptures, Hannah led Charleen to the Lord.

The next day, she led Otis and his two sisters in a song as Charleen played the piano, and at first, it seemed hopeless. Otis could not keep up with the rhythm, and Charleen hit two wrong notes to every right one. After an hour, however, they began to sound better. Before the end of the week, Charleen played perfectly and Emily and Emma did fine, but Otis still had trouble. Hannah thought of just the twins singing, but decided that would never do because Otis was more excited than anyone. What difference would it make if he was a little off key?

That night when the family gathered around the supper table, it was he who said, "Daddy, I'm going to sing with Emma and Emily at church. Will you come?"

Before Garrett could answer, Emily chimed in, "Please come, Daddy. We've worked so hard."

"Yes," added Emma, "you have to come."

"Can you guess who will play the piano?" Charleen asked.

"I have no idea," Garrett replied.

"Me."

"You!" He acted very surprised. "This I have to see . . . and hear." He pretended not to believe any of them.

Otis and the twins loved it and Charleen said enthusiastically, "Then be there!"

"I will," Garrett promised his children, and Hannah knew he would not let them down. She gave him a big smile.

In the predawn hours of Sunday morning, Hannah awoke and heard a faint rumble of thunder. Her anxiety had already caused her to wake up several times through the night, but the sound of thunder upset her, even though it was far away. If it rained, people would get wet and muddy, if they came at all, but worrying would not change one thing, so she turned over and went back to sleep. God was in control, and if it was his will for it to rain, then they would do the best they could.

The rain, however, did not come, and when Hannah awoke that morning, the sun shined brightly. She dressed quickly and ran downstairs for a cup of coffee before she woke Otis and his sisters. Rosie hummed a spiritual tune as she cooked breakfast.

"Good morning, Rosie," said Hannah.

"Moaning, Mis Hannah. Hit's sho a mighty fine day fo de Lawd."

"Yes, Rosie," Hannah agreed, "hit sho is!"

The white in Rosie's eyes stood out in her black face as she cut them around at her, but Hannah didn't see, for she was already out the door.

Later that morning, she sat at her mother's piano and played soft music as worshippers entered the building. The slaves came early and filled the back pews. Big Bo sat among them and deserved credit for many of the others being there. A few visitors came from nearby plantations, and some came all the way from Charleston. Mr. Overteer was there with all of his family.

Mr. and Mrs. Leander came with Dolly and Jim, and Ben and Julie were right behind them, but where was the rest of the Rey family? Hannah had gotten Otis ready, and Reneka had helped the twins, so what could be keeping them?

It was time for the service to start, and all eyes were on Hannah, but she didn't know what to do. She looked at Ben, and he raised his eyebrows and shrugged one shoulder to say, "I don't know where they are."

Finally he stood and walked to the back of the sanctuary to

close the door, but to Hannah's relief, he had to step aside to let his family enter. He closed the door and ushered them to a front pew.

He gave a warm welcome to everyone before the congregation broke up into small groups for Bible study. They reassembled an hour later and sang some hymns. When Hannah stood from the piano, Charleen knew it was time to take her place there, and Otis and the twins came forward.

The girls were nervous, but Otis stood between them with a big smile on his face and didn't appear to be a bit nervous. Hannah waited until she had their attention before she nodded her head for Charleen to begin. When she raised her hand, the young voices began to sing. Otis opened his mouth wide and was so adorable that no one noticed he was off key. After the second song, Hannah stepped aside to present the three vocalists. The congregation seemed pleased, and Garrett was very proud.

Ben preached a message on salvation, and Julie played the piano softly at the end of his sermon. Charleen was the first to rise from her seat, but others followed her down the aisle. Ollie came with Reneka at his side, for support; she had already accepted Christ as her Savior. Tears came to Hannah's eyes when Otis walked down the aisle. He looked so small standing there alone until, to her surprise, Garrett followed him and took his and Charleen's hand. Hannah pictured Catherine rejoicing in heaven with the angels.

The service was long, but no one seemed to mind. When it was over, Hannah lingered in the building after everyone else had left. She straightened the music at the piano and looked around the room and thought of ways to improve its beauty and warmth. Perhaps some curtains over the windows and a rug for the altar. Mostly, however, she stayed behind to thank God. She knelt to her knees at the altar and whispered, "Thank you, Lord, for allowing my vision to come to be, that thou light might shine on Reybrook soil as a beacon to the lost and a place of worship for those who will come. In the name of Jesus I pray. Amen."

When she finally walked out the door, she closed it carefully behind her and turned to see Garrett sitting on the church steps.

"Garrett! I thought you left with the others."

"I waited for you."

"I'm sorry I was so long. If I had known you were waiting—"

"That's okay; I figured you would like some time alone. That's why I waited out here."

"I wanted to thank God for allowing my vision of a church established on the plantation to come to be."

"How long have you had the vision?"

"I began to think about it not long after I came to Reybrook, when Ben told me that the nearest church was in Charleston."

He looked into her eyes and nodded his head.

"Garrett, did you talk to Ben about staying on here to preach at the church and help you on the plantation?"

"Yes, and he said he'd already thought of it, but didn't know how the church could afford to build a building."

"God provided a way."

"Well, he feels bad that you paid for everything and wants me to give the land. I promised him I would try again to persuade you to take the four hundred dollars. We'll talk about it later; right now I have something else to say. Come sit down beside me."

She took a seat on the steps.

"Hannah, you've done so much for my family."

"I told you, Garrett, you're like family to me. You're the only family I have, and it will be hard to leave you, but now that the church building is completed, I should go."

He placed his hand under her chin and gently lifted her face to his. "Hannah, will you marry me?"

Her eyes opened wide, but she was too shocked to speak.

"Ah . . . Garrett . . . I . . . I can't marry you!" she stammered.

"Why not?"

"Well . . . I . . . we don't love each other, for one reason. You still love Catherine and I love Nathan." She began to tremble and her breathing came hard. Garrett realized how great a shock his proposal had been and began to talk to her calmly.

"Yes, I still love Catherine, but she will never come back, and it doesn't look like Nathan will come back. I know I'm a lot older than you, but I'll be good to you and treat you with respect. You're so good to my youngest children and the only woman who could take their mother's place. You need a home, Hannah, and someone to take care of you, and I . . . well, I need someone to take care of."

"Oh, Garrett, what would Charleen and Ben think?"

"I talked to Charleen before church."

"What did she say?"

"It upset her at first, when she thought about her mother, but then she remembered how much Catherine loved you. She said it would be all right if . . ." he hesitated.

"If what?"

"If Nathan wasn't coming back."

"What about Ben? Have you talked to him?"

"No. I haven't told Ben. I don't think it will be all right with him."

"Garrett . . . I—"

"I know you can't give me an answer now, but please think about it."

She sighed deeply. "All right, I will think of it."

The family came together for the noon meal. Hannah sat quietly at her usual place as the others talked of the worship service. Ben was happier than she had seen him in a long time, and Charleen let her joy of salvation show. She felt Ben's eyes on her, several times, but could not look at him, and after eating a small amount of food, she asked to be excused.

She spent the afternoon in her room and tried to catch up on paper work that had been neglected. School had been dismissed for two weeks, but she'd not recorded final marks on her students' end of year report. It was difficult for her to stay focused on the work, as she kept thinking of Garrett's proposal. It was absurd, she told her herself, but then—on the other hand— Garrett had treated her kindly since she returned to Reybrook, and it was true that she had developed affectionate feelings toward him. She didn't love him . . . but she did need a home.

Later, she stood at her window and watched the sun go down with an awful ache in her heart. As soon as it was dark, she went to bed, and as every night, she thought of Nathan and wondered why he had not returned for her. That night she saw him in a dream, and he stood at the front of a beautiful cathedral. Its high walls were so white that they gleamed, and lovely paintings adorned its ceiling. His eyes were fixed on a lady that walked down the aisle toward him; he smiled at her. The lady wore a beautiful white dress with a long train that glittered.

When Hannah awoke from the dream, she could still see Nathan's face as he smiled at the beautiful lady in the wedding dress, and Jeff's words came to her again. "You know how wealthy he is and that he must know a lot of wealthy girls. Do you really believe he'll come back for you?"

She rose from the bed and looked out her window as the dawn began to break. Her plans had been to leave Reybrook soon, but now she didn't know what to do. I'll talk to Ben, she thought, and perhaps . . . if he really loves me . . .

Ben would be up early since it was the busy season. Hannah opened the armoire and took out one of the new dresses that she had bought for her wedding trip. She looked in the mirror to make her face pretty and then slipped the dress on and tied a new ribbon in her hair. The mirror told her that her youthfulness had begun to fade, but her beauty was still there and she wanted Ben to notice.

He was already in the kitchen, pouring himself a cup of coffee, when she entered the room. He reached for another cup and poured it full of the steaming hot coffee.

"Good morning, Hannah. You're up awfully early this morning."

"Good morning, Ben."

"You sure look pretty. Is that a new dress you're wearing?"

"Yes," she smiled. He had noticed.

"I hope you're feeling better. Dad said you felt bad when you left the dinner table yesterday."

"I'm all right, but I need to talk to you about something."

"Okay, and I have something to tell you. Let's sit down. What's on your mind?"

"You first," she said. "What did you want to tell me?"

"I asked Julie to marry me last night, and she said, 'Yes.'"

Hannah had lifted the hot coffee to her lips, and at Ben's words, it suddenly spilled out over her hand and ran down her arm and to the front of her new dress. Her skin was burned, but she didn't feel it.

Ben jumped to take the cup of hot coffee from her. He quickly turned around for a cloth napkin to wrap her hand, but when he turned back, Hannah had disappeared through the kitchen door.

"Hannah, your hand!"

"It's okay," she called to him and ran down the hall, feeling like a complete fool.

"Wait! What did you want to talk to me about?"

"I don't remember."

She met Charleen on the stairs.

"Hannah, what's wrong with your hand?" She noticed that it was very red and that Hannah was upset.

"It's okay," Hannah mumbled. She ran up the stairs and to her room.

"What did you do to Hannah?" Charleen taunted her brother as she entered the kitchen.

"Nothing. She said she wanted to talk to me about something, but when I told her I had asked Julie to marry me, she spilled the hot coffee on her hand and then ran off."

Charleen smiled.

"Why are you smiling?"

"I know what she wanted to talk to you about." Ben waited for her to tell, but her lips were sealed.

"Well, are you going to tell me or not?"

The smile suddenly left Charleen's face, and for once, she was serious with her older brother.

"Daddy asked her to marry him."

"Charleen, will you be serious?"

"I am serious! Our dad asked Hannah to marry him, yesterday after church. He talked to me about it before the service. That was why we were late getting there, and it was why she was upset at dinner, although he made an excuse and said she felt bad."

Ben suddenly felt sick and had to sit down. She wanted to ask me about it, he thought. He remembered how nice she had looked and realized that she wanted to know if he still cared. What an awful time for him to tell her of his proposal to Julie. With his elbows on the table and his eyes closed, he leaned his forehead against his fist and sighed deeply.

After he had given it some thought, Ben looked up at Charleen. "Do you want Dad to marry Hannah?" he asked.

"I don't know. She loves Nathan, but has decided that he's not coming back. I really don't know what to think of it, and I suppose she doesn't either. What will she do if Nathan doesn't come back? Her life will be wasted here, as mine." She made a face. "I had hoped Nathan would return, with Jason, but if he doesn't . . . well, I just don't know. I don't think Hannah ever thought of marrying . . . Dad." Their eyes met, and Ben understood what she meant.

"I've gotta talk to her." He jumped from the chair and hurried upstairs to her room. "Hannah," he called from her open door, but she didn't answer. He saw the new dress where it had been tossed on her bed and knew there was only one reason why she would change clothes. He made a dash for the barn.

Hannah tried to saddle Star with one hand.

"Hannah."

She dropped the cinch strap and it dangled from Star's side.

"What do you want, Ben?"

"I won't let you marry my dad." He spoke firmly.

She turned to face him. "What difference should it make to you?"

"Please, Hannah," he pleaded, "I know Julie is the one God has for me, but I can't be happy unless you're happy."

"All right, Ben, I'll be happy." There was sarcasm in her voice.

"You won't be if you marry my dad. You don't love him!"

"No," she sighed, "I don't, and he doesn't love me. He'll always love your mother, but she'll never come back, and he needs a wife. I love Nathan, but he hasn't returned for me, and I need a home."

"I know Nathan loves you," Ben spoke carefully. Perspiration broke out on his face and neck. He couldn't let her make such a mistake with her life.

"I saw him in a dream," she said, "at his marriage to a lady in a beautiful gown. They were in a large church and she looked so wealthy."

"You only dreamed that because of the thoughts you've had. You must not think that he's gone home and married someone else because I know he hasn't. Before Nathan left Charleston, he told me that to leave you was the hardest thing he'd ever had to do in his life. It was when he asked me to take care of you. The night he came to Reybrook with the British soldiers, his eyes searched for you and when they found you, I saw in his face how much he loved you. That was when I realized I could never have you. When I saw him on the battlefield in New Orleans, his first words were, 'How is Hannah?'"

"Oh, Ben, I love him."

"I know you do, and I won't let you make this mistake. Something has kept him from coming, but it's not another woman. We'll write letters to the British Navy and to his mother."

Ben removed the saddle from Star's back, and Hannah returned to the house with him. She felt better after she had talked to him; her spirits had been retrieved.

That night in her bed, she thought of the night Nathan asked her to marry him. She remembered exactly how it was on the deck of the *Monarch* with the moon shining above them, then in her cabin.

"Will you wait for me, darling?" he had asked.

"Yes," she had answered, "You know I will."

"How long will you wait?"

"Until you return."

"What if I don't return?"

"Then I shall wait forever."

She sat straight up in bed when she remembered her promise. How could she have forgotten? Was this why Nathan had not written? She had promised she would wait, no matter how long he was in coming.

She felt a renewed hope, but whether Nathan ever came or not, she must wait. She would return to Charleston and wait for him there. Perhaps in the fall there would be another job in the public schools. Now that she knew what she must do, a peace came over her.

She got up and lit her lamp and then pulled the large box from underneath her bed and brushed the dust from it before she lifted its top. The white dress was so beautiful; her fingertips carefully touched its soft material.

Julie would need a wedding dress and there was no use in this one just collecting dust. She would take it to her tomorrow . . . right after she told Garrett that she could not marry him.

CHAPTER 39

Dr. Ramirez bent over Jason with a stethoscope in his hand. Nathan stood at the other side of the bed, anxiously awaiting the doctor's diagnosis. He had summoned him to his friend's bedside because his condition had taken a turn for the worse. He feared Jason had pneumonia.

The two rooms he'd rented in the old tenement house were dark and damp and not a good place for Jason's convalescence. He would have looked for other lodging, had Josey not lived right across the hall. She brought them food and other necessities. It kept him off the streets of New Orleans, and he didn't have to leave Jason alone. He wasn't sure how he could have managed without her and had decided that when he returned to England, he would send her enough money to live on until she received a medical degree.

"I'm afraid it's just as you thought, Nathan," said the doctor. "I feel sure he has pneumonia and must return to the hospital. I'll send someone for the two of you."

After the doctor left, Jason tried to sit up. Nathan helped him to a sitting position and propped him with pillows.

"I'll be all right," he said. "I want you to go on to South Carolina. It's been nearly five months since the war was over, and Hannah will think you're not coming. She won't wait forever."

"I won't leave you, Jason. If a hostile person found out you're here, he might try to kill you, and you're too weak to defend yourself. Hannah promised to wait forever, if need be; besides, I wrote her the letter."

Jason sighed and lay back on the bed with his eyes closed. His forehead felt awfully hot, so Nathan went across the hall to borrow Josey's thermometer. He knocked lightly on her door and heard her say, "Who is it?"

"It's Nathan. May I borrow your thermometer?"

"Come in, Nathan."

He opened her door and she called from the back room, "Have a seat. I'll be right out."

He didn't want to have a seat. Jason was too ill to be left alone, but it seemed he would be forced to wait if he wanted the thermometer. He crossed the room to the divan and sat down beside a small box. He didn't mean to pry when he glanced down at the box and saw papers concerning Josey's business. He looked away quickly, but something had caught his eye. A second look revealed his handwriting on an envelope addressed to Miss Hannah Thornton. He reached for it, but before his hand could grasp the envelope, Josey snatched the box from in front of him.

"Let me put this away," she said.

"Josey!"

"I'll only be a moment."

Nathan reached the doorway before her and blocked the exit from the room. He reached his hand into the box and brought out his letter to Hannah. He was confused as to how it could have gotten there until he saw the look on Josey's face.

"Why, Josey?" She didn't answer. "Did you not mail any of my letters?"

"Yes," she mumbled, "I mailed the others."

"Then why not this one?" He turned it over and saw that it had been opened. Josey's head was bowed and she refused to speak.

"Answer me, Josey!"

"I—I wanted you to stay in New Orleans."

"Why?"

She lifted her eyes to his. "Because . . . I'm in love with you." She spoke barely above a whisper and a tear trickled down both cheeks. "I thought if she didn't answer your letter, you would think she didn't care."

At first, Nathan was furious and felt like taking quick leave of the room, but when he saw the agony in Josey's face, his fury gave way to compassion. He sighed and put his arms around her.

"I'm sorry, Josey. I've been so concerned about Jason until I just didn't think. You've been so much help to me, and I don't know how I could have managed without you."

She raised her parted lips to his, and he understood that she wanted him to kiss her. "Josey, I love the girl in South Carolina. We're engaged to be married, if I can ever get back to her."

She put her arms around him and bowed her head to his chest. He held her a moment, caressing her long black hair, then gently forced her arms from around him and left her standing alone with her head still bowed.

He folded the letter and put it into his pocket; he didn't want Jason to see it. While he waited for someone to come from the hospital, he administered cool wet towels to bring his temperature down, and as he worked, he thought of Josey and decided it best not to see her again. He was glad he had not told her he would send the money.

For the next two weeks, Jason's illness was critical. Nathan was with him around the clock and did everything humanly possible to help him get well, but when Jason's condition worsened, he committed him to God a second time.

A few days later, Jason's health took a turn and began to improve so quickly it was nothing short of a miracle. Dr. Ramirez could not explain it. At the end of that week, he walked into Jason's room with his stethoscope around his neck.

"Um-huh, um-huh," the doctor talked to himself as he moved his instrument from one place to another across Jason's bare chest. Finally he let go of the stethoscope and stood straight.

"What, Doctor?" Nathan could hardly wait.

"His chest is clear," he said. "He's going to be all right."

"I told you I would be, Nathan." Jason grinned.

Nathan was so happy he wanted to hug both of them.

The doctor looked at Jason. "How do you feel?" he asked.

"I'm fine, but I'm hungry."

"Well, that's a good sign," the doctor laughed. "Two more weeks and you'll be ready to travel."

"Two weeks! Doctor, I'm ready to go now."

"You must build up your strength."

"Awe man!"

Nathan laughed. It had been so long since he had heard Jason use his favorite expression.

The doctor started to leave the room, but stopped and turned to Nathan. "I almost forgot," he said. "Some mail was delivered to the hospital for you, yesterday."

"For me?"

"Yes. It's in my office. I'll get it for you."

In a few minutes, the doctor returned and handed Nathan a large brown envelope from the British Department of Defense and two smaller envelopes. There was a letter from his mother and one from Jason's dad. A bank draft, made out to him, was enclosed in both letters. Jason's dad had sent more than enough to cover Jason's medical expenses, plus money for both their passages back to England.

Nathan handed Jason the letter from his dad, and he read the one from his mother.

March 30, 1815

Dearest Nathan,

No words can explain the joy I felt when I received your letter. I've been so worried since we were informed that you and Jason were missing. News of the Battle of New Orleans was very frightening and so many families grieve the loss of a son. I pray that Jason's health has improved and you may both return home soon.

All of your family, as well as Jason's, join me in saying that it was a very heroic deed that you did, to stay behind with him. I'm thankful you were able to get him to a hospital and for the kind Americans who helped you in this endeavor.

James returned home from the war with only a few scars and has resumed his job at the bank. I'm so very thankful to have both my sons alive after the war and will be even more so when you and Jason arrive home safely. I pray daily for both of you.

Enclosed you will find a bank draft to cover your expenses. Please let me hear from you again soon.

Good news is that the crew of the *Monarch* was released by the Americans and has returned to Liverpool, but I've not heard from Hannah in many months.

Love,
Mother

In the brown envelope, Nathan found papers that released Jason and him from the British Royal Navy. He walked to the window and looked out. It had been a good day. He was thankful that Jason had recovered from pneumonia, that his brother's life had been spared, and for money received just in the nick of time.

Only one thing kept him from being completely happy. Would Hannah wait as she had promised? Since Josey had not mailed his letter, he could only imagine what was going through her mind? Would she believe that he'd returned to England and married a wealthy girl as Jeff had implied? Was this why she had not written to his mother? Ben was in love with her, and she had been at Reybrook for three years, whereas they were on the *Monarch* only three months.

The war had taken its toll on the shipping industry of England, and he didn't know if Jason's dad had been able to protect his fortune or not. He feared he was no longer wealthy. If not, how would Hannah take the news? He thought of the small diamond ring he had given her and of his plan to have a special one made in London. If he used the money his mother had sent, he could buy her a large one, but it would take all of it.

Nathan made a decision, and when the doctor came later that night, he asked, "Dr. Ramirez, do you know a jeweler whom I can trust? I need a diamond ring."

The doctor scratched his head. "*Sí* . . . I do." He looked confused.

"I hope to get married when I get to Charleston. I intended to buy a ring in London, but I won't be going that way."

"I happen to know the best and most honest jeweler in New Orleans. If Jason feels like walking, we'll go there tomorrow. It's not far and there is a restaurant next door."

On June 15, only one week later instead of two, Nathan and Jason boarded a ship bound for Charleston. Every evening Nathan stood on the main deck of the ship and thought of Hannah as he watched the sun go down. Did she still wait for him? He had seen her for only ten or fifteen minutes in the three years since they had parted, but he remembered how wonderful the few minutes alone with her had been. What would he do if she had married or fallen in love with someone else? For the entire time they had been apart, he'd lived for the day they would be reunited.

The ship sailed into Charleston Harbor during the night of June 29. Nathan and Jason rose early the next morning and dressed for the trip to Reybrook. They ate breakfast in a restaurant and rented two horses at a nearby stable.

On the way out of town, several carriages passed them, but they thought nothing of it, for it was a Saturday morning, and one would expect to see many people out. When they were half a mile from town, they speeded their horses to a gallop. The carriages still rolled along the same way and Nathan noticed that the people were dressed in fine clothing. Most of the men wore suits and the ladies wore nice dresses and bonnets. Finally he pulled his horse up beside one of the carriages.

"Where is everyone going?" he shouted at the man with the reins.

"To Reybrook Plantation," the man shouted back.

"For what?"

"A wedding."

Nathan's heart took a sudden dive, and he stopped the horse so abruptly that he reared into the air. He and Jason looked at each other, but neither spoke. When his horse settled down, he caught up with the carriage again.

"Who is getting married?" he shouted.

"Ben Rey, the plantation owner's son."

"To whom?"

"A young lady who works on the plantation. I don't remember her name."

Nathan pulled on the horse's reins until he came to a complete stop.

"We have to go on, Nathan," said Jason. "If it's Hannah, you have to know."

Nathan's hand shook as he lifted it to his head. "What if it's her and I show up at such a time? What will it do to her?"

"What if it's not her and you never show up? What will that do to her? Besides, I'm going to see Charleen and you're going with me."

It was the longest ride Nathan had ever ridden in his life. When they finally reached Reybrook, they saw the church and the many horses and carriages in front of it.

"I won't go in, Jason, but I'll wait out here until it's over."

"All right; I'll wait with you."

While Nathan and Jason waited in the shade of the trees, Ben stood at the front of the church, and Jim, who would soon be his brother-in-law, stood proudly beside him. Ben had helped Jim and Dolly recite their marriage vows at a small service the Saturday before.

Hannah played a soft melody on the piano as guests were seated. Ben turned his eyes toward her and felt pain in his heart when he saw her head bent over the keys. Sadness covered her face. Her things were packed, and Reneka and Ollie would take her to Charleston as soon as the wedding was over. What if Nathan never came? Perhaps he'd been too hasty on insisting that she not marry his dad. She didn't love him, but she loved Reybrook. When she began to play the wedding march, he realized that Julie had begun her walk down the aisle. She was beautiful . . . in Hannah's wedding dress.

Pastor Richard had a message for Julie and Ben before the wedding vows were spoken to each other, and it made the service run longer. As soon as it was over, Otis jumped from his seat and ran from the church. He couldn't sit still another minute. On the way down the church steps, he saw two men on horses at the edge of the woods and ran to investigate.

Nathan quickly dismounted his horse. "Hi, Otis," he called, "do you remember me?"

To his surprise, Otis answered, "Sure, Nathan, but what'ja doing out here?"

"Who got married, Otis?"

"Ben."

"Who is the bride?" He hesitated then asked, "Is it Hannah?"

"No!" Otis replied in his squeaky voice. "Hannah played the piano. Julie's the bride."

Nathan was so relieved that he picked Otis up and held him high in the air. Otis squealed with delight, but when Nathan put him down, his feet hit the ground running and Nathan went back to his horse. He and Jason remained at a distance until the bride and groom came out of the church with the guests close behind them.

Friends and family surrounded Ben and Julie to wish them well, but out of the corner of his eye, Ben noticed the two men on horseback. Who were they? He watched them dismount, and then his heart skipped a beat. Could it be . . . yes, it was! He asked to be excused from the crowd and went to meet them.

"Hello, Ben. Congratulations," said Nathan. He and Jason held out a hand to him.

"Thanks, Nathan; hi, Jason. I'm glad to see you two."

"I'm glad to be back," Nathan remarked. "Is Hannah here?"

"Yeah, she's still inside. Come on, I'll take you to her." He looked at Jason and said, "Charleen is around someplace."

"You two go ahead. I'll find her."

Nathan and Ben entered the church that was now empty except for Hannah. She stood at the piano and picked up sheets of music to straighten them.

"Hannah," Ben called from the back of the church, "there is someone here to see you."

"Please show them in, Ben." She spoke without looking up, as she thought it was someone interested in the new church.

"He's here," Ben answered.

Nathan watched her face as she looked up and her eyes met his. She blinked and then gasped. A soft cry escaped her lips, and the sheets of music dropped to the floor. As their arms went around each other, Otis ran inside, but Ben caught him by the back of his collar.

"Outside, Otis!" he commanded.

"But I want to tell Hannah something!"

"It'll have to wait." Ben lifted his little brother and took him toward the door with his legs kicking. He put Otis down and turned to close the door. Hannah and Nathan stood in the middle of the church with their lips sealed together. Ben smiled and mumbled, "Hannah knows all that she needs to know right now."

"I love you, Hannah. I love you, darling," Nathan whispered between kisses.

"Oh, Nathan, I love you." Her hand trembled as it touched his face. There was the twinkle in his eyes . . . his wonderful smile . . . the gentle touch of his hands. It was hard to believe he was there. "I thought you weren't coming back," she said. "At first, I was afraid you'd been killed in the battle at New Orleans, but Ben said he saw you after the battle and you were fine. Why have you been so long in coming?"

Before answering, he took her hands in his and looked down at them. The only ring he saw was the small one he had placed there, but he had to know for sure. "You're not married, are you?"

"No, darling, but I feared that you had returned to England and married a wealthy girl . . . an aristocrat like yourself."

"Did you not remember how much I love you?"

"It's been so long, and I was afraid your love for me had faded. I didn't know what to do until I remembered that I had promised to wait forever. Please tell me why you have just now come when the war has been over for months."

"I never left New Orleans. Jason was hit in the chest with shrapnel and almost died. I removed it on the battlefield and managed to get him to a hospital. I've been with him all this time. I was afraid he would die from the wound or someone would kill him if I left him. I just couldn't."

"Of course you couldn't. If I had only known."

"I wrote you a letter."

"I didn't receive one from you."

"I know, and I know what happened to it. It's a long story. I'll tell you everything, but right now I want to know when we can get married."

"When do you want to?"

"As soon as possible."

"What about . . . right now?"

His eyes lit up. "Do you think we can?" he asked.

"I don't know why not. The pastor is here with the guests and you and me. Whom else do we need?"

"No one," he laughed, "but first, I have to tell you something. May we sit down?"

He led her to a church pew, then took her hands in his and told her of his family's misfortune. "I have very little money with me," he said, "perhaps not enough for our passage back to England. My mother sent me a bank draft, but . . . well . . . I spent it. There was something I wanted to buy. I'm not sure of the size of my fortune in the banks of England. It depends on the state of the company when it failed. I have no way to find out, but I know Jason's dad protected my investments and represented the Barrington family with the best of his ability. I owe Ben money and should pay him before we leave. Did you need the money I deposited in the bank for you?"

"No, but Ben won't take any money from you. There is, however, something you can give him."

"What?"

"The rifle. Give him the rifle."

"Well, sure, I'd like for him to have it. It'll be a gift from both of us."

"Thank you. He'll be so proud of it. You don't have to worry about money; it's not a problem. My grandmother died and left me her entire fortune, including her mansion and everything she owned in Northern Ireland. I'm very wealthy now."

Nathan was silent. He studied her face, but didn't know what to say. He now understood how she must have felt when she found out who he was. He looked down at the floor and mumbled, "I can't take money from you."

"Look at me, Nathan. I love you, and you just said that you wanted to marry me."

"I do, sweetheart, but—"

"When we're married," she interrupted him, "what is mine is yours, and what is yours is mine. Don't you understand? We'll be as one. Is that not the way you felt when you asked me to marry you?"

"I love you, Hannah."

"Then come, before the guests begin to leave."

"Wait. Are you sure you want to get married today? If you need time . . . I've been gone so long and must seem like a stranger to you."

She looked into his brown eyes. "Do you need time, Nathan? Are you sure you still want to marry me?"

"I've never been surer of anything in my life. I'm as sure as I was the night I asked you. I want to get married now, but I can wait . . . if you want to."

"I don't want to wait another day."

He smiled. "Neither do I."

"Then come; we must hurry!"

As soon as they stepped out the door of the church, Garrett came to meet them. He held out a hand to Nathan and expressed his happiness for Hannah.

"Thank you, Garrett. We want to get married now, while everyone is here. Do you think it can be arranged?" she asked.

"I don't know why not. I'll talk to the pastor and take care of everything. You two get ready."

Nathan looked around the churchyard. "I need to find Jason," he said.

"Now that might be a problem," Garrett chuckled. "I saw Charleen link her arm through his and they disappeared. I'll send Otis to look for them."

Otis already knew that his sister and Jason were behind the church. He had seen them kiss each other and was more than happy to fetch them at his dad's command. Due to his quick action, within moments Jason stood at the front of the church beside Nathan and watched as guests reassembled for another wedding.

Hannah took longer, however, and Nathan began to worry that something was wrong. Julie came from a back room and sat down at the piano and began to play soft music. He couldn't be sure, but did she have on Hannah's dress? Yes . . . and he understood why when his bride appeared at the far end of the aisle in a beautiful wedding dress. Julie began to play the wedding march, and the guests stood for Hannah to begin her long awaited walk down the aisle.

"Awe man!" Jason whispered. Nathan smiled, but he was speechless and never took his eyes from Hannah.

Pastor Richard repeated the words he had spoken to Ben and Julie, and then Nathan and Hannah pledged their love as they spoke the wedding vows to each other. The pastor was uncertain as to what he should say when it came time for the bride and groom to exchange rings. Under the circumstance, he wasn't sure if either had purchased one. He didn't want to embarrass him, so he whispered to Nathan, "Have you a ring?"

Nathan nodded his head and the pastor said aloud, "You may place the ring on your bride's finger."

Hannah removed the small ring on her left hand and lifted it to Nathan. She almost fainted when she saw the size of the diamond in the ring that he placed on her finger. Nathan put his hands under her arms to steady her, and Pastor Richard gave her a moment to catch her breath before he asked, "Do you have a ring for the groom?"

"No, but I have this." She lifted Nathan's gold chain from around her neck for the first time since he returned it there the night they prayed together. "Until I return with your ring," she reminded him of his words and placed the Barrington coat of arms around his neck where it belonged.

"You may kiss your bride," the pastor announced to Nathan. But Otis couldn't wait that long and was out the church door before the kiss was ended. To sit through two weddings in the same day had been almost unbearable for him.

He circled the family carriage that had been driven to the front of the church and eyed the sign that read "just married" across the back of it. He laughed and clapped his hands when everyone threw rice at Ben and Julie as they climbed onto the front seat and waved good-bye.

"I didn't rent a carriage," Nathan apologized to Hannah. "I never dreamed we could get married today. I'll return to Charleston for one, while you get ready to go."

"Darling, can't we stay at Reybrook, tonight? We're both tired and will need more time to get ready for such a long trip. And Charleen will not want Jason to leave."

"Well, it's fine with me, sweetheart. Jason does need to rest before traveling again. Do you think it will be all right with Garrett and Catherine?"

Hannah's face flinched. Her hand went to her mouth and her eyes opened wide.

"What, Hannah?"

"You had no way of knowing."

"No way of knowing what?"

"Come with me." She led him to the cemetery.

Nathan knelt reverently beside Catherine's grave. He touched his fingertips to her name and let them trace over the dates carved in the stone. "I wondered why she wasn't at the church," he said quietly. "How hard it must have been when she died."

"It was so terrible. Garrett went through an awful time, and he'll never get over her. I knew everyone loved her, but I didn't realize how much until her death. She loved the church and attended every Sunday that she was able. The new building is in memory of her, so people will remember her for generations to come."

"I noticed the name over the door."

Hannah wanted to tell him of Garrett's proposal of marriage and of Ben's love, but it would have to wait. She would tell him everything when there was time. For now, they should return to the guests. When the last family left, she asked Garrett's permission for them to remain at Reybrook that night.

"This is your home, Hannah," he reminded her. "Both of you will always be welcome to stay as long as you will. Besides, Charleen won't let Jason leave anytime soon."

Hannah smiled. "Thank you, Garrett."

"Thank you, Hannah. You returned here and helped my family and me get through an awful time. I hope you'll always be happy; I'm happy for you."

Rosie cooked a special supper, but Hannah found it hard to eat. She couldn't believe everything that had happened that day and that Nathan—her husband—sat beside her. It was almost dark by the time the meal was over, and Nathan went to make sure that his and Jason's horses had been taken care of. While he was gone, Hannah hurried upstairs and got out the white box from THE LADIES' SHOP. She undressed quickly and slipped the lily-white silk gown over her head and let the sheer robe hang loosely about her shoulders. She took the clasp from her hair and ran a brush through it as she heard someone climb the stairs. There was a light knock at her door and then

"Hannah." Nathan called her name softly the way she remembered on the *Monarch*.

"Come in, Nathan."

He opened the door and saw her standing in the soft glow of the lamp light; just like the night she had stood in the doorway of her cabin in a white robe. It was a mental picture he had carried with him for so long. Now she stood before him again, almost the same way . . . and she was his wife. His heart raced as he crossed the room and lifted her in his arms. The robe fell from her shoulders and dropped to the floor.

While his eyes feasted upon her, he undressed and blew out the lamp and then eased beneath the cover and took her in his arms. "My beautiful wife," he whispered in her ear. "I love you; I'll always love you."

"Would you rather be called Mrs. Barrington or Lady Barrington?" Nathan asked Hannah, later that night, for neither could sleep.

"I'd rather be called Hannah, but you may call me whatever you prefer. I'm so happy, Nathan, but it's still hard to believe that you're here with me."

"I am here, sweetheart, and I don't ever want to leave you again, but . . ." he hesitated.

"But what?" She rose to her elbows and leaned her face close to his.

"Do you remember that I told you we would make plans for the future when I returned?"

"Yes."

"I thought then that I would be part owner of a thriving shipping company, but I'm not, and I'm not sure what I'll do. I know I don't want to spend my life working in a bank."

"Nathan, I have something to show you."

"What is it, sweetheart?"

"Let me light the lamp."

"I'll light it." He jumped from the bed.

As soon as there was light in the room, Hannah slipped from beneath the cover and went to her dresser where she opened the top drawer and took out all the land deeds that she had acquired. She laid the papers on her table and then lifted the lamp with one hand and pulled the table near the bed with her other hand. The lamp was returned to the center of the table, and when the two of them were seated on the side of the bed, Nathan began to browse through the papers. He held them close to the lamp and realized they were land deeds . . . and each one was in Hannah's name.

"Hannah . . . do you own all this land?" he queried.

She nodded her head. "I bought it for you."

"For me?"

"Yes. Some of it is swampland, but there is good timber on all of it except for two hundred acres. Mr. Overteer helped me buy it at a good price and thought it was a good investment; I wanted you to have the timber for building ships."

Nathan looked over the papers silently, but Hannah heard a soft whistle when he came to the deed for 5,000 acres. She waited anxiously to hear what he thought. Would he be upset that she had invested so much money in the timberland or would he be glad?

After he'd studied the papers for quite some time, Nathan breathed in a deep breath and lifted his face with a big smile on it. "Wow!" he exclaimed, "I married a real business lady! What would you think if we started our own shipping company right here in Charleston? We'll build our own ships!"

"I think it's a wonderful idea." She knew she had done a good thing when she heard the excitement in his voice.

"I'll ask Jason to be a partner . . . if that's okay with you."

"Yes, of course. The two of you are so close."

"I'll send for Scott. He should be finished at the art school by now, and I know he'll work for us . . . if he can go home often." They both laughed.

Nathan began to talk fast. "I'll write letters to Murray and

Robert and Sam. I'll write to all the crew of the *Monarch* and to Michael Sutterfield." He thought of Jeff, but didn't tell Hannah about his death or that his last words were of his love for her. He would wait until there was time to be sad. He wanted nothing to mar her happiness on this night.

"We'll build a large fleet of the best ships on the seas," he said, "and sail them all over the world!"

She laughed as his excitement escalated. He still voiced his plans for the new business when she forced him backward on the bed and covered his lips with hers.

"Oh-h-h," he groaned and then lifted his body and gently laid her backward and pressed his lips harder to hers. She thought he was completely engrossed in the kiss and had forgotten everything else when his head suddenly shot up and he asked, "Why did you buy two hundred acres without any timber on it?"

"Oh, Nathan," she laughed. "We'll go there tomorrow and you can see for yourself." She reached her hand to the back of his head and forced his lips back to hers.

BVG